The Legal Framework of the Church of England

THE LEGAL FRAMEWORK
OF THE CHURCH OF ENGLAND

A Critical Study
in a Comparative Context

NORMAN DOE

Lecturer in Law
University of Wales College of Cardiff

CLARENDON PRESS · OXFORD
1996

Oxford University Press, Walton Street, Oxford OX2 6DP
Oxford New York
Athens Auckland Bangkok Bombay
Calcutta Cape Town Dar es Salaam Delhi
Florence Hong Kong Istanbul Karachi
Kuala Lumpur Madras Madrid Melbourne
Mexico City Nairobi Paris Singapore
Taipei Tokyo Toronto
and associated companies in
Berlin Ibadan

Oxford is a trade mark of Oxford University Press

Published in the United States
by Oxford University Press Inc., New York

British Library Cataloguing in Publication Data
Data available

ISBN 0-19-826220-5

Library of Congress Cataloguing in Publication Data
Doe, Norman.
The legal framework of the Church of England: a critical study in
a comparitive context/Norman Doe.
p. cm.
Includes bibliographical references.
1. Church of England–Government. 2. Ecclesiastical law–Great Britain.
3. Church and state–Church of England.
KD8642.D64   1996   262.9'8342–d20   95-48474
ISBN 0-19-826220-5

1 3 5 7 9 10 8 6 4 2

Typeset by J&L Composition Ltd, Filey, North Yorkshire
Printed in Great Britain on acid-free paper by
Bookcraft Ltd., Midsomer Norton, Avon

Preface

It may be thought presumptuous for an organist in the Church in Wales to write a book comparing the law of the Church of England with that of the Roman Catholic Church. However, that a project of this sort should be undertaken is not surprising. No attempt has previously been made to compare the laws applicable to these churches. Moreover, given the current ecumenical climate the project may be considered legitimate, particularly at a time when the study of church law is experiencing a genuine renaissance. Both the Church of England, not least through the Ecclesiastical Law Society, and the Roman Catholic Church, through the Canon Law Society of Great Britain and Ireland, are contributing immensely to this revival. For the Church of England, the revision of canon law in the 1960s and the introduction of synodical government in 1970, and for the Roman Catholic Church, the promulgation of the new Code of Canon Law in 1983, have stimulated a vast literature on the respective legal systems of these churches, but largely along separate albeit parallel paths. This book seeks to elucidate the relationship between these two substantial legal systems, and their relative positions with respect to the secular state and its law.

I came to the subject after studying late medieval common law, upon which the influence of canonists and canon law has for a long time been a matter of debate. My studies, which carefully avoided this debate, were limited to the development of medieval law and jurisprudence until around 1500. I wondered where all that canon law had gone. One Sunday afternoon in 1988 (after playing the organ) I read an issue of the *Ecclesiastical Law Journal*, produced by the Ecclesiastical Law Society and then in its infancy. With encouragement and support from that Society, in particular from my colleague the Revd. Thomas Watkin and from the Revd. John Masding, convenor of the Society's Working Party on Education in Ecclesiastical and Canon Law, and his predecessor the Ven. Hughie Jones, in 1991 the LL M in Canon Law was introduced at Cardiff. This collaborative venture, between the Cardiff Law School and St. Michael's Theological College, Llandaff, through its Warden, the Revd. Canon John Rowlands, has been a great success. It was from seminar discussions with the first intake of students on this course that the idea of a book emerged. The course thrives and this book is a direct result of it. To the many students who have already undertaken the course I owe much, not least for their tolerance with the inevitable process of experimentation.

I have relied heavily on the kindness and expertise of many who read draft chapters. For their invaluable comments and suggestions I owe a special debt of gratitude to Brian Hanson, Ingrid Slaughter, the leading lawyers at Church House, Westminster (also for their cheerful help with intrusive telephone calls for materials), to Mark Hill, Oswald Clark, Hughie Jones, Philip Barrett, John Masding, Jeffrey Gainer, Stephen White, George Spafford, Nicholas Ritchens, Timothy Belben, and Susan Mansell. From Sir John Owen, Rhidian Jones, Steven Kirk, Bill Pritchard, David Sherwood, and Jonathan Redvers Harris, students in the first intake on the LL M at Cardiff, I learnt much about the practicalities of church life, law, and administration. A special debt is due to Michelle Gooden who, while a research assistant at Cardiff, helped tirelessly with the references. I also owe a great deal to very many Diocesan Registrars and Secretaries in the Church of England for their assistance in providing handbooks of pastoral regulations from the dioceses. A list of the diocesan documents consulted appears in the Table of Abbrevations; this also indicates which pastoral regulations in 1995 were being revised at the time of writing. I have endeavoured to describe the law as it stood in June 1995 though I have also tried to keep abreast of developments to the date of this preface. Over the next few years major changes in the law on the administrative organization of the Church of England are likely as a result of the report of the Turnbull Commission, *Working as One Body*, published this month; an attempt has been made to describe the key recommendations of this report where appropriate. Any errors in the book are, of course, solely my responsibility.

Whilst producing the typescript was relatively painless with the aid of a word processor, special thanks are given to Julia Craske at the Cardiff Law School and to many other colleagues for their help and support. Similarly, I wish to thank the staff at Oxford University Press, especially Margaret Shade and Anna Rayne, for their patience with and painstaking treatment of the typescript. It was some years ago that I first mooted the possibility of a book such as this to Richard Hart, Senior Law Editor at the Press. To him I am deeply indebted for his inspiration and continued faith in the project. Finally, I should like to thank for their constant kindness and support, my family: my mother, father, and brother, my parents-in-law, and above all my wife Heather and our children Rachel, Elizabeth, and Edward who, far more than myself, enjoy an enduring patience with canonical problems.

C.N.D.
Cardiff,
25 September 1995

Contents

Part III: Ecclesiastical Ministry

Abbreviations

Complete citations are to be found in the Bibliography. For the purposes of footnotes, normally the abbreviations listed below for Measures of General Synod are used, unless the context is not obvious in which case, for the sake of clarity, the full title is given. The documents of the Second Vatican Council may be found in A. Flannery (ed.), *Vatican Council II, Vatican Collection*, Volumes 1 and 2 (New York, 1982, 1988).

Acts of Convocation A. F. Smethurst, H. R. Wilson, and H. Riley (eds.), *Acts of the Convocations of Canterbury and York* (London, 1961)

AR The Thirty-Nine Articles of Religion (1562, confirmed 1571)

ARCIC Anglican-Roman Catholic International Commission

ASB The Alternative Service Book (1980)

AT: HS G. R. Evans and J. R. Wright (eds.), *The Anglican Tradition: A Handbook of Sources* (1991)

BCP The Book of Common Prayer (1662) (edn.: Cambridge University Press, including amendments to 1968)

BDM Diocese of Bradford, *Diocesan Manual* (1987)

BRDSEI Diocese of St Edmundsbury and Ipswich, *Bishop's Regulations* (1993)

c. A canon contained in the Roman Catholic Code of Canon Law (1983)

CA Court of Appeal

CAD Province and Diocese of Canterbury, *Archbishop's Directions* (1994)

CBC General Synod, Board and Council Constitutions 1996–2001, GS. misc. 460.

CCEJM Care of Churches and Ecclesiastical Jurisdiction Measure 1991

CCEJMCP Care of Churches and Ecclesiastical Jurisdiction Measure 1991, *Code of Practice*

CCL: TC J. A. Coriden, T. J. Green and D. E. Heintschel (eds), *The Code of Canon Law: A Text and Commentary* (1985)

CD Catholic Directory (1994) (Published for the Bishops' Conference of England and Wales, Manchester, 1994)

CDH Diocese of Carlisle, *Diocesan Handbook* (1990)

CDSMH Chelmsford Diocesan Synod Members' Handbook (1986, as amended 1994)

CEA(P)A Church of England Assembly (Powers) Act 1919

CE(WD)M Church of England (Worship and Doctrine) Measure 1974

CEYB Church of England *Yearbook* (1995)

CF Diocese of Chelmsford, *The Chelmsford File* (1991)

Ch Diocesan Chancellor, Church of England

CIC Codex Iuris Canonici, The Code of Canon Law of the Roman Catholic Church, promulgated by Pope John Paul II 1983

CLJ Cambridge Law Journal

COCLA E. Caparros, M. Thériault, and J. Thorn (eds.), *Code of Canon Law Annotated* (Montreal, 1993)

Con. Ct. Consistory Court

CPR Diocese of Chichester, *Pastoral Regulations* (1987)

CRR Church Representation Rules (1995 edition), Synodical Government Measure 1969, Sched. 3

DAC Diocesan Advisory Committee

Dale, *LPC* Sir William Dale, *The Law of the Parish Church* (6th edn., 1989)

DCPM Draft Church Property Measure (1992)

DDBF Diocese of Durham, Diocesan Black Folder (1988–92 — under review)

DGBOP Diocese of Guildford, Bishop's Occasional Papers (current but undated edition)

DH Vatican II, Decree, *Dignitatis Humanae* (1966)

DLR Diocese of Liverpool, *Year Book* (1994-5) 163, *Bishop's Regulations* (and Standing Orders for Diocesan Synod, 1991)

DSBN Diocese of Southwell, Bishop's Ad Clerum Notices (1989–93 — under review)

DSPR Diocese of Southwark, Pastoral Regulations (1991 — under review)

ECHR European Convention for the Protection of Human Rights and Fundamental Freedoms (1950)

EDH Diocese of Ely, *Diocesan Handbook* (1991)

EJM Ecclesiastical Jurisdiction Measure 1963

ELJ Ecclesiastical Law Journal

EM Vatican II, Instruction, *Eucharisticum Mysterium* (1967)

FJCE G. H. Newsom, *Faculty Jurisdiction of the Church of England* (2nd edn., 1993)

FJR Faculty Jurisdiction Rules 1992

Flannery See introduction to Abbreviations

GDM Diocese of Gloucester, *Diocesan Manual* (1993)

GES Vatican II, Pastoral Constitution, *Gaudium et Spes* (1966)

GS General Synod of the Church of England

GSRP General Synod, *Report of Proceedings*

GSSO General Synod Standing Orders (October 1995 Edition)

HC House of Commons

H Ct High Court

HDCH Diocese of Hereford, *Clergy Handbook* (1992)

Hill, *EL* M. Hill, *Ecclesiastical Law* (1995)

HL House of Lords

HLE Halsbury, *Laws of England, Vol.14, Ecclesiastical Law* (4th edn., London 1975)

HV Paul VI, Encyclical, *Humanae Vitae* (1968)

IVBCP Incumbents (Vacation of Benefices) Measure 1977, *Code of Practice* (1994)

IVBM Incumbents (Vacation of Benefices) Measure 1977 (as amended 1993)

LBGCP Diocese of Lincoln, *Bishop's Guidance and Memoranda Ad Clerum and Diocesan Code of Practice* (1994)

LDHI Diocese of Lichfield, *Handbook of Information* (1991)

LDR Diocese of London, *Regulations* (1987)

LEP Local Ecumenical Project

LG Vatican II, Dogmatic Constitution *Lumen Gentium* (1965)

LQR Law Quarterly Review

MIECL T. Briden and B. Hanson, *Moore's Introduction to English Canon Law* (3rd edn., 1992)

MLR Modern Law Review

MSODS Model Standing Orders for Diocesan Synods (1990)

NDIB Diocese of Newcastle, *Diocesan Information Handbook* (1992)

NILQ Northern Ireland Legal Quarterly

NLJ New Law Journal

ODYB: IF Diocese of Oxford, *Year Book* (1994) 229–81, Information File

OLAC Legal Opinions Concerning the Church of England (Opinions of the Legal Advisory Commission) (London, 1994)

ORPD Official Report, Parliamentary Debates

PB Apostolic Constitution, *Pastor Bonus* (1988)

PBR Diocese of Peterborough, *Diocesan Regulations* (1992–3)

PC Privy Council

PCC Parochial Church Council

PCC(P)M Parochial Church Councils (Powers) Measure 1956

PDH Diocese of Portsmouth, *Diocesan Handbook* (current edition but undated)

PL Public Law

PMCP Pastoral Measure 1983, Code of Practice

PO Vatican II, Decree, *Presbyterorum Ordinis* (1966)

POWMCP Priests (Ordination of Women) Measure 1993, Code of Practice

RACCL Report of the Archbishops' Commission, *The Canon Law of the Church of England* (1947)

RBG Diocese of Rochester, *Bishop's Guidelines* (1989, as amended 1990–92)

RDL Diocese of Leicester, *Regulations* (1989 revised edition)

Readings J. Hite and D. J. Ward (eds.), *Readings, Cases, Materials in Canon Law* (1990)

Rites The Rites of the Roman Catholic Church, Volumes I and II (New York, 1988 edition)

SADH Diocese of St. Albans, *Diocesan Handbook* (3rd Revision, 1989)

SC Vatican II, Constitution, *Sacrosanctum Concilium* (1964)

SDDH Diocese of Salisbury, *Diocesan Handbook* (1991)

SDH Diocese of Sheffield, *Handbook* (1994)

SGM Synodical Government Measure 1969

SI Statutory Instrument

SO Standing Order

TBF Diocese of Blackburn, *The Blackburn File: A Reference and Resource Manual* (1993)

TDH Diocese of Truro, *Diocesan Handbook* (First Draft, 1994)

UR Vatican II, Decree, *Unitatis Redintegratio* (1965)

WAOB Working As One Body, The Report of the Archbishops' Commission on the Organisation of the Church of England, the Turnbull Commission (1995)

WBRG Diocese of Winchester, *Bishop's Regulations and Guidelines* (1993)

WDHI Diocese of Wakefield, *Handbook of Information* (1989)

WH Diocese of Worcester, *Diocesan Handbook* (1993)

Table of Parliamentary Statutes

Table of Measures of the
Church of England

Table of Canons of the Church of England

SECTION A: THE CHURCH OF ENGLAND

SECTION B: DIVINE SERVICE AND THE ADMINISTRATION OF THE SACRAMENTS

SECTION C: MINISTERS, THEIR ORDINATION, FUNCTIONS AND CHARGE

SECTION D: THE ORDER OF DEACONESSES

SECTION E: THE LAY OFFICERS OF THE CHURCH

SECTION F: THINGS APPERTAINING TO CHURCHES

SECTION G: THE ECCLESIASTICAL COURTS

SECTION H: THE SYNODS OF THE CHURCH

Table of Canons of the Roman Catholic Code

BOOK I: GENERAL NORMS

BOOK II: THE PEOPLE OF GOD

Part I: The Christian Faithful

Part II: The Hierarchical Constitution of the Church

Section I: The Supreme Authority of the Church

Section II: Particular Churches and Their Groupings

Part III: Institutes of Consecrated Life and Societies of Apostolic Life

Part II: Other Acts of Divine Worship

Part III: Sacred Places and Times

BOOK V: TEMPORAL GOODS OF THE CHURCH

BOOK VI: SANCTIONS IN THE CHURCH

Part I: Offences and Penalties in General

Part II: Penalties for Specific Offences

BOOK VII: PROCESSES

Part I: Trials in General

Part II: The Contentious Trial

Table of Cases

Introduction

This book is about the use of regulation in the Church of England. It studies ecclesiastical regulation on three levels: descriptive, evaluative, and comparative. On the descriptive level, the book examines the law created by state institutions on ecclesiastical matters and the law internally made by the church to regulate itself. It is increasingly the case that the internal and formal legal system of the Church of England is being supplemented through regulations created by authorities acting executively at both national and diocesan levels. As well as the church's formal law, the book attempts to describe this ecclesiastical quasi-legislation, operative within the legal framework of the church (and frequently designed to fill gaps in it). On the evaluative level, the study questions critically central areas of church law and practice, particularly in terms of their purpose, clarity, and comprehensiveness. In this context it seeks to elucidate the degree to which areas of church life are regulated, the extent to which they are not the subject of regulation, and the extent to which areas have been de-regulated: in short, it aims to assess whether or not the church employs a minimalist approach to its own regulation. On the comparative level, the book examines both the relationship between internally made law and external state-made law and the relationship between the law of the Church of England and key elements of Roman Catholic canon law, as found principally in that church's Code of Canon Law 1983. Concerning comparisons with Roman Catholic canon law, the study explores and emphasizes substantive similarities and differences, not least in terms of clarity and comprehensiveness, and whether the law and practice of the Church of England present standards equivalent to those appearing in the western canonical tradition represented in Roman Catholic canon law.

Only the central areas of church life and law are examined. The book is not an exhaustive account of ecclesiastical regulation and readers will doubtless find important omissions. In both the formal law and the ecclesiastical quasi-legislation only two general but fundamental sets of legal ideas are investigated: facility and order, and power and its control. Part I attempts to elucidate the main elements of canonical jurisprudence—the nature, forms, and purposes of ecclesiastical regulation. Part II deals with ecclesiastical government—the distribution and control of legislative, administrative, and judicial powers in the church. Part III analyses ecclesiastical ministry—the bishop's central position of oversight and the distribution of individual rights and duties as between ordained and lay people in the church. Part IV examines the law regulating the formation of doctrine, duties of assent to it, and the

formation and control of liturgy. Part V deals with the ministrations of the
church, particularly rights of admission and powers of exclusion, and Part VI
describes regulation of church property and finance.

The book is designed to complement existing literature on the law of the
Church of England, particularly Mark Hill's recent and excellent *Ecclesiastical Law* (1995), a stimulating and trenchant commentary and a wide-ranging
source of materials. Garth Moore's *Introduction to English Canon Law* (1993
edition), edited by Timothy Briden and Brian Hanson, provides an excellent
and up-to-date general and introductory account of the subject's key areas.
Sir William Dale's *Law of the Parish Church* (1989 edition), Kenneth
McMorran, Garth Moore, and Timothy Briden's *Handbook for Churchwardens and Parochial Church Councillors* (1989 edition), and John Pitchford's
An ABC for the PCC (1993 edition) provide first-class accounts of those
subjects. Newsom's *Faculty Jurisdiction of the Church of England* (1993
edition) is a leading work on that subject—observations made in the
following studies on faculty law are deliberately short as a result. Volume
14 of Halsbury's *Laws of England, Ecclesiastical Law* (1975), though still an
important reference work, is in need of general revision. Yet these books are
predominantly descriptive and contain little critical and more often than not
no comparative material. The *Ecclesiastical Law Journal*, the journal of the
Ecclesiastical Law Society founded in 1987, is an invaluable source and its
studies on contemporary church law, especially, represent significant contributions to a more detailed understanding of particular subjects.

An attempt has been made throughout the studies to present both a practical
and a jurisprudential overview of ecclesiastical regulation. Whilst the book is
not intended as an exhaustive analysis of Roman Catholic canon law, com-
plemented as this is by its own abundant, rich, and distinctive literature, it is
hoped that the studies may be of some interest to Roman Catholics and
Anglicans alike. Although the study of comparative canon law has not made
its mark extensively—comparisons of the two churches at a canonical level
have to date not been opened up—the exercise is instructive in so far as it both
exposes the extent to which problems are shared and identifies often common
solutions. In most areas detailed comparisons may be made: sometimes,
however, with respect to each church, comparisons may not be sustained
beyond the conclusion that no equivalent provision exists in the other
church; this vacuum is most evident in relation to property, where the Roman
Catholic Church's code of canon law contains only minimal regulation of
property matters. For the purposes of the Church of England the book is
primarily aimed at the practitioners of church law, not only its users, lawyers
and administrators, but also its planners, at all levels of church government.
Needless to say, it is hoped that conveying the flexibility which law and quasi-
legislation affords in pastoral practice will prove of interest to those engaged in

parochial ordained and lay ministry. Indeed, in the wide sense, the studies here concern the regulation of the church's ministry in nearly all its aspects.

One or two points may be made at this stage concerning the important question of the role of regulation generally within the church, a role which remains, perhaps necessarily, controversial. The church is both a dynamic, spiritual community and a visible organization (but not a business) charged with a mission to society and to the world. In turn, ecclesiastical regulation is an organic function of the church seeking not to hinder but to assist the church in the fulfilment of its mission. A study of regulation in the Church of England, therefore, informs about one way in which the church has decided to organize itself. The following studies explore this, particularly in the light of the church's established position and the occasional ambivalence within its own legal structures between synodical government and episcopal authority and control. Whilst its mission may ideally be effected by prayer and by agreement, the church has chosen to use rules as a means to enable the fulfilment of its mission and as a means to deal with problems arising in the course of so doing. In consequence, although the studies in this book seek to describe, where appropriate, theological and historical themes underlying particular legal arrangements, this is not its main concern. Nonetheless, it is often important to question the theology behind a given rule or to ask whether a rule expresses accurately a particular theological conviction, whether it allows for and facilitates pastoral and spiritual freedom or, rather, whether it is spiritually oppressive or restrictive. To convey the legitimacy of regulation as a function of the church much work still needs to be done on the theological and pastoral roots of ecclesiastical regulation.

What is certain is that the law and practice examined here indicate how the Church of England considers itself, its nature and programme in society and its internal justness. In this respect, however, an evaluative approach is problematic. Needless to say, the Church of England ought to be a just society and its laws ought to be just laws. In so far as the law may be assumed to express a particular, but ever-shifting, idea of ecclesiastical justice, many of the criteria used for criticism here may rightly be seen as subjective. For this reason, criticisms of a moral kind are kept to a minimum: only those expressing formal inequality, discrimination, lack of clarity, or impracticality are considered. The basic assumption is that, as with any legal system, ecclesiastical regulation ought to be characterized by certainty, predictability, coherence, and clarity. It is crucial to determine the workability of ecclesiastical rules and it is hoped that some of the studies here will stimulate a wider debate on this problem. Moreover, beyond questions of internal ecclesiastical justice and utility, as church regulation lives in a wider environment, its standards ought not to fall below those required by the state. The comparative element of the book, therefore, seeks also to set the church's internal rules against the external standards of the civil legal system. The converse is not explored in this book.

On all three levels, descriptive, evaluative, and comparative, the book is intended not to close questions but to open them. The following study is merely an attempt to stimulate a more critical understanding of church law in its comparative context.

PART I
Canonical Jurisprudence

1

The Church and Forms of Regulation

The Church of England, a church by law established, is regulated by a large body of rules located in a multiplicity of different instruments. On one hand, the legal framework of the Church of England subsists in formal legal texts created not only by the church's internal legislators but also by the state, and technical terms have been devised to classify these as canon law and ecclesiastical law. On the other hand, many regulatory instruments governing the church exist outside formal texts legislated by the church and state: these have been devised to supplement the formal system of church law and may be classified as ecclesiastical quasi-legislation. The Roman Catholic Church, which is not formally established in the same sense as the Church of England, is regulated similarly by internally made canon law and by rules legislated by the state. For both churches the degree to which regulatory instruments are binding and enforceable depends on the status of the instrument in question. Jurisprudentially, the fundamental authority underlying internally made church law is conceived by both churches to be divine law.

THE LEGAL POSITION OF THE CHURCH

The Church of England, 'established according to the laws of this realm under the Queen's Majesty, belongs to the true and apostolic Church of Christ'.[1] The Thirty-Nine Articles of the Church of England describe the visible Church of Christ as 'a congregation of faithful men, in which the pure Word of God is preached, and the sacraments be duly administered according to Christ's ordinance in all those things that of necessity are requisite to the same'.[2] Whilst it has been treated judicially as a denomination,[3] as a matter of law

[1] Canon A1.

[2] AR, Art. 19; see also WAOB, 1.1: 'the Church is an integral part of the mystery of God's reconciling work in his world, and an embodiment of the presence of God in his world'.

[3] R v Registrar General, ex p Segerdal [1970] 3 All ER 886 at 887 per Lord Denning; Re Perry Almshouses [1898] 1 Ch 391 at 401 per Stirling J, [1899] 1 Ch 21 at 37 (CA, per Vaughan Williams LJ); whilst the church is established, in law it possesses the marks of a denomination: for these, based on ideas of community and internal organisation, see Walsh v Lord Advocate [1956] 3 All ER 129 at 135 (HL, Jehovah's Witnesses); for religious groups classified as denominations, see Offord v Hiscock (1917) 86 LJKB 941 (Strict Baptist Church), distinguished in Nock v Malins (1917) 87 LJKB 62; Hawkes v Moxey (1917) 86 LJKB 1530 (Church of Jesus Christ of Latter Day Saints); the Seamen and Boatmen's Friends Society (Bratt v Auty (1917) 86 LJKB 305) and the Evangelisation Society (Flint v Courthorpe (1918) 87 LJKB 504) are not denominations.

it was accepted in *Re Barnes, Simpson v Barnes* (1930) that the Church of England may be defined as 'an aggregate of individuals . . . including all persons who adhere and conform to the liturgy and ordinances of the Church of England as by law established, or it may be considered as an organised operative institution'.[4] The Church of England is not a corporation as such, though institutions within it may enjoy the status of corporations sole or aggregate.[5] It may be understood broadly, however, as a 'quasi-corporate institution which carries on the religious work of the denomination whose name it bears' and, narrowly, as 'the institution which ministers religion and gives spiritual edification to the members of the Church of England'.[6] The Church of England consists of 'the lay as well as the clerical members of the community'.[7]

Expressing the relationship between the church and the state,[8] establishment has been understood judicially as meaning action by a state 'to grant legal status, recognition or protection' to a church, 'to confer on a religion or religious body the position of a state religion or a state church', 'to support a church in the observance of its ordinances and doctrines', and 'to found or set up a new church or religion'; full establishment may involve duties on the state and the citizen to maintain the established church as well as legal protection to the exclusion of other religious communities.[9] The Church of England is not an established church in all of these senses.[10] First, whilst there is no 'Establishment Act' as such, the institutional Church of England has been formed at least in part by a series of direct legislative acts of the civil power—though the Reformation legislation of the sixteenth century is often seen as part of a

---

[4] [1930] 2 Ch 80 at 81 *per* Romer J.

[5] As we shall see elsewhere in this study, bodies and persons enjoying legal personality as corporations include incumbents and bishops, parochial church councils, cathedral capitular bodies, diocesan boards of finance, the Church Commissioners, and General Synod's Central Finance Board.

[6] *Re Barnes, Simpson v Barnes*, see fn. 4, at 81, adopting the idea expressed in *MacLaughlin v Campbell* [1906] I IR 588 at 597 *per* FitzGibbon LJ and used in *Re Schoales* [1930] 2 Ch 75 at 78.

[7] *R v Dibdin* [1910] P 57 at 136 *per* Farwell J (CA); for concepts of membership see *post* Ch. 8.

[8] R. Davies, 'Church and state', *Cambrian Law Review*, 7 (1976), 11; A. Vidler, 'The relations of church and state with special reference to England', *Quis Custodiet*, 30 (1971), 6; strictly, there is no legal entity of 'state' in the United Kingdom, though the judges have recognized a 'political organisation which is the basis of civil government' which they describe loosely as 'the state': *D v NSPCC* [1978] AC 171 at 235–6 *per* Lord Simon; for the idea of the Crown as representing the state see *Chandler v DPP* [1964] AC 763.

[9] *AG (Victoria) ex rel Black v Commonwealth* (1981) 146 CLR 559 at 595–7 (H Ct Australia) *per* Gibbs J; relying on *General Assembly of the Free Church of Scotland v Lord Overton* [1904] AC 515 (HL), Barwick CJ explained at 582: 'establishing a religion involves the entrenchment of a religion as a feature of and identified with the body politic . . . [and] the identification of the religion with the civil authority so as to involve the citizen in a duty to maintain it and the obligation of . . . the Commonwealth to patronize, protect and promote the established religion.'

[10] St J. A. Robilliard, *Religion and the Law: Religious Liberty in Modern English Law* (Manchester, 1984) 84 ff; M. H. Ogilvie, 'What is a church by law established?', *Osgoode Hall Law Journal*, 28 (1990), 179.

process which may have begun considerably earlier.[11] Secondly, in consequence, the principle of establishment means that the Church of England,
established by law, is treated legally as 'the public or state-recognised form
of religion'.[12] As explained in *Marshall v Graham*, '[a] Church which is
established is not thereby made a department of State. The process of establishment means that the State has accepted the Church as a religious body in its
opinion truly teaching the Christian faith, and given to it a certain legal
position, and its decrees, if rendered under certain legal conditions, certain
legal sanctions'.[13] Thirdly, as we shall see in the following chapters, the terms
or incidents of establishment are expressed in the fact that state-made law
places upon the Church of England a series of rights and duties which are not
applicable to other churches.[14]

Fourthly, establishment is produced by a fundamental identification of the
Church of England with the state, the monarch being head of each: 'the
Queen's excellent Majesty, acting according to the laws of the realm, is the
highest power under God in the kingdom, and has supreme authority over all
persons in all causes, as well ecclesiastical as civil.'[15] As head of the Church of
England, the sovereign enjoys extensive legal functions, including the executive appointment of candidates to episcopal office and the legislative function
of consenting to some forms of ecclesiastical legislation; the sovereign is not,
however, a minister of the Word of God or of the sacraments.[16] The processes
of royal succession and admission as head of the Church of England are
governed by parliamentary statute. The heir apparent must satisfy the statutory conditions set out principally in the Act of Settlement 1700, the terms of
which are derived from the Bill of Rights 1689: the principal religious
qualification is that only candidates 'being protestants' (which is not
defined) may succeed; in fiercely unecumenical language the statute pre-

---

[11] For a survey of the basic ideas and literature see A. Hastings, *Church and State: The English
Experience* (Exeter, 1991) and C. F. Garbett, *Church and State in England* (London, 1950). For the
principal parliamentary statutes, the Act in Restraint of Appeals 1532, the Submission of the
Clergy Act 1534, the Act of Supremacy 1534, the Act in Restraint of Annates 1534, the
Ecclesiastical Licences Act 1534, see G. R. Elton, *The Tudor Constitution: Documents and
Commentary* (2nd edn., Cambridge, 1982); for an overview: *MIECL*, 10–15 and Archbishops'
Commission Reports, *Church and State* (London, 1916) 5–27, (London, 1970) 1 ff.
[12] *HLE*, para. 334.　　　[13] [1907] 2 KB 112 at 126 *per* Phillimore J.
[14] *Church and State* (London, 1952) 7: rules underpinning establishment 'embrace both "rights
and privileges" and . . . "restrictions and limitations"', though it is 'not always easy to distinguish
them'; for episcopal appointments and the entitlement of some bishops to sit in the House of Lords
see *post* Ch. 6; for parliamentary approval of synodical measures and royal approval of synodical
canons see *post* Ch. 3; whilst legally approved by the state, doctrines may be altered only in
accordance with law (*post* Ch. 9); ordained ministers are disabled from sitting in the House of
Commons (House of Commons (Clergy Disqualification) Act 1801, considered in *Re MacManaway* [1951] AC 161); see also the report of the Select Committee on Clergy Disqualification, HC
200 (1952–3). For duties to offer the church's ministrations to all parishioners see *post* Part V.
[15] Canon A7; *AR*, Art. 37; Act of Supremacy 1558, s. 8; see *Chandler v DPP* [1964] AC 764 for
the idea that the crown personifies the state.　　　[16] *AR*, Art. 37.

scribes that those who 'are or shall be reconciled to or hold communion with
the see or church of Rome or shall profess the popish religion or shall marry a
papist shall be excluded and forever incapable' of succession and therefore of
admission to headship of the church. Successors, who 'shall join in communion with the Church of England as by law established',[17] must declare at
accession that they are faithful Protestants and that they will uphold and
maintain the established church.[18] At the coronation, the successor must
take an oath promising to 'maintain the Laws of God, the true Profession of
the Gospel and the Protestant reformed religion established by Law'.[19] The
duty to administer the oath is placed on either 'the Archbishop of Canterbury,
or the Archbishop of York, or either of them, or any other bishop of this realm,
whom the [Sovereign] shall thereunto appoint, and who shall be, hereby
thereunto respectively authorised'.[20]

Whilst fundamental differences in the respective legal positions of the two
churches may not be overlooked, the position of the Roman Catholic Church
under domestic secular law is in some respects similar to that of the Church of
England in terms of broad concepts of establishment. Theologically and under
its own canon law, the church is conceived as a single complex reality, a
mystery which is both a spiritual and a human society, composed of the people
of God and ordered hierarchically.[21] The pontiff, elected to a position of
primacy, is the successor of Peter, head of the College of Bishops and pastor
of the whole Roman Catholic Church on earth enjoying ordinary, supreme,
full, immediate, and universal authority.[22] According to domestic secular law
the Roman Catholic Church is a denomination, like the Church of England, a
'quasi-corporate institution consisting of those individuals who carry on the

[17] ss. 1, 2, 3; royal marriages of heirs, and the necessary consents, are governed by the Royal
Marriages Act 1770: see *post* Ch. 13.

[18] Accession Declaration Act 1910, Sched: 'I [here insert the name of the Sovereign] do
solemnly and sincerely in the presence of God profess, testify and declare that I am a faithful
Protestant, and that I will, according to the true intent of the enactments which secure the
Protestant succession to the Throne of my Realm, uphold and maintain the said enactments to
the best of my powers according to law'; see P. E. Schramm, *A History of the English Coronation*
(1937).

[19] Coronation Oath Act 1689, s. 3; the successor also promises to 'preserve unto the Bishops
and Clergy of this Realm, and to the Churches committed to their Charge, all such Rights and
Privileges as by Law do or shall appertain unto them, or any of them'.

[20] Ibid., s. 2; it is arguable that an archbishop is obliged to administer the oath if required by the
successor to do so pursuant to the oath of allegiance taken to the Crown; the same applies to a
bishop instructed to do so by the successor or by an archbishop under the obligation of due
obedience to the archbishop: see *post* Ch. 6; though not listed amongst the authorized services of
the Church of England, the essentials of the ancient coronation rite, based on customary practice,
are found in the *Liber Regalis* (in the custody of the Dean of Westminster).

[21] *LG* (1965) I, 1, 7, 8; III; *CIC*, c. 204; see more fully *post* Ch. 2.

[22] *CIC*, cc. 331, 333; the pope acquires office by ordination as a bishop and by his acceptance of
his election by the college of cardinals (c. 332(1)); customarily the pope serves for life but may
freely resign (c. 332(2)); see the Apostolic Constitution *Romano Pontifici eligendo* (1975), I (for
the power of government vested in the sacred college of cardinals during a vacancy in the apostolic
see) and II (for the election procedures): *COCLA*, 1091 ff.

Roman Catholic religion'.[23] As such it exists legally as a consensual society classified as a voluntary religious association whose members are organised and bound together as a matter of contract.[24] Whilst the Holy See enjoys international personality as a non-territorial institution, 'a subject of international law capable of international rights and obligations',[25] there is no formal and express concordat between the Crown and the Roman Catholic Church in England.[26] Yet, whereas domestically the Roman Catholic Church has been recognized both at common law and in parliamentary statute,[27] and may therefore be said (according to judicial definitions) to be established in a loose sense, its precise legal standing remains obscure. The Ecclesiastical Titles Act 1871 prescribes that the church's hierarchy and government, re-introduced in 1850,[28] and its enjoyment of coercive jurisdiction are not rendered lawful by the terms of that statute but depend for their legality upon royal approval.[29] Its present legal position seems to rest, therefore, on the basis of a tacit concordat with the Crown. In any event, most of the legal disabilities which Roman Catholics suffered as a result of the English Reformation have disappeared and the Roman Catholic Church enjoys the same legal freedoms as any other religious community in England.[30] Moreover,

---

[23] *R v Registrar General, ex p Segerdal* [1970] 3 All ER 886 at 887; *Re Schoales* [1930] 2 Ch 75 at 77 *per* Bennett J; for recognition of its 'membership' see *Re Allen, Faith v Allen* [1953] 1 Ch 810 at 821; for membership concepts under its canon law see *post* Ch. 8.

[24] *Buckley v Cahal Daly* (1990) NIJB 8; the notion of the church as a 'voluntary association' also appears in the works of some Roman Catholic canonists: see e.g. J. A. Coriden, 'The canonical doctrine of reception', *The Jurist*, 50 (1990), 58 at 60.

[25] *CIC*, c. 361: 'Apostolic See' or 'Holy See' include the pontiff and the papal Secretariat of State; whilst the Vatican City is a territorial state recognized as such in international law, the Holy See is a non-territorial entity enjoying legal personality: J. G. Starke, *Introduction to International Law* (9th edn., London, 1984) 65, n. 13, 109; P. Ciprotti, 'The Holy See: its function, form and status in international law', *Concilium*, 8(6) (1970), 63; the Holy See is a 'non-typical' subject of international law: G. Schwarzenberger and E. D. Brown, *A Manual of International Law* (6th edn., Professional Books, 1976) 62–3; J. L. Kunz, 'The status of the Holy See in international law', *American Journal of International Law*, 46 (1952), 308.

[26] *CIC*, c. 3 (this recognizes the validity and continuing authority of pre–1983 concordats and their superiority over the terms of the 1983 code); see A. de Jong, 'Concordats and international law', *Concilium*, 8(6) (1970), 104; for doctrinal statements by Vatican II concerning the value of concordats to secure religious freedom and as a compromise between two sovereignties see *DH* (1965) II, 13, *GES* (1965) IV, 76 and J. C. Otero, 'Church-state relations in the light of Vatican II', *Concilium*, 8(6) (1970), 113. There is no concordat in Ireland (see J. Casey, *Constitutional Law in Ireland* (2nd edn., London, 1992) 553 ff; whilst the Roman Catholic Church is not established in Italy, church–state relations are governed by the Lateran Concordat (1984) and the Italian civil constitution: see G. L. Certoma, *The Italian Legal System* (London, 1985) 118–124.

[27] See above nn. 23, 24 and *post* Chs. 9, 13, and 16 for statutory recognition (under e.g. the Sharing of Church Buildings Act 1969 and the Marriage Act 1949).

[28] For the process of re-introduction up to 1850 see e.g. E. R. Norman, *Roman Catholicism in England* (Oxford, 1985), J. Bossy, *The English Catholic Community* (London, 1975).

[29] Preamble and s. 1, repealing the Ecclesiastical Titles Act 1851; *AR*, Art. 37: 'The Bishop of Rome hath no jurisdiction in this Realm of England.'

[30] Roman Catholics may under the Roman Catholic Relief Act 1829 hold seats in parliament (with the exception of priests in the Commons: House of Commons (Clergy Disqualification) Act 1801, s. 2) and under the Roman Catholic Charities Act 1832 they may hold property for religious, educational, or charitable purposes; Roman Catholic priests are exempted from jury service (Juries Act 1974, s. 1, Sched. I, Pt. 1); see generally St J. A. Robilliard, *Religion and the Law* (1984) 199–203.

whilst the Roman Catholic Church and the Church of England are not in full communion with each other,[31] both churches recognize each other's ministries for certain purposes.[32]

The expressions *canon law* and *ecclesiastical law*, classically employed to designate law applicable to the church, have been used so inconsistently that the definition of each is now extremely problematic. Definitions have been constructed around a variety of criteria, including subject-matter, sources, the institutions which create, administer, or enforce canon or ecclesiastical law, and ecclesiological propositions about the purposes for which the church exists. The absence of agreed criteria has resulted in a plethora of divergent definitions. In point of fact, inconsistency is present in both Roman Catholic and Church of England usage.

Canon Law One usage in the Church of England and the Roman Catholic Church treats 'canon law' as that law which a church creates, through its law-making bodies, for its own internal management. For the Roman Catholic Ladislas Örsy, '[c]anon law is principally concerned with the practical life of the Church and of every Christian' and contains 'norms of action for the whole community and for each member'; 'it springs from the will of Christ, but its minute and detailed rules come from human agents . . . that is, the pope and the bishops'.[33] According to James Coriden '"Canon law" is a . . . descriptive title for the rules which govern the public order of the Roman Catholic Church' comprising those 'norms which describe the basic structures of the Church' and 'individual regulations' which constitute 'church discipline'.[34] The Scottish Court of Session in *Daly v The Commissioners of Inland*

---

[31] See Common Declarations of Pope Paul VI and Archbishop Donald Coggan, 29 Apr. 1977, and of Pope John Paul II and the Archbishop of Canterbury Robert Runcie, 29 May 1982 (*Flannery*, I, 452f); see *Final Report* (1982) of the Anglican–Roman Catholic International Commission (ARCIC I), established following the 1982 meeting to enable dialogue to resolve outstanding doctrinal differences between the two churches, and ARCIC II, *Salvation and the Church* (1987), *Church as Communion* (1991); for the purposes of Roman Catholic canon law full communion is effected by joining in the visible structures of the church in its governmental, sacramental, and teaching life: see *post* Ch. 8; the Church of England possesses no formal canonical concept of communion (see, however, *post* Ch. 7).

[32] Whilst there is no legislation as such promulgated by the Roman Catholic bishops of England and Wales for local ecumenical activity, see the Church of England's *Ecumenical Relations Code of Practice* (1989) 37 for the Roman Catholic bishops' official response to the *Ten Proposals for Christian Unity* (1977); for the Roman Catholic Church's denial of Anglican orders see *post* Ch. 7; for liturgical ecumenism see *post* Ch. 10 and Part V; ecumenical activity is also exhorted by Vatican II: *UR* (1964) and by *Ecumenical Collaboration* (1975) published by the Vatican's Secretariat for Promoting Christian Unity: *PB*, Arts. 135–8, *COCLA*, 1241.

[33] 'Towards a theological conception of canon law', *Readings*, 10 at 11.

[34] *An Introduction to Canon Law* (London, 1991) 3–4.

Revenue (1934) adopted the proposition in relation to the Roman Catholic Church that '[t]he government of the Church, the acquisition of property by the Church, the administration of Church property and income, and the rights and duties of priests, are regulated by (first) canon law'.[35] Roman Catholic canonists also subscribe to the idea that canon law governs 'the external order of the church, the public life of the faith community'—it does not 'attempt to measure or compel personal conscience or moral judgments'.[36] In the Church of England 'canon law' has been understood narrowly as 'the domestic law of the Church—the code of faith, morals and discipline',[37] subsisting simply in the canons promulged by the Convocations of Canterbury and York in 1964 and 1969 and by the General Synod from 1970,[38] as 'directives for the guidance of the Church in ecclesiastical matters'.[39] By way of contrast, Garth Moore has defined 'canon law' widely 'as so much of the law of England as is concerned with the regulation of the affairs of the Church of England'; Moore's lists of sources comprising 'canon law' include both church-made and state-made law applicable to the Church of England as well as divine law.[40] Sometimes canon law is treated judicially as part of the law of the land; sometimes the two are distinguished.[41]

Ecclesiastical Law Several different meanings have been assigned to 'ecclesiastical law' by commentators, by common law judges, and by the ecclesiastical judges without, needless to say, any agreed definitional criteria. First, ecclesiastical law has been defined as *law created for the church by God and by the church.* For the Roman Catholic Georg May '[e]cclesiastical law is distinguished according to its origin either as divine or as human law', divine law composed of that set of 'norms . . . laid down by God' for the church and '[h]uman law (purely ecclesiastical law) is either the result of legislation or custom'.[42]Roman Catholics sometimes use the terms

[35] [1934] 18 Tax Cas 641, [1934] SC 44.

[36] Coriden, *Introduction*, 4; *CIC*, c. 130: 'The power of governance is normally exercised in the external forum, but sometimes it is exercised in the internal forum only, but in such a way that the effects which its exercise normally has in the external forum are not acknowledged in this forum except as is established by law in certain instances'; see *post* Chs. 9 and 12 for exceptions to the general rule.

[37] Bishop of Chester, debate on Holy Table Measure 1964, HL Debs, Vol 256 (1964) 1131.

[38] *Bland v Archdeacon of Cheltenham* [1972] 1 All ER 1012; *Re Atkins* [1989] 1 All ER 14 at 16. [39] *HLE*, para. 308.

[40] *MIECL*, 2, 8.

[41] For pre-Reformation canon law as part of the law of the land see *Bishopwearmouth (Rector and Churchwardens) v Adey* [1958] 3 All ER 441. For the distinction between canon law and common law see *Merker v Merker* [1963] 3 All ER 928 (relating to pre-Reformation canon law and common law on marriage); *AG v Trustees of the Howard United Reformed Church, Bedford* [1975] QB 41; *R v Cripps, ex p Muldoon* [1984] 1 QB 68; *Holy Trinity Church v Commissioners of Customs and Excise* (1984) (Manchester VAT Tribunal) MAN/83/58, Transcript 26/1/84; the Manchester Con. Ct. in *Re Holy Innocents, Fallowfield* [1983] Fam 135 considered uses of church buildings as 'not contrary either to the law of the land or to canon law'.

[42] 'Ecclesiastical law', in K. Rahner (ed.), *Encyclopedia of Theology* (London, 1981) 395.

ecclesiastical law and canon law interchangeably. For May: '[e]cclesiastical law, or canon law, [is] the entirety of the norms of the law laid down by God and by the church'.[43] Both Pope John Paul II and the Roman Catholic code of canon law itself employ 'ecclesiastical law' to denote the whole of the internal law of the church,[44] within which Ladislas Örsy distinguishes '"[m]erely ecclesiastical laws" . . . human laws enacted by an ecclesiastical legislator' from 'ecclesiastical laws which are also articulations of divine laws'. So: many norms for the celebration of the Eucharist are mere ecclesiastical laws; that the Church should celebrate the Eucharist is a divine law'.[45] Secondly, ecclesiastical law has been defined as *law created by the state for the church*, a European practice favoured by some Anglican canonists: as Thomas Watkin suggests, in this respect 'ecclesiastical law made by the State for the [Church of England] therefore encompasses the canon law as well'.[46] However, the Roman Catholic Peter Huizing distinguishes the 'internal public ecclesiastical law or the basic juridical relations within the Church' and the 'external public ecclesiastical law or the juridical relations between Church and State', the latter being law created by the state for the church, 'the law made by the civilian legislator which deals with the ecclesiastical associations existing in that territory'.[47] Thirdly, some writers distinguish ecclesiastical law from law made for the church by the state: for Georg May 'laws of the state which regulate church affairs', most especially if the church is established, 'are civil and not ecclesiastical law'.[48]

Fourthly, ecclesiastical law has been defined as *the law of the Church of England* to the exclusion of all other law applicable to other churches. Defined widely, '[t]he term "ecclesiastical law" . . . means the law relating to any matter concerning the Church of England administered and enforced in any court', temporal or ecclesiastical.[49] This definition was employed in *AG v Dean and Chapter of Ripon Cathedral*: for Uthwatt J ecclesiastical law is a single body of law although 'jurisdiction as to its enforcement is divided between the ecclesiastical courts and the temporal courts. . . . The unity and coherence of the law is not affected by the division of jurisdiction as to its enforcement.'[50] One consequence of this understanding, the enforceability of ecclesiastical law in both civil and church courts, is the principle, enunciated by the Court of Appeal in *Kirkham v Chief Constable of Manchester*, that

---

[43] 'Ecclesiastical law', in K. Rahner (ed.), *Encyclopedia of Theology* (London, 1981) 395.
[44] Apostolic Constitution *Sacrae Disciplinae Leges* (1983) issued on the promulgation of the 1983 Code (*COCLA*, 47 at 55); *CIC*, Bk I, Title 1 (*de legibus ecclesiasticis*).
[45] *CCL: TC*, 31.
[46] T. G. Watkin, 'Vestiges of establishment: the ecclesiastical and canon law of the Church in Wales', *ELJ*, 2 (1990), 110 at 111; for this view see also Q. Edwards, 'The canon law of the Church of England: its implications for unity', *ELJ*, 1(3) (1988), 18.
[47] 'Church and state in public ecclesiastical law', *Concilium*, 8(6) (1970), 126.
[48] 'Ecclesiastical law', 395.   [49] *HLE*, para. 301.
[50] [1945] Ch 239 at 245; adopted in *Re St Mary of Charity, Faversham* [1986] 1 All ER 1 at 9.

'ecclesiastical law . . . is part of the general law of England'.[51] As Lord Blackburn explained in *Mackonochie v Lord Penzance*, 'ecclesiastical law is not a foreign law. It is part of the general law of England—of the common law—in that wider sense'.[52] The principle has been adopted judicially on several occasions.[53] Ecclesiastical law has also been defined narrowly 'in the sense of law administered by ecclesiastical courts and persons', in the Church of England, 'and not by the temporal courts'.[54] On other occasions, however, judges have described the law applied by church courts generally as 'canon law',[55] whilst some treat ecclesiastical law as distinct by virtue of the special sanctions and remedies available on its breach.[56] As well as confusing the distinction between ecclesiastical and canon law,[57] the use in these definitions of a concept of actual judicial enforcement suggests that any rule of ecclesiastical (or canon) law not enforced ceases to enjoy the status of law: this is untenable, as any rule enjoying a formal mark of validity which is capable of enforcement by judicial or executive action possesses the quality of law; moreover, many legal arrangements are merely facultative or descriptive by nature and the question of their enforcement does not ordinarily arise.[58]

General Law A third category of law operative in the ecclesiastical context is *general law*, law created by the state which is applicable to a religious community in both its internal affairs and its relations with outside bodies. This idea was used in *AG v Dean and Chapter of Ripon Cathedral* with respect to the Church of England: general law is 'a body of law concerning the Church of England which does not form part of ecclesiastical law'.[59] State-made law applicable to the Roman Catholic Church according to these definitions is therefore general law and not ecclesiastical law, though sometimes the general law may have developed from internally made church law.[60]

---

[51] [1990] 2 QB 283 at 292 *per* Lloyd LJ.   [52] (1881) 6 App Cas 424 at 446.

[53] *R v Millis* (1844) 10 Cl & Fin 680; *Hyde v Tameside Area Health Authority* [1981] *Times* 15/4/81; *Secretary of State for Trade and Industry v Langbridge* [1991] Ch 402.

[54] *AG v Dean and Chapter of Ripon Cathedral* [1945] Ch 239 at 244; adopted in *R v Chancellor of St Edmondsbury and Ipswich, ex p White* [1948] 1 KB 195 at 221 *per* Evershed LJ.

[55] *Hadkinson v Hadkinson* [1952] P 285 (CA: 'a rule of canon law which was adopted by the ecclesiastical courts'); *R v Imam of Bury Park* (1991) *Independent* 13/9/91 (the consistory court was spoken of as 'a body . . . concerned with canon law').

[56] A. T. Denning, 'The meaning of "ecclesiasical law"', 60 *LQR* (1944) 235.

[57] J. H. Blunt, *The Book of Church Law* (London, 1899) 12: 'The Canon Law. This is the distinctively ecclesiastical law, consisting of the canons which have been passed in national and provincial synods, and of such foreign canons of the same description as have been adopted by custom and common law into our domestic system.'

[58] The idea is a standard one in civil jurisprudence; see e.g. C. Munro, 'Laws and conventions distinguished', *LQR*, 91 (1975), 218; for the purposes of canon law and the *cessante causa cessat lex* principle, see *post* Ch. 2.

[59] See fn. 54, at 244–5; for the distinction between 'ecclesiastical law' and 'general law' or 'common law' see also *Tithe Redemption Commission v Welsh Church Commissioners* [1944] 1 All ER 710 (HL).

[60] *R v R* [1992] 1 AC 599 (CA: the pre-existing marital exemption concerning rape within marriage under common law was treated as 'derived from the canon law'); *Rance v Mid-Downs*

For the purposes of understanding generally, and ecumenical dialogue in particular, the inherited confusion surrounding the technical definitions of canon law, ecclesiastical law, and general law poses a special problem. In the remainder of this book, therefore, laws are designated by their source, form, and juridical authority. The term 'church law' is used to cover both internal church-made law and secular state-made law: the term 'ecclesiastical law' is generally avoided. The expression 'law of the Church of England' is used to mean only law made internally by the Church of England, classified according to the various forms of regulatory instrument described in the following section. With respect to the Roman Catholic Church, the term 'canon law' is used to signify internal law as stated in the 1983 Code; any provision found outside the Code is described according to the classification given by the church authority responsible for making it. From the foregoing observations, and from those about the purpose of ecclesiastical regulation described in Chapter 2, the definition of church law in modern legal vocabulary ought to include references to the following properties: *institutional sources*: church law is law made for a church by itself, by the state, or by God; *purposes*: church law is law which seeks, depending on the intent of its makers, to facilitate and order the organization and management of a church; *subject-matter*: church law is law which deals with the public, constitutional, pastoral, doctrinal, sacramental, economic, and proprietorial aspects of church life; *nature*: church law is a hierarchical system of rules, principles, and norms, expressed as prescriptive or descriptive, mandatory or directory, duty-imposing or rights-conferring, normative or facultative; *enforceability*: church law is that law which is enforceable judicially and executively and alongside which many regulatory instruments operate in the form of ecclesiastical quasi-legislation, the enforceability of which is often unclear.

FORMS OF ECCLESIASTICAL REGULATION: JURIDICAL AUTHORITY

Whilst the life of the church ought not to be defined simply as compliance with or deviation from a series of legal categories,[61] often it is crucial to be able to determine with certainty whether a person or body is *bound* to perform an act (or to refrain from acting) and whether a right may be vindicated formally. Whether rights and duties are binding and enforceable depends in part at least

---

Health Authority [1991] 1 QB 587 (elements of civil law on abortion were derived from canon law); *Vervaeke v Smith* [1981] Fam 77 (canonical roots of elements of contract law); for canonical influences in marriage law see e.g. *Szechter (Otherwise Karsov) v Szechter* [1970] 3 All ER 905; *Lazarewicz (Otherwise Fadanelli) v Lazarewicz* [1962] P 171; *Marczuk v Marczuk* [1956] 1 All ER 657.

[61] Pope Paul VI, Allocution to the Second International Congress of Canon Law, Rome, 17 Sep. 1973, *Origins*, 3(17) (1973), 272.

on the juridical status and authority of the regulatory instrument which contains them.[62] In recent years both the Church of England and the Roman Catholic Church have introduced a large body of regulatory instruments which do not appear in the formal sources comprising the central legal systems of these churches. For the Church of England, this corpus of regulatory instruments, including regulations, codes of practice, and guidelines, may be classified as ecclesiastical quasi-legislation, designed to supplement the church's internally made central legal system as well as, in some cases, law created by the state.

The Church of England: Law and Quasi-Legislation

Law Secular law applicable to the Church of England includes public and private law,[63] primary legislation enacted by the Queen in Parliament, secondary legislation created by bodies under the authority of parliamentary statute, rules of the common law found in judicial decisions, fundamental guiding principles, and European law.[64] With regard to the internally made sources of the Church of England's central legal system, on one hand, rules may be properly classified as laws. Chief amongst these are *synodical measures*, the highest form of internal church law, enacted by the Church of England's central legislative body, the General Synod; they enjoy the same authority as parliamentary statutes if given state approval in the form of parliamentary and royal assent.[65] As part of the law of the land, measures bind those to whom they are addressed (both members of the church and non-members) and are enforceable judicially (in civil and ecclesiastical courts) and executively (for example by means of an episcopal order). In the resolution of cases the *decisions of ecclesiastical judges* possess the status of law. Ordinarily the *ratio* of a higher ecclesiastical court decision binds lower ecclesiastical courts, though not all decisions are law for the whole church: a provincial court decision binds only that province, a diocesan court decision only that diocese. The decisions of the ecclesiastical courts generate judicially and executively enforceable rules. However, in a conflict between a judicially made rule and a synodical measure (or parliamentary statute) the latter prevails (although clear

---

[62] It also depends on the jurisdictional competence of the proposed agent of enforcement (see *post* Part II) and the words of the instrument (see *post* Ch. 2).

[63] The distinction between 'public' and 'private' law, though difficult to draw, is much used and discussed today: H. Woolf, 'Public law—private law: why the divide?', *PL* (1986), 220; J. Beatson, '"Public" and "Private" in administrative law', *LQR*, 103 (1987), 34; the Church of England is ordinarily governed e.g. by the law of contract, the law of trusts and so on.

[64] See P. Moore, 'Legal references: a simple guide', *ELJ*, 3 (1994), 183.

[65] Measures are classed here as internal church law: their preambles present them as legislation of General Synod, not as state-made law ('A Measure passed by the General Synod of the Church of England'). For the governing legislation, the Church of England Assembly (Powers) Act 1919 and the Synodical Government Measure 1969, see *post* Ch. 3.

and express words are generally required). If there is a conflict between ecclesiastical common law and secular judge-made common law, ecclesiastical judges are not strictly bound by the latter.[66] Some sources, which are recognized as fundamental to ecclesiastical order but cannot be traced back clearly to legislation or decisions of the ecclesiastical courts, may be classified as *general* or *fundamental guiding principles*. The constitutional ideas of the 'separation of powers' and the 'rule of law', by which ecclesiastical government must be carried out according to law, and the 'doctrines of judicial precedent' have been treated judicially as if they were law of the Church of England.[67] Some fundamental principles may have the status of legal fictions.[68]

Within the terms of the Church of England's own legal system, *canons* are pieces of delegated or secondary legislation created with royal assent by the General Synod under the power conferred upon it by measure. As such, canons ordinarily enjoy an authority inferior to synodical measures: if a canon conflicts with a measure, the measure prevails; primarily, canons bind only the clergy and are enforceable both judicially (in the ecclesiastical and civil courts) and executively.[69] In addition to canons a wide range of other forms of secondary legislation may be created by bodies under the authority of a parent synodical measure in the form of 'rules', 'regulations', 'schemes', 'orders', and other instruments enjoying the same status as Statutory Instruments or Orders in Council under secular law. Although these usually have an inferior status, they sometimes enjoy the same authority as a synodical measure.[70] The central *doctrinal and liturgical documents* of the Church of England, the Thirty-Nine Articles of Religion, the Book of Common Prayer, and other service books, contain rules and rubrics imposing obligations and conferring rights. In so far as these texts have been approved by synodical measure or canon, the rules and rubrics they contain are enforceable executively and judicially, although their norms are sometimes described as directory rather than mandatory. Doctrinal and liturgical norms in these texts will be overriden

---

[66] *Re St Mary's, Banbury* [1985] 2 All ER 611 at 615 *per* Boydell Ch (Oxford Con. Ct.): 'Although Acts of Parliament may directly override the common law or the canon law, the courts have generally held that clear and express words are required to do so'; *R v Chancellor of St Edmundsbury v Ipswich Diocese, ex p White* [1948] 1 KB 195 at 204 *per* Wrottesley LJ: 'the ecclesiastical courts are not bound by the decisions of the common law courts'; see generally *post* Ch. 5.

[67] See e.g. *Re St Mary's Barnes* [1982] 1 All ER 456 at 458 *per* Moore Ch; *R v Archbishop of Canterbury* [1944] 1 All ER 179 at 182 *per* Greene MR.

[68] See e.g. *post* Ch. 13 for the so-called 'right to marry in the parish church' and Ch. 16 for the fiction of consecration concerning centres licensed for worship.

[69] Synodical Government Measure 1969, ss. 1,2; canons will be overriden by general law and measures only if this is expressly provided for: *Re St Mary's, Banbury* [1985], see fn. 66, at 615; *R v Dibdin* [1910] P 57 at 120; see Chs. 7 and 8 for the binding effect of canons on clergy and lay office-holders.   [70] See *post* Ch. 3.

by conflicting synodical measures or canons.[71] Finally, some of the central law of the Church of England is found in the *pre-Reformation canon law* whose continuing authority and applicability is dependent upon conformity with the royal prerogative, the laws, statutes, and customs of the realm, and its incorporation (through recognition and continuous usage) into the laws of the land; if incorporated the rule is enforceable in both civil and ecclesiastical courts as *custom*.[72]

Quasi-Legislation On the other hand, the Church of England has a large body of regulatory instruments, created as a matter of administrative practice, which do not *prima facie* exhibit the formal marks of law possessed by the sources described above. Increasingly in the Church of England, authorities are regulating subjects not by means of laws comprising the orthodox sources of the church's central legal system but by 'regulations',[73] 'codes of practice',[74] 'circulars',[75] and 'guidelines'[76] issued by a host of ecclesiastical authorities either centrally or at diocesan level. Commonly these instruments, dealing with an extensive range of ecclesiastical matters (from clergy appraisal and sacramental discipline to property matters), contain rules, principles, and

[71] For rubrics treated as statutory rules see *Kemp v Wickes* (1809) 3 Phillim 264 at 269; *Martin v Mackonochie* (1882) 7 PD 94; cf. the distinction between directory and mandatory rubrics used in *Bishopwearmouth (Rector and Churchwardens) v Adey* [1958] 3 All ER 441; see however *R v Dibdin* [1910] P 57 at 138 *per* Farwell J (rubrics have parliamentary sanction and if a rubric and a canon conflict, the rubric prevails).

[72] *RACCL*, 362ff; *Mackonochie v Lord Penzance* (1881) 6 App Cas 424 at 446; *R v Millis* (1844) 10 Cl & Fl 534; *Bishop of Exeter v Marshall* [1868] LR 3 HL 17; see *post* Ch. 3 for criteria of validity.

[73] For diocesan regulations see Table of Abbreviations; the phenomenon has been recognized as one which may best be put on the footing of an Act of Synod: *York Journal of Convocation* (Westminister, 1976) 48 *per* Canon P. H. Boulton: 'if . . . nearly all the bishops already use diocesan regulations for areas of ecumenical experiment or cooperation, then why not pool this experience of the diocesan churches and produce a set of regulations which could be debated and issued as a non-legislative Act of Synod? This would be a classic instance of the method the Synod might adopt for the formation of Canon Law by custom and consent'; for regulations of General Synod's House of Bishops, see e.g. Bishops *Regulations for Reader Ministry*, published on behalf of the House of Bishops by the Advisory Board of Ministry (ABM Paper No. 2, 1991).

[74] Whilst these supplement synodical measures, the measure itself does not usually authorize their creation expressly: see Pastoral Measure 1983, *Code of Recommended Practice* (1983); Church of England Ecumenical Relations Measure 1988, *Ecumenical Relations: Canons B43 and B44: Code of Practice* (1989 edn.); Care of Churches and Ecclesiastical Jurisdiction Measure *Code of Practice* (1993) (4: 'The measure for which this is the Code of Practice is a major part of an agreement reached between the General Synod and the Department of the Environment' and the code here is described as a legal document); Priests (Ordination of Women) Measure 1993, *Code of Practice* (1993); cf. Incumbents (Vacation of Benefices) Measure 1977, *Code of Practice* (s. 1(1): 'It shall be the duty of the House of Bishops to draw up rules of guidance . . . and to promulgate the rules of guidance in a Code of Practice').

[75] Churches Main Committee, *The Taxation of Ministers of Religion* (Guidance Notes, Revised 1991, Circular No. 1991/15).

[76] *Public Worship in the Church of England* (1986), issued 'by the authority' of the Standing Committee of General Synod; *Liturgical Texts for Local Use: Guidelines and Copyright* (1988); Board of Mission Inter-Faith Consultative Group, *Guidelines for the Celebration of Mixed-Faith Marriages in Church* (1992).

norms imposing duties and conferring rights in order to supplement the terms of the church's central legal system, particularly to fill gaps in it. This developing ecclesiastical practice mirrors the phenomenon of 'quasi-legislation', already familiar in the secular field of administrative law, in which administrative bodies are permitted to create rules and norms either by virtue of express or implied legal authority or where there is no legal prohibition against their creation.[77] Whilst the precise extent to which ecclesiastical quasi-legislation gives rise to judicially or executively enforceable rights and duties remains unclear, in the secular field the civil judges have in recent years shown a clear willingness to treat quasi-legislation as enforceable.[78] A piece of quasi-legislation will bind both its maker and the person to whom it is addressed if it satisfies the tests laid down by the common law: it will bind if this is the intention of its maker,[79] and intent to bind may be presumed if the language used in the instrument is clearly expressed in mandatory terms,[80] and if the terms of the instrument are capable of enforcement (by executive order, for instance),[81] and if the instrument displays a mark of legitimacy in the sense that it has been approved by a public body lawfully enjoying a governmental position and role.[82] Equally, the civil courts may challenge the legality of quasi-legislation in the form of regulations, standing orders, 'blanket resolutions', policy, directions, circulars, guidance, and resolutions.[83] Judges may also intervene if the body in question disregards the terms of quasi-legislation of its own making; the publication of quasi-legislation may generate a legitimate expectation in those affected by it that its terms will be fairly and properly applied.[84] If a document is classified simply as 'guidance', although *prima facie* there may be no obligation to follow it there may be an obligation

---

[77] G. Ganz, *Quasi-Legislation: Recent Developments in Secondary Legislation* (London, 1987); R. E. Megarry, 'Administrative quasi-legislation', *LQR*, 60 (1944), 125.

[78] R. Baldwin and J. Houghton, 'Circular arguments: the status and legitimacy of administrative rules', *PL* (1986), 239.   [79] *Payne v Lord Harris* [1981] 1 WLR 754.

[80] *R v Secretary of State for Home Affairs, ex p Hosenball* [1977] 1 WLR 766; *British Oxygen Co Ltd v Board of Trade* [1971] AC 610.

[81] *R v Board of Visitors of Hull Prison, ex p Germain* [1979] 1 QB 425.

[82] *Patchett v Leathem* [1949] 65 TLR 69; *R v Chief Immigration Officer Heathrow Airport, ex p Bibi* [1976] 1 WLR 979.

[83] *Lees v S/S for Social Services* [1985] AC 930 (regulations); *Raymond v Honey* [1983] 1 AC 1 (standing orders); *R v Herrod, ex p Leeds City Council* [1978] AC 403 (blanket resolution); *Re Findlay* [1985] AC 318 (policy); *R v S/S for the Home Department, ex p Brind* [1991] 1 AC 696 (directive); *Royal College of Nursing for the UK v DHSS* [1981] AC 800 (circular); *R v S/S for the Environment, ex p Nottinghamshire County Council* [1986] AC 240 (guidance); *R v Legal Aid Board, ex p Bruce* [1992] 1 WLR 694 (resolution). See generally M. Fordham, *Judicial Review Handbook* (Chichester, 1995) 52–3.

[84] *R v Criminal Injuries Compensation Board, ex p Lain* [1967] 2 QB 864; *R v S/S for Foreign and Commonwealth Affairs, ex p Everett* [1989] 1 All ER 655; for the effects of publication see *AG for Hong Kong v Ng Yuen Shiu* [1983] 2 AC 629; *R v S/S for the Home Department, ex p Khan* [1984] 1 WLR 1337; a rule may be set aside if it is so unreasonable as to be manifestly unjust or oppressive or partial and unequal in its operation as between classes: *R v Immigration Appeal Tribunal, ex p Manshoora Begun* [1986] Imm AR 385.

to have regard to or consider it;[85] but, like other forms of quasi-legislation, guidance which is erroneous in law will have no legal effect.[86] Quasi-legislation in the Church of England is commonly expressed in mandatory terms.[87]

Whereas the legal effect of diocesan regulations or norms and national codes of practice in the Church of England has not been the subject of general judicial consideration, some forms of ecclesiastical quasi-legislation have been treated by the courts.[88] The Convocations of Canterbury and York and the General Synod are empowered to create *Acts*: an 'Act of Convocation', a resolution passed by both Houses of the Convocation, has been judicially determined as having only moral and no legal force.[89] However, it is possible that failure by a cleric to obey an executive episcopal order to comply with an Act of Convocation or Synod may give rise to legal proceedings and thus indirectly render the terms of the Act judicially enforceable.[90] The same applies to 'guidelines' laid down by the ecclesiastical judges in the course of judicial proceedings, though if subsequently adopted and absorbed into the *ratio* of a decision these will acquire binding force.[91] Ecclesiastical authorities may frequently enter *contracts* with outside institutions and parties, and sometimes the regulations governing an ecclesiastical body itself will constitute the terms of a contract. Whilst not strictly 'law' these regulations will contain rights and duties which are enforceable under the secular law of contract.[92] Finally, a source of

---

[85] *Laker Airways Ltd v Department of Trade* [1977] QB 643 at 699 (considering Civil Aviation Act 1971, s. 3 in which, as compared with 'direction', '"guidance" . . . did not denote an order or command'.

[86] *Gillick v West Norfolk and Wisbech Area Health Authority* [1986] AC 112 at 193–4 *per* Lord Bridge.

[87] *SDDH*, I, Annex D (readers regulations, concerning selection and training: 'The Bishop expects *a strict adherence* to the regulations both by the readers and by their incumbents'); *RBG*, B.7 ('Applicants for the position of pastoral assistants *must* have the backing and support of their Incumbents and PCC'); *CF*, C.3 ('Extended Communion . . . This practice is not authorised'); *GDBOP*, 6.1 (concerning circulars issued under the Children Act 1989: authorities 'are required to take these into account').

[88] *Re St James, Shirley* [1994] Fam 134 (the Con. Ct. gave effect to a 'Response by the House of Bishops to Questions raised by the Diocesan Chancellors'); for refusals to grant faculties when diocesan regulations have been violated see *Re St Breoke, Wadebridge* [1990] *ELJ*, 3 (1993), 59; *Re St Chad, Bishop's Tachbrook* [1991] *ELJ*, 3 (1993), 60; *Re St Michael and All Angels, Thornhill* [1993] *ELJ*, 3 (1994), 189.

[89] *Bland v Archdeacon of Cheltenham* [1972] 1 All ER 1012 at 1018; *York Journal of Convocation* (Westminster, 1976) 47: an Act of Synod is 'a type of regulatory instrument, possessing moral authority but not legal force'; see *post* Ch. 3.

[90] See *post* Ch. 7 for the scope of canonical obedience.

[91] *Re Holy Innocents, Fallowfield* [1982] 3 WLR 666 at 667 *per* Spafford Ch; *Re St Mary's, Banbury* [1987] 1 All ER 247 at 254 *per* Sir John Owen Dean of Arches; *Re St Luke the Evangelist, Maidstone* [1994] 3 WLR 1165.

[92] For church sharing agreements see *post* Ch. 16; the memorandum and articles of association of e.g. a diocesan board of finance constitute the terms of a contract made between the company and its members: Companies Act 1985, s. 14(1), *Hickman v Kent and Romney Marsh Sheep Breeders Association* [1915] 1 Ch 88; *Salmon v Quin and Axtens Ltd* [1909] 1 Ch 311 at 318.

non-legal rules for ecclesiastical government is to be found in unwritten practices which might be described as *ecclesiastical conventions*. Whilst they are not judicially enforceable, the courts may take cognizance of ecclesiastical conventions and extra-legal consequences may flow from their breach.[93]

The Roman Catholic Church: Canon Law and Administrative Norms

Though there are formal differences as to sources the Roman Catholic Church, like the Church of England, employs a wide variety of regulatory instruments. Like the canons of the Church of England, the canons of the Roman Catholic Church must not be repugnant to the royal prerogative, statute, and common law. Also, like the Church of England, Roman Catholic canon law is protected by the state and is, in certain circumstances, enforceable in the secular courts, but for reasons different from those applicable to the Church of England. Moreover, like the Church of England, the central legal provisions of the Roman Catholic Church are supplemented by a large body of ecclesiastical quasi-legislation.

Much but not all Roman Catholic canon law is found in the Code of Canon Law 1983, replacing the *Codex Iuris Canonici* of 1917 and promulgated as a result of the revision process following the Second Vatican Council.[94] The canon law contained in the Code is binding upon those to whom it is addressed and is enforceable administratively or judicially within the Roman Catholic Church.[95] The Code distinguishes universal laws and particular laws. *Universal laws* are written laws formally enacted by bodies possessing legislative power for the whole church (such as a 'general decree' of the pope, which may introduce new law having universal applicability (c. 29)). They are binding on the whole church unless specifically limited to a class of individuals within it: '[a]ll persons for whom universal laws were passed are bound by them everywhere' (c. 12). Some laws located outside the Code have universal

---

[93] See *post* Ch. 3 for the convention that parliament will not legislate on a matter of doctrine, and Ch. 6 for the monarch being bound to follow ministerial advice as to the appointment of bishops; for the basic principle of their judicial non-enforceability, see C. Munro, 'Laws and conventions distinguished', *LQR*, 91 (1975), 218; N. Doe, 'Non-legal rules and the courts: enforceability', *Liverpool Law Review*, 9 (1987), 173; see generally G. Marshall, *Constitutional Conventions* (Oxford, 1984).

[94] For the process of revision see J. A. Alesandro, 'The revision of church law: conflict and reconciliation', *The Jurist*, 40 (1980), 1; G. Nedungatt, 'The title of the new canonical legislation', *Studia Canonica*, 19 (1985), 61; R. Potz, 'The concept and development of law according to the 1983 *Corpus Iuris Canonici*', *Concilium*, 185 (1986), 14; F. Morrisey, 'Is the new code an improvement for the law of the Catholic Church?', ibid., 32.

[95] The Code affects only the the western Latin Church (*CIC*, c. 1); for the *Codex canonum ecclesiarum orientalium*, (1991) see T. J. Green, 'Reflections on the Eastern Code revision process', *The Jurist*, 51 (1991), 18; G. Nedungatt, 'The title of the oriental code', *Studia Canonica*, 25 (1991), 465.

applicability. 'Authentic interpretations' of a legislator 'communicated in the form of a law' enjoy universal applicability and have 'the same force as the law itself' (c. 16(2)). *Particular laws* are formally enacted written laws made for a 'portion of the people of God', by either a universal legislator (the pope or the College of Bishops, for instance) or a particular legislator (such as a 'general decree' of a diocesan bishop (c. 29)). The 'portion' might be distinguished by location in a particular territory (a diocese, for example) or by class (sacred ministers, for instance) (c. 13). Particular laws, promulgated in the manner determined by their legislator and taking effect from the date of promulgation (unless the legislator fixes another) (c. 13), will not be suppressed by a universal law unless express provision is made for this (c. 20).[96] Particular laws include: diocesan legislation; legislation promulgated by national episcopal conferences; and constitutions, statutes, and ordinances created for or by universities, associations, hospitals, and religious institutes.[97] *Customs* are unwritten usages of a particular community which impose obligations on those to whom they are addressed.[98]

The juridical authority of many instruments (some of which may be created under powers conferred by the Code) is not so readily recognized.[99] *General executory decrees* (issued by those with administrative power) may be used to determine how laws are to be implemented; whilst not technically laws they have an inferior juridical authority and cannot derogate from laws—if they purport to do so they lack force.[100] *Instructions*, similarly, may be issued by bodies (such as pronouncements of the Roman curia) to explain or clarify laws and to fix a method for their implementation. Though they oblige, instructions are inferior to laws and may not override them.[101] *Declarations* are technically not new laws and must be interpreted in the context of existing law.[102] The Code also allows for the creation of a host of normative individual administrative instruments directed to individuals or groups including *individual decrees and precepts* (duty-imposing administrative acts giving a decision and ordering a person to do or to refrain from doing something),[103] and *rescripts* (rights-conferring administrative acts granting a privilege, dispensation, or other favour).[104] *Liturgical laws*, which may be universal or particular,

---

[96] For conditions for validity see *post* Ch. 3.

[97] R. J. Austin, 'The particular church and the universal church in the 1983 Code of Canon Law', *Studia Canonica*, 22 (1988), 339; for an analysis of the historical sources of Roman Catholic canon law see R. Ombres, 'Faith, doctrine and Roman Catholic canon law', *ELJ*, 1(4) (1989), 33 at 37–9.   [98] *CIC*, cc. 23–8; for criteria of validity see *post* Ch. 3.

[99] F. G. Morrisey, 'Papal and curial pronouncements: their canonical significance in the light of the 1983 code of canon law', *The Jurist*, 50 (1990), 102.

[100] *CIC*, cc. 31–3.   [101] Ibid., c. 34.

[102] F. Morrisey, 'Papal and curial pronouncements', 117   [103] *CIC*, cc. 48–52.

[104] Ibid., cc. 59–75; for privileges see cc. 76–84.

are treated as laws but are distinguished strictly from 'canon law'.[105] Other forms of quasi-legislation are not contemplated expressly by the Code. Papal *solemn professions of faith*, *decretal letters*, and *encyclicals* are primarily teaching documents and therefore do not bind as law, but in conjunction with canonical duties they may require obedience.[106] Some papal pronouncements, such as an *address*, a *constitution*, or a *motu proprio*, may enjoy juridical authority and be closer in substance to legislative documents. However, curial pronouncements such as *circular letters*, *directories*, and *notifications* which contain norms may nonetheless resemble 'guidelines' rather than binding laws.[107]

Roman Catholic canon law may be enforceable at civil law in four ways. First: given that the Roman Catholic Church has been judicially classified as a voluntary religious association organized on a consensual basis, its internal rules are enforceable in the secular courts as the terms of a contract. In *Buckley v Cahal Daly* a Roman Catholic priest sought *inter alia* a declaration that the Bishop of Down and Connor had removed him unlawfully from his position, stipend, and residence in so far as the bishop had not acted in accordance with 'the rules and regulations of the Roman Catholic Church'.[108] The High Court, dismissing the action on the basis that the priest lacked *locus standi*, classified the church as a voluntary association. As such, according to well established principles, its rules exist in law as the terms of a contract.[109] For Campbell J, though a court would not ordinarily recognize or enforce the internal rules of a voluntary association, it may do so in some circumstances. Relying on *Forbes v Eden*,[110] Campbell J held that '[a] court of law will not interfere with the

---

[105] Ibid., c. 2: for the most part the Code does not define the rites which are to be observed in celebrating liturgical actions, and current liturgical norms retain their force unless contrary to the canons of the Code; for liturgical norms see *post* Ch. 10. [106] See *post* Ch. 9.

[107] F. Morrisey, 'Papal and curial pronouncements', 107–9, 118–21.

[108] [1990] NIJB 8 (Belfast); see also the Australian case of *Scandrett v Dowling* (1992) 27 NSWLR 483: the plaintiffs, relying on a non-property contract argument, obtained an interlocutory injunction to restrain Bishop Dowling from ordaining women priests; however, the CA considered that the rules of the Australian Anglican Church did not constitute a binding contract as there was no intention to create legal relations—its rules bound only in conscience; the matter would have been justiciable, however, if property rights had been involved: see S. Fisher, 'Judicial intervention in church affairs in New South Wales', *Law and Justice* (1992), 51 and (1993), 128.

[109] *Long v Bishop of Capetown* (1863) 1 Moore PCNS 411 at 461–2; *Conservative & Unionist Central Office v Burrell* [1982] 1 WLR 522 at 525 *per* Lawton LJ; *Baker v Jones* [1954] 2 All ER 553 at 558 *per* Lynskey J; *Warnes v Trustees of Cheriton Oddfellows Social Club* [1993] IRLR 58 *per* Knox J.

[110] (1867) LR 1 HL Sc & Div 566 at 588 *per* Lord Colonsay (see also 581 *per* Lord Cranworth: 'Save for the due disposal and administration of property, there is no authority in the Courts either of England or Scotland to take cognizance of the rules of a voluntary society entered into merely for the regulation of its own affairs. If funds are settled to be disposed of amongst members of a voluntary association according to their rules and regulations, the Court must necessarily take cognizance of those rules and regulations for the purpose of satisfying itself as to who is entitled to the funds'.)

rules of a voluntary association unless to protect some civil right or interest which is said to be infringed by their operation'. Lord Templeman's statement in *Davies v Presbyterian Church of Wales* was cited with approval: '[t]he law imposes on the church a duty not to deprive a pastor of his office which carries a stipend, save in accordance with the procedures set forth in the book of rules'; and '[t]he law imposes upon the church a duty to administer its property in accordance with the provisions of the book of rules'.[111] In determining whether the priest had *locus* Campbell J appealed to and applied the provisions of the 1983 Code of Canon Law relating to incardination, the process by which a priest is tied to a diocese.[112] Had Buckley been incardinated into the diocese then the bishop would have been bound by the Code's procedures governing removal.[113] Analysis of these canonical provisions and of a decision from 1978 of the Apostlic Signatura did not satisfy the Court that Buckley had been incardinated.[114]

Secondly, Roman Catholic canon law may acquire force under secular law by virtue of its incorporation in a trust deed.[115] Thirdly, it may be enforceable when its operation is expressly provided for by parliamentary statute.[116] Finally, Roman Catholic canon law may be understood, more speculatively, as foreign law.[117] As a general principle of international law, the civil courts will recognize a law as a 'foreign law' if it forms part of a legal system prevailing in the territory of a foreign state; foreign law must be established as a question of fact by the evidence of expert witnesses.[118] As the Holy See is for the purposes of international law a non-territorial state, an international person, the code of canon law may be classified as the legal system of a non-territorial state. The assumption that Roman Catholic canon law is a foreign

---

[111] [1986] 1 WLR 323 at 329; for other examples of the legal duty on members of religious bodies to act according to their internal rules see *Capel v Child* (1832) 2 Cr & J 588; *Bonaker v Evans* (1850) 16 QB 162. [112] *CIC*, cc. 265–72.

[113] Ibid., cc. 1742 ff.

[114] Similar use was made of Roman Catholic canon law contained in the 1917 code and particular decrees of the Scottish Provincial Church in *Daly v Commissioners of Inland Revenue* (1934) 18 Tax Cas 641 (the Scottish Court of Sessions appealed to and applied internal canon law and concluded that a priest, who as administrator of revenues was in receipt of certain benefits from the church (cc. 134, 476, 1473, 1496, 1519–20) was not liable to assessment for statutory income tax; he was liable for his 'salary' of £50.

[115] *R v Trustees of the Roman Catholic Diocese of Westminster, ex p Andrews* (1990) 2 Admin LR 142 at 151 (CA) (the practices of the school 'shall in all respects be according to the principles and subject to the regulations and discipline of the Roman Catholic Church'; see also *Le Cras v Perpetual Trustee Co* [1967] 3 All ER 915 (PC); *Chapelle v Chapelle* [1950] 1 All ER 236.

[116] *MaGrath and O'Ruairc v Trustees of Maynooth College* (1979) *Irish Law Reports Monthly* 166: the statutes were made under the Maynooth College Establishment Act 1795; see also *post* Ch. 16 for Roman Catholic discipline provided for under the Sharing of Church Buildings Act 1969.

[117] The assumption was made in J. H. Blunt, *The Book of Church Law* (1899) 18 ff.

[118] See generally P. M. North and J. J. Fawcett (eds.), *Cheshire and North Private International Law* (12th edn., London, 1992).

law has been made in a series of cases;[119] it was also expressed in the Reformation legislation.[120]

FUNDAMENTAL AUTHORITY: CHURCH LAW, THEOLOGY AND DIVINE LAW

The concepts of divine law and natural law have occupied a central position in the historical development of canonical jurisprudence. Whilst the rich literature contains various models of divine and natural law, each is conceived as issuing from the will of God: broadly, divine law having been understood as ascertainable by revelation and natural law by means of reason. Both concepts have been used as criteria of validity for human law, and theories have ranged from the idea that human law in conflict with the law of God is no law at all to the idea that, whilst retaining its status as law, human law offensive to the law of God ought not to be obeyed.[121] Inheriting this legal tradition, both the Church of England and the Roman Catholic Church today employ concepts of divine law in two ways: as a fundamental source for human-created church law and as a criterion of validity for both church-made and state-made church law.

Divine Law as a Superior Source

For canonists in both the Church of England and the Roman Catholic Church, canon law derives its fundamental authority from the revealed will of Christ as expressed in scripture, both of which are often conceived as having a power-conferring and duty-imposing juridical character.[122] In the Church of England, whilst little jurisprudence has been developed concerning the relationship between divine law and humanly created church law, the Archbishops' Commission on canon law in 1947 concluded that '[t]he right of the Church

---

[119] *The Sussex Peerage Case* (1844) 11 Cl & Fin 85; *R v Savage* (1876) 13 Cox CC 178; *R v Illich* [1935] NZLR 90; *Buckley v Cahal Daly* (1990) NIJB 8; *Daly v Commissioners of Inland Revenue* (1934) 18 Tax Cas 641; *MaGrath and O'Ruairc v Trustees of Maynooth College*, see fn. 116.

[120] The thrust of the Reformation legislation was, of course, to oust the 'foreign power and jurisdiction' of the Roman pontiff and to prevent appeals 'out of this realm . . . to the Bishop of Rome'; the legislation uses the expressions 'foreign inhibitions . . . suspensions, excommunications . . . judgments . . . from the see of Rome': Act in Restraint of Appeals 1533, Act of Supremacy 1559; the assumption survived in the Ecclesiastical Titles Act 1871.

[121] For general introductions to the medieval antecedents, based on earlier ideas, see J. A. Brundage, *Medieval Canon Law* (London, 1995) 156 f and N. Doe, *Fundamental Authority in Late Medieval English Law* (Cambridge, 1990).

[122] *MIECL*, 1: 'In the study of moral theology we are concerned with the whole of God's law in so far as it is immediately relevant to man. In the study of canon law we are concerned with so much of the moral law as is enforced, directly or indirectly'; J. A. Coriden, *Introduction*, 7 ff; for the idea in modern theology that God places upon the church demands which comprise the divine law, see P. S. Minear, *Commands of Christ* (Edinburgh, 1972) 12–15; J. Knox, *The Ethic of Jesus in the Teaching of the Church* (London, 1961) 48–51, 97–99; J. Mahoney, *The Making of Moral Theology* (Oxford, 1987) Ch. 6 (on the language of law).

to make rules and regulations for its own members, or *ius statuendi* as it is called, rests upon the commission given by our Lord to His Apostles to "bind" and "loose", [that is] to "declare forbidden" and to "declare allowed"'.[123] For Garth Moore 'God's revealed will is law' and 'our Lord both implicitly and explicitly delegated His law-making authority to what today we should call a subordinate legislature'; the church is 'the inheritor of the whole law of God in so far as that it may at any moment be relevant' and it is this divine law which is the principal and parent of canon law.[124] The divine law is immutable.[125] Although the expression divine law does not itself appear in the modern canons of the Church of England, a general concept of divine law is incorporated into many canons in such a way that the canons themselves are presented as being declaratory of divine law.[126] The concept also surfaces in the Thirty-Nine Articles.[127] Moreover, as a matter of ecclesiastical practice, theological principles are of course commonly employed to justify the creation and administration of internal church law.[128]

The concepts of divine law and natural law have been developed more fully in Roman Catholic jurisprudence by reference to the relationship between theology and canon law. On one hand some writers stress the connection. For Teodoro Urresti, a direct source of authority for canon law is theology: as the study of the nature of the church, as instituted by Christ, is primarily a theological study, so '[t]he results of this theological study will form the data for the discipline of Canon Law'. Suggesting that there is a 'theology of canon law' and a 'theology in canon law',[129] Urresti maintains that ideas derived

---

[123] *RACCL*, 3; the scriptural texts most commonly claimed to authorize the use of canon law are Matt. 16: 19, 18: 18, 19: 28, 28: 18; Luke 10: 16, 22: 28–30; John 20: 21; see also H. Box, *The Principles of Canon Law* (Oxford, 1949) 10.   [124] *MIECL*, 2.

[125] *Ray v Sherwood* (1837) 1 Moo PCC 353 *per* Sir Herbert Jenner Fust: concerning 5 & 6 Will 4, c. 54 (on former marriages of persons within the prohibited degrees).

[126] See e.g. Canons A2–A5 on the doctrine of the church as conforming to or not repugnant to the Word of God; A6: the government of the church is 'not repugnant to the Word of God'; B30: holy matrimony is 'according to our Lord's teaching'; B29 requires the baptized 'to examine their lives . . . by the rule of God's commandments').

[127] Arts. 9,17 (of predestination and election: 'we must receive God's promises in such wise, as they are generally set forth to us in holy Scripture: and, in our doings, that Will of God is to be followed, which we have expressly declared unto us in the Word of God'; Art. 22 (the doctrine of purgatory is 'repugnant to the Word of God'); Art. 24 (it is repugnant to the Word of God to have public prayer or to minister the sacraments 'in a tongue not understood of the people'); Art. 25 (the sacraments of baptism and the Lord's Supper are 'ordained of Christ our Lord in the Gospel'); Art. 27 (baptism of children is 'most agreeable with the institution of Christ'); Art. 28 ('Transubstantiation . . . is repugnant to the plain words of Scripture'); Art. 30 (the cup 'is not to be denied to the Lay-people; for both parts of the Lord's Sacrament, by Christ's ordinance and commandment, ought to be ministered to all'); Art. 32 (bishops, priests, and deacons are 'not commanded by God's Law' to abstain from marriage); Art. 34 deals with traditions which are 'not repugnant to the Word of God'.

[128] N. Doe, 'Toward a critique of the role of theology in English ecclesiastical and canon law', *ELJ*, 2 (1990–92), 328.

[129] See also R. Ombres, 'Faith, doctrine and Roman Catholic canon law', *ELJ*, 1 (1989) 33; for the 'theology of canon law' see *post* Ch. 2.

from the theological science of ascertaining the nature and purposes of God and the church have 'to be given particular shape by the positive rulings of the hierarchy [of the church] itself, by the rulings of ecclesiastical law'; '[t]heology studies revealed data: its aim is to formulate revealed truth; it moves on a level appropriate to this truth, and defines it with doctrinal judgements', and canon law 'receives these theological data in generic form as they concern the basic social structure of the Church, and particularizes them in its laws'. In short, 'theology studies what is the will of Christ, while canon law prescribes how this will of Christ is to be fulfilled in the socio-ecclesial field, that is to say, it studies the will of the Church, which has to be upheld within the will of Christ'.[130] In this context, many Roman Catholic writers view theology as concerning judgment based on knowledge and canon law as imposing a decision based on that judgment.[131] Some see canon law as *ordinatio fidei*, a legal system born of faith.[132] On the other hand, sometimes theology and canon law are disconnected: for Wilhelm Bertrams, focusing on the nature of ecclesiastical institutions, theology deals with the internal structures of institutions and canon law with their external disposition; the Navarra School sees ecclesiastical authority, rather than theology, as the direct basis of canon law: the science of canon law is primarily dependent on the religious authority that makes and sustains it; consisting in the main of canon lawyers teaching 'ecclesiastical law' in faculties of civil law, the Italian School accepts canon law as a proper subject of juridical science but disregards its connection with theology: anything not contained in the legal system is outside the field of proper legal study.[133]

In Roman Catholic jurisprudence divine law, ascertained by revelation and theological reflection, is composed of the natural law and the divine positive law. *Natural law*, 'the root and rule of canon law', is 'a source of law in those cases where its precepts are common to all mankind', having 'God as its author' so 'in its own way [it] is a kind of divine law'; *divine positive law* is 'established by God and made known to us by revelation'.[134] According to the teaching of Vatican II, the ascertainment of the divine and natural law is

---

[130] T. Urresti, 'Canon law and theology: two different sciences', *Concilium*, 8 (1967), 10; see also T. Urresti 'The theologian in interface with canonical reality', *Journal of Ecumenical Studies*, 19 (1982), 146.

[131] L. Örsy, *Theology and Canon Law* (Collegeville, 1992) 137: in a survey of ideas concerning the relation between theology and canon law, from the 'disturbed' to the 'downright nonexistent', Örsy concludes: 'The most important among [the principles of their relation] is that every single piece of the law in the church must be in the service of values either defined or at least controlled by theological reflection'; 165: theology 'contains a body of organised knowledge obtained through revelation and reflection of what was revealed; [canon law] consists of a system of norms of action issued by an ecclesiastical authority'.

[132] E. Corecco, *The Theology of Canon Law: A Methodological Question* (Duquesne UP, Pittsburgh, 1992); see also Myriam Wijlens, *Theology and Canon Law: The Theories of Klaus Morsdorf and Eugenio Corecco* (Lanham, Md, 1992).

[133] For an overview of these approaches see L. Örsy, *Theology and Canon Law*, 179–82.

[134] R. Ombres, 'Faith, doctrine and Roman Catholic canon law', 33 at 38; G. May, 'Ecclesiastical law', 395.

within the competence of the church's teaching authority.[135] For many Roman Catholic writers, whether or not something is of divine institution depends *inter alia* on its irreversibility and its indispensibility for the continuation of that which Jesus established; this may be either expressed in scripture or a decision arrived at by the church led by the Holy Spirit.[136] Thus the church is obliged to fulfill and facilitate the operation of the commands in scripture to repent and lead a holy life, the command to baptize, the duty to celebrate the Eucharist, the precept to love one's neighbour, the prohibition against falsifying the teaching of Christ, the command to teach, and the call for discipline in the church.[137] Whilst the immediate authority underlying the 1983 Code of Canon Law is that of the pontifical office,[138] the Roman Catholic Church presents the right to govern itself as one of divine institution;[139] commonly, canons are presented expressly as being derived from divine law or as being divine in institution.[140]

Divine Law and Validity

The connection between human-created church law and divine law has radical implications for the question of the validity of the former. For the Church of England, there appears to be a dissonance between canonical theory and legal practice. On one hand is the principle presented in the Thirty-Nine Articles: 'it is not lawful for the Church to ordain any thing that is contrary to God's Word written'.[141] According to the 1947 Archbishops' Commission, '[t]he Church

---

[135] *HV* (1968) I, 4 (natural law); *DH* (1965) I, 3: 'the highest norm of human life is the divine law itself—eternal, objective and universal, by which God orders, directs and governs the whole world and the ways of the human community according to a plan conceived in his wisdom and love. God has enabled man to participate in this law so that . . . many may be able to arrive at a deeper and deeper knowledge of unchangeable truth.'

[136] K. Rahner, 'Reflections on the concept of *ius divinum* in Catholic thought', *Theological Investigations*, Vol. V (Baltimore, 1966) 219; A. Dulles, '*Ius divinum* as an ecumenical problem', *Theological Studies*, 38 (1977), 681; C. J. Peter, 'Dimensions of *ius divinum* in Roman Catholic theology', *Theological Studies*, 34 (1973), 227.

[137] Paul VI, 'Justice in the Service of the Gospel', 28 Jan. 1978, *The Pope Speaks*, 23 (1978), 158; see also W. Steinmuller, 'Divine law and its dynamism in Protestant theology of law', *Concilium*, 8 (1969), 13 at 20: '*ius divinum* is the original law; compared with it, *ius humanum* is only a shadow image of law'; in consequence, '[b]ecause divine Church law is a law of the Spirit, a law of grace and love, the ecclesiastical lawgiver has a corresponding legal obligation to mirror this material structure in his human Church law in so far as he can; thus he will provide a model for the world'.

[138] Apostolic Constitution, *Sacrae Disciplinae Leges*, COCLA, 47 at 51.

[139] *CIC*, cc. 129, 331.

[140] *CIC*, c. 1249: all Christ's faithful are obliged by divine law—*ex lege divina tenentur*—to do penance; c. 207: *ex divina institutione*, among Christ's faithful there are sacred ministers and lay people; see also c. 210: holy life; c. 349: baptism; c. 211: to spread the gospel; c. 222: to promote social justice.

[141] Art. 20; Art. 7: 'no Christian man whatsoever is free from the obedience of the Commandments which are called Moral'; see *supra* n. 19 for the monarch's duty to uphold the law of God. For the concepts in Hooker see *The Laws of Ecclesiastical Polity* (1594), Books I to IV, edited by R. Bayne (New York), Bks. II and III.

has no authority from our Lord to alter the way of faith and the way of life and the sacraments which He has entrusted to its care. It cannot make a rule that Christians need no longer believe in our Lord's bodily Resurrection or come to the Holy Communion.'[142] The same approach was used by Garth Moore: arguing that the church's legislative competence is delegated by Christ, law 'has validity only within the framework of its principal and parent, the divine law'; for example, whilst 'it is within the competence of the Church to make and adopt rules concerning the incidentals of marriage and to vary them from time to time and from place to place . . . it is *ultra vires* the Church to vary the nature of marriage, for that is already determined by the divine law within the framework of which alone the Church's delegated authority can operate'.[143]

On the other hand, whilst the civil courts have accepted the possibility that humanly created church law may be based on divine law, the adoption of the positivist philosophy of law results in the invulnerability from judicial challenge of ecclesiastical legislation enacted by General Synod or by the Queen in Parliament.[144] The approach is typified by a statement of Sir Herbert Jenner Fust in *Ray v Sherwood*: 'The law of God cannot be altered by the law of man. The legislature may exempt the parties from punishment; it may legalize, humanly speaking, every prohibited act, and give effect to any contract, however inconsistent with the Divine law, but it cannot change the character of the act itself, which remains as it was, and must always so remain, whatever be the effect of the act of parliament'.[145] At the same time, however, secular courts do sometimes treat such matters as justiciable and apply a natural law outlook in limited circumstances: unreasonable domestic secondary legislation and custom, and foreign law which constitutes a grave infringement of human rights, are deemed not to exist.[146] Nevertheless, it is not open to a priest of the Church of England, in proceedings for criminal damage, to argue that the secular courts 'received their ultimate authority from God and the role of a priest of the established church is to help to ensure the agreement of human law with divine law by teaching the Christian faith and delivering the word of the Lord'.[147]

---

[142] *RACCL*, 3.   [143] *MIECL*, 2–3.

[144] *R v Dibdin* [1910] P 57; *Harries v Church Commissioners for England* [1992] 1 WLR 1241 (see *post* Ch. 17 for the rejection of a challenge to the investment policies of the Church Commissioners on the basis of moral argument); in the case of *Logan*, Times 28/4/95, the Scottish Court of Session decided that ministerial action in purported violation of divine law was justiciable in disciplinary proceedings in the courts of the Church of Scotland and not in the secular courts.

[145] (1837) 1 Moo PCC 353.

[146] *Oppenheimer v Cattermole* [1976] AC 249; *Williams & Humbert Ltd v W&H Trade Marks* [1986] 1 All ER 129 HL accepting the view of Nourse J at first instance that such laws are 'by a legal fiction, deemed not to exist'; [1985] 2 All ER 213; *Settebello Ltd v Banco Totta and Acores* [1985] 1 WLR 1050 at 1056 *per* Donaldson MR; see generally N. Doe, 'The problem of abhorrent legislation and the judicial idea of legislative supremacy', *Liverpool Law Review*, 10 (1988), 113.

[147] *Blake v DPP* (1992), Hill, *EL*, 13; see also *R v Senior* [1899] 1 KB 283 and *R v Blaue* [1975] 3 All ER 446.

As in the Church of England, Roman Catholic jurisprudence also holds that the church may never waive the laws of God,[148] and the task of theology, discovering the will of Christ, is to 'deliver judgements (of theological valuation) on whether canon law is being faithful or not . . . in order to decide whether its reform is necessary'.[149] Although the 1983 Code does not apply the basic principle to all forms of internal church law, '[n]o custom which is contrary to divine law can acquire the force of law'.[150] Similarly, though the doctrine of canonization provides that secular law is deemed to be incorporated into canon law when a matter is not provided for by canon law, incorporation occurs only in so far as civil law is consistent with divine law.[151] A radical approach has been taken to the effect of human law offensive to divine law by the Roman Catholic Church with regard to secular law permitting abortion, understood by the church as an abominable wrong and a violation of the right to life, forbidden by the faith, by the church's teaching, by canon law, and by divine and natural law.[152] According to a declaration on procured abortions, issued by the Sacred Congregation for the Doctrine of the Faith in 1974, whereas 'civil law cannot expect to cover the whole field of morality or to punish all faults . . . it cannot act contrary to a law which is deeper and more majestic than any human law; the natural law engraved in men's hearts by the creator as a norm which reason clarifies and strives to formulate properly . . . which it is always wrong to contradict'; '[h]uman law can abstain from punishment, but it cannot declare to be right what would be opposed to the natural law, for this opposition suffices to give the assurance that *a law is not a law at all*' (emphasis added). For the Sacred Congregation, '[i]t must in any way be clearly understood that a Christian can never conform to a law which is in itself immoral, and such is the case of a law which would admit in principle the liceity of abortion'. Not only should Christians not 'campaign in favour of such a law, or vote for it', but they 'may not collaborate in its application'.[153]

CONCLUSIONS

The approaches of the Church of England and of the Roman Catholic Church to the nature of ecclesiastical regulation have much in common. Both churches are treated in secular law as quasi-corporate institutions and both

[148] R. Ombres, 'Faith, doctrine and Roman catholic canon law', 41.
[149] T. Urresti, 'Canon law and theology: two different sciences', *Concilium*, 8 (1967), 10.
[150] *CIC*, c. 24.   [151] Ibid., c. 22.
[152] *GES*, II, 1, 51; *HV* (1968); *Familiaris consortio* (1981); *Veritatis Splendor* (1993); see also N. St J. Stevas, *The Agonising Choice: Birth Control, Religion and the Law* (London, 1971) 188; M. J. Coughlan, *The Vatican, the Law and the Human Embryo* (London, 1990) 42 ff; P. Hannon, *Church, State, Morality and Law* (Dublin, 1992); see also *post* Ch. 9
[153] *Quaestio de abortu* (18 Nov., 1974), *Flannery*, II, 441.

are 'established' in the loose legal sense of being recognized and protected by the state, though the Church of England is established to a greater extent than the Roman Catholic Church in so far as the terms of its position as a church established by law and its close relation with the state and the sovereign generate greater benefits and burdens for the church. The secular legal position of the Roman Catholic Church is that of a voluntary association whose members are bound together consensually. Both churches are subject to the overriding legal supremacy of the Queen in Parliament: the canons of both churches must not be repugnant to the law of the state. Whilst for the Roman Catholic Church canon law is defined as internal ecclesiastical regulation, (sometimes synonymous with ecclesiastical law) for the Church of England there is no agreed, clear understanding of the terms 'canon law' and 'ecclesiastical law': the expressions are confused, and unless a European-style distinction between ecclesiastical law as state-made law applicable to the church and canon law as church-made law is adopted, it is submitted that they ought to be discarded in favour of the title 'church law', to include both internal church-made law and external state-made law. For the purposes of the Church of England, church law is composed of both law created by the church and law created by the state. Regulatory instruments made within the church consist of laws properly so called, binding and enforceable executively and judicially, and also of instruments which may be classified as ecclesiastical quasi-legislation, itself binding provided the common law tests are satisfied. Regulation in the Roman Catholic Church is likewise based on the church's internal central legal system, the 1983 Code, particular law, and a host of administrative norms. Like the Church of England, but in more limited circumstances, regulations of the Roman Catholic Church may be enforced in the secular courts. For both churches, divine law, ascertained by revelation and theological investigation, operates as a superior source for church law, but the role of divine law as a criterion of validity for humanly created church law is less well developed in the Church of England than in Roman Catholic jurisprudence.

2

The Purposes of Ecclesiastical Regulation

A teleological view of ecclesiastical regulation made an early appearance in the development of canonical jurisprudence.[1] The idea that ecclesiastical regulation is functional, having ends and objectives, exercises modern canonists in the Roman Catholic Church far more than in the Church of England. On one hand, regulation exists to enable the church to fulfill its mission in the world. At the heart of abstract, general theories, devised around concepts of facility and order, lie ecclesiological propositions about the nature and purposes of the church itself. On the other hand, at a more practical level, purposes are entirely dependent on the intent of the legislator—and the intent of the state in legislating for the church, needless to say, may be very different from that of the ecclesiastical legislator—and on the structure of the regulatory instrument in question, and the subject it addresses. In this sense, general theories about purpose are merely classifications of legislative motives. Whilst general theories supply justifications for ecclesiastical regulation, the main practical reasons for identifying purposes are: to enable legislators to determine whether a matter ought to be regulated, and whether the design of the regulatory instrument achieves the intended purpose, and to enable judicial and executive bodies to determine whether its application serves the purposes for which it was made.

THE FACILITY THEORY

In a House of Lords debate on the Sharing of Church Buildings Bill 1969 Lord Brooke of Cumnor observed: 'sometimes laymen like myself are appalled at the extent to which the original work of Christianity has become overlaid with legal structure.'[2] Regulation in the church is seen by many as coercive, imposing a rigidity, whereas ecclesiastical life ought to be governed by the Holy Spirit, the faithful living under grace rather than under a series of humanly made commands and prohibitions.[3] It is this view which has

---

[1] J. A. Brundage, *Medieval Canon Law* (London, 1995) 70 f, 98 ff; for the use of similar ideas in the medieval common law see N. Doe, *Fundamental Authority in Late Medieval English Law* (Cambridge, 1990) 47–51.

[2] *ORPD*, 5th Series, HL Deb., Vol. 298, 30 Jan. 1969, 1279 at 1295.

[3] For Rudolf Sohm (1841–1917) there is a fundamental antithesis between law and the church as a community bound together by love: for Sohm's *Kirchenrecht* (1892) see A. V. Dulles, *Models of the Church* (Dublin, 1976); cf. Adolf Harnack's response in *The Constitution and Law of the Church in the First Two Centuries*, trans. F. L. Pogson (London, 1910).

militated against acceptance of regulation as a legitimate function of the church's right to manage itself.[4] One of the achievements of modern secular jurisprudence has been to move away from the classical positivist view of law as a series of commands, issued to subjects by a sovereign legislator, obedience to which is secured by means of the threat of sanction. Contemporary notions of law stress instead its facilitative nature. Law exists to 'provide individuals with facilities for realizing their wishes'.[5] This analysis is applicable equally to the church.

The primary function of internal regulation is to serve the purposes for which the church exists. Consequently, propositions about the purpose of regulation will depend in large measure upon views held about the nature and objectives of the church. In other words the aim of regulation in the Church of England rests, on the ecclesiology which the church has constructed for itself. Regulation is then seen as programmatic. This points to the elusiveness of a general theory of purpose. The Church of England has developed various ecclesiologies for itself, some associated with its legal position as an established and national church. Historically, it has been seen as a Christian commonwealth seeking a unity between church and society, and today many understand it as a spiritual servant ministering to the whole nation.[6] It is seen as part of the universal and catholic church, as an apostolic community, with the episcopacy as its focus, a worshipping and missionary community of believers, existing to learn and teach the faith, to evangelize the unconverted, and as an ecumenical community in dialogue with other churches.[7] Aspects of these ecclesiologies are reflected, to lesser or greater extents, in the Church of England's doctrinal and liturgical formulae.[8]

Concepts about the purpose of ecclesiastical regulation are, in turn, built on these ecclesiologies: regulation exists to serve the church in the fulfilment of its mission. The Archbishops' Commission on canon law (1947) proposed the

---

[4] For Anglican ideas of the church's right to create law for itself see *RACCL*, 3; for Roman Catholic ideas see *CIC*, cc. 129, 330, 331, and *CCL: TC*, xxiv–vi.

[5] H. L. A. Hart, *The Concept of Law* (2nd edn., Oxford, 1994) 27. For classical positivism and the idea of laws as commands see J. Bentham, *Of Laws in General*, edited by H. L. A. Hart (London, 1970) Chs. 1 and 2; J. Austin, *Lectures on Jurisprudence*, edited by R. Campbell (London, 1880) Pt. I, sec. I, ch. 1; see also e.g. J. Raz, *The Concept of a Legal System* (Oxford, 1970) esp. Chs. 6 and 7.

[6] P. Avis, *Anglicanism and the Christian Church* (Edinburgh, 1989) 47ff., 300–12.

[7] *WAOB*, 1.7: 'The fundamental task and aims of the Church of England are those of the one, holy, catholic and apostolic Church. They are given by divine commission.' See also J. Draper (ed.), *Communion and Episcopacy: Essays to Mark the Centenary of the Chicago–Lambeth Quadrilateral* (Oxford, 1988); C. F. Garbett, *The Claims of the Church of England* (London, 1947); S. Neill, *Anglicanism* (Harmondsworth, 1958); S. W. Sykes, *The Integrity of Anglicanism* (London, 1978); *Believing in the Church: The Corporate Nature of Faith*, A Report by the Doctrine Commission of the Church of England (London, 1981) 26ff.

[8] *AR*, Art. 14; *BCP* and *ASB* both include prayers for the nation; see also ARCIC II, *Church as Communion* (1991).

simple ecclesiology that '[t]he Church exists to help men to follow out the way of faith and the way of life which our Lord brought to the world, and in the finding of which men realize the meaning of true happiness'. Accepting that law is 'a necessary element in any corporate life, whether it serves a temporal or a spiritual end', the Commission considered that canon law aims to promote the Church's 'purpose as an institution for the help of men in their following of our Lord'. To this end 'in its legislative activities the Church is guided by the criterion of utility . . . to have such laws in force as to assist it in its work of training up the followers of our Lord'.[9]

The concept of facility is commonly used by legislators within the Church of England as a practical reason for the creation of actual forms of regulation: to enable the church to serve God and the people;[10] to enable the 'full participation of the laity in decisions about the use of forms of worship';[11] to enable 'the drawing together of those whom in the old language we called High Church and Low Church' and to reconcile the 'tensions between them';[12] to enable the exercise of conscientious objection;[13] and 'to give . . . permissive freedom'.[14] Regulatory instruments, accordingly, reflect these ideas. Some are designed to provide structures to remove pastoral breakdowns which 'impede the promotion . . . of the whole mission of the Church of England, pastoral, evangelistic, social and ecumenical'.[15] Some structures for property management are designed to enable church buildings to be used as centres of worship and mission.[16] Some institutions are created as facilities to promote 'the whole mission of the Church, pastoral, evangelistic, social and ecumenical'.[17] Rights are distributed to ensure that the church makes its ministrations available to the whole community, notably with regard to baptism, marriage, and burial.[18] Whilst the ecclesiastical judges face a particular problem in determining the

---

[9] *RACCL*, 3–5.

[10] The Archbishop of Canterbury understood the draft Prayer Book (Alternative and Other Services) Measure 1965 as 'enabling . . . reforms in public worship, so that the worship of God in our parish churches may be as worthy as we can make it, and intelligible to the people of our time' and as 'enabling the Church to serve God and the people': *ORPD*, 5th Series, HL Deb., Vol. 263, 18 Feb. 1965, 651–8. The 1965 measure was repealed by the Church of England (Worship and Doctrine) Measure 1974.

[11] On the draft Church of England (Worship and Doctrine) Measure 1974, ibid., HL Deb., Vol. 354, 14 Nov. 1974, 867 at 869; see ibid., HC Deb., Vol. 764, 9 May 1968, 727 at 728, for the proposed Pastoral Measure 1968 enabling consultation in the making of diocesan reorganization schemes; ibid., HL Deb., Vol. 489, 29 Oct. 1987, 704 on the draft Church of England (Legal Aid and Miscellaneous Provisions) Measure 1987; see also *York Journal of Convocation* (Westminster, 1976) 44: 'the draft Canon B43 . . . was an enabling canon'.

[12] Prayer Book Measure 1965 debate: *ORPD*, HL Deb., Vol. 354, 14 Nov. 1974, 867 at 870.

[13] Concerning the proposed marriage regulations on divorcees: *GSRP*, 16(1) (1985) 204 at 216.

[14] Church of England (Worship and Doctrine) Measure 1974: *ORPD*, 5th Series, HL Deb., Vol. 256, 24 Mar. 1964, 1131 at 1134.

[15] See the debate on the Incumbents (Vacation of Benefices) Measure 1977, s. 19A, at ibid., HL Deb., Vol. 382, 2 May 1977, 808 at 810.   [16] *CCEJM* 1991, s. 1.

[17] *SGM* 1969, s. 5(3)(b); *PCC(P)M* 1956, s. 2(2)(a).   [18] See *post* Part V.

intent of the law-maker,[19] judicial statements commonly mirror the notion of regulation as facility: rules will be applied because they enable individuals to carry out their wishes,[20] or because they enable a parish to function harmoniously;[21] equally, judges may decline to intervene on the basis that intervention will not serve the interests of the church.[22] The concept of facility may also be the motivation for state-made law applicable to the Church of England,[23] although state-made church law, when the product of political aims,[24] may sometimes also be disabling rather than enabling.[25]

Sophisticated concepts of facility are found in Roman Catholic jurisprudence, built in part around ideas, shared with the Church of England, of the church as communion.[26] Before Vatican II the prevailing official view of the church was that of *societas perfecta*, a society subordinate to none other, possessing all that was needed for its own completeness and working.[27]

[19] For the myth of discovering 'parliament's intention' in secular jurisprudence (in which legislative intent is ultimately based on individual intents), see R. W. M. Dias, *Jurisprudence* (4th edn., London, 1976) 219; N. J. Jamieson, 'Towards a systematic statute law', *Otago Law Review* (1976) 568. Cf. F. Bennion, *Statutory Interpretation* (London, 1984) 226–8, 230–7.

[20] See e.g., concerning a faculty for the disinterment of remains from consecrated ground, *Re Matheson (Deceased)* [1958] 1 All ER 202 at 204 *per* Steel Ch. (Liverpool Con. Ct.): 'the primary function of the court is to keep faith with the dead. When a man nears his end and contemplates Christian burial, he may reasonably hope that his remains will be undisturbed, and the court should ensure that, if reasonably possible, this assumed wish will be respected. In all these cases the court must and will have regard to the supposed wishes of the deceased.' For principles developed to take into account the wishes of parishioners in exercising faculty jurisdiction see *post* Ch. 16.

[21] *Re St. Thomas, Lymington* [1980] 2 All ER 84 at 87; *Burridge v Tyler* [1992] 1 All ER 437 at 442; see *Hayward and Another v Challoner* [1967] 3 All ER 122 at 126 *per* Davies LJ, for civil courts reserving judgment in order to allow consideration of a matter by church authorities (CA).

[22] *Re St Luke's, Chelsea* [1976] 1 All ER 609 at 627 (see 623–4 for the parishioners, the purposive approach to legislation, and the 'legislative intent' formula) *per* Newsom Ch.; *Re St. Hilary, Cornwall* [1938] 4 All ER 147.

[23] *ORPD*, 5th Series, HC Deb., Vol. 722, 17 Dec. 1965, 1624 at 1626; the practice was described as a 'custom' at 1625; see also *Re St Mary's, Banbury* [1987] 1 All ER 247 at 249, 253 for the enabling effect of a 1790 parliamentary statute.

[24] The political motives of the Reformation legislation are well documented: G. R. Elton, *Policy and Police: The Enforcement of the Reformation in the Age of Thomas Cromwell* (Cambridge, 1972); G. R. Elton, *Reform and Reformation: England 1509–1558* (London, 1977); N. L. Jones, *Parliament and the Settlement of Religion* (London, 1982); S. E. Lehmberg, *The Reformation Parliament, 1529–1536* (Cambridge, 1970); J. J. Scarisbrick, *Henry VIII* (London, 1968); L. Stone, 'The political programme of Thomas Cromwell', *Bulletin of the Institute of Historical Research*, 24 (1951), 1.

[25] For the view that the Welsh Church Act 1914 was designed to redress grievances felt by Nonconformists rather than for the good of the Church of England in Wales, see O.W. Jones, 'The Welsh church in the nineteenth century', and D. Walker, 'Disestablishment and independence', in D. Walker (ed.), *A History of the Church in Wales* (Penarth, 1976, reissued, 1990); K. O. Morgan, *Rebirth of a Nation: Wales 1880–1980* (2nd edn., Oxford, 1982); *Tithe Commission v Welsh Church Commissioners* [1943] 1 Ch 183 at 196 *per* Lord Goddard: 'its object was to divert the tithe from the Church and to apply it to secular purposes so that the tithe payer would not be supporting an ecclesiastical institution with which he was not in sympathy.'

[26] An Agreed Statement by the Second Anglican–Roman Catholic International Commission (ARCIC II), *Church as Communion* (1991).

[27] A. V. Dulles, *Models of the Church* (2nd edn., Dublin, 1988) 34ff.

Vatican II moved away from this view, presenting not one but many concepts of the church. On one hand, the church is a spiritual community, the 'mystical body of Christ', existing 'in the nature of a sacrament—a sign or instrument . . . of communion with God and of unity among all men',[28] a communion of people 'brought into unity from the unity of the Father, the Son and the Holy Spirit' with 'the mission of proclaiming and establishing among all peoples the kingdom of Christ and of God'.[29] In the church 'the life of Christ is communicated to those who believe and who, through the sacraments, are united in a hidden and real way to Christ'.[30] On the other hand, the church is also a visible hierarchical institution existing to teach, sanctify, and govern.[31] However, 'the society structured with hierarchical organs and the mystical community, the earthly Church and the Church endowed with heavenly riches, are not to be thought of as two realities . . . they form one complex reality which comes together from a human and divine element',[32] directed by the Holy Spirit and having as its first law the salvation of souls:*salus animarum suprema lex*; the church is a community 'both holy and sinful, as needing repentance and reform',[33] whose 'original reason for being . . . is that of service'.[34] It is within these ecclesiologies that canon law plays its part. For Pope Paul VI canon law is 'the law of a society that is indeed visible but also supernatural',[35] established 'for the guidance and salvation of the people of God'.[36] As Pope John Paul II has stressed, 'it is sufficiently clear that the purpose of the Code is not in any way to replace faith, grace, charisms and above all charity in the life of the church or of Christ's faithful', but to operate as 'an effective instrument by the help of which the Church will be able to perfect itself in the spirit of the second Vatican Council and show itself ever more equal to carry out its salvific role in the world'; to this end, canon law concerns 'the renewal of christian life' and 'must be truly in accord with the salvific mission entrusted to the Church'.[37]

---

[28] *LG* (1965) 1I, 1,7 (I Cor. 10: 17, 12: 12); Y. Congar, *The Mystery of the Church* (Baltimore, 1960); see also K. Rahner, 'The concept of mystery in Catholic theology', *Theological Investigations* (Baltimore, 1966) Vol. 4, 36–73; for the idea of the church as sacrament, see T. O'Dea, 'The church as *sacramentum mundi*', *Concilium*, 8(6) (1970), 36.

[29] *LG*, I, 4,5; J. Hamer, *The Church is a Communion* (New York, 1964).

[30] *LG*, I, 7; H. Kung, *The Church* (London, 1968) 203–59; R. McBrien, 'The church: sign and instrument of unity', *Concilium*, 8(6) (1970), 45.

[31] *LG*, III; B. C. Butler, *The Idea of the Church* (Baltimore, 1962) 39ff; A. Greeley, 'Sociology and church structure', *Concilium*, 8(6) (1970), 26.

[32] *LG*, I, 8; see also Pius XII, Encyclical *Mystici Corporis* (1943).

[33] *LG*, I, 8, II; see also E. Bianchi, *Reconciliation: The Function of the Church* (New York, 1969); *CIC*, c. 1752: the salvation of souls is the supreme law.

[34] Paul VI, 27 Jan. 1969, in *The Pope Speaks*, 14 (1969–70), 40.

[35] F. Morrisey, 'The spirit of canon law and the teachings of Pope Paul VI', *Readings*, 17.

[36] *The Pope Speaks*, 14 (1969–70), 40; see also his Allocution of 28 Jan. 1972: 'A community without law, far from being or ever being able to be, in this world, the community of charity, has never been and will never be anything else than a community of the arbitrary' (W. H. Woestman (ed.), *Papal Allocutions to the Roman Rota 1939–1994* (Ottawa, 1994) 112).

[37] *CCL: TC*, xxiv ff.; see also W. Aymans, 'Ecclesiological implications of the new legislation', *Studia Canonica*, 17 (1983), 63–93 and *Readings*, 118–44.

Within this framework, canon law is seen as assisting in the spiritual life of the church.[38] According to Pope Paul VI, '[t]o limit ecclesial law to a rigid order of injunctions would be to violate the Spirit who guides us toward perfect charity in the unity of the Church'; the first concern is 'to deepen the work of the Spirit which must be expressed in the church's law' which itself 'responds to a need inherent in the church as an organised community' and 'devotes the first place to the spirit which is its supreme law'.[39] Similarly, for Robert Ombres the end of church law is 'the government of the Church and the guidance of the faithful to sanctification and ultimately to eternal life';[40] 'law can contribute to sustaining and expressing the freedom of the children of God, to their doing the truth in love because it is part of our experience of love and reality, part of our sense of community and part of our critical judgment'.[41] In short, as John Alesandro explains, '[t]he Code does not masquerade as the means of salvation [but] . . . represent[s] for the people of God part of the contemporary way of '‘putting on Christ'’, the Church's vision of itself at this moment in history'.[42] In these senses, as was suggested by Pope Paul VI, 'the church's juridical activity is . . . a sacramental sign of salvation . . . [which] can have no other aim but to manifest and serve the life of the Spirit'.[43] This approach was employed by those engaged in the revision of the Code after Vatican II: law takes on the nature of a sacrament or sign of the supernatural life of the Christian faithful and 'must be in accord with the supernatural end or purpose of the church'.[44] The general idea is summed up by George Lobo: '[c]hurch law plays the positive role of drawing attention to some demands of the Christian vocation. It provides for the spiritual well-being of the faithful.'[45]

The pastoral dimension of canon law is crucial in modern Roman Catholic jurisprudence, and many writers, such as John Alesandro, argue that pastoral care should be its essential purpose: canon law is 'not meant to be a text for academic rumination but an effective instrument to guide the life of the people of God . . . its practical intent . . . the promotion of pastoral renewal and reform'.[46]

---

[38] G. May, 'Ecclesiastical law', K. Rahner (ed.), *Encyclopedia of Theology* (London, 1981) 395 ff: 'God is not the God of confusion but of peace' (I Cor. 14: 33); '[t]he activity of the Holy Spirit in the Church does not exclude the need for law in the maintenance of right order'; '[t]he Spirit of God . . . enables [the faithful] to recognise the precepts and prohibitions of the law as the way of the Spirit and fulfill the demands of the law from inner conviction'; see also P. M. Boyle, 'The relationship of law to love', *The Jurist*, 25 (1965), 393.

[39] 29 Jan. 1970, *The Pope Speaks*, 15 (1970–71), 56

[40] R. Ombres, 'Faith, doctrine and Roman Catholic canon law', *ELJ*, 1(4) (1989), 33 at 33, 37.

[41] R. Ombres, 'Why then the law?', *New Blackfriars* (1974), 296 at 304.

[42] *CCL: TC*, 22.

[43] 8 Feb. 1973, *The Pope Speaks*, 18 (1973–4), 77; see also D. J. Vella, 'Canon law and the mystical body', *The Jurist*, 22 (1962), 412–32.   [44] *Readings*, 84 at 85–92.

[45] G. Lobo, 'The Christian and canon law', *Readings*, 30 at 31.

[46] *CCL: TC*, 6, 20–2; J. Alesandro, 'Pastoral opportunities', *Chicago Studies*, 23 (1984), 97–118.

Consequently, for those involved in the revision of the Code, in 'directly promoting pastoral care' canon law must express 'the spirit of charity, temperance, humaneness, and moderation, which as so many supernatural virtues distinguish the laws of the Church from every human or profane law'. As such '[a] reasonable amount of discretionary power and authority should be left in the hands of pastors and those having the care of souls to determine the duties of the faithful and to strike a happy balance between the duties of each individual and the conditions and circumstances surrounding his or her life'.[47] Paul Winninger adopts 'pastoral' in its broadest sense 'as practically synonymous with mission', 'evangelization or strictly missionary activity, outward-looking . . . and inward-looking pastoral work . . . teaching, worship and the building up of the People of God'. For Winninger, whether canon law is pastoral depends on it being *an evangelical law*, based on 'the duty to refer to and return to the gospel', a *realistic law*, capable of application, a *coherent law*, providing the means for mission, a *catholic law*, 'adapted to the customs and traditions of the various nations, linked with a common centre which must ensure the unity of the constitutive institutions of the Church', an *experimental law*, and an *ecumenical law*, coming as close as possible to the institutions of the other churches.[48]

THE ORDER THEORY

A second general theory focuses on internal regulation as disciplinary or coercive, a juridical expression of the values of ecclesiastical order and control. The order theory is presented less emphatically in the Church of England than in Roman Catholic jurisprudence. Whilst on one hand, as the Archbishop of Canterbury observed in 1965, 'in a spiritual society order and unity are created not by law alone, but by something more spiritually compelling . . . [by] a spirit of good will and common loyalty',[49] on the other the Archbishops' Commission considered that canon law exists to 'prevent anything creeping into [the Church's] life that may hinder it from performing its proper functions'.[50] Regulatory instruments are made in the church, as Archbishop Garbett put it, 'for its spiritual welfare and for the sake of its good

---

[47] *Readings*, 84 at 86–7.

[48] P. Winninger, 'A pastoral canon law', *Concilium*, 8(5) (1969), 28; see also A. Tuche, 'The code of canon law of 1983 and ecumenical relations', in M. Theriault and J. Thorn (eds.), *The New Code of Canon Law*, Proceedings of the Fifth International Congress of Canon Law, 2 vols. (Ottawa, 1986) I, 401.

[49] Debate on the Prayer Book (Alternative and Other Services) Measure, *ORPD*, 5th Series, HL Deb., Vol. 263, 18 Feb. 1965, 651 at 654.

[50] *RACCL*, 3; for an early statement of the order theory see Richard Hooker, *The Laws of Ecclesiastical Polity* (1594), Books I-IV, edited by R. Bayne (New York, 1907), Bk. IV; see also *WAOB*, 1.4 ff.

order'.[51] For some in the Church of England this expresses 'the ancient tradition of Canon Law as synodically accepted norms by which the household of God lives out its life in the Spirit'.[52] Consequently, internal church law is designed to create institutions and offices within the church, to distribute functions to these for the service of the church (by the conferral of enabling powers and rights and by the imposition of limitations on their exercise), to define the relationship between institutions and offices (thereby providing systems of oversight and control over the use of powers and the discharging of duties), and to distribute rights to individuals not holding office in the church (by providing structures for their protection and dealing with occasions of disagreement).[53] Using the concept of order, ecclesiastical legislators commonly devise regulations 'to deal with the situation when, for one reason or another, relationships . . . have completely broken down and it has become impossible for any effective pastoral care to be exercised'.[54] The fundamentals of the order theory were presented by the Deputy Dean of the Arches in *Re St Hilary Cornwall*: '[w]here a number of people are united in a community . . . such as the Anglican Church . . . the mutual rights, obligations and duties of the members of the community must be measured and determined by rules of some kind'; in this community 'when people are robbed of the rights which the law accords them, and which the law is supposed to protect, and, if necessary enforce', the use of formal methods of control will be inevitable.[55] The need for order is based on the assumption, accepted by the Archbishops' Commission, that since 'the Church is for the most part made up of ordinary frail human beings, the rules and regulations must be something more than exhortations, which anyone is at liberty to set aside when he thinks fit, or directions

---

[51] C. F. Garbett, *Church and State in England* (London, 1950) 228; Hill, *EL*, 1–2: 'The purpose of the law of the Church . . . is to regulate the functioning of the Church and the conduct of its component members by a combination of commands, prohibitions and permissions. . . . Superficially, the law is concerned only with order and discipline, but a closer analysis reveals that it touches upon spiritual, theological, pastoral and evangelistic concerns at the heart of the Christian faith.'

[52] *York Journal of Convocation* (Westminster, 1976) 45 *per* Canon P. H. Boulton.

[53] For ideas of protection see e.g. *Norfolk County Council v Knights and Ors and Caister-on-Sea Joint Burial Committee* [1958] 1 All ER 394 at 396 *per* Ellison Ch. (Norwich Con. Ct.); *Hargreaves and Ors v Church Commissioners of England* [1983] 3 All ER 17 (PC) at 20 *per* Lord Scarman: 'a [pastoral] scheme . . . will represent . . . the fully considered view of those charged by law with providing the cure of souls in the diocese and with protecting, as far as practicable, the traditions, needs and characteristics of individual parishes'; *Re St Mary's Balham* [1978] 1 All ER 993; see also for protection against public ecclesiastical disorder (in a Methodist church) *Abrahams and Ors v Cavey* [1967] 3 All ER 179 and the references in it to *Girt v Fillingham* (1900) 64 JP 457 and *Palmer v Roffey* (1824) 2 Add 141; for law used to clarify previous laws see *Re St Nicholas's, Baddesley Ensor* [1982] 2 All ER 351 at 352 *per* Aglionby Ch. (Birmingham Con. Ct.) (concerning the intention behind the Church of England (Miscellaneous Provisions) Measure 1976).

[54] Debate on the Incumbents (Vacation of Benefices) Measure 1977 *per* Bishop of London, *ORPD*, HL Deb., Vol. 382, 2 May 1977, 808 at 809.

[55] [1938] 4 All ER 147 at 152 *per* Stable Dep. Dean.

which can be disobeyed with impunity—otherwise members of the Church will obey only when it is convenient'.[56]

In the context of non-compliance with church law, the employment of sanctions is seen as justified in order to commend obedience, to deter disobedience, and to correct indiscipline.[57] Sanctions are not seen, however, as expressing vindictive punishment: as Lord Selbourne explained in *Mackonochie v Lord Penzance*, '[t]he ecclesiastical law . . . even in those proceedings which are called (and in some sense are) criminal and penal, has for its object, not the punishment of individual offenders, but the correction of manners, and the discipline of the Church'.[58] Ordinarily, as Herbert Box explains, '[t]he sanctions the Church possesses and the penalties it can inflict are purely spiritual'; '[o]bedience is to be enforced, not positively by material means, but negatively by exclusion from spiritual privileges'.[59] In addition, however, modern church law provides for the imposition of a variety of material sanctions.[60] Finally, a key limitation in Anglican jurisprudence is that it is *not* the purpose of church law to order or correct the private lives of individuals, except in so far as private conduct may impinge upon the performance of public ecclesiastical functions.[61] Whilst the concept was not fully developed, the 1947 Commission emphasized that canon law concerns not the 'private spiritual affairs' of individual members of the Church, but the latter's 'public spiritual affairs': canonical rules exist for 'the ordering of the public spiritual affairs of the Church of God'.[62]

The order theory is more elaborately expounded in Roman Catholic jurisprudence. First, canon law seeks to establish a just order for the church. As 'the communion of all in Christ is such that all have a right to justice and an obligation to provide it',[63] so canon law seeks to effect a 'responsible autonomy of the individual against all eventual interference and abuse' in

---

[56] *RACCL*, 4.

[57] Ibid.: 'they must be laws with penalties attached in the case of their non-observance, where those who are accused of disobeying the laws of the Church can be tried'; *York Journal of Convocation* (Westminster, 1976) 45 *per* Canon P. H. Boulton: 'If we say there is no need for law and order in the Church or if we try to make the Church's law loose and something easily circumvented, then we are in no position to take any kind of stand about breaches of the law in other areas of life, like dishonesty, vandalism and violence.'

[58] (1881) 6 App Cas 424 at 433; the word 'penalty' is still used, however: *Bland v Archdeacon of Cheltenham* [1972] 1 All ER 1012 at 1017; for the principle that the faculty jurisdiction is not to be employed punitively see for e.g. *Re St Mary's, Tyne Dock No. 2* [1958] 1 All ER 1 at 8 *per* Moore Ch. (Durham Con. Ct.): 'The removal of candlesticks would be in the nature of a punishment of the petitioners which is not the concern of the faculty jurisdiction'; for a recent use of this idea see also *Re St. Mary's, Balham* [1978] 1 All ER 993.

[59] H. Box, *The Principles of Canon Law* (Oxford, 1949) 25.

[60] *Re St Thomas à Becket, Framfield* [1989] 1 All ER 170 at 173 (financial liability of churchwardens for failure to obtain a faculty); see *post* Part VI for injunctions and recovery of debts owed to the church.

[61] See *post* Ch. 7 on public scandal caused by practising clerical homosexuality; *post* Chapter 12 for public scandal from private conduct resulting in excommunication.   [62] *RACCL*, 5.

[63] *Readings*, 17 at 18–20, 22; 4 Oct. 1969, *The Pope Speaks*, 14 (1969–70), 374.

order 'to promote the growth of the community and, at the same time, the capacities for initiative and enrichment of the individual members'.[64] As 'a pastoral means of constantly fostering and preserving peace' canon law seeks to control the use of arbitrary power as 'proof against the weaknesses caused by attention to special interests'.[65] In its contribution to the establishment of ecclesial justice, canon law assumes an educative role: James Coriden suggests that it 'spells out the expectations of members . . . and the ideals of religious life . . . to lead the people to a virtuous life, not simply an external compliance with rules'; it 'challenges the church to strive toward love as its goal'.[66] Secondly, therefore, canon law seeks to provide structures for the settlement of ecclesiastical disputes. The Spanish canonist José Setien treats canon law as fixing the bounds of ecclesial tensions, the 'institutionalization of tensions': '[t]ension can be said to be institutionalized when rights are assigned to different members of the community, thereby guaranteeing them a sphere of competence and action, by virtue of the juridical protection implied in the assignation of rights. This permits the community to utilize its creative forces within the limits of the higher imperative of the common good'.[67]

Thirdly, canon law distributes and protects rights and duties: '[t]he principal and essential object of canon law is to determine and safeguard the rights and obligations of each individual person with respect to the rights and obligations of others and of society at large'.[68] To this end, for James Coriden, canon law exists 'to articulate the rights and duties of the faithful, and to provide means for their protection'.[69] Fifthly, therefore, some canon law may be coercive: the church as 'made up of ordinary humans, will inevitably contain some who from time to time will deviate from the rules and commit [ecclesiastical] crimes; in the interests of due order, it may therefore be necessary to impose sanctions'.[70] The Code claims for the church an inherent right to constrain the faithful with penal sanctions,[71] but '[p]enalties are to be established only in so far as they are really necessary for the better maintenance of ecclesiastical discipline'.[72] Sanctions, to be used as a last resort after pastoral measures have failed,[73] are justified for the purpose of deterrence,[74] and, for Alesandro, to

---

[64] 4 Feb. 1977, *The Pope Speaks*, 22 (1977), 177; ibid., 15 (1970–71), 55.

[65] 4 Feb. 1977, *The Pope Speaks*, 22 (1977), 179; 30 Jan. 1975, *The Pope Speaks*, 20 (1975–6).

[66] *Introduction*, 6.

[67] J. Setien, 'Tensions in the church', *Concilium*, 8(5) (1969), 35; see also K. Matthews, 'Procedures of compromise for the resolution of conflict', *Studia Canonica*, 18 (1984), 55.

[68] *CCL: TC*, 5–7.

[69] *Introduction*, 5; see also P. J. Cogan, 'The protection of rights in hierarchical churches: an ecumenical survey', *The Jurist*, 46 (1986), 205; J. H. Provost, 'Protecting and promoting the rights of Christians: some implications for church structure', ibid., 289.   [70] *Readings*, 99 at 111.

[71] *CIC*, c. 1312.

[72] Ibid., c. 1317; *CCL: TC*, 897–900; L. Gerosa, 'Penal law and ecclesial reality: the applicability of the penal sanctions laid down in the new code', *Concilium*, 185 (1986), 60.

[73] *CIC*, c. 1341; see also J. H. Provost, 'Revision of Book V of the code of canon law', *Studia Canonica*, 9 (1975), 135.   [74] *CIC*, c. 1326.

help the faithful to appreciate the disparity between their attitudes and actions and the values of the Gospel as proclaimed by the church, 'to bring about personal repentance and reconciliation with the community'.[75] According to Thomas Green sanctions exist 'to protect the integrity of the community's faith, communion and service': it is 'imperative that there be some kind of framework to restore peace and order and to integrate the offending party within the life of the community'; if the church has no reaction to 'significant breaches of its faith and order . . . its identity as a sign of God's kingdom would be seriously jeopardized'.[76] Peter Huizing echoes the idea: the church cannot be taken seriously, cannot be respected and comment on secular disorder, if its own life is not characterized by discipline.[77] In the Code itself, penalties are classified as either 'medicinal', emphasizing reconciliation of the offender to the community, or 'expiatory', to restore the community's order, to repair scandal, and to deter.[78]

A THEORY OF MUTUALITY: RULES, PRINCIPLES, AND NORMS

Ideas of facility and order are not mutually exclusive. On one hand, ecclesial order itself may be construed as a facility: the church is able to fulfill its mission more effectively when the community is obliged to act or refrain from acting and when it has a clear framework of structures within which to do so. Moreover, prescriptive and coercive regulation may enable the enjoyment of ecclesiastical facilities: the imposition of a legal duty on a body or person may generate *for others* rights to facilities which that body or person is legally required to provide as bearer of that duty. Much regulation in the Church of England may be analysed in terms of the commanding of facilities: duties to consult, to present reports, to give notice of decisions, for example, all aim to provide facilities for those affected by these decisions.[79] On the other hand, the provision of facilities may generate or necessitate order, typically when structures provide a facility to a body or person for the purpose of conferring power to control. Moreover, regulation designed to facilitate may be effective only if accompanied by coercive arrangements: rights-conferring rules are

[75] *CCL: TC*, 19.

[76] Ibid., 893 ff.; see also T. J. Green, 'Penal law revisited: the revision of the penal law schema', *Studia Canonica*, 15 (1981), 135.

[77] 'Crime and punishment in the church', *Concilium*, 8(3) (1967), 57.

[78] *CCL: TC*, 906–9. The code seeks to move away from the earlier idea of penalties as retributive: E. Taunton, *The Law of the Church* (London, 1906) 539–40: '[p]unishment is the vengeance for evil doing, and it is devised for the amendment of man'; canonical censures 'are sometimes used as vindictive punishments'. For the relation of sanctions to principles of forgiveness see N. Doe, 'A facilitative canon law: the problem of sanctions and forgiveness', N. Doe (ed.), *Essays in Canon Law* (Cardiff, 1992) 69.   [79] *Burridge v Tyler* [1992] 1 All ER 437 at 442.

frequently accompanied or supported by rules protective of those who might be affected by the bearer's exercise of a right.[80]

Whether arrangements effecting facility and order are binding and capable of being enforced depends not only on the authority of the regulatory instrument in question but also upon the intent of its maker as expressed in the language of the instrument itself. On one hand, the employment of regulatory instruments in the form of law properly so called, typified with synodical measures, may be understood as an exercise by the Church of England of *imperium*, or coercive power, in so far as rights and duties contained in these instruments are clearly court-enforceable. On the other hand, the use of quasi-legislation, typified with codes of practice, may be understood as the exercise by the church of *dominium* or regulation by persuasion; when it is intended to bind, quasi-legislation may also be understood as an exercise of *imperium*.[81] Species of ecclesiastical regulation, from whatever source, are expressed in the form of rules, principles, and norms or standards; these in turn will be either rights- or power-conferring, enabling or entitling a body or person to act, or duty-imposing, obliging a body or person to act or to refrain from acting.[82] With regard to many forms of ecclesiastical regulation, however, it is often difficult to determine whether an entity is a rule, a principle, a norm, or a standard—and, therefore, whether its purpose is to bind.

With regard to *rules*, these are formulated with precision and expressed in the form 'if X, then Y'; the first part, 'if X', known as the *protasis*, is descriptive and sets out the scope and conditions under which the rule applies, and the second part, 'then Y', the *apodosis*, is prescriptive, stating whether the conduct regulated by the rule is prohibited, commanded/required, or permitted.[83] Analysis of structure elucidates whether the entity is a rule, and therefore its purpose: rules exist to bind, to prohibit, to command, or to permit;[84] but whether the prohibition, precept, or right may be enforced, executively or judicially, depends on the instrument in which it is published. Rules are found in all instruments of ecclesiastical regulation, and the entity constituting the rule will usually be expressed with such sequences of words as 'must/shall/may not', 'must/shall' or 'may'.[85] Interestingly, structures

---

[80] The Archbishop of Canterbury understood the draft Synodical Government Measure 1969 as facultative and ordering: *ORPD*, 5th Series, HL Deb., Vol. 302, 16 June 1969, 842 at 843; *AG v Dean and Chapter of Ripon* [1945] 1 All ER 479 at 482 (the passage does not appear in the report [1945] P 239 at 244) (*per* Uthwatt J: the Cathedrals Measure 1931 provided a constitution to 'define the powers and duties of the bishop and of the dean and chapter and the manner in which the dean and chapter are to conduct their internal affairs'.

[81] For *imperium* and *dominium* regulation in secular jurisprudence, see T. Daintith, 'Legal analysis of economic policy', *Journal of Law and Society*, 9 (1982), 191.

[82] For the concepts in secular jurisprudence see H. L. A. Hart, *The Concept of Law* (2nd edn., Oxford, 1994)

[83] W. Twining and D. Miers, *How to Do Things with Rules* (2nd edn., London, 1982) 136 ff.

[84] See R. Cotterrell, *The Politics of Jurisprudence: A Critical Introduction to Legal Philosophy* (London, 1989) Ch. 4.

[85] Canon B22(2): 'If the minister shall refuse . . . to baptise any such infant, the parents . . . may apply to the bishop . . . who shall . . . give such directions as he thinks fit'.

appearing in national and diocesan quasi-legislation are often expressed as rules, giving rise to a presumption that they bind.[86] Sometimes, however, whilst they may be expressed in imperative language, such formulae contain no obvious *protasis*.[87] In this sense, many formulae may be classified simply as *principles*, prohibitions, precepts, and permissions expressed at a higher level of generality,[88] or simply descriptive general statements.[89] Some formulae are expressed as *norms*,[90] directory or aspirational in nature rather than mandatory; norms typically contain the words 'ought' or 'should'.[91] The nature, and therefore the purpose, of some formulae is ambiguous;[92] even the expression 'rules of guidance' appears in one notable modern synodical measure.[93] In line with the commonly accepted meaning of κανον,[94] the canons themselves have been understood simply as expressing standards, exhortations of a directory nature, and statements of general principle not having the object of binding in an enforceable obligatory sense.[95]

[86] *SDDH*, B27: 'All requests for lay persons, other than readers . . . to preach in parish churches at statutory services or otherwise must be referred direct to the Area Bishop for his express permission'.

[87] Canon B26(2): 'All parents and guardians shall take care that their children receive . . . instruction' in the doctrine, sacraments, and discipline of Christ; Canon A8: 'it is the duty of clergy and people to do their utmost not only to avoid occasions of strife but also to seek in penitence and brotherly charity to heal such divisions'.

[88] See J. Raz, 'Legal principles and the limits of law', *Yale Law Journal*, 81 (1972), 823; SGM 1969, s. 4(1): '*Diocesan synods shall be constituted for all dioceses* in accordance with Part IV of the Church Representation Rules contained in Schedule 3 to this Measure' (emphasis added): whilst expressed in preceptive terms, the first part of this formula assigns no consequence for the non-constitution of a synod; by reference to the second part, the formula may be re-cast as a rule (if a synod is constituted, then it must be constituted in accordance with the schedule).

[89] Canon B25: 'The Church of England has ever held and taught, and holds and teaches still, that the sign of the Cross used in baptism is no part of the substance of the sacrament'. Some interpretation sections in synodical measures, whilst ordinarily descriptive, contain prescriptive rules: EJM 1963 s.66: '"diocese" means a diocese in the province of Canterbury or a diocese . . . in the province of York and "diocesan" *shall* be construed accordingly' (emphasis added).

[90] J. Raz, *The Concept of a Legal System* (Oxford, 1980) 44–50.

[91] *SDH*, V, C.2: 'All clergy should take a day off each week (or two days each fortnight) and again parishes should help to make this possible'; again, this may be re-cast in the nature of a rule: if a cleric wishes to take a day off, then the parish should assist; *BCP*, 288: 'It is expedient that every person, thus baptized, should be confirmed by the Bishop so soon after his Baptism as conveniently may be; so that he may be admitted to the holy Communion.'

[92] *SDDH*, B.28: where a lay person other than a reader is asked to conduct a family service, 'written approval should first be sought from the Area Bishop. Before giving that permission the Area bishop *will* wish to satisfy himself' *inter alia* that the person has received sufficient training.

[93] Incumbents (Vacation of Benefices) Measure 1977 (as amended 1993), s. 1(1) (referring to the Code of Practice).

[94] J. A. Coriden, *Introduction*, 3; see Gal. 6: 16; for the use of equivalent terms in the New Testament see e.g. H. Ridderbos, *Paul: An Outline of His Theology* (1975) for *taxis*, τάξις (order, Col. 2: 5), *phulaxes*, Øυλακή (rule, 1 Tim. 5: 19), *parangelia*, παραγγελιά (calling, commanding, 1 Thess. 4: 2; 1 Tim. 1: 18) *diatassein*, διατάσσειν (ordinance, 1 Cor. 7: 17).

[95] *York Journal of Convocation* (Westminster, 1976) 44 (standards), 46 (canons as norms); cf. 48 ('directory instruments which, by the authority of the issuing body, will command obedience'); 55, *per* Rev K. J. T. Elphinstone: 'certain canons . . . cannot really be called law at all, if you mean by "law" something which has a sanction or a penalty attached to its breach' (in this sense the canons are not law as they do not bind the laity: see *post* Ch. 8).

Roman Catholic jurisprudence contains a coherent theory of mutuality as between facility and order.[96] In the Apostolic Constitution *Sacrae Disciplinae Leges* (1983) Pope John Paul II states simply that the purpose of the 'juridical formulae' in the Code is to 'serve the whole Church' and in so doing it 'looks towards the achievement of order in the ecclesial society'; canon law 'facilitates . . . an orderly development in the life both of the ecclesial society and of the individual persons who belong to it' and is regarded 'as the essential instrument for the preservation of right order, both in individual and social life and in the Church's zeal'.[97] As such, for Pope John Paul II, '[s]ince the Church is established in the form of a social and visible unit, it needs rules, so that its hierarchical and organic structure may be visible'. Regulation is needed so that 'its exercise of the functions divinely entrusted to it, particularly of sacred power and of the administration of the sacraments, is properly ordered'. Facility and order are also provided: through canon law 'the mutual relationships of Christ's faithful are reconciled in justice based on charity, with the rights of each safeguarded and defined'. Lastly, canon law is needed so that 'the common initiatives which are undertaken so that christian life may ever be more perfectly carried out, are supported, strengthened and promoted'.[98]

These ideas have been developed by Roman Catholic canonists. Robert Ombres stresses that law is necessary to bind the church as a society: 'inherent in the notion of law is that it binds and gathers, it is an integrative mechanism', existing 'to promote the common good'.[99] For James Coriden canon law operates 'to facilitate the attainment of the purpose or common good of the society', helping the community 'to be what it is meant to be, and to carry out its mission in the world'. In this respect canon law affords stability for the church as a society; it aims 'to provide good order, reliable procedures and predictable outcomes'. Leaders need to be elected, the sacraments to be celebrated, the Word of God to be preached, decisions to be made, and property to be administered: '[t]he canons govern these functions, which are vital as well as stabalizing'.[100] For Francis Morrisey the purpose of canon law

---

[96] Roman Catholic jurisprudence frequently identifies duties with rights: see e.g. *CIC*, c. 211: 'All the Christian faithful have the duty (*officium*) and the right (*ius*) to work so that the divine message of salvation may increasingly reach the whole of humankind in every age and in every land'; c. 229: 'Lay people have the duty (*obligatione tenentur*) and the right (*iure gaudent*) to acquire the knowledge of christian teaching'; c. 232: 'it is the duty (*officium*) and the proper and exclusive right (*ius*) of the Church to train those who are deputed to sacred ministries'; to the common lawyer, this identification of duties (based on 'must') with rights (based on 'may') is a difficult concept: see *post* Ch. 13; see also J. P. McIntyre, 'The acquired right: a new context', *Studia Canonica*, 26 (1992), 25.

[97] *CCL: TC*, xxiv–vi; J. Neumann, 'The specific social nature of the church and its consequences for canon law', *Concilium*, 8(5) (1969), 7; see also G. Robinson, 'Law in the life of the church', *Studia Canonica*, 17 (1983), 47.

[98] *CCL: TC*, xxvi. For a comparison of the 1917 and 1983 Codes see F. Morrisey, 'Is the new code an improvement for the law of the Catholic Church?', *Concilium* (1986), 32.

[99] R. Ombres, 'Why then the law?', *New Blackfriars* (1974), 296.   [100] *Introduction*, 5–6.

is to act as 'a bond of unity . . . to help structure Christian institutions by seeing to order and promoting concord'.[101] This role for canon law also serves the purpose of enabling the church to exist as a communion which consists, as Eugenio Corecco puts it, 'in the fact of postulating the total immanence, and the inseparability, of all the elements that make up the Church'; canon law reflects and contributes to this *communio* 'in the structural relationship of reciprocity between sacrament and Word, between the common and the ministerial priesthood, between the faithful and the Church, between duties and rights, between universal and local Church'.[102] Michel Lejeune accepts that the idea of communion is not itself a 'juridical notion', but goes rather to the inner life of the church—yet canon law has a part to play in assisting relations within the communion: '[s]tating that the Church is a communion also means that all its members have a place in it and a role to play in its life.' In this respect, canon law also distributes responsibilities to those sharing in the communion,[103] and its structures are clearly represented as either duty-imposing or rights-conferring.[104]

FLEXIBILITY: THE RELAXATION OF RULES

Whilst in the Roman Catholic Church canon law must as a fundamental principle be applied,[105] unless it has been made unlawfully,[106] the relaxation of rules may occur in five ways. First, the canons sometimes allow administrators and judges to disapply canon law by virtue of exceptions built into the canons themselves: relaxation is often based on a concept of necessity.[107] Secondly, canonical equity enables the relaxation of law: according to Paul VI, 'in canon law it is equity which governs the application of norms to concrete cases, with the salvation of souls as the goal. . . . Equity takes the form of mildness, mercy and pastoral charity and seeks not a rigid application of the law but the true welfare of the faithful'.[108] Appeal is made to canonical

---

[101] *Readings*, 23.

[102] 'Ecclesiological bases of the code', *Concilium*, 185 (1986), 3 at 7 ff.

[103] M. Lejeune, 'Demythologizing canon law', *Studia Canonica*, 21 (1987), 5.

[104] See e.g. J. Koury, 'From prohibited to permitted: transitions in the code of canon law', *Studia Canonica*, 24 (1990), 147; 'Hard and soft canons continued: canonical institutes for legal flexibility and accommodation', ibid., 25 (1991), 325; for canon law as a body of norms conveying 'decisions' see L. Örsy, *Theology and Canon Law* (1992) 146.

[105] See e.g. *CIC*, c. 12 (universal laws bind everywhere), c. 135 (ecclesiastical powers of government must be exercised according to law). [106] See *post* Ch. 3.

[107] See *CIC*, e.g. c. 906 (a priest may not celebrate mass without at least some member of the faithful unless for a just and reasonable cause); c. 805 (baptism must be administered according to liturgical books, except for cases of urgent necessity); c. 853 (in baptism water must be blessed except in cases of necessity); c. 860(1) (no baptism in private homes except in necessity); c. 932 (Eucharist must be celebrated in a sacred place, unless necessity demands otherwise); c. 1323 (judges must not impose sanctions on a person who acted out of necessity).

[108] 19 Feb. 1977, *The Pope Speaks*, 22 (1977), 171.

equity to fill a *lacuna legis* or to relax law if its application will result in injustice.[109] The faithful have a right when summoned to a competent authority to be judged according to law which is to be applied *cum aequitate*.[110] When universal or particular laws are silent on a matter 'the general principles of law are to observed with canonical equity'.[111] The use of equity to relax the application of law does not abrogate the law in question.[112] Thirdly, some suggest that, under the doctrine of reception, a law may be neither applicable to nor bind the believing community if it has not been accepted by that community, when it has been promulgated but not yet complied with or acted upon.[113] Fourthly, law will cease to apply, will be abrogated, by its non-usage through the development of contrary custom: contrary custom applies, that is, only where a law has been fully established and subsequently falls into desuetude.[114]

Finally, canon law may be relaxed by means of dispensation. According to the Code, dispensation is 'the relaxation of a merely ecclesiastical law in a particular case'; it may be granted 'within the limits of their competence, by those who have executive power, and by those who either explicitly or implicitly have the power of dispensing, whether by virtue of the law itself or by lawful delegation'; however, laws which define what constitutes juridic institutions or acts cannot be the subject of dispensation.[115] Whereas the Roman pontiff enjoys extensive powers of dispensation (some expressly reserved to him alone),[116] the usual dispensing body is the diocesan bishop (the ordinary) who may dispense with both universal and particular law established by the supreme authority of the church for his territory or his subjects; he may not dispense from procedural or penal laws, nor from those whose dispensation is reserved to the Apostolic See or some other authority. Moreover, the bishop may dispense from the requirements of diocesan law (created by himself) as well as from laws passed by a plenary or provincial council or by the national episcopal conference when this is for the good of the faithful. Pastors (and other presbyters), on the other hand, have no general powers of dispensation from universal or particular law unless this has been

---

[109] Paul VI, 8 Feb. 1973, 'The pastoral nature of church law and canonical equity', W. H. Woestman, *Papal Allocutions* (1994) 115.

[110] *CIC*, c. 221; the principle is repeated for religious (c. 686: *servata aequitate et caritate*; c.702: *aequitatem et evangelicam caritatem*) and for penal transfer cases (c. 1752).

[111] *CIC*, c. 19; for 'natural equity' see c. 271(3) (a cleric moved to one diocese but still incardinated in another may for a just cause be recalled by his bishop 'provided agreements with the other bishop and natural equity [*naturalis aequitas*] are observed').

[112] J. Koury, 'Hard and soft canons continued: canonical institutes for legal flexibility and accommodation', *Studia Canonica*, 25 (1991), 335 at 359.

[113] J. A. Coriden, 'The canonical doctrine of reception', *The Jurist*, 50 (1990), 58.

[114] *CIC*, c. 26 (the *consuetudo contra legem* must have been used for thirty continuous years and not specifically approved by the competent authority; a centenary or immemorial custom prevails over a canon which forbids future customs).   [115] *CIC*, cc. 85, 86.

[116] *CIC*, cc. 87–8; as the pontiff, under c. 1404, may be judged by no one, it is arguable that papal dispensation powers may be used without limitation; see *COCLA*, 872.

expressly granted to them: dispensation power may be delegated executively. The exercise of the power of dispensation is subject to a series of safeguards. Dispensation must not be granted without 'a just and reasonable cause': the dispensing authority must consider the circumstances of the case and the gravity of the law from which dispensation is to be given. Otherwise the dispensation is illicit and, unless given by the legislator himself (or his superior), it is invalid. Yet, when there is doubt about the sufficiency of the reason for dispensation, it is still granted validly and licitly. The power to dispense must be construed restrictively, and a dispensation ceases when the motivating cause has ceased.[117]

Whilst many in the Church of England accept the need for flexible regulation,[118] its modern formal law contains no explicit doctrine of equity similar to that appearing in the Roman Catholic code.[119] Ordinarily, relaxation of rules is dependent on exceptions built into regulatory instruments. Extraordinarily, the doctrine of necessity enables ecclesiastical judges to relax rules, when (through duress of circumstances) the occurrence of a lesser wrong is permitted to prevent the occurrence of a greater wrong.[120] The doctrine has been appealed to by the ecclesiastical judiciary in limited cases,[121] notably with regard to the reservation of the sacrament.[122] However, in those cases where appeal to the doctrine has been made statements have been *obiter*: the doctrine should therefore be classifed merely as an ecclesiastical convention, not a legal principle.[123] In contrast with Roman Catholic canon law, desuetude is not

---

[117] *CIC*, cc. 87–93 (pastors may sometimes dispense from certain laws: cc. 1079, 1196, 1245); see R. G. W. Huysmans, 'The significance of particular law and the nature of dispensation as questions on the rule of papal law', in J. H. Provost and K. Walf (eds.), *Studies in Canon Law* (Leuven, 1991) 37.

[118] *York Journal of Convocation* (Westminster, 1976) 48 *per* Canon P. H. Boulton (citing Dean Addleshaw): 'The nature of the Church, the supernatural aims of its legislation, necessitates a certain fluidity in its laws to meet hard cases, to provide for untoward circumstances and to prevent the law becoming a burden on the conscience. Canonical jurisdiction can never lead souls to heaven if it imitates the rigidity and impersonality of statute law'.

[119] Whether the pre-Reformation doctrines of canonical equity are still operative is a matter of conjecture: for the idea in Lyndwood see F. W. Maitland, *Roman Canon Law in the Church of England* (1898); for pre-Reformation canonical doctrines of equity generally see J. A. Brundage, *Medieval Canon Law* (London, 1995) 154 ff.

[120] *MIECL*, 58, 59, 96, 114, 132; Garth Moore overplayed the extent of its applicablity in secular law: P. R. Glazebrook, 'The necessity plea in English criminal law', *CLJ*, 30 (1972A), 87; indeed, the Law Commission has recommended that the defence of necessity, if it exists at common law at all, should be abolished: Law Com No 83 (1977).

[121] *Hutchins v Denziloe and Loveland* (1792) 1 Hag Con 170 *per* Sir William Scott: churchwardens or private persons may act if a minister is 'guilty of any act grossly offensive', but this is 'a case of instant and overbearing neceesity that supersedes all ordinary rules'.

[122] *Bishopwearmouth (Rector and Churchwardens) v Adey* [1958] 3 All ER 441 (in which Moore Ch recognized necessity as a common law doctrine which 'applies equally to matters ecclesiastical'; he also used it in *Re St Peter and St Paul, Leckhampton* [1967] 3 All ER 1057.

[123] Technically, there was no need for Moore to use the doctrine as reservation had been accepted as permissible, even if strictly illegal, in *Re Lapford (Devon) Parish Church* [1955] P 205 and *Re St Mary Tyne Dock* [1954] 2 All ER 339.

possible when customary usage contradicts what is otherwise applicable under positive law.[124] Some judicial dicta suggest, however, that this is not always the case.[125] This would make sense in so far as it must be determined what status is enjoyed by a rule with which custom is claimed to be inconsistent: clearly a contrary custom will override earlier custom, but contrary custom cannot override synodical measures or canons. A special variant of desuetude arises when laws no longer serve their original purposes, and here there may be no long-term contrary usage. According to pre-Reformation canonical doctrine, a law may be treated as inapplicable by virtue of the fact that the reason for it has ceased to exist (rather than the law in question not being continuously used); the extent to which the *cessante causa cessat lex* principle has survived the Reformation has not been explored.[126]

The place of dispensation in the Church of England is more problematic than that in Roman Catholic Church.[127] As in Roman Catholic canon law, the power of dispensation is treated as the entitlement to authorize executively the relaxation of legal rules in particular circumstances.[128] The structures of rules conferring dispensation powers vary: usually a dispensation is the lifting by one (superior) authority of a duty imposed upon another, and ordinarily bodies or persons do not have power unilaterally to dispense with duties addressed to themselves. There are some exceptions however, in the law of the Church of England, when a body or person upon whom a duty is placed enjoys a discretionary power to relax that duty. Like the Roman pontiff, the Archbishop of Canterbury, '[b]y the laws of this realm' is 'empowered to grant such licences or dispensations as are therein set forth and provided'; 'such licences and dispensations, *being confirmed by the authority of the Queen's*

---

[124] See R. Bursell, 'What is the place of custom in English canon law?', *ELJ*, 1(4) (1989), 12 at 23–4.

[125] *Gore-Booth v Bishop of Manchester* [1920] 2 KB 412 at 424 *per* Lord Coleridge *obiter*: 'Desuetude, if a clerk were accused of illegality in not wearing the vestments prescribed, might well be pleaded. But if the wearing of such vestments had been abandoned, it would be a difficult thing to accuse a clerk of illegality for wearing them, if they had in 1662 been made lawful, and the Act had not been repealed.'

[126] J. A. Brundage, *Medieval Canon Law* (London, 1995) 173 for Gratian, *Decretum*, C. 1 q. 1 c. 41; see H. Krause, '*Cessante causa cessat lex*', *Zeitschrift der Savigny-Stiftung für Rechtsgeschichte*, kanonistische Abteilung, 46 (1960) 81.

[127] C. F. Garbett, *Church and State in England* (London, 1950) 244: 'since the Reformation the practice of granting dispensation has been looked upon in disfavour by the Church of England, and as the field covered by Canon Law has been greatly restricted, there is no longer the same necessity . . . for numerous dispensations from it. It is more in harmony with the spirit of our Church to have as few rules as possible but to require they should be observed faithfully by those they concern.'

[128] See the Report *Dispensation in Practice and Theory with special reference to Anglican Churches* (London, 1942) 159, proposing a measured revival or extension of the practice. For the concept of 'economy' in Orthodox canon law see H. S. Alivisatos who defines it, ibid. 30, as '[t]he suspension of strict enforcement of Canon Law in cases of urgent need and in a spirit of prudent stewardship, condescension and leniency, practised by the Church's leaders, without overlapping the limits of dogma, in order to regularise abnormal conditions, for the salvation of those concerned'.

Majesty, have force and authority not only within the province of Canterbury but throughout all England'.[129] For example, the Archbishop of Canterbury may grant a special licence for the solemnization of matrimony without publication of banns at any convenient time or place.[130] Moreover, each archbishop may remove by faculty the impediment of remarriage imposed on candidates for ordination.[131] As in the Roman Catholic Church, the normal dispensing authority is the diocesan bishop; unlike Roman Catholic canon law provisions, however, his powers are not subject to formal systematic control. Rules conferring episcopal dispensation powers are examples of a superior authority lifting a duty imposed on another. A bishop may dispense with the requirements that no person be authorized to distribute the holy sacrament unless ordained, that a sermon be preached at least once each Sunday, that divine service be conducted in English, and, by common licence, that solemnization of marriage must follow the publication of banns; he may also dispense with the requirement that only those ordained as ministers of the Church of England may conduct services, that candidates (who have been ordained overseas) for ministerial posts take the oath of allegiance, that clergy reside in the area in which they minister, and that a minister must not engage in trade so as to affect the performance of ministerial duties.[132] In none of these areas is there express provision for appeal against the bishop's employment of or refusal to employ the dispensing power in question.

Sometimes dispensation provisions enable the relaxation of duties by those upon whom the duties are imposed. These are designed to accommodate changing needs and circumstances. For instance, morning and evening prayer must be said or sung in every parish church at least on all Sundays and other principal feast days; holy communion must be celebrated similarly.[133] On an occasional basis these 'may be dispensed with' by the minister and the parochial church council acting jointly or, on a regular basis, when authorized by the bishop on the request of the minister and council acting jointly; the exercise of the discretionary power is subject to control to ensure that no church ceases altogether to be used for public worship.[134] Implicit in this scheme is the suspension of rights enjoyed by the laity to the facility of these 'statutory' services and sometimes the law expressly enables the suspension of rights.[135] Indeed, there is a general parallel here between dispensation in these forms and any legal provision which confers a discretion to apply or to relax

---

[129] Canon 17(7) (emphasis added); this suggests, of course, that the power of dispensation is not inherent.   [130] Canon B34(2).

[131] Canon C4(3A).

[132] Canon B12(3) (holy sacrament); B18(1) (sermons: except for some 'reasonable cause' approved by the bishop); B42 (language); B34(1)(a)(3) (banns); C13(2) (the oath); C17(6) (officiants); for residence and occupations see C20(3), 25(1), (2); C28(1).

[133] Canons B11(1), (3), B14(1), (2).   [134] Canon B14A(1).

[135] Pastoral Measure 1983, s. 67; for the bishop's power to suspend patronage rights see *post* Ch. 7.

rules: dispensation is merely a particular discretionary power to relax rules; in this respect the concept underlying dispensation (a concept of conditional duties which may be lifted in exceptional circumstances) is commonly used in the Church of England.[136]

CONCLUSIONS

The purposes of ecclesiastical regulation can be identified by determining the intentions of its makers. General theories of purpose are fundamentally classifications of these intentions. It is difficult to uncover the multitude of reasons for which ecclesiastical authorities create regulation, and the motive of the state legislator in creating law for the church may be very different from motives of church legislators. Broadly, the ecclesiastical legislative intent is to create regulation in order to serve the purposes for which the church exists—law and quasi-legislation are two, formal, methods which the church has chosen to employ as the means of meeting ecclesiastical needs. Ecclesiastical regulation is also devised to produce order in the church. Canonical jurisprudence, both in the Church of England and the Roman Catholic Church, employs the facility theory and the order theory. These theories are closely connected: law and quasi-legislation enable the church to carry out its mission; order, through prescriptive regulation, provides for the efficient and effective enjoyment of ecclesiastical facilities. Whilst legislators commonly employ a confused idea of rules, principles, and norms, to discharge its basic functions effectively the church as a spiritual and human society needs both facility and order: ecclesiastical regulation is intended to make provision for these subject to the overriding value of flexibility, itself expressed in a variety of devices available to ecclesiastical authorities enabling the relaxation of regulatory forms.

[136] See e.g. Pastoral Measure 1983, s. 42(1), (7) (episcopal discretion to constitute a diocesan redundant churches uses committee); ibid., s. 3(1) ('the pastoral committee shall *so far as may be practicable*' ascertain the views of interested parties in drafting pastoral schemes).

PART II

Ecclesiastical Government

3

Legislative Power: Distribution and Control

In the Church of England the development of law designed to enable and regulate the use of legislative power has been closely associated in recent years with the introduction of synodical government and with the process of democratization.[1] Within the structures of synodical government, based on the different units of the church,[2] the legal distribution and control of power in the exercise of the church's legislative ministry operate on all levels of ecclesiastical government. The church's central legal system does not however, provide one constitutional model alone for the creation of law. Several models are employed. These are most clearly defined at the higher and middle levels of church government where legislative power is enjoyed by General Synod and by bodies many of whose principal functions are administrative. At the lower levels they are weakest, particularly in the diocese where there is little systematic provision for law-making. In contrast, Roman Catholic canon law provides for a distribution of legislative powers at *all* levels of the church; based on the hierarchical principle, this is justified theologically (through the concept of the church as the people of God) and juridically (through the doctrine of subsidiarity).[3] Unlike the Church of England, in Roman Catholic

[1] Canon A6: 'The government of the Church of England under the Queen's Majesty, by archbishops, bishops, deans, provosts, archdeacons, and the rest of the clergy and of the laity that bear office in the same, is not repugnant to the Word of God'; *Government by Synod*, Report of the Synodical Government Commission (London, 1966) 14: 'the ultimate authority and right of collective action lie with the whole body, the Church; . . . and the co-operation of Clergy and Laity in Church government and discipline belongs to the true ideal of the Church'; see also H. C. Deb., 11 July 1969, Vol. 786, 1774 and *The York Journal of Convocation* (London, 1976) 46. Cf., however, *WAOB*, 1.16: the church 'is not a democracy, governed by elected representatives responsible solely to its electorate; nor is it a line-management hierarchy, distributing specific powers and responsibility on a command-obedience model. So far as status is concerned, there is none higher than that of being baptised into Christ. The basis of the Church's polity can only be that of the recognition of the many diverse gifts graciously given to God's people, to be used co-operatively to his glory and for the salvation of humanity.'

[2] See *post* Ch. 4. For an overview of the central units and institutions see Hill, *EL*, 18–30 and K. M. MacMorran, E. Garth Moore, and T. Briden, *A Handbook for Churchwardens and Parochial Church Councillors* (London, 1989) Ch. 1; for an assessment of the system see *Synodical Government, 1970–1990: The First Twenty Years*, A Discussion Paper issued on behalf of the Standing Committee of the General Synod, GS Misc 344 (London, 1990).

[3] The practical necessity for the existence of legislative power in the particular church is rooted in part in the Roman Catholic Church's global territorial nature: *LG*, II, III; for subsidiarity as one of the ten principles governing the revision of the Code, see *Readings*, 87; P. Huizing, 'Subsidiarity', *Concilium* (1986), 118; W. Bertrams, 'Subsidiarity in the church', *Catholic Mind*, 59 (1961), 358.

canon law only ordained ministers possess law-making power. In neither church is a judicial challenge to ecclesiastical legislation possible within the church: indeed, the 'Henry VIII clauses' occassionally used in Church of England legislation exclude judicial review by the secular courts.

THE SUPREMACY OF GENERAL SYNOD

Legislative power within the Church of England is concentrated at the highest level in the General Synod. One of the fundamentals of the church's constitutional order is the principle of synodical supremacy. This has two basic components. On one hand, General Synod may in broad terms create for the church in the form of a *measure* any law it pleases and, with the exception of General Synod itself and the Queen in Parliament, no body, legislative, executive, or judicial, may legally deny a synodical measure its status as law. On the other hand, the formal law imposes conditions on General Synod's measure-making power, both substantive and procedural: a key question is whether these conditions create criteria of validity.

The Institution and its Composition

Before 1919 the principal bodies legislating for the Church of England were its own ancient Convocations of Canterbury and York, each consisting of a House of Bishops and a House of Clergy which legislated by canon, and the Sovereign in Parliament, which legislated by statute. From 1919 until 1970 the National Assembly of the Church of England functioned as the church's central legislature, established by parliament, empowered to legislate by measure, and composed of three Houses: the House of Bishops and the House of Clergy, both derived from the Convocations, and the House of Laity.[4] By the Synodical Government Measure 1969 the Church Assembly was reconstituted as the General Synod (though the Convocations survive, performing— as we shall see—limited functions) empowered by the Church Assembly to legislate by both measure and canon. The General Synod of the Church of England—'the Parliament of the Church'—is a representative legislature composed of three Houses: of bishops, clergy, and laity.[5] The House of

[4] Church of England Assembly (Powers) Act 1919, s. 1(1); for Convocation see A. F. Smethurst, *The Convocation of Canterbury* (London, 1949); see also *Government by Synod*, Report of the Synodical Government Commission set up by the Church Assembly (London, 1966).

[5] SGM 1969, Sched. 2, Art. 1; the expression 'the Parliament of the Church' was used by McCowan LJ in *R v Ecclesiastical Committee of Both Houses of Parliament, ex p the Church Society* (1993): see below. *WAOB* affirms 'the continued importance of both the legislative and deliberative functions of the General Synod' (6.15) as embodying a 'corporate' or 'collective' approach to ecclesiastical government (6.8); although the recommended National Council (see *post* Ch. 4) would be able to propose legislation, 'the Synod would have total legislative control . . . where the Council's proposals required legislation' (6.30).

Bishops consists of the members of the Upper Houses of both Convocations (which include the two archbishops and all diocesan bishops as well as bishops elected by and from the suffragan bishops of the two provinces).[6] The House of Clergy consists of members of the Lower Houses of both Convocations, persons representing clergy of the diocese, university clergy, deans and provosts of cathedrals, archdeacons, chaplains of the armed forces, and religious communities.[7] The House of Laity is composed of four classes of communicant lay people: those elected by the diocesan electors of each diocese (that is, members of all deanery synod houses of laity other than co-opted members), lay persons chosen by lay members of religious communities, ex-officio members, and co-opted members.[8]

Whereas the law of the Church of England enables both the laity and the non-episcopal clergy to share at the highest level in the use of legislative power by means of membership of the General Synod, in the Roman Catholic Church canonically it is the episcopate which possesses and exercises 'supreme authority'. The 1983 Code assigns the primary possession of both the function of government (*munus gubernandi*) and the power of government (*potestas gubernandi*) only to ordained ministers. Lay members of the faithful may co-operate in the exercise of power, but they do not possess it.[9] There is no canonical provision, however, for Roman Catholic lay people to participate directly in the exercise of supreme authority, either by way of consent or consultation. This is justified on theological grounds.[10] Supreme authority over the universal church is exercised either by the pope alone or by the College of Bishops, and the pope has 'the right . . . to determine . . . whether [his] office is to be exercised in a personal or collegial manner'.[11]

Legislative Power: Synodical Measures

The nature of the legislative competence of General Synod is ambiguous. Ecclesiastically, General Synod is the supreme legislator *within* the Church of England, occupying a position analogous to the supreme authority of the pope and the College of Bishops to legislate in the Roman Catholic Church.[12]

---

[6] SGM 1969, Sched. 2, Arts. 1, 2; Canon H3, paras. 1, 2.

[7] Canon H2; for the leadership role of the House of Bishops see *WAOB*, 7.1 ff.

[8] *CRR* (SGM 1969, Sched. 3, Pt. V) rr. 35–42.   [9] *CIC*, c. 129.

[10] *LG*, III; J. Provost, 'The participation of the laity in the governance of the church', *Studia Canonica*, 17 (1983), 417.

[11] *CIC*, cc. 330–5 (the pontiff); cc. 336–41 (the College); *LG*, III, 22. For critical material on the college, and its relation to the pope, see the studies in J. Provost and K. Walf (eds.), *Collegiality Put to the Test*, *Concilium* (1990).

[12] Collegial legislation must be approved by the pope: *CIC*, cc. 331–3, 341; c. 333(3): there is neither appeal nor recourse against a decision or decree of the Roman Pontiff; c. 1404: 'The First See is judged by no one'; c. 1405(2): in cases mentioned in c. 1401, '[a] judge cannot review an act or instrument which the Roman Pontiff has specifically confirmed, except by his prior mandate'; c. 1372: a person who appeals from an act of the pontiff to an ecumencial council or to the College of Bishops is to be punished with a censure.

In many respects General Synod's legislative competence is similar to that of the Queen in Parliament at common law, which is, classically, subject to no legal limitations: parliament may make, repeal, or amend any law it pleases and no body may question the validity of a parliamentary statute.[13] The present legal regime enables General Synod to share in parliament's legislative supremacy in ecclesiastical matters. Intending 'to confer powers on the National Assembly of the Church of England . . . in regard to legislation touching matters concerning the Church of England' (Preamble), by the Church of England Assembly (Powers) Act 1919 (the Enabling Act), the Sovereign in Parliament empowered the Assembly to legislate by measure: under Section 4 a measure 'shall have the force and effect of an Act of Parliament on the Royal Assent being signified thereto in the same manner as to Acts of Parliament'. In addition, by Section 3(6), 'A Measure . . . may extend to the amendment or repeal in whole or in part of any Act of Parliament, including this Act'.[14] A '"Measure" means a legislative measure intended to receive the Royal Assent and to have effect as an Act of Parliament in accordance with the provisions of this Act'.[15] This power is now possessed by the General Synod by virtue of the Synodical Government Measure 1969 enacted by the Church Assembly under the 1919 statute.[16]

In the wider context of the civil constitution, however, General Synod's legislative competence is not supreme. First: whereas parliament's legislative supremacy is conceived as having a political origin,[17] that of General Synod derives from a legislative act of the Sovereign in Parliament. Whilst under the civil constitution Roman Catholic canon law does not enjoy the same authority as a synodical measure,[18] this arrangement may be contrasted with the declaration in Roman Catholic canon law that supreme authority in that church issues from a divine commission.[19] Secondly, therefore: as in law General Synod's legislative power originates from parliamentary statute, in

---

[13] The doctrine as enunciated in 1885 by A. V. Dicey, *Law of the Constitution* (10th edn., London, 1959), though subject to criticism, is still the starting point for modern constitutional theorists: see A. W. Bradley, 'The sovereignty of parliament — in perpetuity', in J. Jowell and D. Oliver (eds.), *The Changing Constitution* (2nd edn., Oxford, 1989) 25. However, the doctrine is now subject to qualification through the direct applicability of European Law: see *R v S/S for Transport, ex p Factortame Ltd (No. 2)* [1991] 1 AC 603 (the operation of statute is suspended if in conflict with European law; the statute in question, however, was not treated as void).

[14] See C. K. Allen, *Law and Orders* (London, 1947) 53, 98–9.   [15] CEA(P)A 1919, s. 1(5).

[16] SGM 1969, s. 2(1); see also Canon H1(1): 'the General Synod of the Church of England, being the Church Assembly renamed and reconstituted by the [Synodical Government] Measure'. Like parliamentary statutes, synodical measures may have extra-territorial effect: see e.g. Diocese in Europe Measure 1980 (and for the draft constitution approved under it by Synod in May 1995 see GS 1159); see generally, J. Nurser, 'The European Community and the Church of England', *ELJ*, 3 (1995), 103.

[17] For the idea that it is a 'political fact' rather than 'law' in the orthodox sense see e.g. H. L. A. Hart, *The Concept of Law* (2nd edn., Oxford, 1994) Ch. 6; the judges treat the principle, however, 'as if' it were law: *Blackburn v AG* [1971] 2 All ER 1380 at 1383 *per* L. J. Salmon.

[18] See *supra* Ch. 1.   [19] CIC, c. 331; LG, III, 20.

the enactment of measures it is an inferior legislator under the secular constitution, empowered to share in the parliamentary competence to create legislation for ecclesiastical matters by virtue of a grant of the Queen in Parliament. Parliament has not effected a complete transference of power: it has not abdicated or abandoned its legislative competence over ecclesiastical affairs but, through the common law principle of parliamentary supremacy, retains an unfettered legal power to legislate on such matters.[20] In this sense, although they have the same force and effect as parliamentary statutes, synodical measures may be conceived strictly as species of secondary or subordinate legislation which, to be valid, must be approved by the Queen in Parliament.[21]

Despite the ambiguity of General Synod's legislative power, an important consequence of the principle that synodical measures may repeal parliamentary statutes (and measures) is that General Synod cannot bind itself as to the content of measures. One 'effect' of statutes is that they repeal earlier inconsistent statutes: parliament cannot bind its successors and an earlier statute will not bind if it is contradicted expressly or impliedly by a later statute.[22] Given the equality of force and effect between statutes and measures, this principle is applicable to General Synod: its legislative competence is continuing and not-self embracing.[23] Later synodical measures may repeal earlier parliamentary statutes, later parliamentary statutes may repeal earlier synodical measures, and later synodical measures may repeal earlier synodical measures.[24] Whilst in the secular context parliamentary statute prevails over Roman Catholic canon law, ecclesiastically the same basic principle applies to the supreme authority in the Roman Catholic Church. A later law abrogates a former law 'if it expressly states so, if it is directly contrary to it, or if it entirely re-orders the subject matter of the former law'. However, the principle of implied repeal does not apply to universal law over particular law: particular law is destroyed only if subsequent universal law 'expressly provides' for this.

---

[20] See *R v Ecclesiastical Committee of Both Houses of Parliament, ex p the Church Society* (1994) 6 Admin LR 670; Hill, *EL*, 72 at 74 *per* McCowan LJ quoting the committee's report on the draft Priests (Ordination of Women) Measure 1993: 'to have proceeded by way of Act of Parliament would have been contrary to the long established convention that legislation for the Church of England should be enacted by way of measure'; for the inability of constitutional convention to fetter parliament's legislative supremacy see N. Doe, 'Non-legal rules and the courts: enforceability', *Liverpool Law Review*, 9 (1987), 173.

[21] Report from the Joint Committee on Delegated Legislation, 1971–2 HL, 184, HC 475, x (synodical measures are included as the first example).

[22] E. C. S. Wade and A. W. Bradley, *Constitutional and Administrative Law* (10th edn., London, 1985) 70–5. *Vauxhall Estates Ltd v Liverpool Corporation* [1932] 1 KB 733; *Ellen Street Estates Ltd v Minister of Health* [1934] KB 590.

[23] For the distinction used in relation to the Queen in Parliament see H. L. A. Hart, *The Concept of Law*, 146.

[24] See e.g. Charities Act 1993, Sched. 6, for statutory amendment of synodical measures; Church of England (Worship and Doctrine) Measure 1974, Sched. 2, for repeals of parliamentary statute.

Indeed, in cases of doubt the abrogation of pre-existing law (universal or particular) is not presumed, instead the presumption is of consistency: inconsistency must be proved and reconciliation between laws must be attempted.[25]

Substantive Limitations

Whereas the Queen in Parliament may legislate by statute on any matter, the legislative powers of the General Synod are subject to limitations. Imposed originally by parliament, in the Enabling Act 1919, the principal restriction is that it may create measures 'touching matters concerning the Church of England': '[a] measure may relate to any matter concerning the Church of England'.[26] These terms are not defined.[27] The legislation does not expressly state whether the same restriction applies to synod's power to repeal statutes.[28] A second substantive limitation is that 'a measure shall not make any alteration in the composition or powers or duties of the Ecclesiastical Committee [of Parliament], or in the procedures in Parliament' (discussed below). No such limitations in Roman Catholic canon law prevent the supreme authority of the Roman Catholic Church from legislating on any given subject.[29]

It has not been unequivocally decided whether the secular courts may challenge on substantive grounds the validity of a synodical measure once it has been enacted. Reference to first principles of secular constitutional law allows two views. On one hand, judicial challenge is possible if synodical measures are viewed as subordinate legislation: the courts may challenge secondary legislation if it deals with a subject upon which the delegatee has no power to legislate under the terms of a parent statute; the courts sometimes allow such an instrument to stand but sever from it those parts which are substantively *ultra vires*.[30] The assumption in *R v Ecclesiastical Committee of Both Houses of Parliament, ex parte the Church Society* was that the civil courts could bear a substantive challenge to a *draft* synodical measure.[31] The Church Society sought judicial review on the ground that

[25] *CIC*, cc. 20, 21.

[26] CEA(P)A 1919, Preamble and s. 3(6), operative by virtue of SGM 1969, s. 2.

[27] Synod has created law for members of other churches: e.g. Patronage (Benefices) Measure 1986, s. 30, removal of 'disabilities on patrons practising the Roman Catholic religion'; parochial fees orders made under the Ecclesiastical Fees Measure 1986 fall into the same category.

[28] It is questionable whether only parliamentary statutes relating to the Church of England can be repealed; presumably this was intended, but a literal interpretation suggests, as s. 3(6) actually says, that 'any' statute may be repealed by the measure procedure; in the *Church Society* case, *supra* n. 20, Tuckey J suggested 'There is no reason to suppose from this legislation [the Enabling Act] that any restriction was intended to be placed upon the uses to which this procedure could be put' (Hill, *EL*, 72 at 77).

[29] For the debate on substantive limitations on the supreme authority see P. Granfield, *The Limits of the Papacy* (London, 1987); however, see *supra* n. 12 for the exclusion of recourse against papal decrees.

[30] *R v Inland Revenue Commissioners, ex p Woolwich Equitable Building Society* [1990] 1 WLR 1400.

[31] (1994) Admin LR 670; Hill, *EL*, 72.

the Enabling Act 1919 did not empower General Synod to enact the Priests (Ordination of Women) Measure 1993. The High Court assumed jurisdiction without question, even though the measure was due for consideration by parliament.[32] The Church Society argued that the proposed measure would fundamentally change the church's doctrine and that synod could legislate by measure only on 'matters on the edge of doctrine'. McCowan LJ rejected the distinction, but assumed a substantive limitation: synod may legislate on 'any matter whatsoever *provided it concerns the Church of England*'. The word 'touching'. in the Preamble of the Enabling Act simply meant 'relating or pertaining to' the Church of England: '[o]ne would expect that if a statute says a measure may relate to any matter, it means "any matter".' Whilst it is not certain that he actually approved it, McCowan LJ cited the principle that 'the Church of England has inherent authority to deal with all matters of doctrine, worship and ritual as affecting its own members'.[33] For Tuckey J there was 'no dispute that the proposed Ordination of Women Measure is a measure "concerning the Church of England". The words "any matter" are wide enough to include *any and all matters*; that is their ordinary, natural and quite unambiguous meaning'. The church had been given 'full power to legislate on Ecclesiastical affairs subject only to Parliament's veto'. The Church Society's application was rejected.[34]

On the other hand, the principle that measures have the force and effect of parliamentary statutes suggests that an enacted measure may not be challenged. First, it is well settled that the courts cannot challenge the validity of statutes on grounds of their substance.[35] The judicial doctrine of the appearance of validity is significant here: if a statute appears on its face to be valid it will not be questioned by the courts; once the legislative process is complete, it is for the legislator not the judiciary to cure substantive defects.[36] Synodical measures, equal in authority to parliamentary statutes, are owed judicial obedience as this is one of the 'effects' of statutes: as was said in *R v Legislative Committee of the Church Assembly, ex parte Haynes Smith*, 'there would be no question of the measure being unlawful because, under the 1919 Act, a measure "may relate to any matter concerning the Church of England" and *if passed* by Parliament and given Royal Assent, has the force and effect of an Act of Parliament'.[37] Enactment confirms, so to speak, the legislator's

---

[32] By Art. 9 of the Bill of Rights 1689 no internal proceedings of parliament may be questioned by any court; McCowan LJ stated that the parties were 'mindful' of this.

[33] Report of the Archbishop's Committee, *Church and State* (London, 1916) 50.

[34] McCowan's judgment accorded with the Ecclesiastical Committee's conclusion that 'the ordination of women to the priesthood is not a matter of fundamental doctrine but of ecclesiological order'.

[35] *Cheney v Conn* [1968] 1 WLR 242 at 247: statute 'is the highest form of law . . . it is the law which prevails over every other form of law . . . It is not for the courts to say a parliamentary enactment, the highest form of law in this country, is illegal'.   [36] See *post* nn. 83, 84.

[37] [1928] 1 KB 411; cited by Lord Reid in *Ridge v Baldwin* [1964] AC 40 at 74.

satisfaction that the measure concerns the Church of England.[38] Secondly, the *Church Society* case does not constitute authority for the proposition that the courts can question on grounds of substance the validity of an *enacted* measure, since the case concerned a challenge to a *draft* measure.[39] Thirdly, the Enabling Act does not state that measures *must* relate *only* to the Church of England.[40] Fourthly, the secular courts would be reluctant to engage in a theological inquiry to determine whether a synodical measure concerns the Church of England.[41] Lastly, the matter may be non-justiciable in that the terms of the Enabling Act are in the nature of a 'Henry VIII clause'. Parliamentary statutes sometimes provide that subordinate legislation should take effect 'as if enacted in this Act'; subordinate legislators are empowered to repeal or amend parliamentary statute; and sometimes statutes expressly provide that secondary legislation is not to be questioned in any legal proceedings.[42] Several judicial statements suggest that the courts cannot challenge secondary legislation in such circumstances when the court is satisfied that this was parliament's clear intention.[43] Whilst the Enabling Act does not expressly exclude judicial review, its terms are in the nature of a Henry VIII clause and, for this reason, synodical measures may be unchallengeable: the Henry VIII clause approach was not used in the litigation concerning the Ordination of Women Measure.

[38] See *post* n. 87.

[39] See below for *R v Archbishops of Canterbury and York, ex p Williamson* (1994) in which the court refused to challenge the validity of the *enacted* Priests (Ordination of Women) Measure 1993: it may be understood that the *ratio* of this case is applicable to both substantive and procedural challenges.

[40] In the *Church Society* case McCowan LJ did not address the question of whether this means 'must relate only' to the Church of England; CEA(P)M 1919, s. 3(6) uses the word 'may'.

[41] *Church Society* case, Hill, *EL*, 72 at 76 *per* McCowan LJ: 'I have every confidence that if the task were thrust upon the Courts they would find it possible to form a view on what was fundamental, though with very great reluctance, particularly in the area of doctrine' (though he did not believe that the task was placed on the courts by the 1919 statute).

[42] The use of such clauses has been the source of much controversy: Report of the Committee on Ministers' Powers (Donoughmore Committee) (HMSO, Cmd. 4060, 1932); see C. K. Allen's outstanding but much neglected, *Law and Orders* (Oxford, 1947) 100 ff. and ch. 7; S. H. Bailey, B. L. Jones, and A. R. Mowbray, *Cases and Materials on Administrative Law* (2nd edn., London, 1992) ch. 15.

[43] If an order is *ultra vires*, prohibition may lie to prevent confirmation by a minister: *R v Minister of Health, ex p Davis* [1929] 1 KB 619; if a confirmed order is *ultra vires*, *certiorari* may lie: *R v Ministry of Health, ex p Yaffe* [1931] AC 494. For an emphatic judicial rejection see *R v Minister of Health, ex p Wortley* [1927] 2 KB 229; cf. the HL decision in *Institute of Patent Agents v Lockwood* [1894] AC 347 in which the clause was held to exclude judicial review; generally, see also *R v Home Secretary, ex p Anosile* [1971] 1 WLR 1136; *Royal Mutual Benefit Society v Walker (HM Inspector of Taxes)* [1978] TR 129. In the Scottish case of *McEwen's Trustees v Church of Scotland General Trustees* [1940] SLT 357 it was argued that an order made under the Church of Scotland (Property and Endowments) Act 1925 was to be treated as if made by parliament; Lord Robertson held that the terms of the statute did not oust jurisdiction.

Procedural Limitations

Elaborate procedures for the enactment of measures are to be found in the Enabling Act 1919, in the Synodical Government Measure 1969, in General Synod's Constitution arising thereunder, and in its Standing Orders.[44] First, the rules govern the processing of measures within the three houses of General Synod. A member desiring the introduction of a measure may move in synod to instruct the Standing Committee to introduce a measure to give effect to the proposals specified in the motion.[45] A measure may enact new law or consolidate with corrections and minor improvements enactments relating to any subject.[46] No measure shall be printed and circulated to Synod members at the general approval stage except on the instructions of the Standing Committee, or at any other stage of consideration except on the instructions of the Steering Committee for the measure.[47] A measure may not be considered at any stage unless copies in the form to be considered by synod have been posted or delivered to every member not less than fourteen days before consideration.[48] Before a measure is considered at the general approval stage the Standing Committee must appoint such synod members as it thinks fit to a Steering Committee (which must act in accordance with Standing Orders) which will be in charge of the measure[49]. With regard to legislation not dealing with doctrine and liturgy,[50] every measure must be considered on five successive stages:[51] general approval,[52] revision committee (which reports with amendments and recommendations including advice to withdraw),[53] revision (where the measure is considered clause by clause, including amendments),[54] final drafting,[55] and final approval.[56] Provision exists for the withdrawal of measures as well as their re-introduction.[57] Standing Orders may be suspended (if this is consistent

---

[44] SGM 1969, s. 2(1), Sched. 2, Art. 11(1) confers the power to 'make, amend and revoke Standing Orders providing for any of the matters for which such provision is required or authorised by this Constitution to be made, and consistently with this Constitution, for the meetings, business and procedure of the General Synod'. [45] *GSSO*, SO 45.

[46] Ibid., SO 47.   [47] Ibid., SO 48(a).

[48] Ibid., SO48(b); SO 130: accidental failure, error or omission in the posting or delivery of copies does not invalidate consideration of a measure.   [49] Ibid., SO 49.

[50] See *post* Part IV.   [51] *GSSO*, SO 50.

[52] Ibid., SO 51 (no amendment to the measure is permitted).

[53] Ibid., SO 52–4; SO 52: composed *inter alia* of members of the Steering Committee and such other members as the Standing Committee may appoint; SO 53: synod members have a right to submit proposals for amendment.

[54] Ibid., SO 55–7; SO 57 allows a revision stage without a revision committee stage immediately after general approval; SO 58 enables further revision committee stages and SO 55 further revision stages.

[55] SO 59 (unless the Steering Committee consider that a final drafting stage is unnecessary in which case the Committee must consider the draft measure in respect of its final drafting).

[56] Ibid., SO 61: no amendments are permitted at this stage.

[57] Ibid., SO 62–3: at any time between introduction and final approval, a member of the Steering Committee may move (on giving notice under SO 10) that a measure be withdrawn.

with synod's Constitution) on a motion carried by at least three-quarters of the members present and voting; reasons for suspension must be given.[58]

Secondly, General Synod must refer every proposed measure to its Legislative Committee, appointed by synod from members of all three of its houses,[59] which must take such steps as are prescribed by the 1919 Act, by the 1969 Measure, and by synod's Constitution and Standing Orders.[60] The Legislative Committee has a statutory duty to submit every measure passed by synod to the Ecclesiastical Committee of Parliament, together with such comments and explanations as the Legislative Committee may deem expedient or as it may be directed by General Synod to add.[61] Writs of *certiorari* and prohibition would not lie against the Legislative Committee which, when discharging its deliberative functions, does not act judicially.[62]

Thirdly, the Ecclesiastical Committee reports to Parliament. The Committee (similar to a parliamentary joint committee) consists of fifteen members of the House of Lords nominated by the Lord Chancellor and fifteen members of the House of Commons nominated by the Speaker.[63] The powers and duties of the Committee may be exercised and discharged by any twelve members and the Committee is entitled to transact its business whether parliament is sitting or not; subject to the Enabling Act, the Committee may regulate its own procedure.[64] It has a duty to 'consider the measure so submitted to it and may, at any time during such consideration, either of its own motion or at the request of the Legislative Committee, invite the Legislative Committee to a conference to discuss the provisions thereof, and thereupon a conference of the two committees shall be held accordingly'.[65] After considering the measure, the Ecclesiastical Committee must draft a report to parliament 'stating the nature and legal effect of the measure and its views as to the expediency thereof, especially with relation to the constitutional rights of all [Her] Majesty's subjects'.[66] Arguably, in examining its 'legal effect' the Committee would have to determine whether it is *intra vires* under the Enabling Act,

[58] SGM 1969, Sched. 2, Art. 11(1A); *GSSO*, SO 38.

[59] *GSSO*, SO 114. *Ex officio* members are the presidents, the convocation prolocutors, the chairman and vice-chairman of the House of Laity, the Dean of the Arches, and the Second Church Estates Commissioner; of elected members, 1 is from the House of Bishops, 2 from the House of Clergy, and 3 from the House of Laity; appointed members include no more than 3 members of the synod who are members of either House of Parliament and appointed by synod's Standing Committee.

[60] As constituted under CEA(P)A 1919, s. 1(3); SGM 1969, s. 2(2); Sched. 2, Art. 10(1).

[61] CEA(P)A 1919, s. 3(1).

[62] *R v Legislative Committee of the Church Assembly, ex p Haynes-Smith* [1928] 1 KB 411: these remedies were sought to prevent the Committee from proceeding with the Prayer Book Measure 1927.

[63] CEA(P)A 1919, s. 2(1), (2). Members are appointed at the commencement of each parliament and serve for its duration; casual vacancies by reason of the death, resignation, or incapacity of a member are filled by nominees of the Lord Chancellor or the Speaker as the case may be.

[64] S. 2(3).   [65] S. 3(2).   [66] S. 3(3).

though it has been suggested judicially that there is no strict duty to do so.[67] It is not clear in the Enabling Act whether the Committee *must* or simply *may* examine the general desirability of a measure, in terms of policy and merits, as a matter of 'expediency'.[68] In practice, the Committee has 'not confined itself to the technical legal aspects of the Measures before it, and has reviewed a wide range of policy considerations'.[69]

The Ecclesiastical Committee must then communicate its report in draft to the General Synod's Legislative Committee but must not present it to parliament until the Legislative Committee signifies its desire that it should be presented.[70] At any time before presentation to parliament, synod's Legislative Committee may on its own motion, or on synodical direction, withdraw a draft measure from consideration by the Ecclesiastical Committee. However, synod's Legislative Committee 'shall have no power to vary a measure' either before or after conference with the Ecclesiastical Committee.[71] The report together with the text of the measure must be laid before both Houses. When a measure is laid before parliament, if the Chairman of Committees in the House of Lords and the Chairman of Ways and Means in the House of Commons are of the opinion that the draft deals with two or more different subjects which might be better divided, they may by joint agreement subdivide the measure, and each separate measure will be laid before parliament separately. On 'a resolution being passed by each House of Parliament directing that such

---

[67] In the *Church Society* case (see n. 20) McCowan LJ held that 'legal effect' simply meant 'the legal results that the measure would have if passed into law'; '"expediency" did not cover "lawfulness"'. The provision in s. 3(3) simply expressed 'an intention that the Ecclesiastical Committee should protect the constitutional rights of all subjects by keeping an eye open for any measure which might affect those rights, and, in such an event, reporting it to the Houses of Parliament'. There was no duty on the Committee to determine whether the proposed measure was *intra vires* the 1919 statute: '"The majority of the Committee emphatically reject the suggestion that the measure is unlawful . . ." [having regard to s. 3 of the 1919 statute] . . . In my judgment it was strictly unnecessary for the Committee to say what it said in this passage.'

[68] For an excellent and detailed discussion of the words 'expediency' and 'constitutional rights' in the statute see I. E. Slaughter, 'Functions of the Ecclesiastical Committee under section 3(3) of the Church of England Assembly (Powers) Act 1919', unpublished, Church House, 20 Apr. 1989, LC(89)12: in a survey of parliamentary debates from 1919 Miss Slaughter suggests that the Committee is simply 'expected to "detect" unexpected or undesirable results' p., 11); the study surveys the use of the word in a wide range of parliamentary statutes and judicial decisions, in which 'expedient' is often understood as '"advantageous" or, possibly, "fit", "proper" or "suitable for the circumstances"', and 'inexpedient' is sometimes understood as 'unjust' (*Canada Enterprises Corporation v McNab Distilleries Ltd* [1981] Com. LR 167 at 168) (ibid., 11–17).

[69] Slaughter, 'Functions of the Ecclesiastical Committee', 33: the Committee 'has not been willing to act as a kind of select committee, hearing evidence from opponents to the Measure' (the Committee has allowed and refused parties to appear before it including members of parliament: p., 21); in the main, the Committee has examined the measure's effect 'as part of English law, and not its effect within the Church viewed as a purely religious body', notably on matters of internal administration and questions of doctrine and liturgy.   [70] CEA(P)A 1919, s. 3(4).

[71] S. 3(5); GSSO, SO 63: in case of withdrawal by the Legislative Committee from consideration by the Ecclesiastical Committee, the former must report this (stating reasons) to General Synod.

measure in the form laid before Parliament should be presented to [Her] Majesty, such measure shall be presented to [Her Majesty]' for assent.[72] In the entire system, the General Synod is under no duty to consult lower levels of the church.[73]

The procedures in the 1983 Code applicable to the supreme authority in the Roman Catholic Church in making universal law are far less detailed than those applicable to General Synod under the law of the Church of England.[74] Whilst the pope may legislate unilaterally, and papal consent must be given to universal law created collegially, canon law made by the supreme authority is valid only when promulgated in the *Acta Apostolicae Sedis*.[75] Roman Catholic canon laws must be prospective and not retrospective unless special provision is made for this; there is no such general provision in the Church of England.[76] Laws which invalidate acts or render a person incapable of acting are invalid unless they do so expressly.[77] If the terms of a law are so unclear that its meaning cannot be determined, the law does not bind.[78] There is no provision in the Code for these high-level legislators to consult lower levels of the hierarchy in their exercise of law-making power, nor for participation by the laity. In Roman Catholic canon law there is no scope for judicial challenges to legislative acts: control is effected vertically within the legislative hierarchy.[79]

Procedural Challenge in the Secular Courts

Whether judicial review of a synodical measure is possible if procedures have been violated in its enactment is a matter of debate. It is arguable that the secular courts are able, for a variety of legal reasons, to question measures in the event of procedural irregularity. First, as we have seen, measures may be conceived strictly as species of secondary legislation. Judicial decisions from secular law indicate that failure on the part of a subordinate legislator to comply with procedural requirements set out in the parent statute may result in secondary legislation being invalid. The judges draw a distinction between mandatory and directory statutory procedures: if the former (such as the duty to consult) are not complied with the legislation will be illegal; if there is

---

[72] S. 4.

[73] Different procedures apply for certain matters concerning doctrine and liturgy: see *post* Part IV.

[74] The requirement of express parliamentary and royal approval for synodical measures in the Church of England (an incident of establishment) produces an effect applicable, though in a different way, to the Roman Catholic Church in England and Wales; whereas General Synod's measures require *express* approval by the state's legislature, Roman Catholic canon law needs the state's *tacit* approval. Roman Catholic canon law, in the civil legal environment, cannot be effective if it conflicts with statute or common law: see *supra* Ch. 1.   [75] *CIC*, cc. 7, 8.

[76] C. 9.   [77] C. 10.   [78] C. 14.

[79] See e.g. *CIC*, c. 446 (papal review of decrees from the particular church); c. 587 (review of constitutions of religious); c. 754 (papal approval of collegial legislation); see *supra* n. 12 for exclusion of internal judicial review; the conditions apply to all forms of law-making: c.7 ff.

substantial compliance with the latter the legislation will be lawful, although minor non-compliance with directory procedures will not invalidate. The question is one of statutory interpretation and judicial classifications depend largely on the gravity of the procedural defect and its effects on those involved.[80] In relation to statutory instruments, failure for example, to follow the procedures on numbering, printing, and availability will not invalidate.[81]

Secondly, a key question is whether a procedural challenge is possible *despite* the 1919 statutory provision that measures have the same force and effect as statutes. There is some evidence that the courts would be prepared to challenge a parliamentary statute when parliament has failed to follow a procedure contained in a *statute* for the future enactment of statutes. In *Manuel v AG*[82], concerning the legality of the Canada Act 1982, the court assumed that parliament was bound by the provisions of section 4, the Statute of Westminster 1931: when legislating for a dominion a parliamentary statute must recite that the dominion had requested and consented to that legislation. As Slade LJ said: 'the sole condition precedent *which has to be satisfied* if a law made by . . . Parliament is to extend to a Dominion . . . is to be found stated in the body of the Statute of 1931 itself (section 4)'; it was a condition which 'must be satisfied' by parliament. A statutory procedural requirement may, therefore, be treated judicially as binding parliament in its enactment of statute: this is a possible exception to the principle that parliament cannot bind its successors. By analogy, if a synodical measure (equal in status to statute) is enacted in contravention of the procedures laid down in the Enabling Act 1919 and the Synodical Government Measure 1969, it may be procedurally *ultra vires* even though enjoying the force and effect of a statute. This approach accords with the principle enunciated in a series of persuasive Privy Council decisions, typified in *Bribery Commissioner v Ranasinghe* (1965), that '[w]here a legislative power is given subject to a certain manner and form, that power does not exist unless and until the manner and form is complied with'; '[a] legislature has no power to ignore the conditions of law-making that are imposed by the instrument which itself regulates its power to make law'.[83] In short, as the courts have assumed that parliament must in its enactment of statutes satisfy a procedure prescribed by an earlier parliamentary statute, so

[80] *London and Clydeside Estates Ltd v Aberdeen DC* [1980] 1 WLR 182 at 189–90 *per* Lord Hailsham. No general duty to consult is imposed by common law: *Bates v Lord Hailsham* [1972] 1 WLR 1373; for the mandatory duty to consult, see *Agricultural, Horticultural and Forestry Training Board v Aylesbury Mushrooms Ltd* [1972] 1 WLR 190 (in which the invalidity was limited: a rule may still be valid in relation to those who have not complained); if the applicant makes no real complaint about the substance of the rule, but only about the failure to consult, *certiorari* may not lie: *R v S/S for Health, ex p United States Tobacco International Inc* [1991] 3 WLR 529. See also *R v Secretary of State for the Home Office, ex p Leech* [1993] 4 All ER 539.
[81] *R v Sheer Metalcraft Ltd* [1954] 2 WLR 777.
[82] [1983] Ch 77, 95. It was held that the Canada Act was valid.
[83] [1965] AC 172; see also *AG for New South Wales v Trethowan* [1932] AC 526; *Harris v Minister of Interior* (1952) (2) SA 428.

too must statutory procedures for the enactment of synodical measures (instruments having the same force and effect as statutes) be complied with.

However, there are problems with this analysis. It is a fundamental principle of constitutional law that the courts may not inquire beyond the face of a statute into internal parliamentary procedures, and nor therefore can they challenge a parliamentary statute for lack of internal procedural regularity. Lord Campbell stated in *Edinburgh & Dalkeith Railway v Wauchope*[84] that 'if it should appear that a bill has passed both Houses and received Royal Assent, no court . . . can inquire into the *mode* in which it was introduced'. Similarly, Lord Reid explained in *British Railways Board v Pickin* (1974) that: '[t]he court has no concern with the manner in which Parliament or its officers carrying out its Standing Orders perform these functions'.[85] For a number of legal reasons the courts cannot investigate the internal proceedings of parliament.[86] Indeed, the decision in *Manuel* was in line with these approaches: the court did not have to inquire beyond the face of the Canada Act 1982 to determine whether the condition precedent in section 4 of the 1931 statute had been met. The prohibition against a judicial inquiry into the internal proceedings of parliament, then, is partly an 'effect' of statute. The basic principle, therefore, may apply equally to measures. If a procedural irregularity within parliament is complained of after the measure has left synod, the courts could not inquire into those proceedings. If the measure *appears* valid the courts could not challenge it as procedurally *ultra vires*; the procedural defect is not for the judiciary but for the legislature to cure.

Whether the courts could inquire into a procedural irregularity occurring in General Synod itself is, however, unclear. With regard to a breach by General Synod of its own Standing Orders applicable to the processing of measures, the matter has not been decided judicially. As one of the 'effects' of a parliamentary statute is that the courts cannot look beyond its face (as described in the previous paragraph) it may be that this principle applies similarly to measures; it would be for General Synod and not for the courts to cure the defect. With regard to procedures contained in the General Synod's Constitution—appended to the 1969 Measure—again, the appearance of validity principle may apply.[87] Indeed, it is arguable that the Constitution itself actually excludes

---

[84] (1842) 8 Cl. and F. 710; see also *Lee v Bude & Torrington Railways Co* (1871) LR 6 CP 577 at 582 *per* J. Willes.

[85] [1974] AC 765 (HL); cf. the approach of the CA: [1973] QB 219.

[86] These include the law concerning parliamentary privilege (see *Clarke v Bradlaugh* (1881) 7 QBD 38; (1884) 12 QBD 271) and the doctrines of separation of powers: see *R v HM Treasury, ex p Smedley* [1985] 1 QB 657.

[87] It is likely that synod's non-compliance with its own constitution's procedures would be a breach of *statutory* procedures: the constitution is appended to SGM 1969. However, a court would have to be satisfied that s. 2(1) of the Measure 'clearly' incorporates the constitution into the body of the Measure: for schedules and incorporation see *Ellerman Lines Ltd v Murray* [1931] AC 126 (HL).

the possibility in certain circumstances of judicial consideration of non-compliance with internal procedures imposed by that Constitution. In relation to the enactment of measures dealing with doctrine, the services or ceremonies of the church, or with administration of the sacraments, any question as to whether the procedural requirements apply, or whether they have been complied with, is to be 'conclusively determined' by the Presidents and Prolocutors of the Houses of the Convocations and the Prolocutors and Pro-prolocutor of the House of Laity (Art. 7(3)). There are similar provisions allowing for internal 'conclusive determination' in relation to measures providing for permanent changes in the services of baptism and holy communion or in the Ordinal, and for schemes affecting inter-church relations (Art. 8(2)). Moreover, as a general principle, '[a]ny question concerning the interpretation [of the synod's constitution] *shall be* referred to and *determined* by' the archbishops (Art. 12(2)). Whether these provisions exclude judicial review has not been decided; if litigated this would be a matter for the courts to decide. In civil law the clearest language is required to oust the jurisdiction of the courts and to render the matter non-justiciable. Generally, similar provisions appearing in other statutes ('finality' or 'conclusive evidence' clauses) have been construed restrictively, though on occasions courts have understood their jurisdiction to be ousted.[88]

With regard to this issue, some support for the proposition that the civil courts would *not* treat as invalid an enacted synodical measure by reason of procedural irregularity is to be found in *R v Archbishops of Canterbury and York, ex parte Williamson* (1994). Opponents of the ordination of women as priests sought leave in the Court of Appeal to move for judicial review to challenge the legality of the *enacted* Priests (Ordination of Women) Measure 1993 and Canon C4B promulged under it. The Court of Appeal had to determine whether the issues raised by the applicant were arguable so as to justify the grant of leave for judicial review. The applicant argued that Canon C4B had been promulged unlawfully, since the 1993 measure was *ultra vires* the Enabling Act 1919 in that it purported to make fundamental changes to the doctrines of the church. Whilst stating that 'the merits of the religious controversy are a matter on which this court is not entitled to hold any opinion', the Master of the Rolls rejected the submission that the Enabling Act 1919 could not authorize fundamental doctrinal changes. Appealing to the *Church Society* case, Sir Thomas Bingham concluded that the terms of the

---

[88] A 'finality clause' in the National Insurance (Industrial Injuries) Act 1946, s. 36(3) did not oust in *R v Medical Appeal Tribunal, ex p Gilmore* [1957] 2 WLR 498 CA (*certiorari* lay). Cf. *R v Registrar of Companies, ex p Central Bank of India* [1986] QB 1114: CA decided that a 'conclusive evidence' clause precluded it from considering evidence adduced to show non-compliance with the requirements for registration. Even an express provision that a matter 'shall not be called into question in any court of law' was held in *Anisminic Ltd v Foreign Compensation Board* [1969] 2 AC 147 not to exclude review of a decision resulting from a jurisdictional error of law.

Enabling Act 1919, authorizing the enactment of a measure relating to 'any matter concerning the Church of England', were 'as wide as any language could possibly be'; it was not possible 'to read into it any limitation as to the scope of matters concerning the Church of England which could form the proper subject of a Measure'; the Measure had a peculiar protection accorded by statute which immunized it from challenge as to validity. Although the applicant's case was effectively an attack on the content of the legislation, the Master of the Rolls commented on the consequences of an alleged procedural irregularity. Once a measure has received royal assent it is 'to be treated as if it were an Act of Parliament' and 'it enjoys the *invulnerability* of an Act of Parliament and it is not open to the courts to question *vires, or the procedure by which it was passed,* or to do anything other than interpret it'.[89]

Dissolution of General Synod

The life of General Synod, and therefore its legislative competence, terminates upon its dissolution. Dissolution may result from operation of law or an executive act of the monarch. The rules are similar to those in Roman Catholic canon law concerning papal prerogatives to dissolve an ecumenical council of the College of Bishops.[90] In the Church of England, as a basic rule General Synod comes into being on the convening of the Convocations and is dissolved automatically on their dissolution.[91] Under the Church of England Convocations Act 1966 convocations may be called or dissolved at such times as Her Majesty may determine without reference to the time at which parliament is summoned or dissolved (s. 1(1)). Unlike the monarch's personal prerogatival power to dissolve parliament (the exercise of which is governed by constitutional convention), the power to dissolve the Church of England's legislature is statutory and may be exercised '[n]otwithstanding any custom or rule of law to the contrary' (s. 1(1)). In any event, and regardless of executive royal dissolution, the statute provides that convocation, and therefore also synod, is dissolved five years after the date for which it was convened, unless dissolved earlier (s. 1(2)).

---

[89] Hill, *EL*, 77 at 80 (emphases added); see also *Williamson v The Archbishop of Canterbury and Ors* (1994) *Independent*, 14 Dec. 1994: challenges to the validity of the Measure were questions of public law and the plaintiff had no standing to commence or to seek determination of these issues in Chancery Division proceedings. The proceedings were struck out *inter alia* as vexatious: *per* Lightman J, Ch. Div).

[90] *CIC*, c. 338: it is the pope's 'prerogative . . . alone to summon an ecumenical council, to preside over it personally . . . [and] to suspend or dissolve the council'. If the papal office becomes vacant during a council it is suspended by operation of law until a new pontiff orders it to continue or dissolves it (c. 340).

[91] SGM 1969, Sched. 2, Art. 3(2); under Art. 3(3) business pending does not abate.

MIDDLE-LEVEL LAW-MAKING

The model of law-making applicable to the enactment of measures of General Synod is based on the concept of consent, both parliamentary and royal. Ordinarily no legal duty is placed on General Synod to consult with lower levels in the church in the creation of measures.[92] However, different law-making models exist in relation to the many other species of law operative in the Church of England (outlined in Chapter 1). Whilst General Synod's power to create canons is based on a consent model, legislative powers enjoyed by the church's middle-level legislators, many of whose functions are primarily administrative,[93] are based on a variety of law-making models. It is with these bodies, whose law-making powers are delegated (usually by General Synod by means of measure), that the formal law allows for consultation. Whereas such bodies do not ordinarily enjoy the quasi-supremacy of General Synod, synodical measures occasionally contain Henry VIII clauses which confer upon middle-level legislators the power to amend primary legislation, and which sometimes expressly exclude challenges in legal proceedings to the delegated legislation in question. Given the general antipathy in civil jurisprudence towards such arrangements, these ecclesiastical schemes are surprising. One characteristic of the formal law is that, even with regard to consultation models, it seeks to safeguard and centralize the supervisory role of General Synod (and sometimes of parliament) over the exercise of power by middle-level legislators: the requirement to consult interested parties is commonly accompanied by a requirement of General Synod's consent.

In broad terms, and with the exception of consultation, these arrangements are not dissimilar to those operating in the Roman Catholic Church. In Roman Catholic canon law, whilst the supreme law-making authority resides in the pope and College of Bishops, subordinate legislative power is also granted ito several middle-level ecclesiastical authorities. The Code safeguards the primacy of the pontiff, and the operative model is that of papal consent. The synod of bishops and curial bodies may legislate, albeit only in a limited way (and rarely practised), for the universal church, but their legislation must be approved by the pontiff.[94] Whilst provincial government has become less important in recent years, the provincial and particular councils do possess legislative power, though their decrees also must be sent to Rome for approval.[95] The national conference of bishops, introduced as a result of

---

[92] See *post* Part IV for consultation with regard to legislation affecting doctrine and liturgy.

[93] See *post* Ch. 4; the term 'middle-level law-making' is used here for the sake of convenience: whilst many bodies are organized in tiers below General Synod, the Church Commissioners, for example, do not fit neatly 'below' General Synod (see *post* Ch. 17).

[94] *CIC*, c. 342 (functions); cc. 341, 343 (decrees need papal approval); see J. G. Johnson, 'The synod of bishops: an exploration of its nature and function', *Studia Canonica*, 20 (1986), 275.

[95] For papal control over these see *CIC*, cc. 439, 446.

Vatican II,[96] is perhaps the most important middle-level legislator. The conference, which must be held at least annually, is able to legislate by general decree over matters designated by universal law or by special papal mandate. For a decree to be enacted at a plenary meeting it must receive at least two-thirds of the votes of conference members possessing a deliberative vote. Such decrees do not bind until they have been subject to a review (*recognitio*) of the Apostolic See and lawfully promulgated. There is no obligation to consult horizontally prior to the exercise of legislative power by a conference, but there is a duty subsequently to communicate decrees to neighbouring conferences.[97] In addition, the general conditions in the Code applicable to the making of law must be complied with: there is no scope for review of middle-level legislation by the church's tribunals.[98]

The Consent Model: Synodical Canons

Until the enactment of the Synodical Government Measure 1969, the power to legislate by canon vested in the Convocations of Canterbury and York; the Enabling Act 1919 did not empower the Church Assembly to legislate by canon, dealing only with measures. By the 1969 Measure, the Convocations of Canterbury and York transferred their power to legislate by canon to General Synod.[99] Though convocation has a limited power to create 'instruments' containing rules, *prima facie* these do not enjoy the force of law.[100] The 1969 Measure prescribed that the canon effecting the transference was to have 'full force and effect'.[101] General Synod may make canons of general application, 'for the Church of England as a whole'.[102] Unlike measures, canons do not (normally) have the same force and effect as parliamentary statutes. Today, canons on specific subjects are usually but not invariably made under the

---

[96] See H. Teissier, 'Bishops conferences and their function in the church', *Concilium* (1986), 110; S. Wood, 'The theological foundation of episcopal conferences and collegiality', *Studia Canonica*, 22 (1988), 327.

[97] *CIC*, cc. 447–59, esp. c. 455; see *COCLA*, 1335–41 for legislation promulgated by the conference of bishops of England and Wales.

[98] For the jurisdiction of church courts see *post* Ch. 5.

[99] SGM 1969, s. 1(1); the transference was effected by Canon H1(1).

[100] Canon H1(2): convocation functions must be exercised 'consistently with the exercise of functions by the General Synod and, in the event of any inconsistency, the provision made by the General Synod shall prevail'. Convocations have power to create rules (governing election) made under the canon: see Canon H3(1). Convocation resolutions and regulations are published as Acts of Convocation and require Archiepiscopal approval (Canon C17(5)). They have no legal but only moral force: *Bland v Archdeacon of Cheltenham* [1972] 1 All ER 1012 at 1018; see *post* Chs. 9, 10 for the involvement of convocations in the development of liturgical and doctrinal law; see Canon H1(3) for the power to make Standing Orders.

[101] SGM 1969, s. 1(1) and Sched. 2, Art. 6(a): to make provision 'by Canon made, promulged and executed with the like provisions and subject to the like restrictions and having the like legislative force as canons heretofore made, promulged and executed by the Convocations'.

[102] S. 1(2).

authority of a parent measure, empowering synod to legislate by canon for a specific purpose.[103] There appears to be no legal obligation upon General Synod specifically to enable itself to create a canon each time it wishes to legislate by such an instrument. As the Synodical Government Measure 1969 and Canon H1 seem to confer a general power to create canons without the need for a prior and specific parent measure, the modern practice of using an enabling measure would seem to be based on ecclesiastical convention only.[104]

Under the Synodical Government Measure 1969 the power to create canons 'shall be exercisable' by General Synod in accordance with its Constitution (s.1(2)). Both substantive and procedural limitations on synod's canon-making competence are to be found in the primary legislation of 1969, in the synod's Constitution, and in its Standing Orders. For canons to be operative, two basic requirements must be satisfied.[105] The first is *substantive*. Under section 1(3)(b) of the 1969 Measure 'no Canons are to be made or put in execution . . . which are contrary or repugnant to the Royal prerogative or the customs, laws or statutes of the realm'. As this provision is contained in a measure it is equivalent to a statutory requirement. Canons, like measures, are subject to the explicit substantive restriction that they may relate only to matters concerning the Church of England.[106] By reference to the general principles (described above) allowing courts to challenge secondary legislation on grounds of substance, it seems that a canon will be invalid if it contains rules dealing with subject-matter with which it is forbidden to deal; if a canon contradicts the terms of a statute, the laws and customs of the realm (the common law), or the royal prerogative it will be invalid. Since synodical measures enjoy the same authority as parliamentary statutes, we might add that a canon is invalid if it contradicts the terms of a pre-existing measure. As Fletcher Moulton LJ explained in *R v Dibdin*, 'If there is anything in the Canons inconsistent with

[103] For an example of the formula used, see Priests (Ordination of Women) Measure, 1993, s. 1(1): 'It shall be lawful for the General Synod to make provision by Canon for enabling a woman to be ordained to the office of priest'. Whilst there was no precise or express statutory prohibition against the ordination of women as priests, it is commonly understood that a custom existed to this effect; a canon alone would not have sufficed to reverse this: a measure was required to authorize such a canon, to comply with the Submission of the Clergy Act 1533 and SGM 1969, s. 1(3).

[104] *Brown and Ors v Runcie and Anor* (1991) *Times* 20 Feb. 1991; Hill, *EL*, 68 *per* L. J. Dillon; a measure is often required, however, by virtue of the Submission of the Clergy Act 1533, s. 3 as applied to General Synod by SGM 1969, s. 1(3); the assumption here is that a measure may authorize a canon to be inconsistent with royal prerogative, statute, and common law (see below): where this is not the case Synod legislates directly by canon under the 1969 Measure and Canon H1.

[105] Ss. 1 and 3 of the Submission of the Clergy Act 1533 are, by SGM 1969, s. 1(3), applied to the making of canons; Synod is under a statutory duty (under the 1533 Act) to act within these limitations, a duty applied to it by the 1969 Measure.

[106] SGM 1969, Sched. 2, Art. 6(a)(ii): one function of Synod is 'to consider matters concerning the Church of England and to make provision in respect thereof . . . by Canon'; for another substantive limitation, made under the legislation in question, see e.g. Church of England (Worship and Doctrine) Measure 1974, s. 1(1)(b) which forbids synod to alter by canon the rules about publication of banns of marriage; for this and s. 4 see *post* Part IV.

the statute law the Canons are so far invalid and of no force or effect'.[107] It may even be possible for a court to challenge a canon as unreasonable.[108] Ordinarily, however, if General Synod legislates *intra vires* parent legislation the courts cannot question a canon's validity. In *R v Archbishops of Canterbury and York, ex parte Williamson*[109], although the Court of Appeal entertained the possibility of judicial review of a canon (Canon C4B 'Of Women Priests') claimed to be *ultra vires* the parent legislation, the court actually declined to impugne the validity of the canon for want of *vires*: in creating Canon C4B General Synod was doing 'no more than giving necessary and obvious effect' to what was provided by the Priests (Ordination of Women) Measure 1993.

The second requirement relates to *procedure*. Under the Synodical Government Measure 1969 the Queen's assent and licence is required for the 'making, promulging and executing' of synodical canons (s. 1(3)(a)). Parliamentary approval is not required. Additional procedures are to be found in General Synod's Standing Orders. Save as expressly provided in the Standing Orders 'or where the context clearly indicates a contrary intention', the rules governing the processing of measures apply *mutatis mutandis* to canons.[110] Special procedures apply to the drafting of canons. A draft of a proposed new canon or of an amendment (including an amendment for the repeal) of an existing canon must be introduced into General Synod by the Standing Committee. Synod members have a right to move a motion instructing or inviting the Standing Committee to introduce a draft canon. Before any motion for the final approval of a draft canon is moved in synod, 'the Presidents shall cause to be prepared for adoption by the Synod a petition for Her Majesty's Royal Assent and Licence to promulge and execute the Canon proposed to be approved'.[111] If before promulgation the Standing Committee considers that a canon should be reconsidered, a member of the Committee at the Committee's request may move that the canon be reconsidered and that member then moves the amendment or the withdrawal of any paragraph.[112]

---

[107] [1910] P 57 at 120; this is the ordinary position: extraordinarily, if it is enacted in a measure that a canon is to enjoy the same status as a measure, and if the measure authorizes a canon to be inconsistent with royal prerogative, statute, or common law (or a pre-existing measure), a lawfully made canon will not be invalid; this is, of course, the reason why a measure is frequently needed to authorize a canon. See below for canons enjoying the same status as measures and statutes.

[108] The courts are able to invalidate unreasonable by-laws (*Kruse v Johnson* [1898] 2 QB 91). It is unclear whether a statutory instrument could be challenged for unreasonableness: see *Maynard v Osmond* [1977] QB 240 and *R v Immigration Appeal Tribunal, ex p Manshoora Begum* [1986] Imm. AR 385 (2 cases concerning regulations not published as SIs). It is also unclear whether the requirement to lay a statutory instrument before parliament is mandatory or directory: *Starey v Graham* [1899] 1 QB 406,412 (directory only). When a canon enjoys the same status as a measure or statute, the unreasonableness argument is ineffective.

[109] *Times*, 19 Mar. 1994; Hill, *EL*, 77.   [110] GSSO, SO 64.

[111] Ibid., SO 65; SO 66 governs procedure for enactment.

[112] Ibid., SO 67(a). No other member may move such a motion or amendment without the permission of the chairman 'and the general consent of the Synod').

When General Synod proposes to legislate by canon with regard to matters of doctrine and liturgy, special procedures apply and a degree of participation by lower levels of the church is required. These are dealt with more fully in Part IV. In outline; under the Church of England (Worship and Doctrine) Measure 1974, no canon dealing with doctrine or worship may be submitted for royal licence and assent unless finally approved by synod with not less than a two-thirds majority in each house (s. 3). According to the synod's constitution, a canon dealing with doctrine, church services or ceremonies, or the administration of the sacraments must, before being approved by the synod, be referred to the House of Bishops. The form of the canon presented to the Synod for final approval must be that approved by the bishops. However, the two convocations (or either of them) or the House of Laity may also insist on the provision being referred to them before final approval by synod. Neither canons making permanent changes in the services of baptism or holy communion or in the Ordinal, nor canons creating constitutional union (or changes in relationships) with other churches, may be finally approved by synod unless approved by a majority of diocesan synods. Only in these circumstances is General Synod legally obliged to involve lower levels of the church in the creation of canons.[113]

Ordinarily, the courts may entertain a challenge to a canon because of the way it was made, for want of proper compliance with statutory procedures. A procedural attack on a *draft* canon occurred in *Brown and Others v Runcie and Another*[114]. The case concerned the legality of Canon C4(3A) empowering the archbishops to permit the ordination of persons divorced and remarried, or married to a divorced person whose former spouse is still living. A declaration was sought that the canon, passed in synod by a simple majority but not yet having received royal assent, had not been processed in accordance with the procedures (outlined above) contained in the Worship and Doctrine Measure 1974. Under this measure, when synod legislates by canon on 'any matter . . . to which any of the rubrics contained in the Book of Common Prayer relate' (s. 1(1)(b)), the special majority procedures apply (s. 3). The plaintiffs argued that the Prayer Book rubric in the service for the ordination of deacons, which provides that 'if any . . . impediment be objected, the Bishop shall surcease from ordering that person', was to be construed widely as embracing an impediment concerning divorce, and that any provision in a canon about impediments fell within sections 1(1)(b) and 3 of the 1974 Measure. Dillon LJ rejected this wide interpretation: the rubric related not to the definition of 'impediment' but to procedure on a claim of an impediment. As such, Canon C4(3A) was not within s.1(1)(b) of the 1974 Measure and did not

---

[113] SGM 1969, Sched. 2, Arts. 7,8; *GSSO*, SO 67(c), (d),81–94 with regard to Article 7 and 8 canons; see *post* Part IV for qualifications to this general principle.

[114] *Times* 20 Feb. 1991; Hill, *EL*, 68 (it was argued by counsel that canons were pieces of 'primary legislation').

require a special majority. For Dillon LJ the operative impediment concerning divorce and ordination derived from the Clergy (Ordination and Miscellaneous Provisions) Measure 1964, s. 9. This, he held, had been lawfully altered by the Clergy (Ordination) Measure 1990 which itself authorized the creation of Canon C4(3A) without restriction as to special procedures: the canon had been lawfully passed, not under the 1974 Measure, but under the 1990 Measure. Dillon LJ contrasted this with the creation of Canon C4, promulged under the Deacons (Ordination of Women) Measure 1986: both had required and received a special majority under the 1974 Measure because they made provision about worship in the Church of England. The clear inference from this case is that when a proposed canon falls within the terms of the 1974 Measure the statutory procedures for its creation must be followed.

Consent and Other Subordinate Synodical Instruments

The conditions under which General Synod may regulate the church by means of subordinate legislation and quasi-legislation are to be found in its Constitution and Standing Orders. Under its constitution, General Synod may confer upon itself by measure or by canon the power to create several forms of subordinate legislation. One function of synod is to consider matters concerning the Church of England and 'to make provision in respect thereof . . . by such order, regulation or other subordinate instrument *as may be authorised by Measure or Canon*'.[115] Whilst this provision implicitly imposes both a substantive and a procedural limitation, with respect to these documents there is no general requirement of royal assent. However, in some circumstances parliamentary consent is required. When a measure empowers synod to create subordinate legislation which affects the legal rights of individuals, the parent measure must require the laying of the instrument before parliament. This is not a statutory requirement but arises under General Synod's Standing Order 46, which deals with 'Measures providing for Subordinate Legislation': 'no Measure as finally approved by the Synod shall contain any provision empowering *an authority* to make a subordinate instrument having the force of law of general, as distinct from local, application unless [the measure] also provides' as follows. The instrument must be approved or deemed to be approved by synod; any member may give notice that he wishes the instrument to be debated on a motion for its approval; the instrument (not being a scheme to be approved by Her Majesty in Council), 'if it affects the legal rights of any person, shall be laid before both Houses of Parliament and be subject to

---

[115] SGM 1969, Sched. 2, Art. 6(a)(iii) (emphasis added). See e.g. Canon B12(3): bishops may authorize a person to distribute holy communion 'under such regulations as the General Synod may make from time to time': these regulations, made by the Church Assembly in November 1969, remain in force and have not been revoked or amended by General Synod; SGM 1969, s. 4(6): power to make regulations dealing with functions of diocesan synods.

approval or annulment in pursuance of a resolution of either House as may be determined by that Measure'.[116] "Subordinate instrument" means 'any regulation, rule, order, scheme or other instrument which may be authorised by Measure, but does not include a Canon'.[117]

A less formal rule-making mechanism available to General Synod under its constitution is the power to create an 'Act of Synod, regulation or other subordinate instrument or proceeding as may be appropriate in cases where provision by or under a Measure or Canon is not required'.[118] When synod regulates in these ways, otherwise than under the direct authority of a parent measure or canon, the resultant document may be classified as ecclesiastical quasi-legislation. Although such instruments may be made only in relation to a matter concerning the Church of England, synod's constitution is otherwise silent about the conditions which must be satisfied for these to acquire validity. Instead, conditions are provided by synod's Standing Orders operative with regard to 'any instrument of the Synod' (not being a measure or canon or instrument made pursuant to a measure or canon) or 'any resolution of the Synod' (not being for the approval of or pursuant to a measure or canon). If it is desired to give solemn and formal publication to an instrument or resolution 'as the embodiment of the will or opinion of the Church of England as expressed by the whole body of the Synod, it shall be affirmed and proclaimed as an Act of Synod' in the prescribed form.[119] Final approval of an Act of Synod must be construed as referring to General Synod's final approval of the contents of the Act 'and not to the formal promulgation thereof'.[120] There is no requirement for parliamentary or royal approval and the common opinion is that an Act of Synod does not have binding force.[121] With regard to these

---

[116] *GSSO*, SO 46; see also SO 68 (consideration) and 69 (procedure for deeming); e.g. under the Ecclesiastical Judges and Legal Officers Measure 1976, ss. 5, 8 the House of Bishops is empowered to make regulations with respect to the maximum number of registrarships in a diocese: these must be approved by synod and take effect 'as if they were a statutory instrument' subject to annulment in pursuance of a resolution by either House of Parliament; see also the Ecclesiastical Jurisdiction Measure 1963 s. 2A (concerning diocesan chancellorships) and the Ordination of Women (Financial Provisions) (Appeals) Rules 1993 made by the GS Standing Committee as an SI under the Ordination of Women (Financial Provisions) Measure 1993, s. 10(5) (to ensure that the negative resolution procedure applies in Parliament).

[117] Whilst SO 46 does not define 'an authority', here it is assumed that the principle applies to General Synod itself when exercising the power under Art. 6(a)(iii) of its constitution. There seems to be no provision in Standing Orders for the rules contained in SO 46 to apply to 'subordinate instruments' made under a *canon* as contemplated by Art. 6(a)(iii): the standing order states that it applies only to subordinate instruments created under measures.

[118] SGM 1969, Sched. 2, Art. 6(a)(iv).

[119] *GSSO*, SO 40(a). SO 40(b): either of the presidents shall with the concurrence of the other and the Standing Committee move 'That (Short Title) be solemnly affirmed and proclaimed an Act of Synod'. Under SO 40(c) if the motion is carried and the presidents ratify and confirm the same for their respective provinces, either of them with the agreement of the other must then read to synod the customary form of proclamation and transmit the Act of Synod to the diocesan synods.

[120] SGM 1969, Sched. 2, Art. 12(1).

[121] *HLE*: para. 398, n. 5; e.g. the Episcopal Ministry Act of Synod 1993, dealing with the ordination of women; for a full discussion of the status and effect of such rules see *supra* Ch. 1.

subordinate instruments, including Acts of Synod, there is no general legal obligation on the General Synod to consult lower levels in the church prior to their creation.

The Consultation Model

Between the top and bottom tiers of synodical government, between General Synod and diocesan synods, are located a plethora of bodies, many of whose principal functions (as we shall see in Chapter 4) may be classified as administrative. To these bodies General Synod, by means of measure (and less typically by means of canon), has also given extensive powers to create subordinate legislation. When synod does so by measure, the matter is governed by Standing Order 46 (described in the previous section): no parent measure may empower an authority to make a subordinate instrument *having the force of law* of general (as opposed to local) application 'if it affects the legal rights of any person', unless it provides for parliamentary approval or annulment; this synodical duty is '[s]ubject to any express statutory provision' to the contrary, by which the operation of the Standing Order is excluded.[122]

In delegated law-making powers the notable device of the consultation model is employed. Whilst examples may be found in which legislation is to have national application, the consultation model is most often seen in relation to legislation applicable at local levels in the church. The duty to consult is woven into parent legislation and, as it enhances wider participation in the church's law-making activity, may be welcomed as part of the process of democratization. However, this technique is developing only piecemeal: no general duty to consult is imposed by synodical measure which applies to all middle-level ecclesiastical bodies with power to make subordinate legislation. Furthermore, the consultation model operates within the general scheme of synodical supremacy and is invariably accompanied by the requirement of approval by General Synod. These subordinate laws usually take effect as Statutory Instruments or Orders in Council. The duty to consult and the pre-condition of synodical consent appear in several notable synodical measures. The following arrangement is typical in both its requirement of consent and the duty to consult.

Under the Dioceses Measure 1978 the Dioceses Commission is empowered to formulate 'reorganization schemes' for dioceses.[123] The diocesan bishop may, with the consent of General Synod's Standing Committee, submit to the

---

[122] *GSSO*, SO 46(a).

[123] S. 3: the scheme may make provision for the foundation of a new bishopric (including if necessary the dissolution of an existing diocese), the transfer of the whole area of a diocese to another diocese (and the dissolution of the first mentioned diocese), the transfer of parts of any diocese to another diocese (and if necessary the dissolution of the first mentioned diocese), and the transfer of a diocese from one province to the other; see *post* Ch. 4 for the general functions of the Commission.

Commission proposals for a reorganization scheme; the proposals must be prepared by the bishop 'after preliminary consultation with the diocesan synod'.[124] On receiving proposals, the Commission must prepare a draft scheme (with such amendments, if any, as the Commission thinks should be made), or report to General Synod's Standing Committee and the bishop of every affected diocese 'that it has decided not to proceed with the preparation of such a scheme, giving the reasons for that decision'.[125] When the Commission decides to proceed the duty to consult arises: 'it shall send a copy of the draft scheme and of the financial estimate to every interested party together with a notice stating that written representations with respect to the draft scheme may be made to the Commission no later than a date specified in the notice'.[126] The interested parties to be consulted at the lower levels are the diocesan bishop, every suffragan bishop, every archdeacon, the diocesan and deanery synods concerned, the incumbent or priest-in-charge, the parochial church council of any parish 'which would be particularly affected by the implementing of any such provision', and 'such other persons, if any, who would be so affected as the Commission thinks fit'.[127] The Commission is under a duty to consider the representations and after considering these it must either proceed with or abandon the scheme. If it decides to abandon the scheme it must report to General Synod's Standing Committee and to every bishop concerned giving reasons for its decision. If it decides to proceed 'it shall then submit the draft scheme to the diocesan synod of every diocese which would be affected by the implementing of that scheme for its *consent*'.[128] If the diocesan synod consents to a draft scheme the Commission must lay the draft scheme before General Synod for its approval.[129] As soon as possible thereafter the Commission must submit the scheme for confirmation by Order in Council.[130]

Sometimes, however, the parent measure does not impose a duty to consult.[131]

---

[124] S. 4. If the proposals affect 2 or more dioceses, they must be prepared by the bishops of those dioceses after preliminary consultation by each of them with the diocesan synods involved; s. 4(4), SGM 1969 is not to be taken 'as permitting the consultative functions of a diocesan synod under this section to be discharged on its behalf by the bishop's council and standing committee of that synod': see *post* Ch. 4.   [125] S. 5(2).

[126] S. 5(3).

[127] S. 5(1). It must also consult the Church Commissioners and the Charity Commissioners, and where the scheme involves the transfer of a diocese to the other province, the archbishop of that province; the consenting body of the cathedral is also an interested party.   [128] S. 5(4), (5).

[129] S. 6.

[130] S. 7; under s. 8 a reorganization scheme may be varied or revoked by a subsequent reorganization scheme, and any Order in Council confirming a reorganization scheme may revoke any Order in Council confirming a scheme made thereunder.

[131] Ecclesiastical Fees Measure 1986, ss. 2, 5 (draft parochial fees orders made as a statutory instrument by the Church Commissioners must be approved by General Synod and the SI is subject to annulment by a resolution of either House of Parliament); Church of England (Pensions) Measure 1988, s. 16 (Pensions Board orders require the consent of the Church Commissioners and General Synod); see also Care of Cathedrals Measure 1990, ss. 16, 18.

For example, the Rule Committee enjoys powers under the Care of Churches and Ecclesiastical Jurisdiction Measure 1991 'to make rules' nationally for carrying into effect this and other pieces of legislation with a view, *inter alia*, to regulating the procedure and practice of church courts and the appointment and duties of their officers: '[a]ny rules made . . . shall be laid before the General Synod and shall not come into force until finally approved by the General Synod, whether with or without amendment.' They are to have effect 'as if' statutory instruments subject to annulment by parliamentary resolution.[132] Consultation duties apply to appointment to the chairmanship of the committee but there is no formal duty to consult diocesan chancellors directly in exercising its rule-making power.[133]

Judicial Review and Its Exclusion

Sometimes the law of the Church of England itself provides a judicial process for challenging middle-level legislation. This model is exceptional and such provisions exist only with respect to legislation in draft form. For example, cathedral constitutions and statutes are operative by means of 'schemes' made under the Cathedral Measures 1963 and 1976. Schemes for new constitutions and statutes, or amendments to these, are dealt with by the Cathedral Statutes Commission. Under the 1976 Measure, the Commission can only prepare a draft scheme after consultation with the 'consenting body' (broadly, the administrative authority) of the cathedral church to which the new scheme relates. It must submit the draft scheme to the bishop, the Church Commissioners, and 'so far as is practicable, every other person who appears to the Commission to be affected'. Notice of the preparation of the draft scheme must also be published in the diocese stating *inter alia* that the Commission will consider any written representations duly made before a specified date. After considering written representations and making amendments, if any, the draft scheme must be submitted to the bishop and the consenting body for their respective consents. On obtaining their consents, the Commission must then submit the draft scheme to General Synod which may reject or approve it. If accepted the scheme is implemented by Order in Council. A right of appeal lies against a draft scheme. Any person who has duly made written representations to the Commission may appeal with leave to Her Majesty in Council for

---

[132] Ss. 25, 26, 27

[133] S. 25(4): the chairman must be the Dean of Arches and Auditor unless he declines or is unable to act in which case the chairman must be such other member of the committee as is nominated by the Dean of Arches and Auditor 'after consultation with the Archbishops of Canterbury and York' (given its membership under s. 25, which includes 1 archdeacon from each of the provinces, 2 diocesan chancellors, and 2 diocesan registrars from the provinces, it may be thought that direct consultation is unnecessary); s. 25(1): the committee is composed *inter alia* of 2 diocesan chancellors nominated by the archbishops; s. 25(5): the committee may regulate its own procedures.

an order that the appeal be heard by the Judicial Committee of the Privy Council. The Judicial Committee reports and Her Majesty in Council may allow the appeal (in which case the scheme is of no effect), dismiss the appeal (whereby the scheme is confirmed), or return the scheme to the Commission for reconsideration. If returned for reconsideration, the Commission may withdraw the scheme or amend it with the agreement of the bishop and the consenting body.[134] On the authority of a recent decision of the Judicial Committee of the Privy Council concerning a draft pastoral scheme made pursuant to the Pastoral Measure 1968, containing an appeal arrangement similar to that in the Cathedral Measure 1976, on an appeal the merits of a draft scheme may in serious cases be considered: a change of circumstances or the emergence of fresh evidence could in a proper case constitute grounds for allowing an appeal even though there was no question of any erroneous judgment on the part of church authorities; if these had weighed up the respective merits and had cogent reasons for their decision, however, an appeal would probably fail.[135]

In addition, as a general principle of civil administrative law, whenever subordinate legislation is enacted *ultra vires* parent legislation, its legality can be challenged in the secular courts. Failure to satisfy a statutory duty to consult, for instance, may render enacted subordinate legislation invalid.[136] As we have seen in relation to synodical canons, the same principle is applicable to ecclesiastical subordinate legislation. In some circumstances, however, judicial review may not be possible once ecclesiastical subordinate legislation has been enacted. Whereas the Queen in Parliament employed a Henry VIII clause in the Church Assembly (Powers) Act 1919 with respect to measures of the Church of England, the General Synod likewise has occasionally used this device to enable middle-level legislators within the church to repeal primary legislation by means of subordinate legislation which itself, if lawfully made, then *ex necesitate* enjoys the same force and effect as primary legislation. Although, as we have seen with regard to synodical measures, the

---

[134] Ss. 2, 3; see s. 3(1), (2) for the right of appeal; there are substantive limits: 1963 Measure ss. 6–12; a power is conferred by s. 13 to create rules or bye-laws; leave for an appeal is required under Church of England (Miscellaneous Provisions) Measure 1992, s. 9.

[135] See e.g. Pastoral Measure 1983, s. 9(1) (leave is required). For an appeal to the Privy Council under the (now repealed) Pastoral Measure 1968, s. 8(2) see *Hargreaves v Church Commissioners of England* (1983) 3 All ER 17 (the right under s. 8 gave rise to a genuine appeal process rather than mere judicial review and the appellant was therefore entitled to have the appeal heard on its merits; it was held that the church authorities had acted lawfully in considering the merits and their reasons were cogent; the appeal was dismissed). For the power of the Privy Council to dissent from the recommended scheme only for 'the most cogent reasons', see *Elphick v Church Commissioners* [1974] AC 562 at 566 *per* Lord Diplock. The formula accepted in *Hargreaves* (and expressed in *Holy Trinity, Birkenhead, Parochial Church Council v Church Commissioners* (6 May 1974, unreported) was that confirmation of a scheme would not be refused 'unless for irregularity of procedure, for excess of jurisdiction, or on cogent evidence of erroneous judgment': *per* Lord Scarman at 21.   [136] See *supra*, n. 80.

civil courts take a restrictive view of Henry VIII clauses, if the courts are satisfied that this is the clear intention of the legislator the provision will have the effect of ousting the jurisdiction of the civil courts.[137] The principle of non-justiciability surfaces both expressly and impliedly in several forms of ecclesiastical subordinate legislation.

Exceptionally, a synodical canon prescribed by measure enjoys the same status and effect as a measure or statute. For example, the Church of England (Worship and Doctrine) Measure 1974 states that the principle that 'no Canons shall be contrary to the Royal Prerogative or the customs, laws or statutes of the realm . . . shall not apply to any rule of ecclesiastical law relating to any matter for which provision may be made by Canon in pursuance of this Measure'.[138] Likewise, canons promulged under the Deaconesses and Lay Ministry Measure 1972 operate 'notwithstanding . . . *any* rule of ecclesiastical law'.[139] A similar provision is found in the Church of England (Miscellaneous Provisions) Measure 1976 in relation to rules contained in those canons dealing with declarations of assent at ordination.[140]

The Clergy Pensions (Amendment) Measure 1972 permits synodical regulations (taking effect as statutory instruments) to 'amend, repeal and revoke any of the provisions of the Clergy Pensions Measures 1961 to 1969 and this Measure'.[141] Similarly, the Church Commissioners are empowered under the Ecclesiastical Fees Measure 1986 to prepare a draft Parochial Fees Order which, when approved by General Synod, takes effect as if a statutory instrument.[142] When an order is inconsistent with a private, local, or personal Act of Parliament which affects the parish, the parochial church council, or if there is none the incumbent or minister, may apply to the commissioners requesting them to prepare an order 'providing for the amendment or repeal of that Act in order to permit the Parochial Fees Order to apply to the parish'. Provision for consultation is included. On receipt of an application the commissioners must send the draft order to the diocesan bishop, the parochial church council (if any), and the incumbent or minister whose written representations, if any, the commissioners must consider. The commissioners must also publish notice of the draft order in the parish and consider any written representations submitted in response. The order once sealed by the commissioners takes effect as a statutory instrument.[143] Whilst in this arrangement only an express order can effect the amendment or repeal of a parliamentary

---

[137] See *supra* nn. 42, 43.   [138] S. 6(1).   [139] S. 1(2).

[140] S. 1(3). Sometimes measures provide that a canon created under a repealed measure is to retain its validity e.g. Church of England (Worship and Doctrine) Measure 1974, Sched. 3, para. 4: 'The repeal by this Measure of any provision of an Act or Measure shall not affect the validity of any Canon made under or by virtue of that provision'.

[141] S. 6, as amended by the Church of England (Pensions) Measure 1988 s. 16. These regulations cannot, however, alter the provisions mentioned in s. 6(3).   [142] S. 1.

[143] Sched. 1. Rules contained in cathedral schemes have the same force and effect as synodical measures or parliamentary statutes: *AG v Dean and Chapter of Ripon* [1945] Ch 239 at 244 *per*

statute, under the Episcopal Endowments and Stipends Measure 1943 inconsistency between an order of the Church Commissioners and the terms of an Act of Parliament above results in the automatic repeal of the latter. Under this Measure the Church Commissioners are empowered to prepare a scheme with respect to endowments and stipends of bishops. The scheme, if and when confirmed by Order in Council, 'shall have the force of law'. The commissioners are under a duty to consult with the bishop and the diocesan board of finance in the preparation of the scheme. However, 'so much of any Act of Parliament, Measure, Order in Council, trust deed or any other instrument as is inconsistent with any provision of the scheme shall cease to have effect in relation to the see to which the scheme relates'.[144] In 1993 General Synod repealed a Henry VIII clause in the Incumbents (Vacation of Benefices) Measure 1977 providing that synodical 'rules' (taking effect 'as if' statutory instruments) 'may amend, replace, or revoke any of the provisions of the Schedule to this Measure'.[145]

The terms of the Pastoral Measure 1983 are more draconian. The pastoral committee of a diocese has power to review arrangements for pastoral supervision in the diocese and may make recommendations to the bishop in this connection. Before making recommendations the committee must 'so far as is practicable' ascertain the views of interested parties including incumbents, archdeacons, and parochial church councils; the diocesan synod has a right to indicate any matters of diocesan policy to which the committee must have regard. If the bishop approves, the draft is submitted to the Church Commissioners who may make a scheme or order giving effect to the proposals with any amendments (with the agreement of the bishop given after consultation with the pastoral committee) as appear to them desirable. As well as provisions for publication and notice, there is a right of appeal against a draft scheme to Her Majesty in Council. A pastoral scheme must be confirmed by and takes effect as an Order in Council and a pastoral order is made when sealed by the bishop.[146] However, 'the validity of a scheme made and confirmed by Order in Council . . . or of any order made under this Part, shall not be questioned in any legal proceedings'.[147] This may also be the effect of the provision in the Dioceses Measure 1978 (outlined above) that a draft reorganization scheme

Uthwatt J. See also Cathedrals Measure 1976, s. 2(8) for a 'conclusive evidence' clause. The Church of England (Worship and Doctrine) Measure 1974, s. 4(1): 'The final approval by the General Synod of any such Canon or regulation [dealing with new services] . . . or amendment thereof shall conclusively determine that the Synod is of such opinion' that the legislation does not depart from the Church of England's doctrines. [144] S. 9.

[145] S. 18(2). This provision was repealed by the Incumbents (Vacation of Benefices) (Amendment) Measure 1993.

[146] Ss. 1–10; for a more detailed discussion of the procedure and the effects of pastoral schemes and orders see *post* Ch. 4.

[147] S. 11(1); schemes may also provide for matters forbidden by Parsonages Measure 1938, under s. 33(5).

proposed by the Dioceses Commission, once signed by the commission's chairman or by two nominees, 'shall be conclusive evidence that the provisions of this Measure relating to the draft scheme have been complied with'.[148]

LOW-LEVEL LAW-MAKING: THE DIOCESE

It is at the lower levels of ecclesiastical government that the law of the Church of England differs most radically from that of the Roman Catholic Church. In Roman Catholic canon law at diocesan level a general law-making power is vested in the bishop; it cannot be delegated (c. 391). The bishop may exercise his legislative power within or outside the diocesan synod. He may convoke a synod but must consult the presbyteral council—a body representative of the diocesan clergy—before doing so (c. 461).[149] Provision is made for both ordained ministers and lay faithful to be members of the synod (c. 463). However, synod members have only a consultative role in the making of diocesan legislation: decrees are promulgated on the bishop's authority, not on that of the synod (c. 466).[150] The synod simply assists the bishop in exercising his legislative power. The bishop must communicate to the metropolitan and to the Conference of Bishops, any laws enacted, but their approval is not needed for diocesan laws to become operative (c. 467). The pastoral council of the parish has no power to legislate, though it does have power to create rules governing its internal matters (cc. 511, 512). There is no specific provision for the bishop to consult the parish council in his use of legislative power.[151]

The main lower-level bodies in the Church of England's system of synodical government are the diocesan synod (and other quasi-statutory diocesan administrative bodies), the deanery synod, and the parochial church council. Under the formal law these institutions possess no express *general* legislative power, their functions being primarily administrative.[152] However, as we have seen,

---

[148] S. 6(5).

[149] For the presbyteral council see *CIC*, cc. 495–502 (it has the power to create internal statutes with episcopal approval: c. 496).

[150] C. 466: 'The diocesan bishop is the sole legislator in the diocesan synod. Other members of the synod have only a consultative vote. The diocesan bishop alone signs the synodal declarations and decrees, and only by his authority may these be published.'

[151] On the diocesan synod see L. Jennings, 'A renewed understanding of the diocesan synod', *Studia Canonica*, 20 (1986), 319; for a US example of a model parochial constitution see R. G. Howes, *Creating an Effective Parish Pastoral Council* (Collegeville, Minnesota, 1991) 67–72.

[152] Generally, their internal constitutions are imposed by General Synod in the parent measure, though commonly they also have powers to create norms governing internal procedure: see *post* Ch. 4; one function of diocesan synods, however, is to consider matters concerning the Church of England 'and to make provision for such matters in relation to their diocese' (SGM 1969, s. 4(2)(a)), and a similar formula is used with regard to deanery synods to make provision for deaneries (SGM 1969, s. 5(3)(a). These provisions may certainly be construed as conferring a power of informal rule-making (quasi-legislation) but they do not expressly confer a law-making power; see also *WAOB*, 10.11 for a hint of this assumption.

there is some scope for diocesan authorities occasionally to participate in the creation of law by higher and middle-level legislators: the diocesan synod has rights of consent and consultation in the making of reorganization schemes processed by the Dioceses Commission and so has the bishop in the law-making process, initiated by the Pastoral Committee, resulting in a pastoral scheme; a majority of diocesan synods is directly involved in the creation of synodical measures and canons concerning doctrinal and liturgical matters.[153] Only rarely does primary legislation confer upon the bishop a power to legislate unilaterally,[154] or indeed to exercise an executive power of dispensation.[155] In the absence of a general power to legislate, authorities in the dioceses of the Church of England, particularly bishops, resort as a matter of practice to the making of quasi-legislation in the form of pastoral regulations, guidelines, and other species of diocesan norm.[156]

In terms of formal law-making the contemporary process of democratization has not fully reached this level. The only *general* associated power, at diocesan (or parish) level, is the (ancient) power of the community to create customary law. Yet, as in the Roman Catholic Church, popular custom is no longer an important source of law. In Roman Catholic canon law communities are empowered to create customary law (through long usage) subject to a series of limitations, both substantive and procedural. Custom introduced by a community of the faithful has the force of law if it has been approved by the legislator in accordance with the following canons.[157] No custom contrary to divine law can acquire the force of law; a custom contrary to or apart from canon law cannot acquire the force of law unless it is reasonable and a custom which is expressly reprobated in the law is not reasonable.[158] No custom acquires the force of law unless it has been observed, with the intention of introducing a law, by a community capable at least of receiving a law.[159] Unless specifically approved by the competent legislator, a custom contrary to canon law currently in force (or one which is apart from canon law) acquires the force of law only if it has been lawfully observed for thirty continuous years; only a centennial or immemorial custom may prevail over canon law which carries a provision forbidding future customs.[160] Custom is the best interpreter of law.[161] A custom (whether contrary to or apart from law) is

---

[153] *Supra* and, for liturgy and doctrine, *post* Part IV.

[154] Parochial Church Councils (Powers) Measure 1956, s. 9(1): subject to the provisions of the Measure and the constitution under the Schedules to SGM 1969, '[t]he bishop may . . . make rules for carrying this measure into effect within the diocese'; Churchwardens (Appointment and Resignation) Measure 1964, s. 11(1)(a): to make 'provision' for any matter 'herein not provided for'. [155] See *post* Ch. 4.

[156] See *supra* Ch. 1.

[157] *CIC*, c. 23; *CIC: TC*, 38–40: the 1983 Code incorporates the classical doctrine as appearing in the 1917 Code; L. Örsy is of the opinion that a parish would be too small a community to create custom: ibid., 39. See also L. Örsy, *Theology and Canon Law* (1992) 87. [158] *CIC*, c. 24.

[159] C. 25.   [160] C. 26.   [161] C. 27.

revoked by a contrary custom or law; however, unless the law makes express mention of the custom it does not revoke centennial or immemorial custom, nor does a universal law revoke particular custom.[162] The Conference of Bishops of England and Wales has recently promulgated legislation confirming particular customs and long established practices.[163]

Similar conditions exist in the Church of England. Pre-Reformation canon law continues to operate in the Church of England by means of incorporation into the common law on condition that it is not repugnant to royal prerogative, statute, or common law.[164] Beyond this general requirement, more specific conditions are difficult to ascertain. As is the case in secular law, a custom must be reasonable before it is judicially recognized and enforceable; it must also have enjoyed continuous usage from time immemorial.[165] A rule will not be operative as customary law if in conflict with positive law. According to the Privy Council in *Ridsdale v Clifton* (1876), 'Usage, for a long series of years, in ecclesiastical customs especially, is entitled to the greatest respect; it has every presumption in its favour; but it cannot prevail against positive law, though, where doubt exists, it might turn the balance'.[166] As a general rule, therefore, custom *contra legem* is invalid and inoperative; customary non-usage of a statutory rule, for example, does not destroy the statutory rule's status as law.[167] For pre-Reformation canon law to be incorporated as custom, it must be pleaded and proved to have been recognized, continued, and acted upon since the Reformation. The purpose of this 'rule of practice' is to show that the custom has been received and adopted as part of the ecclesiastical law recognized by the common law. In *Bishop of Exeter v Marshall*, according to Lord Westbury, for custom to be operative as law it must have been 'continued and uniformly recognised and acted upon by the bishops of the Anglican Church since the Reformation'.[168] This requirement for episcopal approval did not appear in Lord Dunboyne's formulation of the rule of practice, in the Commissary Court decision of *Re St. Mary's Westwell*: 'no directive, rule or usage of pre-Reformation canon law is any longer binding on this court unless

---

[162] C. 28.

[163] *COCLA*, 1335: 'The existing customs in regard to ecclesiastical dress are well founded and are to be continued, in accordance with c. 284'; 1335: 'In view of the long-established practice in England and Wales, a register of confirmation is to be kept in each parish rather than in a central register at the diocesan curia, in accordance with c. 895'; 1341: 'The long-standing customs obtaining in the diocese of England and Wales, by which the faithful support the work of the Church in financial matters and which have proved themselves over many years, now obtain the force of law in accordance with c. 1262'; see also *Briefing*, 85, 114.

[164] Submission of the Clergy Act 1533, s. 3; SGM 1969, s. 1(3)(b); see R. Bursell, 'What is the place of custom in English canon law?', *ELJ*, 1(4) (1989), 12.

[165] *Kruse v Johnson* [1898] 2 QB 91.   [166] (1876) 1 PD 316 at 331.

[167] *Kensit v Dean and Chapter of St. Paul's Cathedral* (1905) 2 KB 249; see also *Westerton v Liddell* (1857) Moore's Special Report 1; for desuetude see *Gore-Booth v Bishop of Manchester* [1920] 2 KB 412; *In re Rector of West Tarring* [1954] 1 WLR 923.

[168] (1868) LR 3 HL 17 at 53–6.

pleaded and proved to have been recognised, continued and acted on in England since the Reformation'.[169] This suggests that custom may validly arise without episcopal consent. Custom must have operated from time immemorial.[170] Custom which operates where the formal law is silent, custom *praeter legem*, may obtain validity.[171] Similarly, custom *secundum legem*, designed to implement the terms of formal church law, is permitted.[172] Whilst it is unclear to what extent these conditions apply to the establishment of modern custom in the contemporary church, the principle of supremacy allows General Synod to destroy or approve a community's customary law. The revised canons of the Church of England occasionally refer to and 'adopt' customs. They do so in different ways. First, sometimes the canons *recognize* the operation of custom as the basis of a rule contained in the canons: in this sense the canon is declaratory of the custom which is itself treated as having binding force.[173] Secondly, the canons recognize that customs may confer rights,[174] or impose duties and liabilities.[175] Thirdly, on one occasion canon allows the operation of a custom *contra legem*.[176] Occasionally, measures confirm and allow the continuing operation of custom.[177]

CONCLUSIONS

As a broad statement of principle, the current legal regime applicable to the Church of England, when the will exists, does not hinder the church in creating binding laws for itself. Only synodical measures have to be expressly approved by the Queen in Parliament. In this sense the Roman Catholic Church is in a similar position, in so far as its rules, to be operative in the wider legal environment, must enjoy the tacit approval of the state and must not conflict with state law. With regard to the Church of England, express parliamentary approval is not required for the making of canons and whether it is required for other species of subordinate legislation depends on the terms of the parent

---

[169] [1968] 1 WLR 513.   [170] See e.g. *Bryant v Foot* (1867) LR 2 QB 161.
[171] *Marson v Unmack* [1923] P 163 at 167–8.
[172] *Read v Bishop of Lincoln* (1892) Roscoe's Reports 1 at 17.
[173] Canon C1(3), concerning canonical obedience: the canon is declaratory of 'ancient law and usage'.   [174] See e.g. Canons C3(3) and C19(1)).
[175] Canons C5(5), C17(4), E1(4) and F13; Canons C17(2) and C18(2) provide for exemptions based on existing custom.
[176] Canon F1(2): there is a canonical duty to ensure that '[t]he font shall stand as near to the principal entrance as conveniently may be . . . except there be a custom to the contrary'.
[177] Pastoral Measure 1983, s. 2(3)(b): the pastoral committee, in making schemes, must 'have regard also to the traditions . . . of individual parishes', ordinarily traditions regarding churchmanship; Churchwardens (Appointment and Resignation) Measure 1964, s. 12(2): 'In the case of any parish where there is an existing custom which regulates the number of churchwardens or the manner in which [they] are chosen, nothing in this Measure shall affect that custom'; s. 13: '"existing custom" means a custom existing at the commencement of this Measure which has continued for a period including the last forty years before its commencement')

measure. As with canons of the Church of England, under the civil constitution the canons of the Roman Catholic Church must not be repugnant to state-made law. Though some of the legal distribution of legislative powers in the Church of England is the result of piecemeal development, most is the result of a systematic reorganization over the last twenty years based around the introduction of synodical government and the application of concepts of democracy to church life. Institutions in the church possessing the power to create *legal* rules exist on a variety of levels similar to the hierarchical ordering of legislative bodies in the Roman Catholic Church. In the Church of England it is the church's central legal system which distributes legislative powers to these. Different models of law-making operate at the different ecclesiastical levels and generally (unlike the Roman Catholic Church) both clergy and laity are involved at all these levels. Whereas General Synod may by measure, subject to parliamentary approval, make any law it pleases, no general law-making power exists at diocesan level: in contrast with the Roman Catholic Church, the diocesan bishop possesses no express general law-making power. At the middle level, extensive powers exist to create subordinate legislation. Controls limiting the exercise of these take different forms. Procedural law is used to effect both vertical and horizontal control usually reserving to General Synod a supervisory position. The consultation model, a relatively recent development, operates only in some areas. The possibility of judicial review is in many key areas not clear. The employment of Henry VIII clauses is not uncommon in ecclesiastical legislation with the result that many pieces of legislation (in addition, it is submitted, to enacted synodical measures) are, as is also the case within the Roman Catholic Church, judicially unchallengeable.

4

Administrative Power:
Organization and Accountability

Outside the processes of legislation and adjudication, the general activities of the Church of England's structures of synodical government might be classified as administrative.[1] It is in this area, rather than in law-making, that these structures are most active.[2] The administrative business of implementing church law, of discussing, formulating, and executing policies which have not been given a legal expression, the management of property and the administration of liturgical matters are carried on by a host of ecclesiastical institutions and persons. Much if not most of the remainder of this book is devoted to the legal regulation of the church's administration. This Chapter examines the administrative organization of the Church of England in terms of its institutions, the functions of central and local bodies exercising executive power, arrangements for delegation, and provisions to facilitate control. The study analyses traditional modes of accountability, through visitatorial powers, complaints systems, and judicial review, as well as the degree to which church structures are characterized by a principle of open government. As a constitutional fundamental, each body must exercise its administrative powers according to law, within the legal authority committed to it. Though both churches employ similar structures of organization and control, many of the administrative models operative in the Church of England find no direct parallel in Roman Catholic canon law.

CENTRAL ADMINISTRATION

Whereas in the Church of England central administration is organized around the General Synod, in the Roman Catholic Church it is primarily the responsibility of the bishops. In addition to the executive functions of the pontiff and

---

[1] For the artificiality of distinctions between legislating, adjudicating, and administering see e.g. S. H. Bailey, B. L. Jones, and A. R. Mowbray, *Cases and Materials on Administrative Law* (2nd edn., London, 1992) Ch. 1.

[2] For recommendations for the future see generally *WAOB* (references to this are made in the following discussion where appropriate); see also B. McHenry, 'The future of synodical government in the Church of England', *ELJ*, 3 (1993), 86.

curial bodies located in Rome,[3] bodies which administer 'the universal church', the principal administrative bodies of the Roman Catholic Church in England and Wales are centred around the Episcopal Conference. The Conference itself, however, has only modest administrative functions, mainly of discussion as a preliminary to the exercise of its legislative functions, though the statutes of the Conference (a permanent institution) must provide not only for plenary meetings but also for a permanent bishop's council, a general secretary, and other offices and commissions.[4] It is these which handle the administrative business of the Conference, a network of departments (composed of and subdivided into committees),[5] consultative bodies,[6] and agencies,[7] co-ordinated by the general secretariat and constituted to perform prescribed functions. With the obvious difference that central administration is in the keeping of the bishops of the Roman Catholic Church, in terms of organization much the same might be said of the General Synod of the Church of England. Like the Roman Catholic Conference, synod has a policy-making function and a power to discuss, but its administrative work is carried on by a cluster of executive bodies.[8] General Synod is empowered to consider matters concerning the Church of England and 'to consider and express their opinion

[3] *CIC*, c. 360; for norms applicable to curial bodies see the apostolic constitution *Pastor Bonus* (1988) (*COCLA*, 1166). For the various curial commissions, councils, congregations, tribunals, and secretariats see J. Muthig, 'The Roman curia: how the church is run', *Readings*, 221; *CD*, 84. For the synod of bishops, enjoying only a consultative role and a power to discuss, see *CIC*, cc. 342, 343: it has no power 'to resolve [questions] or to issue decrees about them'; J. G. Johnson, 'The synod of bishops: an exploration of its nature and function', *Studia Canonica*, 20 (1986), 275; see also for an authentic interpretation (1991) of c. 402, *COCLA*, 1287 (bishops emeriti may be members of the synod of bishops).

[4] For provincial councils, *CIC*, cc. 377, 445, 952, 1264 and for the episcopal conference see *supra* Ch. 3; *CD*, 88 ff.

[5] *CD*, 102: the departments are Christian Life and Worship, Mission and Unity, Catholic Education and Formation, Christian Responsibility and Citizenship, and International Affairs (each composed of committees).

[6] Ibid., 105, comprising the National Conference of Priests, the Conference of Religious, the National Council for the Lay Apsotolate, the National Board of Catholic Women, the Catholic Union of Great Britain, and the Canon Law Society of Great Britain and Ireland.

[7] Ibid: e.g. the Catholic Education Service, the Diocesan Vocations Service, the National Missionary Council, and the National Catholic Fund.

[8] *WAOB* recommends a radical reorganization of central administration; see App. B for the Commission's illustrative draft measure: a National Council, a body corporate chaired by the two Archbishops, would comprise *inter alia* the Secretary General, the Prolocutors of the two Convocations, the chairman and vice-chairman of the House of Laity, two members of the House of Bishops, and three others nominated by the Archbishops and approved by General Synod. The functions of General Synod's Standing Committee, the Central Board of Finance, and some functions of the Church Commissioners would be transferred to the National Council which would function 'to co-ordinate, support and generally further the work and mission of the Church of England'. General Synod's present subordinate bodies would be reshaped into four National Council departments dealing with resources for ministry, mission, heritage, and legal services and finance.

on any other matters of religious or public interest'.[9] Transaction of business by synod itself is regulated directly by its Constitution and Standing Orders, the latter being kept under review by the Standing Orders Committee;[10] these govern agenda, notice of business, the powers and duties of the chairman, debate, motions and amendments, addresses, and voting. Synod's Standing Committee must settle the agenda to which the joint presidents may direct additions with priority given to listed matters. Notice of new business must be included on the agenda; length of notice depends on the matter in question. One-fifth of the members of each house forms a quorum of synod and every member has a right to speak in debate subject to limitations.[11]

Beyond this, central administration of the Church of England is carried on by a plethora of bodies, which can be classified broadly as 'statutory' and 'non-statutory'. The work of the major statutory bodies, established and regulated directly by synodical measure, relates in the main to the administration of property and finance and is discussed fully in Part VI. These bodies include the Church Commissioners, the Pensions Board, the Cathedral Fabric Commission, and the Legal Aid Commission. The following sections focus on central 'non-statutory' bodies which play an increasingly important part in the administrative life of the church. Though established by General Synod through 'statutory' power conferred by the Synodical Government Measure 1969 (and by synod's constitution appended to it), the bodies considered here are treated as 'non-statutory' in the sense that, though established directly by synod, they operate without *direct* control by the church's central legal system. Functions are given and control is effected otherwise than by synodical measure.

Subordinate Bodies of General Synod

General Synod is empowered to appoint a Standing Committee 'and such other Committees, Commissions and bodies, which may include persons who are not members of the Synod, and such officers as they think fit'.[12] Today, synod's

---

[9] Synodical Government Measure 1969, s. 2(1), Sched. 2, Art. 6(a), (b); each convocation may consider in relation to its province matters concerning the church and provide by instrument for these; it has a power to refer matters to General Synod, limited administrative power, and is required to meet to consider any matter referred to it by General Synod (Canon H1(2)); see also *supra* Ch. 3.   [10] SGM 1969, s. 2(1), Sched. 2; *GSSO*, SO 117.
[11] General Synod of the Church of England, *Standing Orders* (1995 edn); agenda, SO 4–9; notice of business, SO 10–12; chairman at sittings, SO 13–14; debate, SO 16–21; motions and amendments, SO 22–4; amendments, SO 25–8; special procedural motions, SO 29–34; voting, SO 35–7.
[12] SGM 1969, Sched. 2, Art. 10(2); Art. 11(1) allows synod to make, amend, and revoke Standing Orders for its own meetings, business, and procedure; under Art. 10(3) each house may appoint or provide by Standing Orders for the appointment of such committees of their members as they think fit; under Art. 11(2) each house may make, amend, and revoke Standing Orders for matters falling under Art. 10(3) for the separate sittings, business, and procedure of that house; Art. 11(3): subject to the Constitution and Standing Orders, business and procedure at any meeting of synod or of each house is regulated by the chairman of the meeting.

administrative work is done by a group of 'subordinate bodies', permanent and temporary advisory committees and commissions, performing the functions not only of advising synod but also of implementing ecclesiastical legislation and synodical policy. Standing Orders directly regulate the subordinate bodies. A 'subordinate body' is 'a body (other than the Crown Appointments Commission) which is, or as far as it is, responsible to and subject to direction by the Synod, or a body which is, or so far as it is, responsible to and subject to a subordinate body as so defined'.[13]

The functions of the Standing Committee are, *inter alia*: to keep under review the overall needs of the church; to propose to synod such action as seems appropriate; to advise synod on such matters of policy as the committee may think fit; to 'co-ordinate all work done in the Synod's name, including the policies and activities of all permanent and temporary bodies responsible to the Synod'; and 'to take such action as may be necessary to ensure that the decisions of the Synod are implemented and that its work is carried on between groups of sessions'.[14]

Concerning subordinate bodies generally, General Synod may constitute any number of these as it thinks fit as well as 'make such other provisions as it thinks fit in regard to the constitution, powers and duties of any subordinate body'. Synod determines the size of each body, whether all or some of the members are to be members of Synod, the mode of appointment of members, and, if these are to be elected, the number to be elected by Synod or by its Houses. Synod may also determine the power of any subordinate body to co-opt such members as Synod may direct.[15] Before 1995 subordinate bodies were classified under Standing Orders either as commissions or as advisory committees;[16] this classification has been removed from Standing Orders though the bodies themselves retain these titles.

The Constitutions of Subordinate Bodies

General Synod determines 'the Constitution and terms of reference of each subordinate body and may at any subsequent time revoke or amend them'.[17] Beyond status and title, internal constitutions of subordinate bodies, designed by General Synod,[18] share the same basic terms. The chairman is appointed by the presidents of synod after consultation with synod's Standing Committee.[19] A member's term of office is usually five years with a prohibition against

---

[13] *GSSO*, SO 131; for an outline of the recommendations of the Turnbull Commission see above n. 8 and *WAOB*, App. C.   [14] SO 116.
[15] SO 119.   [16] Hill, *EL*, 22.
[17] SO 119(b); SO 120–1 contain general provisions concerning election, business, procedure, and the power to regulate their own procedure.
[18] Synod has recently completed a review of these: see *General Synod: Board and Council Constitutions: Quinquennial Review*: Report by the Standing Committee, *GS* 1136 (taking effect in 1996).   [19] *CBC* (1996–2001), GS misc 460, 3, 6, 9, 12, 15, 22, 26, 30, 31.

serving for more than two successive terms.[20] Each body regulates its own business and procedure subject to synod's standing orders and directions.[21] Each body must appoint committees as may be agreed in consultation usually with the Standing Committee.[22] Constitutional functions (and ordinary membership) vary as between the subordinate bodies.

First, the *advisory committees*. The Advisory Board of Ministry is '[t]o advise the bishops and the General Synod on all matters concerning the ministry of the church, to make recommendations as required, and to take such action as may be authorised'. It must consult with the Doctrine Commission and the Faith and Order Advisory Group as necessary on theological issues related to ministry and, in conjunction with the Standing Committee (through the Policy Committee), it must promote ministry concerns in the work of all Boards and Councils of General Synod. It is obliged to work in close collaboration with *inter alia* the Church Commissioners, the Pensions Board, the Central Board of Finance, and the clergy appointments adviser. It must advise dioceses in working out ministerial deployment policy 'which takes account of the variety of forms of ministerial resources available to the church'. The board also investigates new patterns of ministry, advises on policy for the selection of candidates, and reviews training programmes.[23] The constitution of the Board of Education prescribes two basic functions: to advise synod and the dioceses on all matters relating to education and to take action (in the name of the church and synod) on such occasion as is required.[24] The function of the Board for Social Responsibility is to 'promote and co-ordinate the thought and action of the Church in matters affecting the lives of all in society'. It works through a plethora of committees, advisory committees, and *ad hoc* working parties operating within 'terms of reference' imposed by synod.[25] The Board of Mission exists to stimulate and encourage theological reflection, in consultation with the Doctrine Commission, on issues and proposals concerning mission, evangelism, renewal, and inter-faith relations, and to advise synod and the dioceses on these matters.[26] Under its constitution the Council for Christian Unity must foster ecumenical work nationally and in the dioceses, acting in consultation with the Doctrine Commission and the Faith and Order Advisory Group, and advise the Standing Committee on unity issues and proposals; in conjunction with the Standing

---

[20] Ibid.; 4, 6, 9, 12, 16, 22, 27, 30, 32.

[21] *CBC*; in the absence of such regulation *GSSO*, SO 121 applies.

[22] *CBC* (usually through the Policy Committee), 4, 7, 10, 13, 16, 23.

[23] Ibid., 1–4 (chairman must be a member of the House of Bishops; members include persons chosen by the House of Bishops and 7 members elected by synod).

[24] Ibid., 5–7 (its committees include a Schools Committee, a Further and Higher Education Committee, and such others agreed consulting the Standing Committee).   [25] Ibid., 8–10.

[26] Ibid., 11–13; in conjunction with the Standing Committee (through the Policy Committee) it promotes mission concerns in the work of all synod boards and councils.

Committee it must promote unity and ecumenical concerns in the work of all boards and councils of General Synod.[27]

Secondly, the *commissions* are also regulated by synod's standing orders and by internal constitutions. The Doctrine Commission exists to consider and advise General Synod's House of Bishops on doctrinal questions referred to it by that house as well as make suggestions to that house as to what in its view are doctrinal issues of concern to the Church of England.[28] The Liturgical Commission performs similar functions with regard to liturgy.[29] The principal function of the Hospital Chaplaincies Council is to consider questions (referred to it by synod) relating to spiritual ministration to patients and staff in medical establishments and community care programmes, and to act as liaison between civil health agencies and the Church of England concerning these matters. The council must monitor and co-ordinate chaplaincy work and arrange appropriate training for those in chaplaincy ministry.[30] By way of contrast, the Council for the Care of Churches, a synod commission, is subject to some 'statutory' regulation in addition to its internal constitution.[31] The council's principal function is to advise General Synod on all matters relating to the use, care, and planning or design of places of worship.[32] The Crown Appointments Commission of the Synod, consisting *inter alia* of synod's presidents (*ex officio*), elected members, and non-voting elected members,[33] has three functions: to consider vacancies in diocesan bishoprics and candidates for appointment; to agree on two names for submission on the commission's behalf to the Prime Minister; and to report to synod from time to time as the commission deems expedient on matters of general concern within the area of its responsibility.[34] General Synod is also assisted by many other bodies which are not constituted under Standing Orders.[35]

[27] *CBC* (usually through the Policy Committee), 14–16; on behalf of the standing committee it is the principal link between synod and *inter alia* the Anglican Consultative Council; the House of Bishops may, in consultation with the Standing Committee, seek the advice of the council when the council must report directly to that house (ibid., 16).

[28] Ibid., 31–2: it has a chairman and other members not exceeding 15 of whom at least 3 must be synod members; members are appointed by the synod presidents after consulting the Standing Committee.

[29] Ibid., 29–30: it has a chairman and of its other members at least 2 must be members of the House of Bishops and 4 synod members; members are appointed by synod's presidents after consulting with the Standing Committee; see also *post* Ch. 10.

[30] *CBC*, 25–8; as well as the chairman at least 4 must be synod members and at least 1 a part-time hospital chaplain; others include those appointed by the Standing Committee with 'a knowledge of the Health Service'. [31] See *post* Ch. 16.

[32] *CBC*, 20–4; the chairman is appointed by the presidents after consulting the Standing Committee; others, appointed by the Standing Committee, must have expertise in this field.

[33] *GSSO*, SO 122(a); the Archbishop of Canterbury is chairman and the Archbishop of York vice-chairman (SO 122(b).

[34] SO 122(d) (the report procedure is contained in SO 95–6); the Commission is not classified as a 'subordinate body' under SO 131.

[35] These include the Committee for Black Anglican Concerns, the Communications Committee, the Central Board of Finance (see Ch. 17 *post*), and the Legal Advisory Commission (see *post* Ch. 5).

DIOCESAN AND DEANERY ADMINISTRATION

Local administrative bodies are organized on the basis of dioceses, and those of the diocese on the basis of archdeaconries, deaneries, and parishes.[36] Administrative functions cover both policy-making and the implementation of law. As in Roman Catholic canon law,[37] in the Church of England the law enables a high degree of delegation. This section examines the main functions of these bodies; ancillary functions (added by synodical measure and dealing with specific subjects) are discussed where appropriate elsewhere in this book.

Diocesan Organization and Episcopal Oversight

The Dioceses Commission is a central 'statutory' body established under the Dioceses Measure 1978 and is appointed by General Synod's Standing Committee. The Commission has a duty (on the instructions of synod, the Standing Committee, or the House of Bishops) to advise on matters affecting diocesan structures in the two provinces and on action which might be taken 'to improve the episcopal oversight of any diocese . . . or the administration of its affairs'. One of its functions is to participate in the process (outlined in Chapter 3) of making diocesan reorganization schemes. Where it appears to the Commission that there is any such matter on which it might usefully advise, 'it may bring that matter to the attention of the General Synod or the Standing Committee with a view to receiving instructions'. The Commission must be available to be consulted by any diocesan synod or bishop on any action which might be taken under the measure in relation to the diocese. The Commission may appoint committees consisting of such members and having such functions as it may designate.[38]

Diocesan Administration: The Diocesan Synod

The principal administrative body of the diocese is the synod.[39] It is assisted in its work by a range of executive bodies. The diocesan synod consists of a

---

[36] Ecclesiastical Commissioners Act 1836, Preamble; see *WAOB*, 10.1 ff. for recommendations concerning the relationship between the dioceses and the proposed National Council (particularly co-operation and the 'dissemination of good practice' by the Council) and for the standardizing of regional groupings; the Commission recommends that 'over time some relaxation of the statutory framework which governs diocesan administration' should be effected (10.10) and that 'the size of many [diocesan] boards should be reduced, that staff should be given greater executive authority (and be held accountable for it) and that a greater reliance should be placed on *ad hoc* working groups comprising members selected for their expertise' (10.11).

[37] The diocese is treated as the primary reality of the universal church: *CCL: TC*, 316 (*CIC*, c. 369: a diocese is a portion of the people of God entrusted to a bishop).

[38] Dioceses Measure 1978, ss. 1, 2.

[39] SGM 1969, s. 4(1); for alteration of diocesan boundaries under a pastoral scheme see Pastoral Measure 1983, Sched. 3, para. 16; when a diocese contains an 'episcopal area' under a reorganization scheme, provision exists for it to have an 'area synod' to which a diocesan synod may delegate specified functions: Dioceses Measure 1978, s. 17.

house of bishops, a house of clergy, and a house of laity.[40] The house of bishops is composed of the diocesan bishop, every suffragan bishop of the diocese, and such other persons in episcopal orders working in the diocese as the diocesan bishop, with the concurrence of the provincial archbishop, may nominate.[41] The house of clergy consists of *ex officio* members, members elected by the houses of clergy of the deanery synods, and not more than five co-opted ordained members.[42] The house of laity consists of *ex officio* members, members elected by the houses of laity of deanery synods, and not more than five co-opted members who must be actual communicants.[43] As president of the synod[44] the bishop may nominate ten others, clerical or lay, as members of the appropriate houses.[45] The synod has a discretionary power to vary by scheme its membership to secure better representation of clergy or laity or both.[46] It must make standing orders, to regulate procedure, providing *inter alia* that the bishop need not be chairman at meetings and that nothing be deemed to have synod's assent unless the three houses assent; standing orders must also provide for a secretary and for a specified number of not less than two meetings in each year.[47] There must be a bishop's council and standing committee of the diocesan synod with such membership as is prescribed by standing orders.[48]

The diocesan synod is primarily a deliberative, advisory, and consultative body.[49] Its functions, which General Synod may extend by canon or by regulation,[50] are to consider matters concerning the Church of England, to make provision for such matters in relation to the diocese, to consider and express its opinion on any matters of religious or public interest (but it cannot in so doing 'issue . . . any statement purporting to declare the doctrine of the Church of England on any question'), and to advise the bishop on any matters on which he may consult the synod.[51] The bishop must consult the synod on matters of general concern and importance to the diocese.[52] Subject to standing orders and its own directions, the synod may delegate its advisory

---

[40] *CRR*, r. 30(1).   [41] *CRR*, r. 30(2).

[42] *CRR*, r. 30(4): *ex officio* members are any bishop not nominated to the House of Bishops, the dean or provost of the cathedral, the archdeacons, the proctors elected from the diocese to the lower house of convocation, the diocesan chancellor (if ordained), and the chairman of the diocesan board of finance (if ordained).

[43] *CRR*, r. 30(5); *ex officio* members are the diocesan chancellor (if a lay person), the chairman of the board of finance (if lay), and members elected to the House of Laity of General Synod (excluding the registrar if so elected); elections are governed by rr. 31, 32.

[44] Canon C18(4); *CRR*, r. 30(3).   [45] *CRR*, r. 30(6).   [46] *CRR*, r. 33.

[47] *CRR*, r. 34; business is decided by votes of all members present and voting.

[48] *CRR*, r. 34(1)(k).

[49] For its legislative role concerning doctrinal and liturgical development see Chs. 3, 9, 10.

[50] SGM 1969, s. 4(6); General Synod has created rules which may be adopted by diocesan synods: GS, *Model Standing Orders for Diocesan Synods* (1990); for functions under the Repair of Benefice Buildings Measure 1972 and Inspection of Churches Measure 1955 see *post* Ch. 15.

[51] SGM 1969, s. 4(2)(a),(b); *OLAC*, 107: this applies 'whether or not the motion involves only the reaffirmation of the statement of doctrine'.   [52] SGM 1969, s. 4(3).

and consultative functions to the bishop's council and standing committee (which then act on synod's behalf), but 'the bishop or the body so appointed may require any matter to be referred to the synod'; the synod 'may delegate executive functions to deanery synods'.[53] Questions as to whether a matter falls within the functions of a diocesan synod must be decided by the bishop.[54] Finally, the bishop may summon a conference of persons appearing to him to be representative of diocesan clergy and laity on such occasions and for such purposes as he thinks fit.[55]

Diocesan Administrative Bodies

Diocesan administration is carried out by both statutory and non-statutory bodies, subject and accountable directly or indirectly to the diocesan synod. Though practices vary, functions of non-statutory executives are regulated by diocesan norms and internal constitutions—there is no general regulation by the church's central legal system—and the subjects with they deal are similar to those dealt with by General Synod's subordinate bodies, commonly including ministry training, education,[56] mission, stewardship,[57] social responsibility, faith in the city (where appropriate), and communications.[58] The main bodies established by synodical measure are as follows.

The diocesan *pastoral committee*, under the general direction of the bishop, must review the arrangements for pastoral supervision in the diocese. When the committee decides on its own initiative to review arrangements for pastoral supervision in the diocese, it must consult the bishop and give him particulars of the matters which it intends to consider and of the benefices which will be affected. It is this committee which must make recommendations to the bishop regarding pastoral reorganization or any other matter for which a pastoral scheme or order may need to be made. Further, the committee, which must act in accordance with its statutory constitution, must present annually to the diocesan synod a report of its activities during the preceding year. At all times the committee must have particular regard to the making of provision for the cure of souls in the diocese as a whole (including the provision of appropriate spheres of work and conditions of service for those engaged in the cure of

[53] Ibid., s. 4(4), (5): these plan synod business, prepare its agenda, circulate to members information about matters for discussion, initiate proposals for action by synod, and advise synod on matters of policy, transact its business between meetings, and appoint members of committees or nominate persons for election.

[54] Ibid., s. 4(6), including functions allocated by synodical canon or regulation.

[55] Ibid., s. 4(7); the conference is a vestige of the diocesan conference which was replaced by the diocesan synod.

[56] *SADH*, B: constitutions and terms of reference for the education committee, the board of mission and the stewardship committee and for the diocesan synod and bishop's council); *TDH*, Y1–8: statutory bodies; and Y21–4: non-statutory bodies; *WDHI*, Chs. 1, 3, 5.

[57] *TBF*, 12.1; *SDH*, VII, C.9; *GDM*, B.11. [58] *SDH*, VII, C.8, 9; *GDM*, B.12.

souls and reasonable remuneration for such persons). In so doing it must consider the traditions, needs, and characteristics of individual parishes. Importantly, the diocesan synod may from time to time indicate to the pastoral committee any matters of diocesan policy to which the committee must have regard. There is apparently no statutory duty to comply with these instructions, simply to consider them.[59]

Each diocesan synod must establish a *diocesan board of finance*, a registered company the activities of which are regulated by both civil company law and synodical measure. Its memorandum and articles of association must empower the board to hold property and transact business for purposes connected with the Church of England. The diocesan synod may augment the board's powers if necessary or expedient in view of the requirements of the diocese. The board consists of the diocesan bishop and not less than three-quarters of other members who must be elected by the diocesan synod or, if allowed by the memorandum or articles, wholly or partly by the diocesan deanery synods; the remainder must be elected, nominated, or co-opted as prescribed by the company's memorandum and articles ensuring that not less than two-thirds of those elected are members of the diocesan synod and that a majority are lay persons. The diocesan board of finance is subject to the direct control of the diocesan synod for which it acts as a committee: it 'shall in the exercise of its powers and duties comply with such directions as may from time to time be given to the board by the Diocesan Synod'.[60] The role of the board in property and financial management, particularly its powers to consent to transactions involving the acquisition, disposal, and management of church property, is discussed in Part VI.

The diocesan *parsonages board* deals with questions relating to the provision, care, and maintenance of clergy residence houses and related property. Every diocesan synod must provide by scheme either for the appointment of a parsonages board or for the diocesan board of finance to discharge the functions of a parsonages board. A body corporate, the board is composed of all diocesan archdeacons as well as clerics (elected by beneficed and unbeneficed diocesan clergy) and lay persons. The purpose of the board is to further the work of the Church of England by the exercise of its functions under the Repair of Benefice Buildings Measure 1972 and related legislation. To this end, the board is empowered to enter contracts, hold property, borrow money, execute works, and has such other powers as may be provided by schemes created by the diocesan synod. The board's constitution and procedure must be prescribed by scheme of the diocesan synod; provision may be

---

[59] Pastoral Measure 1983, ss. 1, 2 for its constitution and composition see Sched. 1.

[60] Diocesan Boards of Finance Measure 1925, ss. 1, 3; *OLAC*, 105; ibid., 106 for model standing orders, issued by General Synod (the board 'shall be the financial executive of the [Diocesan] Synod and responsible for the custody and management of the Synod's funds and the employment of all persons in receipt of salaries paid directly from those funds').

made for the appointment of committees, the exercise of functions by them, and for the appointment of officers and other staff, their remuneration and terms of service. The parsonages board must present an annual report (and accounts) to the diocesan synod and it must 'comply with any such directions as may be given to [it] by resolution of the diocesan synod'.[61]

Every diocese must have an advisory committee for the care of churches (the *diocesan advisory committee*) regulated by a constitution provided by the diocesan synod under the Care of Churches and Ecclesiastical Jurisdiction Measure 1991. It is under a duty to report annually on its work and proceedings to the diocesan synod with a copy sent to the Council for the Care of Churches.[62] The committee is composed of a chairman appointed by the bishop (who must consult, in so doing, the bishop's council, the diocesan chancellor, and the Council for the Care of Churches), the diocesan archdeacons, and not less than twelve other members (two appointed by the bishop's council from elected members of the diocesan synod, not less than ten appointed by the bishop's council, and such others as may be co-opted).[63] The committee's primary function is to advise on matters affecting places of worship in the diocese in relation to the granting of faculties, the architecture, archeology, art and history of places of worship, the use, care, planning, design, and redundancy of these, and the use and care of their contents, churchyards and burial grounds. The committee must advise when requested by the bishop, the diocesan chancellor, the archdeacons, parochial church councils, faculty applicants, the pastoral committee, persons engaged in the planning, designing, or building of new places of worship, and 'such other persons as the committee may consider appropriate'. Lastly, the committee reviews developments, keeps records of these, encourages care and maintenance, and has 'such other function as may be assigned . . . by any enactment, by any Canon . . . or by resolution of the diocesan synod or as the committee may be requested to perform by the bishop or the chancellor'.[64]

Rather different regulation applies to the diocesan *redundant churches uses committee*. Constituted by the diocesan bishop 'to make every endeavour to find suitable alternative uses for redundant buildings', the committee has a chairman appointed by the bishop and members appointed by the diocesan board of finance, the pastoral committee, the diocesan advisory committee (after consulting the Council for the Care of Churches), and not more than three other members as the bishop's council and standing committee may appoint; the secretary is appointed by the diocesan board of finance. This body is not accountable to or subject to the direction of the diocesan synod:

---

[61] Repair of Benefice Buildings Measure 1972, s. 1; its work under the Parsonages Measures 1938 to 1947 and the Endowments and Glebe Measure 1976 is considered *post* Part VI; for a parsonages committee see e.g. *SDH*, V, A.3.

[62] Care of Churches and Ecclesiastical Jurisdiction Measure 1991, s. 2; Sched. 1.

[63] Sched. 1, paras. 2–4 (see para. 5 for qualifications). [64] Ibid., Sched. 2.

it is answerable to and must submit its reports to the Church Commissioners; the bishop may suspend the committee until needed if satisfied that there are no redundant churches in the diocese.[65]

Finally, every diocese must have a *patronage board* regulated by the constitution prescribed by the Patronage (Benefices) Measure 1986. The board consists of the diocesan bishop, three clerics (beneficed or licensed to a parish in the diocese) elected by the house of clergy of the diocesan synod, five lay persons elected by the diocesan synod's house of laity, and, for the purpose of transacting business relating to a particular benefice, the appropriate archdeacon and both chairmen of the deanery synod of the area in which that benefice is situated.[66] Subject to the provisions of the measure and to any directions given by the diocesan synod, the board may regulate its own procedure.[67] Patronage has been the subject of considerable reform under this measure and the board exists for the purpose of acquiring and exercising rights of patronage.[68] When a new benefice is created under a pastoral scheme, this may make provision as to patronage but if it does not do so expressly the diocesan board of patronage is patron.[69] The functions of the diocesan registry, the vacancy in see committee,[70] and the diocesan board of education are discussed later.[71]

Roman Catholic Diocesan Organization

Diocesan structures in the Roman Catholic Church are not dissimilar in their essentials: bodies enjoy powers of consultation, recommendation, and implementation of law and policy.[72] However, whilst formally in the Church of England diocesan bodies are broadly responsible to and under the direct control of the clerical and lay diocesan synod, in the Roman Catholic Church control is reserved to the bishop. Other than a power to discuss,[73] the *diocesan synod* has no day-to-day executive functions. The diocesan *pastoral council* (a new institution broadly similar to the diocesan pastoral committee in the Church of England) has a consultative role and is composed of sacred

---

[65] Pastoral Measure 1983, s. 42, Sched. 5, para. 5 ff.

[66] Patronage (Benefices) Measure 1986, s. 26(1),(2), Sched 3. para. 1(1); the bishop may nominate a suffragan or assistant to act in his place; the board must elect as its chairman a person other than the bishop.					[67] Sched. 3, para. 7.

[68] S. 27(1)-(4) It may acquire, hold, and transfer any right of patronage and exercise any right of presentation held by the board; transfers are effected only with the consent of the parochial church council; see generally *post* Ch. 7.					[69] Pastoral Measure 1983, s. 32.

[70] See *post* Chs. 6 and 8.

[71] For the Diocesan Boards of Education Measure 1991 see *post* Ch. 9; *SDH*, VII, C.6; *BF*, 10.1; *GDM*, B.8; *DDBF*, C/1–3/88 (b).

[72] For the role of the bishop, and in a vacancy the diocesan administrator (*CIC*, c. 416 ff.) see *post* Ch. 6; for the subdivision of dioceses into pastoral areas see e.g. the Diocese of Westminster, *Parish Administration Manual* (1993) 1.1.2.

[73] See *supra* Ch. 3; *CIC*, c. 465; proceedings must be based on 'free discussion'.

ministers, religious, and lay persons designated in a manner determined by the bishop so that the whole diocese is represented. It investigates and considers pastoral matters and advises the bishop on these proposing practical courses of action; the bishop convokes the council at least once a year and must make public its proceedings and recommendations.[74]

The diocesan *presbyteral council* (a new institution 'like a senate of the bishop') is composed of sacred ministers representative of the diocesan clergy (half are elected by the diocesan presbyterate, some are *ex officio*, and others are appointed by the bishop). It has a power of discussion and recommendation to assist the bishop and promote the pastoral welfare of the people of God in the diocese. The council is regulated by its own statutes approved by the bishop in the light of norms issued by the national episcopal conference. The bishop convokes the council, presides over it, determines its agenda, and receives proposals from its members. The council enjoys a consultative vote and the bishop must consult it 'on matters of greater moment' and on specific matters (such as creating, suppressing, or altering parishes). From the council, the bishop must appoint between six and twelve priests to constitute a *college of consultors*, established for a five-year term and presided over by the bishop; its major responsibilities relate to finance and arise when the diocese is vacant or impeded.[75] The conference of bishops may commit its functions to the cathedral chapter, a body charged with the administration of the diocesan cathedral.[76] The bishop must also establish a *finance council*—similar to the Church of England's diocesan board of finance—to assist him in the management of diocesan finances; its functions are examined in Chapter 17.

It is the *diocesan curia* which is most directly involved in administration, existing to assist the bishop in the governance of the entire diocese, especially in directing pastoral activity and in providing for its administration.[77] Its officers are appointed by the bishop and must promise to act faithfully, and to observe secrecy, according to the manner determined by canon law or by the bishop.[78] The diocesan bishop retains oversight: he must ensure that all matters of diocesan administration are duly co-ordinated and arranged for the good of the people of God in the diocese. To this end, the bishop may whenever expedient appoint a moderator of the curia (who ought to be a priest) who, under the authority of the bishop, co-ordinates the exercise of administrative

---

[74] *CIC*, cc. 511–14: members must be in full communion, of proven faith, good morals, and outstanding prudence.

[75] *CIC*, cc. 495–502. Its functions may be committed by the conference of bishops to the cathedral chapter: c. 502(3)); see *COCLA*, 1289 for an authentic interpretation (1984) of c. 502(1) (a member of the college of consultors who ceases to be a member of the presbyteral council may remain in office as consultor).   [76] *CIC*, cc. 503–10.

[77] *CIC*, c. 469; for diocesan organization in the 22 dioceses in England and Wales see *CD*, 115 ff. (diocesan administrative bodies include, typically, commissions and committees for education and formation, liturgy and ecumenism, and Christian responsibility).   [78] *CIC*, cc. 470, 471.

responsibilities and ensures that curial members fulfill their functions.[79] In order to acquire validity, curial acts must be signed by the ordinary.[80]

The Deanery Synod

In the Church of England, while archdeaconries define the territorial jurisdiction of the archdeacon as an ecclesiastical person with a particular ministry,[81] the deanery is an administrative unit composed of a group of parishes,[82] roughly equivalent to the diocesan *vicariates forane* in the Roman Catholic Church.[83] In contrast to Roman Catholic canon law, in which there is no express provision for vicars forane to hold a synod,[84] each deanery in the Church of England has a synod consisting of a house of clergy and a house of laity. The house of clergy is composed of beneficed or licensed deanery clergy, extra-parochial clergy licensed to an institution in the deanery, any clerical members of General Synod or diocesan synod resident in the deanery, and any other clergy licensed and resident or working in the deanery. The house of laity is composed of parochial representatives elected to the synod by the annual meetings of deanery parishes, any lay members of General Synod, the diocesan synod or an area synod whose names are entered on the electoral roll of a deanery parish, lay representatives (chosen in a manner approved by the bishop) of any community of persons in the deanery who are in the spiritual care of a chaplain licensed by the bishop, and deaconesses and lay workers licensed by the bishop to work in any part of the deanery.[85] Members, being actual communicants, may be co-opted.[86] The deanery synod may make provision to ensure that the total number of its members does not exceed 150 and is not less than fifty; but the maximum may be exceeded so that the house of laity is not less in number than the house of clergy.[87] Moreover, the diocesan synod may vary by scheme composition rules to meet the special circumstances of the diocese or the deaneries and to secure better representation of clergy or laity or both in the deanery synod. The diocesan synod may also make a scheme for the representation of cathedral clergy and laity.[88]

The diocesan synod is obliged to make rules for deanery synods which must provide the following. The rural dean and a member of the house of laity

---

[79] c. 473; the bishop may appoint as moderator the vicar general; he may if expedient also appoint an episcopal council (composed of the vicars general and the episcopal vicars).

[80] c.474; they must be counter-signed by the chancellor and curial notary, but if not this does not affect their validity; the chancellor must inform the moderator concerning these acts.

[81] See *post* Ch. 7; *WAOB* does not deal with deanery administration (10.17).

[82] SGM 1969, s. 9(2). Technically, 'deanery' means rural deanery; a pastoral scheme or order may provide for the creation, alteration, or dissolution of a deanery (or archdeaconry): Pastoral Measure 1983, s. 19.   [83] *CIC*, c. 374(2).

[84] Ibid., c. 555; for deanery councils see *CCL: TC*, 433.   [85] *CRR*, r. 24(6).

[86] SGM 1969, s. 5(1),(2), Sched. 3, *CRR*, r. 24(7); the number of co-opted members must not exceed 5% of the total members of the house co-opting.   [87] *CRR*, r. 25(6).

[88] Ibid., rr. 26, 27; elections are governed by r. 25.

(elected by that house) are to be joint chairmen of the synod and there must be a secretary. A specified minimum number of meetings must be held each year. On such matters and in such circumstances as may be specified in these rules, voting must be by houses but otherwise decisions must be taken by a majority of synod members present and voting. The deanery synod must have a standing committee with such membership and functions as provided by the rules of the diocesan synod. Under the rules, the deanery synod must prepare and circulate to all parochial church councils in the deanery a report of its proceedings. To the diocesan synod is reserved the power to provide for such other matters consistent with these rules as it thinks fit. Subject to the rules, the deanery synod has power to determine its own procedure.[89]

The deanery synod's principal functions, like those of the diocesan synod, are to consider matters concerning the Church of England, to make provision for such matters in the deanery, and to consider and express opinion on any other matters of religious or public interest. Like the diocesan synod, it cannot issue any statement purporting to declare the doctrine of the church on any question. Also, unlike the diocesan synod, it must bring together the views of the parishes on common problems and discuss and formulate common policies on these. Unlike the diocesan synod, an express function of the deanery synod is to foster a sense of community and interdependence among the parishes and generally to promote in the deanery the whole mission of the church: pastoral, evangelistic, social, and ecumenical.[90] In discharging its functions, the deanery synod must obey instructions issued by the diocesan synod, 'to make known and so far as appropriate to put into effect any provision made by the diocesan synod'. It is under a duty to consider the business of the diocesan synod, in particular matters referred to the diocesan synod by General Synod, and 'to sound parochial opinion whenever [it is] required or consider it appropriate to do so'. The deanery synod may raise such matters as it considers appropriate with the diocesan synod.[91] Moreover, the deanery synod has a right to be informed by the diocesan synod of 'the policies and problems of the diocese' and of the diocesan synod's business, as the diocesan synod has a right to be informed through the deanery synod of 'events and opinion in the parishes'.[92] If the diocesan synod delegates to the deanery synod 'functions in relation to the parishes . . . the deanery synod shall exercise those functions'.[93] General Synod may by canon or regulation extend, amend, or further define the functions of deanery synods.[94] The two houses of the deanery synod may each elect their members to the diocesan synod's houses of clergy and laity respectively; members of the houses of laity of all the deanery synods in the diocese (other than co-opted members and any non-members of the Church of

---

[89] Ibid., r. 28.   [90] SGM 1969, s. 5(3).   [91] Ibid.   [92] s. 4(5).
[93] s. 5(4); for synod's power to delegate executive functions to the deanery synod see s. 4(5).
[94] s. 5(5); see *Model Rules for Deanery Synods* (1990).

England) are the diocesan electors for the purposes of elections to the house of laity of the General Synod.[95] Lastly, the deanery synod has a limited power to instruct parochial church councils.[96]

For both the Church of England and the Roman Catholic Church, parishes, including new and altered parishes, constitute the most localized unit for administrative purposes. In the Church of England there are other units (short of deaneries), 'clusters' of parishes or areas analogous to a parish whose administrative structures may be correspondingly different from those of the parish. Some of these arrangements find direct parallels in the Roman Catholic Church.

The Parish: Conciliar Government

Although the meaning of 'parish' depends on the context of its use, and legal definitions vary accordingly,[97] it can broadly be described as an ecclesiastical district assigned to the charge of a minister whose responsibility for the cure of souls of everyone in it is shared with the diocesan bishop.[98] Designed around the twin concepts of territoriality and the cure of souls, as a general classification parishes, constituting a separate cure of souls, are either ancient or new.[99] A rather different understanding operates in Roman Catholic canon law: a parish is a definite community of the Christian faithful established on a stable basis within a particular church, the parish being generally territorial and its pastoral care being entrusted to a pastor as shepherd under the authority of the diocesan bishop—a parish enjoys juridic personality and the bishop alone is competent to erect, suppress or alter parishes (after consulting the presbyteral council and without any obligatory consultation with the laity).[100]

---

[95] *CRR*, rr. 30, 31, 35.   [96] See below.

[97] For the purposes of *CRR* r. 54(1), a parish is an 'ecclesiastical parish' and 'a district which is constituted a ''conventional district'' for the cure of souls'; for the purposes of the Pastoral Measure 1983, a parish means 'a parish constituted for ecclesiastical purposes, and does not include a conventional district' (s. 86(1)); see also *OLAC*, 70; under the Extra-Parochial Ministry Measure 1967, s. 3, parish means 'an ecclesiastical parish or district the Minister of which has a separate cure of souls, and includes a conventional district to the charge of which a separate curate is licensed'.

[98] See I *Bl. Comm* (14th edn.) 10: a parish is that circuit of ground committed to the charge of one person or vicar or other minister having the cure of souls therein.

[99] New Parishes Measure 1943, s. 29(1); historically, parishes were created not for the benefit of the cleric but for the people in them: *Britton v Standish* (1704) Holt KB 141.

[100] *CIC*, c. 515; c. 518: as a general rule a parish is territorial embracing all the Christian faithful in that territory, but 'personal parishes' may also be established according to rite, language, or nationality within some territory or 'even upon some other determining factor'; see generally R. Carlson, 'The parish according to the revised law', *Studia Canonica*, 19 (1985), 5; J. A. Coriden, 'The rights of parishes', *Studia Canonica*, 28 (1994), 293.

In the Church of England, parochial administration is classically centred on the incumbent and the parochial church meeting and council. In every parish there must be held (no later than 30 April in each year) an annual parochial church meeting. The right to attend and take part in proceedings is vested in all lay persons whose names are entered on the electoral roll of the parish, as well as clerks in holy orders who minister or are resident in the parish.[101] The duty to convene the meeting and chairmanship is placed ordinarily on the minister of the parish.[102] The meeting's function is to receive and discuss freely various documents from the parochial church council.[103] The meeting has power to adjourn and to determine its own rules of procedure, and any person entitled to attend has a right to ask any question about parochial church matters and to bring about a discussion of any matter of parochial or general church interest by moving a general resolution or by moving to give any particular recommendation to the council in relation to its duties.[104] The meeting has a duty to elect in every third year parochial representatives of the laity to the deanery synod, to elect parochial representatives of the laity to the parochial church council, and to elect sidesmen.[105]

The parochial church council is composed of all beneficed and licensed clergy in the parish and, *inter alia*, churchwardens, readers, lay members of the deanery, diocesan and general synods, parochial representatives elected at the annual parochial church meeting, and, if the council wishes, co-opted members not exceeding one-fifth of the elected lay representatives.[106] General provisions dealing with officers, meetings, and proceedings may be varied by the council with the consent of the diocesan synod.[107] The minister ordinarily

[101] SGM 1969, Sched. 3, *CRR*, r. 6: beneficed or licensed to the parish or to any other parish in the area of the benefice; if the parish is in the area of a group ministry, the incumbent of any benefice in the group; any resident but unbeneficed or unlicensed cleric. For qualification for entry on the electoral roll see *post* Ch. 8.

[102] *CRR*, r. 7; during a vacancy, the duty to convene is on the vice-chairman of the parochial church council, or if there is none or he is unwilling or unable to act, on the secretary or some other person appointed by the council: r. 7(3); r. 8: if the minister is not present the chair is occupied by the vice-chairman of the parochial church council or, if not present, a chairman chosen by the annual meeting itself; in the case of an equal division of votes the chairman has a second or casting vote, but no clerical chairman has a casting vote in the election of the parochial representatives of the laity; *OLAC*, 6: failure to convene should be reported by the rural dean to the bishop under *CRR*, r. 53(5) who may appoint someone to convene under r. 53(1)(b).

[103] Ibid., r. 9; these include a copy of the electoral roll, the annual report of the council, the annual report on parish finances, the audited accounts of the council, an audited statement of the funds and property of the council, a report on the fabric, goods, and ornaments of the church(es) in the parish, and a report on the proceedings of the deanery synod.

[104] R. 9(6), (7); it may adjourn and determine its own rules of procedure.

[105] R. 9(4); r.18 provides for representation of congregations at annual meeting when a parish has 2 or more churches or places of worship; r. 10 sets out the qualifications of persons to be chosen or elected at annual meetings; r.11 deals with conduct at elections; r.12 governs variations of method of election.

[106] R. 14; elected lay representatives hold office from the conclusion of the one annual meeting to the conclusion of the next: r. 16; the annual meeting may limit the number of years during which a lay member may hold office: r.17.   [107] R.15; general provisions are contained in App. 2.

being chairman, a lay member must be elected as vice-chairman; during a vacancy or when the chairman is incapacitated by absence, illness, or any other cause, or when the minister invites him to do so, the vice-chairman must act as chairman.[108] The chairman convenes the council which must hold not less than four meetings in each year; however, the chairman may convene a meeting 'at any time'; if he refuses or neglects to do so within seven days after a requisition for that purpose presented to him (signed by not less than one-third of the council's members) those members may convene a meeting.[109] The meeting must be quorate (one-third of its members must be present) and only business specified on the agenda can be transacted unless three-quarters of the members present decide otherwise.[110] The council's business must be decided by simple majority vote and the chairman has a second or casting vote.[111] The council must have a standing committee, with not less than five persons, empowered to transact council business between meetings, and subject to directions which the council may give.[112] The council may appoint other committees, not necessarily composed of council members, for the purposes of church work in the parish.[113] Proceedings of the council cannot be invalidated by any vacancy in the membership of the council or by any defect in the qualification or election of its members.[114] Any question concerning the interpretation of these provisions must be referred to the diocesan bishop and any decision given by him (or any person appointed by him) is final.[115]

As to governance, the minister and the parochial church council are under a duty imposed by both measure and canon to consult together on matters of general concern and importance to the parish.[116] The council's functions are

---

[108] App. 2, para. 1 (concerning r. 15(1)); the council may appoint a secretary, treasurer, electoral roll officer, and auditors.

[109] App. 2, paras. 2, 3; the archdeacons may convene extraordinary meetings, *CRR*, r. 23 on written representation with sufficient cause by at least half of the PCC or by one-tenth of persons on the electoral roll.   [110] App. 2, para. 6.

[111] Ibid., paras. 10, 11; minutes must be kept: para.12.

[112] Ibid., para. 14; see also *OLAC*, 200.

[113] App. 2, para. 15; the minister is *ex officio* member of all committees.

[114] Ibid., para. 16.

[115] Ibid., para. 17; the extent of the bishop's powers under the *CRR* is governed by r. 53(1)—he may: make provision for any matter not therein provided for; appoint a person to do any act in respect of which there has been any neglect or default on the part of any person or body charged with any duty under the rules; give effect 'to the intention of these rules' by extending or altering the time for holding any meeting or election or modify the procedure laid down in these rules in connection therewith (but the power cannot be exercised in relation to the conduct of elections under rr. 39 and 48); 'in any case in which any difficulties arise, [the bishop may] give any directions which he may consider expedient for the purpose of removing the difficulties'. However, the powers of the bishop under this rule shall not enable him 'to validate anything that was invalid at the time when it was done', or 'to give any direction that is contrary to any resolution of the General Synod' (r. 53(2)).

[116] Canon C24(7) (priest); Parochial Church Councils (Powers) Measure 1956, s. 2(1) (incumbent); see also *Re St Peter, Roydon* [1969] 2 All ER 1233: the processes of consultation and co-operation must not be a 'solemn farce'; the council must pay 'proper regard' to the wishes of the minister and it must be 'free to differ from him if in their view the honest discharge of the particular duty requires them to do so'.

governed in the first instance by the Parochial Church Councils (Powers) Measure 1956.[117] The functions of the council, a body corporate,[118] in co-operation with the minister, are to promote in the parish 'the whole mission of the Church, pastoral, evangelistic, social and ecumenical'.[119] It must consider and discuss matters concerning the Church of England or any other matters of religious or public interest, but it cannot make a 'declaration of the doctrine of the Church on any question'.[120] It must make known and put into effect any provision made by the diocesan synod or the deanery synod, 'but without prejudice to the powers of the council on any particular matter'.[121] It gives advice to the diocesan and deanery synods on any matter referred to the council and raises such matters as the council considers appropriate with these bodies.[122] In exercising its functions the council 'shall take into consideration any expression of opinion by any parochial church meeting'.[123]

Moreover, the council has '[t]he like powers, duties and liabilities' as were formerly assigned to the vestry of the parish or the churchwardens concerning the financial affairs of the church, the care, maintenance, preservation, and insurance of the fabric of the church, its goods and ornaments, and the care and maintenance of churchyards.[124] The council is empowered to acquire, hold, administer, and dispose of certain classes of real and personal property as well as having powers over the acquisition, holding, administration, and expenditure of finance.[125] These functions, along with those concerning liturgy, the closing of churches, church sharing agreements, and clerical appointments, are dealt with elsewhere in this book. Importantly, the bishop has a power, subject to the 1956 Measure and the constitution operative under the Synodical Government Measure 1969, to 'make rules for carrying this Measure into effect within the diocese'.[126] If any act required to be done by any person is not done within such time as the bishop may consider reasonable, it may be done by or under the authority of the bishop.[127] If a council and minister are unable to fulfill their duty to agree on any matter for which their agreement or joint action is required, 'such matter shall be dealt with or determined in such manner as the bishop may direct'.[128]

---

[117] Curiously, the governing formula, '[t]he functions of [councils] shall include', does not specify when these 'functions' are 'duties' and when they are 'powers': Parochial Church Councils (Powers) Measure 1956, s. 2(1) as substituted by SGM 1969, s. 6 (which contains, unlike the 1956 measure, a reference to 'general functions'). The word 'powers' in the title of the measure may suggest that the 'functions' listed in s. 2(2) are not 'duties' but 'powers'; the measure clearly contemplates both duties and powers (when it employs the words 'power' (s. 5), 'duty' (s. 2(1)), and 'liability' (s. 4(1)). There is no definition of 'functions' as 'powers or duties' such as exists in other measures e.g. Cathedrals Measure 1963, s. 52(1).   [118] PCC(P)M 1956, s. 3.

[119] S. 2(2)(a); whether this imposes a duty to promote, or a power to promote, is unclear; see n. 117.   [120] S. 2(2)(b); for *OLAC*, 107 see *supra* n. 51.

[121] PCC(P)M 1956, s. 2(2)(c).   [122] S. 2(2)(d), (e).

[123] S. 2(3); *CRR*, r. 9(6): the annual meeting may make recommendations to the council.

[124] S. 4(1).   [125] Ss. 5–7; see *post* Chs. 15–17.   [126] S. 9(1).   [127] S. 9(2).

[128] S. 9(3); during a vacancy the bishop's powers are to be exercised by the guardian of spiritualities. S. 9(4): see *post* Ch. 6; see e.g. *GD: BOP*, 1.6 for full-time parochial administrators and the duty to inform the diocesan secretary concerning their appointment.

Whereas the Church of England has a single council at parochial level, acting in co-operation with the incumbent, in the Roman Catholic Church the parish has two: the pastoral council and the finance council. After the bishop has consulted the diocesan presbyteral council, and if he judges it expedient, a pastoral council is to be established in each parish. The pastor presides and through it the Roman Catholic faithful assist in fostering pastoral activity. In contrast to the Church of England, the council has a consultative vote only and is governed by norms determined by the diocesan bishop. It is commonly understood, though the Code is silent, that the pastor must ratify the recommendations of the council before these might be implemented. Unlike the Church of England, there is no formal duty in the Code for the council and pastor to co-operate, but this idea surfaces in the commentaries.[129] In addition, each parish must have a finance council. This is regulated by the Code and by norms issued by the diocesan bishop and in it the faithful, selected according to norms determined by the bishop, must aid the pastor in the administration of parish goods. The pastor has general oversight: he represents the parish in all juridic affairs, in accord with the norms of law, and he must ensure that the temporal goods of the parish are administered in accordance with the canons.[130]

New Parishes and Unions: Joint Councils

As a result of changing needs the Church of England has frequently legislated to modify territorial arrangements and to facilitate the creation of new parishes.[131] Today the matter is governed principally by the Pastoral Measure 1983. The power to initiate the process for the creation of a new parish or to alter existing parishes vests in the diocesan pastoral committee. The committee must consult prescribed 'interested parties' and submit its recommendations to the diocesan bishop who may make such amendments as he considers desirable (but only with the agreement of the committee).[132] The bishop may reject *in toto* the recommendations but if he approves with or without amendment then he must submit these to the Church Commissioners; he must inform the pastoral committee that he has done so and the committee must, in turn,

---

[129] *CIC*, c. 536; for the theological background see W. Dalton, 'Parish councils or parish pastoral councils', *Studia Canonica*, 22 (1988), 169; A. Anandarayar, 'Parish and its pastors in the new code of canon law', *Readings*, 271; benefices do not exist in England and Wales: *COCLA*, 1341.   [130] *CIC*, cc. 532, 537.

[131] Church Buildings Acts 1818 and 1884, New Parishes Acts 1843 to 1884, repealed or modified by the New Parishes Measure 1943 and the Pastoral Measures 1968 to 1983.

[132] Pastoral Measure 1983, s. 3 (see *supra* for other substantive limitations under s. 2); interested parties include *inter alia* the incumbents, patrons, and parochial church councils of affected benefices, the priests-in-charge and councils of affected conventional districts, the archdeacons and rural deans of archdeaconries and deaneries affected, and the local planning authority (s. 3(2)).

send the proposals as approved to the interested parties. The commissioners must (after consultation with prescribed parties) make a draft pastoral scheme which is sent back to the diocesan bishop for his acceptance or rejection. If the bishop consents the commissioners submit the document for confirmation by Order in Council.[133] Alternatively, some forms of reorganization may be effected by the shorter pastoral order procedure; this is available where the interested parties consent.[134] If the bishop is of the opinion after consultation with the pastoral committee that proposals should be submitted to the Church Commissioners (and the interested parties have consented), the bishop may of his own motion submit such proposals to the commissioners and a pastoral order to give effect to them is prepared by the commissioners and made by the bishop.[135] The position is similar, though less detailed, in Roman Catholic canon law, in which the power to erect, suppress, or alter parishes is vested in the diocesan bishop who, in exercising this power, must first consult the presbyteral council; no lay consultation is required.[136]

The law of the Church of England carefully regulates the content of pastoral schemes and orders. The scheme or order may create (by union or otherwise), alter, or dissolve existing benefices, parishes, and extra-parochial places. A pastoral scheme must name every new benefice, or parish created under it and it may alter the name of any existing benefice or parish. A scheme which unites two or more benefices may provide for uniting all the parishes within a new benefice or for uniting some but not all of those parishes, or it may leave them as separate parishes. Moreover, a pastoral scheme may provide for the creation of a new parish with full parochial status even if the parish so created will have no parish church.[137] A pastoral scheme may also authorize the making of church sharing agreements and provide for the holding of benefices in plurality.[138] Dissolution of an archeaconry must be by scheme, not by pastoral order.[139] Incumbents dispossessed by reorganization are entitled to be considered for compensation.[140] An appeal against a draft scheme lies to the Privy Council,[141] but once confirmed by Order in Council its validity cannot be questioned.[142] These structures find a point of contact in the Roman Catholic Church: the code recognizes 'quasi-parishes', equivalent to a parish and a definite community of the Christian faithful entrusted to a priest, which has, due to particular circumstances, not yet been erected as a parish.[143]

In the Church of England the administrative structures of reorganized parochial units vary depending on the reorganization in question. A pastoral scheme or order creating a new parish may make provision (or authorize the

---

[133] Pastoral Measure 1983, ss. 3(9), (10), 4, 5–9.
[134] S. 37; for holding in plurality see s. 18.   [135] Ss. 8(4), 14.   [136] *CIC*, c. 515(2).
[137] Pastoral Measure 1983, s. 17(1)-(4); the parish has a 'centre of worship'.
[138] S. 17(5).   [139] S. 14(1); *PMCP*, A10.   [140] See *post* Ch. 17.
[141] S. 9; *Hargreaves v Church Commissioners* (1983) 3 All ER 17.
[142] S.11; see also *supra* Ch. 3.   [143] *CIC*, c. 516.

bishop to do so by instrument) to ensure that the congregation of every church (or place of worship) in the new parish will have its own elected lay representatives on the parochial church council of that parish.[144] When two or more parishes are comprised in the area of a single benefice, or two or more benefices are held in plurality, the scheme or order may make provision for establishing a *joint parochial church council* for all or some of the parishes of the benefice(s). Alternatively, the scheme or order may authorize the bishop by instrument (with the concurrence of the incumbent of the benefice(s)) to establish a jount council. Moreover, such arrangements may provide for the chairmanship, meetings, and procedure of the joint council, as well as for functions of the parochial church council of any such parish to be delegated to the joint council.[145]

Team Ministries: Chapters and Councils

In addition to classical (or reorganized) parochial structures, the law enables the establishment of a team ministry by pastoral scheme. This is an arrangement by which the parish or parishes of a single benefice are under the pastoral care of those who have the cure of souls together with members of the team.[146] Some matters for which schemes make provision are mandatory and others are discretionary. The scheme itself must provide for the sharing of the cure of souls in that area by the incumbent of the benefice, the rector, and one or more other ministers who have the title of vicar and a status equal to that of an incumbent. Arrangements must be made in the scheme for pastoral care in that area by those sharing the cure of souls together with all other persons from time to time authorized by a provision contained in a licence or permission of the bishop to serve as members of the team. Those sharing the cure of souls in a team ministry (not including those licensed or permitted to serve) are under a duty to constitute a team chapter; the chapter and those licensed and permitted to serve together constitute the team.[147] The rector, responsible for leadership of the team, must convene meetings of the team at regular intervals to discuss and reach a common mind on all matters of general concern or special interest to the team ministry unless the scheme provides otherwise; he presides at

---

[144] Pastoral Measure 1983, Sched. 3, para. 12(1); an annual parochial church meeting may make similar provision by scheme (*CRR*, r. 18).

[145] Sched. 3, para. 13(1); *CRR*, r. 19: the annual meetings of all or some of the parishes may make a joint scheme to establish a joint council composed of ministers and representatives of each of those parishes (functions under the Patronage (Benefices) Measure 1986, Sched. 2 and Priests (Ordination of Women) Measure 1993, s. 3 cannot be delegated).

[146] Pastoral Measure 1983, s. 20; *PMCP*, B4(1): a team ministry may be established for an existing benefice or the area of a new benefice formed by union or other reorganization of existing benefices; a benefice for which a team ministry has been established may be included in a group ministry.

[147] Pastoral Measure 1983, s. 20(1) as amended by the Team and Group Ministries Measure 1994; see also Pastoral (Amendment) Measure 1994.

meetings and in his absence a vicar appointed by him as deputy chairman presides.[148] The annual parochial church meeting and parochial church council must continue to operate in each area of a benefice for which a team ministry is established but if the area comprises more than one parish, a team council must be constituted.[149] The scheme (or episcopal licence) may assign to a vicar the duties (or a share in them) of chairmanship of the annual parochial church meeting and the parochial church council of the parish or any of the parishes in the area of the benefice for which the team ministry is established.[150]

When a team ministry is established for the area of a benefice which comprises a parish in which there are two or more churches (or places of worship), the pastoral scheme may provide (or authorize the bishop with the concurrence of the rector to provide) for ensuring due representation of the congregation of each church (or place of worship) on the parochial council of the parish. A discretion exists to provide for the election of a district church council for any district in the parish in which such church (or place of worship) is situated and for the constitution, chairmanship, and procedure of that council. Similarly, the scheme can arrange for the functions of the parochial church council of the parish to be delegated to the district church council.[151] A scheme regulating functions may also be made by the annual parochial church meeting.[152] When a pastoral scheme establishes a team ministry for the area of a benefice comprising more than one parish, the scheme may provide (or authorize the bishop to provide by instrument with the concurrence of the rector) for the establishment of a team council. Arrangements can be made to regulate the team council's chairmanship, meetings, procedure, and those functions of the parochial church council of each parish in the area which are delegated to the team council.[153] Similar provisions may be contained in a scheme made jointly by the annual parochial church meetings of the parishes in the team area.[154] A team ministry may be terminated, revoked, or amended.[155] Similar arrangements are permitted in the Roman Catholic Church. When circumstances require, the pastoral care of a parish or of several parishes can be entrusted to a team of priests *in solidum* with one acting as moderator; the moderator should direct combined activity and answer for it to the bishop. The team ministry may apparently be assisted by a parish council enjoying a consultative role.[156]

---

[148] Pastoral Measure 1983, s. 20(7), (10A); any team member has a right to request in writing the rector to convene and the member may convene if the rector fails to do so.
[149] S. 20(11).   [150] Sched. 3, para. 4(1) (for absence).
[151] Ibid., para. 4(2); *CRR*, r. 14(5).   [152] *CRR*, r. 18.
[153] Pastoral Measure 1983, Sched 3, para. 4(3).
[154] *CRR*, r. 20; functions under Patronage (Benefices) Measure 1986, Sched. 2 and Priests (Ordination of Women) Measure 1993, s. 3 cannot be delegated; *PMCP*, B4(6).
[155] Pastoral Measure 1983, s. 22.
[156] *CIC*, cc. 516, 517; for qualifications and functions of team members see cc. 542, 543; see c. 140 for acts *in solidum*; for team ministry vacancy see c. 544; for impeded or vacant parishes and the role of the parish administrator see cc. 539–41.

Group Ministries: Chapters and Councils

As an alternative to both the classical parish and the team ministry, it is possible in the Church of England to establish by pastoral scheme a group ministry. As compared with a team ministry, a group ministry is a looser grouping of benefices whose incumbents are to make the best possible provision for the cure of souls throughout the area of the group.[157] To this end, duties are placed on all incumbents to assist each other in the cure of souls,[158] and the incumbents must meet as a group chapter to discuss and reach a common mind on all matters of general concern or special interest to the group ministry. If the scheme does not provide for chairmanship of the chapter, the members must elect a chairman (normally for a term of three years). It is the duty of the chairman to convene meetings of the group chapter at regular intervals; he presides but if absent a deputy chairman appointed by the meeting presides.[159] Special rules apply to group councils.[160] These can be established by the scheme itself or, if the scheme so authorizes, by the bishop through instrument made with the concurrence of all the members of the group.[161] Arrangements may deal with the chairmanship, meetings and procedure of a group council. Functions of the council of each parish in the group area may be delegated to the group council.[162] Similar arrangements may be made by schemes devised by annual parochial church meetings.[163] Provision exists for the amendment, renewal, and termination of a pastoral scheme establishing a group ministry.[164]

CATHEDRAL ADMINISTRATION

For the purposes of administration, cathedrals of the Church of England are subject, broadly, to separate bodies of law distinct from those operating at diocesan or parochial level.[165] Cathedrals fall into two general classes: 'dean and chapter cathedrals' and 'parish church cathedrals'. As we saw in Chapter 3, a dean and chapter cathedral is governed by its own statutes and constitution as well as by the church's central legal system. The statutes and constitution must provide for the performance of executive functions by an administrative

---

[157] Pastoral Measure, s. 21; *PMCP*, B4(1), (2).   [158] S. 21(1)-(3).   [159] S. 21(4).
[160] S. 21(5).
[161] Though incumbents must assist each other, each retains full responsibilities and rights with regard to his own benefice and parish.   [162] Sched. 3, para. 4(4); *CRR*, r. 14(4).
[163] *PMCP*, B4(8); *CRR*, r. 21; functions under the Patronage (Benefices) Measure 1986, Sched. 2 and the Priests (Ordination of Women) Measure 1993 s. 3 cannot be delegated.
[164] Pastoral Measure 1983, s. 22.
[165] For the Cathedral Statutes Commission (not within the scope of General Synod's *Quinquennial Review* of constitutions) see *supra* Ch. 3 and *Heritage and Renewal*, The Report of the Archbishops' Commission on Cathedrals, the Howe Commission (London, 1994) 67, 68–9, 199.

chapter or by the general chapter (the capitular body, the dean and canons) acting through an administrative committee. The dean and chapter may establish a committee composed of members from the general chapter and any other persons (whether clerical or lay) to which functions concerning the administration of property and finances of the cathedral may be delegated.[166] When a new diocese is created a parish church is normally designated as the cathedral and its incumbent and his successors become provosts.[167] The provost, canons, and archdeacons constitute the parish church cathedral chapter (the capitular body) and, like the dean and chapter cathedral, the cathedral must be governed according to its statutes and constitution. These must provide for administrative functions to be carried out by a cathedral council, or by an administrative chapter, or by an administrative committee to which the cathedral chapter delegates such of its functions as it may determine. Where administrative functions are performed by an administrative chapter or by the cathedral chapter, provision must be made for lay representation and for the appointment of a committee handling the administration of finance and property.[168] The constitution and statutes may arrange for the transference to the administrative body of all functions formerly exercised by the parochial church council.[169]

In Roman Catholic canon law, the central administrative body of a cathedral is the chapter of canons, the erection, change, or suppression of a cathedral being reserved to the Apostolic See. The chapter is regulated by its own statutes, created, altered, or abrogated with the approval of the diocesan bishop. The statutes must define the schedule of meetings in which the business of the cathedral is transacted as well as the conditions required for the valid and legitimate transaction of cathedral business. One of the canons is elected by the chapter to preside and the election must be confirmed by the bishop. A capitular cathedral may at the same time be a parish church and a pastor is assigned independently of the chapter.[170]

MALADMINISTRATION: ACCOUNTABILITY AND CONTROL

Both churches have established complex mechanisms to control the action and inaction of institutions possessing administrative power.[171] The following discussion deals with accountability and control effected by access to

---

[166] Cathedrals Measure 1963, s. 7.

[167] It is possible by scheme for a parish church cathedral to become a dean and chapter cathedral: Cathedrals Measure 1963, s. 14.   [168] Ibid., s. 8.

[169] Ibid., s. 12; s. 10 abolishes archdeacons' and rural deans' jurisdiction and transfers their powers to the administrative body.   [170] *CIC*, cc. 503–10.

[171] The discussion presented in this section is not exhaustive; many key powers exercised by administrative bodies in relation to ministry and property are discussed in Parts III and VI; see *supra* Ch. 2 for the executive power of dispensation.

information, visitatorial powers, and those rules which enable complaint short of and including review by the civil courts.

The Absence of General Norms

The law of the Church of England possesses no central body of rules governing administration[172] with a view to its *general* control regardless of the body in question, similar to those appearing in the Roman Catholic Church. The 1983 Code contains general norms applicable to all executive acts and requires all executive power to be exercised lawfully.[173] Although the Code does not define the term, an 'administrative act' is one which executes the law through interpretation, implementation, and completion by those enjoying administrative rather than judicial or legislative authority.[174] Executive power 'can be delegated both for a single act and for all cases unless the law expressly provides otherwise', but no 'subdelegated power can be again subdelegated, unless this has been expressly granted by the one delegating'.[175] Ordinary executive powers, and executive powers delegated for all cases, are to be broadly interpreted: a delegatee is empowered to do whatever is necessary to exercise that power.[176] Unless other legal provision is made, when a person approaches a competent authority (even a superior one) this does not suspend the executive power (ordinary or delegated) of another competent authority; but a lower authority cannot interfere in cases submitted to a higher authority except for a grave and urgent reason.[177] Delegated power ceases by fulfilment of the mandate, by lapse of time, by cessation of the final cause of delegation, by revocation, and by resignation of the delegatee accepted by the delegator. It does not cease by expiration of the authority of the delegator, unless this is clearly provided for in the delegation.[178] Ordinary executive power ceases by

---

[172] This may not be surprising given the 'common law' approach (see *supra* Ch. 1) and the fact that administrative structures are constituted by an amalgamation of corporations sole and aggregate.

[173] *CIC*, c. 135(4); see generally, F. Urrutia, 'Administrative power in the church according to the code of canon law', *Studia Canonica*, 20 (1986), 253.

[174] See M. Moodie, 'The administrator and the law: authority and its exercise in the code', *Readings*, 444.

[175] *CIC*, c. 137(1), (4); executive power delegated by the Apostolic See may be subdelegated unless delegation was granted in view of the special qualifications of the delegate or unless subdelegation was expressly prohibited; if executive power is delegated for all cases it can be subdelegated only for individual cases; if delegated for a single act or for determined acts it cannot be subdelegated except by the expressed grant of the one delegating: c. 137(2), (3); see generally, F. Urrutia, 'Delegation and the executive power of governance', *Studia Canonica*, 19 (1985), 339.

[176] *CIC*, c. 138.

[177] c. 139: the lower authority must notify immediately the superior authority; c. 140: when several persons have been delegated *in solidum* to transact the same business, the one who first undertakes it excludes the others from acting, unless thereafter that person is impeded or does not wish to proceed; c. 141: if several persons have been successively delegated, that person should transact the business whose mandate is prior to the others.   [178] C. 142.

loss of office and can be suspended, unless the law provides otherwise, if privation or removal from office is legitimately effected.[179]

Special norms apply to *individual administrative acts* of juridic persons. Whether competence to act exists is to be determined broadly according to the proper meaning of the words and the common usage of speech. Administrative acts dealing with lawsuits, threatening or inflicting penalties, restricting the rights of a person, injuring acquired rights, benefitting private individuals and those (such as dispensations) which relax the law, must be interpreted strictly.[180] When conditions are attached, non-compliance invalidates the act.[181] Administrative acts dealing with the external forum must be in writing, but if not validity is not affected.[182] A juridic person who executes an administrative act before receiving the letter of verification functions invalidly, unless prior notice of the letter is given.[183] An executor may refuse to execute an administrative act if it is manifestly null, if it cannot be upheld for serious cause, or if the conditions attached to it have not been met.[184] Unless the law expressly provides otherwise, an administrative act does not cease with the termination of the authority of its author, though its revocation by another act of a competent authority takes effect only from the moment the latter has been made known to the person for whom it has been given.[185]

Open Government: Disclosure of Information

It is a common assumption in civil law that administrative accountability and control are facilitated by access to information upon which government bodies base their decisions and actions.[186] The assumption may equally be applied to ecclesiastical government. To regulate disclosure of information, the Church of England extensively employs duties to report, to consult, to obtain consent, and to publicize (examples of which we have already met) as well as powers to investigate (typically visitatorial powers, discussed below). The report model is commonly used in Roman Catholic canon law: the permanent council of the Episcopal Conference must ensure that Conference decisions are properly

[179] C. 143.   [180] Cc. 35, 36; see *supra* Ch. 3 for rescripts, decrees, and precepts.
[181] C. 39.   [182] C. 37.   [183] C. 40.

[184] C. 41: if the execution of the act appears inopportune due to circumstances of person or place, the executor must delay execution and inform immediately the authority issuing it; c. 42: the executor must proceed according to law and execution is invalid if the essential conditions have not been fulfilled or if the executor has not substantially observed procedural formalities; c. 45: if execution is in error, the act may be implemented again.

[185] Cc. 46, 47; see cc. 48–75 for special rules applying to individual decrees, precepts, and rescripts; e.g. in relation to decrees, c. 50 imposes the duty to hear those whose rights may be injured 'insofar as this is possible' and c. 51 imposes a duty to give reasons; with regard to rescripts, on a refusal a competent authority to whom recourse is had must not grant the favour unless he has obtained the reasons for the refusal: c. 65.

[186] N. Lewis, 'De-legalisation in Britain in the 1980s', in P. McAuslan and J. F. McEldowney, *Law, Legitimacy and the Constitution* (London, 1985) 107.

implemented, the president must send the minutes of Conference plenary sessions to the Apostolic See, and its general secretary must report on its proceedings to neighbouring conferences; the bishop must communicate the texts of synodal decisions to the metropolitan and to the Conference of Bishops; the decisions of the diocesan curia must be submitted to the ordinary.[187]

In the Church of England the duty to report is often listed amongst the functions of administrative bodies. Whilst the model is employed at all levels of the administrative hierarchy, the terms and scope of duties to report vary as between bodies; sometimes the duty is found in the central legal system, sometimes not. Standing Orders of General Synod, regulating its subordinate bodies, impose directly on the secretary of each body the duty to report to the Secretary General 'such details of its business, procedure, and activities as the Standing Committee may from time to time direct'.[188] Every permanent body responsible to General Synod must lay before synod annually 'a concise report relating to the previous year's activities', including a schedule detailing membership changes and the number of meetings held'.[189] Members of General Synod have a right to ask questions of designated persons (including the chairmen of subordinate bodies) and if the person to whom a queston is addressed for oral answer is a synod member 'he shall reply personally unless he sees fit to authorise another member . . . to reply on his behalf'.[190] Standing orders of diocesan synods provide for notice of business to be circulated to members in advance.[191] In addition to the bishop's duty to consult with the diocesan synod on matters of general concern and importance to the diocese,[192] the diocesan synod itself must keep the deanery synods of the diocese informed of the policies and problems of the diocese and of the business which is 'to come before meetings of the diocesan synod',[193] and one of the functions of the deanery synod is to consider the business of the diocesan synod.[194] Standing orders of diocesan synods require the secretary to prepare and circulate after a meeting, to the secretaries of all diocesan deanery synods, a report of proceedings.[195]

---

[187] *CIC*, cc. 446, 456–8, 467, 474.

[188] *GSSO*, SO 121(b); see e.g. for reporting under the internal constitutions, *CBC* (1990–95) 13, 16; for the advisory board for redundant churches, see Pastoral Measure 1983, s. 41(3).

[189] *GSSO*, SO 96(a) (except the Crown Appointments Commission and those excluded by the Standing Committee); SO 116(g): the Standing Committee must report on such agenda matters as the committee thinks fit; consequently, constitutions do not fix reporting duties: *CBC* (1990–95).

[190] *GSSO*, SO 105–9; these also govern content, admissibility, procedures in reply, and circulation of questions; *OLAC*, 216: synod proceedings must normally be open to the public (see SO 129); its Standing Committee chooses to conduct its proceedings in private.

[191] *CDSMH*, SO 28–31; the bishop's council is 'to receive and approve recommendations from its Standing Committee and any other of its sub-committees for the agenda items to be placed before Synod and to circulate to members information about matters for discussion'.

[192] SGM 1969, s. 4(3).   [193] Ibid., s. 4(5).   [194] Ibid., s. 5(3)(d).

[195] *CDSMH*, SO 31; *OLAC*, 107: the diocesan synod may exclude the press: like the PCC, it is not included in the lists under the Public Bodies (Admission to Meetings) Act 1960: a right to attend exists only if authorized; see e.g. *DLR*, Standing Orders for Diocesan Synod, SO 117.

Similarly, diocesan synod committees are required by standing orders to report to the synod on their activities at such times and in accordance with such procedure as may be determined by the bishop's council.[196] When it delegates functions to the deanery synod, the diocesan synod must keep itself informed, through the deanery synod, of events and opinion in the parishes, and it must give opportunities for discussing at its meetings matters raised by deanery synods and parochial church councils.[197]

Diocesan executive bodies have specific duties to report on their activities to diocesan and central bodies. The pastoral committee must present annually to the diocesan synod a report of its activities during the preceding year and it must consult the bishop and give him particulars of matters which it intends to consider and of the benefices that will be affected by its work.[198] The diocesan parsonages board must present an annual report and accounts to the diocesan synod and the synod must, in turn, submit a copy of these to the Church Commissioners.[199] The Church Commissioners may seek information from the board concerning its functions and the board 'shall provide such information'.[200] The diocesan board of finance may demand information from those engaged in the administration of diocesan property,[201] and it must supply information to the diocesan synod when so directed.[202] The diocesan redundant churches uses committees must make to the Church Commissioners in each year a report of their proceedings in the preceding year.[203] Similarly, the diocesan advisory committee, as soon as practicable after the end of each year, must prepare a report of 'its work and proceedings' during that year and cause it to be laid before the diocesan synod; the secretary of the synod is required to send a copy of the report to the Council for the Care of Churches.[204]

Although the parochial church council is under no direct duty to report on its proceedings and activities to the deanery or diocesan synods, a limited report may be required indirectly. The deanery synod must 'make known' any provision made by the diocesan synod and it must bring together the views of the parishes.[205] One of the council's functions is to make known and put into effect 'any provision' made by the diocesan or deanery synods and to advise these on any matter referred to it by them.[206] Yet, standing orders of diocesan synods sometimes simply provide that the synod 'may invite' deanery synods and parochial councils 'to supply information within their

---

[196] *CDSMH*, SO 97; see also Pastoral (Amendment) Measure 1994, s. 1 for reports of advisory board for redundant churches (amending Pastoral Measure 1983, s. 41).
[197] SGM 1969, s. 4(5).   [198] Pastoral Measure 1983, ss. 1(3), 2(2).
[199] Repair of Benefice Buildings Measure 1972, s. 1(7).
[200] S. 24; under s.23 the incumbent must furnish the board with details of benefice property.
[201] See e.g. the Endowments and Glebe Measure 1976, s. 16.
[202] Diocesan Boards of Finance Measure 1925, s. 3.   [203] Pastoral Measure 1983, s. 42(5).
[204] Care of Churches and Ecclesiastical Jurisdiction Measure 1991, s. 2(7).
[205] SGM 1969, s. 5(3)(b), (c).   [206] PCC(P)M 1956, s. 2(2) (c), (d).

knowledge' or 'to report to the diocesan synod by a specified date'.[207] When a matter is referred to it by the diocesan synod, the deanery synod's function is 'to consider' this and 'to sound parochial opinion whenever they are required or consider it appropriate to do so'.[208] The parochial church council must publish its accounts,[209] and it must obtain the consent of diocesan authorities with regard to the acquisition, holding, and disposal of most property.[210]

Access to Personal Information

Both the Church of England and the Roman Catholic Church hold and process an abundance of material containing information relating to individuals. Rights of access to this material vary depending on the type of information in question. In the Church of England special rules apply to documents held as part of diocesan archives. Parochial registers and records (including baptismal and burial records), containing personal information about living (and dead) individuals, and access to them, have been the subject of some internal ecclesiastical legislation. Provision exists for depositing records and registers in the diocesan record office,[211] as well as for the correction of erroneous entries.[212] Those having care and custody of any parochial register books or records may deposit them for a limited period in the diocesan record office or other suitable and safe place approved by the bishop for exhibition or research or for enabling copies or lists to be made.[213] This may be done on request but, whether or not a request is made, the custodian (if not the parochial church council) may do so only with the consent of the council. If a request is refused, or the parochial church council refuses to consent to deposit, the applicant may request the bishop to order them to be deposited for a period specified at the diocesan record office or some other suitable place; the bishop must give the council (and/or custodian) the opportunity to make representations.[214] Similar provision exists with regard to records already deposited in the diocesan records office.[215] In both cases, the expenses incurred in the transfer, deposit, or return of records are met by the person making the request.[216]

Whilst the law of the Church of England frequently generates the creation and use of personal files by ecclesiastical authorities, internal legal regulation is undeveloped. *Prima facie* the subject is governed by the civil law, though

---

[207] *CDSMH*, SO 106.   [208] SGM 1969, s. 5(3)(d).

[209] PCC(P)M 1956, s.8(3); *OLAC*, 7: the council cannot bind its successors as to procedure and the annual parochial church meeting must give notice of major matters of principle.

[210] See *post* Chs. 15–17.

[211] Parochial Registers and Records Measure 1978 (as amended by the Church of England (Miscellaneous Provisions) Measure 1992, s. 4, Sched. 1) s. 7.   [212] S. 4.

[213] S. 16(1).   [214] S. 16(2), (3).   [215] S. 17.   [216] S. 18(2).

sometimes this clearly does not apply[217] and sometimes its scope is narrow.[218] The relevant legislation is the Data Protection Act 1984. This applies to computerized personal data which embrace factual information or opinion (including data concerning religious belief, health, and sexual life) relating to a living individual. The data must by the statutory principles be obtained lawfully and fairly, must be held for a specified and lawful purpose, must not be used or disclosed in any manner incompatible with those purposes, and must be adequate, relevant, accurate, and not excessive. The data-subject has rights of access and correction. All data-users must be registered (unless exempt) or else a criminal offence is committed. The data protection registrar maintains the register, and makes entries containing, *inter alia*, the name and address of users, a description of the personal data, the purpose(s) for which they are held, and a description of sources and recipients; access is had only with the data-subject's consent. Certain categories of information are exempt and the data-user must be satisfied that an exemption exists. Personal data held only for the purpose of distributing or recording the distribution of articles or information to individuals are exempt from the requirement to register. Strict conditions stipulate that data can be used only for this purpose and individuals must be asked whether they object to the holding. Disclosure is lawful only when the individual authorizes it or if it is required by law: payroll, pensions, and accounts are exempt from the duty to register. A subject has no right of access to data held for enforcing the criminal law, assessing or collecting tax, or to data 'held for the purpose of discharging statutory functions'.[219]

Three key areas involve the creation and use of files: selection and appointment, discipline, and property. First, candidates for ecclesiastical office may be obliged by law to furnish authorities with personal information. Every ordination candidate must exhibit to the bishop 'testimony of his former good life and behaviour from persons specified by the bishop'.[220] Files containing

[217] With the Access to Personal Files Act 1987, and secondary legislation created under it, dealing with information held in manual documentary form, no special provision has been made for churches (but the statute confers a power to legislate for 'any authority keeping records containing personal information' (s. 1(1)).

[218] The Access to Medical Reports Act 1988, operating in the area of 'employment', clearly applies to those seeking a contract of employment with church authorities; s. 1 gives a right of access to medical reports supplied by medical practitioners 'for employment purposes'; under s. 3 disclosure may occur only with the data-subject's consent: it is not clear whether this applies to holders of or applicants for ecclesiastical office; under s. 2(1) the statute applies whether employment arises 'under a contract of service or not': see *post* Ch. 7; see also Access to Health Records Act 1990.

[219] Data Protection Act 1984, ss. 1–5 for 'data', the protection principles, and registration); s. 2(3) governs data on racial origin, political opinions, religious or other beliefs, physical or mental health, sexual life, and criminal convictions; ss. 21–5 (rights of data-subject); ss. 26–35 (exemptions, esp. s. 28 for exclusion of data held for the prevention or detection of crime and data held 'for the purpose of discharging statutory functions').

[220] Canon C6 (e.g. files of the Archbishops' Appointments Adviser and the Prime Minister's Patronage Secretary).

personal information on divorced and re-married ordination candidates (which may include information provided by former spouses) may be opened by the diocesan bishop or his representative.[221] To ensure that selection panels enjoy a degree of doctrinal balance and impartiality (e.g. with female ordination candidacy),[222] files might contain personal information about the relgious beliefs of potential selectors. If held and processed in a computerized form it is likely that such data would fall within the ambit of the civil law giving rise to a duty to register and a right of access.[223] Secondly, personal information may be acquired and processed in connection with discipline. Files may be compiled on potential 'assessors' in the consistory court.[224] When a serious breakdown of pastoral relations in a parish results from the conduct of the incumbent or parishioners, a request for proceedings 'shall contain particulars of the facts which appear to the person or persons making the request to justify an enquiry'.[225] Norms regulating the periodic appraisal of clergy may generate the creation and holding of files.[226] Once more, if computerized data contains personal information it may come within the terms of the civil law.[227]

Thirdly, personal information may be gathered and used in relation to church finances. It has been advised recently that any administrative data held on computer at parish level should be registered in the name of the parochial church council; similarly, a cleric holding personal data relating to parishioners would need to be registered separately as a data-user.[228] As the electoral roll of a parish is a public document required by law, personal information contained on the roll and computerized is exempt from registration; but if data is added to the computerized roll the user must register.[229] If a parochial authority computerizes covenanting or other fund-raising administration using personal data of parishioners, the user must register.[230] Keeping accounts relating to any business or other activity carried on by a data-user or keeping records of purchases, sales, or other transactions or for the purpose of making financial or management forecasts are exempt from registration.[231]

---

[221] Canon C4(3A); these may be sent to the archbishop. [222] See *post* Ch. 7.

[223] These may be exempt under s. 28(2)(a) as data held for the purpose of discharging statutory functions.

[224] It is arguable that, as part of the process of administering the church's criminal jurisdiction, this would be exempt under s. 28 of the 1984 statute. [225] S. 1.

[226] See e.g. *SDH*, V, E.

[227] If arrangements such as these were classified as the discharging of a statutory function, they would be exempt under s. 28(2)(a).

[228] Office of the Data Protection Registrar, *A Local Church of England Parish and Registration*, compiled by S. Rowland (1994).

[229] *CRR*, rr. 1, 2; *OLAC*, 118–19 (on s. 34(1) of the 1984 statute); S. Rowland, *A Local Church*: if the law requires personal data to be made public, an exemption from registration arises; if extra data not made public is added, a duty to register arises; if electoral roll information is computerized, this is exempt; any additional information computerized is not.

[230] S. Rowland, *A Local Church*.

[231] Data Protection Act 1984, s. 32(1) (this provides exemption from the provisions of Part II and from ss. 21,24 on subject access rights).

Holding telephone numbers or descriptions of the 'talents' of parishioners would give rise to a duty to comply with the statutory provisions.[232]

Similar issues arise with regard to the Roman Catholic Church in which, likewise, internal recognition of rights of access is minimal. No one is permitted to damage unlawfully the good reputation of another or to violate a person's right to privacy.[233] Documents in diocesan curial archives, dealing with both spiritual and temporal affairs, 'must be protected with the greatest care' and can be disclosed only with the consent of the bishop or of both the moderator and the chancellor. However, it is 'the right of interested parties to obtain personally or through their proxy an authentic written copy or a photocopy of documents which are public by their nature and which pertain to the status of such persons'.[234] Documents may also be deposited in the diocesan curia's secret archives to which there is no right of access; the bishop only has the 'key' and documents must not be removed. Whilst the Code does not categorize the documents to be held in the secret archives, it does require the destruction of documents relating to 'matters of morals in which the criminal has died or in which ten years have passed since the condemnatory sentence'; but 'a brief summary of the case with the text of the definitive sentence is to be retained'.[235] In relation to both churches, when computerized personal files are held and processed by ecclesiastical authorities the provisions of the civil law will ordinarily apply unless an exemption can be established. Though computerization in the church is increasing, in practice these provisions ensure no effective control in so far as files are held and processed manually.[236]

---

[232] *OLAC*, 119.

[233] *CIC*, c. 220; it is a right which can be vindicated in the church tribunals (c. 221); the right appears in many different contexts (cc. 642, 1548(2), 1674, 1697).   [234] *CIC*, cc. 482, 486–7.

[235] Cc. 489–90; documents commonly held include matrimonial dispensations in the non-sacramental internal forum (c. 1083), the register for secret marriages (c. 1133), dispensations for impediments and irregularities to orders (cc. 1047, 1048), decrees of dismissal from religious institutes (c. 700), and documents relating to loss of clerical state (cc. 290–3); see K. E. McKenna, 'Confidential clergy matters and the secret archives', *Studia Canonica*, 26 (1992), 191.

[236] See N. Doe, 'Churches in the United Kingdom and the law of data protection', in G. Robbers (ed.), *Europaisches Datenschutzrecht und die Kirchen* (Berlin, 1994) 167–83: the Council of Ministers adopted in Feb. 1995 a Common Position on a proposed European directive; the directive, which must be incorporated into domestic law within 3 years of its final adoption, deals with both computerized and manual personal data filing systems; under Art. 8 member states must prohibit the processing of data revealing religious belief unless the data-subject gives explicit consent; however, this does not apply where 'processing is carried out in the course of its legitimate activities with appropriate guarantees by a foundation, association or any other non-profit-seeking body with a . . . religious . . . aim and on condition that the processing relates solely to the members of the body or to persons who have regular contact with it in connection with its purposes and that the data are not disclosed to a third party without the consent of the data subjects'. A key problem for Catholic canon law concerns the processing of data by matrimonial tribunals, which under *CIC*, c. 1592 may take place without further collaboration by the respondent.

Visitatorial Powers

Visitation, the policing of administrative activities, is treated as a pastoral exercise; its purposes are investigation, prevention and cure.[237] Visitatorial power must be derived from and exercised according to law.[238] It is vested in and exercisable only by ordained ministers,[239] by archbishops, bishops, and archdeacons, but in the Church of England visitatorial power beyond that of the archdeacon is rarely used.[240] Every 'archbishop, bishop and archdeacon has the right to visit, at times and places limited by law or custom, the province, diocese or archdeaconry committed to his charge, in a more solemn manner'. Each has the right 'to perform all such acts as by law or custom are assigned to his charge in that behalf for the edifying and well-governing of Christ's flock, that means may be taken thereby for the supply of such things as are lacking and the correction of such things as are amiss'.[241]

The archbishop has throughout his province at all times metropolitical jurisdiction 'to correct and supply the defects of other bishops' and 'during the time of his metropolitical visitation, jurisdiction as Ordinary, except in places and over persons exempt by law or custom'.[242] When visiting his province, the archbishop usually visits first his own cathedral and diocese; when visiting a diocese, he begins with the cathedral and proceeds subsequently to any place he pleases.[243] In the Roman Catholic Church the arrangement is rather different: the metropolitan must visit the diocese only if the diocesan bishop neglects to do so; the metropolitan must first submit his reasons to and obtain the approval of the pontiff. Whether an archiepiscopal visitation of a diocesan bishop is permissible has recently been the subject of debate.[244]

---

[237] Historically, the visitation process has been described as judicial and the visitation itself as a court: *Re Dean of York* (1841) 2 QB 1 at 39; *Reconciliation Sentence and Service in St Paul's* (1891) 7 TLR 276 at 277; the original aim of detecting and correcting offences against ecclesiastical law seems now to be obsolete with the visitor's role conceived as pastoral rather than coercive and judicial: *Report of the Archbishop's Commission on Ecclesiastical Courts* (1951) (London, 1954) 51; for the Roman Catholic Church, the new Code does not spell out the purposes of visitation, unlike the 1917 Code in which (c. 343) visitation existed to preserve doctrine and morality, to correct abuses, and to promote peace and piety in both clergy and laity.

[238] *Dean of York's Case* (1841) 2 QB 1; *Whiston v Dean and Chapter of Rochester* (1849) 7 Hare 532, for discussion of prohibition as lying to prevent an act in excess of jurisdiction; *AG v Dean and Chapter of Ripon Cathedral* [1945] 1 Ch 239 at 248.

[239] See Ch. 16 for quasi-visitatorial powers vested in lay people, concerning accounting and inspection.

[240] P. Smith, 'Points of law and practice concerning ecclesiastical visitation', *ELJ*, 2 (1990–92), 189 at 204 (n.171); 207.

[241] Canon G5 (during the time of the visitation 'the jurisdiction of all inferior ordinaries shall be suspended save in places which by law or custom are exempt': para. 2).   [242] Canon C17(2).

[243] *HLE*, para. 431; by agreement the Archbishop of Canterbury does not visit the diocese of London: *Gobbet's Case* (1634) Cro Car 339.

[244] *CIC*, c. 436; see J. P. Beal, 'The apostolic visitation of a diocese: a canonico-historical investigation', and J. Provost, 'Suggested operative principles for apostolic visitation', *Jurist*, 49 (1989), 341, 543.

The diocesan bishop has the right (but no duty) to hold 'visitations at times limited by law or custom to the end that he may get some good knowledge of the state, sufficiency, and ability of the clergy and other persons whom he is to visit'.[245] The bishop may visit places and persons in the diocese including the cathedral. In relation to cathedrals, the bishop may visit either under his ordinary visitatorial jurisdiction or under special visitatorial jurisdiction conferred by cathedral statutes and constitutions.[246] These must provide: that the bishop is the visitor of the cathedral; for the exercise of his functions as visitor as well as specify the occasions upon which, and the conditions subject to which, the bishop is to have the right to officiate in or use the cathedral church.[247] The bishop has, however, no duty to visit the cathedral at 'regular intervals' notwithstanding anything to the contrary in those statutes or in any rule of ecclesiastical law.[248] The capitular body of a cathedral must take care that the law 'and such as shall be enjoined by the bishop of the diocese in his visitation. . .shall be diligently observed'.[249] If a bishop believes the cathedral's administrative body may have committed or be intending to commit an act in contravention of the rules governing alteration of cathedral fabric[250] he shall interview its members and then, if necessary, order a special visitation to inquire into the matter.[251] A written statement with reasons for the visitation must be sent to the administrative body. When in these circumstances a special visitation is held, the administrative body has no power to act in respect of the matter under inquiry without the written approval of the bishop.[252] The bishop is empowered to give interim instructions before holding the special visitation and may give such directions as he thinks fit to avoid a contravention or to restore the position so far as possible to that which existed before the act was committed. The directions must be usually given in writing; in cases of urgency they may be given orally; oral instructions must subsequently be confirmed in writing.[253] When he considers it necessary or expedient, the

---

[245] Canon C18(4); Cathedrals Measure 1963, s. 1(1)(a): the bishop is the visitor of the cathedral church and may do all such things as belong of right to the office of visitor; for recent consideration of cathedral visitation see *Heritage and Renewal* (1994) 66–7.

[246] See *Boyd v Phillpotts* (1874) LR 4 A&E 297, *Phillpotts v Boyd* [1875] 6 PC 435: an appeal lies to a superior ecclesiastical court from an episcopal determination arising from an exercise of ordinary jurisdiction; *R v Dean and Chapter of Chester* (1850) 15 QB 513 at 519: the special jurisdiction may give rise to a right in the visitor to interpret the cathedral statutes in cases of ambiguity and is not subject to an appeal.   [247] Cathedrals Measure 1963, s. 6.

[248] Ibid., as added by the Church of England (Miscellaneous Provisions) Measure 1976, s. 4; statutes and constitutions need not provide for 'periodical episcopal visitations'.

[249] Canon C21(2).   [250] A contravention of the Care of Cathedrals Measure 1990, s. 2.

[251] Care of Cathedrals (Supplementary Provisions) Measure 1994, s. 1.

[252] The bishop may not order a special visitation if satisfied that the body intends to apply to the Cathedral Fabric Commission or if there are exceptional reasons: s. 2(2); a special visitation is not treated as an episcopal visitation for the purposes of the cathedral's statutes and constitutions 'restricting the ordering of such visitations': s. 2(4).

[253] The administrative body must comply with the directions: s. 3(6); see also *AG v Dean and Chapter of Ripon* [1945] 1 Ch 239 at 248 *per* Uthwatt J: 'If circumstances so demand, he may admonish or make orders, and disobedience to the orders of the Visitor will . . . be the ecclesiastical offence of disobedience to the lawful orders of the Ordinary'.

bishop may also authorize a commissary to institute proceedings on his behalf against the administrative body to obtain an injunction or restoration order or both.[254] In Roman Catholic canon law, the bishop has a duty to visit some parts of the diocese (in person or by delegatee) annually so that every five years the whole diocese is covered. He must visit places, Roman Catholic institutions, sacred things, and persons in the diocesan territory. He must complete this pastoral visitation with due diligence ensuring that no one is burdened with unnecessary expenses. The bishop must report every five years to the pontiff on the state of the diocese and during the year of the report he must make an *ad limina* visit to Rome. As we have seen, if the diocesan bishop fails to make the visitation the metropolitan must do so.[255]

The archdeacon has a general duty to 'see that all such as hold any ecclesiastical office within the [archdeaconry] perform their duties with diligence, and shall bring to the bishop's attention what calls for correction or merits praise'.[256] In contrast to the bishop's right to visit, the archdeacon has a duty to hold yearly visitations, save when inhibited by a superior ordinary.[257] The archdeacon must survey in person (or by deputy) all churches, chancels, and churchyards and give directions for the amendment of all defects in the walls, fabric, ornaments, and furniture of the same as well as discharge 'the powers conferred on him by the Inspection of Churches Measure 1958'.[258] A similar function is performed by the Roman Catholic vicar forane who must visit parishes, with regard to lay and clerical discipline and property, in accordance with regulations made by the diocesan bishop.[259]

Visitation procedure is as follows. Every archbishop, bishop, and archdeacon, 'and every other person having ecclesiastical jurisdiction' must deliver or cause to be delivered to the minister and churchwardens of every parish (or to some of them) 'such articles of inquiry' as the archbishop, bishop, or archdeacon shall require.[260] The articles contain questions relating to the administration of the parish, the state of buildings, arrangements for services, and the life and health of the parish generally.[261] The minister and churchwardens must render their account (their 'presentment') upon these articles.[262] The minister and churchwardens may be examined orally and in private,[263] but it is unclear whether they are under a duty to answer questions not included in

---

[254] S. 4; the vicar-general of the province has original jurisdiction to hear and determine the proceedings: ss. 5, 6; failure to comply is a contempt of court: s. 6(9).

[255] *CIC*, cc. 396–400; for visitation of religious, see cc. 397(2), 628, 683.

[256] Canon C22(4); see also F18: duty to survey churches, chancels, and churchyards at least once every three years, either in person or by the rural dean.   [257] Canon C22(5).

[258] Ibid.   [259] *CIC*, c. 555(4).   [260] Canon G6(1).   [261] *OLAC*, 8.

[262] Canon G6(1); with the articles must be delivered a form of declaration which must be made by the minister and churchwardens before the presentment, so that they have time to frame the presentment 'advisedly and truly according to their consciences': G6(2). For the continuing duty on churchwardens to report to the bishop, see *post* Ch. 8.

[263] Burn, *Ecclesiastical Law*, IV, 30.

the articles, although in the opinion of the Legal Advisory Commission they 'are at liberty to include in their response any further matters affecting the parish which may be relevant'.[264] The information contained in the account is not intended to be restricted to the archdeacon—he may communicate it to other authorities even if it 'were marked "confidential"'.[265] The presentments are made by the retiring churchwardens as, customarily, the visitor admits new churchwardens to office at the annual visitation.[266]

Those enjoying visitatorial jurisdiction may investigate whether clergy and certain lay office-holders are in breach of church law in order to provide information for use as the basis of further judicial or executive proceedings.[267] The visitor must determine whether the parochial church council and officers are discharging their duties concerning the care and maintenance of the church, the churchyard, and their contents and an order may be made to correct the effects of neglect.[268] The visitor must preach a sermon,[269] and delivers a charge to those attending surveying needs and proposing objectives.[270] On old authority, the visitor may be able to compel attendance (by citation) of the clergy and churchwardens (and perhaps sidesmen), but not of the laity generally.[271]

Complaints and Remedies

In civil administration, recent years have seen the development of a plethora of procedures conferring rights of complaint, notably to the parliamentary commissioner, against administrative decisions and activities of government departments (central and local), social services, and the professions.[272] In the Roman Catholic Church the right to complain is found in the principle

---

[264] *OLAC*, 47: 'Such presentments include any gross neglect of duty or impropriety of life on the part of the incumbent and, if made in good faith, are privileged communications'.

[265] Ibid., 8, 9: to the bishop, the chancellor, the pastoral committee, or the diocesan board of finance, for example. 'He may also feel obliged to take action himself ... e.g. by calling a meeting of the PCC or by presenting a petition for a faculty'; if communication were malicious, this may be restrained; see *post* Ch. 12 for the equitable doctrine of confidence.

[266] *R v Sowter* [1901] 1 KB 396, usually the archdeacon, but the bishop may do so at his visitation, the archdeacon thereby being inhibited.

[267] *Re Dean of York* (1841) 2 QB 1 at 40: the archbishop was prohibited from summarily depriving the dean at a visitation; legal proceedings had to be instituted separately under the Church Discipline Act 1840 (repealed); *Sanders v Head* (1843) 2 Notes of Cases 355 (at 368). Proceedings would now be instituted under the Ecclesiastical Jurisdiction Measure 1963.

[268] For the council's property duties (and the archdeacon's powers to remove items) see *post* Ch. 16; the archdeacon may 'give such direction for the amendment of all defects in the fabric, ornaments, and furniture' of churches, chancels, and churchyards: F18.

[269] *R v Williams* (1828) 8 B & C 681; this may it seems be a duty which he can delegate to the minister: *Huntley's Case* (1626), Burn, *Ecclesiastical Law*, IV, 27.

[270] *Laughton v Bishop of Sodor and Man* (1872) LR 4 PC 495 (a privileged communication); see *post* Ch. 12.   [271] *Anon* (1608) Noy 123.

[272] J. F. McEldowney, *Public Law* (London, 1994) Ch. 14; J. Wadham (ed.), *Your Rights: The Liberty Guide* (London, 1994) Ch. 5.

of hierarchical administrative recourse. This is the process of complaint against an administrative act, and its consequences, to the superior of the actor or to an administrative tribunal; administrative acts cannot be challenged in the church's courts.[273] There are three stages. First, before an aggrieved party appeals to the superior every effort ought to be made to mediate with the administrator to reach an amicable solution; the Code empowers the conference of bishops to set up conciliation agencies. Secondly, if this fails a reconsideration of the administrative act may be sought within ten days of notification, the aggrieved party petitioning the administrator to revoke or modify the act. The petition may be addressed directly to the diocesan bishop. Thirdly, if this fails, the complainant may make recourse to the superior for any just reason within fifteen days of the notice of the original action or of the response to the request for re-consideration. Alternatively, the complainant may make recourse directly to the superior or instruct the administrator to communicate it to the superior; the complainant has a right to counsel. The appropriate hierarchical superior has power to confirm, rescind, or modify the original executive act.[274]

In the Church of England it is difficult to identify or construct a right to complain.[275] Outside the annual archdeacon's visitation,[276] the right to complain about parochial administration may arise indirectly through various duties. By and large, the bishop is not the first channel for complaints, though no formal rule forbids a right of access to the bishop directly as 'chief pastor of all that are within his diocese, as well laity as clergy'.[277] As an officer of the ordinary, a parochial complainant may have a right to compel a churchwarden to communicate a complaint to the bishop under the churchwarden's duty of 'representing the laity'.[278] A right of complaint to the archdeacon may exist given his continuing duties to ensure that those holding ecclesiastical office perform their duties with diligence.[279] Similarly, the rural dean may be used as a channel for complaint: he is under a duty to report to the bishop any matter in any deanery parish which it may be necessary or useful for the bishop to know.[280]

---

[273] *CIC*, c. 1400(2); c. 1732 prohibits recourse against administrative acts of the pontiff or the College of Bishops; see also K. Matthews, 'Extra-judicial appeal and hierarchical recourse', *Studia Canonica*, 18 (1984), 95.

[274] *CIC*, cc. 1735–9; *COCLA*, 1287 (authentic interpretation 1988: a 'group' of the faithful have no recourse against a decree of a diocesan bishop but individuals within it may have (collectively they lack juridical personality under c. 299).

[275] When complaint becomes conflict, the conflict may be dealt with by the use of those quasi-judicial or judicial powers described in Ch. 5 *post*.

[276] *OLAC*, 8: presentments 'may include sensitive material e.g. complaints by the incumbent or churchwardens about each other's conduct or complaints about individual parishisioners'.

[277] Canon C18(1).   [278] Canon E1(3).   [279] Canon C22(4).

[280] Canon C23(1); C23(2): rural deans must report failures to prepare or maintain electoral rolls, to form or maintain PCCs, or to hold annual parochial meetings.

In connection with diocesan and central church authorities[281] a distinction must be made between complaints against individual officers and those against the executive bodies themselves. Within the schemes for responsibility described earlier in this chapter, the proper forum for a serious complaint against the deanery synod or its officers would be its joint chairmen or the diocesan synod, and for those against the diocesan synod, its president (the bishop), General Synod, or its Standing Committee. Complaints against diocesan administrative bodies (such as the parsonages board) and their officers ought to be made to the diocesan synod or its president (the bishop). Diocesan norms do not contain separate and general provision concerning complaints; the absence of regulation is most conspicuous in relation to non-statutory diocesan executives. Complaints against General Synod's administrative bodies would be properly made to the synod itself (or its Standing Committee) to which they are responsible.[282] Some of constitutions of subordinate bodies make general provision for this.[283] Complainants may, of course, approach members of these bodies to raise issues by means of questions. The right to ask questions in these assemblies is subject to regulation by their standing orders. With diocesan synods, the degree to which questions are answered often depends on whether the person asked is responsible for that subject, and standing orders often entitle the person asked to refuse to answer 'without reason given'.[284] With General Synod (and its executive bodies) the right of members to ask questions is conferred and regulated by standing orders.[285]

Recourse to the civil courts, as an extra-ecclesiastical complaints process,[286]

---

[281] For implicit and explicit rights to appeal against administrative action see e.g.: *CRR*, r. 43 (electoral roll disputes); concerning appointments to benefices see Patronage (Benefices) Measure 1986, s. 13(5); see Chs. 3, 5 for appeals against executives acting legislatively and quasi-judicially.

[282] See above.

[283] *CBC* (1996–2001) : board of ministry: 'to represent the views of deaf people to the Church'; 5: board of education, 'to promote educational concerns in the work of all Boards and Councils of the General Synod'.

[284] *CDSMH*, SO 74: questions after due notice to synod officers 'provided that the person asked may, without reason given, refuse to answer that question') ibid., SO 75 (based on the GS model): 'A question, if addressed to an officer, shall relate to the duties assigned to him and, if addressed to the chairman of any body to the business of that body. Questions shall not ask for an expression of opinion or for the solution of either an abstract legal question or a hypothetical problem and shall be otherwise in order'.

[285] *GSSO*, SO 105: questions may be asked by any member of the secretary, the financial secretary, the chairman of any subordinate body, and the chairman of any church body on which the synod is represented; SO 106 governs content of questions (and is similar in form to that described in n. 284 above); SO 107, supplementary questions; SO 108, procedure on reply to questions for oral answer; and SO 109 circulation of questions and replies.

[286] For Henry VIII clauses see *supra* Ch. 3. No obvious provision exists for complaints to the ombudsman under the Parliamentary Commissioner Act 1967 or the Local Government Act 1974, ss. 25, 26.

may be made in serious and appropriate cases.[287] With judicial review (the jurisdiction of the superior civil courts to review the decisions, acts, and omissions of public authorities) the courts' function is to determine whether the body (typically statutory) has exceeded, abused, or failed to perform functions legally assigned to it. The grounds for judicial review, and the availability of discretionary remedies, fall broadly between action substantively *ultra vires* and action which fails to comply with procedures imposed by statute.[288] As judicial review of General Synod's legislative activity has been entertained by the civil courts in recent years (see Chapter 3), so too have the courts entertained judicial review of ecclesiastical administrative action.[289]

However, judicial review may not be appropriate in relation to many ecclesiastical executives. Judicial review depends not only upon an alternative remedy not being available but also upon whether or not the function of the body in question is a public one.[290] If the body is established and regulated by statute its administrative activities will *prima facie* be reviewable. When, however, the body against which review is sought is a non-statutory body its functions may be classified as public, and therefore reviewable, provided there is evidence that if the body had not taken on the function in question the state would have done so.[291] As we have seen, although many bodies are non-statutory, most of the Church of England's central and local executive bodies were established directly or indirectly through powers derived from synodical measure. Their functions are analogous to statutory functions, measures having same authority as parliamentary statutes. It is upon this basis that the civil courts may proceed to review functions not carried out in accordance with the terms of parent ecclesiastical legislation. With respect to the Church of

---

[287] For other forms of process see e.g. *OLAC*, 98–104: a 'risk of a [diocesan advisory committee] being found liable does exist in law' (liability for damages if a person suffers loss through reliance on negligent advice given); this contains discussion of the applicability of *Saif Ali v Sidney Mitchell Co Ltd* [1980] AC 198 (HL) and *Murphy v Brentwood DC* [1991] 1 AC 398 (HL).

[288] For a statement of general principle see *Council of Civil Service Unions v Minister for the Civil Service* [1985] AC 374 (HL) (illegality, irrationality, and procedural impropriety); see S. H. Bailey, B. L. Jones, and A. R. Mowbray, *Cases and Materials on Administrative Law* (London, 1992) Chs. 6–10; J. F. McEldowney, *Public Law* (London, 1994) Ch.16 (for remedies); judicial review is brought by way of an application under Order 53 of the Rules of the Supreme Court.

[289] See e.g. *Hargreaves v Church Commissioners for England* (1983) 3 All ER 17; for *Harries v Church Commissioners* (1991) see *post* Ch. 17.

[290] *R v East Berkshire Health Authority, ex p Walsh* [1984] 3 All ER 425; see also D. Pannick, 'What is a public authority for the purposes of judicial review', in J. Jowell and D. Oliver (eds), *New Directions in Judicial Review* (1988) 5,23.

[291] Judicial review was denied for want of sufficient public element in *R v Chief Rabbi of the United Hewbrew Congregations of Great Britain and the Commonwealth, ex p Wachmann* [1992] 1 WLR 1036 and *R v Imam of Bury Park, ex p Sulaiman Ali* [1992] COD 132; cf. *R v Rabbinical Commission, ex p Cohen* (unreported, 14 Dec. 1987, CA) (the exercise of statutory licensing functions under the Slaughterhouses Act 1974 was subject to review).

England's non-statutory executives, where the public element is not so obvious, the applicability of judicial review is more problematic.[292]

CONCLUSIONS

Administrative structures of the Church of England, built around the institutions of synodical (and conciliar) government at all levels, are regulated principally by rules contained in the church's central legal system. However, the advent of functions exercised by 'non-statutory' executives at all levels of the church has given rise to complex administrative schemes not directly regulated by the church's central legal system. These are governed by a plethora of norms contained in instruments (constitutions and standing orders) operating alongside this. Basic administrative organization is not dissimilar to that in the Roman Catholic Church. The general principle, operative from central through to parochial administration, is that these bodies must exercise their functions and discretionary powers in accordance with law and with executive directions of those superior bodies to which they are responsible. The central legal system, and the norms of the supplementary instruments, control the possibility of maladministration in a prospective or preventative manner. Duties to report, rights of access to information, and visitatorial powers have been devised to effect accountability. Beyond the area of parochial administration, however, visitatorial powers remain undeveloped, as do procedures for complaint and questioning of administrative action. Though these structures are very similar to those regulating administrative action in the Roman Catholic Church, the Church of England has no formal equivalent of the Roman Catholic principle of recourse to a hierarchical administrative superior.

---

[292] Given sufficient public element, non-statutory bodies may also be the subject of judicial review: see e.g. *R v Panel on Take-Overs and Mergers, ex p Datafin PLC* [1987] 1 All ER 564.

5

Judicial Power: The Settlement of Disputes

In addition to the possibility of challenges in the civil courts to the use of ecclesiastical legislative and administrative powers, the law of the Church of England provides two basic forms of internal adjudication and settlement of disputes: by the church's courts and by bodies, whose functions are predominantly administrative, exercising quasi-judicial power. In fact, the use of arrangements enabling quasi-judicial settlement is increasing and, in this respect, the position of the courts in the Church of England has been radically altered in recent years. In effect the courts have been marginalized; the power to adjudicate is now more widely dispersed in the church. With the exception of faculty matters, and even here the role of the courts has been altered recently, the law avoids trials and recourse to the courts is rare. Moreover, when the courts do adjudicate their exercise of power is limited by rights of appeal, by rules about the interpretation of ecclesiastical legislation and by the doctrines of precedent. This Chapter traces these arrangements in the Church of England and seeks to draw out similarities to and differences from Roman Catholic canon law.

QUASI-JUDICIAL SETTLEMENT: ENQUIRIES AND TRIBUNALS

In the secular field, alongside the state's court system, the resolution of disputes is a function commonly allocated to bodies and persons whose principal tasks are administrative.[1] An area that has undergone significant development in recent years, it is now commonly understood that any decision involving the resolution of a dispute and affecting the rights, duties, or legitimate expectations of individuals is subject to the principles of natural

---

[1] For the wide range of dispute-related functions subject today to judicial review see M. Fordham, *Judicial Review Handbook* (Chichester, 1995) 51 ff. A 'judicial' decision is a binding resolution of a dispute between two or more parties concerning facts or legal rights/duties, by ascertaining the facts and by determining and applying law to those facts; a 'quasi-judicial' decision is one with a significant judicial element, resolving a dispute by recourse to policy considerations and not necessarily to law: see P. Cane, *An Introduction to Administrative Law* (2nd edn., Oxford, 1992) 26, 27. The distinction between 'truly judicial decisions' and 'quasi-judicial decisions', appearing in the Report of the Committee on Ministers' Powers, The Donoughmore Committee, Cmnd. 4060, April 1932, Section III, 2 had been much criticized (see e.g. W. A. Robinson, *Justice and Administrative Law* (3rd edn., 1951) 446) and technical difficulties over these terms have now become less important: see *post* n. 2.

justice and a general duty to act fairly.[2] Similarly, the law of the Church of England enables the determination of internal disputes by bodies and persons in an administrative setting where the decision in question contains an adjudicative element. Though rights of appearance, representation, and legal aid are evenly distributed,[3] the distribution of rights of appeal and duties to give reasons for decisions seems haphazard, being dependent on the terms of the legislation in question, and the question of whether the common law principles of natural justice and fairness are applicable to the Church of England is not assumed and must frequently be established. Several adjudication models are employed of which the following are typical.

Adjudication Models

First, in a manner similar to the principle of hierarchical recourse in Roman Catholic canon law,[4] the central legal system of the Church of England sometimes provides (most commonly without an express right of appeal) for referral to the diocesan bishop of matters of disagreement and doubt. The episcopal resolution of the problem may necessarily require the ascertainment of facts, the application of rules or policies, and the giving of directions. Powers containing an element of adjudication are conferred both by the canons[5] and by measures.[6] Moreover, the bishop enjoys specific powers

---

[2] *Ridge v Baldwin* [1964] AC 40; *R v Liverpool Corporation ex p Liverpool Taxi Fleet Operator's Association* [1972] 2 QB 299; *Council of Civil Service Unions v Minister for the Civil Service* [1985] AC 374; see generally e.g. S. H. Bailey, B. L. Jones, and A. R. Mowbray, *Cases and Materials on Administrative Law* (2nd edn., London, 1992) Ch. 9.

[3] Indeed it is arguable that the provision of legal aid, in most of these arrangements, raises the presumption of the 'judicial' character of these functions: for legal aid see *post* Ch. 17.

[4] See *supra* Ch. 4.

[5] The allocation of quasi-judicial functions is clearly envisaged in several canons dealing with liturgical matters: see e.g. Canon B3(4): referral to the bishop 'for his decision'; B5(4): referral to the bishop for 'pastoral guidance, advice or direction as he may think fit'; B15A(3): admission to holy communion, referral to the bishop, and duty to 'follow his guidance'; B16(1): exclusion from holy communion, duty to obey the bishop's 'order and direction'; B22(2): refusal or undue delay in baptism, application to the bishop 'who shall . . . give such directions as he thinks fit'; B38(6): burial, 'the minister shall refer the matter to the bishop and obey his order and direction'. Ministers are under a general duty to comply with such episcopal directions: for canonical obedience, see *post* Ch. 7.

[6] *CRR*, r. 53(1). In carrying out these rules 'the bishop shall have power . . . (d) . . . in any case in which any difficulties arise, to give directions which he may consider expedient for the purpose of removing the difficulties'; see Churchwardens (Appointment and Resignation) Measure 1964, s.11 (1)(e) for a similar provision; Parochial Church Councils (Powers) Measure 1956, s. 9(3): [i]n the event of a council and a minister being unable to agree as to any matter in which their agreement or joint action is required under . . . this Measure, such matter shall be dealt with or determined in such manner as the bishop may direct'; Benefices Measure 1972, s. 1(2), for a right of appeal to the archbishop (against episcopal refusal to admit a presentee); for the adjudicative power of the bishop under the Care of Cathedrals (Supplementary Provisions) Measure 1994, s. 3 see *supra* Ch. 4. For episcopal powers generally see *post* Ch. 6.

concerning the revocation of licences granted to those engaged in ministry.[7] The exercise of such powers will of course necessarily affect the rights of the holder of the licence and it has been understood judicially in civil law that the revocation of licences may involve a process of adjudication.[8] The bishop may, for example, by notice in writing revoke summarily 'and without further process' any licence granted to a deaconess 'for any cause which appears to him to be good and reasonable'. There is no express duty on the bishop to give reasons for the revocation. The bishop is under a duty, however, to give her 'sufficient opportunity of showing reason to the contrary'. The bishop must notify the deaconess of her right of appeal, within twenty-eight days from the date of receipt of notice, to the archbishop. The archbishop, after hearing the appeal personally or delegating this function to a bishop, may confirm, cancel, or vary the revocation of the licence as he considers just and proper. The appeal must be conducted in accordance with rules approved by the two archbishops; 'there shall be no appeal from the decision of the archbishop' and legal aid is available only in relation to the appeal.[9]

Secondly, the right to appeal against a decision to a 'tribunal' is increasingly used in ecclesiastical legislation. For instance, the incumbent of a benefice dispossessed by a pastoral scheme made under the Pastoral Measure 1983 is entitled to compensation for any consequential loss suffered. The right to and the amount of compensation is determined in the first instance by the diocesan pastoral committee, and if either of these is disputed the claimant has a right of appeal to a tribunal established under the Measure for each province.[10] The Dean of Arches and Auditor is the chairman of the Appeal Tribunal and the Vicar-General of each province acts as deputy chairman; one of the three (but not more than one) sits on and presides over each appeal.[11] Rules prescribing the procedure to be followed in claiming and determining rights to and amounts of compensation (including proceedings before the Appeal Tribunal) may made by the Church Commissioners. Costs incurred in proceedings are recoverable from the Legal Aid Fund.[12]

[7] For Canons C12 (licensing of ministers under seal), E6 (readers), and E8 (lay workers) see *post* Chs. 7 and 8; for the availability of legal aid under the Church of England (Legal Aid) Measure 1994, Sched. 1 see Ch. 17.

[8] *R v Huntington District Council, ex p Cowan* [1984] 1 WLR 501, duty to specify substance of objections and to allow reply; *R v Bristol City Council, ex p Pearce* [1984] 83 LGR 711, duty to give opportunity to comment.

[9] Canon D3(3A): any appeal must be conducted in accordance with rules approved by the two archbishops; for legal aid see Church of England (Legal Aid) Measure 1994, Sched. 1; for appeals from decrees of the bishop in Roman Catholic canon law see *supra* Ch. 4.

[10] S. 26; Sched. 4, paras. 1, 6, 15(1); the functions of the pastoral committee cannot be delegated to a sub-committee (para. 14(1)).

[11] Ibid., para. 15(1). These are assisted for each appeal by 4 persons nominated from a panel of 12 appointed by the Lower House of Convocation of the province in question, and by 2 from a panel appointed by the House of Laity of General Synod.

[12] Ibid., para. 16. The rules, which must be approved by General Synod and laid before parliament, take effect as as a statutory instrument; see SI 1970 No. 1009; for legal aid, para. 17 and Church of England (Legal Aid) Measure 1994, Sched. 1.

A similar but rather more refined tribunal arrangement is to be found in the Ordination of Women (Financial Provisions) Measure 1993, designed to make provision for the relief of hardship incurred by persons resigning from ecclesiastical service by reason of opposition to the ordination of women as priests. Compensation is paid by the Church of England Pensions Board. An applicant who is aggrieved by the determination of the Board has a right of appeal to a tribunal consisting of five persons nominated by the chairmen of the General Synod's three houses.[13] The tribunal has power to affirm the board's determination or to make any other determination which could have been made by the Board. The Board must give effect to the tribunal's determination. The tribunal must not vary the Board's determination unless satisfied that (a) the Board has exercised its discretion on a basis on which no reasonable determination could have been made, or (b) the Board has failed to take into account some material matter, or has taken into account some irrelevant matter, where in either case in acting properly the determination of the Board would or might have been significantly different. In any event the tribunal may vary the Board's determination if in all the circumstances not doing so would or might result in injustice to the applicant or cause significant financial hardship.[14] Though legal aid is available,[15] the Measure contains no right of appeal against the tribunal's decision nor does it impose a duty to give reasons. General Synod's Standing Committee may make rules regulating the tribunal's procedure and practice; these have now been made in the form of a Statutory Instrument.[16] The appellant has a right to object to the membership of the tribunal and 'the secretary shall determine whether the objection is reasonable and should be allowed, and his decision shall be final' (r. 5), as well as a right to make written representations (r. 6), and a right to notice of the hearing (r. 7). The chairman of the tribunal may give such directions as appear to him to be appropriate 'for the just and convenient conduct of the appeal' (r. 8) and the tribunal may authorize a member thereof (or the secretary) to carry out enquiries into facts in dispute or issues arising and report these to the tribunal (r. 9). The appellant and a representative of the Pensions Board are entitled to appear before and be heard by the tribunal, to give oral evidence, and to call witnesses. The appellant may be represented by a barrister or solicitor (or assisted by a friend) and the tribunal 'may require oral evidence by any person to be given on oath' (r. 10). Subject to the provisions of these rules, the tribunal

---

[13] S. 10(1), (4).

[14] S. 10(2), (3); *R v Northumberland Compensation Appeal Tribunal, ex p Shaw* [1952] 1 All ER 122 (CA), erroneous tribunal decision quashed. The provision about irrelevant considerations (not listed) is declaratory of the common law: *Roberts v Hopwood* [1925] AC 578; *Associated Provincial Picture Houses Ltd v Wednesbury Corporation* [1948] 1 KB 223 (CA); *Cannock Chase District Council v Kelly* [1978] 1 All ER 152 (CA).

[15] Church of England (Legal Aid) Measure 1994, Sched. 1.

[16] S. 10(5); see Ordination of Women (Financial Provisions) (Appeals) Rules 1993, SI No. 2847.

may from time to time determine its own procedure (r. 15). Importantly, '[n]on-compliance with any of these Rules shall not affect the validity of the proceedings except insofar as the tribunal so directs' (r. 18).[17]

Thirdly, provision is sometimes made made for adjudication processes to be held in public. Under the Patronage (Benefices) Measure 1986 the diocesan registrar must compile and maintain a register indicating the patron of every benefice in the diocese. No person is to exercise the functions of a patron unless registered. The Measure contains specific provisions about the exercise of rights of presentation and about the determination of disputes. If the registrar decides, amongst other things, that any person is not entitled to be registered, he must serve notice on that person informing him of the decision. The person may appeal by sending the registrar notice of appeal. The registrar refers the appeal to the diocesan chancellor who must decide whether to uphold or dismiss the appeal. Proceedings on appeal to the chancellor must be held in public and any party to such proceedings is entitled to appear; no provision seems to exist for legal aid.[18] The Patronage (Appeals) Committee, consisting of the Dean of the Arches, one chancellor and one diocesan registrar nominated by the archbishops, and two nominated by the Standing Committee of General Synod, are empowered to make rules regulating appeal procedure and practice.[19]

Fourthly, the law sometimes provides for initial determination by an administrative body with subsequent appeal to a church court. The Care of Cathedrals Measure 1990 empowers the administrative body of a cathedral to propose alterations to cathedrals. The Fabric Advisory Committee has power to approve specified proposals. If an application made by the administrative body for the approval of the Fabric Advisory Committee is refused, appeal lies to the Cathedrals Fabric Commission which may reverse, confirm, or vary the decision of the Advisory Committee.[20] If the appeal is unsuccessful, the administrative body has a right of further appeal to a Commission of Review, which may reverse, confirm, or vary the Fabric Commission's decision. The decision of the Commission of Review 'shall be final'.[21] Occasionally, however, ecclesiastical legislation provides for no right of appeal against an initial determination. The Church of England (Legal Aid) Measure 1994 regulates applications for legal aid to assist in specified ecclesiastical proceedings. The Legal Aid Commission, appointed by the Standing Committee of General Synod, is charged with administering the

---

[17] The remaining rules deal, *inter alia*, with evidence, findings, and service of documents.

[18] Parts I and II and Sched 1, paras. 7–9; these proceedings are not listed in the Church of England (Legal Aid) Measure 1994, Sched. 1; see also Ordination of Women (Financial Provisions) (Appeals) Rules 1993, r. 12 (discretion as to private or public hearing).

[19] Sched 1, paras. 10–12.   [20] S. 9.

[21] S. 10(1)-(7); see *supra* Ch. 4 for the quasi-judicial nature of visitations generally and for visitation of cathedrals in particular.

church's legal aid fund. Before deciding whether to grant legal aid, the Commission must consider the resources of the applicant. The Commission cannot grant legal aid if it appears that the applicant could afford to proceed without legal aid and 'unless that person shows that he has reasonable grounds for taking or defending the proceedings or being a party thereto'. Synod's Standing Committee may make such rules as it considers necessary for giving effect to or for preventing abuses and the rules may provide for procedure to be observed in relation to applications.[22] No right of appeal against a refusal is contained in the measure.

Serious Breakdown of Pastoral Relations

Sophisticated arrangements for out-of-court settlement are to be found under the Incumbents (Vacation of Benefices) Measure 1977 (as amended in 1993), designed to deal with a situation in a parish where 'it has become impossible for any effective pastoral care to be exercised'.[23] The legislation applies when there has been 'a serious breakdown of the pastoral relationship between incumbent and the parishioners to which the conduct of the incumbent or of the parishioners or of both has contributed over a substantial period' (s.1A(1)). A 'serious breakdown of the pastoral relationship' is 'a situation where the relationship between an incumbent and the parishioners of the parish in question is such as to impede the promotion in the parish of the whole mission of the Church of England, pastoral, evangelistic, social and ecumenical'.[24] The measure provides for the establishment of an enquiry into the pastoral situation. A right to request an enquiry is vested in the incumbent, the archdeacon, a majority of not less than two-thirds of the lay members of the parochial church council or, when the incumbent is also the archdeacon, a majority of the members of the bishop's council and standing committee of the diocesan synod (s.1(1)). An enquiry may be undertaken only after the persons concerned have had an opportunity to resolve the pastoral difficulty. Accordingly, the request cannot be made unless notice of intention to make the request has been given by the person(s) concerned to the diocesan bishop at least six (and not more than twelve) months before the request is made (s.1A(1A)). The request, which must be written and state the facts which justify an enquiry, has to be sent to the bishop and the secretary of the diocesan synod (s.1(2)). Provision exists for the withdrawal of the request (s.1(7)).

The bishop is to direct the archdeacon to take such steps as the former considers appropriate to promote better relations in the parish and to remove the 'cause of their estrangement'; the archdeacon may decline if 'it would not

---

[22] Ss. 2, 4; SI 1995 No. 2034; for judicial review of a resolution of the secular Legal Aid Board see *R v Legal Aid Board, ex p Bruce* [1992] 1 WLR 694; see also *post* Ch. 17.
[23] HL Deb., Vol. 382, 2 May 1977, 808 at 809 *per* Bishop of London.   [24] S. 19A.

be right and expedient for him to act in the case'; the bishop may then appoint another (s.2(3), (4)). The archdeacon must report to the bishop on whether an enquiry should be instituted. In making his report the archdeacon must have regard to the extent to which the Code of Practice (discussed below) has been complied with. The archdeacon is to recommend an enquiry if he considers this to be in the best interests of the incumbent and the parishioners (s.2(5)). On the archdeacon's recommendation the bishop may, if he thinks fit, direct the secretary of the diocesan synod to institute an enquiry (s.3(1)). An enquiry will not be necessary if the incumbent resigns, and the bishop may accept resignation if he considers that 'it would be in the interest of the Church to do so' (s.4(1)).

The enquiry must be conducted by a provincial tribunal composed of five persons appointed by the Vicar-General of the province in which the parish in question is situated;[25] the incumbent concerned has a right to object (giving reasons) to the tribunal's membership.[26] The bishop is also empowered to instruct the secretary of the diocesan synod to institute an enquiry (conducted by the provincial tribunal) as to whether the incumbent is unable to discharge his duties by reason of infirmity of mind or body.[27] The incumbent may apply for legal aid with regard to the proceedings.[28] The provincial tribunal determines whether in its opinion there has been a serious breakdown and whether the incumbent and/or the parishioners have contributed to it and, in a disability case, whether this was due to the age or infirmity of the incumbent. This is fundamentally an adjudicative function in so far as the tribunal must determine the facts and, by applying the statutory definition described above, the legal question as to serious breakdown. The tribunal must report with recommendations to the bishop (s. 9). The bishop may issue a temporary inhibition (in effect suspending the incumbent from the exercise of his office) in disability cases if it appears to him that this is 'desirable in the interests of the Church of England'.[29] When the enquiry results in a report that a pastoral breakdown exists, the bishop may (if the tribunal so recommends) execute a declaration of avoidance, declaring the benefice vacant.[30] If the enquiry finds that the incumbent's conduct has contributed over a substantial period to the break-

---

[25] S. 5; the constitution of provincial tribunals is set out in Sched. 1, para. 1: of the 5 appointed, 1 (the chairman) must be either a diocesan chancellor in the province—other than of the diocese where the parish is situated—or a Queen's Counsel who is a communicant member of the church; 2 must be clerks in holy orders chosen from a panel appointed from members of the lower house of the province's convocation, and 2 from a panel appointed from members of General Synod's House of Laity; para. 2: a person may refuse to accept appointment 'if in his opinion it would not be right for him to serve'.

[26] Sched. 1, para. 3. This is determined by the Vicar-General whose decision is final.

[27] S. 6; s. 7A: the tribunal may direct that the incumbent should undergo a medical examination; if the incumbent fails to do so, the tribunal may draw such inferences (if any) from that fact as appear proper in the circumstances.

[28] Church of England (Legal Aid) Measure 1994, Sched. 1.   [29] S. 9A.

[30] S. 10(2); for compensation see *post* Ch. 17.

down, the bishop has a discretion to rebuke and may, if he thinks fit, disqualify the incumbent from performing his rights and duties for a specified period.[31] The bishop may also rebuke parishioners if they contributed to the breakdown and may, if he thinks fit, disqualify such of them as he thinks fit (for a period not exceeding five years) from being a churchwarden or member or officer of the parochial church council of the parish in question or of other parishes in the diocese.[32] In disability cases, if the breakdown is due to the incumbent's age or infirmity, the bishop may request *inter alia* resignation, but only if this is recommended by the enquiry. The bishop has power to declare the benefice vacant if the incumbent refuses to resign.[33]

The framework contained in this legislation has been supplemented recently by rules enacted by General Synod (in the form of a Statutory Instrument) and by a Code of Practice formulated by synod's House of Bishops. Under the Incumbents (Vacation of Benefices) Rules 1994,[34] the chairman of the provincial tribunal is to give directions as to (amongst other things) the submission of statements by the parties, production of documents, interviewing, procedure, and 'the holding of a preliminary hearing in order to consider and determine points of law or jurisdiction' (r. 5). The rules prescribe that the parties to the proceedings 'shall be entitled to appear before, and be heard by, the tribunal and to give oral evidence' (r. 8(1)). The tribunal may require oral evidence to be given by any person on oath (r. 8(3)). Proceedings must be held in private, unless the incumbent requests a public hearing or the tribunal 'so directs in the interests of justice or for any other good reason' (r. 10). Similar provisions operate in relation to disability cases (rr. 14–23). The rules do not, however, confer enforceable rights: 'Non-compliance with any of these Rules shall not affect the validity of the proceedings except insofar as the tribunal so directs' (r. 30). Neither the measure nor the rules incorporate a right of appeal against the bishop's decision. Nor is there specific provision for the tribunal to give reasons, though there seems to be discretion to do so.[35]

Generally, these legislative arrangments are to be used as a last resort. The Code of Practice, operative when the bishop receives notice of intention to make an enquiry request, is designed to promote better relations between the incumbent and the parishioners and to remove the causes of their estrangement.[36] Every effort should be made by the incumbent and parishioners, by the bishop, the archdeacon, the rural dean, 'and all others acting on the bishop's behalf' to effect a reconciliation; this should be done, if possible, without

---

[31] S. 10(5).

[32] S. 10(6). The bishop may revoke the disqualification of both incumbent and lay office-holders: s. 10(9). [33] S. 11.

[34] S. 18 (Vacation of Benefices Rule Committee).

[35] R. 26; the tribunal determines its own procedure.

[36] Incumbents (Vacation of Benefices) Measure 1977 (as amended), s. 1; see *supra* Ch. 1 for the enforceability of these 'rules of guidance'.

recourse to formal procedures contained in the legislation.[37] When the bishop receives a notice of intention to request an enquiry, 'he should as soon as possible interview the "parties"—that is, the incumbent and the lay members of the parochial church council—at least once together and once separately'.[38] If the interviews fail to effect reconciliation the bishop should appoint a person (other than the archdeacon) responsible for (a) explaining the consequences of invoking the measure (including financial implications) and (b) appointing (if possible) a conciliator (other than the archdeacon) acceptable to both parties.[39] The conciliator is to interview any parishioners concerned and the incumbent separately giving them an opportunity to express their respective views and bringing them into dialogue to further a reconciliation.[40] Once the reconciliation (or attempted reconciliation) process is completed, the conciliator should make a 'factual report' to the bishop, copies being sent to the parties involved. The report should not apportion blame but should state, if this is the case, that a particular party has refused to discuss the matter with the conciliator or the other party.[41] If the conciliator's attempts prove unsuccessful, it is for the bishop to decide, in the light of the conciliator's report, whether to initiate any further steps towards reconciliation.[42]

If and when the bishop receives a formal request for an enquiry and directs the archdeacon to report to him whether an enquiry is necessary, the archdeacon must in making his report have regard to the extent to which the procedures contained in the Code of Practice have been complied with.[43] If the bishop orders an enquiry, he should be guided by the recommendations in the archdeacon's report (or any information which the archdeacon subsequently provides) 'unless there is some substantial reason for not doing so'.[44] If a tribunal sits and reports, in deciding what action is to be taken 'the bishop should in all cases consult his diocesan registrar about the extent of his legal powers in the particular circumstances'.[45] The Code of Practice recognizes a discretion in the bishop to publish the report or extracts from it. In exercising this discretion the bishop should have regard to the following: whether the enquiry or part of it took place in public; 'the interests of justice and the importance of ensuring that justice must be seen to be done'; pastoral considerations and the interests of the parties involved (if the incumbent is to continue, whether publication would help or hinder his future ministry there); and the bishop's own position (if he has decided to implement the tribunal's

---

[37] *IVBCP*, para. 4.   [38] Para. 6.

[39] Para. 7; the episcopal appointee, someone other than diocesan registrar, may also be the conciliator; if unable to find an acceptable conciliator, the person should report to the bishop with copies to the parties.

[40] Para. 8. Para. 9: process should if possible be completed within 6 months of notice of intent to request an enquiry; if successful, the parties may agree to co-operate for a 'trial period' of up to 6 months.   [41] para. 10; it 'should be treated as confidential'.

[42] Para. 11.   [43] Para. 12; IVBM 1977, s. 2(5).

[44] *IVBCP*, para. 14, e.g. the incumbent wishes to resign, there has been a change in circumstances, or the bishop feels a disability enquiry would be more appropriate.   [45] Para. 16.

recommendations, it may well be helpful to make those recommendations public).[46] In addition to securing reconciliation, the bishop, archdeacon, and rural dean 'should at all stages have regard to the need to ensure that the incumbent (and his family), any other ministers in the parish and the laity all receive proper pastoral care and any necessary support until the problems in the parish can be resolved'.[47] A finding of a serious pastoral breakdown is not to be taken as necessarily showing that the incumbent has acted in a blameworthy manner; even in cases where the incumbent is deprived that should not be regarded as debarring him from further ministry elsewhere in the church.[48]

All three bodies of rule (the provisions of the 1977 Measure as amended, the rules contained in the secondary legislation, and those in the code of practice) are designed to provide the fullest opportunity in pastoral breakdown cases for flexible attempts to secure reconciliation in the conflict. They are also designed to give the bishop a discretion in all cases and to locate enquiry beyond the diocese so that it may not be seen 'as prosecutor, judge and jury in its own cause'.[49] Nevertheless, despite the impartial nature of the tribunal, the ultimate decision rests with the bishop: this may render the 'outsider' element nugatory.

Judicial Review of Quasi-Judicial Action

The arrangements described here must be seen in their wider legal environment, particularly in view of the fact that, like in the Roman Catholic Church, the courts of the Church of England generally possess no jurisdiction to question the use of the quasi-judicial powers outlined in this section.[50] In the secular sphere, enquiries and tribunals play an increasingly important role in modern government.[51] Normally, tribunals are appellate bodies, their function is adjudicative, to hear and determine appeals against discretionary administrative decisions: to review the substance, not the legality, of those decisions. The civil courts may be more prepared to entertain judicial review against an administrative decision when there is no provision for appeal to a tribunal.[52] Nevertheless, under the Tribunals and Inquiries Act 1992, specified tribunals have to give reasons for their decisions.[53] Generally, even if there is no statutory duty to give reasons, the common law may impose a duty to do so under the principles of procedural fairness and legitimate expectation.[54] Moreover, the Tribunals and Inquiries Act 1992 enables an appeal to the High Court

---

[46] Para. 17.   [47] Para. 19.   [48] Para. 3(b).

[49] *Report of the Legislative Committee of General Synod*, 15 Apr. 1992, para. 6.

[50] See below for jurisdictional limits; cf. *supra* the power of the Commission of Review under the Care of Cathedrals Measure 1990; it may be possible for proceedings in the church courts to treat a failure to perform duties surrounding the exercise of episcopal powers (for neglect of duty, see below).   [51] See generally J. Peay, *Tribunals on Trial* (Oxford, 1989).

[52] *Glynne v Keele University* [1971] 1 WLR 487; improper determinations of the Church of England's Legal Aid Commission (against which the governing measure provides no appeal) may fall into this category (see *supra* n. 22).   [53] S. 10.

[54] *R v Civil Service Appeal Board, ex p Cunningham* [1991] IRLR 297.

on a point of law; the court may substitute its decision for that of the tribunal.[55]
The civil courts may challenge an enquiry or tribunal decision when it is made
in excess of its jurisdiction,[56] or 'when the decision of the tribunal is unreasonable in the sense that no tribunal . . . could reach that decision'.[57] If the
tribunal is (or appears to be) biased, or if the individual has been given no
reasonable opportunity to be heard, then its decision may be upset as contrary
to the principles of natural justice.[58]

It may be thought that the duty to give reasons (as we have seen, not
generally incorporated into ecclesiastical legislation) and the possibility of
judicial review *ought* to be applicable equally to the Church of England's
new model adjudicative tribunals, but these do not appear in the lists contained
in the Tribunals and Inquiries Act 1992[59] and the matter has not been litigated.
Moreover, given the application of the common law principles of natural
justice and the general duty to act fairly to adjudicative and administrative
decisions of bodies vested with statutory powers,[60] and provided the civil
courts are satisfied that the matter contains a sufficient public element,[61] it
is submitted that the availability of judicial review to control the work of the
Church of England's tribunals is certainly arguable; vested by synodical
measure, their powers are the product of public law approved by the state.[62]
The civil courts have in the past entertained litigation against bishops[63] and, it
is submitted, these principles are applicable equally to episcopal powers of
adjudication conferred by *measure* (such as those enjoyed under the Incumbents (Vacation of Benefices) legislation). However, it is less clear whether
episcopal adjudicative functions, including archiepiscopal powers to hear
appeals, conferred by *canon* (such as powers dealing with the revocation of
licences) would be subject to judicial review.[64] Since the civil courts in recent

[55] S. 11.   [56] *R v Blackpool Rent Tribunal, ex p Ashton* [1948] 2 KB 277.
[57] *R v Preston Supplementary Benefits Appeals Tribunal, ex p Moore* [1975] 1 WLR 624.
[58] *R v London Rent Assessment Panel, ex p Metropolitan Properties Co Ltd* [1968] 3 All ER 304
(CA).
[59] Sched. 1 lists tribunals; these are under the general supervision of the Council on Tribunals.
[60] See *supra* n. 2.   [61] See *supra* Ch. 4.
[62] The public element may indeed be presumed by parliament's involvement in the approval of
the structures discussed in this section and, under the adjudicative structures described here,
judicial review is nowhere expressly excluded; moreover, as seen in Ch. 3, the civil courts have
entertained judicial review of *legislative* action within the church.
[63] For the use of natural justice, see *Capel v Child* [1832] 2 C & J 558; *Bonaker v Evans* [1850]
16 QB 163; *Rice v Bishop of Oxford* [1917] PD 181. For other examples of supervision of quasi-
judicial episcopal power by the courts see *Rugg v Bishop of Winchester* (1868) LR 2 PC 233;
Marquis of Abergavenny v Bishop of Llandaff [1888] 20 QBD 460; *Notley v Bishop of Birmingham
No. 2* [1931] 1 Ch 529 (*quare impedit*: court order to bishop to admit nominee).
[64] In so far as canonical powers exist by virtue of synodical measure (see *supra* Ch. 3) it may be
argued that they are at least analogous to statutory powers. The courts have, after all, applied these
principles to bodies whose adjudicative powers have been derived from both non-statutory
instruments (see *Glynne v University of Keele* [1971] 1 WLR 487) and, *via* a statute, from
secondary legislation: *Cinnamond v British Airways Authority* [1980] 1 WLR 582; see also *Chief
Constable of North Wales v Evans* [1982] 1 WLR 1155.

years have frequently entertained review of statutory powers vested in public authorities to revoke licences, as they have of non-statutory powers vested in voluntary self-regulatory organizations, judicial review would seem possible.[65] In the civil context, when revocation has an effect on a person's livelihood, procedural standards of fairness, including the duty to give reasons, have been applied.[66] Indeed, the civil courts have even altered the classical doctrine that they are unable to question the use of non-statutory prerogatival powers vested in the Crown;[67] around the idea that they are to be exercised for the public good, the courts are now prepared to review some prerogatives (such as the issuing or revoking of passports, essentially licences) to ensure that these are used fairly, including the duty to give reasons.[68] The extent to which these developing standards apply to the episcopal power to revoke licences has not been the subject of judicial consideration.[69] Though the Church of England's legal standards governing its administrative adjudicating bodies are complex and generally well developed, given the lack of clarity concerning judicial review of adjudicative powers vested in bishops by canon, it cannot be said that the threat of litigation averts its actuality.[70]

---

[65] If revocation is out of proportion to the mischief which occasions it, the revocation may be unlawful: for the doctrine of proportionality, see *R v Barnsley Metropolitan Borough Council, ex p Hook* [1976] 1 WLR 1052; *McInnes v Onslow-Fane and Another* [1978] 3 All ER 211 (British Boxing Board of Control).

[66] *R v Wear Valley District Council, ex p Binks* [1985] 2 All ER 699 (duty to give reasons). There may, however, be no general duty to give reasons: *McInnes v Onslow-Fane and Another* [1978] 3 All ER 211; cf. Roman Catholic canon law: *CIC*, cc. 51, 1742.

[67] *China Navigation Co Ltd v AG* [1932] 2 KB 197; *Chandler v DPP* [1964] AC 763.

[68] *R v Secretary of State for Foreign and Commonwealth Affairs, ex p Everett* [1989] 1 All ER 655 (CA), applying *Council of Civil Service Unions v Minister for the Civil Service* [1985] AC 374.

[69] The courts may be reluctant to be involved in a religious matter of this type: see *R v Chief Rabbi, ex p Wachmann* [1992] 1 WLR 1036, and *R v Immam of Bury Park Jame Masjid, Luton, ex p Sulaiman Ali* [1994] COD 142 (Immam's determination that the applicants were not eligible to vote in the election of the executive committee of a mosque was not reviewable). Cf. *R v Rabbinical Commission, ex p Cohen*, unreported, 14 Dec. 1987 (decisions of commission reviewable in exercise of statutory functions under Slaughterhouses Act 1974, Sched. 1); *Buckley v Cahal Daly* (1990) NIJB 8 (HC entertained review by RC priest against his bishop). Cf. also the general exclusion of judicial intervention in spiritual matters under the Church of Scotland Act 1921: see generally F. Lyall, *Of Presbyters and Kings: Church and State in the Law of Scotland* (Aberdeen, 1980) Ch. 5.

[70] M. Beloff, 'Judicial review in the sporting world', *PL* (1989) 95; the problem of episcopal powers of dismissal is closely related to the principle that clergy are not employed (see *post* Ch. 7), though today the civil courts are prepared to recognize that an obligation to observe the principles of natural justice is implied into a contract of employment when the employee is categorized as a 'servant', particularly when that person may be treated as a public officer having responsibilities towards the public as well as towards the employer: *Stevenson v United Road Transport Union* [1977] ICR 893 (trade union offiical); *R v British Broadcasting Corporation, ex p Lavelle* [1983] 1 WLR 23 (employee); see F. P. Davidson, 'Judicial review of decisions to dismiss', *NILQ*, 35 (1984) 121.

The legal framework of the Church of England, like that of the Roman Catholic Church, seeks to avoid litigation and trials. In the Roman Catholic Church the judicial process is treated very much as a last resort, even once this process has begun: disputants are under a canonical duty to settle amicably, promptly, and equitably out of court.[71] The conference of bishops is encouraged to establish permanent offices in every diocese to resolve disputes without going to trial.[72]

The Legal Advisory Commission performs a similar role in the Church of England. Its functions are to respond to enquiries and to give legal advice to General Synod (to which it submits an annual report), its houses, boards, councils and commissions, the Church Commissioners, and others (including diocesan chancellors and registrars and other clerical and lay officers).[73] The Commission cannot normally advise on contentious matters but it recognizes 'the importance of avoiding unnecessary litigation within the Church'. It may give an opinion on a contentious matter in three circumstances: if the facts are agreed by all parties to the dispute; if the matter is referred to the Commission for an opinion by all parties to the dispute; and if the matter is not, and is not expected shortly to become, the subject-matter of proceedings in the courts.[74]

The court system of the Church of England underwent considerable reform with the enactment of the Ecclesiastical Jurisdiction Measure 1963 as a result, in the main, of the Lloyd Jacob Report (1954).[75] As in the Roman Catholic Church, the courts of the Church of England are ordered hierarchically. There are elaborate provisions both for pre-trial settlement and for the protection of rights to challenge decisions by way of appeal. The organization of the courts is based on the broad distinction between their 'civil' work (the faculty jurisdiction) and their 'criminal' work (dealing with offences against the ecclesiastical law, unbecoming conduct, and serious neglect of duty on the part of the clergy).

Faculty Cases

Whereas courts in the Roman Catholic Church are most active in the area of matrimonial canon law,[76] the busiest courts of the Church of England are the

---

[71] *CIC*, c. 1446. If the issue is about the private good of the parties, the judge is to discern whether an agreement or a judgment by an arbitrator, in accordance with the norms of cc. 1713–16, might serve to resolve the controversy.

[72] C.1733; the episcopal conference of England and Wales has not, as yet, introduced these: *COCLA*, 1335–41; see also K. Matthews' studies on the history of the resolution of disputes in Roman Catholic canon law in *Studia Canonica*, 18 (1984), 55.

[73] The Commission was established under SGM 1969, Sched. 2, Art. 10(2); Legal Advisory Commission, *Annual Report* (1994) GS 1150, 1.1, 1.2.   [74] Ibid., 1.3.

[75] For background to the legislation, see HL Deb., Vol. 249, 16 May 1963, 1435; HC Deb., Vol. 680, 1–9 July 1963, 1158; Vol. 681, 16 July 1963, 344.

[76] G. Read, 'The Catholic tribunal system in the British Isles', *ELJ*, 2 (1991), 213: in 1988 58,797 marriage nullity cases were decided worldwide, 1,295 in Britain and 663 in Ireland.

diocesan courts exercising faculty jurisdiction concerning church property.[77] Exceptionally, in relation to faculties, the law actually generates litigation: as a basic principle, if any alterations, additions, removals, or repairs are proposed to be made to the fabric, ornaments, or furniture of the church the minister and churchwardens must obtain a faculty or licence.[78] Faculty petitions, unopposed or opposed,[79] are ordinarily entertained only by recourse to the Diocesan or Consistory Court, the court of the bishop presided over by the diocesan chancellor.[80] However, provision now exists for the diocesan chancellor to delegate faculty jurisdiction to the archdeacon in cases of unopposed faculty petitions, thereby by-passing the need for the formal involvement of the courts.[81] The bishop may hear faculty cases with the chancellor or alone 'if, and insofar as, provision . . . is made in the letters patent by which the chancellor . . . is appointed'.[82] In most dioceses there is no such reservation and it has been suggested that it would be a breach of the separation of powers for a bishop to insist on trying cases personally.[83]

The consistory court's principal original jurisdiction is to determine faculty cases authorizing acts related to consecrated diocesan land, or to anything on or in such land, for which the decree of a faculty is required.[84] The court has power to make a variety of orders including the power to issue injunctions and

---

[77] In many respects, the faculty system itself contains a strong administrative element similar to functions performed by local planning authorities; for the mixture of judicial and administrative elements see J. D. C. Harte, 'Church *v.* State in listed building control, 1: the faculty jurisdiction: a case for conservation', *Journal of Planning Law* (1985), 611 at 616.

[78] Canon F13(3); see *post* Ch. 16 for the need for faculty structures in view of the problem of 'ecclesiastical exemption'; for a detailed discussion see G. H. Newsom and G. L. Newsom, *Faculty Jurisdiction of the Church of England* (London, 1993) Ch. 2. [79] See *post* nn. 81, 87.

[80] Ecclesiastical Jurisdiction Measure 1963, ss. 1(1), 2 (the Commissary Court in the diocese of Canterbury).

[81] Care of Churches and Ecclesiastical Jurisdiction Measure 1991, s. 14. The diocesan chancellor shall confer upon the archdeacon the jurisdiction of the consistory court in faculty matters relating to the archdeaconry to such an extent and in such manner as may be prescribed; the archdeacon has power to grant faculties falling to be considered by him which are unopposed; if the archdeacon refuses, or considers the matter should be dealt with as a matter of urgency without reference to the Diocesan Advisory Committee, or if the faculty is opposed, he must refer the matter to the diocesan chancellor. The archdeacon may not issue an injunction or make a restoration order. See also Care of Churches and Ecclesiastical Jurisdiction Measure *Code of Practice* 1993, 86 (special cases and alternatives to faculty procedure): for this and the diocesan chancellor's duty to give guidance as to what does not requires faculty (under CCEJM 1991, s. 11(8)) see *post* Ch. 16.

[82] EJM 1963, s. 46(1); see *post* Ch. 8 for qualifications and rules concerning appointment and removal of chancellors.

[83] *Re St. Mary's, Barnes* [1982] 1 WLR 531 at 532 *per* Moore Ch. Reservations were recognized by CA in *R v Tristram* [1902] 1 KB 816.

[84] EJM 1963, s. 6; CCEJM 1991, s. 11: the court has jurisdiction over all parish churches and churchyards in the diocese, including unconsecrated buildings licensed for public worship by the bishop; however, in relation to the latter the bishop may exclude the court's faculty jurisdiction (s. 11(3)).

to make restoration orders.[85] A right of access to the court by way of faculty petition is vested in the archdeacon of the archdeaconry in which the parish concerned is situated, the minister and churchwardens and any other person appearing to the court to have a sufficient interest in the matter; any person whose name is entered on the electoral roll of the parish but who does not reside therein is deemed to have an interest as though he were a parishioner.[86] The following have a right to object to the proposed faculty being granted: a person resident in the parish or entered on the electoral roll, the archdeacon, the parochial church council (its consent to a petition not in law being required), the local planning authority, one of the named national amenity Societies, and 'any other body designated by the chancellor . . . and any other person or body who appears to the chancellor to have a lawful interest in the proposals'.[87] Whether a person has *locus standi* is a matter for the diocesan chancellor.[88] In addition to ensuring that the church and everything belonging to it is properly cared for, in exercising faculty jurisdiction the adjudicating body must have regard to the role of the church as a local centre of worship and mission.[89]

Generally, concerning the granting or refusal of faculties, no appeal lies to the bishop from the decision of the chancellor. Rights of appeal operate within the judicial hierarchy to the appropriate appellate court. The legal distribution of these rights is systematic and comprehensive. If the matter does *not* involve doctrine, ritual, or ceremonial, appeal lies to the Provincial Court: the Court of the Arches in the Province of Canterbury or the Chancery Court in the Province of York. These appellate courts may give any judgment or direction which ought to have been given by the consistory court or may order a re-hearing.[90] Appeal lies from the provincial courts, at the instance of any party, to the Judicial Committee of the Privy Council.[91] If the matter involves doctrine, ritual, or ceremonial then appeal lies not to the provincial courts but to the Court of Ecclesiastical Causes Reserved. This may overturn the consistory court's decision or order a retrial. It is for the chancellor to decide

---

[85] The faculty may authorize work to be done or confirm what has been done before the petition: ibid., ss. 12, 13 (injunctions and restoration orders and the power to impose condition, to make restoration orders). Contempt of court is certified to the High Court which may enquire and proceed as if the contempt were committed in respect of itself (EJM 1963, s. 81 as substituted by the CCEJM 1991, Sched. 4, para. 10); *R v Daily Herald, ex p Bishop of Norwich* [1932] 2 KB 402.

[86] CCEJM 1991, s. 16(1), (2). If the archdeaconry is vacant, or the archdeacon is incapacitated by absence or illness, or in the opinion of the bishop the archdeacon is for any other reason unable or unwilling to act—or it would be inappropriate for him to act—such other person as the bishop appoints has power to act in place of the archdeacon: s. 16(3).   [87] *FJR*, r. 15.

[88] For the detailed rules about *locus standi* see Newsom, *FJCE*, Ch. 2; the approach is liberal but subject to the general principle that 'It is not the law that anyone can confer upon himself a sufficient interest to be a litigant in the consistory court merely by deciding that he wants to do something to a church or churchyard in the diocese': *Re St Luke's, Chelsea* [1976] P 295 at 305.

[89] CCEJM 1991, s. 1; see *post* Ch. 16 for a fuller statement of the principles involved.

[90] EJM 1963, s. 47(1).   [91] S. 8 (for leave, see below).

whether the matter concerns doctrine, ritual, or ceremony.[92] A further appeal lies from the Ecclesiastical Causes Reserved Court to a Commission of Review, which is assisted by a panel of advisers. The commission's decision is by a majority and each member must state his opinion on the question under review.[93] The judges in each appellate court must be communicant members of the Church of England.[94] As a matter of judicial convention, throughout the hierarchy, reasons are given.

Criminal Proceedings

Concerning offences against the ecclesiastical law (the substantive elements of which will be dealt with in Chapter 7), a distinction is made between 'conduct' cases (such as neglect of duty) and 'reserved' cases (involving doctrine, ritual, and ceremonial). Proceedings against an archbishop or bishop are instituted by way of complaint laid before the provincial registrar; those against priests or deacons by way of complaint laid before the diocesan registrar.[95] With regard to proceedings against priests and deacons, the right to complain belongs only to an authorized person. If the complaint is against an incumbent of a benefice, it must be made by six or more persons of full age whose names are on the electoral roll; complaints against a stipendiary curate licensed to a benefice can be made only by the incumbent of the benefice.[96] If the complaint is against an archbishop and relates to his duties as such, it must be made by any two diocesan bishops of his province; if it relates to the archbishop's duties as a diocesan bishop, by not less than ten persons five of whom must be incumbents in the diocese and five members of the diocesan synod.[97] In the case of a diocesan bishop, the right to complain is vested in a person authorized by the archbishop or not less than ten persons five of whom must be diocesan incumbents and five members of the diocesan synod.[98]

Conduct cases are determined at first instance by the consistory court. Crucially, the law enables the resolution of the matter without going to trial.

---

[92] S. 10(1), (3); s.10 (4), (5): the Arches Court and the Ecclesiastical Causes Reserved Court may transfer to enable process in the appropriate court regardless of the diocesan chancellor's certification.   [93] S.48.

[94] This religious qualification was the cause of some objection when the draft measure was considered by the House of Commons: HC Deb., Vol. 680, 9 July 1963, 1179 ff.

[95] EJM 1963, s. 18; see also Ecclesiastical Jurisdiction (Discipline) Rules, 1964, SI No. 1755. The case of *The Right Revd Conner v The Very Revd Jackson, Dean of Lincoln* (1995) has stimulated calls for reform of disciplinary proceedings and a working party of the General Synod is at present investigating the question.

[96] S. 19. An authorized complainant is a person authorized by the bishop or archbishop: s. 66(1)).   [97] S. 20(a).

[98] S. 20(b); (c): in the case of a suffragan, the complaint may be laid by the commissioning bishop, or by an authorized person or by 5 incumbents and 5 members of the diocesan synod; (d): in the case of any other bishop, by the diocesan bishop, or an authorized complainant, or, if he is an incumbent, by 6 or more persons of full age appearing on the electoral roll.

In the cases of priests and deacons, the power of the consistory court to try a conduct case may be ousted by an episcopal decision (made after a private interview with the complainant and accused) that no further steps should be taken. The retention of the bishop's veto had not been recommended by the Lloyd Jacob Report.[99] There is no provision for an appeal against the bishop's decision nor is he required, by the governing measure, to give reasons. Indeed, if the bishop decides not to exercise his veto, if he decides that the complaint should be prosecuted, the matter is committed to an examiner who determines whether there is a case to answer. The accused and the complainant have a right to be represented at the enquiry and may lay before the examiner such evidence as they think fit; provision exists for evidence to be given on oath. If the examiner decides there is no case to answer then 'no further step shall be taken'. The examiner is under a duty to communicate his decision to the accused and to the bishop.[100] In some circumstances, when a cleric has been convicted or is subject to specified orders made by a secular court, without further trial the bishop must refer the matter to the archbishop who has a discretion to order deprivation and to disqualify from holding preferment.[101] Similarly, when the accused consents, and after consultation with the complainant, the bishop may dispose of the case summarily.[102] If a matter proceeds to trial, the consistory court has the power to demand attendance, examine witnesses, and inspect documents. The case is tried by the chancellor and four assessors, two clerical and two lay people, who are judges of fact, performing the same function as that of a jury in the Crown Court. The assessors are drawn by ballot from a panel of six priests and six communicant lay people approved by the diocesan synod. The assessors must be unanimous in order to convict, if they are not the chancellor directs either a re-trial or an acquittal.[103] The court has the power to impose a variety of sanctions (discussed in Chapter 7).[104] There is a right of appeal to the provincial court and from there to the Judicial Committee of the Privy Council.[105]

In a conduct case against an archbishop or bishop committal proceedings occur before an episcopal committee composed of the archbishop and two diocesan bishops, assisted by a legal assessor. The committee has power to veto a prosecution or to commit for trial and shall declare its decision, reduce it to writing, and send a copy to the accused; in the case of complaints against a bishop a copy is also sent to the upper house of convocation of the relevant province.[106] The court of trial is a commission of convocation composed of the

---

[99] S. 23; for objections to this see HL Deb, Vol. 249, 1963, 1435 at 1455–70; HC Deb, Vol. 680, 1963, 1164 ff., Vol. 681, 343 at 350 ff.

[100] S. 24. While evidence must ordinarily be given by affidavit, the examiner must on application of either party or on his own motion request attendance to answer questions on oath; the bishop then appoints a fit person to promote the complaint (s. 25).

[101] S. 55; s. 56: deprivation of archbishops; for the effect of secular court decisions see *post* Ch. 7.   [102] S. 31.

[103] Ss. 28–30.   [104] S. 49; see *post* Ch. 7.   [105] Ss. 7, 8.   [106] S. 33.

Dean of the Arches (or Auditor) and four diocesan bishops of the accused's province. Trial is in the form of that of the Crown Court and the public may be excluded. The commission cannot impose a censure but may refer the matter to convocation to do so. A censure of deprivation cannot be imposed without confirmation by Orders in Council.[107]

Reserved cases, concerning doctrine, ritual, or ceremonial, are dealt with at first instance in the Court of Ecclesiastical Causes Reserved.[108] Once more, if the accused is a priest or deacon the law enables the bishop to settle the matter by private interview. The bishop may veto further proceedings, but if he does not do so then the matter goes for examination to a committee composed of a bishop, two members of the lower house of convocation, and two diocesan chancellors. If the committee decides there is no case the matter is dismissed. It may also dismiss the case if the matter is trivial, if there are extenuating circumstances, or if prosecution is not in the interests of the church; dismissal may be made on these grounds only after considering representations made by the accused and the bishop. The committee must then report its decision with reasons to convocation. The trial in the Court of Ecclesiastical Causes Reserved is conducted in the same way as that in the consistory court with the assistance of five advisers selected from a panel of eminent theologians and liturgiologists. The court may exclude from proceedings such persons as it determines. Decision is by majority and the court may pronounce such censure as is warranted. There is a right of appeal from the Court of Ecclesiastical Causes Reserved to a Commission of Review consisting of three Lords of Appeal who are communicant members of the church and two bishops (who sit as members of the House of Lords). Proceedings against a bishop in reserved cases are similar to those against a priest or deacon, the archbishop conducting an initial review.[109] Examination is by a convocation committee and the court of trial is the Court of Ecclesiastical Causes Reserved. Appeal from this lies to a Commission of Review.[110] An important element of these arrangements is the right of parties to legal aid and the judicial power to demand costs.[111]

Grounds of Appeal

Under the Ecclesiastical Jurisdiction Measure 1963, in a criminal suit appeal from the consistory court to the provincial court lies at the instance of any party on a question of law and at the instance of the defendant on a question of fact. Appeals against decisions of convocation commissions or the Court of Ecclesiastical Causes Reserved may be made by any party to the proceedings on a question of law and by the defendant on a question of fact. In a civil suit,

---

[107] Ss. 35–7.   [108] The following rules are found in ss. 38, 42, 45.
[109] S. 40; in the case of complaint against an archbishop the matter is referred directly for enquiry (s. 41).   [110] S. 48.
[111] See *post* Ch. 17.

whilst appeal lies at the instance of any party to the proceedings, leave must be obtained from the consistory court or, if this refuses leave, from the Arches Court.[112] The superior church courts may challenge the decision of a lower court on grounds of substance or for want of procedural propriety. The appellate court may draw inferences of fact which might have been drawn by the lower court and it may reverse a decision if the lower court's decision was founded on an erroneous evaluation of the facts.[113] An unjustified delay in expediting criminal proceedings against the accused may result in the dismissal of a case.[114] Acting in excess of jurisdiction or improper or mistaken interpretation of ecclesiastical law may result in the overturning of a decision.[115]

Procedural impropriety was considered on appeal to the Arches Court in *Burridge v Tyler* (1992), a case in which the Chichester Consistory Court found a clergyman guilty of conduct unbecoming a clerk in holy orders.[116] Before trial, and unknown to the chancellor, the accused visited a canon, a fellow priest, with whom he discussed the evidence relating to the allegations. It was established that on this occasion the canon had suspended judgment as to where the truth lay. The canon subsequently visited the accused forming a preliminary view adverse to the accused, but he did not communicate this to the accused. The diocesan registrar wrote to the accused's solicitor asking whether he wished to be present at the ballot for assessors. Accepting legal advice the accused did not attend. The canon was chosen as an assessor; he had not informed the registrar about his discussions with the accused or that he had formed a view. The canon did, however, inform the accused that he had been chosen, asking whether the accused wanted him to withdraw. The accused did not object. The canon convinced himself after prayer that he could judge the matter impartially and objectively. Convicted, the accused appealed to the Arches Court. The Dean formulated two tests: would a reasonable and fair-minded person sitting in the trial court, knowing the facts, have had a reasonable suspicion that a fair trial was not possible, and: was there evidence from

---

[112] Ss. 7, 11.

[113] For Arches Court appeals see: *Re St Edburga's, Abberton* [1961] 3 All ER 429 (the approach to appeals was that of the CA as set prescribed in *Benmax v Austin Motor Co Ltd* [1955] AC 370); *Re St Gregory's, Tredington* [1971] 3 All ER 269; *Re St Helen's, Brant Broughton* [1974] 3 All ER 386; *Re St. Mary's, Banbury* [1987] 1 All ER 247; for appeals to the Court of Ecclesiastical Causes Reserved: *Re St. Michael and All Angels, Great Torrington* [1985] Fam 81; *Re St Stephen's Walbrook* [1986] 2 All ER 705. [114] *Jenkins v Barrett* (1827) 1 Hag Ecc 12.

[115] *Bland v Archdeacon of Cheltenham* [1972] 1 All ER 1012 (for the consistory court's misunderstanding of 'neglect of duty'); see also *MacAllister v Bishop of Rochester* (1880) 5 CPD 194; *Combe v De la Bere* (1881) 6 PD 157.

[116] [1992] 1 All ER 437 at 442 *per* Sir John Owen: 'In the circumstances we must decide that fairness and justice demand that the verdicts against Mr Tyler cannot stand. Of course it is a matter of regret that the Church has been put to considerable wasted expense but justice is more important than financial considerations'; the suit was based on EJM 1963, s. 14(1)(b)(ii).

which a proper inference might be drawn that the accused might have been prejudiced? Both of these were satisfied, the verdict was unsafe and unsatisfactory and a re-trial was ordered before fresh assessors. *Per curiam*, the Dean added that a diocesan registrar 'should' reveal to any assessor the accused's identity and likely witnesses and ask for details of any acquaintance. It is for the chancellor to disqualify potential assessors.

Supervision by the Secular Courts

The degree to which the courts of the Church of England are autonomous is fairly well settled. As a basic principle, the church's courts are subject to the supervisory jurisdiction of the civil courts. Nothing in the Ecclesiastical Jurisdiction Measure 1963 affects, by means of discretionary remedies, 'any power of the High Court to control the proper exercise by ecclesiastical courts of their functions'.[117] Oversight is possible in limited circumstances: overall, there seems to be a presumption that the ecclesiastical courts act within their jurisdiction.[118] An ecclesiastical court must be satisfied about its competence to determine a matter.[119] If an ecclesiastical court acts in excess of its jurisdiction prohibition may lie.[120] Similarly, if an ecclesiastical court fails to observe the common law principles of natural justice, it will act outside its jurisdiction.[121] In the case of an ecclesiastical court's refusal to exercise jurisdiction in a case in which it should do so, the High Court may issue *mandamus* compelling the assumption of jurisdiction.[122] Whether the High Court has power to issue *certiorari* to quash a decision of an ecclesiastical

---

[117] S. 83(2)(b) (nor, under s. 83(2)(a), 'any prerogative of Her Majesty the Queen').

[118] *Mackonochie v Lord Penzance* (1881) 6 App Cas 424 at 446; *Hallack v Cambridge University* (1841) 1 QB 593; *R v Twiss* (1869) LR 4 QB 407.

[119] *Re St Mary's, Barton-on-Humber* [1987] 2 All ER 861 at 864; *Re Escot Church* [1979] Fam 125 at 127; for non-assumption of jurisdiction, see e.g. *Re St Andrew's, Thornhaugh* [1976] 1 All ER 154; *Re St. Martin le Grand, York* [1989] 2 All ER 711 at 721; see *AG v Dean and Chapter of Ripon Cathedral* [1945] Ch 239 for non-assumption of jurisdiction by the civil courts.

[120] *R v Tristram* [1902] 1 KB 816 (CA); *ex p Story* (1852) 12 CB 767; a common law action against the chancellor or bishop may also lie: *Beaurain v Scott* (1812) 3 Camp 388; *Ackerley v Parkinson* (1815) 3 M&S 411; prohibition may not lie for error (rather than excess) of jurisdiction: *R v Judicial Committee of the Privy Council, ex p Smyth* (1835) 2 CM&R 748; *Proud v Price* (1893) 69 LT 664 at 665 (CA); for the possibility of prohibition against the Privy Council acting in excess of its ecclesiastical jurisdiction see *Mackonochie v Lord Penzance* (1881) 6 App Cas 424.

[121] *R v North, ex p Oakey* [1929] 1 KB 491: a consistory court order—in a faculty case—against a cleric to pay for restoration without a special citation was in excess of jurisdiction: 'the order being a breach of the fundamental principle of law, that a person is entitled to have notice of a claim against him and to be heard before he can be deprived of his property': *per* Atkin LJ); for determination of a matter by the application of rules which are contrary to the common law: *Veley v Burder* (1841) 12 Ad & El 265 at 311–12.

[122] *R v Archbishop of Canterbury* (1856) 6 E&B 546; *R v Arches Court Judge* (1857) 7 E&B 315; *R v Bishop of London* (1889) 24 QBD 213 (CA); *Allcroft v Lord Bishop of London, Lighton v Lord Bishop of London* [1891] AC 666 (HL).

court is less clear.[123] With regard to pre-trial review and examination, it is submitted that, in so far as powers enjoyed by bishops, examiners, and commissions in criminal suits are conferred by public law, the principles of natural justice and fairness are applicable.[124] Finally, it is notable that the European Commission of Human Rights has recently entertained (but rejected) a complaint against a decision of the Church of England's courts.[125]

A Comparison with Roman Catholic Courts

The courts of the Roman Catholic Church are treated as a last resort; as we have seen, there is a canonical duty to settle conflicts out of court, and the judicial process itself is treated as very much a pastoral matter.[126] Moreover, the principle of hierarchical recourse substantially marginalizes the courts from the resolution of conflict: complaints against administrative acts are settled within the administrative hierarchy (see Chapter 4). With regard to the judicial process, the object of a trial is to prosecute or to vindicate the rights of physical or juridic persons, to declare juridic facts, or to declare the penalty for offences (c.1400). Judicial power is possessed by judges or judicial colleges and must be exercised in the manner prescribed by law; it cannot be delegated, except to carry out acts which are preparatory to a decree or a decision (c.135). Once jurisdiction is established, anyone (whether baptized or not) can bring an action before a church court (c.1476). The faithful have access to the courts to vindicate or defend their rights (c.221) and there is a legal action to defend every right (c.1491). According to Canon 1401, the courts have jurisdiction (a) over cases concerning spiritual matters or connected with the spiritual and (b) over the violation of ecclesiastical laws and all

---

[123] *R v Chancellor of St Edmundsbury and Ipswich Diocese, ex p White* [1948] 1 KB 195. CA simply held that the lack of a precedent to issue *certoriari* justified refusal; in the light of developments in judicial review in recent years, it might not be thought out of the question for *certiorari* to lie on evidence of a serious breach of the rules of natural justice, for example.

[124] Although, *after trial*, earlier pre-trial procedural impropriety may be a ground of appeal within the church, with regard to *pre-trial settlement*, effected by means of statutory powers (under EJM 1963), a failure to give reasons for proceeding or any failure to allow appearance may be a proper ground for judicial review: see *supra* for judicial review of quasi-judicial decisions.

[125] *Re Thomas Tyler*, ELJ, 3 (1994), 348 (European Commission of Human Rights, Application No. 21283/93); the applicant was unsuccessful as the Commission was not satisfied that 'the charge of ''conduct unbecoming a priest'' [under EJM 1963] is not inherently criminal in nature' within the meaning of ECHR, Art. 6(1); however, with regard to 'civil rights and obligations' before an 'independent and impartial tribunal' (Art. 6(1)) the Commission did suggest that it might be prepared to process a case to the European Court of Human Rights given clear evidence of actual bias; for Revd. Williamson's ECHR Art. 9 application concerning the ordination of women legislation, see *Church Times*, 7 July 1995, 17.

[126] W. H. Woestman (ed.), *Papal Allocutions to the Roman Rota, 1939–1994* (Ottawa, 1994) 83 ('The ecclesiastical judge's pastoral role', Paul VI, 25 Jan. 1966), 105 ('Judicial authority in the contemporary church', Paul VI, 28 Jan. 1971), 123 ('The sacred naure of judicial authority and activity in the church', Paul VI, 31 Jan. 1974), and 176 ('Judge, interpreter and servant of the law', John Paul II, 26 Feb. 1983).

those cases in which there is a question of sin in respect to the determination of culpability and the imposition of ecclesiastical penalties.[127]

As in the Church of England, the courts before which cases are brought, the 'competent fora', are ordered hierarchically. The tribunal of first instance is the diocesan court, presided over by the bishop who may exercise judicial power personally (if he does not have a direct interest) or through others (c.1419). The bishop's judge is the judicial vicar (*officialis*) who may be assisted by adjutant judicial vicars; these exercise ordinary and not delegated power and must be priests (c.1420). Lay members of the church may participate in the exercise of judicial power (c.129) and the conference of bishops may appoint lay judges to assist the judicial vicar (c.1421). With papal approval dioceses may group together and operate a single court for that diocesan group: the interdiocesan tribunal (c.1423). Specified cases, concerning dismissal from the clerical state and contentious matrimonial cases, are reserved to a collegiate tribunal of three judges (c.1425). Provision is made for oral hearings (except in marriage cases), but proceedings are invariably conducted in writing (cc.1601–18). Cases must be concluded within a year (c.1453).

Also with the Church of England, Roman Catholic canon law has an elaborate system of rights of appeal. The tribunals of second instance are the Metropolitan Court, the court of a province (c.1436), constituted in the same way as the diocesan court. Appeal may be made to this from the diocesan court. The metropolitan court is also a court of first instance for some cases. A court competent to determine first instance cases acts invalidly if it hears a case of second instance. The Apostolic See has two judicial bodies: the Rota is the appeal court and the Apostolic Signatura is a supervisory court (dealing, for example, with disputes about administrative acts and questions about the competence of lower courts).[128] In some cases a direct appeal may be made from the diocesan court to the Roman Rota (c.1444), but usually appeals to the Rota are from the metropolitan court. The Rota also enjoys a first instance competence in prescribed cases, such as the trial of bishops in contentious cases (c.1405). The pope is the supreme judge for the universal church and the Code reserves certain cases to the pontiff (c.1405): the incompetence of other judges to try reserved cases is absolute (c.1406(2)). Any of the faithful is free to bring a case before the Holy See at any time (c.1417). There is no appeal against a papal judicial decision (c.1404). Parties may be asked to contribute to costs (c.1649).

THE INTERPRETATION OF ECCLESIASTICAL LEGISLATION

In the Roman Catholic Church a set of basic norms governs the interpretation of all canon law: laws are 'to be understood in accord with the proper meaning

[127] See generally H. F. Doogan (ed.), *Catholic Tribunals: Marriage Annulment and Dissolution* (Newtown, Australia, 1990).   [128] *CIC*, cc. 1419, 1438–9, 1442–5; cc. 1645–8 (restitution).

of the words . . . in their text and context'; if the meaning remains doubtful and obscure, recourse is to be taken to parallel passages, to the circumstances of the law, and to the mind of the legislator.[129] Similar approaches are employed by the courts of the Church of England.[130] A basic duty is imposed on judges of the Church of England by the Interpretation Act 1978 [s. 22] which provides that the canons of construction employed in secular law in relation to parliamentary statutes shall apply to all measures passed by the General Synod. The Interpretation Measure 1925 defines only a small number of key terms.[131] This does not, of course, impose a general duty upon the ecclesiastical judiciary (or upon anyone called upon to interpret law) to interpret *all* synodical measures in the same way as parliamentary statutes though, commonly, General Synod enacts interpretation sections within measures giving rise to a particular duty to interpret according to the meaning specified in the Measure 'unless the context otherwise requires'.[132] However, the principles of interpretation operating in secular jurisprudence with regard to parliamentary statutes—by which the courts must discover the intent of the legislator—apply equally to measures.[133] Ecclesiastical courts frequently employ a literal interpretation of church legislation, although sometimes they employ a different construction when they feel that this is more appropriate.[134] Frequently, moreover, they employ a purposive approach examining historically the circumstances or problems (theological and pastoral) giving rise to the enactment of the legislation.[135] The judges

[129] Ibid., c. 17; see generally L. Örsy, *Theology and Canon Law* (1992); see *Buckley v Cahal Daly* [1990] NIJB 8, for use by H Ct. of an Apostolic Signatura decision of 1978 and expert evidence as to the meaning of incardination in the 1983 Code.

[130] Interpretation is also a function of the Legal Advisory Commission: *Annual Report* 1994, 2.1, 2.2; for actual interpretations see *OLAC*.   [131] Ss. 2, 3.

[132] Some are extremely elaborate (CCEJM 1991, s. 31) and some very short (Clergy Pensions (Amendment) Measure 1972, s. 7).

[133] This may indeed be a general duty: as this is one of the 'effects' of parliamentary statute so, given their equality of authority (see Ch. 3), the scheme applies also to synodical measures; for civil law principles see J. Bell and G. Engle (eds.), *Cross on Statutory Interpretation* (2nd edn., London, 1987); in *R v Archbishops of Canterbury and York, ex p Williamson* (1994) Hill *EL*, 77 at 80 appeal was made to *Pepper v Hart* [1993] AC 593 enabling in exceptional secular cases recourse to evidence derived from debates in the legislative process.

[134] *R v Ecclesiastical Committee of Both Houses of Parliament, ex p Church Society* (1993) Hill, *EL*, 72 *per* McGowan LJ on 'any matter' in Church Assembly (Powers) Act 1919, s.3(6); see also *Gorham v Bishop of Exeter* (1850) 15 QB 73 at 74 *per* Lord Campbell: 'Were the language of the statute obscure, instead of being clear, we should not be justified in differing from the construction put upon it by contemporaneous and long-continued usage' (followed in *Ridsdale v Clifton* (1877) 2 PD 276 at 331: 'It would in the opinion of their Lordships, be contrary to well-settled principles of law to admit private opinions to control the legal interpretation of public documents . . . but it may be not without advantage to point out the circumstances under which the opinions of these writers appear to have been expressed': ibid., 332–3); see also *In Re Robinson, Wright v Tugwell* (1897) 1 Ch 85.

[135] *Hebbert v Purchas* [1872] LR 4 CP; *Ridsdale v Clifton* (1877) 2 PD 276 at 278; *Re St Luke's, Chelsea* [1976] 1 All ER 609 at 627; *Re St Nicholas, Baddesley Ensor* [1982] 2 All ER 351; *Crisp v Martin* (1876) 2 PD 15 at 27–28; in *Re Flenley* [1981] Fam 64, in the light of complexities under the Incumbents (Vacation of Benefices) Measure 1977 the ecclesiastical tribunal suggested that a reform in the law be effected by General Synod.

have adopted both literal and purposive approaches to the interpretation of canons, often reading them in the light of doctrinal and liturgical documents.[136] Today, literal interpretations of liturgical rubrics are uncommon: the favoured approach is more liberal with judges sometimes distinguishing mandatory and directory requirements.[137] Occasionally ecclesiastical judges interpret ecclesiastical legislation restrictively, for example if the legislation abridges the common law.[138] When ecclesiastical judges find it difficult to understand the terms of ecclesiastical legislation, they may appeal to a host of extra-legal materials.[139]

THE DOCTRINES OF PRECEDENT

In the Roman Catholic Church a series of basic principles militates against the operation of a doctrine of binding judicial precedent. In part these principles also supply justifications for the absence of a precedent system. It is commonly said that Roman Catholic canon law employs a 'no-precedent' system: the decision of a judge in a particular case 'is nothing more than a weighty opinion of an expert who has sought to interpret and apply ecclesiastical, divine positive and natural law'.[140] A judicial *decision* does not have the status or force of law: it binds only the parties to it and it affects only the matter for which it was given.[141] The principle is implicit in the *purpose* of the judicial process: to prosecute or vindicate rights, to declare juridic facts, or to impose penalties: the function of the court is to adjudicate, not to legislate.[142] Nor do judicial *interpretations* enjoy the status of law: the only authentic and binding interpretation of a law which itself possesses the quality of law is that as promulgated by the legislator, and this is treated merely as a descriptive,

---

[136] *Re Atkins* [1989] 1 All ER 14 at 15: in construing Canon B38, the answer was to be found in 'the rites and ceremonies of the Church of England . . . [which] must be taken to represent the intention of the church and its members'. On the meaning of 'table' under Canon F2, cf. the approaches of the consistory court (narrow) [1986] 2 All ER 705 at 709 and that of the Court of Ecclesiastical Causes Reserved (wide) in *Re St Stephen's, Walbrook* [1987] 2 All ER 578; see *post* Ch. 9 for judicial use of Lambeth Conference documents.   [137] See *post* Ch. 9.

[138] *Re St Mary's, Banbury* [1985] 2 All ER 611 at 615; see also *Ridsdale v Clifton* (1877) 2 PD 276 at 327; for an historical survey of the canonical principle *statutum contra ius commune stricte interpretandum est*, see R. H. Helmholz, *Roman Canon Law in Reformation England* (Cambridge, 1990) 167.

[139] See *R v Ecclesiastical Committee of Both Houses of Parliament, ex p Church Society* (1993), Hill, *EL*, 72, for McGowan LJ's use of the Ecclesiastical Committee's understanding of the legality of the draft measure under review and for his use of the Church of England Assembly (Powers) Act 1919 Preamble (following the canon of construction enunciated in *AG v Prince Ernest Augustus of Hanover* [1957] AC 436); see *Re St Martin le Grand, York* [1989] 2 All ER 711 for extensive use of commentators (Halsbury, Phillimore and Gale); *Ridsdale v Clifton* (1877) 2 PD 276 at 323 (for use of a statutory preamble); see *Combe v De La Bere* (1881) 6 PD 157 at 164 for the Arches Court's use of Jacob's *Law Dictionary* (1744) ('a book not without authority': *per* Lord Penzance).

[140] *CCL: TC*, 12.

[141] *CIC*, c. 16(3). A judicial decision does not come within the Code's definition of law under cc. 7, 9.   [142] C. 1400 (and c.135).

declaratory, or confirmatory statement of existing law.[143] Furthermore, when a judge appeals to materials (which may include judicial decisions) to assist in interpretation, he is not obliged to *follow* these, he is simply obliged to *consult* them: they are of merely persuasive authority.[144] Closer to a doctrine of precedent is the canonical requirement that, unless the matter is penal, if the law is silent on a point 'the case is to be decided in the light of . . . the jurisprudence and praxis of the Roman Curia'.[145] Again, this casts a duty to consult the jurisprudence of the curia—to take cognizance of it—but not an obligation to follow it: there remains a discretion as to whether or not it will be applied or enforced. It may bind not as *law* (if not also the subject of a legislator's authentic interpretation), but only in the loose sense that it is something which must be *considered* as a possible lawful *solution*. A judicial decision of a curial body does not bind directly *proprio vigore*.[146]

In practice, decisions of Roman Catholic courts in matrimonial cases time and time again contain appeals, for varying reasons,[147] to the decisions of other judicial bodies: decisions of the Rota and the Apostolic Signatura are regularly published for the guidance of lower courts.[148] Most importantly, these decisions are actually followed or adopted. The Rota frequently uses previous rotal decisions, and diocesan tribunals frequently employ rotal decisions.[149] Indeed, when a rotal decision is an authentic and promulgated interpretation it enjoys the canonical authority of a binding legal precedent.[150] In addition, even in those cases when appeal is made to rotal decisions as guidance or as persuasive authority, for the parties to the instant case the rotal decision, woven into the lower court's actual decision, has a direct binding

[143] C. 16(1), (2); see also L. Örsy, *Theology and Canon Law*, 47; the Pontifical Council for the Interpretation of Legal texts (set up by the Apostolic Constitution *Pastor Bonus* 1988) gives authentic interpretations with papal authority. These are listed in *COCLA*, Appendix II.

[144] *CIC*, c. 17.

[145] C.19; W. H. Woestman, *Papal Allocutions* (1994) 165 ('The magisterium and jurisprudence of the tribunals of the Apostolic See', John Paul II, 24 Jan. 1981) and 181 ('Importance of the new code and rotal jurisprudence', John Paul II, 26 Jan. 1984).

[146] N. Doe, 'Canonical doctrines of judicial precedent: a comparative study', *The Jurist*, 54 (1994), 205.

[147] Reasons for appealing to decisions vary: in a rotal case *coram* Burke (15/11/90), a decision *c.* Egan (1986) was used to *explain* the reason for the principle in Canon 1598(1): see *Studia Canonica*, 25 (1991), 509. Appeal to rotal decisions *c.* Burke (11/6/1992) seemed simply to augment the authority of Pope John Paul II's address to the Rota (1989) concerning the right of defence.   [148] Both *The Jurist* and *Studia Canonica* carry these.

[149] See *Studia Canonica*, 26 (1992), 490 at 491 for the rotal decision *c.* Cormac Burke (11/6/92) relying on rotal decisions *c.* Mattioli (26/2/1954), *c.* Wynen (9/3/1955), and *c.* Brennan (27/11/1958); ibid., 22 (1988) 485 for a decision of the Dublin Regional Marriage Tribunal, *c.* Rev. A. McGrath (13/6/88) and his use of the rotal decision *c.* Egan (29/5/1976)—this decision is interesting for the reliance on an earlier decision of the Dublin Regional Marriage Tribunal, *c.* Kelly (4/3/1980).

[150] See the decision of the court of the Diocese of Rockville Centre, New York, *c.* K. Boccafola, *Garcia-Costa* (1980), *The Jurist*, 43 (1983): 'We may legitimately come to such a conclusion based on c.1069 and its legitimate and authoritative interpretation as illustrated in the rotal decision *coram* Pinto . . . 1974'.

effect on the parties.[151] In short, in Roman Catholic canon law, whereas there is no formal system of binding precedent, earlier decisions, which if relevant must be consulted, are in practice followed. Though the doctrine of binding precedent applies in the Church of England, it is around this practice (the adoption of persuasive decisions) that the approaches of the Roman Catholic Church and the Church of England find a direct point of contact.

The rationale for the doctrines of precedent in the Church of England is based on the models of secular jurisprudence—certainty, internal consistency and coherence, predictability for the ecclesiastical citizen, and ensuring that judicial power is not exercised arbitrarily.[152] The doctrines have two main elements, one duty-imposing and preceptive, the other facilitative. On one hand, through the principle of *stare decisis*, judges are bound to keep to earlier decisions of the court in which they sit or to decisions of courts superior in the hierarchy because these enjoy the status or authority of law.[153] The entire decision of a court is, however, not always binding: only the *ratio decidendi* represents the law, the rule which was used as the reason for or as the determinant of the decision.[154] Judicial statements made in passing (*obiter dicta*), statements of law which are not determinants in the instant case, enjoy only persuasive authority. Moreover, not *all* judicial decisions are binding: the decisions of lower courts, for example, will not be binding on higher courts. On the other hand, therefore, as in Roman Catholic canon law, an integral element of the doctrines of precedent is the idea that the judiciary has in some circumstances a right, not a duty, to follow previous decisions. Indeed, the status of decisions of many courts in the Church of England's hierarchy remains unsettled.

Previous decisions of a Commission of Review are binding on the Commission, an obligation imposed by legislation.[155] It is probably the case (though this has not yet been decided) that its decisions are binding on all lower courts in matters of doctrine, ritual, and ceremonial. It has not been decided but, as an appellate court on the civil side, the Court of Ecclesiastical Causes Reserved may be bound by its own earlier decisions and those of the Commission. It has not been settled, but it is likely that its decisions are binding on all lower courts in both provinces. It has also been pointed out that it is unclear what binding effect a decision of this court has when it acts as a first instance court in exercising its criminal jurisdiction in matters of doctrine, ritual, and ceremony.[156] Decisions

---

[151] *CIC*, c. 16(3); L. Örsy, *Theology and Canon Law*, 49, n. 13: in practice the impact of rotal on diocesan tribunals jurisprudence goes 'well beyond what the theory would allow'.

[152] For secular models see R. Cross and J.W. Harris, *Precedent in English Law* (4th edn., Oxford, 1991).   [153] See *supra* Ch. 1.

[154] There is a considerable degree of uncertainty as to what, precisely, constitutes the *ratio* of a case: see R. Cross, *Precedent*, Ch. 2; *HLE*, para. 1271: 'There is reason to think that cases cited as authorities in writings on ecclesiastical law have sometimes been given undue weight, partly through failure to observe the distinction between the ratio decidendi and an obiter dictum'.

[155] EJM 1963, s. 48(6).   [156] *HLE*, para. 1271, n. 4.

of the Judicial Committee of the Privy Council are binding on the Arches and Chancery Courts in faculty cases *not* involving doctrine, ritual, and ceremony.[157] It is not settled whether Privy Council decisions are binding on consistory courts in matters involving doctrine, ritual, and ceremony, but they are not binding on the Ecclesiastical Causes Reserved Court in these matters.[158] The decisions of provincial courts bind only in that province. The Arches Court is not bound by decisions of the Chancery Court, nor is the Chancery Court bound by the Arches Court's decisions.[159] The Arches Court is bound by its own previous decisions, as is the Chancery Court.[160] Decisions of the Arches Court bind consistory courts only in the Province of Canterbury; those of the Chancery Court bind consistory courts only in the York Province.[161] Most importantly, because in practice this court is the most active, a consistory court is bound by its own previous decisions.[162] However, a consistory court in one diocese is *not* bound by the decision of a consistory court in another diocese.[163]

Although several key elements remain unsettled, these arrangements represent the preceptive aspects of the precedent doctrines. There is also a softer, more benign and liberal side giving the ecclesiastical courts a freedom to depart from an earlier decision which would otherwise be binding. The Privy Council may depart from its own earlier decisions as may the Arches and Chancery Courts if there is a strong reason so to do.[164] An Arches Court decision is of persuasive authority for the Chancery Court and vice versa, and decisions of lower courts may be persuasive authorities for superior courts.[165]

[157] There is no direct authority on this point. However, as under EJM 1963, s. 8(2) the Privy Council is the court of appeal from the Arches and Chancery Courts, this is the likely position; see *Sherwood v Ray* (1837) 1 Moo PCC 353 for PC overruling an Arches Court decision.

[158] EJM 1963, s. 45(3). Nor is the Commission bound by Privy Council decisions on these matters (s. 48(5).   [159] *HLE*, para. 1271 (no authority is given).

[160] *Re Lapford (Devon) Parish Church* [1955] 3 All ER 484.

[161] *Re St. Mary, Tyne Dock No. 2* [1958] 1 All ER 1; see also *Re St. John the Divine, Richmond* [1963] 1 All ER 818 at 820; *Stephenson v Langston* [1804] 1 Hag Con 379.

[162] *Rector and Churchwardens of Bishopwearmouth v Adey* [1958] 3 All ER 441; see also *St. Mary, Aldermary* [1985] 2 All ER 445 for the London Con. Ct.'s use of its own previous decisions in *Re St. John's, Chelsea* [1962] 2 All ER 850 and *Re St Paul's, Covent Garden* [1974] Fam 1; see also *Grosvenor Chapel, South Audley Street* (1913) 29 TLR 286 (Kempe Ch. bound even when in disagreement).

[163] *Re Rector and Churchwardens of St. Nicholas, Plumstead* [1961] 1 All ER 298; for the technique of distinguishing see: *Re St. Stephen Walbrook* [1987] 2 All ER 578 (Sir Ralph Gibson in the Ecclesiastical Causes Court distinguishes (and disapproves) Arches decision in *Re St. Mary Banbury* [1987] 1 All ER 247); *Re St. Martin le Grand, York* [1989] 2 All ER 711 at 720; see also *R v Abney Park Cemetery Co* (1873) 8 LR 515 at 520.

[164] For the PC see *Read v Bishop of Lincoln* [1892] AC 644; *Ridsdale v Clifton* (1877) 2 PD 276 at 306–7; for the provincial courts, see the suggestion in *Re Lapford (Devon) Parish Church* [1955] 3 All ER 484 (no 'sufficient reason' for Arches Ct. to depart from its own previous decision in *Capel St Mary Suffolk* [1927] P 289).

[165] For the use of the Arches Court decision of *Re St. Edburga's, Abberton* [1961] 2 All ER 429 by the Court of Ecclesiastical Causes Reserved, see *Re St. Michael, Torrington* [1985] 1 All ER 993; for the Arches Ct. acting in the absence of a binding rule see *Re St Gregory's, Tredington* [1971] 3 All ER 269 at 273.

In practice, the ecclesiastical judges sitting in consistory courts employ in the main the benign form of the precedent doctrines. They frequently follow earlier decisions of other consistory courts when strictly they are not obliged to do so; this might be described as a doctrine of adoption.[166] In short, the doctrine of persuasive precedent is the dominant doctrine in practice. Finally, civil courts are not bound to follow the decisions of the courts of the Church of England, nor are ecclesiastical courts bound to follow decisions of the civil courts.[167]

CONCLUSIONS

The legal organization of judicial powers in the Church of England has undergone radical reform in recent years, not least in their wider distribution beyond the ecclesiastical courts. With the exception of the faculty jurisdiction, the settlement of disputes is effected today by a wide range of enquiries, tribunals, and the exercise of episcopal powers, not by the hierarchy of courts. Adjudication processes of these bodies are closely regulated by law (and by codes of practice). Rights of appeal are commonly built into ecclesiastical legislation. The precise extent to which the church's developing system of enquiries and tribunals is subject to judicial review has not been tested. The church's legislation does not contain adequate provision for the giving of reasons in the process of adjudication by these bodies. In relation to the hierarchy of courts, as in Roman Catholic canon law and its court hierarchy, the law of the Church of England has been designed to avoid trials. This is the case with regard to both civil and (where there are elaborate provisions for pre-trial settlement) criminal proceedings. When a court is required to exercise jurisdiction, its decisions are subject to a systematic arrangement of appeals, general supervision by the secular courts, the canons of construction, and the doctrines of precedent. Indeed, whereas there are fundamental formal differences between the two approaches, Roman Catholic and Church of England canonical doctrines of judicial precedent actually meet in the practical sphere around the concept and use of persuasive authorities.

---

[166] In *Re All Saints, Harborough Magna* [1992] 4 All ER 948, the Coventry Con. Ct. judge was prepared to 'adopt and accept' the unreported Rochester Con. Ct. decision of *Re Rusthall, St. Mark's, Biggin Hill* (13 May 1992); in the Court of Ecclesiastical Causes Reserved case *Re St Stephen Walbrook* [1987] 2 All ER 578 at 591, Sir Ralph Gibson treated that court's earlier decision in *Re St. Michael, Great Torrington* [1985] 1 All ER 993 as having 'adopted and applied the statement of law by Sir Henry Willink' in the case of *Re St. Edburga's, Abberton* [1961] 2 All ER 429, and this he was prepared to follow. See also the Arches Ct. decision *Re Rector and Churchwardens of Capel St Mary* [1927] PD 289 at 296; *Poole v Bishop of London* (1859) 5 Jur NS 522 was 'not in strictness an authority' and it was distinguishable.
[167] *Mackonochie v Lord Penzance* (1881) 6 App Cas 424 at 431, 447, 460; *AG v Dean and Chapter of Ripon* [1945] 1 Ch 239 at 246; *Chancellor of St. Edmundsbury and Ipswich Diocese, ex p White* [1948] 1 KB 195 at 204; see also *Notley v Bishop of Birmingham* [1931] 1 Ch 529 at 536, 538.

PART III
Ecclesiastical Ministry

6

Episcopal Ministry: The Offices of Bishop

Bishops in the Church of England are involved directly or indirectly in all aspects of ecclesiastical life: pastoral, governmental, doctrinal, liturgical, and proprietorial. The ministry of the episcopate, one of the Church of England's three clerical orders, is pivotal: associated theologically with charismatic power and leadership, it is a ministry ordered and facilitated by law.[1] The episcopal order itself is generic, but the Church of England has in recent years introduced a variety of different episcopal offices principally with a view to giving assistance to the diocesan bishop. As well as exploring the terms under which the new offices of bishop are regulated, this Chapter explores the law applicable to all episcopal offices with regard to appointment, consecration, basic functions, retirement, resignation, and discipline. The entire legal framework of the Church of England, like that of the Roman Catholic Church, though sometimes in radically different ways, is one which protects and enhances the centrality of the episcopal ministry as an instrument of continuity and authority within the church.[2]

CANDIDATURE: NOMINATION AND SELECTION

The law of the Church of England recognizes three types of episcopal office: archbishop, diocesan bishop, and suffragan bishop. There are two archbishops: one has jurisdiction over the Province of Canterbury and all of England, and

---

[1] Canon C1(1): 'The Church of England holds and teaches that from the Apostles' time there have been these orders in Christ's Church: bishops, priests, and deacons'; see also *BCP*, 553; *ASB*, 338; it is in part the purpose of this Chapter to study the applicability today (particularly in view of the introduction of synodical government) of the claim in *Bishop of St Alban's v Fillingham* [1906] P 163 at 179 that 'The Church of England is subject to episcopal government'. The same theological stance is employed in the Roman Catholic Church: 'The orders are the episcopacy, the presbyterate, and the diaconate' (*CIC*, c. 1009(1)).

[2] J. Draper (ed.), *Communion and Episcopacy: Essays to Mark the Centenary of the Chicago–Lambeth Quadrilateral* (Oxford, 1988); for an historical analysis of the word *episcope* as oversight see *Episcopal Ministry*, Report of the Archbishops' Group on the Episcopate (London, 1990) Part I, 5; for these ideas appearing in diocesan norms see e.g. *LDHI*, IV, 1.1; *SDDH*, A.1; *BDM*, A.1; *TDH*, E.1. See generally, M. Santer (ed.), *Their Lord and Ours* (SPCK, London, 1982); J. Halliburton, *The Authority of a Bishop* (SPCK, London, 1987). *WAOB* seems to recommend an enhanced role of leadership for General Synod's House of Bishops, including the issuing of guidance and pastoral letters particularly in the fields of doctrine and worship (5.31, 7.1 ff.)

the other over the Province of York.[3] The diocesan bishop, having jurisdiction over the diocese,[4] may be aided by suffragan bishops who enjoy specified forms of jurisdiction, either throughout the whole of the diocese or only in a particular area of it, depending on the terms of the instrument by which they are commissioned.[5] The diocesan or the suffragan, either separately or jointly, may also be given episcopal oversight of an area in the diocese, in which case they may be known as 'area bishops'.[6] An ecclesiastical practice has developed by which suffragans and other bishops resident in the diocese, who may assist the diocesan, are styled 'assistant bishops', 'honorary assistant bishops', or 'auxiliary bishops'.[7] A recent creation resulting from the rules developed to implement to new legislation dealing with women priests is the 'regional bishop' (or 'flying bishop') and the 'episcopal visitor'.[8] With the exception of these, a similar division is found in Roman Catholic canon law: bishops are either diocesan, having care of a diocese, or titular: titular bishops, either auxiliary bishops or coadjutor bishops, are assistants to the diocesan;[9] the archbishop, or metropolitan, presides over an ecclesiastical province.[10]

With regard to qualifications for admission to the episcopal order, the law of the Church of England is considerably less well defined than that of the Roman Catholic Church.[11] For both archbishops and bishops, a candidate must be at least thirty years of age (thirty-five in Roman Catholic canon law),[12] and

---

[3] Canon C17(1): 'By virtue of their respective offices, the Archbishop of Canterbury is styled Primate of All England and Metropolitan, and the Archbishop of York, Primate of England and Metropolitan.'   [4] Canon C18(2); for jurisdiction see below.

[5] Suffragan Bishops Act 1534; Dioceses Measure 1978, s. 10 (temporary delegation by episcopal instrument); *HLE*, para. 493: 'Strictly speaking all the bishops of a province are suffragans or helpers to the archbishop, but the term "suffragan" is now only applied to bishops who assist the diocesan bishop.'

[6] Dioceses Measure 1978, s. 11: permanent provision for episcopal areas by means of a reorganization scheme.

[7] For legal recognition of the office of 'assistant bishop' in (since repealed) legislation, see Church of England (Miscellaneous Provisions) Measure 1976, s. 3(1) (appointing as deputy 'a suffragan bishop, assistant bishop or archdeacon'); for example, the diocese of Oxford has 3 area bishops (suffragans) and 8 honorary assistant bishops (*ODYB: IF*, 19, 20). The title 'assistant bishop' is often given to retired bishops; Birmingham has a suffragan (Aston) and an assistant bishop; the diocese of Europe has a suffragan and the diocesan bishop may, at his discretion, authorize persons in episcopal orders to act as auxiliary bishops (Diocese in Europe, Draft Constitution (as approved by the diocesan synod, May 1995) GS 1159 8, 11); the Episcopal Ministry Act of Synod 1993, s. 4(3) refers to a 'full-time stipendiary assistant bishop' (which is distinguished from a suffragan).   [8] Episcopal Ministry Act of Synod 1993, ss. 2, 4.

[9] *CIC*, c. 376; auxiliary bishops are requested by a diocesan (c. 403(1)) or imposed on a diocesan (c. 403(2)); a coadjutor is an auxiliary bishop whose appointment confers a right to succeed (c. 409(1)).

[10] *CIC*, c. 435; for the assumption of titles and the Ecclesiastical Titles Act 1871 see *post* n. 50.

[11] *CIC*, c. 378: candidates must have a good reputation, be outstanding for their solid faith, good morals, zeal for souls, wisdom, prudence, and human virtues, and possess all the other talents necessary to fulfill the office.   [12] Canon C2(3); *BCP*, 554; *CIC*, c. 378(1), (3).

'godly and well-learned' (vouched as such by two bishops).[13] A woman cannot, at present, be consecrated bishop.[14] There is no express requirement in the Church of England, equivalent to that in Catholic canon law, that a candidate for episcopal orders must be a priest (of at least five years), nor that the candidate must possess prescribed academic qualifications.[15] As in Roman Catholic canon law, where the definitive judgment as to suitability of a candidate belongs to the pope, so in the Church of England, legally, this lies with the monarch as head of the church.[16]

In the Church of England, the admission procedure has three basic elements: nomination, election (and confirmation, discussed in the next section), and ordination or consecration. With the exception of nomination, scope for the laity's participation in the process is minimal. Though persons are appointed as bishops by the monarch as head of the church, the procedures for nomination vary as between the different episcopal offices. The subject is governed by both law and ecclesiastical convention. With regard to the appointment to the office of diocesan bishop, each diocese has by synodical regulation a Vacancy in See Committee designed to represent both the diocesan laity and clergy.[17] The committee has a power to discuss the names of persons who might be considered for episcopal appointment, although there is no duty to do so.[18] The committee may submit its suggested nominations to the Crown Appointments Commission, composed of both lay and clerical members elected from General

---

[13] *BCP*, 588; *ASB*, 387; birth out of lawful wedlock does not disqualify (Canon C2(4), Clergy (Ordination and Miscellaneous Provisions) Measure 1964, s. 8); a candidate must not have attained age 70: Ecclesiastical Offices (Age Limit) Measure 1975, s. 1(1), Sched. (which lists archbishops, diocesans, and suffragans); see below for retirement; the rules governing the ordination of divorced persons to the priesthood have not been expressly applied to candidates for episcopal office but may apply indirectly (see *post* Ch. 7).

[14] Priests (Ordination of Women) Measure 1993, s. 1(2): '[n]othing in this Measure shall make it lawful for a woman to be consecrated to the office of bishop'; see below n. 126 for the ministry of women bishops consecrated as such overseas.

[15] *CIC*, c. 378(1)(5): at least a licentiate in sacred scripture, theology, or canon law is required.

[16] *CIC*, c. 378(2): this gives an opportunity for judgments about suitability at a lower level e.g. by the conference of bishops. For the Church of England see *R v Archbishop of Canterbury* (1848) 11 QB 483; *R v Archbishop of Canterbury* [1902] 2 KB 503.

[17] Vacancy in See Committees Regs. 1993: the committee, which draws up a 'diocesan profile', has *inter alia* the diocesan bishop or suffragan as *ex officio* members, 2 clerics beneficed in the diocese or episcopally licensed elected by the House of Clergy of the diocesan synod, and not fewer than 2 actual communicant lay persons whose names are on the electoral roll of a parish in the diocese elected from the House of Laity of the diocesan synod (r. 1); it is the understood that *ex officio* members of the committee also have a right to stand for election to it: *OLAC*, 227 citing *R v Wimbledon Local Board* (1882) 8 QBD 459 and *R v Bishop of Salisbury* [1901] 1 KB 573 at 579; it must be ensured that every archdeaconry in the diocese will be adequately represented, but no procedure or test is posited: this is left in the discretion of the diocesan synod (r. 1(b)) and in practice it is often represented by the archdeacon.

[18] *OLAC*, 227: 'the committee could decide not to discuss such names and could resolve accordingly or, without a vote, could simply refrain from doing so. Its discretion is absolute' (under r. 5(d)); the committee is rarely mentioned in diocesan norms: see, however, *SDH*, VII, C.14; *SDDH*, V.18–19; *SADH*, B.16.

Synod as well as four members from the diocesan vacancy-in-see committee.[19] The Commission, in turn, is under a duty to agree upon two names which the appropriate archbishop submits to the prime minister, 'such names to be given in the order decided by the Commission'.[20] Pursuant to a prime ministerial statement of 1976, the prime minister has a right to recommend either name to the monarch or, indeed, to ask the Commission for further nominations.[21] There is no legal duty on the prime minister to act upon the nominations of either the diocesan committee or the Commission. The same procedures apply to the nomination of candidates for appointment as archbishop.[22] By Act of Synod no person shall discriminate against candidates for appointment to senior office in the Church of England on the grounds of their views or positions about the ordination of women to the priesthood.[23]

With regard to suffragans the right to nominate two candidates, deriving from parliamentary statute, rests with the diocesan bishop. The diocesan petitions the monarch who has a statutory power to appoint one of those named.[24] In exercising the right to nominate, the diocesan bishop is under no general legal duty to consult the laity or clergy of the diocese.[25] However, when a new suffragan see is to be created (or when the suffragan see has been vacant for five years or more) the diocesan's right to petition may be exercised only with the approval of both the diocesan synod and General Synod after consultation with the Dioceses Commission.[26]

Appointment to other episcopal offices from existing pools of persons

[19] Vacancy in See Committees Regs. 1993, r. 5(d); *GSSO*, SO 159 (3 members are elected from the House of Laity and 3 from the House of Clergy).

[20] *GSSO*, SO 122(d); it has a duty to report to synod from time to time 'as [it] deems expedient'.

[21] See *Senior Church Appointments* (London, 1992) para. 5.1 ff.; see also St. A. Robilliard, *Religion and the Law* (Manchester, 1984) 91: 'there is clearly no constitutional convention that the state must accept the first choice of the Church'; *Episcopal Ministry* (1990) para. 507; B. Palmer, *High and Mitred: Prime Ministers as Bishop Makers, 1837–1977* (London, 1992).

[22] *GSSO*, SO 159(b),(c); when the Commission considers a vacancy of the Archbishopric of Canterbury, the chairman is appointed by the prime minister, and when a vacancy of the Archbishopric of York, by synod's Standing Committee).

[23] Episcopal Ministry Act 1993, s. 1.

[24] Suffragan Bishops Act 1534, s. 1; for prime ministerial advice see *Senior Church Appointments* (1992) para. 5.1; the normal practice is for one to be the diocesan bishop's preference and the other to be a 'sleeping partner': there is precedent for the second name having to be changed to secure the appointment the diocesan wanted, when the sleeping partner was known well and admired by the prime minister (*Episcopal Ministry* (1990), para. 507, n. 22).

[25] Diocesan practices vary: usually the bishop's council, the diocesan synod, and the appropriate archbishop are consulted: *Senior Church Appointments*, paras. 5.4, 6.2 f., recommending, *inter alia*, the creation of an 'appointing group' to consider the needs of the diocese and the qualities needed for a suffragan: para. 6.2 ff.

[26] Dioceses Measure 1978, s. 18; the Howick Commission on Crown Appointments (1964) recommended that the archbishop and diocesan should nominate together with only one name submitted to the monarch; the Chadwick Commission (1970), 139, recommended that its proposed systems of appointment of diocesans should also apply to the appointment of suffragans coupled with a requirement for the diocesan's consent: see generally *Senior Church Appointments* and, for the case for change, ibid., para. 4.1 ff.

already admitted to the episcopal order may be made without recourse to the monarch. The appointment of 'flying bishops' is regulated by Act of Synod designed to provide pastoral arrangements in a diocese for those opposed to the promulgation of the canon enabling the ordination of women as priests. Its object is to ensure that the highest possible degree of communion be maintained within each diocese and that the integrity of differing beliefs and positions concerning the ordination of women to the priesthood be recognized and respected.[27] The appropriate archbishop is to designate a region (an area comprising two or more dioceses in a province) the bishops of which (diocesan, suffragan, or full-time stipendiary assistant bishops) acting jointly shall nominate from within their region one or more bishops who are opposed. The nominated bishop is to act as bishop for those in any parish opposed.[28] The archbishop, it seems, has no right to veto the nomination.[29] Furthermore, the Act of Synod provides for the appointment of bishops entrusted with the pastoral care of those opposed at a provincial level. A duty is placed on each archbishop to secure the appointment of additional suffragan bishops for his province (one or two for Canterbury and one for York) 'to act as a provincial episcopal visitor'.[30] When a vacancy occurs in the office of episcopal visitor, the right to appoint a successor vests in the archbishop. However, before appointing a successor the archbishop shall consult the other provincial episcopal visitor(s) and all other bishops directly concerned.[31] The act confers a right upon the parochial church council to petition the diocesan bishop for episcopal duties within the parish to be carried out by the regional bishop or episcopal visitor; the diocesan, after consultation with the minister and parochial church council, 'shall make' the appropriate arrangements.[32]

Finally, the diocesan bishop has a legal power, in the diocesan's illness or absence, to appoint by instrument an episcopal delegate to discharge all or any of the diocesan's functions. The instrument must specify all functions delegated. This appointment can be made without the consent of the diocesan synod but he must consult the bishop's council and standing committee.[33] Formally, with regard to selection of all types of episcopal office, the system allows for the direct participation of the laity only in relation to the nomination of diocesans. Furthermore, whereas rights to nominate and appoint diocesans, suffragans, and episcopal delegates derive from law, rights to appoint regional

---

[27] Episcopal Ministry Act 1993, Preamble, (3) and s. 12(1); the first two 'flying bishops' were not taken from the pool of existing bishops but were both archdeacons. For a cautionary reaction in the context of an historical survey see R. Turner, 'Bonds of discord: alternative episcopal oversight examined in the light of the nonjuring consecrations', *ELJ*, 3 (1995), 398.

[28] Ss. 12(1), 2(b) and 4

[29] S. 4(2): 'Each bishop so nominated shall . . . be approved by the archbishop of the province'.

[30] S. 5(1), (2). It has been proposed that a diocesan bishop should be empowered to invite a provincial episcopal visitor to be a member of the diocesan synod where he resides: draft Church Representation (Amendment) Resolution 1995, GS 1174X.   [31] S. 6.

[32] Ss. 7, 8(1).   [33] Church of England (Miscellaneous Provisions) Measure 1983, s. 8.

bishops and episcopal vicars, conferred by Act of Synod, may not *prima facie* be legally enforceable.[34]

EPISCOPAL AUTHORITY: ELECTION AND CONSECRATION

Though governed by parliamentary statute, episcopal appointments in the Church of England are made by the monarch acting on the advice of the prime minister, advice which, by constitutional convention, the monarch is ordinarily bound to accept.[35] With regard to archbishops and diocesan bishops, the monarch grants a licence (a *congé d'élire*) and a letter missive, containing the name of the candidate, authorizing an election which is carried out by the dean and chapter of the cathedral of the vacant diocese. If the dean and chapter do not act with all speed and celerity but defer the election beyond twelve days of delivery of the licence and letter missive, the monarch has a power to nominate by letters patent (to the provincial archbishop) and to present such person as she considers suitable to fill the vacancy. Once a certification of the election is made to the monarch the person elected takes the title of lord elect of the bishopric.[36] With respect to archbishops, the monarch must signify the election to the other archbishop and two bishops and the election is then confirmed.[37] With respect to bishops, the monarch signifies the election to the appropriate archbishop commanding him to confirm the election; the archbishop commissions the vicar-general to effect confirmation.[38] At confirmation the archbishop takes an oath of allegiance to the crown, as does a bishop who also takes an oath of obedience to the archbishop.[39] In relation to suffragans, the monarch appoints one of the diocesan's two nominees and sends letters patent to the appropriate archbishop requiring him to consecrate that person within three months unless he is already a bishop.[40] In the entire process, the only opportunity for lay participation is the negative one of

[34] See *supra* Ch. 3.

[35] The conventional duty to follow ministerial advice applies classically to the exercise of prerogative power (G. Marshall, *Constitutional Conventions* (Oxford, 1984) Ch. 1); as the monarch's power to appoint is derived from statute (Appointment of Bishops Act 1534) the royal power is not, strictly, a prerogatival power, but a statutory power (see generally *Council of Civil Service Unions v Minister for the Civil Service* [1985] AC 374); see also *AG v De Keyser's Royal Hotel* [1920] AC 508; *R v Secretary of State for the Home Department, ex p Fire Brigades Union* [1995] 2 All ER 244 for the displacement of prerogative by statute; it is arguable, therefore, that technically any conventional rule which requires 'blind' appointments (fettering the use of this statutory power) is illegal (for fettering of discretion see *post* Ch. 13, n. 159); though it contains a review of the role of convention, this point is not considered in *Senior Church Appointments* (1992): paras. 5.19–5.25.   [36] Appointment of Bishops Act 1533, s. 3.

[37] Ibid., ss. 3, 4.

[38] Ibid., s. 4; Canon C17(4): 'to [the archbishop] belongs the right of confirming the election of every person to a bishopric.'   [39] Ibid., and Canons C13, C14.

[40] Suffragan Bishops Act 1534, ss. 1, 3; Suffragan Bishops Act 1898, s. 1; see also Suffragan Nominations Act 1888.

objection at confirmation of the election, on the grounds that the election was defective as to form or that the person presented for confirmation was not the royal appointee.[41] The process has been the subject of considerable criticism in recent years.[42]

The legal position of the Church of England is not dissimilar to that of the Roman Catholic Church, in which bishops are appointed by the head of the church. An office in the church is acquired either by conferral or by election,[43] and the pope freely appoints bishops or confirms their election by others.[44] The first stage of the process is designation, of which there are two types. The bishops of a province or the episcopal conference have a duty to draw up in secret a list of presbyteral candidates every three years.[45] The list is sent to the Holy See and the pope selects. Alternatively, the pontifical legate may propose and transmit names of candidates.[46] It is the legate's duty to gather information and opinions from the metropolitan, the suffragans of the province, the president of the episcopal conference, and members of the college of consultors and of the cathedral chapter, and to communicate these, 'together with his own preference', to the pontiff.[47] Importantly, the legate has only a discretion, if he judges it expedient, to obtain individually and in secret the opinion of other members of the clergy 'as well as of the laity who are outstanding for their wisdom'; there is no duty to discern the views of the laity.[48] Similarly, there is no duty on a diocesan bishop to consult the clergy or laity in exercising the right to request an auxiliary bishop when proposing a list of at least three suitable priests to the Apostolic See.[49] The Code expressly provides that '[n]o rights and privileges of election, nomination, presentation, or designation of bishops are hereafter granted to civil authorities'.[50]

---

[41] *Mandamus* does not lie to compel the archbishop to hear and determine objections on grounds of unsoundness or doctrine: *R v Archbishop of Canterbury* [1902] 2 KB 503 at 562–3.

[42] For analysis of the many recommendations that have been made see *Senior Church Appointments* (1992): two suggestions were made, one introducing an advisory committee, the other an electoral board, both composed of the 2 archbishops, 6 members of General Synod (including at least 3 lay people, 1 diocesan), 4 members of the vacancy-in-see committee of the diocese involved, and the dean or provost of the diocesan cathedral. *GSRP*, Feb. 1982, Feb. 1983, Nov. 1984, and Feb. 1985 (for debates on the Appointment of Bishops Measure which was rejected by the House of Commons). [43] *CIC*, c. 147.

[44] C. 377(1).

[45] C. 377(2): individual bishops also have a right to propose names; on the episcopal conference see *CD*, 20.

[46] The legate is an apostolic delegate whose function is to strengthen the bonds between the Apostolic See and the particular church (*CIC*, c. 364). [47] C. 377(3).

[48] Ibid.; the canonical rationale is found, arguably, in c. 211 (the right to be involved in the church's mission), c. 212(3) (the right to express an opinion), and c. 119 (what touches all must be approved by all). For criticism of these structures see the studies in G. Alberigo and A. Weller (eds.), *Election—Consensus—Reception, Concilium*, 7(8) (1972), and in P. Huizing and K. Walf (eds.), *Electing Our Own Bishops, Concilium* (1980). [49] *CIC*, c. 377(4).

[50] C. 377(5); when the title of bishop is not already legally appropriated on behalf of the Church of England, the title of bishop may be used by the Roman Catholic Church as connected with some place in the realm: Ecclesiastical Titles Act, 1871, Preamble.

In addition to the rules allowing appointment by conferral, the Code provides the possibility of electing bishops, but the election must be confirmed by the pope and the practice is not extensive.[51] When a see is impeded (physically or legally),[52] the coadjutor (if there is one) succeeds automatically, but if not the college of consultors selects a priest to govern the diocese.[53] If a see is vacated by death, resignation, deprivation, or transfer the coadjutor succeeds; if there is none, an administrator is elected by the college of consultors.[54] Metropolitans are not elected but are designated as such by the pontiff.[55]

In both churches, for admission to episcopal orders a person must be consecrated and ordained bishop. Roman Catholic canon law prescribes that, unless there is a legitimate impediment, whoever is promoted to the office of bishop must receive consecration within three months of the receipt of the apostolic letter effecting or confirming appointment. A papal mandate is required for episcopal consecration.[56] Before taking possession of the diocese, the appointee must make a profession of faith and take an oath of fidelity to the Apostolic See.[57] Valid episcopal ordination occurs only when effected by a consecrated bishop and, unless a dispensation has been granted by the pope, the consecrating bishop must be assisted by at least two other consecrating bishops.[58] The common opinion is that, in terms of validity, the consecration of a bishop by one bishop is valid, but in terms of liceity co-consecrators are required.[59] The episcopal consecration 'should take place' on a Sunday 'when a large number of the faithful can attend'. The participation of the laity is minimal: they simply assent to an appointment already made.[60] Liturgical norms recommend that the ordination be accompanied by a celebration of the Eucharist and they command the reading of the papal mandate. The liturgy stresses that the bishop-elect has been chosen by God to fulfill the charism of leadership within the church; the laying-on of hands confirms the gift of leadership conferred by the Holy Spirit and effects the individual's acceptance into the College of Bishops.[61] According to the Code it is through the Holy Spirit given to them that bishops are successors to the apostles by divine institution: by episcopal consecration they receive the episcopal function.[62]

---

[51] *CIC*, c. 377(1); in e.g. Germany and Switzerland cathedral chapters (cc. 503–10) still enjoy rights of election: see R. Trisco, 'The variety of procedures in modern history', in W. Bassett (ed.), *The Choosing of Bishops* (Hartford, 1971) 33.   [52] *CIC*, cc. 412, 415.

[53] C. 413: normally, on taking office, the diocesan draws up a list of coadjutors to cover the eventuality of impediment. The college of consultors is involved if there is no list; the pontiff must be informed. Members of the college of consultors are selected by the diocesan and drawn from the presbyteral council (c. 502).

[54] Cc. 418, 421; the episcopal conference may delegate the college of consultor's right to elect to the cathedral chapter (c. 503); if the college fails to act the metropolitan may do so (c. 436).

[55] C. 435.   [56] Cc. 379, 1013.

[57] C. 380 (for taking canonical possession see c. 382).

[58] Cc. 1012, 1013, 1014; see also *Rites*, Vol. 2, 87.

[59] *CIC: TC*, 719, n. 41; a bishop who consecrates without a papal mandate (c. 1013) is excommunicated (c. 1382).

[60] *Rites*, Vol. 2, 89; see also the apostolic constitution *Pontificalis Romani* (1968).

[61] *Rites*, Vol. 2, 94–6; *LG*, 21.   [62] *CIC*, c. 375.

Episcopal ordination confers an indelible character and expresses the fullness or totality of the sacrament of orders.[63]

A similar scheme operates in the Church of England. After confirmation the bishop-elect must be consecrated: '[n]o person shall be consecrated to the office of bishop by fewer than three bishops present together and joining in the act of consecration'. One of the bishops must be the archbishop of the province (as 'the chief consecrator') or a bishop appointed to act on his behalf.[64] If the chapter refuses to elect, the appropriate archbishop must consecrate the person nominated and presented.[65] Episcopal consecration must be carried out in the form prescribed by the authorized liturgies.[66] The decision as to which form of service is to be used rests solely with the appropriate archbishop.[67] The liturgy is built around the presentation of the bishop-elect, the reading of the royal mandate, and the required declarations of assent to the church's doctrine. The ordination itself is effected by the laying-on of hands, the recital of the words of consecration, and the sending down of the Holy Spirit.[68] Following consecration, the new bishop is installed in the bishopric and pays homage to the monarch.[69]

EPISCOPAL FUNCTIONS: BASIC POWERS AND DUTIES

Theologically, episcopal authority is in a fundamental way conceived by both churches to be charismatic, a gift of the Holy Spirit and recognized as such in the liturgies of episcopal consecration. The purpose of legislation is merely to define, organize, recall, and facilitate the exercise of the charism of leadership.[70] The law achieves this by attaching to episcopal ministry particular functions and responsibilities. Their nature and extent are dependent on the episcopal office in question.

[63] *LG*, 21; J. W. M. Hendricks, 'On the sacramentality of the episcopal consecration', *Studia Canonica*, 28 (1994), 231.

[64] C2(1); consecration must take place on a Sunday or Holy Day, unless the archbishop 'for urgent and weighty cause' appoints another day (C2(2)); see also C17(4). As archbishops are translated from another see, there is no consecration as when a bishop is translated from one diocese to another: *HLE*, paras. 429, n. 3, 471.   [65] Appointment of Bishops Act 1533, s. 4.

[66] Canon B1; see *post* Ch. 10.   [67] Canon B3(5).

[68] *BCP*, 593 ff.; *ASB*, 382 ff.; the idea occasionally surfaces in diocesan norms: see e.g. *LDHI*, IV, 1.1: 'the authority to exercise episcopal responsibility is vested in each diocese in one person, the Bishop of that diocese, who is the focus of that authority which is derived from God and given to the church'; for scriptural material on episcopal charisms see *Episcopal Ministry* (1990) paras. 31 ff.

[69] Appointment of Bishops Act 1533, s. 5; see below for the oath of allegiance and exceptions to it.

[70] This relation between charismatic authority and juridical authority poses a fundamental problem for canon law: see e.g. J. H. Casado, 'Renewal and effectiveness in canon law', *Studia Canonica*, 28 (1994), 5 at 9, and *supra* Ch. 2.

Archbishops

There are subtle differences between the roles of archbishops in each church: in the Church of England the archbishop is to correct defects in diocesan episcopal ministry; in the Roman Catholic Church the archbishop is to report these for correction by the pontiff. It is the duty of the Catholic metropolitan to ensure that the faith and discipline of the dioceses entrusted to him are preserved and to inform the pontiff of abuses. He is to perform the canonical visitation if the diocesan neglects to do so and may be invested by the pope with special duties and powers.[71] He has a right to receive synodal declarations and decrees from the diocesan and to suggest candidates for episcopal appointment.[72] It is for the metropolitan to convoke, preside over, set the agenda of, and dissolve the provincial council; these he can do only with the consent of the majority of diocesan bishops of the province.[73] If a diocesan is prohibited from exercising his functions, the metropolitan must make recourse to Rome for the Holy See to make appropriate arrangements for episcopal oversight in the diocese.[74] Beyond this function of vigilance, the metropolitan has no power of governance within the suffragan diocese.[75]

In the Church of England, the archbishop has throughout his province at all times 'metropolitical jurisdiction', as 'superintendent of all ecclesiastical matters', 'to correct and supply the defects of other bishops'.[76] Within his province, the archbishop is the 'principal minister'; generally, there is equality in the respective legal positions of the two archbishops.[77] Like the Roman Catholic metropolitan, the archbishop presides over the provincial convocation; unlike the Roman Catholic metropolitan, the archbishop possesses the right to confirm the election of diocesans, to be chief consecrator at an episcopal consecration, and to hold metropolitical visitations.[78] The archbishop has a right to permit any minister who has been ordained priest or

---

[71] *CIC*, c. 436. For his powers when a see is vacant, and when the college of consultors has failed to act, see c. 421; if a diocesan is for more than six months absent unlawfully from the diocese, the metropolitan must inform the Apostolic See (c. 395(4)).   [72] Cc. 467, 377.

[73] C. 442.   [74] C. 415.

[75] C. 436(3). He may, however, perform liturgical functions in any church within a suffragan diocese, but in the cathedral only after informing the diocesan; the *pallium* signifies his authority (c. 437).

[76] C17(2); each archbishop has his own diocese: in post–1925 measures ' 'bishop' ' in relation to the diocese of the archbishop means "archbishop" (Interpretation Measure 1925, s. 3; SGM 1969, s. 2(2)). The archbishop's jurisdiction is exercised by the archbishop himself, or by a vicar-general, official, or other commissary to whom authority has been formally committed by the archbishop (C17(3)).

[77] The Archbishop of Canterbury enjoys several special privileges: to crown the monarch; to grant in both provinces licences, dispensations, and faculties formerly belonging to the pope (Ecclesiastical Licences Act 1533, ss. 2, 4; C17(7), see *supra* Ch. 2); he is chairman of the Church Commissioners (see Ch. 17 *post*); the Archbishop of York has the privilege to crown a Queen Consort and both archbishops have a seat in the House of Lords: see *HLE*, paras. 433, 434.

[78] C17(4); the two archbishops are joint presidents of the General Synod; for visitations see *supra* Ch. 4 and for the archbishop's judicial role, Ch. 5.

deacon by an overseas bishop, or a bishop of a church not in communion with the Church of England (but whose orders are recognized or accepted by the Church of England), to officiate within the province.[79] He also has a statutory right to consecrate persons (British subjects and others) to be bishops in 'any foreign country'.[80] Like the Roman Catholic metropolitan, the archbishop possesses certain functions concerning vacant sees. On a vacancy the archbishop automatically becomes 'guardian of the spiritualities' of a diocese[81] and as such must exercise the spiritual jurisdiction of the diocese.[82] Importantly, the archbishop's right to obedience from bishops is the general basis of his disciplinary powers over them.[83] The archbishop has an extensive range of rights and responsibilities both with regard to doctrine and liturgy and in the legislative, administrative, and judicial processes of the Church of England.[84]

Diocesan Bishops

In the Roman Catholic Church the bishop's functions (*munera*) are to sanctify, to teach, and to govern, functions received at episcopal ordination and exercisable only when the bishop is in hierarchical communion with the pontiff.[85] As an ordained minister, a bishop is bound by law to show reverence and obedience, and by oath to show fidelity, to the pontiff.[86] In his diocese, the bishop possesses all the ordinary, proper, and immediate power required for the exercise of his pastoral office,[87] an office which extends to all, Christians and non-Christians, in the diocese.[88] The bishop possesses legislative, executive, and judicial power to govern the diocese, which must be exercised in accordance with the norm of law (c. 391); he oversees the discipline of both the diocesan clergy and the laity (c. 392) and also administers, or oversees the administration of, property within the diocese (cc. 1276,

---

[79] C17(6); and the Overseas and Other Clergy (Ministry and Ordination) Measure 1967, s. 1(2)): 'such minister shall possess all such rights and advantages and be subject to all such duties and liabilities as he would have possessed and been subject to if he had been ordained by the bishop of a diocese in the province of Canterbury and York.'

[80] Bishops in Foreign Countries Act 1841, s. 1; he may also dispense with the oath of canonical obedience of a such a person: Colonial Clergy Act 1874, s. 12; C14(2).

[81] C19(2); he (or his nominee(s)) acts as diocesan guardian if by prescription or composition this role does not belong to the dean and chapter of the cathedral church. In the diocese of Durham the dean and chapter claim and exercise guardianship: *MIECL*, 26. During a vacancy of a metropolitical see the dean and chapter of the metropolitical cathedral possess guardianship of both the province and diocese: C19(1). The crown is guardian of temporalities: *HLE*, paras. 358, 488 and *Covert's Case* (1600) Cro Eliz 754.

[82] C19(3): including the giving of institution to benefices, the granting of licences for solemnization of marriage without banns, and the granting of commissions for ordination; he may not, however, present to benefices of which the bishop is patron: this role belongs to the crown 'by royal prerogative': see *OLAC*, 21 and *post* Ch. 7.   [83] See *post* n. 91.

[84] See Parts II and IV.   [85] *CIC*, c. 375; *LG*, 20–1.   [86] Cc. 273, 380.

[87] C. 381 (except those reserved to a superior ecclesiastical authority).

[88] C. 383; he is to attend to the presbyters 'with special concern' (c. 384) and to foster vocations in the diocese (cc. 385, 394).

1287). The bishop represents the diocese in all juridic affairs (c. 393). As teacher, the bishop must protect, present, and explain the doctrine of the faith, preach frequently, and oversee the ministry of the word and catechetical formation (c. 386). As sanctifier, the bishop must set a personal example of holiness, to promote the holiness of the faithful and to ensure that the faithful 'grow in grace through the celebration of the sacraments' (c. 387) and he must celebrate mass for the people regularly (c. 388).[89] He must reside within the diocese for at least eleven months each year (c. 395), conduct a pastoral visitation of the diocese at least once every five years (cc. 396–8), and report on the condition of the diocese to the pope every five years (c. 399), as well as appearing before the pontiff during the same year as he submits his report (c. 400).

In the Church of England episcopal functions vary between the different episcopal offices. The rights and duties of diocesan bishops are scattered and defined throughout the canons, synodical and parliamentary legislation, and judicial decisions.[90] Every person to be made diocesan bishop must take the oath of 'due obedience' to the archbishop and his successors as well as an oath of allegiance to the monarch as head of the church.[91] As in the Roman Catholic Church, according to the canons the bishop is 'the chief pastor of all that are within his diocese, as well laity as clergy, and their father in God'. His office is one of teacher ('to teach and to uphold sound and wholesome doctrine'),[92] governor (to 'maintain quietness, love, and peace', and to exercise 'jurisdiction as ordinary'),[93] and principal minister (having the right 'of conducting, ordering, controlling, and authorising all services in churches').[94] This three-fold ministry is commonly presented in descriptive diocesan norms which

---

[89] See T. J. Green, 'Rights and duties of diocesan bishops', *Readings*, 229; T. J. Green, 'The pastoral governance role of the diocesan bishop: foundations scope and limitations', *The Jurist*, 49 (1989), 472.

[90] For the theological setting of episcopal functions see J. Tiller, *A Strategy for the Church's Ministry* (London, 1985) 89 ff., and generally *Episcopal Ministry* (1990).

[91] C14(1); the *BCP* form is: 'In the name of God, Amen. I, A.B., chosen bishop of the Church and See of . . . do profess and promise all due reverence and obedience to the Archbishop and to the Metropolitical Church of . . . and to their Successors: So help me God, through Jesus Christ'; the oath of allegiance to the monarch is set out in C13(1): 'I, A.B., do swear that I will be faithful and bear true allegiance to Her Majesty Queen Elizabeth II, her heirs and successors, according to law: So help me God'; under C13(2) the oath of allegiance is not required to be taken by any subject or citizen of a foreign state whom either archbishop (calling to assist him such bishops as he thinks fit) consecrates to officiate as a bishop in any foreign state. For declarations of assent to the church's doctrine see *post* Ch. 9.

[92] C18(1); for the Church of England Advisory Council on the Relations of Bishops and Religious Communities see the norms contained in *A Directory of the Religious Life* (4th edn., London, 1990).

[93] C18 (1), (2) (except those places and persons exempt by law or custom); C18(3): jurisdiction is to be exercised by himself or by a vicar-general, official, or other commissary to whom he has formally committed authority; the bishop is a corporation sole: *HLE*, para. 458; for a discussion of episcopal jurisdiction see *Episcopal Ministry* (1992) paras. 324–8.   [94] C18(4).

often stress episcopal ministry as being shared with that of the whole church.[95]

Within this general canonical framework the diocesan bishop's actual and potential workload, imposed or empowered by law, is enormous and perhaps excessive: its size has recently been the subject of considerable criticism.[96] The diocesan is obliged to involve himself in almost every aspect of life in the Church of England, from national to parochial level. The diocesan bishop's rights and duties within the diocese are summarized in Canon C18. As prescribed by canon his general rights include celebrating ordination and confirmation, granting faculties concerning diocesan property, consecrating churches, churchyards, and burial grounds, and instituting to all vacant benefices (whether of his own collation or of the presentation of another). He is empowered to admit by licence to all other vacant ecclesiastical offices, to hold visitations, and to be president of the diocesan synod.[97] As prescribed by canon his general duties include: assenting to resolutions of the diocesan synod (an assent which he may withhold for 'grave cause'), ensuring (as much as in him lies) that there shall be suitable and sufficient priests to minister the word and sacraments to the people, correcting and punishing, according to law, 'all such as be unquiet, disobedient, or criminous, within his diocese', residing within his diocese except for the performance of duties of his office outside the diocese.[98]

As may be seen from the other studies in this volume, in addition to these functions generally fixed by canon innumerable and more detailed functions are allocated to the diocesan by synodical measure. With respect to the diocese: though his powers of law-making and dispensation are very limited, in practice the diocesan is directly involved in the creation of executive norms and in visitatorial, adjudicative, and disciplinary processes. With regard to diocesan administration, as well as his obligatory involvement in the work of diocesan administrative bodies, including work concerning financial and property matters, he has extensive powers of veto over diocesan and parochial reorganization schemes and appointments.[99] With respect to the Church of England nationally, as well as state-related functions, the diocesan may be

---

[95] *LDHI*, IV, 1.3: 'The Bishop has clearly to lead his diocese, to articulate the truths of the faith and the gospel and to be the kind of prophetic voice which inspires, enthuses and encourages the People of God'; *PDH*, I.A: the bishop's functions include 'preserving the unity of the Church . . . safeguarding its faith, and guiding its morals'; 'the episcopate is responsible for Christian Belief, the Christian Way and the Christian Community'; for a similar formula see *SDDH*, A.1–2; *CF*, A.1.1; see *TBF*, 1.1(a) for the 'right of direct access to the Diocesan Bishop'.

[96] *Episcopal Ministry* (1990) paras. 383–7.

[97] C18(4); whether a bishop's charge to his clergy enjoys absolute privilege, ousting the possibility of an action for libel, has not been decided judicially: see *Laughton v Bishop of Sodor and Man* (1872) LR 4 PC 495 (at 504, it was held to be a 'privileged' communication in the ordinary sense of the term, but its publication in a local newspaper may not be: at 502).

[98] C18(5)–(8).

[99] These subjects are treated elsewhere in this study in the appropriate chapters; for the doctrine of 'bishop-in-synod', see *Episcopal Ministry* (1990) para. 825 and e.g. *LDHI*, IV, 1.3.

involved in a wide range of collegial acts performed in concert with the other diocesans. From the General Synod's House of Bishops the diocesan participates directly in the process of legislating (by measure and canon) and in the creation of norms issuing from that House by way of guidelines. Collegially, a bishop enjoys a power of veto over law-making when special procedures are required. Individually, consultation with the diocesan is required for the making of a host of quasi-legislative instruments. He may also be called upon to perform judicial functions in the church's superior courts as well as executive functions through membership of the many subordinate bodies of General Synod and, *ex officio*, as a Church Commissioner.[100] In short, in the contemporary church the operative doctrine of episcopal oversight as reflected in actual law is one which demands direct personal participation and management rather than vicarious and general responsibility for the life of the ecclesiastical community.[101]

Suffragan and Other Assistant Bishops

Given the extent of the diocesan's functions, sharing episcopal ministry is crucial; indeed, delegation itself may be conceived as more readily enhancing a doctrine of episcopal oversight in which the diocesan retains overall responsibility for management effected by others. In addition to the plethora of diocesan bodies and persons fulfilling executive and advisory roles,[102] the diocesan may be assisted by other bishops within the diocese. Episcopal functions, as a general rule, may be delegated only horizontally, so to speak, to those in episcopal orders, principally to suffragan bishops.[103]

The suffragan's position is subordinate to that of the diocesan: the rights and duties of suffragans are designed both by law and by the diocesan seeking his appointment. Though he takes no oath of obedience to the diocesan, the suffragan has a duty to execute faithfully such things pertaining to the episcopal office as shall be delegated to him by the diocesan bishop; his only general right is to exercise or discharge this duty as the terms of episcopal office permit and as the diocesan directs.[104] The Dioceses Measure 1978 deals with the terms of delegation, and diocesan norms commonly

---

[100] See Chs. 3, 4, 17; for theological aspects of collegiality see *Episcopal Ministry* (1990) para. 303.

[101] For a call to review 'episcopal priorities . . . with a view to freeing bishops for the work which properly falls to them alone' see *Episcopal Ministry*, para. 387. The Bishops of London, Durham, and Winchester sit *ex officiis* in the House of Lords, along with 21 other bishops in order of seniority of appointment: *HLE*, paras. 351, 479; for recommendations that other churches should be similarly represented see *Episcopal Ministry* (1990) para. 501; see generally G. Drewry and J. Brock, 'Prelates in parliament', *Parliamentary Affairs*, 14 (1971) 222.   [102] See *supra* Ch. 4.

[103] For exceptions, where persons other than those in episcopal orders may share in episcopal ordinary jurisdiction, see *supra* n. 93 (for diocesans) and n. 76 (for archbishops).

[104] C20(1) and (2); Suffragan Bishops Act 1534, s. 4.

contain lists of functions exercisable by suffragans, some stressing the principle of shared episcopal ministry, others the principle of episcopal collegiality, and some underlining the ultimate supremacy of the diocesan.[105]

The diocesan bishop has a power, with the consent of the diocesan synod, to delegate by instrument to a suffragan any of the diocesan's functions (and the instrument must specify all functions delegated) subject to such conditions as are specified in the instrument; he may delegate by instrument the functions of administering confirmation and ordination without the consent of the diocesan synod. The instrument specifies whether these functions can be discharged throughout the diocese or only in a particular area, and whether they may be exercised independently by the suffragan or jointly with the diocesan.[106] The suffragan's delegated powers cease when, *inter alia*, the diocesan or the suffragan cease to hold office; the diocesan has the power to vary or revoke an instrument with the consent of the diocesan synod; its consent is not required, however, if the instrument simply delegates functions of ordination and confirmation.[107] Delegation to a suffragan does not divest the diocesan of any of his functions.[108] The suffragan must reside within the diocese, except with the licence of the diocesan.[109] He has a specific right to be elected to the Upper House of Convocation, and therefore to membership of General Synod's House of Bishops.[110] Whilst these provisions confer on the diocesan a considerable degree of flexibility, there may be no uniformity of practice between dioceses.[111]

More permanent arrangements for the delegation of episcopal functions may be made when a diocese is the subject of a reorganization scheme and is divided into areas.[112] The scheme must provide for episcopal oversight to be vested in the diocesan, or in a suffragan, or to be shared by them jointly: it is the scheme, which must be approved by General Synod, that defines which functions attaching to the diocesan are to be discharged by the suffragan of the 'episcopal area'.[113] The scheme may impose conditions including the obligation, when the oversight of the diocese is shared by more than two bishops, to meet together periodically in an episcopal chapter.[114] A right is reserved to the

---

[105] *TDH*, E.5; *WBRG*, A.1; *LDHI*, IV, 1.4. Turning to the suffragan does not 'preclude any clergyman from looking for direct pastoral or other advice from the Diocesan Bishop nor the Bishop from giving it'; *SDDH*, A.1 (collegiality), I, A.4 (delegation lists); *TBF*, 1.1(b); *CF*, A.1.2,1.6; *LBGCP*, 2.

[106] Dioceses Measure 1978, s. 10(1)–(4); s. 24(1): 'functions' includes 'powers and duties'.

[107] S. 10(6), (8)–(10).   [108] S. 10(13).

[109] C20(3): the canon does not specify the form or terms of the licence; Suffragan Bishops Act 1534, s. 6 proviso.

[110] Canon H3(1); he is an *ex officio* member of the diocesan synod's House of Bishops (*CRR*, r. 30(2)) and pastoral committee (Pastoral Measure 1983, Sched. 1, para. 3).

[111] *Episcopal Ministry* (1990) para. 420; see also para. 426 for concern over the theology of suffragans 'as an anomoly born of pastoral necessity'.   [112] See *supra* Ch. 4.

[113] Dioceses Measure 1978, s. 11(1), (2), (4).

[114] S. 11(3), (5); for the chapter in diocesan norms see e.g. *CF*, A.1.5 (it must meet on no less than six occasions each year).

diocesan to propose amendments to or revocation of the scheme, but once a
scheme is made it shall bind the bishop of the diocese and his successors.[115]
Though episcopal functions may be redistributed, still the diocesan can perform any of the delegated episcopal functions.[116] With regard to revocation of
both temporary and permanent delegation arrangements, there are no express
provisions for reasons to be given or for a right of appeal against revocation.[117]

The rights and duties of 'flying bishops', ministering to those opposed to the
ordination and ministry of women as priests, are governed by Act of Synod. Its
rules are rudimentary and in general reserve to the diocesan a considerable
degree of oversight and control. The regional bishop is to carry out for any
parish in the opposed region such duties as the diocesan concerned may
request.[118] There is no express obligation for the diocesan and regional to
meet together. The episcopal visitor, who also must carry out those duties
which the diocesan requests, is under a duty to work with the diocesan in
enabling extended pastoral care and sacramental ministry to be provided, to
act as spokesman and adviser for those opposed, and to assist the archbishops in
monitoring the operation of the Act of Synod.[119] The synodical act makes no
detailed provision for the diocesan to specify the terms of the functions of the
regional bishop or the episcopal visitor, nor does it expressly reserve to the
diocesan the right to perform his episcopal functions to those opposed.[120] When
a see is vacant, or a diocesan is absent or incapacitated through illness, the
diocesan's functions are exercisable by the archbishop of the province.[121]

'Assistant bishops', 'honorary assistant bishops', and 'auxiliary bishops',
resident in the diocese but not falling within the formal categories discussed
above, act only with the direct permission of the diocesan and sometimes
provision is made to ensure that they act in an episcopal capacity only through
prior consultation with the diocesan.[122] The position of the ministry in England

---

[115] S. 13(2). It must be approved by the diocesan synod: s. 13(5); "amendment" includes
revocation: s. 13(7); s. 11(6).   [116] S. 11(7).
[117] It is possible that the common law principles of natural justice and procedural fairness apply:
for these see *supra* Ch. 5.
[118] Episcopal Ministry Act of Synod 1993, s. 4(2); *Code of Practice* (1993), App. A.
[119] S. 5(3), (4).
[120] It does, however, state that '[t]he diocesan bishop shall make arrangements so far as possible
within his own diocese for appropriate care and oversight of the clergy and parishes in the diocese'
(ibid., s. 3); for the effect of parochial resolutions see *post* Ch. 7. A diocesan also has the right, with
the consent and licence of the appropriate archbishop, to request and commission in writing the
assistance of an overseas bishop, or a bishop consecrated in a church not in communion with the
Church of England (whose orders are recognized and accepted); the assisting bishop may ordain
persons and perform other episcopal functions (which are not specified): Overseas and Other
Clergy (Ministry and Ordination) Measure 1967, s. 4(1); see *OLAC*, 192–3.
[121] For vacancy, see C19; in relation to absence or illness, this arrangement is also provided for
in specific circumstances, e.g. *CRR*, rr. 53(6) ff., Ecclesiastical Offices (Age Limit) Measure 1975,
s. 5.
[122] For the notion of episcopal ministry as shared amongst these see e.g. *LDHI*, IV, 1.3; *PDH*,
I.A; *SDDH*, A.1–2; *CF*, A.1.2; for their episcopal action as permitted by the diocesan see *TDH*,
E.5: they 'have the Bishop's permission to perform episcopal duties within the Diocese. The
Bishop should always be consulted before they are asked to perform such duties.'

of a visiting woman bishop, consecrated as such overseas in a province in the Anglican Communion,[123] has not been the subject of explicit legal regulation in the Church of England. The matter is dealt with under pastoral guidelines resulting from the Eames Commission 1989 incorporating a resolution affirmed by the Lambeth Conference: in a diocese other than their own, visiting bishops should not exercise episcopal ministry 'without first obtaining the permission and invitation of the ecclesial authority thereof'.[124] However, though they are to be owed 'respect' and 'courtesy',[125] according to a recent archiepiscopal statement, a diocesan bishop cannot at present permit or invite a woman bishop to perform episcopal functions in England as the episcopal ministry of women within the Church of England has not been legally recognized.[126]

There are direct parallels with Roman Catholic canon law: when a diocesan requests the appointment of an assistant, 'when the pastoral needs of the diocese warrant it', the auxiliary's canonical function is to help the diocesan.[127] As in the Church of England, the auxiliary's role must be fulfilled 'without prejudice to the unity of the diocesan administration or to the authority of the diocesan bishop'.[128] Unlike the Church of England, Roman Catholic canon law provides for the imposition of assistant bishops. The imposed auxiliary with special faculties (without a right of succession) and the imposed coadjutor with special faculties (with a right of succession) have those rights and responsibilities defined in their letters of appointment and they are to aid the diocesan 'in the entire governance of the diocese and take his place if he is absent or impeded' (c.405). They are not simply helpers but sharers (c. 407(3)) in the threefold function of teaching, sanctifying, and governing; the diocesan is to appoint them as vicar-general (or at least as episcopal vicar) (c. 406). The diocesan, the auxiliary, and the coadjutor are under a duty to consult with each other on matters of major importance (c. 407). Though the papal letter of appointment may reserve to the assistants a

---

[123] Overseas and Other Clergy (Ministry and Ordination) Measure 1967, s. 6: an 'overseas' bishop means 'a bishop of the Church of England or a Church in Communion with the Church of England having a diocese or office elsewhere than in the province of Canterbury . . . or York, Ireland, Wales or Scotland'.

[124] Eames Commission (1989), Pastoral Guidelines, 56–78: for this and a discussion of the ecclesiological issues, particularly with regard to communion, see *Episcopal Ministry*, Part II, 13.

[125] Ibid., Eames Commission, paras. 69–72.

[126] In a statement to General Synod in 1989, the Archbishop of Canterbury (also speaking on behalf of the Archbishop of York) explained: 'it seems clear enough that the Church of England does not canonically accept the ministry of either women priests or bishops of other Churches, unless and until the ecclesiastical law is changed specifically to allow this or to allow the Church of England itself to ordain women to the orders of priest or bishop' (reproduced in *ELJ*, 1(5) (1989), 9 at 11). The law has changed with regard to the former, but not the latter: see *supra* n. 14.

[127] *CIC*, c. 403(1); beyond this the Code does not specify the conditions under which an appointment may be made; reasons include 'the great size of the diocese, the number of inhabitants, some special pastoral problem, or for some other reasons': Vatican II decree, *Christus Dominus*, 25. [128] *Christus Dominus*, 25.

decision-making power independent of the diocesan, as a basic principle the auxiliary and coadjutor are bound to perform those functions which the diocesan requests (c. 408(1)).[129] The coadjutor and auxiliary are under a duty to reside within the diocese and are not to leave the diocese except for a short time, unless they are fulfilling some other office outside the diocese or are on vacation (not to exceed one month) (c. 410).

RETIREMENT, ACCOUNTABILITY, AND CORRECTION

In connection with the Church of England, the common opinion is that a bishop is not an employee and does not, therefore, fall within the terms of civil employment protection legislation; the bishop is an office-holder.[130] Functions attaching to episcopal office cease either by operation of law or as the result of a lawfully executed decree, that is by vacation of office or when the bishop is the subject of disciplinary action.[131] The person concerned may retain the title (and order) of bishop but cannot exercise episcopal functions. On retirement, resignation, or vacation as a result of disciplinary action, bishops have a cluster of rights to financial provision.[132]

Vacation of Office: Retirement and Resignation

In the Church of England, a bishopric becomes vacant by the translation, retirement, resignation, death, or deprivation of its holder. A bishop must vacate his office on the day on which he attains the age of seventy.[133] An archbishop, if he considers that there are special circumstances, has a right to authorize a diocesan to continue, and a diocesan has a right to authorize a suffragan to continue; in either case, the continuance must not exceed one year.[134] When a diocesan or suffragan is required to vacate the archbishop must declare the bishopric vacant, but the declaration does not take effect unless and until confirmed by Her Majesty in Council.[135] As for archbishops, not less than six months before the required date of vacating an archbishop must tender his resignation to the monarch who declares the archbishopric

---

[129] On a vacancy the coadjutor immediately becomes bishop of the diocese provided he has legitimately taken possession of it (c. 409(1)). For taking possession, see c. 404. He retains all his powers of vicar-general (or episcopal vicar) until a new bishop takes possession of the diocese (c. 409(2)).   [130] *OLAC*, 120 ff.

[131] See above for revocation of delegated powers enjoyed by suffragans.

[132] See *post* Ch. 17.   [133] Ecclesiastical Offices (Age Limit) Measure 1975, s. 1(1), (3).

[134] S. 3(1). It seems the continuance may be renewed; the diocesan may exercise his powers in relation to a suffragan only after consultation with the appropriate archbishop: Bishops (Retirement) Measure 1986, s. 11.

[135] Ecclesiastical Offices (Age Limit) Measure 1975, s. 4(2); see also Bishops (Retirement) Measure 1986, ss. 2, 4.

vacant.[136] The monarch has statutory power to authorize an archbishop to continue in office after that date, for not more than one year, if she considers there are special circumstances, and as she may 'in her discretion determine'.[137]

Bishops have a qualified legal right to resign their office before the age of seventy. An archbishop wishing to resign must tender resignation to the monarch, in a written instrument, who by Order in Council declares the archbishopric vacant.[138] A diocesan or suffragan wishing to resign must first consult with the archbishop and then tender resignation to the archbishop in a written instrument. The archbishop can accept or refuse the resignation. If accepted, the archbishop shall within twenty-eight days of receiving the instrument by endorsement on the instrument declare the bishopric vacant.[139] The law is silent as to the circumstances in which the archbishop might reject a resignation tender; nor does the bishop have a specific right of appeal against his refusal. No express right is conferred upon a diocesan to request the resignation of a suffragan, though the diocesan (as we have seen) does have power to revoke the delegation.[140] No provision exists in the Act of Synod 1993 for the resignation of regional bishops and episcopal visitors.[141]

Different rules apply in cases of physical or mental disability.[142] The archbishop has a right to request (by written instrument) the diocesan or suffragan to resign when physical or mental disability renders either unable to discharge the due performance of episcopal duties. The archbishop must obtain the concurrence of the two senior diocesan bishops of the province and shall send to the bishop concerned notice of his intention to request resignation; the bishop has a right to demand a medical examination and the archbishop must not request resignation until the report of it has been considered by the archbishop and the two senior bishops. The archbishop may then declare the bishopric vacant. If the diocesan or suffragan refuses or fails to tender his resignation within two months of receiving the archiepiscopal request, or is prevented by infirmity from so doing, the archbishop has a right to declare the bishopric vacant by written instrument.[143]

Similarly, with regard to the physical or mental disability of an archbishop, the right to request resignation (which the archbishop must tender to the

---

[136] Ecclesiastical Offices (Age Limit) Measure 1975, s. 4. It is declared vacant as from that date or such date determined as a matter of discretion under s. 2.   [137] Ibid., s. 2.

[138] Bishops (Retirement) Measure 1986, s. 4.

[139] Ibid., s.1(1); s.1(2): the vacancy runs from the date proposed by the diocesan in the instrument or such other date as agreed between them.

[140] Dioceses Measure 1978, Sched. 6 (a reorganization scheme may provide for the vacating of office by a suffragan).   [141] For vacancies in the office of episcopal visitor see *supra* n. 31.

[142] Bishops (Retirement) Measure 1986, s. 3.

[143] Choice of medical practitioner must be agreed by both sides and, failing agreement, the examination is to be carried out by the President of the Royal College of Physicians (ibid., s. 10(1)).

monarch) is vested in the two senior bishops of the province who must act with the concurrence of the archbishop of the other province. The archbishop has a right to demand a medical examination. If the archbishop refuses or fails to resign, or is prevented by infirmity from so doing, the two senior bishops with the concurrence of the other archbishop may petition Her Majesty to declare (by Orders in Council) the archbishopric vacant.[144]

The same basic principles apply in Roman Catholic canon law: a diocese is vacated when the bishop dies, resigns, is transferred, or is deprived of office (c. 416). Episcopal resignation can only be voluntary and must be submitted to the authority responsible for the provision of the office, that is the pope; a resignation which is not based on a just and proportionate cause cannot be accepted (c. 189). A diocesan bishop who has completed his seventy-fifth year of age is requested to present his resignation to the pontiff who is to make provision after he has examined all the circumstances (c. 401(1)). Moreover, a bishop is earnestly requested (*enixe rogatur*) to offer resignation when he has become less able to fulfil his office due to ill health or other serious reason; canon law recommends but does not require resignation (c. 401).[145] Though a refusing bishop cannot be forced to resign—a forced resignation is invalid—the pontiff may, of course, ask for a bishop's resignation.[146]

Episcopal Discipline

Episcopal indiscipline may take a variety of forms and procedures, for correction and remedies, depend upon the indiscipline in question. Episcopal acts in excess of jurisdiction or the exercise of powers in violation of the common law principles of natural justice and procedural fairness may give rise to proceedings in the civil courts.[147] Within the church, as an overriding principle, it belongs to the archbishop 'to correct and supply the defects of other bishops'.[148] Theoretically episcopal wrongdoing may come to light by means of archiepiscopal visitation (though rare) or else pressure may be brought upon a bishop to render an account, and perhaps to take amendatory action, as a result of questions within the various assemblies of the church.[149] Complaints about the use of episcopal powers and discretions are in many circumstances dealt with by means of express rights of appeal to the archbishop, but there is no general provision at diocesan level for the settlement of problems, short of judicial proceedings, analogous to pastoral breakdown at

---

[144] Choice of medical practitioner must be agreed by both sides and, failing agreement, the examination is to be carried out by the President of the Royal College of Physicians (ibid., s. 10(1)). Ibid., s. 6.

[145] *CIC*, c. 402: he retains the title of bishop emeritus of his diocese (and has a right to a place of residence there if he desires, unless the Apostolic See makes special provision, and a right to decent support).

[146] C. 401(1); a resignation submitted out of grave fear unjustly inflicted or fraud, substantial error, or simony is invalid (c. 188).   [147] See *supra* Chs. 4 and 5.

[148] C17(2).   [149] See *supra* Ch. 4.

parochial level.[150] Serious cases (non-performance of episcopal duties, breaches of the ecclesiastical law, failure to effect due obedience to the archbishop) may give rise to legal proceedings within the church courts under the Ecclesiastical Jurisdiction Measure 1963; and in these circumstances the law reserves the correction of bishops (and archbishops) to the episcopate itself.[151] In most cases, it may be presumed, occasions of episcopal indiscipline are remedied executively and privately, so to speak, within the framework provided by the rules (described above) concerning resignation.

Executive episcopal correction, reserved to the pontiff, is treated more elaborately in the Roman Catholic Church. A bishop may be subject to internal disciplinary action for breach of those duties imposed by the Code,[152] and for breach of the oath of obedience to the pope,[153] if moderating the bishop's function serves the common good of the church (c. 223(2)). Episcopal wrongdoing may come to light as a result of an apostolic visitation or after a complaint made by way of administrative hierarchical recourse.[154] It is the right of the pontiff alone to judge bishops in penal cases, and that of the Roman Rota to try them in contentious cases; the College of Bishops and the metropolitan enjoy no coercive power over bishops.[155] Penalties are treated as a last resort; an attempt must first be made, as with any other, to reform a bishop executively by 'fraternal correction, rebuke and other ways of pastoral care' (c. 1341). Non-penal correction, therefore, includes the issuing of a decree, rebuke, resignation justly pressured, or the imposition of a penance or an auxiliary.[156] The pope has a right to propose to transfer a bishop to another diocese; if the bishop refuses, the pope, subject to the procedures, may transfer against the bishop's will for a grave reason.[157] The pontiff may remove a bishop short of deprivation. Removal by an administrative decree must be carried out according to the correct procedure; there must also be a grave reason for it, such as ineffective or detrimental episcopal ministry,

---

[150] See e.g. Canons D3(3A), E6(3), E8(5).

[151] See *supra* Ch. 5; if any overseas bishop performs any episcopal function in a diocese in the province of Canterbury or York, otherwise than in accordance with the provisions of the Overseas and Other Clergy (Ministry and Ordination) Measure 1967, s. 4, he shall be, by s. 4(3) of this measure, subject to proceedings under the Ecclesiastical Jurisdiction Measure 1963 for an offence against the laws ecclesiastical.

[152] CIC, cc. 221(3),1321: no penalty except according to law, for violation of law imputable to that person by reason of malice or culpability.   [153] CIC, cc. 212, 273, 380, 1371.

[154] See *supra* Ch. 4.

[155] CIC, c. 1405; see generally J. M. Huels, 'The correction and punishment of a diocesan bishop', *The Jurist*, 49 (1989), 507; the right of a curial body to do so, such as a sacred congregation, is possible only with the pope's approval.

[156] For decrees (precepts) see c. 49 (and the formalities required under cc. 48–58, including the right to a hearing and the duty to give reasons); for rebuke and penance, cc. 1339,1340; for 'pressured resignations' see P. C. Augustine, *A Commentary on the New Code of Canon Law* (St. Louis, 1922) 8: 72 (where he argues that a resignation can be 'justly' pressured and therefore not invalid).

[157] CIC, c. 190; the Code does not contain special rules for the transfer of a bishop; those dealing with involuntary transfers of pastors apply: see *post* Ch. 7 for cc. 1748–52.

incompetence or a permanent infirmity of mind or body, loss of good reputation, grave neglect of duties, or poor administration of temporal goods.[158] As in the Church of England, penal processes against bishops are rare. A bishop may be the object of a medicinal censure (excommunication, interdict, or suspension) but this may be remitted if the bishop reforms and repairs the harm done.[159] The pope has a right to impose expiatory penalties, which may continue regardless of whether the bishop reforms; deprivation occurs only after a judicial process and can be issued only by the pope for grave reasons; it does not destroy the bishop's power of order, but his right to exercise it.[160]

CONCLUSIONS

In both churches, the appointment of a bishop lies with the head of the church. In the Roman Catholic Church, though a right to nominate is vested in the episcopate (not the laity), the pope freely appoints. In the Church of England, laity and clergy at diocesan and provincial level have a right to nominate, but appointment belongs to the monarch who, by constitutional convention, acts on prime ministerial advice; election is ceremonial. These arrangements take the appointment of archbishops and diocesan bishops out of the control of the church. It is only with regard to assistant bishops that the church more directly controls episcopal appointments which, generally, are in the keeping of the episcopate; lay involvement is minimal. Episcopal functions, which find a direct parallel in the Roman Catholic Church's threefold episcopal ministry of governing, teaching, and ministering, are organized and distributed legally according to office though it may be thought that episcopal oversight is actually hampered by the multiplicity of functions falling upon the diocesan. The Roman Catholic metropolitan's powers are considerably less than those of the Church of England archbishop. Today, possibilities for shared episcopal ministry at diocesan level have been built into the church's legal system. The diocesan bishop's power of delegation may create a distribution of episcopal functions to suffragans varying unequally from diocese to diocese and the law effects a subordination of the suffragan to the diocesan. There is no clear equivalent in the Church of England to imposed bishops in the Roman Catholic Church. The right to effect episcopal resignation and discipline vests, unlike in Roman Catholic Church, in the archbishops. Outside judicial proceedings, there is no systematic and public provision in the Church of England, unlike in Roman Catholic canon law, for broadly executive episcopal correction similar to that operative at parochial level in cases of a serious breakdown of pastoral relations.

---

[158] Cc. 192, 193, 1740, 1741; see cc. 1742–7 for procedures for removal of pastors.
[159] Cc. 1331–5.   [160] C. 1336(1).

7

The Ordained Ministry of Priests and Deacons

The diaconate and the presbyterate are ministries of service: deacons and priests are treated theologically as called by God to work as servants and shepherds to the faithful.[1] Legal arrangements in the Church of England reflect both this and the idea that the ministries of priests and deacons are shared with those of the bishop and the laity in partnership. This Chapter examines the process of ordination, ministerial appointments, and functions, which vary depending on the position held, pastoral care for clergy, ministerial discipline, and termination of ministry. There are many parallels with Roman Catholic canon law: in both churches, as a general principle, the ministry of priests and deacons is subordinate to that of the episcopate; all aspects of their ministry are in the keeping of the bishops. It is within the framework of the canonical ministry of priests and deacons that the use of supplementary executive norms operating at diocesan level is most evident.

ADMISSION TO THE ORDAINED MINISTRY

Admission to the clerical orders of the presbyterate and the diaconate,[2] unlike admission to the episcopate, rests wholly in the keeping of the church. A complex of ecclesiastical quasi-legislation operates at provincial and diocesan levels alongside the general canon and ecclesiastical law applicable in both provinces of the Church of England.

The Process of Ordination

In the Church of England, the diocesan bishop has a canonical duty to provide, 'as much as in him lies', sufficient priests to minister the word and the

[1] *BCP*, 553; *ASB*, 344, 356; A. Russell, *The Clerical Profession* (London, 1980); J. Tiller, *A Strategy for the Church's Ministry* (London, 1985) 52 ff.; for the Roman Catholic position see *CIC*, c. 1008; for a critical study see E. Schillebeeckx, *Ministry—A Case for Change* (London, 1981); see also the agreed statement on *Ministry and Ordination* (1973) and its elucidation (1979); Anglican-Roman Catholic International Commission, *The Final Report* (London, 1982) 29–45; *Baptism, Eucharist, Ministry*, World Council of Churches (Geneva, 1982) 20–32.
[2] The order of deaconess may be not one of the 'holy orders' but, rather, an 'order of ministry' (Canon D1(1)) (Canon D1(5): deaconesses may accept membership of any lay assembly of the Church of England); *CIC*, c. 1009.

sacraments; there is no canonical equivalent to the provision in the Roman Catholic Church that the fostering of vocations to the ordained ministry is the responsibility of the whole community.[3] In common with Roman Catholic canon law,[4] a person shall not be taken to be a lawful priest or deacon unless tried, examined, and admitted to those orders according to the authorised liturgies.[5] In addition to canonical structures, candidature is regulated by norms at diocesan level; these often differ particularly with regard to consultation. Typically selection is processed, in the first instance,[6] by the incumbent who refers the candidate to the diocesan director of ordinands.[7] After interview the director reports to the bishop (usually an area bishop) who in turn decides whether or not to sponsor the candidate for a bishop's selection conference carried out by the Advisory Board of Ministry at national level.[8] The Board makes a recommendation to the bishop who then decides whether to proceed with training; in the case of rejection some norms provide for a reassessment of the individual's ministry.[9] It is the policy of some dioceses to recommend only candidates with a 'strong case' and often the structures are organized so that the decision, particularly refusal, is seen as that of the diocese and not of the bishop personally.[10] Some norms indicate upper age limits for candidature.[11] Financial support for families of candidates recommended for training is given at the discretion of the diocese.[12]

As in the Roman Catholic Church, the right to determine suitability for ordination belongs to the diocesan bishop, but his discretion is not absolute.[13]

---

[3] C18(6); *CIC*, c. 233.   [4] *CIC*, cc. 242, 1027, 1028, 1050(1).   [5] C1(1).

[6] *LDHI*, II, 1: the incumbent's role is discernment, nurture, and encouragement; *TBF*, 3.6–7: the incumbent tests potential and suitability; *PDH*, B.1–2: the incumbent must seek out candidates; *WH*, B.P.12: diocesan vocation advisers must foster vocations; for the diocesan board of ministry and vocations, *SADH*, B.11.

[7] *PBR*, I.9 (the director must establish whether vocation is 'sufficiently formed'); *SDDH*, Part I, Annex E: the director must obtain support from the incumbent, the parochial church council and the churchwardens; *RBG*, B.1: the director must consider the incumbent's advice; *PDH*, B.1–2: the director is assisted by assessors; *WH*, B.P.11: the director must obtain written representations from the rural dean; the archdeacon should interview; appeal lies to the director and the archdeacon together.   [8] *SDDH*, Part I, Annex E; *LDR*, 5 ff. (interview by area bishop).

[9] See *supra* Ch. 4 for the board's functions. *WAOB*, App. C proposes the transference of these to the National Council's Resources for Ministry Department which would be responsible to the House of Bishops for managing the national policies of the church with respect to vocation, selection, and training; *CF*, E.3 (for reassessment); *PDH*, B.1.2 (the bishop's decision 'in all these matters is binding and final'; a recommendation to train 'does not commit the church to the ordination of those it trains').

[10] *SDH*, III, A.1,2; *PBR*, I.9; *Guildford Diocesan Directory* (1994–95), Regulations, 91: the bishop must have regard to educational qualifications and health.

[11] Ibid., (normally up to 35 for stipendiary ministry, and 50 for non-stipendiary); *LDR*, 5 ff. (50) *EDH*, B.8 (48 for stipendiary ministry and 50 for non-stipendiary ministry); *RBG*, B.1 (50); for the normal selection process see *CEYB* (1995).   [12] See e.g. *SDH*, III, A.3; *PDH*, B.1–2; *CF*, E.3.

[13] Cf. *HLE*, para. 657 citing *R v Archbishop of Dublin* (1833) Alc & N 244; Hill, *EL*, 217–18; he may be said to have an absolute discretion in so far as he cannot be compelled to ordain anyone if he chooses not to do so; *CIC*, c. 1029 (the bishop must be satisfied the candidate has an integral faith, a right intention, the required knowledge, and a good reputation); see also P. Smith, 'Lack of due discretion and suitability for ordination', *Studia Canonica*, 21 (1987), 125.

In contrast to Roman Catholic canon law, both women and men may be ordained to the orders of deacon and priest.[14] The bishop has a duty to examine candidates carefully and diligently and may require the assistance of the archdeacons and other ministers appointed for this purpose.[15] As in Roman Catholic canon law,[16] the diocesan must be satisfied so that he knows himself, or by sufficient testimony, that the candidate has been baptized, confirmed, and sufficiently instructed in holy scripture and the doctrine, discipline, and worship of the church. If not satisfied, he has no discretion but must exclude.[17] With regard to the candidature of those in a sexually active homophile relationship, a pattern of life which the church does not commend, '[o]rdinarily it should be left to candidates' own consciences to act responsibly', though in the process of selection it would not be 'right to interrogate on their sexual lives, unless there are strong reasons for doing so'.[18] In contrast with Roman Catholic canon law (where the ages are twenty-four and twenty-five respectively), in the Church of England candidates for the diaconate must be at least twenty-three years of age and for the priesthood at least twenty-four; in both cases the Archbishop of Canterbury may by faculty dispense with these requirements.[19] As in Roman Catholic canon law,[20] promotion from diaconate to priesthood is not automatic: a deacon may not be ordained priest for at least one year, unless the bishop has good cause to ordain earlier, 'so that trial may be made of his behaviour in the office of deacon'.[21]

The distinction in Roman Catholic canon law between irregularities (permanent disqualification) and impediments (temporary disqualification) to ordination finds some parallels in the law of the Church of England.[22] First, the diocesan bishop must not admit if the candidate is suffering or has suffered

---

[14] For female deacons see Deacons (Ordination of Women) Measure 1986 s. 1(1) and Canon C4A(1); for female priests see Priests (Ordination of Women) Measure 1993, s. 1(1) and C4B(1); *CIC*, c. 1024: 'Only a baptized male validly receives sacred ordination.'

[15] Clergy (Ordination and Miscellaneous Provisions) Measure 1964, s. 1(1); C7.

[16] *CIC*, cc. 1023–7.

[17] C4(1) requires the candidate to be of virtuous conversation, of good repute, and a wholesome example and pattern to the flock of Christ; C6(1),(2): the candidate must submit a testimony, from those specified by the bishop, of former good life and behaviour; Clergy (Ordination and Miscellaneous Provisions) Measure 1964, s. 1(1).

[18] *Issues in Human Sexuality*, A Statement by the House of Bishops (1991, GS Misc 382) 5.22.

[19] C3(5), (6); also, for priests, Clergy (Ordination and Miscellaneous Provisions) Measure 1964, s. 2); *CIC*, c. 1031).   [20] *CIC*, c. 1030.

[21] C3(8); during a vacancy in see, this is exercised by the archbishop; no one can be ordained both deacon and priest on the same day unless by faculty of the Archbishop of Canterbury: CE(7); taking part in illegal ritual does not automatically disqualify: *Kensit v Dean and Chapter of St Paul's* [1905] 2 KB 249.

[22] *CIC*, c. 1041. Irregularities include insanity, apostasy, heresy, schism, attempted suicide, and procurement of abortion); c. 1042 (impediments include marriage—except annulled or dissolved by death—and holding incompatible offices (cc. 285, 286); c. 1043 requires the faithful to expose impediments; c. 1047: the pope may dispense from all irregularities reserved to him and a bishop may dispense from irregularities and impediments not reserved to the pope; see J. P. McIntyre, 'Optional priestly celibacy', *Studia Canonica*, 29 (1995), 103.

from any physical or mental infirmity which will prevent the ministering of the word and sacraments or the performance of 'the other' ministerial duties.[23] The candidate is given no specific right to an independent medical examination and, in any event, it is 'the opinion of the bishop' which is the determinant.[24] Secondly, the diocesan bishop must not admit a person who has remarried and has a former spouse still living or who is married to a divorced person whose former spouse is still living.[25] However, recent legislation enables former divorcees to be ordained if certain conditions are met: what was unlawful may now be lawful in so far as this impediment may be removed by archiepiscopal faculty. The diocesan bishop (or his appointee) is under a duty, arising from archiepiscopal directives, to interview the applicant, present spouse, and two referees (one of whom should be aware of the circumstances surrounding the breakdown of the first marriage), and to make appropriate inquiries of the former spouse unless this proves impossible; he must also discuss the application with the incumbent or priest-in-charge of the parish where the applicant usually worships.[26] The diocesan bishop (or his representative) is empowered to interview any other person (subject to their consent) whom he deems appropriate; there is no duty to seek the applicant's permission to do so.[27] If the enquiries are conducted by the bishop's representative, a written report must be submitted to the diocesan setting out the recommendations. After interview and enquiry the diocesan must decide whether or not to apply to the archbishop for a faculty and must inform the applicant of his decision;[28] there is no duty to give reasons for a rejection. The archbishop has a canonical discretion to grant or reject an application but his discretion must be exercised according to the archiepiscopal directions.[29] The archbishop may make further enquiry, as he thinks fit, and his decision must be communicated in writing to the diocesan bishop who must in turn inform the applicant.[30] No provision is made for the applicant to make direct

---

[23] Blindness may no longer bar: *Kensit v Dean and Chapter of St Paul's* [1905] 2 KB 249 at 257; a medical examination is usually part of the selection process involving the Advisory Board of Ministry.   [24] C4(2); ordination cannot be refused for birth out of wedlock (C4(4)).

[25] C4(3); *OLAC*, 108: 'a faculty is not required in the case of a person . . . married twice [where] both . . . marriages have ended in divorce; but that does not . . . mean that the candidate's marital history should not be taken into account in assessing his or her suitability for ordination.'

[26] Directions (13 Sep. 1991), dd. 2, 3, 4; if interview/enquiry of referees or former spouse is not possible, the bishop (or his representative) must arrange for these to be carried out by the bishop of the diocese where the referee or former spouse resides (d. 4); a diocesan cannot delegate his episcopal functions to a suffragan: Clergy (Ordination) Measure 1990, s. 2.

[27] Directions (1991), d. 5: the diocesan or his representative 'may seek the applicant's permission'.

[28] Ibid., d. 7; the diocesan must specify the possibility of any scandal and the type of ministry appropriate for the applicant should he/she be ordained: d. 8.

[29] C4(3A) promulged under the Clergy (Ordination) Measure 1990, s. 1.

[30] Directions (1991), d. 9; when the archbishop is the diocesan the interview and enquiry are carried out by his representative (d. 10); when the bishopric or archbishopric is vacant, the application goes into abeyance (d. 11).

representations to, or to appear before, the archbishop, nor does the applicant have a right of appeal against the archbishop's decision.

As in the Roman Catholic Church,[31] before proceeding to the service of ordination a candidate for the diaconate or priesthood must submit to the diocesan bishop various documents: a birth certificate, testimonials,[32] and a certificate that ecclesiastical office is provided within the diocese 'wherein he may attend the cure of souls and execute his ministry'.[33] Moreover, whilst their Roman Catholic counterparts take an oath of allegiance to the pope,[34] candidates in the Church of England must prior to ordination make various declarations: an oath of allegiance recognizing the ecclesiastical supremacy of the monarch,[35] a declaration of assent (to the doctrine, and to use only the lawful forms of worship, of the church),[36] and an oath of canonical obedience to the bishop.[37] No person can be admitted by any bishop other than the bishop of the diocese in which that person is to exercise ministry.[38]

The service of ordination must take place on prescribed days or on a day which the diocesan on urgent occasion shall appoint.[39] It must be in the diocesan cathedral church or other church or chapel at the discretion of the bishop, and the candidate must be presented by an archdeacon or his deputy.[40] Ordination must be celebrated according to the authorized liturgies, the choice of which lies with the bishop conducting the service.[41] According to liturgical norms, a person is ordained deacon when he consents and by prayer and laying on of hands by a bishop.[42] At ordination to the priesthood, the priests taking part must together with the bishop lay their hands upon the head of every

[31] *CIC*, c. 1050 (including certification of studies completed, baptism, and confirmation).
[32] C6.
[33] C5(1); a deacon should at least be licensed to the office of assistant curate; C5(2) lists specific positions to which a bishop may admit.
[34] *Rites*, II, 54 (deacons), 64 (priests); for profession of faith see *CIC*, c. 833; for canonical duties of obedience (*CIC*, cc. 273, 274) see below.
[35] Clerical Discipline Act 1865, s. 4; C13(1).   [36] C15(4); see *post* Chs. 9 and 10.
[37] C14(3).
[38] C5(4): except either he brings letters dimissory from the bishop of that diocese or is a fellow in a college or hall in the Universities of Oxford or Cambridge: C5(4), (5); a person to be ordained priest must also exhibit letters of orders (C6(2)); suffragan bishops may do so when this function is delegated by the diocesan (C20); it is not clear whether the same applies to area bishops and it may be that C5(4) needs amending in the light of C20.
[39] C3(1): on Sundays immediately following Ember Days, or on St Peter's Day, Michaelmeas Day, or St Thomas' Day (or within the week following each of these); if on another day, this must be a Sunday, a Holy Day, or one of the Ember days.
[40] C3(2), (3); alternatively, presentation may be by such persons as by ancient custom have the right to do so.
[41] C1(1), B3(5); *ASB*, 338, Note 4: the bishop is to determine 'having regard to tradition and local custom'; the archbishops may jointly authorize forms of service for the ordination of deaconesses as deacons: C4A(4).
[42] *BCP*, 553f.; *ASB*, 338; 'holy orders' suggests 'episcopal ordination': *Bishop of St Albans v Fillingham* [1906] P 163.

person receiving the order.[43] At both ordinations, candidates declare their acceptance of the church's doctrine and discipline.[44] The bishop has a right to invite ministers of other churches to participate in elements of an ordination service.[45]

The Ordination of Women as Priests

These general principles apply equally to the ordination of women as priests.[46] However, the Priests (Ordination of Women) Measure 1993 expressly excludes the effects of the Sex Discrimination Act 1975 from the process of ordaining women as priests.[47] At the date of the promulgation of the canon enabling the ordination of women, to enjoy protection the bishop must have made a written declaration that a woman is not to be ordained within the diocese to the office of priest; the bishop has a right to withdraw this.[48] It is an ecclesiastical offence to contravene a declaration.[49] When a bishop ceases to hold office, the declaration continues in force for six months after succession by another as bishop of the diocese.[50]

By Act of Synod, when a diocesan bishop has indicated that he is opposed (and unwilling to make a declaration), ordinations of women from the relevant diocese must be carried out by the archbishop personally or through a bishop acting as his commissary.[51] The archbishop must do so either at the request of the opposed diocesan or in pursuance of his metropolitical jurisdiction. However, the archbishop 'shall not so act unless he is satisfied that the diocesan bishop concerned has no objection'; in short, the diocesan can veto the ordination.[52] Moreover, the archbishop cannot do so 'where the bishop of a diocese has made arrangements for the ordination of women to the priesthood

---

[43] C3(4); *POWMCP*, para. 5; a diocesan who has not made a declaration must 'respect the views of suffragan, area and assistant bishops . . . in the diocese and will not expect or require any bishop to act against his conscience'.   [44] *ASB*, 345, 358.

[45] Canon B43, paras. (1), (3). An invitation 'to perform . . . any duty in connection with a service of ordination', whilst loosely drafted, may not presumably include laying on of hands.

[46] Canon C4B(1): 'A woman may be ordained to the office of priest if she otherwise satisfies the requirements of Canon C4 as to the persons who may be ordained as priests.' Since most existing women deacons have now been priested, some of the following provisions are nugatory: whilst the Priests (Ordination of Women) Measure 1993 made certain provisions for the ordination of existing women deacons, for most purposes the same procedures now apply to both male and female ordinands.

[47] S. 6: 'Without prejudice to section 19 of the Sex Discrimination Act 1975, nothing in Part II of that Act shall render unlawful sex discrimination against a woman in respect of (a) her ordination to the office of priest in the Church of England'; D. McClean, 'Women priests: the legal background', *ELJ*, 1(5) (1989), 24 at 27; *quaere* whether a bishop discriminating against men in the ordination process is also protected.

[48] S. 2(2), (3); copies must be sent, *inter alia*, to the monarch and the provincial archbishop (s. 2(4)); *POWMCP*, para. 6 imposes a duty to inform area, suffragan, or assistant bishops.

[49] S. 5(a); s. 2(6): the declaration binds those discharging episcopal functions under Dioceses Measure 1978, ss. 10, 11.   [50] S. 2(5).

[51] Episcopal Ministry Act of Synod 1993, s. 11(1).   [52] S. 12(2); *POWMCP*, para. 4.

... to be carried out by another bishop'.[53] A code of practice and guidelines issued by the House of Bishops regulate testing and discernment of vocation and preparation for ordination of women as priests. A lay woman or a woman deacon must, in any diocese where an episcopal declaration is not in force, apply to her diocesan bishop. In dioceses with a declaration in force, the bishop of a neighbouring diocese should be approached and, in the case of a deacon, 'she must first inform her own bishop of her intention to do this'.[54] A bishop to whom application is made, if prepared to pursue it, 'shall inform the bishop of the candidate's own diocese . . . and invite the bishop to let him have any observations on the candidate'.[55] If accepted for training, 'the candidate will be sponsored by the bishop to whom the application was made'.[56] In order to establish 'parity between dioceses', though the process should not involve central selection, all women candidates 'should undergo some formal process of testing. Ordination to the priesthood should not be regarded as an automatic right.'[57] The process of testing should include early consultation with the deacon's incumbent or other person to whom she is directly responsible, at least one interview with her bishop, and a review of past and present ministry, 'her gifts and sense of vocation to the priesthood'.[58] The bishop may allow, refuse, or delay the candidate to or from proceeding to ordination.[59] There can be no 'initial training requirement' for existing women deacons and each diocese has a responsibility to ensure that they have access to the training necessary to exercise priesthood.[60]

The conduct of ordination services is a matter for the diocesan bishop: he determines who will ordain, and with the ordaining bishop decides (after due consultation) where and when individuals are ordained and which priests should be present and take part in the laying on of hands. In an ordination to the diaconate, and the same sensitivity must be applied to ordinations to the priesthood, 'it would be inappropriate to exclude candidates of one sex from a particular ordination service, or to arrange a separate service for ordinands opposed to the ordination of women to the priesthood'.[61] The ministry in England of women ordained to the priesthood overseas, in a province in the Anglican Communion, has not as yet been formally addressed in the Church of England.[62] Short of invoking in exceptional cases the doctrine of conditional

---

[53] S. 12(3).   [54] *POWMCP*, paras. 8, 9.

[55] Ibid., para. 10; when the bishop has decided whether or not to sponsor for a selection conference he must inform the other bishop accordingly.

[56] Ibid. The bishop 'will accept the same financial responsibility for training as for that of all other candidates he sponsors'.   [57] Ibid., App. B, para. 1.

[58] Ibid., para. 3; some diocesan norms have a single director for both male and female candidates (e.g. *WDHI*, Ch. 3 (at 183) whilst others have one male and one female director dealing with candidates of each sex (e.g. *EDH*, B.8).

[59] *POWMCP*, App. B., para. 3(ii)-(iv); para. 5 covers retired women deacons wishing to test vocation to the priesthood.

[60] Ibid., paras. 7–10 (para. 11: these aspects of preparation should not involve 're-entering a diocese's "post-ordination training" programme').   [61] Ibid, paras. 13–15.

[62] See *supra* Ch. 6.

ordination, the orders of both male and female priests in the Church of England are technically not recognized by the Roman Catholic Church.[63]

Ordained ministries in the Church of England, from which priests and deacons attend the cure of souls or otherwise exercise service, may be classified according to the status of the minister or office occupied, the location of the ministry, the degree to which the ministry enjoys security of tenure, and whether the ministerial post attracts remuneration.[64] Archidiaconal ministry, parochial or sector ministry, and stipendiary ministry are amongst the many different types of service. Broadly, powers of appointment are concentrated, as with ordination, in the diocesan bishop.[65] Several appointment models exist, depending on the ministry in question; there are no general norms applicable to all appointments to ecclesiastical office, such as those in Roman Catholic canon law.[66]

Beneficed Appointments

A benefice is an office (such as that of a rector or vicar of a parish or parishes), with cure of souls, to which a freehold attaches.[67] The equivalent office-holder

---

[63] *Apostolicae Curae*, Apostolic Letter of Pope Leo XIII on Anglican Orders (1896). Para. 40: the Letter 'shall be now and for ever in the future valid and in force, and that it is to be inviolably observed both judicially and extrajudicially by all persons of whatsoever degree or pre-eminence'; the Commission advising the Supreme Sacred Congregation of the Holy Office prior to the publication of the Letter was not unanimous in its recommendations: of its 8 members, 4 claimed Anglican orders were invalid, 2 that they were valid, and 2 claimed doubtful validity: *COCLA*, 559. For conditional ordination (invoked to enable the recognition of Bishop Graham Leonard, by virtue of the participation of old catholic bishops in his ordination) see *CIC*, c. 845 and *Reuniting Anglicans and Rome*, *The Messenger of the Catholic League*, No.254 (1994) 40 ff. See generally J. J. Hughes, *Absolutely Null and Utterly Void: The Papal Condemnation of Anglican Orders 1896* (London, 1968) and J. J. Hughes, *Stewards of the Lord: A Reappraisal of Anglican Orders* (London, 1970). For the teaching that priestly ordination is reserved to men see the Apostolic letter *Ordinatio sacerdotalis* (1994); see also 'Ordination and reception of Dr. Graham Leonard', a statement from Cardinal Hume, Canon Law Society *Newsletter*, No. 98 (1994), 54 and n. 1 *supra* for the relevant ARCIC I statements.

[64] The first two categories are examined here: for remuneration see *post* Ch. 17.

[65] Concentration often surfaces in diocesan norms: *NDIB*, III.33(2) ('The ministerial posts in the Diocese are established by the authority of the Bishop either directly or on the advice of the Diocesan Pastoral Committee. No minister may be appointed without his prior approval'); *SDH*, III, E; *TBF*, 3.5.; *PDH*, E.3; *Issues in Human Sexuality*, A Statement by the House of Bishops (1991, GS Misc 382) 5.19: with regard to clergy openly 'homophile in orientation, but . . . committed to a life of abstinence', 'We greatly regret the way in which candidates for appointment who are open in this way are often rejected by parishes and others solely on these grounds'.

[66] *CIC*, cc. 149, 150: the appointee must be qualified, in communion, and if carrying the cure of souls the office cannot be held by a non-ordained person; appointment is by free conferral and presentation followed by installation or election and confirmation; see c. 522 for the appointment of pastors.   [67] Pastoral Measure 1983, s. 86(1).

in Roman Catholic canon law is the pastor, an episcopal appointee who exercises pastoral care in the parish community entrusted to him.[68] In the Church of England, the procedure for appointing to a benefice is governed by the Patronage (Benefices) Measure 1986. It has three basic parts: presentation, admission or institution, and induction. A candidate must be presented to the bishop for admission. The right to present, vested in the patron,[69] may be exercised when the benefice is vacated.[70] The bishop must notify the diocese's designated officer of a vacancy who, in turn, must notify the registered patron and the secretary of the parochial church council.[71] The parochial church council must prepare a statement describing the conditions, needs, and traditions of the parish and appoint two lay members to act as representatives of the council in the selection process. It must also decide whether to request the patron to consider advertising the vacancy, whether to request a meeting between the council, bishop, and patron, and whether to request a written statement from the bishop describing the needs of the diocese and the wider interests of the church.[72] No offer of the benefice can be made to a candidate until approved by the council's representatives and the bishop.[73] These have a right of veto and a duty to state grounds of refusal; the patron may request the archbishop to review a refusal; once an offer is made and accepted, the patron sends notice presenting the nominee for admission.[74] If there has been no presentation at the expiration of nine months after vacancy, the right to present is exercisable by the archbishop who is under a duty to consult the bishop and

---

[68] *CIC*, c. 519 (for impeded and vacant parishes see cc. 539–40); in England and Wales there are no beneficed appointments: *COCLA*, 1341 concerning c. 1272. For incardination, the process of tying a cleric to a diocese (*CIC*, cc. 265 ff.) see P. R. Calvo and N. J. Klinger (eds.), *Clergy Procedural Handbook* (Washington, 1992) Ch. 1.

[69] Patronage, a form of property, is transferrable but cannot be sold: Patronage (Benefices) Measure 1986, s. 3(1); a register of patrons must be kept and all transfers recorded; no right of patronage may be exercised without registration; the bishop's consent is required for a transfer and the parochial church council must be allowed to make representations: ss. 1–6. Sched. 1 contains rules governing registration of patrons; s. 23 and Sched. 2 contain special provisions applicable to benefices comprising two or more parishes, benefices in which the parochial church council is the registered patron, and benefices held in plurality. The 1986 Measure has simplified the earlier law: for this see *HLE*, paras. 776–841.

[70] When there is no registered patron the Diocesan Board of Patronage becomes the patron (s. 25); for composition and procedure, see Sched. 3; Roman Catholics may be patrons (ibid., s. 30).

[71] Patronage (Benefices) Measure, s. 7 (designated officer means such person as the bishop, after consulting the bishop's council, may designate or, if no person is designated, the secretary of the diocesan pastoral committee. The patron (or his representative) must make a declaration of his status within 2 months of notification of vacancy (s. 8); C9(1); if there is no PCC, notification must be postponed until a council is constituted: *King v Bishop of Truro* [1937] P 36.   [72] S. 11(1).

[73] S. 13; for joint meetings of council, bishop, and patron see s. 12; supplementary norms are sometimes added: see e.g. *SDH*, III, C.5: the bishop notifies the parish representatives of his own candidate and they have 2 weeks to approve or refuse; if they do not do so within that time, approval is assumed.

[74] S. 13(4), (5); the archbishop need not hold a full quasi-judicial enquiry: *R v Archbishop of Canterbury, ex p Morant* [1944] 1 All ER 179 (CA).

the parish representatives.[75] Similarly, if the patron or the parochial church council fail to comply with prescribed elements of the process, the bishop himself may offer the benefice.[76]

The bishop has a power to suspend the right of presentation for a period not exceeding five years. He can, however, only do so with the consent of the diocesan pastoral committee and after consulting the patron, the rural dean, the parochial church council, and the lay co-chairman of the deanery synod. When consulting the bishop must give the reasons for the proposed suspension.[77] It is not clear whether the pastoral committee's consent must be obtained before or after the consultation process; in any event, evidence derived from the consultation process must be duly considered.[78] Suspension may be terminated by the bishop with the consent of the diocesan pastoral committee and may be renewed for a further period(s) with the same consent and consultation.[79] Moreover, if the making of a pastoral scheme (which may itself contain provision as to patronage) is pending, the right of presentation cannot be exercised without the consent of the diocesan pastoral committee and the bishop. The right is lost until the scheme is implemented, withdrawn or rejected, or three years elapses.[80]

Admission to a benefice, open only to those ordained priest,[81] is in the keeping of the diocesan bishop—nothing in the procedures described above may be taken 'as affecting the power of a bishop . . . to refuse to institute or admit a presentee to the benefice'.[82] If a person was ordained by a bishop other than the appointing diocesan, the bishop is forbidden to admit or institute without first receiving evidence of ordination by another bishop, nor can he appoint unless the person appears on due examination to be of sufficient learning.[83] The bishop has wide powers of refusal: he may refuse if not more than three years have elapsed since the presentee's ordination as deacon, if the priest is unfit by reason of physical or mental infirmity or incapacity, pecuniary embarrassment of a serious character, grave misconduct or neglect of duty in an ecclesiastical office, or evil life (having caused grave scandal concerning his moral character since ordination).[84] The bishop may

---

[75] S. 16(1), (5). If there has already been a refusal by the bishop and the parish representatives within the 9 months, the archbishop cannot offer without the consent of the bishop and parish representatives.

[76] Ss. 14,15 (if the patron does not comply with s. 9 and the council with ss. 11 and 12).

[77] Pastoral Measure 1983, s. 67(1), (3).

[78] *PMCP*, B14(1): 'It will be apparent that the bishop should not have made up his mind before carrying out these statutory consultations.'				[79] Pastoral Measure 1983, s. 67(4), (5).

[80] Ibid., s. 69(1); for pastoral schemes and patronage see s. 32 and *PMCP*, B11.

[81] C10(1).

[82] Patronage (Benefices) Measure 1986, s. 17(1); where the patron is the bishop, the process of institution is known as collation: *HLE*, paras. 842, 846.

[83] C10(1), (2): the appointee must show Letters of Orders or other suffcent evidence and the bishop may require testimony of former good life and behaviour.

[84] C10(3)(a); see *Marriner v Bishop of Bath and Wells* [1893] P 137 at 146 (poor character); *Bishop of Exeter v Marshall* (1868) LR 3 HL 17 at 39, 51 (morals); *Walsh v Bishop of Lincoln*

refuse, in the case of those who have not previously held a benefice (or the office of vicar in a team ministry) in the absence of experience (or less than three years' experience) as a full-time assistant curate or curate-in-charge licensed to a parish.[85] No provision is made as to how the bishop should determine these matters. However, the bishop must signify in writing the refusal and the ground to both presentee and patron. Moreover, the presentee may appeal against refusal to a tribunal which may either uphold the bishop's decision or direct him to institute or admit.[86] Where refusal is based on lack or insufficiency of experience, the bishop must signify in writing the refusal and ground to the patron and presentee either of whom may, within one month after signification, appeal in writing to the provincial archbishop alone who may either uphold the refusal or direct institution or admission.[87] Though a parish has no right to veto an episcopal appointment, before admission or institution, the bishop must give notice of appointment to the secretary of the parochial church council: the bishop must not admit or institute until three weeks have expired from the date of notice.[88] Institution into the spiritualities is followed by induction into the temporalities of the benefice, usually at a service in the parish church.[89]

(1875) LR 10 CP 518 (fitness); *Heywood v Bishop of Manchester* (1883) 12 QBD 404 at 418 and *Gore-Booth v Bishop of Manchester* [1920] 2 KB 412 (orthodoxy).

[85] C10(3)(b); Benefices Measure 1972, s. 1(1).

[86] By s. 18 of the Patronage (Benefices) Measure 1986 (No.3), s. 3 of the Benefices Act 1898 as amended has effect (the appellate tribunal consists of the archbishop and the Dean of the Arches and Auditor; proceedings must be in public and there is a right to legal representation). Particulars of the deficiency must be stated and the adequacy of the grounds given may be subject to judicial review: *Willis v Bishop of Oxford* (1877) 2 PD 192 (insufficiency of learning); for the possibility of compulsion to act by court order see *Notley v Bishop of Birmingham No. 2* [1931] I Ch 529.

[87] Benefices Measure 1972, s. 1(2). Where the diocesan is an archbishop, appeal lies to the other archbishop.

[88] C10(4); C10(5): the bishop must as speedily as possible give institution to the priest; C10(7): the bishop himself must institute, or for grave and urgent cause shall delegate the power to do so to a commissary in holy orders. For the ceremony see *HLE*, para. 845, n. 1; C10(6): a written instrument (with episcopal seal attached) is delivered to the presentee; C10(8): the provisions of this canon are wihout prejudice to the right of a patron or a presentee to appeal against an episcopal refusal to institute; the institution of a person not in holy orders is null: *R v Ellis* (1888) 16 Cox CC 469.

[89] C11: the bishop directs the archdeacon or 'other the person to whom induction belongs' to induct the priest 'into possession of the temporalities of the benefice'; the archdeacon may authorize the rural dean or any other minister beneficed or licensed in the archdeaconry to make the induction; diocesan norms often provide for choice of service: see e.g. *SDDH*, H.1–5 (using the form 'Celebration of a New Ministry'); *BF*, 3.5 (Diocesan Order for Institution Services); *SDH*, III, D; *BDM*, B5 (attendance at institutions within the deanery should be regrded as 'obligatory'). On a vacancy in see, as a matter of ecclesiastical convention the archbishop admits, though strictly the guardianship of the spiritualities rests (under C19(2)) in the dean and chapter of the cathedral church of the diocese (see B. Till, *York Against Durham: The Guardianship of the Spiritualities in the Diocese of Durham Sede Vacante* (York, 1993) 25).

Rather different models of appointment exist with regard to senior beneficed offices. The right to appoint an archdeacon, broadly equivalent to the office of vicar-general or episcopal vicar in the Roman Catholic Church,[90] usually vests in the diocesan bishop who admits by collation; the bishop cannot appoint until the candidate has completed six years in priest's orders.[91] There is presently no legal requirement for the bishop to consult before appointing an archdeacon, though in practice diocesan bishops do consult.[92] The right to appoint a rural dean (usually a beneficed cleric), equivalent to the dean or archpriest in Roman Catholic canon law,[93] resides in the bishop acting under the episcopal seal, although diocesan norms commonly provide for consultation.[94] It is lawful for a deacon to be appointed as a rural dean, as a residentiary or non-residentiary canon.[95] Special rules apply to the appointment of cathedral staff: to be appointed dean, provost, or canon a person must have been in the priesthood for at least six years.[96] The monarch appoints the dean,[97] the diocesan bishop appoints provosts of a parish church cathedral[98] and, in most cases, cathedral canons.[99]

---

[90] *CIC*, c. 475. The vicar-general is appointed by the bishop to assist him in the governance of the entire diocese; c. 476: episcopal vicars are appointed by the bishop to assist in the governance of a particular area in the diocese.

[91] C22(1); when the archdeaconry is in the gift of a layman, the patron presents to the bishop: *Sale v Bishop of Coventry and Lichfield* (1590) 1 And 241; induction is by the dean and chapter and he must make the necessary declaration and oath of canonical obedience to the bishop.

[92] *Senior Church Appointments* (1992) para. 6.42 and App. II, recommending that an agreed procedure be established by the House of Bishops providing for explicit consultation with e.g. all suffragans, archdeacons, and diocesan synod chairmen: para. 6.43; see ibid., 6.10 ff. for changes recommended in appointments of those discussed in the following paragraph.

[93] *CIC*, c. 374 (deans, 'vicars forane', who oversee 'vicariates', groups of parishes in the diocese, are appointed by the bishop after consultation with priests of the vicariate: c. 553).

[94] For consultation in diocesan norms see e.g. *DSBN*, Ad clerum notice, 1989/12.; the rural dean will be a member of the deanery synod, which implies that he must qualify for membership thereof in accordance with *CRR*, rr. 24, 28(1)(a). See also the Report on Rural Deans, presented to the Lower House of the Canterbury Convocation 1948, No. 665.

[95] Church of England (MIscellaneous Provisions) Measure 1992, ss. 14, 15, 16.

[96] Ecclesiastical Commissioners Act 1840, s. 27 and C21(1) (except where the canonry is annexed to a professorship, headship, or other office in any university); under the Church of England (Miscellaneous Provisions) Measure 1995, s.5 a candidate for the position of dean or provost must have been in holy orders for at least 6 years; by the Pastoral Measure 1983, s. 85(3), no person can hold a cathedral preferment (i.e. the office of dean, provost, residentiary or stipendiary canon) in more than one cathedral, nor a cathedral preferment with a benefice or 2 or more benefices unless the cathedral statutes allow this (s. 85(2)).

[97] Cathedrals Measure 1963, s. 10(1)(a); the prime minister's secretary for appointments draws up a list of candidates after consultation with (amongst others) the bishop and the chapter from which the prime minister recommends to the monarch: see *Senior Church Appointments* (1992) App. II, paras. 21 ff. For the exceptions see *HLE*, para. 641.

[98] The incumbent of the benefice for which the cathedral is parish church: Cathedrals Measure 1963, s.10(1)(b); the Patronage (Benefices) Measure 1986 therefore applies, enabling the lay representatives of the parochial church council to participate in the selection process.

[99] Cathedrals Measure 1963, s.10(1)(c): appointment is according to the cathedral's constitution and statutes.

Unbeneficed Appointments: Licences

The power to appoint to unbeneficed offices, held by those not having the status of incumbent and to which no freehold attaches, vests in the diocesan bishop. Appointments may be made with or without request. Assistant curates, usually deacons or members of the non-stipendiary ministry, are appointed by the diocesan on the nomination of the incumbent.[100] The appointment of curates or ministers-in-charge, responsible for a parish lacking an incumbent, is made by the diocesan bishop.[101] There is no general legal requirement for the diocesan to consult in the process of appointing unbeneficed clergy; the requirement that the bishop must consult the parochial church council and, if reasonably practicable, the patron, before appointing a priest-in-charge to a suspended benefice is exceptional.[102] However, diocesan norms commonly provide for consultation by the bishop with his senior staff (and sometimes the diocesan director of ordinands) prior to the placement or movement of deacons and other assistant curates; norms sometimes contain criteria to be used in determining deployment as well as procedures for the giving of notice, in the case of requests, so that incumbents and parochial church councils are included in the allocation process.[103] Though it is difficult to generalize about appointments to specialist and sector ministries, broadly, appointment is regulated by rules and practices of the institution or body in which the minister is to serve. Appointment of chaplains in the army, navy, and air forces, for instance, is arranged by the Queen's Regulations governing those forces.[104] Chaplains in schools, universities or colleges, hospitals, and prisons will be appointed under the rules and practices of these institutions: the general practice is that appointments are to be approved by the bishop.[105]

---

[100] *PBR*, III.10.

[101] Act of Uniformity 1662, s. 10 (unrepealed) forbids anyone other than an episcopally ordained priest to be admitted 'to any Parsonage Vicarage Benefice or other Ecclesiastical Promotion or Dignity whatsoever'; s. 10 notwithstanding, a deacon can be appointed to office of rural dean, residentiary or non-residentiary canon: see *supra* n. 95; by Pastoral Measure 1983, s. 68, when presentation rights are suspended, priests only may be appointed. For the applicability of natural justice (which requires the incumbent to be heard) in the appointment of a curate when the incumbent is neglectful, see *Capel v Child* [1832] 2 C & J 358.

[102] Pastoral Measure 1983, s. 68, *PMCP*, B14(3); B14(4) recommends that the pastoral committee, to allay 'apprehension about the use of the power of suspension', furnish particulars of the use of the power in its annual report to diocesan synod.

[103] For consultation see *TBF*, 3.6; *SDH*, III, E; *SDDH*, F.8, F.9; *PDH*, B2.4, B3.1–2 (B.2.7, for the provincial Clergy Appointments Adviser); *WDHI*, Ch. 3 (at 157): deacons are placed according to the criteria of training rather than parochial needs; *CF*, E.6: placement of deacons for first and second curacies and criteria.

[104] *HLE*, paras. 728, 729: the Home Secretary may appoint army or air force chaplains (Army Chaplains Act 1868, s. 2); service chaplains are licensed to the Archbishop of Canterbury and the Bishop of the Armed Forces exercises pastoral supervision on his behalf; chaplains may also receive permission to officiate from their local diocesan bishop.

[105] Canon B41(2); the office of prison chaplain is statutory: Prison Act 1952, s. 7(1). The Church of England cleric is appointed by the home secretary who must notify the nomination to the

Whereas beneficed clergy are licensed to exercise ministry by admission or institution, unbeneficed appointees must be admitted to serve within the diocese by episcopal licence (under the bishop's hand and seal) or by written permission to officiate.[106] Regulation of the bishop's decision to license or permit is minimal, far less detailed than that concerning his powers to institute beneficed clergy. If coming from another diocese the candidate must produce to the bishop Letters of Orders (or other sufficient evidence of ordination) and a testimonial from the bishop of the other diocese.[107] No stipendiary curate may be licensed to serve in more than one church or chapel, unless they are churches of a united benefice held in plurality, or the chapel is dependent on the parish church.[108] There is no general duty on the bishop to give reasons for refusing to grant a licence or permission.[109] With both ministers-in-charge and assistant curates, candidates must make the declarations and take the oaths required by canon.[110]

Different rules apply to appointments to a team ministry.[111] Although the pastoral scheme may designate the first team rector (the leader), if the bishop was the sole patron of the benefice(s) for which the team ministry was established, he will continue as patron and collate future rectors unless the scheme provides for the rector to be chosen by a special patronage board or by the diocesan board of patronage. If the right to patronage was exercisable by anyone other than the bishop, and that person (or body) wished to relinquish their interest to the bishop, the scheme could provide for the bishop to collate the rector. In any other case presentation lies with the patronage board specially constituted by the scheme or with the diocesan patronage board.[112] First team vicars may be designated by the scheme and subsequent team vicars may be chosen by the bishop and rector jointly or, where the rector is chosen by the specially constituted patronage board or by the diocesan patronage board, the scheme may provide for team vicars to be chosen in the same way.[113] With respect to a group ministry, the pastoral scheme may designate

---

diocesan bishop: s. 9(2); see e.g. *DSBN*, Ad clerum notice 1989/7 (hospital chaplains: 'although his appointment is approved by the Bishop, [he] is appointed by the Department of Health and Social Security and is responsible to that department'); see also *PDH*, B.6.1–3 for episcopal representation on appointing panels in educational institutions and hospitals; for the position in Roman Catholic canon law see *CIC*, cc. 565, 566.

[106] C8(3); for exceptions (including extra parochial ministry) see below.

[107] C12(2). This also requires testimony of 'his honesty, ability, and conformity to the doctrine, discipline and worship of the Church of England'.   [108] C12(4).

[109] *R v Bishop of London* (1811) 13 East 419; *Bishop of Down v Miller* (1861) 11 I Ch R App 1; *R v Bishop of Liverpool* (1904) 20 TLR 485.   [110] *OLAC*, 10.

[111] Pastoral Measure 1983, s. 20(2): the office of team rector is to be either a freehold office or for a term of years specified in the scheme; under the Team and Group Ministries Measure 1994, s. 1, with regard to cases following the coming into force of this Measure, a team rector does not hold a freehold office but holds office for a term of years (thereby producing parity with team vicars).

[112] Pastoral Measure 1983, s. 20(4), Sched. 3, para. 3(1); *PMCP*, B4(4).

[113] S. 20(4)(b), Sched 3, para. 2(1): The rector and every team vicar has a right to attend and vote at the board's meetings considering concerning presentation: para. 2(2).

the first person (who may be the existing incumbent) to hold any benefice as a benefice in the group; otherwise the incumbent is to be presented or collated to the benefice by the patron with the approval of the bishop who must consult the other incumbents and any priests-in-charge in the group before reaching his decision.[114]

Appointment of Women Priests

The Priests (Ordination of Women) Measure 1993 contains special rules applicable to appointments of women priests to ministerial posts. An episcopal declaration (described above) may provide that a woman is not to be instituted or licensed to the office of incumbent or priest-in-charge of a benefice, or of team vicar for a benefice, within the diocese, and that a woman is not to be given a licence or permission to officiate as a priest within the diocese.[115] However, a declaration cannot prevent a woman from being allowed to officiate as a priest in a church or chapel for one period of not more than seven [consecutive] days in any period of three months without reference to the bishop or other ordinary.[116] According to the code of practice, before licensing a priest to a college, hospital, prison, or other institution (under the Extra Parochial Ministry Measure 1967) 'a bishop consults with the appropriate authorities of the institution': these consultations 'will cover the question of the acceptability of a woman priest where such an appointment is contemplated'.[117]

A parochial church council may pass a resolution that it would not accept a woman as the incumbent or priest-in-charge of the benefice or as a team vicar for the benefice.[118] It cannot do so, however, unless its secretary has given four weeks' notice of the meeting at which the motion proposing the resolution is to be considered and the meeting is attended by at least half of the members of the council entitled to attend.[119] The administrative body of a cathedral may also resolve that it would not accept a woman as the dean of the cathedral church.[120] Both the parochial church council and the cathedral's administrative body may rescind the resolution.[121] While in force, the resolution is binding on

---

[114] S. 21(3), Sched. 3, para. 3; *PMCP*, B4(7): the rector and every vicar has the right to attend and vote at meetings of the patronage board at which vicars are chosen; see e.g. *DSBN*, Ad clerum notice, 1993/1 for procedures for renewal of team vicar licences; for cathedral appointments see Cathedrals Measures 1963 and 1976 and C21.   [115] S. 2(1)(b).

[116] S. 2(7): *POWMCP*, para. 23: 'The House of Bishops would regard it as an abuse of Section 2(7) . . . and of canon C8, for an incumbent to use those powers to further a policy of a regular ministry of women priests in the parish(es) of his benefice.'

[117] Ibid, para. 27; the Hospital Chaplaincies Council has issued guidance on the matter: see ibid., App. D.

[118] S. 3(1); Sched. 1 (Resolution B); *POWMCP*, App. C: a PCC cannot delegate its functions to a team or group council or to a joint PCC. For clarification of the terms of resolutions see *ELJ*, 3 (1994), 247.   [119] S. 3(4).

[120] S. 4(1); Sched. 2.   [121] Ss. 3(2), 4(2).

specified classes. Those discharging any function in relation to the parish or benefice must not contravene a parochial resolution; those discharging any function concerning the conduct of services in a cathedral church or in relation to the appointment of the dean must not contravene a cathedral resolution.[122] Nor shall any bishop, priest, or deacon contravene or permit any act in contravention.[123] Though refusals to appoint a woman as dean, incumbent, priest-in-charge, team vicar, or assistant curate are expressly excluded from the sex discrimination legislation, it does not seem that the same protection is given to these resolutions.[124]

Under the code of practice, when a parish is part of a larger unit comprising a single benefice, or contains several churches, and in cases such as group ministries, 'especial sensitivity will be required in making appointments'. Effectively, the passing of a resolution by any one parochial church council prevents the appointment of a woman as incumbent of the benefice. This position must be respected, but each parochial church council within such a benefice should recognize the effect and implications that passing a resolution will have for the benefice as a whole. Similar considerations apply in cases of parishes containing churches of different traditions: '[i]t would be inappropriate to seek to appoint a woman as incumbent of a parish which contained a church whose congregation found her ministry unacceptable'; the same would apply to appointments of women as a team vicar or assistant curate whose area of responsibility would include that church.[125]

MINISTERIAL FUNCTIONS: CANONICAL MINISTRY

As in the Roman Catholic Church, the Church of England systematizes ministerial functions in two basic ways: they are distributed generally to all ordained ministers, priests and deacons alike, exercising their ministry in any field; and they are distributed according to particular ministries. Specific rights and duties are dealt with elsewhere in this study; the following is a description of the basic framework.

Basic Principles: Legal Status

Generally, clergy do not exercise ministry under a contract of employment—they are not employees.[126] Though admission to ordination and appointment to a

---

[122] Ss. 3(6), 4(5).   [123] S. 5(b),(c); C10(2A).   [124] S. 6: the resolutions are not listed.
[125] *POWMCP*, paras. 26–9.
[126] Employment Protection (Consolidation) Act 1978, s. 153(1): "employee" is defined as an individual who has entered into or works under a contract of employment. In *Re Tyler* the European Commission of Human Rights considered that 'the applicant's functions as a priest [of the Church of England] are more in the nature of public service than they are of private professional practice' (Application No. 21283/93).

ministerial post are based in a fundamental way upon agreement, clergy are treated legally as holders of an ecclesiastical office.[127] The expression 'office' commonly occurs in ecclesiastical legislation as denoting an order of ministry generically or a particular ministerial position created by law.[128] The underlying rationale is commonly understood to be that vocation to the ordained ministry and the spiritual nature of ministerial functions render the holding of ecclesiastical office incompatible with the existence of a contract of employment.[129] There may also be incompatability between the concept of contract and that of service.[130] Clerical functions, accordingly, are not defined in a contract but arise by operation of church law: this applies to both beneficed and unbeneficed clergy.[131] On the other hand, some ministries may be contractual and those engaged in them may be employees: functions pertaining to specialist sector ministries are normally determined by a contract of employment.[132] However,

[127] *OLAC*, 121 ff.; *Clergy Conditions of Service: A Consultative Paper* (1994, GS 1126) para. 27; *Great Western Railway v Bater* [1920] 3 KB 266 *per* Rowlatt J: an office is 'a subsisting, permanent, substantive position which had its existence independently from the person who filled it, which went on and was filled in succession by successive holders'; see also *Rogers v Booth* [1935] 2 All ER 751: Salvation Army officers; *Home Office v Robinson* [1982] ICR 31: prison officers; *AG for NSW v Perpetual Trustee Co Ltd* [1955] AC 451: trustees; for functions dictated by conscience and not law see *Van Roosmalen v Bestuur*, *Times* 29 Oct. 1986 (ECJ).

[128] See e.g. C4B (office of priest); C12(1)(b) (licence to perform some office); C22(4) (archdeacon's office); C26 (ministerial office); Pastoral Measure 1983, s. 20(2),(3) (offices in team ministry); see e.g. *DSBN*, Ad clerum notice, 1991/2 for 'job descriptions' applicable to non-stipendiary ministers.

[129] *Methodist Conference President v Parfitt* [1984] QB 368 (CA) (whilst no contract could be found, Lord Dillon nevertheless agreed that 'the spiritual nature of the work . . . and the spiritual discipline to which that person is subject may not necessarily, in an appropriate context, exlcude a contractual relationship . . . *A fortiori* it would be possible to draft a legally binding offer and a legally binding acceptance'; *Davies v Presbyterian Church of Wales* [1986] 1 All ER 705 (HL) (see generally, J. Bowers, *Employment Law* (London, 1990) 16–17); D. R. Howarth, 'Church and state in employment law', *CLJ*, 45 (1986), 404; A. N. Khan, 'Employment of church minister', *Solicitors Journal*, 131 (1987), 38; the statement in *OLAC*, 121 that '[t]he same reasoning applies with equal force to incumbents of the Church of England', may be criticised insofar as in these two cases ministerial functions were not, as in the Church of England, prescribed by the law of the land.

[130] There may be an analogy here with civil servants as servants of the Crown whose status, classically, is not contractual: *IRC v Hambrook Bros* [1956] 2 QB 641; however, recent cases suggest that a contract of some sort exists: *Kodeeswaran v AG for Ceylon* [1970] 2 WLR 456; *Malins v Post Office* [1975] ICR 60; *R v Civil Service Appeal Board, ex p Bruce* [1988] ICR 649, approved by CA [1989] ICR 171 and applied in *McLaren v Home Office* [1989] ICR 550.

[131] *Re National Insurance Act 1911, Re Employment of Church of England Curates* [1912] 2 Ch 563: an assistant curate is not an employed person but an office-holder, cited with approval in the cases referred to in n. 129 but doubted in *Barthorpe v Exeter Diocesan Board of Finance* [1979] ICR 900; *Turns v Smart, Carey and Bath and Wells Diocesan Board of Finance* (Employment Appeal Tribunal No. EAT 510–90, 11 June 1991) and *Fane v Bishop of Manchester* (Industrial Tribunal No. 8–229–232, 27 Feb. 1990); see *OLAC*, 122. See also *Coker v Diocese of Southwark* (unreported IT judgment, 24 Feb. 1995, London South): the chairman, Prof. R. W. Rideout, rejected the incompatability argument, holding that an assistant curate may be employed *Independent*, 16 Mar. 1995.

[132] For sector ministry in which a person will normally be an employee and for matters to be included in written particulars of employment for sector minister/employee see *OLAC*, 122–3,126–7; for the civil law tests see *Ready Mixed Concrete (South East) Ltd v Minister of Pensions and National Insurance* [1968] 2 QB 497.

those engaged in sector ministries may sometimes be both employees and office-holders.[133]

In one sense, regulation of ministry by law produces a fundamental tension in the concept of ministry itself: theologically ministers are treated as called by God to serve the community, yet the church wills its ministers to serve in the manner prescribed by law. Admission to the ordained ministry may be a voluntary response to vocation, but legally service is required. For this reason we might speak of a priest or deacon's *canonical ministry*. Whereas canon law articulates what the church defines as ministry, the minimal terms and conditions under which service is effected, ministerial rights and duties are particularized by synodical measures and executive norms, often adding to the canonical ministries (such as the ministry of healing or deliverance). Many rules are applicable to all ordained clergy regardless of the actual ministry in which they serve. Every minister ordained deacon or priest must exercise ministry in accordance with the law of the Church of England and may only do so after receiving authority to do so from the bishop of the diocese or other ordinary.[134] Every minister has a canonical duty to say daily morning and evening prayer, privately or openly, and to celebrate or to be present at the Eucharist on prescribed days; as in Roman Catholic canon law, all ministers have a duty to be diligent in daily prayer and intercession, to examine their consciences and to study scripture and such other matters pertaining to their ministerial duties.[135]

Not only do priests and deacons promise at ordination to do no work inconsistent with their ministry, but also they must not engage in occupations, habits, or recreations as do not befit their sacred calling, are detrimental to the performance of the duties of their office, or tend to be a just cause of offence to others. Similar rules exist in Roman Catholic canon law where, importantly, ministers are as a general rule forbidden to engage in political activity.[136]

---

[133] *OLAC*, 123: 'It is possible for someone to be both an office holder receiving a stipend [under the Diocesan Stipends Funds Measure 1953, s. 5, substituted by the Endowments and Glebe Measure 1976, s. 9] and engaged at the same time as a sector minister on a salary; for some purposes he would be an office holder and for others an employee, depending on which "job" was in view.'

[134] *AR*, Art. 23: 'It is not lawful for any man to take upon him the office of public preaching, or ministering the Sacraments in the Congregation, before he be lawfully called, and sent to execute the same'; C8(1),(2),(3): 'The bishop confers such authority on a minister either by instituting him to a benefice, or by admitting him to serve within the diocese by licence under his hand and seal, or by giving him written permission to officiate within the same.' The exceptions are listed in C8(2), including ministers of a church or chapel, sequestrator in a vacancy, members of cathedral chapters, those holding archiepiscopal licences to preach, and those performing funeral services under Church of England (Miscellaneous Provisions) Measure 1992, s. 2.

[135] C26(1); *CIC*, cc. 276, 277, 279; see *post* Ch. 10.

[136] C26(2): 'at all times he shall be diligent to frame and fashion his life and that of his family according to the doctrine of Chirst, and to make himself and them, as much as in him lies, wholesome examples and patterns to the flock of Christ'; *CIC*, cc. 285–9. For permanent deacons who may be married see cc. 1031 ff.

According to a statement of the House of Bishops, clergy should not engage in sexually active homophile partnerships: whereas 'intrusive interrogations' to determine this ought not to be undertaken, steps may be taken 'to avoid public scandal and to protect the Church's teaching'; however, 'all clergy who give no occasion for public scandal' must be treated with 'trust and respect'.[137] Beneficed and licensed clergy, and those holding cathedral preferment or any curacy or lectureship, are forbidden by parliamentary statute to farm (above eighty acres) for profit without written episcopal permission.[138] Nevertheless, it is lawful for a minister to engage in a trade or any other occupation if this is authorized by statute or by episcopal licence; ministers must inform the bishop of proposed extra-ministerial occupations.[139] With parochial ministry, a diocesan bishop may grant or refuse a licence only after consultation with the parochial church council; a right of appeal is exercisable within one month of the refusal to the appropriate archbishop.[140] Trading contracts entered into illegally are enforceable in civil law as if the contracting party had not been an ordained minister.[141] Finally, ordained ministers cannot be elected to the House of Commons though they are not disqualified with regard to local government;[142] clerics are eligible to vote at general and local government elections and enjoy exemption from jury service.[143]

The Deacon's Ministry

Criticism has been made recently in the Church of England that the diaconal order lacks a distinctive ministry: there is too great an emphasis on its transitional nature, as an apprenticeship to priesthood, and its generality.[144]

---

[137] *Issues in Human Sexuality*, A Statement of the House of Bishops (1991, GS misc. 382) 5.18. The steps to be taken are not specified.

[138] Pluralities Act 1838, s. 28 (he forfeits £2 p.a.; recoverable against unbeneficed clergy in the High Court: s. 117) and against beneficed clergy in the consistory court (EJM 1963, s. 6(1)(d)), *Rackham v Black* (1846) 9 QB 691); see also Residence of Incumbents Act 1869.

[139] Clergy (Ordination and Miscellaneous Provisions) Measure 1964, s. 11(1), which operates notwithstanding the Pluralities Act 1838; C28(1); exceptions are listed in the 1838 statute including, *inter alia*, tutors.

[140] Clergy (Ordination and Miscellaneous Provisions) Measure 1864, s. 11(2); C28(2), (3). The archbishop may confirm or overrule the diocesan's decision 'as may seem good to him'; during a vacancy-in-see the archbishop exercises the diocesan's powers: C28(4); for treatment in diocesan norms see e.g. *DSBN*, Ad clerum notice 1989/6: disregarding the basic prohibition is an ecclesiastical offence; for relaxation of the rule with regard to non-stipendiary ministry see e.g. *BF*, 3.8.

[141] Pluralities Act 1838, s. 31 (ministers illegally trading may be suspended and, for a third offence, deprived); see also *Lewis v Bright* (1855) 4 E&B 917.

[142] House of Commons (Clergy Disqualification) Act 1801, s. 1 (*Re MacManaway* [1951] AC 161; the Local Government Act 1972, s. 80 omits clerics from the categories of those disqualified.

[143] They are not disqualified under the Representation of the People Act 1983, s. 1; Juries Act 1974, s. 1, Sched. 1, Part I, Group C.

[144] See J. Tiller, *A Strategy for the Church's Ministry* (London, 1983) 107–14; for recommendation that the Church of England 'make provision for . . . an ordained distinctive diaconate' see *Deacons in the Ministry of the Church*, A Report to the House of Bishops of the General Synod of the Church of England (1988, GS 802); see also L. Leeder, 'The diaconate in the Church of England: a legal perspective', in C. Hall (ed.), *The Deacon's Ministry* (Leominster, 1992) 123.

The impreciseness of the ministry of deacons, much of which may be performed by the laity, is reflected in the formal structures of the church. The ministry is presented liturgically as one of service: to serve the church, to care for the disadvantaged, to strengthen the faithful, to preach, to assist the priest in leading worship, and to do such pastoral work as is entrusted.[145] Though there is no separate treatment of deacons as such in the canons (and what exists is scant), these ideas surface in law but the requirement that deacons are to care for the poor, the needy, and the sick does not.[146]

The deacon's functions are prescribed directly either by canon law and or by the bishop's licence or written permission.[147] The licence may be general: 'to preach or otherwise to minister' in any parish or ecclesiastical district, or limited: 'to perform some particular office'.[148] With respect to general licences, the deacon cannot exercise ministry (in any place) without the permission (and it is unclear whether this must be express or may be tacit) of the incumbent. However, the deacon has a right, without the consent of the incumbent, to minister at the homes of any persons on the electoral roll or in, *inter alia*, a university, college, school, hospital, or public or charitable institution in which he is licensed to officiate.[149] Licensed deacons qualify as members of the deanery synod's house of clergy, team or group ministry chapters, and parochial church councils.[150] A deacon member of a team ministry may be licensed to perform all such offices and services as may be performed by an incumbent if these are consistent with diaconal office.[151] Deacons have a right to participate in parochial assemblies,[152] to be elected to diocesan and national church assemblies,[153] and may be appointed as rural deans, residentiary and non-residentiary canons.[154] Their liturgical functions are limited: they may lead morning and evening prayer, but cannot pronounce the absolution, and they may assist in the celebration of the Eucharist, but cannot preside.[155] A deacon may baptize, ordinarily only 'in the absence of the priest' or 'when required to do so';[156] finally, with the consent of the incumbent a deacon may officiate at a marriage, but should rarely solemnize a marriage in the first year following ordination.[157] As we shall see elsewhere in this study all these liturgical functions, with the exception of marriage, may be performed by lay people.[158] These diaconal functions find direct parallels in

---

[145] *BCP*, Ordinal; *ASB*, 344.   [146] *OLAC*, 96.   [147] Ibid.
[148] C12(1)(a) and (b).   [149] C8(4).   [150] *CRR*, rr. 14, 20, 21, 24.
[151] Team and Group Ministries Measure 1994, s. 1(5); Pastoral Measure 1983, s. 20(3A).
[152] *CRR*, r. 6(3) (and a right to attend special extraordinary meetings: r. 32).
[153] *CRR*, r. 30(4); Canon H2.   [154] *Supra*, n. 95.
[155] *OLAC*, 4; absolution is reserved to priests (B29).   [156] See *post* Ch. 11.
[157] See *post* Ch. 13.
[158] Generally diocesan norms do not allocate to deacons additional functions, but repeat the basic principle described above (e.g. *RBG*, B.2); see generally *Deacons in the Ministry of the Church* (1988) Ch. 4.

Roman Catholic canon law which, unlike the Church of England, also provides for a permanent diaconate.[159]

The Parochial Ministry of Priests

The canonical ministry of parish priests, having a cure of souls, is to provide the liturgical services of the church, to present the church's doctrine, and to prepare candidates for and to administer the sacraments.[160] Every priest must be diligent in visiting parishioners, particularly the sick, and must be available to parishioners for spiritual counsel and advice.[161] Every priest unable to discharge his duties, whether from non-residence or some other cause, must provide for his cure to be supplied by a priest licensed or otherwise approved by the diocesan bishop.[162] These functions find a direct parallel in Roman Catholic canon law.[163]

Like Roman Catholic pastors, Church of England beneficed parish priests are under a duty to reside in the benefice.[164] They may not be absent in any one year for a period or accumulated periods exceeding three months unless the diocesan bishop licenses the absence or they are exempt from residence by law; a right of appeal lies against an episcopal refusal to the appropriate archbishop.[165] An episcopal licence continues in force until the end of the calendar year during which it was issued though it may be revoked beforehand, the priest having a right of appeal against revocation to the archbishop.[166] If there is no house of residence the bishop may license residence outside the benefice.[167] If a priest fails to reside, the bishop may order residence: if non-

---

[159] The 'distinctive diaconate' is only occasionally treated in diocesan norms in the Church of England (e.g. *PDH*, B.7). For Roman Catholic law see *CIC*, c. 236 and the *motu proprio, Sacrum diaconatus ordinem* (1967) for the permanent diaconate; the ministry of deacons includes baptism (c. 861), blessings if given by law (c. 1169), charitable works (c. 222), diocesan synod participation (c. 463), dispensing powers if given by law (c.89), liturgical roles (cc. 275, 1174), service (c. 207), and marriage (c. 1108); for transitional deacons see cc. 1030, 1031; *COCLA*, 1335, on c. 276, the episcopal conference of England and Wales has enacted that permanent deacons must recite daily morning and evening prayer. [160] C24(1)-(5): see *post* Chs. 9, 10.

[161] C24(6); diocesan norms commonly regulate visiting: e.g. *DSBN*, Ad clerum notice, 1989/7 regulates hospital visiting: it forbids entry of wards without staff permission, examination of admission lists, and passing on confidential information; for regulation of healing ministry and healing services see Canon B36 and *BF*, 11.10, 3.24; *PDH*, H.7; *RBG* A.9. [162] C24(8).

[163] *CIC*, cc. 528–30.

[164] Pluralities Act 1838, ss. 32–51; C25(1); for residence Roman Catholic canon law see *CIC*, cc. 283, 533.

[165] C25(2), (3). The right must be exercised within one month of refusal; the archbishop may confirm or overrule the refusal as seems to him 'just and proper'.

[166] Pluralities Act 1838, ss. 46, 49–51; duties cannot be resumed before the period of non-residence prescribed in the licence expires without episcopal permission: Pluralities Acts Amendment Act 1885, s. 12; see also *Pinder v Barr* (1854) 4 E&B 105; Pastoral Measure 1983, s. 68(3) covers residence when presentation is suspended.

[167] C25(4). The house must be within 3 miles of the church or chapel of the benefice or, if within a city or borough town of market town, within 2 miles.

residence persists, the priest forfeits, depending on the period of absence, part or all, of the emoluments of the benefice.[168]

In the wider church environment, parish priests are entitled to membership of all the parochial church's assemblies, committees, and deanery synod and chapter, but only if elected can they belong to diocesan synod or General Synod. The incumbent is under a canonical duty to consult with the parochial church council on matters of general concern and importance to the parish and is an *ex officio* member and chairman of the parochial church council, responsible for convening its meetings and, as chairman, must observe the laws governing the conduct of meetings; he has a second or casting vote.[169] In addition, parish priests enjoy rights, arising from synodical measures, canons, and diocesan norms, to participate in and to be consulted about a host of appointment and property matters concerning the parish.[170]

Team and Group Ministry

The Roman Catholic Church has little canon law on team ministries.[171] In the Church of England, the rector is the leader of team ministry. The scheme establishing the team ministry may fix the relationship of the rector to the other team members (licensed or permitted) or else the bishop may by licence assign any vicar to a special cure or pastoral responsibility in part of the area in question. In so doing the bishop may also prescribe that the vicar's function shall be independent of the rector's general responsibility which then becomes subject to the arrangements by licence. General responsibility may also be distributed under the scheme or licence between the rector and the vicar. Subject to the terms of the licence, a vicar has authority in the team area to carry out all such ministerial offices and services as may be exercised by an incumbent. The rector must convene meetings of the team chapter at regular intervals to discuss and to reach a common mind on all matters of general concern or special interest to the team ministry.[172]

In a group ministry each incumbent is authorized to perform, within the area of every benefice in the group, all such ministerial functions as belong to the incumbent of each benefice. All the incumbents must assist one another in order to make the best possible provision for the cure of souls in the group area. When operating in the area of a benefice other than his own, each

---

[168] Pluralities Act 1838, ss. 32, 54–6; s. 114 regulates recovery in the consistory court.

[169] C24(7); for *CRR* see *supra* Ch. 4.

[170] See *supra* for appointments and *post* Part VI for property matters.

[171] *CIC*, c. 543; G. Cora, 'Team ministry: theological aspects', *American Ecclesiastical Review*, 167 (1973), 684.

[172] Pastoral Measure 1983 s. 20(1), (7), (8), (10); *PMCP*, B4(1), (6): allocating functions by licence produces a greater flexibility as functions defined under a scheme might be changed only by altering the scheme; diocesan norms usually add no more than appears in the code of practice: e.g. *SDDH*, K.5–12; *PDH*, K.8; Team and Group Ministries Measure 1994, s. 1(11) allows any member of team ministry to convene a meeting of the chapter after notice is given to a rector who refuses.

incumbent is obliged to comply with the directions of the incumbent of that other benefice. Incumbents must meet as a chapter to discuss all matters of concern to the group ministry.[173]

Cathedral Ministries

As a general principle, cathedral schemes, constitutions, and statutes may specify the functions of cathedral staff.[174] Cathedral duties are those duties in connection with the cathedral church or pastoral duties in the diocese which, in the opinion of the cathedral's administrative body, are discharged from the cathedral church as the mother church of the diocese. Two residentiary canons must be engaged exclusively in cathedral duties.[175] The cathedral dean is both head of the general chapter and the administrative chapter of a dean and chapter cathedral, and a cathedral provost is head of the cathedral chapter of a parish church cathedral: both are *ex officio* members of the diocesan synod and may be elected by their fellow deans and provosts to the General Synod's house of clergy.[176] Deans, provosts, and canons residentiary have a general canonical duty diligently to observe the law applicable to cathedrals including the requirements of the statutes and customs of the cathedral and those directions issuing from the bishop as visitor. They must reside in the cathedral, maintain the standards of divine service there, and perform all duties of office unless hindered by weighty and urgent causes. These, along with assistant clergy at cathedrals (unbeneficed and commonly known as minor canons or vicars choral), must also provide, so far as in them lies, that divine service be conducted with reverence, care, and solemnity.[177] Though it has been questioned whether a cathedral dean, provost, or canon has a cure of souls in the diocese at large,[178] staff of a parish church cathedral have the same functions and responsibilities as those in parochial ministry.

Other Specialist Ministries

Subject to the overriding ministry of bishops, archdeacons enjoy full and equal ordinary jurisdiction over a portion of the diocese,[179] an archdeaconry, which

---

[173] Pastoral Measure 1983, s. 21(1), (2), (4); *PMCP*, B4(7); for treatment in diocesan norms see e.g. *SDDH*, K.13; *PDH*, K.9; see also *Good Practice in Group and Team Ministry*, ACCM Occasional Paper No. 39 (Jan. 1991).

[174] Cathedrals Measure 1963, s. 11(1), (2); for chapters of canons, *CIC*, cc. 503–10.

[175] Cathedrals Measure 1963, s. 9(2); these do not include duties performed by *inter alia* a suffragan, assistant bishop, or archdeacon.

[176] *CRR*, r. 30(4)(a)(ii); Canon H2 (convocation); for representation in deanery synods, *CRR*, r. 27 (by scheme); see generally *supra* Ch. 4. [177] Canon 21(1)-(4).

[178] *HLE*, paras. 640, 644; *Ecclesiastical Commissioners v Dean and Chapter of Kildare* (1858) 8 I Ch R 93 (CA).

[179] Ecclesiastical Commissioners Act 1836, Preamble and s. 19; Canon 22(2); the office is a corporation sole: *Tufnell v Constable* (1838) 7 Ad & El 798; whether an archdeacon has a cure of souls as such is unclear: R. Phillimore, *Ecclesiastical Law*, I, 382.

he exercises in person or through an official or commissary to whom authority is formally committed.[180] Like vicars-general and episcopal vicars in the Roman Catholic Church, the archdeacon must assist the bishop in his pastoral care and office, ensuring that duties attaching to all ecclesiastical offices in the archdeaconry are fulfilled diligently, and bringing to the attention of the bishop matters which require correction or deserve praise;[181] he must carry out an annual visitation, survey all church property, and induct priests.[182] Diocesan norms commonly distribute tasks to archidiaconal ministry, in addition to the many key administrative and judicial functions allocated directly or through delegation by the church's central legal system: these emphasize the partnership of bishop and archdeacon in the priestly, pastoral, and teaching ministry of the diocese.[183] Some norms stress that the archdeacon is to represent the bishop's interests in the policy-making and business life of the diocese through *ex officio* membership of the statutory synodical and other major committees of the diocese.[184] An archdeacon is not, however, an intermediary or in a line management role between the bishop and clergy or laity.[185]

The function of a rural dean is supervisory: to report to the bishop any matter in a deanery parish which it may be necessary or useful for a bishop to know; in particular he must report clerical illness or distress, any vacancy of any cure of souls, any measures taken by sequestrators to secure the administration of the word and sacraments and other rites during a vacancy, and any case of a minister from another diocese officiating in the deanery without episcopal authorization. The rural dean must also report to the bishop any failure in a parish to maintain an electoral roll or to form or maintain a parochial church council or annual parochial meeting. Further, if he has reason to believe there is any serious defect in the fabric, ornaments, and furniture of any church or chapel, or that buildings of any benefice are in a state of disrepair, he must report the matter to the archdeacon.[186] The rural dean is joint chairman, with a member of the house of laity, of the deanery synod, and may also be a member of the diocesan synod, the lower house of convocation and the house of clergy of the General Synod.[187] Within the

---

[180] C22(3); see also Church of England (Miscellaneous Provisions) Measure 1983, s. 9: if the archdeacon is absent or ill the bishop may appoint by instrument a priest to perform any or all of his functions.

[181] C22(4),(5); see generally R. L. Ravenscroft, 'The role of the archdeacon today', *ELJ*, 3 (1995), 379 *CIC*, c. 479 for the administrative duties of vicar general and episcopal vicar and c. 480 for the duty to report to the bishop.

[182] C22(4), (5); Inspection of Churches Measure 1955; for his role in the faculty jurisdiction see *post* Ch. 16.

[183] *CF*, A.4.2; *LDHI*, IV, 2: as his officer, the archdeacon is answerable to the bishop; *SDDH*, H.1–5.　　　　　　　　　　　　　　　　　　　　　　　　　　[184] See Chs. 4 and 6.

[185] *CF*, A.4.3; *WH*, BP.4. The archdeacon must maintain close co-operation with the diocesan secretary and is the first line of approach in the consultative process between the parishes and the diocese.　　　　　　　　　　　　　　　　　　　　　　　　　　　　　[186] C23(1)-(3).

[187] C23(4); *CRR*, r. 28(1)(a); r. 30(4)(b): right to be elected from deanery synod to diocesan synod; H2 (convocation)

framework set by the church's central legal system, the rural dean's functions may be further specified by diocesan norms.[188]

It is difficult to generalize about the functions of those in extra-parochial and sector ministry. In addition to basic regulation by synodical measure and canon, functions are prescribed by the terms of the office held (which may be statutory), by the terms of the contract of employment (if there is one), as well as by the terms of the episcopal licence or permission enabling service. Like the episcopally given faculty in Roman Catholic canon law,[189] the bishop of the diocese in which the ministry is served, such as in schools, colleges, hospitals, or prisons, may license a minister to perform such offices and services (with the exception of solemnizing marriages) on any premises belonging to the institution in question as are specified in the licence; the ministry may be exercised without the consent of the incumbent of the benefice in which the ministry is located.[190] Chaplaincy ministries are typical of the multiplicity of forms of regulation available.[191] As an illustration: under parliamentary statute every prison must have a chaplain who, ordinarily, must be an ordained minister of the Church of England; a person cannot be chaplain of two prisons unless the prisons are within convenient distance of each other and together receive not more than one hundred prisoners; the chaplain cannot officiate without licence from the diocesan bishop.[192] The prison governor must supply a list of prisoners belonging to the Church of England whom, with their consent, the chaplain must interview on reception and before release and visit regularly during the period of imprisonment.[193] Chaplains must conduct divine service at least every Sunday and other prescribed days and such celebrations of communion and weekday services

---

[188] *PDH*, App. 9 (dealing with vacancies and planning induction services); *SDH*, VI, D.6. He is responsible for the maintenance of services during a vacancy and for conveying the needs and opportunities of the deanery to the deanery synod; *WH*, BP.3: interviewing candidates for ordination; for deanery chapters see *SDDH*, I.1–8; *LDHI*, IV, 2, *TBF*, 5.2, *BDM*, B.5: these 'should not ne used as an occasion for conducting deanery business which is properly the concern of the deanery synod'; *TBF*, 5.3: to assist ecumenical co-operation in the deanery; *LDHI*, IV, 2: rural dean is subordinate to the archdeacon.

[189] *CIC*, c. 566 (and cc. 567–70 for particular chaplaincy ministries); a chaplain must maintain a close relationship with the pastor: c. 571.

[190] Extra-Parochial Ministry Measure 1967, s. 2; Canons B41(2), (3), C8(4); Army Chaplains Act 1868, s. 6

[191] Extra-Parochial Ministry Measure 1967, s. 2(5); for hospitals see *LDHI*, II, 7: parochial clergy must inform the archdeacon to arrange for cover; *TBF*, 11.6: chaplaincy with deaf people; *CF*, E.9.1–2: industry.

[192] Prison Act 1952, s. 7(1): if in the opinion of the Home Secretary it is large enough, an assistant chaplain may be appointed: s. 7(2)); the Chaplain General of Prisons is the responsible senior cleric; one of General Synod's standing commissions is that for prison chaplains; extra-ordinarily, ministers of other religious denominations may be appointed by the Home Secretary: s. 10.

[193] Prison Act 1952, s. 10(5); Prison Rules 1964, SI No. 388, r. 11: a particular duty exists to visit the sick and those under restraint or cellular confinement, r. 12(1).

as might be arranged.[194] Sector ministries' functions are governed by the terms of a contract of employment (where appropriate), by the terms of an episcopal licence, or written permission and by diocesan norms.[195]

PASTORAL CARE FOR MINISTERS

The Roman Catholic Church has a complex range of canonical duties designed to ensure that sacred ministers are supported by clergy and laity alike.[196] Apart from rights to housing, sickness benefits, stipends, and pensions (described in Part VI) the Church of England has little detailed legal provision for the day-to-day pastoral care of clergy.[197] In the event of incapacity through illness or disciplinary action, diocesan bishops, clergy having cure of souls, and lay officers have a legal responsibility to provide cover.[198] The diocesan bishop has an express canonical duty to safeguard the pastoral welfare of diocesan clergy,[199] and the rural dean must report to the bishop 'any case of serious illness or other form of distress amongst the clergy'.[200] Moreover, at ordination, institution, and induction the people promise to uphold clergy in their ministry.[201] In disability cases at parochial level, the bishop has extensive powers to appoint, with the consent of the incumbent, an assistant curate, and to authorize a leave of absence.[202] In the event of absence through sickness clergy are usually obliged to inform the churchwardens and rural dean to arrange cover.[203]

Clergy care is subject to more detailed regulation by diocesan norms. Though there is no general statutory or canonical right to holidays, diocesan norms recommend that clergy in full-time service take an annual holiday for periods varying between dioceses as well as a day off each week; lay members of parishes should respect these arrangements.[204] Churchwardens are asked to help 'protect' clergy families from undue burdens during periods of illness.[205]

---

[194] Prison Rules, r. 13.   [195] *SDDH*, J.1; *LDR*, 55; *SDH*, VII, C.11.

[196] *CIC*, cc. 275, 281, 283, 384.

[197] The church has many organizations (often with charitable status) giving specialist help: *CEYB* (1995).   [198] See *supra*. For ministers see C24(8).

[199] C18(1); for the bishop as *pastor pastorum* see J. Tiller, *A Strategy for the Church's Ministry* (1985) 91; *Report of the Lambeth Conference 1978* (London, 1978) 44, 77 ff., 94 ff.

[200] C23(1); some dioceses place responsibility for reporting instances of sickness or absence directly upon ministers: *SDH*, V, D.

[201] *ASB*, 344,356; see J. Tiller, *Church's Ministry*, 65 f., and *post* Ch. 8.

[202] Incumbents (Vacation of Benefices) Measure 1977, ss. 6, 11(2).

[203] *GDM*, A.6, G.1–9; *NDIB*, I, 7.1; *BDM*, B.7.2.

[204] *CF*, E.10.2.1, *GDM*, A.7, *BDM*, B.8 (4 wks); *WH*, BP.36 (5 wks); *TBF*, 3.1.3, *PDH*, C.12, App. 1 (6 wks); *RBG*, B; *NDIB*, I, 7.2.

[205] E.g. *SDH*, V, D.1–14: ministers are advised to contact archdeacons who might arrange grant aid during periods of convalescence.

Dioceses operate systems of discretionary grants to be awarded for holidays or sabbaticals arranged by agreement with diocesan authorities.[206] Diocesan norms frequently contain guidance on clergy unemployment and those in sector ministry are advised to ensure the inclusion of terms and conditions relating to holidays in the contract of employment.[207]

For counselling, many diocesan norms confer a right on diocesan clergy to see the bishop privately to discuss pastoral or personal problems,[208] or else to approach the archdeacon under his canonical duty to assist the bishop with pastoral care in the diocese.[209] Dioceses commonly employ procedures and staff (usually appointed by the bishop) to give confidential advice on a range of personal matters,[210] including advice to retired clergy and clergy widows.[211] More particular pastoral care is facilitated by systems of episcopal review or appraisal. Diocesan norms frequently impose a mandatory duty on all clergy following invitation by one of the bishop's senior staff, to attend and take part in the episcopal review, an extended interview, preceded by the completion of a questionnaire, designed to study the cleric's ministry, to assess aims, and to discuss personal or pastoral problems. Following the interview, provision is made for the report (which must remain confidential) to be sent to the diocesan bishop; usually a right is given for the minister to see the report.[212]

MINISTERIAL DISCIPLINE: CANONICAL OBEDIENCE

The basis of clerical discipline in both the Church of England and the Roman Catholic Church is the doctrine of canonical obedience.[213] It has two facets: the duty to obey the law of the church and the duty to obey episcopal directions.

---

[206] E.g. *LDR*, 170; *BDM*, B.8; *SDH*, V, B.　　[207] *OLAC*, 126.

[208] *TBF*, 1.1(a); *RBG*, B; *SDH*, V, E; some dioceses also operate a joint work consultancy scheme by which consultants voluntarily give assistance to clergy; such schemes are usually supervised by the Joint Work Consultancy Working Group under the aegis of a Diocesan Training Committee.

[209] *SDH*, V, F: some dioceses have consultant psychiatrists, a wide range of bodies and fellowships for the clergy, and a 'bishop's visitor' to give practical advice; Broken Rites, for example, is an independent association of divorced and separated wives of Anglican clergy: *CEYB*.

[210] *CDH*, 140; *PDH*, C.27; *GDM*, A.10: unemployment; see also *Clergy Conditions of Service* (1994), para. 133.

[211] *SDH*, V, H, which refers to *What's What*, an annual publication setting out rules and policies affecting the welfare of clergy within the diocese.　　[212] *CF*, A.2; *PDH*, B.14; *WH*, BP.9.

[213] The oath must be taken by ordained priests and deacons, those instituted to a benefice, and those licensed: C13(1); Clerical Subscription Act 1865, ss. 4,59; Promissory Oaths Act 1868, ss. 2, 8; it need not be taken by those consecrated bishop to serve overseas or by overseas clergy under the Overseas and Other Clergy (Ministry and Ordination) Measure 1967, and may be dispensed with by the bishop for those ordained for ministry overseas: C13(2).

Obedience to Law: Ecclesiastical Offences

In common with Roman Catholic canon law,[214] all ministers of the Church of England are under a general duty to obey, and to exercise their particular ministry in accordance with, the laws of the church. This duty is imposed specifically by the law itself[215] and generally by virtue of the status of that law as part of the law of the land.[216] The canons of the church bind the clergy *proprio vigore* in spiritual matters[217] and, if declaratory of the usage and law (including the ecclesiastical law) of the realm, they may bind in temporal matters.[218] Discipline may be enforced executively or by judicial proceedings.

The Roman Catholic Church claims an inherent right (c. 1311) to penalize a wide range of canonical offences being external violations of a law or precept to which a penalty attaches. To penalize, a violation must be gravely imputable to the person by reason of deliberate intention or culpable negligence (c. 1321).[219] The Church of England prohibits, by the Ecclesiastical Jurisdiction Measure 1963, two sorts of offence against the laws ecclesiastical: reserved cases, 'offence[s] against the laws ecclesiastical involving matters of doctrine, ritual and ceremonial'; and conduct cases, 'offence[s] against the laws ecclesiastical, including (i) conduct unbecoming a clerk in Holy Orders; or (ii) serious, persistent, or continuous neglect of duty'. No proceedings may be taken in respect of conduct unbecoming or neglect of duty 'in respect of the political opinions or activities of such person'.[220] The repeal by this measure of any statutory provision under which proceedings could have been taken for an offence against the ecclesiastical law does not prevent the taking of proceedings under this measure in respect of such an offence; except where a contrary intention appears, the repeal of earlier enactments dealing with cleric indiscipline does not affect those offences recognized by the common

---

[214] *CIC*, c. 129(1); the Archbishop's Commission 1947 recommended the creation of a canon in the form: 'The Law of the Church of England is binding upon, and shall be enforceable by and against, the clergy'; any 'infraction of, or neglect to observe, such Canon Law . . . shall be deemed to be an ecclesiastical offence' (draft Canon 9, *RACCL*, 108). For a theological setting of the problem see B. Rogerson, 'Law, grace and liberty and clergy discipline', *ELJ*, 3 (1994), 149.
[215] C8(1).   [216] See *supra* Ch. 3.
[217] *Matthew v Burdett* (1703) 2 Salkeld 412: 'If the King and clergy make a canon it binds the clergy in *re ecclesiastica*'; *Cooper v Dodd* (1850) 7 Notes of Cases 514 at 532 (Dean of Arches considered Canon 68 of the 1603 Canons as binding); *Escott v Mastin* (1842) 4 Moore's Privy Council Cases 104 at 139; *Bishop of Exeter v Marshall* (1868) LR 3 HL 17 *per* Lord Chelmsford and Lord Westbury at 47, 54 (though Willes J was in doubt: 43); *Banister v Thompson* [1908] P 362 at 385 (Arches Court, Dean: 1603 Canons 'bind the clergy re ecclesiastica'); *R v Dibdin* [1910] P 57 at 110 (CA: Cozens-Hardy MR not prepared to express an opinion); *Blunt v Park Lane Hotel* [1942] 2 KB 253.
[218] *Bishop of Exeter v Marshall* (1868) LR 3 HL 17 at 54; *RACCL* (1947) 77–8.
[219] The Code lists specific offences to which particular penalities attach including: offences against religion and the unity of the church (cc. 1365–9) or against church authorities (cc. 1370–7) and offences against particular duties such as engagement in prohibited activities or non-residence (cc. 1392–6).   [220] S. 14(1); HL Deb, Vol. 249, 1435 at 1437 (16 May 1963).

law with respect to ecclesiastical matters.[221] Doctrine offences, including heresy, blasphemy, impious opinions contrary to the Christian religion, depraving the Book of Common Prayer, and maintaining opinions repugnant to the Thirty-Nine Articles, are, it seems, both ecclesiastical offences and offences at common law.[222] Ritual and ceremonial offences involve a violation of the law requiring conformity of worship.[223]

Though no definition of 'conduct unbecoming' appears in the 1963 Measure, the expression has been understood judicially as conduct which offends the canonical requirements (described above) as to an ordained minister's manner of life.[224] Though the Measure does not specify this,[225] according to pre–1963 judicial decisions conduct is unbecoming only if serious, persistent, and continuous. Drunkenness, incontinence, irreverent language in the pulpit, and the solicitation of chastity have been classified as such;[226] *Bishop of Ely v Moore* (1913) decided that 'the occasional use of bad language [would] not justify a charge of its habitual use'.[227] However, writing a single rude or obscene letter, or a series of such letters, to a parishioner may constitute an offence.[228]

Neglect of duty, also undefined in the Measure, which must be serious, persistent, or continuous, has been understood judicially as failure or refusal without due cause to perform an ecclesiastical duty.[229] Failure to make due enquiry of parties' residence or as to impediments prior to solemnization of marriage[230] and failure to observe the requirements of ministerial residence may constitute neglect of duty,[231] as may refusing to admit to Holy Communion,

---

[221] S. 14(2); S. 87, Sched. 5 repeals the Church Discipline Act 1840 and the Incumbents (Discipline) Measures 1947 to 1953.   [222] See *post* Ch. 9.

[223] See *post* Ch. 10: common law offences are still cognizable by the ecclesiastical courts: *HLE*, paras. 1353, 1355.

[224] C26(2); *Burridge v Tyler* [1992] 1 All ER 437; for conduct unbecoming under *CIC*, see c. 285.   [225] See *supra* Ch. 5 for sufficiency of single acts.

[226] For drunkenness see *Bishop of Rochester v Harris* [1893] P 137; *Marriner v Bishop of Bath and Wells* (1878) 42 JP 436 (PC); for incontinence, see *Free v Burgoyne* (1828) 2 Bli NS 65 (HL); *Kitson v Loftus* (1845) 4 Notes of Cases; *Bonwell v Bishop of London* (1861) 14 Moo PCC 395; for solicitation of chastity see *Berney v Bishop of Norwich* (1867) 36 LJ Eccl 10 (PC).

[227] *Bishop of Ely v Close* [1913] P 184 at 195 *per* Dean of Arches (citing *Moore v Bishop of Oxford* [1904] AC 283). The prosecution was founded on the now repealed Clergy Discipline Act 1892.

[228] In *Bishop of Ely v Moore* [1913] P 184 the sending of a single obscene letter to a parishioner was held to constitute an offence (an immoral act signifying unbecoming conduct) under the Clergy Discipline Act 1892, ss. 2, 12; *Bland v Archdeacon of Cheltenham* [1972] 1 All ER 1012 at 1020: *inter alia*, the writing of several rude letters; it is arguable that the Deputy Dean of Arches made the assumption that a single act could constitute an offence: 'the respondent did not choose to rely on each of the six letters as in itself constituting an offence'. 'A single act or omission cannot constitute a series of acts or omissions' when 'the particulars of each offence showed that the offence charged consisted of more than one act'.

[229] *Bland v Archdeacon of Cheltenham* [1972] 1 All ER 1012 at 1015.

[230] Canons B33, B35; *Priestly v Lamb* (1801) 6 Ves 421; *Wynn v Davies and Weaver* (1835) 1 Curt 69; see *post* Ch. 13.

[231] For residence see *Bluck v Rackham* (1846) 5 Moo PCC 305 at 312, 313; for failure to attend a visitation see *Clewer v Pullen* (1684) Rothery's Precedents, No. 79, 36.

refusing or delaying baptism, refusing burial and marriage. In any event refusal must be wilful and without just or lawful cause: a conscientious objection will not excuse in the absence of express legal provision.[232] Acts detrimental to the performance of ministerial duties, such as engaging in a trade or occupation without episcopal licence, may also constitute neglect of duty.[233] Finally, ecclesiastical offences may be committed by performing any ministerial function whilst disqualified by a censure,[234] by officiating in a diocese whilst inhibited or unlicensed, by officiating in a benefice without the consent of the incumbent,[235] by making alterations to the fabric, fittings, or ornaments of a church or churchyard without faculty,[236] or by contravening an episcopal declaration or parochial church council resolution barring the ministry of women priests.[237] Although 'neglect' does not mean 'negligence', and 'neglect of duty' does not mean 'breach of a duty of care',[238] absence of negligence in the non-performance of a duty may excuse.[239] However, in the Church of England there is no equivalent to the list of general defences available in Roman Catholic canon law, nor to the principle that imputability may be presumed.[240]

Obedience to Episcopal Directions

Ministers of the Church of England have a duty to obey the directions of their bishops. The duty flows from a promise under oath by which the minister 'voluntarily submit[s] himself to the authority of the bishop'.[241] According to Canon C14(3) '[e]very person who is to be ordained priest or deacon, or to be

---

[232] For communion see *Banister v Thompson* [1908] P 362; *R v Dibdin* [1910] P 57 (CA); *post* Ch. 12; *Bland v Archdeacon of Cheltenham* [1972] 1 All ER 1012 at 1017, citing the unreported case of *Watkins-Grubb v Hilder* (1965) (Canterbury provincial court): ' . . . it is clear beyond question that when offences are proved it is no defence to allege that the offence was caused by a conscientious objection to the performance of statutory duties or other lawful requirements'. For communion and marriage see *post* Part IV; for burial see *Escott v Mastin* (1842) 4 Moo PCC 104 and *Cooper v Dodd* (1850) 2 Rob Eccl 270. See also *Bishop of St Albans v Fillingham* [1906] P 164 at 176, when the cleric 'having in the first instance deliberately, and after repeated warnings, committed the act complained of, has deliberately, after many months' opportunity for consideration, adhered to his main position as right and justifiable'.

[233] *Re Bartlett* (1848) 3 Exch 28; *Bartlett v Kirwood* (1853) 2 E & B 771; *Bonaker v Evans* (1850) 16 QB 162.   [234] EJM 1963, s. 87.

[235] *Barnes v Shore* (1846) 8 QB 640; *Nesbitt v Wallace* [1901] P 354.

[236] *St Pancras Vestry v Vicar and Churchwardens of St Martins-in-the-Fields* (1860) 6 Jur NS 540; *Lee v Vicar and Churchwardens of Herne* (1892) Trist 217; it is possible for proceedings to be instituted in the High Court for contempt of court: EJM 1963, s. 81(2), (3).

[237] Priests (Ordination of Women) Measure 1993, s. 5.

[238] *Bland v Archdeacon of Cheltenham* [1972] 1 All ER 1012, rejecting the view of Moore Ch in the Con. Ct.

[239] As to residence and marriage, if a cleric has used 'due diligence' and 'reasonable means' in the inquiry, he will not be liable: *Nicholson v Squire* (1809) 16 Ves 259 *per* Lord Eldon.

[240] *CIC*, cc. 1322–4.

[241] *Long v Bishop of Capetown* (1863) 1 Moo PCCNS 411 (PC); 15 ER 756 at 775 *per* Lord Kingsdown; *Barnes v Shore* (1846) 8 QB 640.

instituted to any benefice, or to be licensed either in any lectureship, preach-ership, or stipendiary curacy, or to serve in any place, shall first take the Oath of Canonical Obedience to the bishop of the diocese by whom he is to be ordained, instituted or licensed, in the presence of the said bishop or his commissary'. The sworn oath, similar to that taken in the Roman Catholic Church, is in the form: 'I, AB, do swear by Almighty God that I will pay true and canonical obedience to the Lord Bishop of C and his successors in all things lawful and honest: So help me God'.[242] It has been suggested that there is no objection in law to, for example, a canon or prebendary taking an oath of canonical obedience to the dean and chapter by which that person promises to observe the rules of the capitular body.[243] Moreover, as in the Roman Catholic Church,[244] canon law imposes directly on all clergy a duty to obey episcopal commands after having been authorized to exercise their ministry. Canon C1(3) prescribes that, according to the ancient law and usage of the church and realm, 'the inferior clergy who have received authority to minister in any diocese owe canonical obedience in all things lawful and honest to the bishop of the same'.

Several critical observations may be made about the scope and terms of these arrangements which, it is submitted, are badly drafted and in need of revision. First, one or other of Canon C14 and Canon C1(3) is legally super-fluous: the oath amounts to a promise to fulfil a pre-existing obligation to obey episcopal directions arising by operation of Canon C1(3); the oath has merely symbolic significance.[245] Secondly, there is no definition of 'inferior clergy'.[246] Thirdly, the expression 'who have received authority to minister in any diocese' is ambiguous. Interpreted narrowly, it may mean that a cleric authorized by Bishop X to minister in diocese X1 owes obedience only to Bishop X;[247] indeed, obedience is not owed to all bishops serving in a diocese.[248] However, interpreted widely it may mean that a cleric authorized by Bishop X to minister in diocese X1 owes obedience to Bishop Y when visiting diocese Y1. The expression may also be unnecessary: any minister 'authorized' (by institution or licence) to serve in a diocese will have taken the

---

[242] C14(3); see also Clerical Subscription Act 1865, s. 12: 'Nothing in this Act contained shall extend to or affect the oath of canonical obedience to the bishop'; for the Roman Catholic position see *Rites* I, 54, 64. [243] *OLAC*, 187.

[244] *CIC*, cc. 273, 274; *CIC: TC*, 205.

[245] P. S. Atiyah, *Promises, Morals and Law* (Oxford, 1981) 187–90; C1(3) is general and C14 particular: the general duty is made specific and personal by the oath.

[246] Archdeacons take an oath of obedience to the bishop. Deans do likewise, with the exception of Norwich: P. L. S. Barrett, *Barchester: English Cathedral Life in the Nineteenth Century* (London, 1993) 327, n. 8.

[247] See *HLE*, para. 660, n.10 for the view that although under C14(3) the oath requires obedience to the diocesan bishop who ordained the candidate 'it is unlikely that . . . at an ordination under letters dimissory . . . the oath should be other than to the bishop who issued them'.

[248] A prison chaplain (e.g.) would not owe obedience to the bishop for prisons, nor a minister to a flying bishop or episcopal visitor (*quaere* to a suffragan not acting under power delegated by the diocesan): but respect is due to them under the declaration made at ordination.

Disobedience to lawful and honest episcopal commands may constitute an ecclesiastical offence, perhaps the most serious.[254] In so far as canonical obedience is a ministerial duty, proceedings would be for neglect of duty, and actionable disobedience would have to be serious, persistent, or continuous, wilful, and obstinate,[255] though in *Rugg v Bishop of Winchester* (1868) it was said that disobedience of episcopal directions went 'beyond . . . neglect of duty'.[256] A clerical promise of reform may not be sufficient to prevent proceedings.[257] It is unclear whether a bishop may release a minister whilst still ordained from the sworn oath of obedience; in any event the duty of obedience directly imposed by canon law remains.[258]

Sanctions

When an ecclesiastical offence has been established in the church's courts, the censures which may be pronounced are prescribed by the Ecclesiastical Jurisdiction Measure 1963.[259] Generally, two censures cannot be imposed for a single offence,[260] and if an offender gives a satisfactory assurance of obedience in the future pronouncement of censure is not obligatory.[261] In the absence of any enacted provision to the contrary, the court has a discretion as to the severity of the censure depending on the gravity of the offence and may take into account the interests and wishes of parishioners.[262] Sanctions available in the Church of England are similar to those in the Roman Catholic

or through neglect disobeying lawful commands; lawful commands are those not contrary to English or international law and justified by military law; for disobedience of superior commands not manifestly illegal see *Keighley v Bell* (1866) 4 F & F 763 at 790, 805; *R v Trainer* (1864) 4 F & F 105 at 112.

[254] *Combe v De La Bere* (1881) 6 PD 157 at 172.

[255] EJM 1963, s. 14; *Tuckniss v Alexander* (1863) 32 LJ Ch 794 at 806; see also *Julius v Bishop of Oxford* (1880) 5 PC (HL) at 226 *per* Earl Cairns LC: no action should be taken if the offence is 'of so trifling and insignificant a nature that no one, having any discretion in this matter, ought to allow it to be the subject of litigation'. [256] (1868) LR 2 PC 223 at 235.

[257] *Julius v Bishop of Oxford* (1880) 5 PC (HL) 214 at 226.

[258] *Barnes v Shore* (1846) 8 QB 640 at 671 *per* Lord Denman: 'when he vowed and promised canonical obedience to that Church; from . . . that vow and promise he can be released only by the same authority which . . . enjoined and received' that vow and promise. The effects of the oath lapse on appointment to a different diocese; the duty is contingent on the office held.

[259] S. 49.

[260] S. 49(6) However, suspension and inhibition may be pronounced for the same period.

[261] *Read v Bishop of Lincoln* [1892] AC 644 (PC). The case concerned ritual, doctrine, and ceremonial, and therefore may not be of general applicability.

[262] Ibid., 669; *Martin v Mackonochie* (1882) 7 PD 94 at 99 (PC); *Bland v Archdeacon of Cheltenham* [1972] 1 All ER 1012 at 1016; at first instance, Moore Ch explained: 'it has long been the practice of the courts spiritual to pass sentence *pro salute animae*—for the good of the soul— and I give that a wider interpretation, and say that I think it is my duty to pass sentence *pro salute animarum*—for the good of souls, which includes both the [appellant], the convicted clerk himself, and the souls of those who were committed to his care' (criticized ibid., 1021: the gravity of the offence was the paramount consideration for the purposes of censure).

Church,[263] though there are no equivalents in English canon law to the Catholic distinctions between expiatory and medicinal penalties, penal transfers, or the principle that a person might be penalized, when there is an urgent need to prevent or cure scandal, for offensive conduct not listed as a canonical offence.[264]

Deprivation, which may be imposed for any offence under the 1963 Measure, is *removal* from any preferment held and *disqualification* from holding any other preferment; if no preferment is held at the time, a minister may be disqualified from holding preferment in the future. However, further preferment may be held with the consent of a diocesan bishop, the appropriate archbishop, and the bishop of the diocese where the censure was imposed.[265] When one of a prescribed set of sanctions has been imposed by a secular court, the bishop must refer the matter to the archbishop who has a discretion, without further trial, to impose the censure of deprivation and disqualification; there is no right of appeal against the archbishop's decision.[266] Inhibition disqualifies for a specified time from exercising ministerial functions: it does not not disqualify from future preferment nor ordinarily does it remove from preferment.[267] Suspension is disqualification for a specified time from exercising or performing, without the bishop's leave, any right or duty attached to or incidental to the preferment or from residing in the house of residence of the preferment (or within a specified distance). Suspension may accompany an inhibition for the same period.[268] Suspended or inhibited persons must not interfere with any person appointed to discharge ministerial functions, nor (as a general rule) reside in or occupy the house of residence belonging to the office.[269] Monition is an order to do or refrain from doing a specified act constituting an ecclesiastical offence.[270] The least severe censure is rebuke.[271]

---

[263] *CIC*, c. 1341: sanctions must be a last resort; for removal and deprivation of offices, cc. 192–3, 1336; for suspension cc. 1333–4; for monition and rebuke cc. 1312, 1339.

[264] *CIC*, for excommunication and interdict, cc. 1331–2; medicinal penalties will be lifted after warning to repent and repentance c. 1347; for other forms of suspension of penalties see cc. 1335, 1352–3, 1355, 1357–8, 1361; for the distinction between *ferendae sententiae* (imposed penalties) and *latae sententiae* (automatic penalties) see c. 1314; for penal transfer see cc. 190–1, 1742, 1748, 1751–2.

[265] EJM 1963, s. 49(3): deprivation cannot be imposed for an offence involving doctrine, ritual, or ceremony unless the court is satisfied the offender has already been admonished on an earlier occasion with regard to another offence of the same or substantially the same nature; it must be merited by the gravity of the offence(s) and ought not to be imposed simply to separate an incumbent from his parish: *Bland v Archdeacon of Cheltenham* [1972] 1 All ER 1012 at 1021, 1022.

[266] EJM 1963, s. 55. The secular sanctions are: conviction followed by imprisonment; an affiliation order; a decree of divorce or judicial separation on the ground of adultery, unreasonable behaviour, or desertion; a finding of adultery in a matrimonial cause; wilful neglect by a married person to maintain other party or child—the last are of course determined on the civil standards of proof and result in the imposition of a 'criminal' sanction by the church.

[267] S.49(1)(b); under s.49(6) inhibition may be accompanied by suspension for the same period.

[268] S. 49(6).

[269] S. 74. The bishop may, for 'special reasons', permit residence or occupation: s. 74(2).

[270] S. 49(1)(d); s. 49(3): monition only lies for the first reserved case offence.

[271] Ibid., s. 49(1)(e).

Whether review by a civil court of the censures pronounced would be possible is a matter of debate.[272]

Some censures may be imposed otherwise than after judicial proceedings, though only exceptionally; in the Roman Catholic Church this is not uncommon.[273] When a minister is accused of an ecclesiastical offence, or of a criminal offence under secular law, the bishop may if he considers it in the interests of the church inhibit the minister pending proceedings from performing any services of the church within his diocese. This inhibition *pedente lite* operates until proceedings are concluded or until revoked at the discretion of the bishop.[274] A censure of excommunication may be imposed extra-judicially, disqualifying the minister from any office for which communicant status is required.[275] The censure of monition also, it seems, may be imposed without recourse to the courts.[276] When there has been a serious breakdown of pastoral relationships the bishop may avoid a benefice and disqualify and/or rebuke the cleric.[277]

TERMINATION OF A MINISTRY

When engaged in sector ministry under a contract of employment termination is governed by the civil employment protection legislation; unlawful and unfair dismissal may be challenged in an industrial tribunal.[278] The Legal Advisory Commission has suggested matters for inclusion in written particulars of employment for sector ministers and employees, including length of notice for termination and disciplinary and grievance procedure.[279] Otherwise, the provisions of secular employment law are excluded and termination of ministry varies as between the different ministerial offices held. Ministerial security in the Church of England is the subject of a major recent study.[280]

Loss of Office: Voluntary and Involuntary

In the Roman Catholic Church, ecclesiastical office is lost by lapse of time, by reaching an age determined by law, by resignation, transfer, removal, or

---

[272] *Julius v Bishop of Oxford* (1880) 228, 232, 233.

[273] See *supra* Ch. 4 for hierarchical recourse.   [274] EJM 1963, s.77.

[275] The power to excommunicate was hitherto enjoyed by the courts (*Kemp v Wickes* (1809) 3 Phillim 264 at 271,272); for sequestration see Church of England (Miscellaneous Provisions) Measure 1992, s. 1.

[276] Burn's *Ecclesiastical Law*, III, 191; *Cox v Goodday* (1811) 2 Hag Con 138 at 142; *Mackonochie v Lord Penzance* (1881) 6 App Cas 424 at 433 (HL); *Enraght v Lord Penzance* (1882) 7 App Cas 240 at 247 (HL).   [277] IVBM 1977, s. 10.

[278] See *supra* for *Coker v Diocese of Southwark* (1995).

[279] *OLAC*, 126, 128. For disciplinary and grievance procedure see Employment Protection (Consolidation) Act 1978, s.1 (4)(a)-(c), (5).

[280] *Clergy Conditions of Service* (1994, GS 1126).

privation.[281] In the Church of England, with regard to beneficed clergy, a benefice becomes vacant (is avoided) by the holder's death, retirement, resignation or deprivation, or by an episcopal declaration of avoidance.[282] Ministers retire by operation of law at the age of seventy unless the bishop authorizes continuation in office due to the pastoral needs of the benefice; the bishop may do so only with the consent of the parochial church council.[283] A minister may offer resignation which the bishop may accept or reject.[284] Following a serious breakdown of the pastoral relationship in a benefice, whether resulting from mental or physical disability or the conduct of the incumbent, the bishop may request resignation; failure to offer resignation may result in the bishop declaring the benefice void, effecting an automatic resignation.[285] The incumbent of two or more benefices held in plurality may not resign one benefice only but must resign all except by episcopal licence.[286] Rectors and team vicars in team ministries hold office for the term specified in the pastoral scheme, or as fixed by episcopal licence.[287] Where a group ministry is established, the incumbent is not entitled to resign or withdraw from rights and duties attaching to the office except by resigning the benefice.[288]

An assistant curate may resign on giving three months' notice to the incumbent and bishop.[289] An incumbent may terminate the appointment of an assistant curate on six months' notice with the consent of the diocesan bishop; if the bishop refuses the incumbent has a right of appeal to the archbishop who may confirm or overrule the bishop's refusal.[290] Episcopal licences may be revoked, for good and reasonable cause, summarily or with notice;[291] appeal lies to the archbishop.[292] Where a bishop has granted a

[281] *CIC*, cc. 184–96.

[282] Hill, *EL*, 222; it may also be avoided by exchange, cession (when the incumbent is made bishop or takes another benefice or ecclesiastical dignity or preferment which he cannot hold with it) *HLE*, para. 930.

[283] Ecclesiastical Offices (Age Limit) Measure 1975, s. 1, this may be for a period or further period not exceeding 2 years.

[284] Church of England (Miscellaneous Provisions) Measure 1992, s. 11, Sched. 2: it must be in writing; it may be made at the bishop's request to avoid scandal or legal proceedings: *Reichel v Bishop of Oxford* (1889) 14 App Cas 259 at 268, 269; see also Ordination of Women (Financial Provisions) Measure 1993, ss. 1, 7.   [285] IVBM 1977, ss. 4, 11(2)(a), 12(2).

[286] Pastoral Measure 1983, s. 18(4).

[287] Ibid., s. 20(2), (3): the term may be extended by epsicopal licence: s. 20(6).

[288] Ibid., s. 21(2).

[289] Pluralities Act 1838, s. 97: the bishop may waive the right of notice.

[290] Ibid., s. 95: the incumbent may also give 6 weeks' notice within the first 6 months after his admission.

[291] *OLAC*, 230, a licence may be revoked summarily (in which case no appeal lies to the archbishop) or with notice (when appeal lies).

[292] For Canon C12 see *supra* Ch. 5; *R v Archbishop of Canterbury* (1859) 1 E & E 545; for the finality of the archbishop's decision see *Poole v Bishop of London* (1861) 14 Moo PCC 262; a decision of the archbishop upholding revocation ought to be based on the same grounds as that of the diocesan bishop: *Re Sinyanki* (1864) 12 WR 825.

licence to an assistant curate to minister for a specified term of years, the bishop may revoke that licence before the expiration of the term by the same process and subject to the same right of appeal.[293] A bishop may lawfully revoke a licence for an alleged crime without the minister having been convicted in a secular court.[294]

Archdeacons and deans and provosts of cathedrals must retire at seventy unless authorized episcopally to continue in office.[295] These may be required to retire by reason of mental or physical incapacity at the instance of the diocesan bishop who must, if satisfied that such action is proper, by written notice require a special meeting of the cathedral chapter to consider and report to him whether such a person is incapacitated. The chapter must consider the matter and invite the dignitary and the bishop (or his representative) to confer with it separately or together; the dignitary has a right to be assisted or represented by a friend or adviser at the chapter's meeting. If retirement is recommended by at least two-thirds of the chapter present and voting, and the right of appointment is vested in the monarch, the bishop must within six months of its receipt petition the monarch to declare the office vacant.[296]

Relinquishment of Orders

In the Church of England, as in the Roman Catholic Church, no person admitted to the holy orders of priest or deacon can be divested of the mark of those orders; ordination confers an indelible character.[297] In Roman Catholic canon law ordained status does not exist if orders are not validly conferred: there must be a declaration of invalidity. On dismissal the validity of orders remains but the power to exercise them is lost.[298] The position in the Church of England is similar: the right to exercise orders may be lost in three ways. First, a minister may by legal process voluntarily relinquish orders and use himself as a lay person.[299] Having resigned any and every preferment held, the person must execute a deed of relinquishment.[300] On the recording of the deed, the individual is incapable of officiating, acting, taking, or holding any preferment as a minister, and ceases to enjoy all rights, privileges, advantages, and exemptions attaching to office. Moreover, the minister is discharged from all disabilities, disqualifications, and restraints otherwise imposed and from all

---

[293] C12(6).

[294] *Re Sinyanki* (1864) 12 WR 825; *OLAC*, 230: reaching a given age below retirement age would not be a 'good and reasonable cause' for *summary* revocation.

[295] Ecclesiastical Offices (Age Limit) Measure 1975, ss. 1, 3(1)(b), and Sched.

[296] Church Dignitaries (Retirement) Measure 1949, ss. 1,2(1), 3(2), 12, 13. When a dean, residentiary canon, or archdeacon wishes to resign this must be offered in writing: Church of England (Miscellaneous Provisions) Measure 1995, s. 4.

[297] C1(2); *Barnes v Shore* (1846) 8 QB 640 at 660 (*arguendo*) and 671 (*per* Lord Denman); 115 ER 1021, 1052; *CIC*, cc. 290, 1103, 1159, 1191.   [298] *CIC*, cc. 290(2), 1336, 1364.

[299] C1(2).   [300] Clerical Disabilities Act 1870, s. 3.

jurisdiction, penalties, censures, and proceedings.[301] Secondly, an ordained minister may by legal and canonical process be deprived of the exercise of his orders.[302] Thirdly, he may be deposed from orders after deprivation.[303] The bishop must serve notice of intention to depose; appeal within one month of receipt of notice lies to the archbishop.[304] When a person is deposed the same consequences as relinquishment follow.[305] The effects of relinquishment or deposition cease with the grant of a royal pardon and the person may be restored to any preferment previously held if this has not in the meantime been filled.[306] Alternatively, a petition may be made to the archbishop so that the enrolment of the deed is vacated. After consulting the bishop of the diocese in which the deed was recorded, and whomsoever he deems necessary, the archbishop may in writing request the vacation of the deed. No re-ordination is required or possible. For two years after recording a vacation he may exercise a ministry determined by the bishop; after two years he is capable of holding a benefice or other preferment.[307]

CONCLUSIONS

Whereas in each church the determination of suitability for ordination rests with the bishop, in the Church of England extra-legal norms enable wider participation in the process of selection. Similarly, the power to make ministerial appointments is concentrated in the bishop, though in the Church of England the process of presentation confers rights of lay participation and diocesan norms facilitate consultation but standards vary as between dioceses and particular ministries. In both churches, within the general framework set by canonical ministry (where the terms of service are prescribed by law) the designing of ministerial functions is achieved principally by means of executive episcopal action. The Roman Catholic Church has a more fully developed central law concerning day-to-day pastoral care of clergy, a subject which is generally left to diocesan quasi-legislation in the Church of England. Each church employs a system of ecclesiastical offences and sanctions, though the terms of the oath of canonical obedience are extraordinarily imprecise. Voluntary and involuntary termination of ministry lie in the keeping of the bishop, but in both churches ordination is treated as conferring an indelible character.

---

[301] Clerical Disabilities Act 1870, s. 3. Ibid., s. 4. Liability for dilapidations, debt, or other pecuniary liability is not lifted: s. 8.

[302] See above.   [303] C1(2).   [304] EJM 1963, s. 50.   [305] Ibid., s. 52.

[306] Ibid., s. 53.

[307] Clerical Disabilities Act 1870 (Amendment) Measure 1934, ss. 1, 2: circumstances and reasons for the deed must be set out as must the reasons resuming ministry: s. 1(1).

8

The Ministry of the Laity

As part of its ecclesiology of all the faithful as the people of God, at Vatican II the Roman Catholic Church developed an elaborate understanding of the ministry of the laity: this was one of the central achievements of the Council and a separate section is devoted to the subject in the 1983 Code. In contrast, though theologically the church has moved towards an enhanced view of the laity, emphasizing the partnership of both the ordained and lay ministries, there is no separate treatment of the laity in the law of the Church of England and the rules that exist produce a fundamental imbalance. Rights of lay people are extensive but the Church of England prescribes no comprehensive canonical ministry for the laity: responsibilities and disciplinary processes are minimal. The general distribution of lay rights and duties is based on a distinction between members of the church and non-members, and forms of regulation vary as between those who hold office in the church and those who do not. Much of the law dealing with the many public ministries of office-holders, their appointment, functions and discipline, is supplemented by extra-legal norms operating mainly at diocesan level.

THE LAITY AND CLASSES OF MEMBERSHIP

Legislators in the Church of England and the Roman Catholic Church employ classifications of juridic persons in order to organize (and sometimes to justify) the distribution of rights and duties. In this section we shall examine the classifications of lay persons, and in the next their rights and duties. Roman Catholic canon law uses a concept of membership: the faithful 'incorporated into the Church of Christ through baptism' constitute the people of God; composed of ordained and lay members, the faithful comprise in turn those in full communion with the Catholic Church on earth (those joined with Christ in its visible structures through their profession of faith, their sharing in the sacraments, and their acceptance of ecclesiastical government) and those who are not.[1] Similarly, the Church of England is not the church of 'the clergy or of the laity, but of both'; it consists 'of the laity as well as the clerical members of

---

[1] *CIC*, cc. 96, 204, 205; cc. 207(1) (*laici* and *ministri sacri*) 232, 274; the laity are organized territorially on a diocesan and parochial basis: cc. 372, 518. See Y. Congar, 'What belonging to the church has come to mean', *Readings*, 168; A. Gauthier, 'Juridical persons in the code of canon

the community'.[2] Lay persons are those who are not episcopally ordained ministers in holy orders[3] and as such, given the territorial division into parishes, the parochial laity consists of all non-ordained residents of a parish.[4] It is a person's status as parishioner which generates a basic entitlement to the ministrations of the church.[5] Parishioners, in turn, are classified in law either as members of the Church of England or as non-members. Status as a member entitles to additional rights: only members may hold office in the church.[6] In this respect the concept of membership is of central importance. However, law created by the Church of England does not define 'member' nor does it specify what gives rise to membership.[7] Membership of Christ's Church is effected by baptism, but baptism itself does not confer membership of the Church of England.[8] Membership has, however, been defined in secular law for the purposes of determining certainty of beneficiaries under a trust.[9] Two approaches have been used. First, 'a person who has been baptized . . . confirmed, or is ready and desirous to be confirmed, and is an actual commu-

law', *Studia Canonica*, 25 (1991), 77; J. Komonchack, 'The status of the faithful in the revised code of canon law', *Concilium* (1981), 37; for some comments on reception into the church see J. H. Provost, 'Approaches to Catholic identity in church law', *Concilium* (1994), 15 and A. Borras, 'The canonical limits of catholic identity in some problematic situations', ibid., 47.

[2] *R v Dibdin* [1910] P 57 at 136 (CA) *per* Farwell J; *The Position of the Laity in the Church* (1902), Report of the Joint Committee of the Convocation of Canterbury (London, Reprint, 1952) 62; Resolution of the Lambeth Conference 1930, *AT: HS*, 404.

[3] *CRR*, r. 54(2): 'Any reference in these rules to the laity shall be construed as a reference to persons other than Clerks in Holy Orders, and the expression "lay" in these rules shall be construed accordingly'; see also *Bishop of St Albans v Fillingham* [1906] P 163 at 177; *Walsh v Lord Advocate* [1956] 3 All ER 129 at 139 *per* Lord Patrick (HL); C1(2): on relinquishment of orders a person must 'use himself as a layman'.

[4] For earlier ideas of a parishioner as an 'inhabitant householder' in the parish see *Veley v Burder* (1841) 12 Ad & El 265; *Etherington v Wilson* (1875) 1 Ch D 160 (CA); *The Position of the Laity in the Church* (1902) 50 f. at 54: 'in England "citizen" and "churchman" are no longer convertible terms . . . a "parishioner" is not now so called because he is a member of the Church within a given ecclesiastical area, but because he is a ratepayer in a particular locality; thus compelling the Church to readjust its relation to the civil power, and to find a definition of membership which in this country was unnecessary before'. Today the word is sometimes used without definition: Incumbents (Vacation of Benefices) Measure 1977, s. 1(1); for parishioners as those whose names are entered on the electoral roll, see Churchwardens (Appointment and Resignation) Measure 1964, s. 3(1); the meaning of 'residence' varies according to the context of its use: see e.g. Ch. 13 for marriage.

[5] For a 'parishioner's' rights to baptism, marriage, and burial recognized at common law see *R v Dibdin* [1910] P 57 (CA); for the 'interests of parishioners' in faculty cases see *post* Ch. 16.

[6] *Re St Hilary, Cornwall* [1938] 4 All ER 147; for 'membership' giving rise to rights and eligibility for office see below.   [7] See e.g. Canons A1–3, B15A(1).

[8] Canon B21; *Christian Inititation: A Policy for the Church of England*, A Discussion Paper by M. Reardon, GS Misc 365 (London, 1991) 22–3: baptism confers membership of Christ's Body, the Church, which 'is not fulfilled without personal profession of faith and communion in the Christian community'; *AT: HS*, 513: Japan, Constitution and Canons for the Government of the Nippon Sei Ko Kai (1971) Art. 6: 'A *layman* is a person who has become a member of the Holy Catholic Church by Baptism'.

[9] *Re Allen, Faith v Allen* [1953] 1 Ch 810 at 827: 'the words "a member of the Church of England" are capable of having a definite certain meaning attached to them'.

nicant member, does hold the status of a member of [the Church of England], and would be ordinarily regarded and spoken of as such'.[10] Secondly, baptized and confirmed persons who attend the parish church regularly and conform to the church's discipline would be 'entitled to call themselves members of the Church of England'.[11] Similarly, 'member' has been defined in the commentaries as any 'baptized person giving general allegiance to the ordinances and liturgy of the Church of England as by law established'.[12] In civil legislation the concept of 'belonging to the Church of England' is sometimes used but without precise definition.[13]

Members of the Church of England are classified according to status. First, all persons whose names are entered on a parish electoral roll are members: entry of a name recognizes rather than confers membership.[14] In every parish there must be a church electoral roll, and a lay person is entitled to entry on the roll 'if he is baptised, of sixteen years or upwards, has signed an application form for enrolment . . . and declares himself to be a member of the Church of England, or of a Church in communion therewith resident in the parish', or is a member of the Church of England (or of a church in communion with it) and, not being resident in the parish, has habitually attended public worship in the parish during a period of six months prior to enrolment; a person may also be enrolled if a member in good standing of a church which subscribes to the doctrine of the Holy Trinity (not being a church in communion with the Church of England) and also prepared to declare himself a member of the Church of England having habitually attended public worship in the parish during a period of six months prior to enrolment.[15] The roll is kept and revised annually by or under the direction of the parochial church council which must appoint a church electoral roll officer to act under its direction for the purpose of carrying out its functions with respect to the electoral roll. It is the duty of the electoral roll officer to keep the roll constantly up to date and to cause names to be added or removed and to report such additions and removals at the next meeting of the parochial church council.[16] A name must be removed from

---

[10] *Re Perry Almshouses* [1898] 1 Ch 391 at 400; *Re Barnes, Simpson v Barnes* [1930] 2 Ch 40; *Re Schoales, Schoales v Schoales* [1930] 2 Ch 76.

[11] *Re Allen, Faith v Allen* [1953] 1 Ch 810 at 827; this was approved in *Re Tampolsk (Deceased), Barclays Bank and Another v Hyer and Others* [1958] 3 All ER 479 at 480–1 *per* Dankwerts J; the requirement of regular attendance was doubted in *Marshall v Graham* [1907] 2 KB 112 at 124.   [12] *HLE*, para. 346.

[13] Prison Rules, SI 1964/388, r. 11(2).

[14] *CRR*, App. I: in applying for enrolment a candidate must declare, *inter alia*, 'I am a member of the Church of England'; Canon B15A: 'members of the Church of England who have been confirmed' or are desirous of being confirmed must be admitted to holy communion; see also *Banister v Thompson* [1908] P 362 at 378 *per* Dean of Arches: 'The promoters [of the suit] are members of the Church of England, have been confirmed, and are residents in the parish'.

[15] *CRR*, r. 1(2); a person may be a qualified in any number of parishes: r. 1(4).

[16] Ibid., r. 1(5), (7), (8); rr. 2, 4 govern revision and preparation of new rolls and certification of numbers.

the roll if the person dies, is ordained, signifies in writing a desire that the name be removed, or ceases to reside in the parish (unless he continues habitually to attend public worship there in any period of six months except when prevented from doing so by illness or other sufficient cause); if a person is not resident and has (otherwise than by illness or other sufficient cause) not attended public worship during the preceding six months, or was not entitled to have the name entered initially, again the name must be removed; a removed name may be entered again if the person is or becomes qualified.[17] A right of appeal vests in any person aggrieved against any enrolment or refusal to enroll and against the removal of or the refusal to remove any name on the roll.[18]

Secondly, a person may enjoy the status of an 'actual communicant member': 'a member of the Church of England who is confirmed or ready and desirous of being confirmed and has received Communion according to the use of the Church of England or of a Church in communion with the Church of England at least three times during the twelve months preceding the date on which he makes the declaration of membership'.[19] Thirdly, a member enjoying 'communicant status' is 'a person who has received communion according to the use of the Church of England or of a church in communion therewith at least once within the twelve months preceding the date of his declaration that he fulfils that requirement'.[20] These classes are distinguished, further, from members who are 'regular communicants' and 'habitual worshippers'.[21] Finally, a person 'received' into the Church of England enjoys the status of a member. Reception occurs in six ways. Any person who has not been baptized (or the validity of whose baptism is in question) must be instructed and baptized (or conditionally baptized) 'and such baptism, or conditional baptism, shall constitute the said person's reception into the Church of England'. Those baptized but not episcopally confirmed who desire 'to be formally admitted into the Church of England' must be received (after appropriate instruction) either by confirmation or (if not yet ready to be confirmed) by the parish priest with appropriate prayers. Those episcopally confirmed (with unction or the laying on of hands) must be instructed and, with the permission of the bishop, received into the Church of England according to the Form of Reception approved by the General Synod or with other

---

[17] Ibid., r. 1(9), (10); r. 3 governs procedures for entry and removal of names.

[18] Ibid., rr. 43, 45; *Stuart v Haughley Parochial Church Council* [1936] Ch 32 (CA): the civil courts will not upset a decision of a lay electoral commission unless it was contrary to natural justice.

[19] Patronage (Benefices) Measure 1986, ss. 8(1), 39(1): the registered patron's 'declaration of membership'; see also *CRR*, r. 54(1): under r. 54(5) questions as to whether a church is in communion are determined conclusively for the purpose of these rules by the archbishops.

[20] Ecclesiastical Jurisdiction Measure 1963, s. 66(1).

[21] See e.g. Canon D2(1): deaconesses must be regular communicants; for 'habitual worshipper', *CRR*, rr. 1(2), 31(3).

appropriate prayers.[22] In the Form of Reception a received person promises 'to live as a loyal member of the Church of England'.[23]

In short, there is no precise legal understanding of membership of the Church of England similar to that operative in the Roman Catholic Church, though the law clearly defines different classes of member.[24] Yet communicant status and the other forms of status are marks of membership rather than causes of membership. Whilst both churches deny certain sacramental and governmental rights to excommunicates, in neither church does excommunication deprive a person of membership.[25] In the Church of England there is no equivalent to the Roman Catholic Church's canonical doctrine of formal acts of defection.[26]

THE COMMON MINISTRY OF THE LAITY

The modern theological approach of the Church of England is that, like the ordained clergy, each lay person has 'a ministerial function derived from that of Christ . . . every member has his place and share according to his different capabilities and calling'; diocesan norms often speak of the 'every member ministry'.[27] Moreover, '[t]he ministry of the laity does not consist solely in the service to the Church or in the Church's worship . . . [but] demands witnesses to the Christian gospel through word and deed in the world'; in this sense the service of the Church to the world 'must be discharged mainly by the laity'.[28] However, whereas canon law presents a fundamental ministry for the ordained clergy, canon law offers no guidance as to lay ministry: there is no discreet

---

[22] Canon B28.

[23] Canon B28(1)-(3); for a Form of Reception (1952) see *Acts of Convocation*, 165–9; for membership arising through reception in diocesan norms see e.g. *LDR*, 90; *BRDSEI*, Bii; *WDHI*, Ch. 4, 202.

[24] The problem has been debated recently: J. Tiller, *A Strategy for the Church's Ministry* (London, 1985) 59–64: the Church of England is a 'communal' or 'open' rather than an 'associational' church, which subordinates the concept of membership; C. Lewis, 'The idea of the church in the parish communion', *Crucible* (July-Sept. 1982), 119; E. Harrison, 'The God club', *Times Magazine*, 19 Mar. 1994, 16; see also M. Reardon, *Christian Initiation*, 28–31, 52; *One Body, Many Members*, British Council of Churches (1986); *Christian Initiation and Church Membership*, British Council of Churches (1988) 22.

[25] See below.

[26] A. Stenson, 'The concept and implications of the formal act of defection of Canon 1117', *Studia Canonica*, 21 (1987), 175; in M. Reardon, *Christian Initiation*, 4, it was argued that someone baptized in the Church of England but rebaptized in a church having doctrines inconsistent with those of the Church of England thereby 'negative[s] his adherence to the Church of England'.

[27] Doctrine Commission, *Doctrine in the Church of England* (1938) 114 (*AT: HS*, 421); *WH*, BP.1: 'Nor is ministry any longer the preserve of the ordained. The whole People of God is to be a priestly and ministering community. For this work every member, by vitrue of baptism, has a responsibility'; *SDDH*, I, E.1; *LDR*, 10: 'Christian ministry is a corporate ministry'; *WAOB*, 1.2.

[28] *Message*, Lambeth Conference, 1968: *AT: HS*, 470.

canonical statement of functions, rights, and duties common to all the laity.[29] The task of defining the common lay ministry is performed, at least in part, by liturgical forms and by extra-legal diocesan norms which prescribe that 'all members share in Christ's ministry both in the world, and in the building up of the life of the Church'.[30] In this way, 'the very important conception that a layman is a member of the Church, under the discipline of the body, who has responsibilities as well as rights, has been much obscured'.[31] Lay rights are extensive but lay duties are not: both are organized on the basis of the classifications outlined in the previous section.

Lay Rights

Distributed either expressly or as correlative to duties imposed on the ordained clergy,[32] lay rights are organized according to a person's status; some derive from the canons and others from synodical measure and, exceptionally, from law created by secular authorities.[33] Parishioners, members and non-members, are entitled to instruction in the faith by the ordained ministers,[34] and they have a right to notice of services and to seats at divine service.[35] Parishioners have a right to sufficient priests, provided these might be supplied by the diocesan bishop 'as much as in him lies',[36] as well as, for spiritual counsel and advice, a right of access to and to be visited by their priest.[37] As well as rights to baptism, members and non-members are entitled (subject to satisfying the legal qualifying requirements) to confirmation, confession, marriage, and

---

[29] Lambeth Conference Resolution (1968): 'there is an urgent need for increase in the quantity and quality of training available for laypeople for their task in the world': *AT: HS*, 475; J. Tiller, *A Strategy for the Church's Ministry*, 63, 79–80: proposes a 'ministry roll' by which, in an appropriate liturgical setting, individuals renew baptismal vows and indicate a willingness to engage in ministry programmes.

[30] *WH*, BP.2: 'visiting housebound and bereaved people, bearing Christian witness in home, pub and factory, standing for Christian principles in local affairs, are part of a Christian's vocation'; *BDM*, A.1; for diocesan Boards of Ministry and equivalent organizations see e.g. *CF*, H.7; *TBF*, 3.25; *NDIB*, II, 19; *WDHI*, 31; *LDR*, 55; for Local Ministry Schemes and Teams see e.g. *LDHI*, II, 3 at 17; for education for the laity see e.g. *SDDH*, G.6; *BRDSEI*, Ni.

[31] *The Position of the Laity in the Church*, 63.

[32] Such rights may be classified as 'rights' or 'claim-rights' (where there is a correlative duty) as distinct from 'liberties' (arising where the law is silent), 'privileges' (or 'no-rights') and 'powers' (where there is no correlative duty), and 'immunities': see W. N. Hohfeld, 'Some fundamental legal conceptions as applied in judicial reasoning', *Yale Law Journal*, 23 (1913), 16; R. Stone, *Civil Liberties* (London, 1994) 4–7.

[33] For rights to practise the faith and property rights (such those under a religious trust) given by secular law see *post* Ch. 9 and Part VI.   [34] See *post* Ch. 9.

[35] Canon B7. Parish Notices Act 1837 regulates giving of notices during divine service; Canon F7(1): 'In every church and chapel there shall be provided seats for the use of the parishioners and others who attend divine service'; though seats may be allocated by the churchwardens, allocation of seats to non-parishioners must not interfere with the rights of parishioners to sit in the main body of the church (F7(2), (3)); a person may have a right to a chancel seat by faculty, prescription, or statute: F7(2).   [36] C18(6).

[37] C24(6), esp. the sick.

burial, the last two being recognized at common law. Baptized lay persons confirmed or desirous of confirmation have a right to admission to holy communion; special rights to communion arise in circumstances of sickness and danger of death. A lay person may say or sing morning and evening prayer (but not administer the absolution) if authorized by the diocesan bishop, or by invitation of the incumbent (if the person is a 'suitable lay person'), or, if there is no incumbent through vacancy or incapacity, by invitation of the church-wardens. Lay persons have a canonical right to administer baptism in time of necessity and, if authorized, a right to assist in the administration of the elements at holy communion. A lay person who is a member in good standing of a church in communion with the Church of England may be admitted to and participate in the celebration of services in the Church of England.[38]

Additional rights to participate in ecclesiastical government are enjoyed only by members of the Church of England: these rights vary according to status.[39] Entry of a member's name on the electoral roll generates a right to attend the annual parochial church meeting and qualifies a person to elect parochial representatives of the laity to the parochial church council, to the deanery synod, and to the office of sidesperson.[40] Those on the electoral roll who are actual communicant members of the Church of England are entitled to be elected to the parochial church council and to the house of laity of the deanery synod.[41] Communicants whose names are on the electoral roll of a parish in the deanery are eligible for election to the house of laity of the diocesan synod.[42] They also have a right to elect to and to be elected to General Synod provided thay are actual communicant members.[43] Lay persons on the roll who are lay members of any deanery synod or diocesan synod, or of General Synod may also be members of the parochial church council.[44] Finally, provided they have the required *locus standi*, any lay person is entitled to initiate judicial proceedings with regard to clerical discipline and those resident in a parish may object to a faculty application.[45] Rights to present

---

[38] For Canons B11, 12, 15A, 43, 44 see *post* Chs. 10–14.

[39] Canon A6: 'The government of the Church of England under the Queen's Majesty, by archbishops, deans, provosts, archdeacons, and the rest of the clergy and of the laity that bear office in the same, is not repugnant to the Word of God'; see also the *Message*, Lambeth Conference, 1968, *AT: HS*, 470: 'The laity . . . have a right to a proper share in the government of the Church'.   [40] *CRR*, rr. 6(2), 9(4).

[41] *CRR*, rr. 10, 14, 24(6); if a person is on the electoral roll of 2 parishes he must choose one of those parishes for the purpose of qualification to a deanery syond, a diocesan synod, and General Synod (r. 1(3)); for co-opted members, who must be 'actual lay communicant members', see rr. 14(1)(h), 24(7); a member on the electoral roll has a right of admission as sidesperson (r. 10(2)); no person may be nominated for election to serve on a parochial church council or deanery synod without signifying their consent nor to a parochial church council if disqualified by a bishop under Incumbents (Vacation of Benefices) Measure 1977, s. 10(6) or if diqualified from being a charitable trustee under the Charities Act 1993, s. 72: r. 10(3).   [42] *CRR*, rr. 30(5)(b), 31(3).

[43] *CRR*, r. 35. They are elected by the 'diocesan electors', members of the house of laity of all the deanery synods in the diocese except co-opted members and lay members of a religious community represented in General Synod under r. 35(1)(b).   [44] *CRR*, r. 14(1)(f).

[45] See Chs. 5, 16.

oneself as a candidate for admission to specific and individual lay ministerial offices are discussed below.

Lay Duties

Few legal duties are imposed on the laity: these are distributed generally (and some are imposed equally on the clergy) and to classes. General responsibilities include the canonical duty to avoid schismatic conduct[46] and the canonical duty to observe the Lord's Day, 'particularly by attendance at divine worship, by deeds of charity and by abstension from all unnecessary labour and business'.[47] All persons present at divine service must audibly with the minister make the answers appointed and in due place join in such parts of the service as are appointed to be said or sung by all present.[48] All persons have a canonical and statutory duty not to create a disturbance in church or in the churchyard.[49] It is the canonical duty of baptized persons privately to examine their consciences, to confess, and to repent,[50] and a canonical duty is placed on all those who have been confirmed to receive holy communion regularly, especially at the festivals of Christmas, Easter, and Whitsun.[51] Special duties attach to parishioners seeking baptism, confirmation, confession, marriage, and burial; for the last two there are duties to pay fees.[52]

According to an Act of Convocation (1953), 'the duties of church *membership*', some of which are repeated in the canons, are summed up as follows: to pray every day and to read the Bible regularly; to join in the worship of the church every Sunday and to observe holy days; to receive holy communion regularly after due preparation, and more particularly at the great festivals of the church and on the great occasions of their own lives; to make Fridays and the season of Lent special by acts of devotion and self-denial; to contribute worthily to the work of the church at home and overseas and for the relief of those in need; to uphold the marriage laws of the church; and to bring up children to love and serve the Lord. Convocation stressed that '[t]hese rules do not attempt to cover the whole of the Christian life and conduct . . . they nevertheless are duties which loyal members of the Church of England should include in their personal rule of life'.[53]

---

[46] Canon A8.

[47] Canon B6(1); observance of other feast days and holy days is required by B6(2)-(4).

[48] B9(1); all persons present 'shall give reverent attention in the time of divine service, give due reverence to the name of the Lord Jesus and stand at the Creed and the reading of the Holy Gospel at the Holy Communion. When the Prayers are read and Psalms and Canticles are said or sung, they shall have regard to the rubrics of the service and locally established custom in the matter of posture, whether of standing, kneeling or sitting' (B9(2)).   [49] See below and *post* Ch. 10.

[50] Canon B29.   [51] Canon B15(1).   [52] See *post* Chs. 11–13 and, for fees, Ch. 17.

[53] *Acts of Convocation*, 172–3, drawn up by convocations — Canterbury, 1948, York, 1954 — at the request of the House of Laity of the Church Assembly; these rarely appear in diocesan norms: see exceptionally *BDM*, F.1 ff.

The Canonical Ministry of the Faithful in the Roman Catholic Church

Treatment of the laity in the Church of England might be contrasted in four fundamental ways with Roman Catholic canon law. First, the legal framework of Church of England presents no canonical doctrine of the fundamental equality of all the faithful or of their rights and duties. In Roman Catholic canon law, when incorporated by baptism into the Church of Christ, and constituted a person in it, each member of the faithful has such 'duties and rights which, in accordance with each one's status, are proper to Christians, in so far as they are in ecclesiastical communion and unless a lawfully issued sanction intervenes'; it is from baptismal rebirth in Christ that all members of the faithful, clerical and lay, enjoy within the church 'an equality of dignity and action' to contribute, 'each according to his or her own condition and office, to the building up of the Body of Christ'; the laity are 'bearers in Christ's priestly, prophetic and royal office'.[54] Secondly, the Church of England possesses no equivalent to the Roman Catholic Church's canonical ministry applicable to all the faithful and to the lay faithful in particular. Giving effect to their mission in the world as the people of God, this includes the duty and right to evangelize, to petition, to recommend, to receive the sacraments, to participate in worship and to one's proper spirituality, the right to associate and assemble, the right to participate in the apostolate, the right to a Christian education, and the right to promote social justice.[55] In contrast, as we have seen, lay duties and rights in the Church of England are more introverted and do not touch lay ministry in the secular sphere. There is, however, no lay right to possess the power of governance in the Roman Catholic Church, though the laity may participate in the use of such power by means of deputation and the consultative vote.[56] Thirdly, these rights are treated in Roman Catholic canon law as deriving from the fundamental dignity of the individual as a human person: they are inalienable and inviolable human rights.[57] Fourthly, in the Church of England there is no formal equivalent to the Roman Catholic principle that '[i]n exercising their rights, [the] faithful, both individually and in association, must take account of the common good of the church, as well as the rights of others and their own duties to others': the appropriate '[e]cclesiastical authority is entitled to regulate, in view of the common good, the exercise of rights which are proper to Christ's faithful'.[58]

[54] CIC, cc. 96, 204, 208; F. Morrisey, 'The laity in the new code of canon law', Readings, 323; S. A. Euart, 'Council, code and laity: implications for lay ministry', The Jurist, 47 (1987), 492.
[55] CIC, cc. 208–23: rights and duties of all the faithful, cc. 224–31: rights and duties of the lay faithful; see studies in The Jurist, 46 (1986), and J. A. Coriden, 'A challenge: make rights real', The Jurist, 45 (1986), 1.   [56] CIC, cc. 129, 274: cf. Canon A6.
[57] See supra n. 55
[58] CIC, c. 223; C. Lara, 'Some general reflections on the rights and duties of the Christian faithful', Studia Canonica, 20 (1986), 7.

LAY DISCIPLINE

Modern theology on common lay ministry in the Church of England, summed up as responsibility and partnership,[59] has outgrown the understanding of the civil judiciary that ordained ministers 'set apart in sacred matters are superior to the rest of the religious community, the laity . . . [a] position . . . possessed even by the lowest of the three holy orders, the diaconate'.[60] On one hand, ample structures exist to enable the laity to carry out their ministry by vindicating rights violated by the clergy. On the other hand, there is in the modern church no general and formal mechanism to compel performance of (the few) duties fundamental to lay ministry: lay people take no oath of canonical obedience to their bishops or to other clergy, nor do they promise to maintain the discipline of the church;[61] the promise of those received into the church to live as loyal members 'obeying its rules and heeding its teachings' is exceptional.[62]

Vindication of Lay Rights

Lay rights directly or indirectly deriving from parliamentary statutes, common law, synodical measures, or canons are enforceable executively or judicially. In the absence of a lawful reason for refusal, a duty cast upon a minister creates a correlative right to the performance of acts due by virtue of that duty (such as admission to baptism, communion, or marriage).[63] Provided the matter falls within the terms of canonical obedience, recourse may be had to the diocesan bishop to order executively the performance of a ministerial duty.[64] On the complaint of lay people having *locus standi*, failure to discharge duties on the part of ordained ministers may result in judicial proceedings under the Ecclesiastical Jurisdiction Measure 1963, perhaps leading to an order compelling the performance of the duty, and in serious and appropriate cases judicial review may be available in the civil courts.[65] In cases of a serious breakdown of pastoral relations a majority of not less than two-thirds of actual communicant lay members of the parochial church council may request the institution of proceedings under the Incumbents (Vacation of Benefices) Measures 1977

[59] J. Tiller, *The Church's Ministry*, 79; for instances of mandatory co-operation, see e.g. Canons B3(1): choice of liturgy and C24(7): priests having cure of souls 'and the parochial church council shall consult together on matters of general concern and importance to the parish'.

[60] *Walsh v Lord Advocate* [1956] 3 All ER 129 at 139 *per* Lord Patrick (HL).

[61] This produces a fundamental inequality as between the laity and clergy; for the possibility of lay oaths in principle see *AR*, Art. 39 ('a man may swear when the Magistrate requireth') and *OLAC*, 187 (albeit concerning oaths taken by a canon to a cathedral dean and chapter).

[62] *Acts of Convocation*, 165 at 167.   [63] See *post* Part IV.

[64] C18(7) (or to the archdeacon: C22(4)).

[65] For ss. 19(a), (b), 49(1)(d), 66 and judicial review see *supra* Chs. 5–7; proceedings may be brought under the 1963 Measure to compel a bishop to enforce the church's law if non-enforcement amounts to a neglect of the episcopal duty under C18(7).

and 1993.[66] Finally, failure by ecclesiastical bodies or lay officers to perform legally imposed duties, when this violates a lay right, may also be remedied by internal executive action or by recourse to the civil courts.[67]

Enforcement of Lay Duties

Whether lay duties are enforceable depends on the duty in question, its source, and the proposed method of enforcement, executive or judicial. Before examining these, two basic points may be made. First, executive enforcement, by means of a clerical order, would ordinarily not be supported by sanctions imposed judicially. Ample evidence suggests that it is unlikely that the laity would be disciplined today in either the secular or the church courts even though, with regard to the latter, the Ecclesiastical Jurisdiction Measure 1963 does not expressly destroy jurisdiction over them.[68] Secondly, the possibility of both executive and judicial enforcement is impeded by the basic principle that the canons of the Church of England do not of their own force bind the laity: imperative or prohibitive (duty-imposing) canons cannot be enforced against the laity.[69]

In *Middleton v Crofts* (1736) Lord Hardwicke explained: 'We are all of the opinion that the Canons of 1603, not having been confirmed by Parliament, do not *proprio vigore* bind the laity; I say *proprio vigore*, by their own force and authority.' Nevertheless, if a canon is 'declaratory of ancient usage and law of the Church of England, received and allowed here', it 'will bind the laity'; in this respect, there is 'an obligation antecedent to, and not arising from, this body of canons'.[70] The principle was approved by the Dean of the Arches in *Lloyd v Owen* (1753), by the House of Lords in *Bishop of Exeter v Marshall* (1868), and by the Court of Appeal in *R v Dibdin* (1910).[71] The scope of the principle, however, is not entirely clear as these judicial statements concern only the 1603 canons. Though it applies to post–1969 canons enacted by General Synod under the Synodical Government Measure 1969,[72] it may not

---

[66] IVBM 1977, s. 1(1)(c).   [67] See *supra* Ch. 4 and below.

[68] S. 82(2); their jurisdiction had begun to disappear well before: *Phillimore v Machon* (1876) I PD 481 at 487–9; *Redfern v Redfern* [1891] P 139 at 145 (CA); *Elliott v Albert* [1934] KB 650 at 660 (CA); *Cole v Police Constable 443A* [1937] 1 KB 316 at 333; *Blunt v Park Lane Hotel Ltd* [1942] 2 KB 253 at 256 (CA); *Manchester Corporation v Manchester Palace of Varieties Ltd* [1955] P 133 at 149, 150 (Chivalry Court).

[69] *HLE*, para. 308; H. Jones, 'Omnnis Gallia . . . or, the roles of the archdeacon', *ELJ*, 2 (1990–92), 236 at 238.   [70] (1736) 2 Atkins 650 at 653; *RACCL* (1947) 76–7.

[71] (1753) 1 Lee 434 at 437; (1868) LR 3, HL 17; [1908] P 362 at 385 (*per* Dean of Arches), [1910] P 57 at 85–6 (*per* Bray J, Div. Ct), 111 (*per* Cozens-Hardy MR); [1912] AC 533 (HL). See also *Cox's Case* (1700) 1 P Wms 29 at 32 and *More v More* (1741) 2 Atk 157; a person seeking marriage is under a canonical duty (B31) to satisfy the statutory requirements as to capacity: this is binding in so far as the requirements are duplicated in civil law: see *post* Ch. 13.

[72] SGM 1969, Sched. 2, Art. 6(a)(ii) (post–1969 canons have 'the like force as Canons heretofore made, promulged and executed by the Convocations of Canterbury and York'); see *supra* Ch. 3.

apply to the revised canons of 1964–9.[73] In any event, even though the commonly understood original reason for the principle (the non-representation of the laity in convocation, the canon-making body before 1969)[74] has disappeared, it is submitted that the principle is otiose given the existence of so few lay canonical duties. It has been said that a parliamentary statute or synodical measure would be needed to make the canons binding on the laity: in so far as the principle seems to have been judicially made, there appears to be no legal obstacle to the judiciary reformulating it.[75]

Within this general framework only limited possibilities exist for lay discipline. First, as an overriding principle, the diocesan bishop has a canonical duty 'to correct and punish *all* such as be unquiet, disobedient, or criminous, within his diocese'; nothing legally limits this episcopal power to ordained ministers.[76] It is also the function of churchwardens 'by example and precept to encourage parishioners in the practice of true religion'.[77] Breach of the duty not to disturb divine service, declaratory of duties imposed by parliamentary statute, may be the subject of a ministerial or episcopal executive order and, in addition or as an alternative, proceedings in the secular courts.[78] Secondly, a ministerial decision arising from a ministerial canonical duty or from the exercise of a ministerial canonical right will bind the laity: whenever the canons confer a ministerial right this generates a correlative lay duty. For instance, the decision of a cleric to refuse admission to holy communion, provided refusal is lawful, generates a lay duty to abstain which may be upheld by the courts.[79] Thirdly, the laity may be ordered to fulfil a canonical duty, to do or refrain from doing an act (as with the previous example) by an executive ministerial order: provided the order is lawful disobedience may be treated in the civil courts.[80] Fourthly, in cases where the laity have contributed to a serious pastoral breakdown the diocesan bishop, as he thinks fit, may issue a rebuke or disqualify laity from serving as churchwardens or as members or officers of the parochial church council of

[73] However, it is arguable that a wide understanding of the principle as 'canons created by convocation are not binding on the laity' makes it applicable also to the 1964–9 canons.

[74] *Case of Convocations* (1611) 12 Co Rep 73; *Bishop of St David's v Lucy* (1699) Carth 484; *Matthew v Burdett* (1703) 2 Salk 412.

[75] *HLE*, para. 308, n.10; see also Blunt, *Book of Church Law* (11th edn., 1921) 25; for the ancient principle that 'what is approved by all binds all', see N. Doe, *Fundamental Authority in Late Medieval English Law* (Cambridge, 1990) 17–18.   [76] C18(7).

[77] Canon E1(4).

[78] Ecclesiastical Courts Jurisdiction Act 1860. For a recent use of the statute see *R v Bourne*, *Daily Telegraph*, 15 Apr. 1995; recovery of marriage and burial fees is discussed *post* Ch. 17.

[79] See *post* Part IV.

[80] The principle is, after all, expressed in the form 'the canons do not bind the laity', and not in the form 'decisions based on the canons do not bind the laity'; an incumbent, under a duty to uphold the law, may forbid the commission of illegal acts (*R v Dibdin* [1910] P 57); this may not apply to some illegal acts, however: if X did not participate in liturgy (Canon B9) and a minister ordered participation, it is unclear (and probably unlikely) that the executive order would if disobeyed be enforced in the civil courts.

the parish in question and of such other parishes in the diocese as he may specify during a period of five years.[81] This may be conceived as the application of a censure for breach of the canonical duty of the 'people to do their utmost not only to avoid occasions of strife but also to seek in penitence and brotherly charity to heal such divisions'.[82]

Finally, discipline may be effected by operation of law: failure of a lay person to satisfy canonical or other legal requirements may lead to loss of rights to or qualifications for the church's ministrations;[83] in prescribed circumstances excommunication may be imposed, resulting in loss of communicant status and rights flowing from that status.[84] Disciplinary processes could not result from breach of the duties of church membership deriving from Act of Convocation unless these duplicate duties arising under the schemes described above.[85]

Roman Catholic Canon Law

Unlike the law in the Church of England, the canon law of the Roman Catholic Church is binding on laity baptized or received into the church who enjoy the sufficient use of reason and, unless the law expressly provides otherwise, have completed seven years of age.[86] In pursuance of the church's claimed inherent right to correct offending members with penal sanctions, violation of canonical duties may result, but only as a last resort, in a sanction imposed to effect conversion, repentance, and reconciliation of the offender, the restoration of order, and reparation of scandal.[87] However, only external violations of a law

---

[81] Incumbents (Vacation of Benefices) Measures 1977 and 1993, s.10(6); s.10(6A): where a bishop disqualifies a person who is or becomes a lay member of a deanery synod, a diocesan synod, or General Synod from being a member of a parochial church council during such a period, that person cannot be a member of that council by virtue of that lay membership during that period, notwithstanding *CRR*, r. 14(1)(f).

[82] Canon A8; see also *AR*, Art. 34: '[w]hosoever through his private judgement, willingly, and purposely, doth openly break the traditions and ceremonies of the church, *and be ordained* and approved by common authority, ought to be rebuked openly, (that there may fear to do the like,) *as he that offendeth* against the common order of the Church, and hurteth the authority of the magistrate, and woundeth the consciences of the weak brethren' (emphases added).

[83] For legal requirements concerning e.g. baptism and marriage see *post* Part V.

[84] *CRR*, rr. 10(1)(b), 24(7), 30(5)(c), 37(1)(a); this suggests that an excommunicate does not cease to be a 'member' of the church universal or of the Church of England; however, *AR*, Art. 33 suggests that 'membership' is lost by excommunication but is restored on repentance: 'That person which by open denunciation of the Church is rightly cut off from the unity of the Church, and excommunicated, ought to be taken [out] of the whole multitude of the faithful, as an Heathen and Publican, until he be openly reconciled by penance, and received into the church by a Judge that hath authority thereunto'; see also *Kemp v Wickes* (1809) 3 Phillim 264 at 271, 61 ER 1320 at 1323: 'excommunication . . . is not merely expulsion from the Church of England, but from the Christian Church generally.' It cannot be imposed by the courts: EJM 1963, ss. 49, 82(4); for Canons B16 and B38 see *post* Ch. 12.

[85] As we have seen, few duties are imposed on the laity by primary legislation: see above for e.g. Ecclesiastical Courts Jurisdiction Act 1860.

[86] *CIC*, c. 11.

[87] Cc. 1311, 1341.

or precept (to which a penalty attaches) gravely imputable to the person by reason of deliberate intent or culpable negligence are punishable.[88] Those lacking capacity (such as the use of reason), those whose awareness is diminished (such as those under sixteen), those unaware that their action was a violation, and those acting accidentally, under duress, grave fear, necessity, or in self-defence are not subject to penalties.[89] Similarly, those suffering from a partial impairment of their freedom or awareness may have penalties reduced.[90] The ordinary makes a preliminary investigation and decides whether to proceed administratively or judicially.[91] Penalties may be imposed (*ferendae sententiae*) or arise automatically (*latae sententiae*) depending on the offence in question and extensive provision is made for their suspension.[92] These include excommunication which effects a partial exclusion from the communion of the faithful; excommunicates are forbidden to receive the sacraments and to carry out functions attaching to offices.[93] The faithful can legitimately vindicate and defend their rights before a competent ecclesiastical court in accord with the norm of law; they have the right if summoned to be judged according to law which must be applied with equity; and they have the right not to be disciplined with canonical penalties except in accord with the norm of law.[94]

THE MINISTRY OF LAY OFFICE-HOLDERS

In the Roman Catholic Church, in addition to the canonical ministry of all the faithful, lay persons may participate in the threefold mission of the church by holding ecclesiastical office and by performing functions proper to their own apostolate.[95] Many norms enable and regulate official or public lay activity within the church not reserved to the ordained clergy and authorized by means

---

[88] Cc. 1321; c. 1330: internal forum offences are not punishable.   [89] Cc. 1322, 1323.

[90] C. 1324, e.g. by drunkenness, provocation, or duress.

[91] C. 1717: in either process the accused is given a right to be heard (see cc. 1720, 1723, 1725, 1481).

[92] C. 1314: attempted marriage; for suspension see cc. 1335, 1352–3); for penalties for specific offences, cc. 1365–9, 1370–7; usurpation of functions (cc. 1378–89); falsehood (cc. 1390–1); for a critical assessment see T. J. Paprocki, 'Rights of Christians in the local church: canon law procedures in the light of civil law principles of administrative justice', *Studia Canonica*, 24 (1990), 427.

[93] *CIC*, c. 1331 (an interdict has the same effect with regard to the sacraments but does not exclude from governing functions: c. 1332); see e.g. c. 1398: automatic excommunication for procuring an abortion; A. Stenson, 'Penalties in the new code: the role of the confessor', *The Jurist*, 43 (1983), 406.

[94] *CIC*, c. 221; J. A. Coriden, 'A challenge: make the rights real', *The Jurist*, 45 (1985), 1.

[95] *CIC*, cc. 208, 225, 228, for lay *munera*; c. 145 governs appointment of lay persons to an 'ecclesiastical office', an office stably constituted by divine or ecclesiastical law (*CCL: TC*, 98, 99).

of deputation or designation by a competent ecclesiastical authority.[96] Similarly, the Church of England opens up to qualified lay persons a range of ecclesiastical offices from which to exercise particular ministries. Special rules apply to 'lay officers', defined as 'licensed lay workers, readers, lay judges of consistory or provincial courts, and lay holders of offices admission to which is for the time being regulated by Canon';[97] the last category includes, *inter alia*, legal officers (such as diocesan registrars), administrative officers (such as churchwardens), and liturgical officers (such as organists). Disciplinary processes and powers differ according to the ministry in question, though as a general principle no proceedings may be taken against lay office-holders in the church courts.[98] Ordinarily, discipline of lay officers is effected executively by archbishops, bishops, archdeacons, and incumbents; for readers and lay workers this is reinforced by a declaration of due obedience to the bishop.[99] For the purposes of implementing the Children Act 1989, the House of Bishops of General Synod has recently formulated child protection guidelines to regulate the selection and appointment of persons whose ecclesiastical work involves children and young people; these include the making of a declaration concerning convictions for criminal offences which might be construed as impediments to working with children or young people as well as the church conducting on its own investigations into child abuse.[100] Similar provision has been made at diocesan level.[101]

Judicial and Other Legal Offices

In Roman Catholic canon law judicial office is generally reserved to the ordained clergy though the episcopal conference may permit lay persons to be appointed as a diocesan judge (provided they possess a doctorate or at least

---

[96] S. A. Euart, 'Council, code and laity: implications for lay ministry', *The Jurist*, 47 (1987), 492; E. J. Kilmartin, 'Lay participation in the apostolate of the hierarchy', in J. H. Provost (ed.), *Official Ministry in a New Age* (Washington, 1981); J. M. Huels, 'Another look at lay jurisdiction', *The Jurist*, 41 (1981), 74.

[97] Church of England (Worship and Doctrine) Measure 1974, s. 2(2).

[98] EJM 1963, s. 82(2)(c); see *RACCL*, 108, draft Canon 9: 'The Law of the Church of England is binding upon, and shall be enforceable by and against . . . such of the laity as either hold office in the church or are members of any of the bodies mentioned in Canon CXXX and all other of the laity claiming the benefit of any of the ministrations of the Church.'   [99] See above n. 81.

[100] *Policy on Child Abuse* (1995); for the Roman Catholic Church see *Child Abuse: Pastoral and Procedural Guidelines*, a report from a Working Party to the Bishops' Conference of England and Wales; see also F. G. Morrisey, 'Recent studies concerning clerics and sexual abuse of minors', Canon Law Society *Newsletter*, No. 91 (1992) 6.

[101] Diocese of Ely, *Policy on Child Abuse* (approved by the Bishop's Council, May 1995), and Ely Diocesan Board of Education 'Guidelines for work with children and young people in the parishes' (1995); *Children: the Churches' Care: Policy Guidelines*, Lichfield Diocese, 1993; Diocese of Sheffield, 'Guidelines for parishes appointing persons to work with children and young people' (1991); *DGBOP*, 6.1.

a licentiate in canon law) to assist in a collegial tribunal.[102] The norm is very different in the Church of England. A candidate for the office of diocesan chancellor must be a communicant member of the church, at least thirty years of age, a barrister or solicitor who has a seven-year general qualification under the Courts and Legal Services Act 1990, or a person who has held high judicial office. Appointment is made by the diocesan bishop who must in so doing consult the Lord Chancellor and the Dean of the Arches and Auditor.[103] The chancellor, whose powers are defined by the jurisdiction of the consistory court, sits as ordinary and his decisions are not subject to the control of the bishop.[104] Candidates must take an oath of allegiance to the monarch, 'to deal uprightly and justly . . . without respect of favour or reward', and declare assent to the church's doctrine.[105] Tenure ceases automatically on reaching the age of seventy-two, but the diocesan bishop may authorize continuance in office if he considers it desirable in the interests of the diocese.[106] Though a right exists to offer resignation to the bishop by written instrument, the bishop is empowered to remove the chancellor if the upper house of the appropriate convocation resolves that the chancellor is incapable of acting or unfit to act.[107] A candidate for appointment as Dean of the Arches and Auditor of the Chancery Court must be a communicant member of the church, a person who has ten years' High Court qualification, or who has held high judicial office. Appointment is made by the two archbishops jointly.[108] These courts must also consist of two lay persons being diocesan chancellors.[109] Judicial powers are defined by the jurisdiction of these courts and candidates are required to take the same oaths and declarations as chancellors.[110] Tenure is without limit of time though a provincial judge may resign by written

[102] *CIC*, c. 1421; *COCLA*, 1341: the bishops' conference of England and Wales permits 'suitably qualified faithful, other than clerics, to be appointed diocesan judges in England and Wales'; *Briefing*, 85, 1.

[103] EJM 1963, s. 2(1), (2) (in the diocese of Canterbury, styled Commissary General) as amended by CCEJM 1991, s. 8, Sched. 4, para. 3; Courts and Legal Services Act 1990, s. 71, Sched. 10, para. 17; see also Canon G2 (declaratory of the Measures).

[104] EJM 1963, s. 6; CCEJM 1991, Part III; see *supra* Ch. 5.

[105] EJM 1963, s. 2(5)(a) , Sched 1, Parts I and II and Canon G2(3); s. 4: deputy chancellors may be appointed when the chancellor is ill or temporarily incapacitated or 'for any reason unable to act' and CCEJM 1991, Sched. 4, para. 4.

[106] CCEJM 1991, s. 9, Sched. 4, para. 2; a vacancy-in-see does not terminate the appointment, but when a new bishop is appointed continuing appointment must be confirmed by the capitular body of the diocesan cathedral: s. 2(3).

[107] EJM 1963, s. 4; in Roman Catholic canon law judges cannot be removed 'except for a lawful and grave reason': *CIC*, c. 1422.

[108] EJM 1963, s. 3(1), (2)(a), (3); Courts and Legal Services Act 1990, s. 71; Canon G3.

[109] EJM 1963, ss. 3(2)(c), (4): they are appointed by the chairman of the house of laity of General Synod after consultation with the Lord Chancellor and must have communicant status and such judicial experience as the Lord Chancellor thinks appropriate; under s. 3(2)(b) the courts are also composed of 2 ordained ministers appointed by the prolocutor of the lower house of the appropriate convocation.

[110] For jurisdiction see *supra* Ch. 5; for oaths see EJM 1963, s. 3(6) and Canon G3(6).

instrument offered to both archbishops; the archbishops acting jointly may remove a provincial judge if the upper houses of both convocations resolve that he is incapable of acting or unfit to act.[111] Similar rules apply to an assistant provincial court judge,[112] as well as to those sitting in the other appellate courts.[113]

In Roman Catholic canon law lay people serve in many offices associated with the administration of justice: as auditors, assessors, promoters of justice, and defenders of the bond in matrimonial proceedings.[114] In the Church of England the holder of the statutory office of provincial registrar is appointed by the appropriate archbishop who must, in so doing, consult the Standing Committee of General Synod.[115] Diocesan registrars shall be appointed by the bishop, who must consult the bishop's council and standing committee of the diocesan synod.[116] A provincial registrar acts as legal adviser to the archbishop, and as registrar of the provincial court; both provincial registrars act as joint registrars of General Synod; diocesan registrars act as legal advisers to the bishop and as registrars of the consistory court.[117] By canon, candidates in each case, must be communicants and solicitors, 'learned in the ecclesiastical laws and the laws of the realm', and must take an oath of allegiance to the monarch and declare their assent to the church's doctrine.[118] By measure, registrars must vacate their office on attaining age seventy or at such earlier date as prescribed by regulations made by the House of Bishops.[119] They may offer resignation by written instrument which must be served on the archbishop in the case of provincial registrars and on the diocesan bishop in the case of diocesan registrars.[120] Moreover, the archbishop and the bishop respectively have a power to terminate the appointment by written instrument: with regard to provincial registrars, the other archbishop must consent to termination, and with respect to diocesan registrars, termination must be

---

[111] EJM 1963, s. 3(5).

[112] Ibid., ss. 3(5)(b), (7); *Ex parte Medwin* (1853) 1 E & B 609; *Re Tristram* [1902] 1 KB 816 (CA): the bishop has no right to hear cases personally unless there is a special reservation.

[113] EJM 1963, s. 5 governs lay judges (who must be communicants) sitting in the Court of Ecclesiastical Causes Reserved. [114] *CIC*, cc. 1424, 1428, 1435.

[115] Canon G4(1); Eccleiastical Judges and Legal Officers Measure 1976, s. 3; s. 3(4) provides for the appointment of a deputy.

[116] Ibid., s. 4; Canon G4(1); s. 4(5A) provides for the appointment of a deputy; Hill, *EL*, 348, n. 2 discusses the possibility of making a contract of employment with the diocesan board of finance as a party.

[117] Ecclesiastical Judges and Legal Officers Measure 1976, ss. 3(2), 4(2); SGM 1969, Sched. 2, Art. 4(3).

[118] Canon G4(2), (3); it is unclear whether a person could be deprived for lack of learning: see *Jones v Bishop of Llandaff* (1693) 4 Mod Rep 27 (concerning chancellors); for the oath and declaration see G4(3).

[119] Ecclesiastical Judges and Legal Officers Measure 1976, s. 5(1), (3); the regulations must be approved by General Synod and each House of Parliament (s. 8); no regulation applies to any person who at the date of its coming into force holds the office of registrar (s. 5(4)).

[120] Ibid., s. 5(5).

agreed by the provincial archbishop.[121] There is no express duty to give reasons for the termination, nor a right of appeal against the decision.

Administrative Offices: National and Diocesan

In the Roman Catholic Church lay people serve in many administrative capacities at provincial and diocesan levels: as secretary general of the episcopal conference, as diocesan financial officer, as members of diocesan synods, pastoral, and finance councils.[122] In the Church of England lay people exercise administrative ministries at all levels of the church by virtue of either a statutory office or a contract of employment. The following outlines the major offices and positions. A member of the House of Laity of General Synod may be elected by that House to act as its chairman; during a vacancy in office, or if the chairman is absent or incapable of acting, the Vice-Chairman (also elected) carries out the duties of chairman.[123] The Secretary General of the General Synod, who must be a 'lay person' holding office 'subject to the pleasure of the Synod', performs those functions assigned by synod's Standing Orders and 'such other duties as may be assigned by the Standing Committee or by the Presidents after consultation with the Standing Committee'. The Registrar is the Legal Adviser to General Synod and advises the chairman on the interpretation of Standing Orders and on any other matter affecting the practice and procedure of Synod, its Houses, and Subordinate bodies. The General Synod 'shall be the employer of all persons in receipt of salaries paid from the General Synod Fund . . . employees shall serve under contracts of service made with the Central Board of Finance as financial executive of the Synod . . . their conditions of service shall be prescribed in Staff Regulations issued from time to time by the Central Board of Finance'.[124]

The bishop may appoint a lay person as chairman of meetings of the diocesan synod; only a lay person may be appointed as chairman of the diocesan synod's house of laity: their principal function is to regulate procedure.[125] At its first meeting after each triennial election the synod must appoint a secretary,[126] an assistant secretary, and a treasurer. Of the secretary and assistant, one must be ordained and the other a lay person. Appointees, unless they resign or cease to be qualified, must serve until the conclusion of the meeting at which their successors are appointed.[127] Having

---

[121] Ibid., s. 5(6), (7); s. 4(5C): a bishop who considers that the registrar is unable or unlikely to perform his duties, or that it would not be appropriate for him to do so, may request the provincial registrar to appoint a fit and proper person to perform those duties.

[122] *CIC*, cc. 494, 451, 443, 463, 512, 492, 470, 536.

[123] *GSSO*, App. C 4, 7; for chairmanship and membership of subordinate bodies see *supra* Ch. 4.

[124] *GSSO*, SO 123–7; see *WAOB*, 5.41 ff. for organization of staff on the proposed National Council (and 7.13 ff. for the House of Bishops). [125] *CRR*, r. 34(1)(a); *MSODS*, 7, 8.

[126] *CRR*, r. 34(1)(b). [127] *MSODS*, 11.

overall responsibility for the diocesan office, the diocesan secretary is also secretary to the bishop's council, the diocesan board of finance, its finance committee, and its various sub-committees. The assistant secretary is responsible for day-to-day management of the office and acts as personnel officer for its staff and other diocesan officers.[128] With regard to the many other statutory offices open to the laity, appointment, functions, and discipline vary according to the office in question and the terms of the governing synodical measure.[129] In addition, many diocesan posts—such as youth officer, children's officer, communications officer, and stewardship adviser—may be held by the laity: the diocesan bishop is commonly involved in appointment whilst functions and discipline are effected by means of contracts of employment.[130] In relation to the deanery synod, the lay chairman, as one of its joint chairmen, is elected triennially by the house of laity and holds office (unless he resigns or ceases to be qualified) until the commencement of the next meeting at which his successor is elected; at its first meeting the synod must also appoint a secretary and assistant secretary (one a cleric and the other a lay person) and a treasurer.[131]

Parochial Offices: Churchwardens

Churchwardens, of which there must be two in each parish, occupy a central position in the Church of England's parochial system[132] (there seems to be no obvious equivalent in Roman Catholic canon law). Rules concerning appointment, functions, and discipline are found predominantly in canons and synodical measures; diocesan norms merely repeat these.[133] Candidates must be communicant members (except where the bishop permits otherwise) of at least twenty-one years of age and are chosen from persons resident in the parish or from names on the electoral roll.[134] Unless there is an existing pre–1964 custom (of at least forty years) regulating the number and manner of choosing

---

[128] Ibid.   [129] See *supra* Ch. 4.

[130] See *CF*, H.1 ff.; *TBF*, 9.1: communications officer; *PDH*, M.2: stewardship adviser; *WDHI*, Ch.3; *SDH*, VII, A-C.

[131] General Synod's *Model Rules for Deanery Synods* (1990) 7, 8, 11.

[132] Churchwardens (Appointment and Resignation) Measure 1964, s. 1(1); as by law parishes cannot be without churchwardens, their appointment may be compelled by *mandamus*: *R v Wix Inhabitants* (1832) 2 B & Ad 197. For a memorandum of the Ecclesiastical Law Society for the General Synod's present Working Party on Lay Office-Holders see *ELJ*, 3 (1995) 354; for the report itself see *Working Party on Lay Office-Holders: Report and Proposed Measure and Canon*, GS 1164–6 (London, 1995).   [133] See e.g. *CF*, F.2; *TBF*, 5.1; *BDM*, M.1 f.; *GDM*, F.1–5.

[134] Churchwardens (Appointment and Resignation) Measure 1964, s. 1(2), (3); s. 12(4) provides that nothing in the Measure authorizes selection of a person 'who under the existing law' is disqualified: it seems, therefore, that aliens, Jews, and persons convicted of prescribed offences remain disqualified: *Anthony v Seger* (1798) 1 Hag Con 9.

of churchwardens in a particular parish,[135] selection must be carried out in accordance with the Churchwardens (Appointment and Resignation) Measure 1964 and the canons.[136] The Measure contemplates two selection processes. Ordinarily, candidates must be 'chosen by the joint consent of the minister of the parish and at a meeting of the parishioners'; joint consent is deemed to be present (a) if a motion stating the names of the (two) persons to be chosen (or the name of either of them) is declared to have been carried by the person presiding over the meeting *and* (b) if, concerning the motion, the minister announces his consent to the 'choice'.[137] In short, the minister has a power of veto and no churchwarden can be chosen unless both are chosen at this joint meeting. The Measure covers two forms of disagreement. First, in the event of disagreement between the minister and the parishioners' meeting (that is, if they cannot agree on the choice of both churchwardens) the minister is under a duty to appoint one churchwarden and the parishioners' meeting under a duty to *elect* the other. Secondly, if 'after due opportunity has been given no motions or insufficient motions have been moved', again the minister must appoint one churchwarden and the parishioners' meeting must elect the other.[138] If as a norm, and as a first procedure, the minister were to appoint and the parishioners to elect, this would strictly be contrary to the terms of the Measure, and the law requiring 'joint consent' would be a fiction.[139] Extraordinarily, although there must as a general principle be two churchwardens, where an 'existing custom' regulates the number of churchwardens or the 'manner in which [they] are chosen', the provisions of the Measure 'shall not affect that custom': when there is a custom it must be applied instead of the statutory procedure. However, in the case of any parish where (under a custom) any churchwarden is chosen either 'by the vestry of that parish' or 'jointly with any other person[s]', the churchwarden must be chosen 'by the meeting of the parishioners, either alone or jointly with the other person[s], as the case may be'.[140]

---

[135] Churchwardens (Appointment and Resignation) Measure 1964, s. 12(2); the custom must be clearly proved: *Catten v Barwick* (1719) I Stra 145: the minister chooses one and outgoing churchwardens the other; *Gibbs v Flight* (1846) 3 CB 581: the vestry elects both; *Vicar of Holy Sepulchre v Churchwardens of Holy Sepulchre* (1879) 5 PD 64: custom allows more than 2 churchwardens.   [136] Canon E1(1).

[137] Churchwardens (Appointment and Resignation) Measure 1964, s. 2(2)(a), (b).

[138] Ibid., s. 2(3).

[139] Ibid., s. 2(2): no person is deemed chosen 'unless both . . . have been so chosen'; s.2(1), (2), Canon E1(2): not later than 30 Apr. each year, though the bishop may extend the time: s.11(1)(c), at a time and place appointed by the ordinary; s.3(1): the parishioners are those on the electoral roll or those resident and entered on a register of local government electors.

[140] Churchwardens (Appointment and Resignation) Measure 1964, s. 12(2); *OLAC*, 46: 'The fact that for many years it has been the practice . . . for the incumbent to nominate one warden does not necessarily indicate or prove an "existing custom" [under s. 12(2)] . . . It normally indicates an assumed disagreement between the two appointing parties . . . . In other words, it will be assumed that the joint consent . . . has not been signified and that the alternative procedure . . . will be followed.'

Although these rules afford a degree of subsidiarity to the parochial church
in the selection of its wardens, the governing legislation reserves legislative
and executive powers of oversight to the diocesan bishop. So far as may be
necessary for the purpose of giving effect to the intentions underlying the
Measure, the bishop is empowered 'to modify the procedure laid down' by
it.[141] In any case where there has been no valid choice the bishop may direct a
fresh choice 'and . . . give such directions in connection therewith as he may
think necessary'; in any case in which any difficulty arises the bishop may give
any directions which he considers expedient for the purpose of removing the
difficulty; however, these powers shall not enable the bishop to validate
anything that was not valid at the time it was done.[142]

Churchwardens must appear before the ordinary (or his substitute) for
admission to office after promising to perform faithfully and diligently the
duties of office.[143] According to judge-made law, it seems the ordinary has no
discretionary power to refuse admission to a lawfully and validly selected and
qualified candidate.[144] On admission both churchwardens become officers of
the ordinary,[145] though they take no oath of canonical obedience to the bishop.
Under a canonical duty to 'discharge such duties as are by law and custom
assigned to them', as officer of the ordinary and as guardian of the parish
church, churchwardens share in the leadership of the local church and possess
ministerial functions of a pastoral and governing nature. Their foremost duty is
that of 'representing the laity and in co-operating with the incumbent'; it is
through them as representatives that the laity have access to the ordinary. Their
pastoral and quasi-priestly function is to use their best endeavours by example
and precept to encourage the parishioners in the practice of true religion and to
promote unity and peace among them.[146] In the opinion of the Legal Advisory
Commission, churchwardens must report to the archdeacon any matters which
are amiss or irregular in the parish or about which they feel the archdeacon
should be made aware, and the ordinary has a right to make enquiries of them
at any time.[147] They must attend a visitation, answer questions put to them, and
their presentments should include 'any gross neglect of duty or impropriety of
life on the part of the incumbent and, if made in good faith, [these] are
privileged communications'.[148] They are members of the parochial church

---

[141] Churchwardens (Appointment and Resignation) Measure 1964, s. 11(1)(c).
[142] Ibid., s. 11(1)(d), (e), (2).
[143] Ibid., s.7(1); Canon E1(2); the mode of election is the same as that for the parochial church
council except that the minister has a right to nominate and vote (*CRR*, r. 13); casual vacancies
may be filled by a person chosen in the same way: s.2(5), (6).
[144] *Mandamus* may be the appropriate remedy: *R v Rice* (1697) 1 Ld Raym 136; *R v Bishop of
Sarum* [1916] 1 KB 467.
[145] Canon E1(4). For these purposes the bishop is normally the admitting ordinary and in years
of episcopal visitation it is conducted by him, his chancellor, or surrogate: *R v Sowter* [1901] 1 KB
396 (CA); in other years admission is conducted by the archdeacon as ordinary: *OLAC*, 47.
[146] Canon E1(4).   [147] *OLAC*, 8, 9.   [148] *OLAC*, 47.

council (if actual communicants whose names are on the electoral roll) and of its standing committee, and are joint treasurers where no treasurer is appointed by the parochial church council.[149] Under a duty to maintain order and decency in the church and churchyard, especially during the time of divine service,[150] churchwardens must also protect the church (or chapel) from being profaned at any meeting held there for temporal objects inconsistent with the sanctity of the place.[151] They must not allow any person to behave in the church, church porch, or churchyard during the time of divine service in such a way as to create disturbance, and must restrain those (and if necessary proceed against them according to law) guilty of riotous, violent, or indecent behaviour in any church, chapel, or churchyard, whether in the time of divine service or not, or those disturbing, vexing, troubling, or misusing any minister officiating there.[152] Churchwardens must provide those things necessary for divine worship,[153] including allocation of seats (subject to the ordinary's direction or any rights to seats conferred by faculty, prescription, or statute).[154] As a quasi-corporation,[155] in churchwardens is vested the property in the plate, ornaments, and other movable goods of the church; they must keep an inventory of these to be revised from time to time as occasion may require.[156] Jointly with the minister, they are responsible for ensuring that the requirements are satisfied when a faculty is needed for the care, alteration, or repair of the church.[157] It is commonly understood that churchwardens also have a right of free access to the church and churchyard to discharge their functions.[158]

The churchwardens' one-year tenure continues until they or their successors

---

[149] *CRR*, r. 14(1)(d), App.II, paras. 1(e), 14.

[150] Canon E1(4); they may enlist the assistance of sidespersons: E2(3).   [151] F15(1).

[152] F15(2),(3); see also *Cope v Barber* (1872) LR 7 CP 393 at 404, n. 1; *Cole v Police Constable 443A* [1937] 1 KB 316; a power of arrest is given by Ecclesiastical Courts Jurisdiction Act 1860, s.3; *OLAC*, 220: churchwardens 'cannot exclude an orderly person on the ground that the church is full if he can stand in such a part of the church as will not interfere with the conduct of the service' (no authority is given); it seems they may also restrain a minister if his conduct falls within the terms of F15(3), but the normal course is to inform the ordinary: see *Hutchins v Denziloe and Loveland* (1792) 1 Hag Con 170 at 173, 174 *per* Sir William Scott; *AG v St Cross Hospital* (1854) 18 Beav 601 at 605 ff.

[153] Canon B17(1): with the advice and direction of the minister, they must provide sufficient bread and wine for holy communion; B17A: as agents of the parochial church council, they organize the collection of alms and other offerings at communion.

[154] Canon F7(2); see for the ordinary's direction *Vicar etc. of Claverley v Parishioners etc. of Claverley* [1909] P 195 at 212; they may remove a person intruding on a seat assigned to another, provided they use only necessary force and do not cause scandal or disturb the service: *Reynolds v Monkton* (1841) 2 Mood & R 384.

[155] *Fell v Charity Lands Official Trustee* [1898] 2 Ch 44 at 51, 59 (CA).

[156] Canon E1(5); as owners of the movables, they take proceedings for their recovery if stolen or improperly removed: *Adlam v Colthurst* (1867) LR 2 A & E 30; *Evans v Dodson* (1874) Trist 26; the former duties and liabilities of churchwardens concerning care, maintenance, preservation, and insurance of goods are now vested in the parochial church council: Parochial Church Councils (Powers) Measure 1956, s. 4(1)(ii)(b) (see *post* Ch. 16); the churchwardens have the custody of the church register books during a vacancy: Parochial Registers and Records Measure 1978, s. 6.

[157] Canon F13(2); see *post* Ch. 16.   [158] *OLAC*, 48.

are admitted by the ordinary; a qualified person has a statutory right to stand for reselection on any number of occasions.[159] On vacating office they must deliver to their successors any goods remaining in their hands together with the inventory which must be checked by their successors.[160] They may offer resignation, with the consent of the minister and the other warden(s), to the bishop who may refuse or accept. No other form of resignation is permitted and there is no right of appeal against a refusal, though if accepted the office is vacated forthwith.[161] Although judicial proceedings cannot be taken against them, they may be subject to (for example) rebuke at visitation.[162] No specific provision seems to exist to remove churchwardens in the event of misbehaviour although a diocesan bishop may have a power of removal under the general principle in the 1964 Measure 'to make provision for any matter not herein provided for'.[163] In any event, the diocesan bishop has a general executive power to appoint a person to do any act in respect of which there has been neglect or default on the part of churchwardens.[164]

The law of the Church of England concerning other parochial lay administrators is not so well developed. Though the minister is the chairman of the parochial church council, a lay member must be elected as vice-chairman.[165] A secretary may be appointed by the council from its membership, but if no member is appointed the council must appoint some other fit person with such remuneration (if any) as the council thinks fit; there seems to be no requirement that a candidate be a communicant. The secretary has charge of all documents relating to the current business of the council with the exception (unless he is also the electoral roll officer) of the electoral roll. The secretary must keep the minutes and record all resolutions passed.[166] The council may appoint one or more of their number to act as treasurer solely or jointly and, failing such appointment, the office of treasurer must be discharged jointly by such of the churchwardens as are members of the council; no remuneration

---

[159] Churchwardens (Appointment and Resignation) Measure 1964, ss. 2(1), 7(2), Canon E1(3); by s. 9 of the 1964 Measure the office is vacated if the churchwarden is not resident in the parish and his name is not on the electoral roll.   [160] Canon E1(5).
[161] Churchwardens (Appointment and Resignation) Measure 1964, s. 8.
[162] See *supra* Ch. 4.
[163] Churchwardens (Appointment and Resignation) Measure 1964, s. 11(1)(a); EJM 1963, s. 82(2)(c); hitherto, churchwardens may have been removed from office for misconduct by a church court: *Ritchings v Cordingley* (1868) LR 3 A & E 113 at 117, 118; for removal by resolution of an extraordinary meeting of the parishioners, which may still be possible, see *Parish Clerk* (1601) 13 Co Rep 70; see *supra* n. 81 for the bishop's power to disqualify a person from holding the office of churchwarden.
[164] Churchwardens (Appointment and Resignation) Measure 1964, s. 11(1)(b).
[165] *CRR*, r. 15, App. II, para. 1(b); during a vacancy or when the minister is incapacitated by absence or illness or for any other reason, the vice-chairman acts with the full powers vested in the chairman (ibid., para. 1(c)); these and the following officers are occasionally treated in diocesan norms: see *GDM*, F.9–12.
[166] *CRR*, App. II, para. 1(d). He must also keep the secretary of the diocesan synod and deanery synod informed as to his name and address.

may be paid.[167] The electoral roll officer having charge of the roll must be appointed by the council; if the officer is not a member of the council, the council may pay such remuneration as it thinks fit;[168] again, there is no requirement of communicant status. Auditors are to be appointed by the annual meeting but if they are not, or if they are unwilling to act, the council must appoint auditors who may receive any remuneration paid by the council.[169] The Legal Advisory Commission considers that auditors 'must not be members' of the council.[170] Though it seems that the council can appoint its officers for such term as it thinks fit,[171] there seems to be no provision governing the removal of such people prior to the expiration of the term of their office. Any question arising as to the interpretation of these provisions must be referred to the diocesan bishop and his decision (or that made by his appointee) is final.[172] Prospective sidespersons must be on the electoral roll and are elected by the annual parochial meeting; they must 'promote the cause of true religion in the parish and . . . assist the churchwardens in the discharge of their duties in maintaining order and decency in the church and churchyard, especially during the time of divine service'.[173] By Measure, the parochial church council and the incumbent have a power acting jointly to appoint and to dismiss the parish clerk and the sexton or any persons performing or assisting to perform the duties of parish clerk or sexton (who must be 'fit and proper' persons). If they cannot agree the matter must be settled by the diocesan bishop whose decision is final; the minister and council must determine 'their salaries and the conditions of the tenure of their offices or of their employment'.[174] Again, by canon, the holders of these offices must 'perform such services upon such terms and conditions' as the minister and council think fit.[175] The office of parish clerk may be held by a lay person (or a cleric).[176]

Liturgy and Pastoral Care: Readers and Lay Workers

Since Vatican II Roman Catholic canon law has widened the opportunities for lay people to participate in the teaching and sanctifying functions of the church. Whereas they cannot preside at the Eucharist, absolve, ordain, confirm, or solemnize marriages,[177] lay people can assist the pastor in the parish

---

[167] *CRR*, App. II, para. 1(e). If there is only one churchwarden, he shall be treasurer solely.
[168] Ibid., para. 1(f).   [169] Ibid., para. 1(g); *CRR*, r. 9(4)(d).   [170] *OLAC*, 14.
[171] *OLAC*, 198 (in the absence of any provision to the contrary, the appointment terminates at the first meeting of the parochial church council held after the annual meeting following the officer's appointment).   [172] *CRR*, App. II, para. 17.
[173] Canon E2; *CRR*, rr. 9(4)(c), 10(2); they must consent to serve or there must be sufficient evidence of their willingness to serve: r. 10(3); churchwardens are the proper persons to make the collection, either alone or with the aid of sidesmen or other persons selected by the churchwardens: *OLAC*, 69.
[174] Parochial Church Council (Powers) Measure 1956, ss. 7(iii), 9(3); Canon E3.
[175] Canon E3.   [176] PCC(P)M 1956, s.7(iii); Canon E3; *OLAC*, 194.
[177] See *post* Part V.

catechetical ministry, serve as catechist in missionary work, and teach the sacred sciences at institutions of higher learning, but they cannot give a homily;[178] they may serve as liturgical minister, special minister of the Eucharist, and minister of sacramentals, and a lay man (not a woman) may be installed as lector or acolyte.[179] The law of the Church of England enables the laity to share in liturgical and other ministries by virtue of the offices of reader, lay worker, choirmaster, and organist.

The office of *reader* is sometimes treated as sub-diaconal.[180] Rules concerning appointment, functions, and discipline found in canons, Measures, and in norms issued by the House of Bishops, are commonly supplemented by a host of norms issued at diocesan level providing *inter alia* for the office of Warden to Readers, readership committees, and chapters or associations of readers.[181] A lay candidate must be a baptized, confirmed, and regular communicant member of the church, male or female.[182] A candidate must be nominated to the diocesan bishop by the minister of the parish (or district) or, if appointed to a wider area, by one of the rural deans or archdeacons after consultation with the minister of the parish or district.[183] The person nominating must satisfy the bishop that the candidate is 'of good life, sound in faith . . . and well fitted for the work of a reader, and provide all such other information about the said person and the duties which it is desired that he should perform as the bishop may require'.[184] The bishop cannot admit to the office unless satisfied by examination (personally or by competent appointees) that the candidate possesses sufficient knowledge of holy scripture and the doctrine and worship of the church, is able to read the services of the church plainly, distinctly, audibly, and reverently, and that he is capable of both teaching and preaching.[185] According to regulations issued by the House of Bishops, selection of candidates for reader ministry is the responsibility of the diocese 'exercised usually through a panel of selectors appointed by the Warden in consultation with the bishop'. The process of selection 'should be thorough and rigorous' with candidates assessed in the light of criteria agreed by the diocese. The process should include adequate contact between the candidate and the warden, sufficient interviews with diocesan selectors, and the consultation of referees. The parochial church council (or equivalent)

---

[178] *CIC*, cc. 776, 785, 229(3).   [179] Cc. 230, 910(2), 1168.

[180] *Acts of Convocation*, 52 (1925); a reader is not a 'minister': *OLAC*, 176; for critical studies suggesting that readers are under-used see J. Tiller, *The Church's Ministry*, 152.

[181] *CF*, E.2; *TBF*, 3.10; *PDH*, B.9.3; *LDHI*, II, 4; *SDDH*, I, Annex (there must be 'strict adherence' to the diocesan norms); *BDM*, C.1; *LDR*, 80; *BRDSEI*, Ki; *NDIB*, III, 36; *WDHI*, Ch. 1, 32, Ch. 3, 174, 185; *HDCH*, B.1ff.   [182] Canon E4(1).

[183] Canon E5(1); the modern canons do not employ the distinction appearing in Convocation Acts of 1939 and 1940 between parochial and diocesan readers: *Acts of Convocation*, 55; it has been held judicially that a reader is not a 'regular minister' for the purposes of the Military Service Act 1916 (repealed): *Simmonds v Elliott* [1917] 2 KB 894.   [184] Canon E5(2).

[185] Canon E5(3).

in the place where the candidate is to serve 'must express its approval'. The cost of the selection procedure, excluding candidate's expenses, should be borne by the Diocesan Readers' Board. Provision is made for both pre- and post-admission training.[186]

By canon, on admission and licensing readers must declare assent to the church's doctrine and 'due obedience' to the bishop and his successors in all things lawful and honest.[187] If a reader moves to another diocese admission cannot be repeated,[188] but the reader must be licensed afresh.[189] If the reader is to be stipendiary, the bishop must not license until satisfied that adequate provision has been made as to stipend, insurance, and pension.[190] According to the House of Bishops' regulations, licences held by those under the age of seventy 'should be subject to regular renewal, normally every three years'. Readers exercising office temporarily should do so on the basis of the bishop's written permission rather than a formal licence. On reaching seventy, readers wishing to remain in active ministry should surrender their licence and apply for a bishop's written permission to officiate. With regard to readers licensed to an incumbent, in an interregnum the rural dean or the archdeacon should be substituted.[191]

A reader is obliged by canon to perform those functions prescribed by canon or by Act of Synod,[192] and liturgical functions may be lawfully performed notwithstanding any rubric or direction in the Book of Common Prayer or any rule of ecclesiastical law.[193] Readers have five basic functions.[194] First, as promised at licensing, a reader must endeavour, as far as in him lies, to promote peace and unity, and to conduct himself as becomes a worker for Christ, for the good of his church and for the spiritual welfare of his fellows.[195] Secondly, the licence (or written permission), which will specify functions,[196] may allow a reader to visit the sick, to read and pray with them, to teach in Sunday school and elsewhere, and generally to undertake such pastoral and educational work and to give such assistance to any minister as the bishop may direct.[197] Thirdly, during divine service, it is lawful for a reader to read morning and evening prayer (but not to administer the absolution), to publish

---

[186] *Bishops' Regulations for Reader Ministry* (Advisory Board of Ministry Policy Paper No.2, 1991) para. 3; see also *CBC*, 5, para. 2 for the Advisory Board of Ministry's role in the ministry of readers.

[187] Canon E5(4); E5(5): admission is effected by delivery of the New Testament but without imposition of hands; E4(3): the bishop must keep a register of all readers admitted and licensed in the diocese.

[188] E5(6). Also, the bishop must give the newly admitted reader a certificate of admission.

[189] Canon E6(1), unless its exercise is temporary in which case the bishop's written permission is required.   [190] E6(4).

[191] *Bishops' Regulations* (1991) para. 7.

[192] Canon E4(1); *CRR*, r. 14(1)(e) confers membership of the parochial church council.

[193] Deaconesses and Lay Ministry Measure 1972, s. 1(3).

[194] *Bishops' Regulations* (1991) para. 1.   [195] E6(2).   [196] *Acts of Convocation*, 55.

[197] Canon E4(2)(a).

marriage banns, to read scripture, to preach, to catechize children, and to receive and present the offerings of the people.[198] Fourthly, a reader may lawfully distribute the elements.[199] Fifthly, the bishop may authorize a reader to bury the dead or read the burial service before, at, or after a cremation, but only, in each case, with the goodwill of the persons responsible and at the invitation of the minister.[200] Though General Synod is specifically empowered to enact a canon to this effect, at present a reader ought not ordinarily baptize in the absence of a minister.[201] According to the House of Bishops' regulations, in exercising any function readers must act 'in accordance with what is agreed with the minister to whom they are responsible, and with the written permission of any other minister who is the incumbent or priest in charge of the place where they are to minister'; they must 'assist the minister in undertaking pastoral and educational work as the bishop directs'.[202] With regard to conditions of service, readers should be clearly informed of their duties and rights and they should submit an annual report to the warden or an appointed delegate. Indeed, readers and their incumbent or minister 'should make a written agreement over the duties to be undertaken' taking into account the particular expression of the individual's ministry, the role of the reader in the local ministerial team, and, in relation to the parochial church council, the arrangements for post-admission training and regular attendance at readers' chapters; the agreement should take into account also the balance between their role as reader and the requirements of their family, work, and leisure, as well as arrangements for reimbursement of expenses incurred: this agreement 'should be regularly reviewed, normally at the time of the annual report'.[203]

Discipline of readers is dealt with episcopally. Though no formal provision exists concerning resignation or reliquishment of office, a diocesan bishop may by notice in writing revoke summarily and without further process a licence granted to a reader for any cause which appears to him to be good and reasonable. The rights of readers with respect to revocation, including the right to appeal to the archbishop, are the same as those of licensed ordained ministers.[204]

---

[198] Canon E4(2)(b); for administration of the reserved sacrament under B12(3) see *OLAC*, 4.

[199] Canon E4(2)(c).

[200] Canon E4(2A): 'minister' means a minister of a parish or extra-parochial place within the meaning of the Deaconesses and Lay Ministry Measure 1972, s. 1.

[201] Deaconesses and Lay Ministry Measure 1972, s. 1(1)(b).

[202] *Bishops' Regulations* (1991) paras. 1.2, 3.

[203] Ibid., para. 5. Para. 6: readers who are voluntary and unpaid should not accept a fee for their services.

[204] Canon E6(3). The appointee must be a diocesan bishop or suffragan, who then reports to the archbishop in writing; when the provincial archbishopric is vacant or the archbishop is the revoking bishop, the appeal is heard by the other provincial archbishop or his nominee (a bishop in the appellant's province); appeals must be conducted according to rules approved by the two archbishops; *Bishops' Regulations*, para. 4.6: readers must surrender their licence or written permission if revoked, and where a licence is revoked summarily the reader must be notified of the right to appeal. See Church of England (Legal Aid) Measure 1994, Sched. 1 for legal aid in revocation process concerning 'lay worker or *stipendiary* reader' (emphasis added).

It has not been settled whether a stipendiary reader is employed, with a remedy in an industrial tribunal against an unfair dismissal; nor has it been decided whether and to what extent a reader has a remedy or may be disciplined in the event of breach of a written agreement as to duties made with an incumbent.[205]

Lay persons may also be admitted to the office of *lay worker*.[206] As with readers, candidates must be baptized, confirmed, and regular communicant members; they must have had proper training and possess 'the other necessary qualifications' (undefined).[207] Admission, ordinarily by the bishop, cannot be repeated if the person moves to another diocese.[208] No person admitted may serve unless authorized by the licence or written permission of the bishop of the diocese.[209] Stipendiary lay workers cannot be licensed unless the bishop is satisfied that adequate provision has been made concerning salary, insurance, and pension.[210] By canon a lay worker may, 'under the direction of the minister', lead the people in public worship, exercise pastoral care, evangelize, instruct the people in the Christian faith, and prepare them for the reception of the sacraments; they may also read morning and evening prayer (but cannot administer the absolution), distribute the elements at communion, and read the epistle and gospel. With the authorization of the bishop a lay worker may at the invitation of the minister preach at divine service, church women, (with the goodwill of the persons responsible) bury the dead or read the burial service before or after a cremation, and publish banns of marriage at morning and evening prayer.[211] Prior to admission and licensing the lay worker must make the declaration of assent to the church's doctrine and of due obedience in all things lawful and honest, to the licensing bishop.[212] Disciplinary processes against lay workers are the same as those against readers and licensed ordained ministers.[213]

The liturgical offices of organist, choirmaster, and director of music are in the keeping of the parish.[214] Appointed by a joint act of the minister and the parochial church council, conditions of service are often defined by written agreement.[215] Unless the agreement prescribes otherwise, the organist and choirmaster have no responsibility for the choice of music, nor does canon

---

[205] *OLAC*, 124: 'the law is not clear about this'; in *Barthope v Exeter Diocesan Board of Finance* [1979] ICR 900, the Employment Appeal Tribunal, reversing the decision of an industrial tribunal, decided that a stipendiary reader was employed, and remitted the case to the tribunal to identify the employer; the case was settled before the tribunal gave judgment on the matter.

[206] For diocesan norms see e.g. *CF*, E.1.1, local project lay workers; *TBF*, 3.6; *SDDH*, F.10; *CDH*, 112: candidates must be 30 years of age.

[207] Canon E7(1), made under the Deaconesses and Lay Ministry Measure 1972, s. 1(1).

[208] Canon E8(1), the bishop must certify admission; the certificate is given to the candidate; E8(6): the bishop must keep a register of all lay workers; E7(2): an evangelist is thereby admitted as a lay worker. [209] Canon E8(2).

[210] Canons E7(1); E8(3). [211] E7(3), (4), (5). [212] E8(4). [213] E8(5).

[214] Canon B20(1). The appointment and functions of cathedral musicians may be governed by the statutes and customs thereof: ibid.

[215] B20(1); for model contracts see *OLAC*, 188 (this includes no information as to functions).

law specify duties generally.[216] Canonically, it is the minister who must ensure that only chants, hymns, anthems, and other settings are chosen as are appropriate, both the words and the music, to the solemn act of worship and prayer as well as to the congregation assembled; ministers are under a duty to 'banish all irreverence in the practice and in the performance of the same'.[217] However, if music is chosen the minister is under a canonical duty to pay heed to the advice of the organist or choirmaster in choosing chants, hymns, anthems, or other settings and in the ordering of the music of the church: nevertheless, 'the final responsibility and decision in these matters rests with the minister'.[218] In relation to music at weddings, and in the absence of an agreement to the contrary, the organist or choirmaster has no responsibility for organizing music—this belongs to the minister.[219] If there are disagreements about choice or performance of music, it seems that the matter ought to be referred to the ordinary.[220] The minister, who must obtain the agreement of the parochial church council, may terminate the appointment (presumably only in accordance with any operative contract); in serious cases the archdeacon may facilitate termination of the appointment without the agreement of the parochial church council.[221]

Extra-Canonical Lay Ministry: Parish Assistants

Some key posts at parochial level now exist in the Church of England which are neither statutory nor canonical in origin. Designed to give assistance to the ordained clergy, particularly with regard to pastoral care, these have increasingly become the subject of regulation by diocesan norms justified on the basis of the public nature of the tasks performed.[222] Practices vary: typically selection is in the keeping of the incumbent though the parochial church council ought to be involved in finding and choosing suitable candidates and sometimes candidates are interviewed by a warden for pastoral assistants. After due training and preparation, a person may be commissioned (usually for a prescribed period) by the incumbent of the parish (or the rural dean) to undertake the work of a parish assistant in the parish (or other community). The candidate promises to endeavour to live as a faithful follower of Christ

---

[216] *OLAC*, 189–90: the duties listed here, unless they are terms of the contract, are not mandatory. [217] Canon B20(3).

[218] Canon B20(2).

[219] B35(5): when matrimony is solemnized in any church, it belongs to the minister of the parish to decide what music shall be played and what hymns or anthems sung.

[220] *Wyndham v Cole* [1875] 1 PD 130.

[221] B20(1), although the archdeacon, if he 'considers that the circumstances are such that the requirement as to the agreement of the parochial church council should be dispensed with' may direct accordingly; where the minister is the archdeacon the bishop may dispense with the requirement; see *TBF*, 3.14; *PDH*, J.9.

[222] *WH*, BP.2.1 for 'authorization, accreditation or commissioning' of public liturgical and pastoral tasks.

and to work with the clergy and lay people in the parish. The assistant may be commissioned to perform liturgical (in which case the bishop's permission is required), pastoral, educational, or missionary activity and must work in close association with the incumbent, readers, evangelists, and lay workers. Several dioceses have lay pastoral assistants committees as well as appraisal schemes and structures enabling the bishop to be informed of operative assistance schemes.[223] Lay elders have also been introduced within the concept of 'shared leadership in ministry' and norms sometimes require consultation with the bishop before their appointment.[224]

CONCLUSIONS

The law of the Church of England is lagging behind theological developments which recognize the centrality of the ministry of the laity. It contains no comprehensive statement of common lay rights and duties similar to that in Roman Catholic canon law. In this sense it fails to guide the laity in its ministry. This may be seen as a distinct advantage: the assumption is that the Church of England has chosen to place few duties on the laity and, unlike the Roman Catholic Church, the opportunity for discipline is neglible; the consequence is a greater degree of lay freedom. Lay rights, on the other hand, though scattered, are capable of vindication as in the Roman Catholic Church by both executive and judicial processes. These are enjoyable, unlike in the Roman Catholic Church, by virtue of a person's status as a parishioner rather than as a member. Indeed, whilst the Church of England has no clear understanding of membership, often only members classed according to status are capable of admission to the wide range of offices and posts open to the laity to exercise its ministry. Regulation of appointment, functions, and disciplining of lay ministerial offices and posts is effected by a complex array of legal rules which are increasingly supplemented by norms issued executively.

[223] *LDHI*, B.7; *WH*, BP.2 Appendix (for liturgy of admission); *BDM*, A.4; *LDR*, 75–6; *RBG*, B.7; *SDDH*, V.38–9.
[224] See e.g. *BDM*, A.11 and *BRDSEI*, Li

PART IV

Faith, Doctrine, and Liturgy

9

Faith and Doctrine

Doctrine may be understood as that body of faith or teaching which is received and believed by those comprising a religious community.[1] Legislators in both the Church of England and the Roman Catholic Church have in part reified faith and doctrine, treating them as entities capable of regulation. Doctrinal law has two facets. On one hand it is used to define and protect the faith, to ensure its public presentation, and to empower the church to develop and reformulate the faith. On the other hand, doctrinal law is used to effect assent to the teaching of the church and to regulate and correct dissent. Moreover, in the context of secular society a large body of state-made law exists to protect the Christian faith from scurrilous public attacks, to enable Christians to practise their faith freely, and to facilitate a minimal religious education.

PRESENTATION OF THE FAITH AND THE RIGHT TO INSTRUCTION

The Roman Catholic Church has a set of canons devoted exclusively to the ministry of the word.[2] Its canon law recognizes in all the faithful, lay and ordained, a general duty (and right) to present the Christ-given 'deposit of faith' to the world: the church is 'missionary by its nature' and evangelization is 'a fundamental duty of the people of God' who are 'to work so that the divine message of salvation may increasingly reach the whole of humankind in every age and in every land'.[3] Lay members of the faithful, by reason of

---

[1] This is of course a vulgarization of a complex definitional problem; for a Church of England perspective see *Believing in the Church: The Corporate Nature of Faith*, A Report by the Doctrine Commission of the Church of England (London, 1981) esp. ch. 5; *The Nature of Christian Belief*, A Statement and Exposition by the House of Bishops of the General Synod of the Church of England (London, 1986) 4–16; *AR*, Art.11: 'that we are justified by Faith only is a most wholesome Doctrine'. For the Roman Catholic perspective see General Catechetical Directory, *Ad normam decreti* (1971), On Dangerous Opinions and on Atheism, *Ratione habita* (1967). For doctrine as tenets of belief or faith in civil law see *General Assembly of the Free Church of Scotland v Lord Overton* [1904] AC 515; *Barralet v AG* [1980] 3 All ER 918; *R v Registrar General, ex p Segerdal* [1978] 3 All ER 886; and the Australian case of *Church of the New Faith v Commissioners for Payroll Tax* (1983) 57 ALJR 785 (HC) at 789.

[2] *CIC*, c. 760: in the ministry of the word the mystery of Christ is to be presented in its entirety, based on scripture, tradition, liturgy, the *magisterium*, and the life of the church; cc. 760, 761: every means available is to be used.

[3] *CIC*, cc. 747, 781, 211; *LG*, 33; some commentators treat it as an immutable duty: *CIC: TC*, 143 (Matt. 28: 19–20; Mark 16: 15). See c. 225 for the right of the faithful to work in associations to spread the divine message; c. 227: the faithful cannot pass off their own opinions as the teaching of Christ in questions open to various opinions.

baptism and confirmation, are to be witnesses to the gospel by their words and by the example of their Christian life.[4] Moreover, a special teaching function (particularly through preaching) is assigned to the ordained ministers of the church, notably the bishops.[5] In addition, canon law recognizes the church's right to proclaim moral principles, even with respect to the social order, and to make such judgments about any human matter 'in so far as this is required by fundamental human rights or the salvation of souls'.[6]

In contrast, lay persons in the Church of England are under no canonical duty to present the Christian message.[7] This function is assigned to the ordained clergy and to lay office-holders: bishops, priests, deacons, readers, and lay workers all have specific duties to teach the faith, either formally or by way of example.[8] The duty to preach is central. A sermon must be preached in every parish church at least once each Sunday, except for some reasonable cause approved by the diocesan bishop; ordinarily the sermon is preached by a minister, reader, or lay worker, although at the invitation of the minister having cure of souls 'another person may preach with the permission [given occasionally or generally] of the bishop'; the preacher 'shall endeavour himself with care and sincerity to minister the word of truth, to the glory of God and to the edification of the people'.[9]

The parishioners' general right to a sermon is one of a package of rights to instruction in the faith enjoyed by specific classes of parishioner on the occasion of particular ecclesiastical events. Each minister must 'teach the people from time to time', especially at Christmas, Easter, and Whitsun, so that they come to holy communion prepared.[10] A minister is under a canonical duty to 'take care that the children and young people within his cure are instructed in the doctrine . . . of Christ, as the Lord commanded and as they are set forth in the holy Scriptures, in the Book of Common Prayer, and especially in the Church Catechism'; 'to this end he, or some godly and competent persons appointed by him, shall on Sundays or if need be at other convenient times instruct and teach them in the same'; moreover, all parents

---

[4] *CIC*, cc. 759, 216; for sponsors see c. 872.

[5] See *CIC*, cc. 756–72; c. 756(1): the pope and College of Bishops; cc. 386, 756(2), 763: bishops; cc. 528, 757, 763: presbyters, cc. 757, 763: deacons, cc. 758, 765: religious, c. 784: missionaries; laypersons may be permitted to preach (c. 766).   [6] *CIC*, c. 747.

[7] In contrast, liturgical forms do treat confession of faith: see e.g., concerning baptism for those of riper years, *BCP*, 288: whilst no express promise is made to teach, the candidate is signed with the cross 'in token that hereafter he shall not be ashamed to confess the faith of Christ crucified'; see also *ASB*, 245.

[8] Canon C18(1): bishops must 'uphold sound and wholesome doctrine'; E4(2): readers; E7(5): lay workers; for the duty to teach by example, C18(1): bishops; C26(2): ministers must frame their lives 'according to the doctrine of Christ'; E1(4): churchwardens must 'encourage parishioners in the true practice of religion'; C15(1)(1), Preface to the Declaration of Assent: 'which faith the Church is called upon to proclaim afresh in each generation.'

[9] Canons B18, C24(3); *BCP*, 241 (mandatory sermon at holy communion); *ASB*, 116: 'The sermon is an integral part of the Ministry of the Word. A sermon should normally be preached at all celebrations on Sunday and other Holy Days'.   [10] Canon B15(2).

and guardians shall take care that their children receive such instruction.[11] Ministers are bound to instruct parents or guardians before baptism of an infant; adult candidates must be instructed 'in the principles of the Christian religion', as must candidates for confirmation and those to be received into the church.[12] Whereas enforcement of these duties is usually effected executively by the bishop, a serious clerical violation of the laity's canonical rights may result in judicial proceedings for neglect of duty.[13]

These provisions are similar to those in Roman Catholic canon law: the faithful have a duty and a right to acquire a knowledge of Christian doctrine in order to live in accordance with it, to announce it, to defend it when necessary, and to be able to assume their apostolic role.[14] Parents have a special obligation to proclaim the gospel to their children 'according to the teaching handed down by the Church'.[15] There is, however, no general equivalent in the law of the Church of England to the process of catechesis in Roman Catholic canon law. Catechesis, the ministry of the word directed to those who have responded to the faith, is the process by which 'through doctrinal formation . . . the faith of the people may be living, manifest and active'; the bishop, the conference of bishops, and pastors have special responsibilities to provide catechetical formation.[16] In the Church of England,[17] in addition to canonical duties placed on specified office-holders,[18] evangelization is co-ordinated by the Board of Mission, one of General Synod's subordinate bodies. Its functions include the promotion of theological reflection and study in the area of mission, the stimulation of theological reflection (in consultation with the Doctrine Commission) 'on issues and proposals concerning mission, evange-lism, renewal and inter-faith relations', and giving advice to General Synod and the dioceses on these matters.[19] In addition to the legal duty imposed on deanery synods and parochial church councils to promote 'the whole mission of the Church', which includes its 'evangelistic' mission,[20] norms operating at diocesan level commonly provide structures for evangelization as well as opportunities for the education of lay people and the continuing education of ordained ministers.[21] Rights to religious education under civil law are considered below.

---

[11] Canon B26; B28 confers on persons to be received into the church a right to be instructed.
[12] Canons B22(3), B24(1), B27(2), B28(1).   [13] See *supra* Ch. 7.
[14] *CIC*, cc. 229, 217.
[15] C. 226; c. 1366: parents who allow children to be 'educated in a non-Catholic religion' are subject to a just penalty.
[16] *CIC*, c. 773 ff.; Canon Law Society *Newsletter*, No. 94 (1993) 12–32; for missionary action see *CIC*, cc. 781 ff.
[17] *BCP*, 289, the catechism to be learned before confirmation: see *post* Ch. 12.
[18] Canon E(4), churchwardens; E7(2), (3), lay workers.
[19] *CBC*, 11; *WAOB* recommends the transference of the Board's functions to the proposed National Council's Mission Resources Department (App. C).
[20] SGM 1969, s. 5(3)(b); PCC(P)M 1956, s. 2(1)(a).
[21] E.g. *WDHI*, Ch. 3, 173–4: bishop's adviser on evangelism and director of ministerial training; *NDIB*, V, 51; *LDR*, 70; *PDH*, M.4, P.1, R.4; *TBF*, 3.8, 3.9, 12.1, 12.3; for boards of mission see e.g. *BDM*, I.9, *LDHI*, VI, 3, *SDDH*, V.42–53, 46–7.

The Church of England possesses two species of doctrine in documentary form: what might be described as its 'official' doctrines,[22] namely those which enjoy express legal approval, and its 'persuasive' doctrines. The extent to which the law enables ecclesiastical authorities to develop doctrine depends on these classifications.

The Legally Approved Doctrines

Two bodies of doctrine enjoy the legal status of the official doctrine of the Church of England: the function of the law here is to define ecclesiastical doctrine.[23] The first is that contained in the ancient pre-Reformation formularies: 'the doctrine of the Church of England is grounded in the Holy Scriptures, and in such teachings of the ancient fathers and Councils of the Church as are agreeable to the said Scriptures.' The second body of approved doctrine is contained in the three central post-Reformation documents: '[t]he doctrine of the Church of England . . . [i]n particular is to be found in the Thirty-Nine Articles of Religion, the Book of Common Prayer, and the Ordinal.'[24] The status of these as the church's lawful doctrines has been recognized in the Church of England (Worship and Doctrine) Measure 1974: '[r]eferences in this Measure to the doctrine of the Church of England shall be construed in accordance with the statement concerning that doctrine contained in the Canons of the Church of England.'[25] Moreover, doctrines may enjoy tacit legal approval when contained (perhaps implicitly) in synodical legislation, parliamentary statutes, and the judgments of the courts. It has been suggested that these too may be said to be authoritative, 'not necessarily right, but binding until altered'.[26]

Other documents may contain doctrines of 'persuasive authority'.[27] Formulations of the Doctrine Commission, of other General Synod subordinate

---

[22] The phrase 'official teaching of the Church' was used by the Bishop of Chichester in *Re St Stephen's, Walbrook* [1987] 2 All ER 578 at 561; for 'approval' by the House of Bishops of these see *The Nature of Christian Belief*, A Statement and Exposition by the House of Bishops of the General Synod of the Church of England (1986) 1–2.

[23] *Believing in the Church* (London, 1981): 'Definition of doctrine is necessary to present the gospel to the current generation and to preserve it for future ones.'

[24] Canon A5; cf. the view of the Arches Court *per* Sir Herbert Jenner Fust in *Gorham v Bishop of Exeter* (1849) 2 Rob. Ecc. 1 at 55: '*Prima facie* . . . the Thirty-Nine Articles are the standard of doctrine; they were framed with the express purpose of avoiding a diversity of opinion, and are, as such, to be considered, and, in the first instance, appealed to, in order to ascertain the doctrine of the Church' (ER 163, 1221 at 1241).   [25] S. 5(1).

[26] *MIECL*, 49–50.

[27] Ibid., 50; the problem of identifying doctrine of persuasive authority is increased by the view that there is no distinct Anglican theology: see e.g. *AT: HS*, 345, 401.

bodies, or of the House of Bishops fall into this category,[28] as do those of the Lambeth Conference which has repeatedly asserted that its doctrinal statements are merely guidelines and not binding.[29] Indeed, the courts sometimes appeal to persuasive doctrines in the resolution of disputes: in *St Stephen's, Walbrook* the Bishop of Chichester appealed to the formulations of the Anglican-Roman Catholic International Commission in clarifying doctrines of the holy communion.[30]

Alteration and Evolution of Doctrine: General Synod

The law seeks to strike a balance between preservation and protection of the Church of England's doctrine and its development. The Preface to the Book of Common Prayer 1662 and the Thirty-Nine Articles 1571 establish the principle that ecclesiastical doctrine is reformable.[31] As a matter of law, however, doctrine of an established church may be altered only in accordance with the legal procedures prescribed for alteration. According to the House of Lords in *General Assembly of the Free Church of Scotland v Lord Overton* (1904), 'where the state has by legislative acts established a church identified by certain doctrines, that church cannot, while retaining the benefit of establishment, exercise any power of altering those doctrines without the legislative sanction of the state'.[32] With regard to the Church of England, state approval for the alteration of doctrine has been given with the enactment of the Synodical Government Measure 1969 and the Church of England (Worship

---

[28] E.g. *Believing in the Church*, A Report of the Doctrine Commission (London, 1981); *Abortion and the Church*, A Report by the Board of Social Responsibility (London, 1993) (this report 'has only the authority of the Board by which it was prepared'); *Issues in Human Sexuality* (London, 1991) and *The Nature of Christian Belief* (London, 1986), both statements by the House of Bishops. *WAOB* commends the practice of the House of Bishops as the proper institution ('a college of pastors') to issue papers on doctrine and also recommends that the House of Bishops 'from time to time issue a pastoral letter' (7.5).

[29] See *AT: HS*, 383, 389–390; the 1920 Conference Resolution 44 stated that its Consultative Body, 'created by the Lambeth Conference in 1897 and consolidated by the Conference in 1903 is a purely advisory Body . . . [it] possesses nor claims any executive or administrative power'; its encyclical stated that the Conference 'does not claim to exercise any powers of control or command'; *HLE*, para. 314.

[30] [1987] 2 All ER 578 at 582: the findings of ARCIC had been 'recently approved by the General Synod as consonant in substance with the Doctrines of the Church of England'.

[31] *AR* (1571), Art. 34 states: 'It is not necessary that traditions and ceremonies be in all places one, or utterly alike, for at all times they have been diverse, and may be changed of countries, times and man's manners.' Also, 'Every particular or national Church has authority to ordain, change, and abolish ceremonies or rites of the Church ordained only by man's authority'. See E. J. Bicknell, *A Theological Introduction to the Thirty-Nine Articles of the Church of England* (2nd edn., London, 1925) 376–88; see, however, *AR*, Art.20: 'The Church hath . . . authority in Controversies of Faith; And yet, it is not lawful for the Church to ordain any thing that is contrary to God's Word written, neither may it so expound one place of Scripture, that it be repugnant to another.' [32] [1904] AC 515 at 648.

and Doctrine) Measure 1974: and the doctrines approved by the latter may, in turn, be altered only with an amendment of that Measure.[33]

In this respect General Synod is the only authority within the Church of England competent to alter the legally approved doctrines: no doctrinal development may occur unless the three Houses of General Synod consent to it. Indeed, it has been understood judicially that General Synod possesses *in law* an unlimited power to change the church's fundamental doctrines, provided the required procedures are followed.[34] The procedures are rigorous and, by requiring the participation of the whole church as represented in General Synod, they give juridical expression to the theological principle that doctrines ought to be derived from a *consensus fidelium*.[35] According to General Synod's constitution '[a] provision touching doctrinal formulae shall, before it is finally approved by the General Synod, be referred to the House of Bishops, and shall be submitted for such approval in terms proposed by the House of Bishops and not otherwise'.[36] If they so require, the two Convocations (or either of them) or the House of Laity may insist on the provision being referred to them before final approval by synod. Once referred, no doctrinal provision shall be submitted for final approval by synod unless it has been approved (in the form proposed) by Convocations sitting separately and by the House of Laity.[37] The question of whether a reference is to be made must be conclusively decided by the President and Prolocutor of the respective Houses of Convocation and by the Prolocutor and Pro-Prolocutor of the House of Laity; if, however, before such a decision is taken either House of Convocation or the House of Laity resolves that the provision concerned shall be so referred, or both Houses or the House of Laity resolve that it shall not be so referred, the resolution(s) shall be a conclusive decision that the reference is or is not required by that Convocation.[38] A provision which fails to secure

---

[33] *HLE*, paras. 335, 936, n. 3.

[34] *R v Ecclesiastical Committee of Both Houses of Parliament, ex parte the Church Society* (1993) *per* McCowan LJ, accepting the argument that 'the Church of England has inherent authority to deal with all matters of doctrine . . . as affecting its own members'; the courts had not been given the task of determining, for the purposes of the Enabling Act 1919, what was a fundamental change of doctrine (Hill, *EL*, 72 at 76); *R v Archbishops of Canterbury and York, ex p Williamson* (1994) *per* Sir Thomas Bingham MR: 'I, for my part, can see nothing absurd about entrusting decisions on matters of doctrine and faith to a body of church people, including the Bishops and Clergy, with overall control reserved to a majority in Parliament' (Hill, *EL*, 77 at 80).

[35] *Believing in the Church*, 3–5, 27 ff, 220–9; nor does the law express the idea that a matter be consistent with reason or tradition: for these in Anglican theology see *The Nature of Christian Belief*, 8, n. 4.

[36] SGM 1969, Sched. 2, Art. 7(1); see also *GSSO*, SO 81–94; according to *HLE*, para. 403, n.1, '"Provision" is evidently understood to include not only Measures, but also canons and Acts of Synod': it is submitted that as official doctrine has been approved by the 1974 Measure, it can be altered only by a measure, and not by a canon or Act of Synod—alteration by canon without an enabling measure would be unlawful; see *post* for the idea that canons of their own force cannot depart from, nor therefore alter, doctrine.   [37] Art. 7(2).

[38] Art. 7(3) and (4).

approval on a reference by each of the four Houses of Convocation or by the House of Laity, it is not to be proposed again in the same or similar form until a new General Synod comes into being. However, if one house of one Convocation objects on a reference a second reference may be made to the Convocations. If there is a second objection the provision may be referred to the General Synod's Houses of Bishops and Clergy. The approval of the provision by a two-thirds majority of the members of each of these Houses present and voting is sufficient and operates in lieu of approval by the four Houses of Convocation.[39] As we shall see in Chapter 10, the introduction of new forms of worship may involve doctrinal questions and special rules apply: under the Church of England (Worship and Doctrine) Measure 1974, canons and regulations authorizing forms of service and the liturgies themselves 'shall be such as in the opinion of the General Synod is neither contrary to, nor indicative of any departure from, the doctrine of the Church of England in any essential matter'.[40]

Development of Doctrine by Other Bodies

Whereas diocesan synods, deanery synods, and parochial church councils may discuss matters of religious interest, they cannot 'issue . . . any statement purporting to declare the doctrine of the Church of England'.[41] However, as we have seen, there are several ecclesiastical authorities other than General Synod competent to declare or devise new persuasive doctrines, notably the Doctrine Commission. This is empowered to consider, and to advise the House of Bishops on, doctrinal matters referred to it by that House, to suggest to General Synod what in its judgment constitute doctrinal issues of concern to the Church of England, and to exchange information and advice in doctrinal matters with other Christian churches.[42]

The classical view is that the courts do not possess a power to declare, create, or change ecclesiastical doctrine: 'the courts do not claim to declare true doctrine, but only to state what the law is with regard to doctrine.'[43] In *Gorham v Bishop of Exeter* the Privy Council concluded: '[t]his court has no jurisdiction or authority to settle matters of faith or to determine what ought in any case to be the doctrine of the Church of England.' The duty of the courts

---

[39] Art. 7(5).

[40] S. 4(1) and (2): synod 'shall' determine conclusively; CE(WD)M 1974, s. 2(1): a canon dealing with declarations of assent to the church's doctrine must be passed by a two-thirds majority in each House of General Synod.

[41] SGM 1969, ss. 4(2), 5(3); PCC(P)M 1956, s. 2(2)(b); *OLAC*, 107: this applies 'whether or not the motion involves only the reaffirmation of doctrine'. Whether these provisions are enforced is a matter of dispute: see *post* Part IV for diocesan synod statements concerning baptismal policy and remarriage of divorcees.

[42] *CBC*, 31–2. In so doing it must collabroate with the Liturgical Commission and the Faith and Order Advisory Group.   [43] *MIECL*, 50.

extends 'only to a consideration of that which is by law established to be the doctrine of the Church of England upon the true and legal construction of the articles and formularies'.[44] Similarly, in *General Assembly of the Free Church of Scotland v Lord Overton* Lord Halsbury stressed that 'it is to be remembered that a court of law has nothing to do with the soundness or unsoundness of a particular doctrine'.[45]

What the courts do in relation to doctrine is, it is submitted, a matter of debate. In resolving a legal question a court may clarify a doctrine and settle a doctrinal dispute. In *St Stephen's, Walbrook* the Court of Ecclesiastical Causes Reserved had to determine the legality of a refusal to grant a faculty allowing the introduction of a Henry Moore sculpture because it was not a 'table' within the meaning of Canon F2. The diocesan chancellor refused to exercise his discretion to allow its introduction classifying the sculpture as an 'altar': '"altar" signifie[d] a place where a sacrifice is to be made, a repetition at every Mass of the sacrifice of our Lord at Calvary.' For the chancellor this doctrine had been rejected at the Reformation: the 'theology of Holy Communion' being 'an essential matter', it was not a 'table' under the Book of Common Prayer which 'doctrinally is still normative'.[46] The Court of Ecclesiastical Causes Reserved reversed the decision. Concluding that the matter should be decided in the light of 'the more recent ecumenical developments in the understanding of Christian doctrine', the Bishop of Chichester stated '[i]t is clear . . . that a doctrine of the Eucharistic sacrifice which is not that of a repetition of the sacrifice of Calvary can lawfully be held in the Church of England and consequently that the holy table can lawfully and properly be called an altar'; interestingly *Gorham* was not discussed.[47] There was, as such, no doctrinal obstacle to the introduction of the Henry Moore 'altar'. Indeed, the civil courts have frequently to clarify the doctrines of a community before it might be classed legally as a religion;[48] moreover, decisions of the civil courts can stimulate a change of doctrine within the Church of England.[49]

---

[44] (1850) Moore's Special Reports, 462; (1850) 117 ER 377; this was used in *Williams v Bishop of Salisbury* [1863] 2 Moo. P.C. 375; for the view of the Arches Court in *Gorham* (1849) ER 1221 at 1238: 'I am particularly anxious . . . to have it distinctly understood that I guard myself against being supposed to offer any opinion on the purely theological point at issue between the parties. . . . All that the Court is called upon to do is to endeavour to ascertain whether the Church has determined any thing upon the subject, and, having done so, to pronounce accordingly. . . . The authoritative declaration of the Church constitutes the law which this Court is bound to follow implicitly, without indulging in any opinion of its own as to its correctness or erroneousness. The Court is to administer the law as it finds it laid down.'

[45] [1904] AC 515 at 648; compare in civil law, however, charitable trusts cases concerning doctrines subversive to morality: see *post* Ch. 16.   [46] [1986] 2 All ER 705 at 709.

[47] [1987] 2 All ER 578 at 583.

[48] See e.g. *R v Registrar General, ex p Segerdal* [1978] 3 All ER 886.

[49] For the effect of parliamentary statute, considered in *R v Dibdin* [1910] P 57, and the alteration of the Table of Kindred and Affinity for marriage see *post* Ch. 13.

Comparisons with Roman Catholic Canon Law

The law of the Church of England dealing with doctrine and its development is in some formal respects very different from that of the Roman Catholic Church. According to the 1983 Code the church does not create doctrine but simply declares or enunciates it. Though conceived as a function of the whole church, classically the teaching function (*magisterium*) belongs to the clerical hierarchy in the church.[50] Supreme teaching authority, exercising authentic or authoritative *magisterium*, vests in the pontiff and the College of Bishops; these may declare infallible doctrine, by which faith or morals as a matter of truth is solemnly defined,[51] and they may proclaim truth, as contained in the written word of God or in tradition, which is defined as existing in the deposit of faith entrusted to the church and proposed as divinely revealed.[52] Alternatively, the pope or College of Bishops may proclaim doctrine on faith or morals non-definitively,[53] as might bishops (while not infallible in their teaching) individually or collectively in matters of faith.[54] Though not a canonical body, the International Theological Commission may assist the pontiff in the preparation of doctrinal statements.[55] Whilst the formal law of the Church of England does not possess obvious equivalents to infallibly declared doctrine, its official doctrine contained in the Thirty-Nine Articles, the Book of Common Prayer, and the Ordinal is presented canonically as 'agreeable to the Word of God',[56] and its persuasive doctrines may be analogous to the Roman Catholic Church's non-definitive doctrine.

DOCTRINAL DISCIPLINE

Whilst approaching the question of the effects of doctrine in radically different ways, both churches organize law relating to doctrinal discipline on the basis

---

[50] F. A. Sullivan, 'Magisterium', in J. A. Komonchak, M. Collins, and D. A. Lane (eds.), *The New Dictionary of Theology* (London, 1987) 617; *LG*, 25.

[51] *CIC*, c. 749: the bishops may declare definitively whilst dispersed throughout the world; K. Rahner, 'Magisterium', in K. Rahner (ed.), *Encyclopedia of Theology* (London, 1981) 871. See generally T. Horvath, 'A structural understanding of the magisterium of the church', *Science et Esprit*, 29(3) (1977), 283, and W. M. Thompson, 'Authority and *magisterium* in recent Catholic thought', *Chicago Studies* (1977), 278.   [52] *CIC*, c. 750.

[53] C. 752.

[54] Cc. 753, 386; T. J. Green, 'The church's teaching mission: some aspects of the normative role of episcopal conferences', *Studia Canonica*, 27 (1993), 23.

[55] It is supervised by the Sacred Congregation for the Doctrine of the Faith: its statutes have been papally approved and its members (nominated by its president, a cardinal-prefect) must observe 'professional secrecy' and have 'eminent knowledge, prudence and fidelity toward the magisterium': *CCL: TC*, 297.

[56] Canon A2: '[t]he Thirty-nine Articles *are* agreeable to the Word of God'; *AR*, The Declaration: 'the Articles of the Church of England . . . do contain the true Doctrine of the Church of England agreeable to God's Word'; Canon A3: 'The doctrine contained in the Book of Common Prayer . . . *is* agreeable to the Word of God'; Canon A4: the Ordinal 'is not repugnant to the Word of God'.

of duties of assent, rights to dissent, and procedures designed to ensure the maintenance of doctrinal standards.

The Duty of Assent

In Roman Catholic canon law the faithful must seek the truth in all matters concerning God and the church: when they have found it then by divine law they are bound to embrace and keep it.[57] The faithful are under an absolute duty to give assent, an assent of faith, to infallible doctrine which itself is irreversible: it must be 'held definitively'; doctrine declared to be part of the deposit of faith 'must be believed with divine and catholic faith' and the faithful are 'bound to shun any contrary doctrines'.[58] According to the documents of Vatican II, when the *magisterium* defines a doctrine it must 'be adhered to with the submission of faith'.[59] However, Roman Catholic canonists are not in agreement about the precise obligation which canon law places on the faithful with regard to non-definitive doctrine. The crucial word in the canons is *obsequium*, which has been translated variously as giving rise to an obligation (if not of an assent of faith) of 'respect of intellect and will', or else as an obligation of 'religious submission of intellect and will'.[60] *Lumen Gentium* (1965) stressed that non-definitive doctrines impose the obligation of 'respect and submission of the will and mind' and the duty 'to adhere sincerely'.[61] When a papal encyclical, the usual medium for the expression of non-definitive doctrine on faith and morals,[62] requires conduct or refraining from conduct on the part of the faithful, it possesses a quasi-legal nature and must, by operation of these canonical duties, be (as the case may be) respected or obeyed.[63]

In the Church of England legal duties of assent to doctrine are less obvious. There is no clear legal duty on individuals to believe Holy Scripture, unless perhaps the statement in the Thirty-Nine Articles that 'whatsoever is not read [in Holy Scripture], nor may be proved thereby, is not to be required of any man, that it should be believed as an article of the Faith' impliedly requires an assent of faith to that which is contained in Holy Scripture.[64] The Thirty-Nine

---

[57] *CIC*, c. 748. This is also expressed as a right.

[58] Ibid., cc. 749, 750; B. C. Butler, 'Infallible; authenticum; assensus; obsequium. Christian teaching authority and the Christian's response', *Doctrine and Life*, 31 (1981), 77.

[59] L. Örsy, *The Church: Learning and Teaching* (Wilmington, Delaware, 1987) 82–90; L. Örsy, *The Profession of Faith and the Oath of Fidelity: A Theological and Canonical Analysis* (Wilmington, Delaware, 1990) App. II, 64–71.

[60] F. A. Sullivan, *Teaching Authority*, 158–66; F. A. Sullivan, 'The response due to the non-definitive exercise of magisterium', *Studia Canonica*, 23 (1989), 267.   [61] *LG*, 25.

[62] F. A. Sullivan, *Teaching Authority*, 155.

[63] Ibid., 162: Sullivan is of the view, however, that (a doctrinal document such as) *Humanae Vitae* (1968) 'is not Church law', because law does not require an intellectual response, an acceptance of its moral worth.

[64] I am grateful to Jeremy Burrows for raising this question; *AR*, Art. 6: 'Holy Scripture containeth all things necessary to salvation: so that whatsoever is not read therein, nor may be proved thereby, is not required of any man, that it should be believed as an article of faith, or be thought requisite or necessary to salvation.'

Articles do, however, more clearly require belief in the Creeds.[65] Nor do legal rules clearly impose a duty on individuals to believe the Thirty-Nine Articles, unless the royal declaration preceding the Articles, enjoining 'all Our loving Subjects to continue in the uniform Profession' of the Articles as containing 'the true Doctrine of the Church of England agreeable to the Word of God' gives rise to a legal duty of assent. Rather, and doubtless this makes sense in terms of enforceability, the law provides only for a right to assent: the Thirty-Nine Articles 'may be assented to with a good conscience by all members of the Church of England' as agreeable to the Word of God.[66] Indeed, according to the Thirty-Nine Articles the church 'ought not to decree any thing against [holy Writ], so besides the same [it] ought not to enforce any thing to be believed for necessity of Salvation'.[67] Nevertheless, with regard to the statement that '[t]he Church of England . . . belongs to the true and apostolic Church of Christ', 'no member thereof shall be at liberty to maintain or hold the contrary'.[68] Moreover, with those seeking the ministrations of the church in baptism, confirmation, and holy communion an assent of faith is required liturgically.[69] The position of office-holders in the Church of England is very different. Soundness of faith is a prerequisite to admission to holy orders and various lay ministries.[70]

General Synod is empowered by measure to make provision by canon with respect to the obligations of the clergy and lay officers of the Church of England to assent or subscribe to the doctrine of that Church.[71] At ordination and on admission to office ordained clergy and lay ministers must make a declaration of assent to the faith and doctrine of the Church of England.[72] Archbishops, diocesan and suffragan bishops, archdeacons, priests, deacons, and readers are obliged to *affirm* 'loyalty to this inheritance of faith as [the candidate's] inspiration and guidance under God in bringing the grace and

---

[65] *AR*, Art. 8: 'The Three Creeds . . . ought thoroughly to be received and believed; for they may be proved by most certain warrants of Holy Scripture.'

[66] Canon A2. It is uncertain whether this canonical right is repugnant to the royal prerogatival declaration preceding the Thirty-Nine Articles and therefore what its effect is in the light of SGM 1969, s. 1(3)(b)); see also Canons A3–5; House of Bishop's *The Nature of Christian Belief*, 6: 'Canon A5 . . . from one point of view, is not worded strongly enough. Commitment to the catholic Creeds implies more than commitment to teachings "agreeable" to Scripture. It means accepting as normative on specific points only that interpretative selection of teachings agreeable to Scripture which the Creeds authorise'.   [67] *AR*, Art 20.

[68] Canon A1. Moreover, concerning schisms, 'it is the duty of clergy and people to do their utmost not only to avoid occasions of strife but also to seek in penitence and brotherly charity to heal such divisions': Canon A8.

[69] Liturgical action may of course require an assent of faith, see e.g. *BCP*, 285: 'Wilt thou be baptized in this faith? *Answer.* That is my desire'). Similarly, under Canon B9 the Creed must be recited.   [70] For the testing of faith see *supra* Chs. 7, 8.

[71] Church of England (Worship and Doctrine) Measure 1974, s. 2.

[72] See generally *Subscription and Assent to the 39 Articles*, A Report of the Archbishops' Commission on Christian Doctrine (London, 1968) 12: 'assent' does not mean 'general assent'; '[i]n law, assent must be taken to mean "complete legal acceptance"'.

truth of Christ to this generation and making Him known to those in [the minister's] care'; and they are obliged to 'declare [their] belief in the faith which is revealed in the Holy Scriptures and set forth in the catholic creeds and to which the historic formularies of the Church of England bear witness'.[73] Though it has been understood that the declaration generates a duty of intellectual assent,[74] it remains unclear whether assent means a complete and *ex animo* adherence to every doctrinal statement, or acceptability of their main tenor, or preference for them as opposed to any other doctrinal statement, or else their acceptance as portraying the identity of the Church of England.[75] These arrangements are similar to those appearing in Roman Catholic canon law.[76] The same declaration must be made by ecclesiastical judges and registrars.[77] Unlike the Roman Catholic Church, the Church of England provides for no intellectual response to persuasive doctrines falling outside the terms of the declaration of assent. Whereas these may sometimes prescribe forms of conduct, *prima facie* any obligation to follow these prescriptions is moral rather than legal in nature.[78]

Enforcing Doctrinal Standards: The Right to Dissent

Dissent may involve a private withholding of assent to or a public attack upon doctrine. Whilst ordinarily regulation of dissent in the Church of England is minimal,[79] in serious cases doctrinal discipline may be effected in the first

[73] Canons C15, E5, E6.

[74] House of Bishop's *The Nature of Christian Belief*, 4: 'It is on the basis of this response, made in good conscience and *without private reservation*, that ministers are ordained, commissioned or appointed to particular work, and given authority to teach as officially approved representatives of the Church of England' (emphasis added).

[75] *Subscription and Assent to the 39 Articles* (1968) 33.

[76] *CIC*, c. 833 imposes a duty to make a profession of faith on all those listed therein. See also c. 1029: sound faith is needed for ordination; c. 378: a bishop must have a strong faith; c. 865: baptism of adults.

[77] EJM 1963, s. 2(5)(a) and Canon G2(3): diocesan chancellors; EJM 1963, s. 3(7)(a) and G3(5): Dean of the Arches and Auditor; Canon G4(3): registrars.

[78] *HLE*, para. 314; *AT: HS*, 1920 Lambeth Conference issued a 'warning about the habit of adopting adversarial attitudes in industrial relations' and pointed out that 'they have no place in Christian fellowship'; *Issues in Human Sexuality*, A Statement by the House of Bishops (London, 1991) 5.12 ff.: for the possibility of disciplinary action against clergy who engage in sexually active homosexual relationships, treated as contrary to the doctrine of the church, see *supra* Ch. 7; see also *Bland v Archdeacon of Cheltenham* [1972] 1 All ER 1012: the Deputy Dean accepted that Bland had been influenced (in refusing baptism) by doctrinal ideas 'generally consistent with those expressed in several official reports and decisions of the Convocations and in the report and resolutions of the Anglican bishops at the 1949 Lambeth Conference'. Though refusal to baptize was not itself a 'doctrinal offence' (ibid. 1017), the assessors at Bland's trial did not know about his 'high ideas' of the importance of baptism as based on these doctrinal documents. 'This', said the Deputy Dean, 'would have been highly relevant on the issue of whether the neglect of duty (if any) was serious.'

[79] *AR*, Art. 10: of free will; see *post* Ch. 10 for the principle that ministerial liturgical variation must not be contrary to the doctrine of the Church of England.

instance by the bishop. Canonically, the bishop has a duty 'to uphold sound and wholesome doctrine, and to banish and drive away all erroneous and strange opinions'; he also has a duty to correct 'all such as be unquiet, disobedient, or criminous, within his diocese'.[80] According to a 1986 statement by the House of Bishops, as part of the episcopal duty to 'guard' the faith, bishops are 'guardians of the process of exploration as well as of received truths' and as such are 'to give courage and support to those who are engaged in "proclaiming afresh"' the faith. Bishops must 'not allow themselves to be trapped in purely negative criticism of older ideas which are still spiritually precious and creative for many'; moreover, 'they have at all times the duty to avoid and to warn against the shallow truth, either traditionalist or innovatory, which fails to connect with and penetrate human life'. Bishops, like others, too 'may properly enter into questionings on matters of belief . . . [b]ut must in all ways . . . take care not to present variant beliefs as if they were the faith of the Church'; 'a bishop is obliged not only to refrain himself from statements contrary to the doctrine of the Church of England but also to use all his efforts against such statements, whether made by those under his authority or by others'. However, to 'attempt to monitor and control every piece of doctrinal or moral instruction given by the ministers under [episcopal] care would be repugnant, disastrous and utterly impracticable. Those entrusted with ministry must be trusted . . . . What the bishop can and should do is to foster a continuing process of theological education for all ministers, clerical and lay, and to share and guide, so far as opportunity allows, their reflection on these matters, including reflection on questionings and speculations'; 'when a bishop has done all he can . . . to promote true understanding and presentation of the faith by those who share his authoritative teaching ministry, he will have fulfilled his obligations under Canon Law for the care of both ordained and lay Christians alike'.[81]

[80] C18(1), (7); The *Gravamen* prepared for presentation to Convocations: Bishop David Jenkins' views on the Virgin Birth and Jesus' 'bodily Resurrection' were 'in contradiction to the teachings of the Church of England as set forth in the Holy Scriptures and affirmed in the Apostles' and Nicene Creeds'; this was especially the case as bishops are required 'to set forward and maintain quietness, love and peace among all men. . .to teach and to uphold sound and wholesome doctrine. . .[and to] drive away erroneous and strange opinions' (Canon C18(1)). The *Reformandum* sought to restore confidence and peace. For the synod debates, sparked off by the Jenkins controversy see the General Synod February Group of Sessions 1985 *Report of Proceedings*, Vol. 16, No. 1 (London, 1985) 128–63,171–82. For the Robinson controversy see K. W. Clements, *Lovers of Discord: Twentieth Century Theological Controversies in England* (London, 1988) 178–217; for the enforcement of doctrinal standards and the faculty jurisdiction see Ch. 16.

[81] *The Nature of Christian Belief* (1986) paras. 64–73 (34–7); *WAOB* recommends that the House of Bishops continue the practice of issuing statements on doctrine and, indeed '[a] more clearly focused and regular collective approach by the House of Bishops would not suppress openness of debate or differences of view within the Church' (7.5). For heresy proceedings against a bishop see *In re Lord Bishop of Natal* [1864–5] III Moore NS 114; *Capetown (Bishop of) v Natal (Bishop of)* [1869] VI Moore NS 202; A. Ive, *The Church of England in South Africa: A Study of its History, Principles and Status* (Capetown, 1966) 18 ff.

Given the absence in the Church of England of a general legal duty of assent, the laity enjoy a legal right to private rejection of the church's doctrines.[82] However, according to a statement by the House of Bishops a serious (and presumably public) denial by an ordained person of the church's doctrine may in appropriate cases result in episcopal executive correction, but it is unlikely that disciplinary proceedings would be taken in the church courts.[83] A public sermon, being a matter of public interest, is open to fair public criticism under the civil law of libel.[84] With regard to those who have made a declaration of assent the position is very different. Though the law contains no specific provision, lay-office holders may be disciplined executively but not judicially.[85] As well as executive episcopal correction, judicial proceedings may be instituted against archbishops, bishops, priests, or deacons in pursuance of a complaint under the Ecclesiastical Jurisdiction Measure 1963 for an offence against the laws ecclesiastical involving a matter of doctrine.[86] Proceedings for a doctrinal offence must be brought in the Court of Ecclesiastical Causes Reserved.[87]

Though generalisations may be made as to what constitutes a doctrinal offence, it is difficult to ascertain its precise elements. Maintaining opinions contrary to the Christian religion, depraving the Book of Common Prayer, maintaining doctrines repugnant to the Thirty-Nine Articles, and heresy have all been treated as doctrinal offences.[88] In *Bland v Archdeacon of Cheltenham* the Deputy Dean of the Arches explained that '[c]ertain offences clearly involve a matter of doctrine', including 'a public statement (as in a sermon or a book) denying the doctrine of the Trinity or of the deity of Christ', which 'would be charged as such and would be referred without hesitation to the Court of Ecclesiastical Causes Reserved'. In this case it was decided that refusal to baptize was not a doctrinal offence.[89] In the celebrated case of *Gorham v Bishop of Exeter* the defendant maintained *inter alia* that infants were not incorporated into the Body of Christ at baptism. His presentation and induction were refused by the bishop on the basis that he held 'unsound doctrines, contrary to the true Christian faith, contrary to and inconsistent with the doctrine of the Church of England', and against the Thirty-Nine

---

[82] Canon A2; e.g. if a 'member' publicly maintained or held a view contrary to the statement that the Church of England belongs to the true and apostolic church of Christ: Canon A1; for judicial proceedings see *supra* Ch. 7; see below for blasphemy under secular law.

[83] See *supra* Ch. 8 (for homophile relations).

[84] *Gathercole v Miall* (1846) 15 M & W 319; *Kelly v Sherlock* (1866) LR I QB 686; *Botterill v Whytehead* (1874) 41 LT 588; *Magrath v Finn* (1877) IR II CL 152.

[85] *Reformandum* (1984): 'the doctrine of the Church of England is and remains as defined by Canon A5 . . . and [is] required to be assented to in accordance with canon C15.'

[86] EJM 1963, s. 38.

[87] S. 10(1); for lack of jurisdiction over readers, judges, and registrars see *supra* Ch. 8; for the basic procedure see *supra* Ch. 5.   [88] *HLE*, para. 1354.

[89] [1972] 1 All ER 1012 at 1017.

Articles and the Prayer Book. The decision of the Court of the Arches to uphold the bishop's refusal to induct[90] was reversed by the Privy Council.[91]

It has been understood that proceedings may be brought for heresy if a cleric advances publicly 'a false opinion repugnant to some point of doctrine clearly revealed in scripture and either absolutely essential to the Christian faith or at least of most high importance'.[92] In *Williams v Bishop of Salisbury*[93] the defendant was prosecuted under the (now repealed) Church Discipline Act 1840 for publishing heretical doctrines in contravention of the Thirty-Nine Articles, for *inter alia* describing the Bible as 'an expression of devout reason', 'the written voice of the congregation' and not 'the Word of God', and for his assertion that the offering of Christ was not for the propitiation for the sins of the whole world. Williams was found guilty by the Arches Court. On appeal the Privy Council formulated two basic principles. First, if a standard of faith is not 'expressly and distinctly stated, or which is not plainly involved in or to be collected from that which is written', then 'there is so far freedom of opinion that they may be discussed without penal consequences'.[94] Secondly, in proceedings the articles must distinctly state the opinions which the cleric maintains, the relevant passages of the work in which the heretical statements appear, and the doctrines of the church which the individual's statements are alleged to contravene.[95] Issuing from the Privy Council, the decisions in *Gorham* and *Williams* are not strictly binding on the Court of Ecclesiastical Causes Reserved,[96] and today the use of legal powers to prosecute for doctrinal offences may be fettered by an ecclesiastical convention recognizing doctrinal freedom.[97]

Roman Catholic canon law contains more detailed provision than the Church of England concerning both the right to dissent and the elements of

---

[90] (1849) ER 1221 at 1253.

[91] (1850) Moore's Special Report, 462; (1850) ER 177. The question for the Privy Council was jurisdictional: whether an appeal would lie to it or to the Upper House of Convocation; it held that appeal lay to the Privy Council. For the history of the declaration of assent see *Believing in the Church*, 129; *Subscription and Assent to the 39 Articles* (1968).

[92] Burn, *Ecclesiastical Law*, 304, 305; see T. H. Jones, 'Law and the suppression of heresy in the English Church: an historical survey', University of Wales LL.M. dissertation (Cardiff, 1994).

[93] (1864) 2 Moore PCCNS 375.

[94] The court relied on *dicta* from *Gorham v Bishop of Exeter*.

[95] *HLE*, para. 1354: 'There are . . . many points of doctrine which the church has not decided and which are open to every member of the church to decide for himself according to his own conscientious opinion.' [96] EJM 1963, s. 45(3).

[97] House of Bishops', *The Nature of Christian Belief*, 10: '[t]he questioning and creative process is a necessary part of Christian discipleship'; 37–8: 'if the Church of England does not proceed against its ministers for heresy this comes not from indifference but from a conviction born of experience that such proceedings do more harm than good. It would be foolish to say that there can never be a situation in which it would be right (or, more likely, unavoidable as a last resort) to take such a step. But such cases as there have been in modern times are not encouraging'; N. Doe, 'Obedience to doctrine in canon law: the legal duty of intellectual assent', *Denning Law Journal* (1992) 23.

offences concerning doctrine.[98] Although dissent to infallible doctrine is not permissible (once a doctrine is declared infallibly this 'puts an end to freedom of opinion of the matter'),[99] for non-definitive doctrines the position may be more liberal depending on the meaning (discussed above) of *obsequium*: generally, '[a]ll the Christian faithful are obliged to observe the constitutions and decrees which the legitimate authority of the Church issues in order to propose doctrine and proscribe erroneous opinions'.[100] The Sacred Congregation for the Doctrine of the Faith concluded in 1988 that a right to private dissent from such doctrines exists if there is a 'personal certitude that the teaching of the Church is incorrect':[101] dissent is permissible if the individual has 'reasons that are persuasive (even if inculpably erroneous)' or a 'grave suspicion that the presumption of truth which official teaching enjoys is not verified in this case'.[102] The right is presented explicitly in a variety of forms. According to Canon 748: '[p]ersons cannot ever be forced by anyone to embrace the Catholic faith against their conscience.'[103] The faithful have 'the right and even at times the duty to manifest to the sacred pastors their opinion on matters which pertain to the good of the Church' as well as to the other Christian faithful; in so doing the faithful must have 'due regard for the integrity of faith and morals and reverence towards their pastors, and consideration for the common good and the dignity of persons'.[104] Those engaged

---

[98] The issue of dissent has become important is recent years: the Belgian Edward Schillebeeckx, Professor of Theology at the Catholic University of Nijmegen in Holland, was after publishing *Jesus: An Experiment in Christology* (1974), subjected to a five-year investigation; he was summoned to and exonerated by a 'colloquium' of the Vatican's Congregation for the Doctrine of the Faith in 1979. The Swiss-born Hans Kung's *Infallible? An Inquiry* (1970) resulted in a judgment of the Vatican that he was no longer to be approved as a theologian allowed to teach at the Catholic Theology Faculty at the University of Tubingen. In 1979 Father Johannes Baptist Metz, the liberation theologian, was offered a chair at Munich but the Archbishop of Munich, Cardinal Ratzinger, exercised his power of veto under a 1924 church–state concordat to block the appointment. For censorship in the church see also Canon Law Society *Newsletter*, No. 92 (1992) 58.   [99] Sullivan, *Teaching Authority*, 79–118.

[100] *CIC*, c. 754.   [101] C. E. Curran, *Faithful Dissent* (Kansas City, 1986) 201–2.

[102] The opinion of learned writers has authority under c. 19; for a discussion of D. Palmieri's *Tractatus de Romano Pontifice cum prolegomeno de Ecclesia* (1891), C. Pesch's *Praelectiones dogmaticae* (1924), and L. Lercher's *Institutiones theologicae dogmaticae in usum scholarum* (1951) see Sullivan's article in *Studia Canonica*, 23 (1989), 267 at 276–8.

[103] *CIC*, c. 748; *DH*, Iff.: the right to religious freedom is based on the 'very dignity of the human person'. Though 'endowed with reason and free will', individuals are bound by a 'moral obligation' to seek the truth and 'to adhere to the truth once they come to know it and direct their lives in accordance with the demands of truth'. But individuals cannot be forced to this. 'For this reason the right to this immunity continues to exist even in those who do not live up to their obligation of seeking the truth and adhering to it'; 'It is through his conscience that man sees and recognises the demands of the divine law. He is bound to follow his conscience faithfully in all his activity so that he may come to God . . . Therefore he must not be forced to act contrary to his conscience . . . especially in religious matters. The reason is because the practice of religion of its very nature consists primarily of those voluntary and free internal acts by which a man directs himself to God.'   [104] *CIC*, c. 212(3).

in theological study enjoy the right of free inquiry and expression.[105] According to the International Theological Commission, public dissent is permissible if grounded in a 'true respect for the *magisterium* even while disagreeing with it on a particular point'.[106]

By contrast with the Church of England, the elements of doctrinal offences are more clearly defined in Roman Catholic canon law. The Code creates two categories of doctrinal offence. There are four basic offences against religion and the unity of the Church. *Heresy* is 'the obstinate post-baptismal denial of some truth which must be believed with divine and catholic faith, or it is likewise an obstinate doubt concerning the same'; it may be committed only in relation to those doctrines presented as part of the revealed deposit of faith: it does not apply to a rejection or denial of non-definitive doctrine. *Apostasy* is 'the total repudiation of the Christian faith' and *schism* 'the refusal of submission to the Roman Pontiff or of communion with the members of the Church subject to him'.[107] The penalties for heresy, apostasy, or schism are automatic excommunication for lay people, and for clerics excommunication or suspension, deprivation, or penal transfer.[108] *Blasphemy* is committed by a 'person who uses a public show or speech, published writings, or other media of social communication to blaspheme, seriously damage good morals, express wrongs against religion or against the Church or stir up hatred or contempt against religion or the church [and] is to be punished with a just penalty'.[109] With regard to offences against church authorities, a person who teaches a doctrine condemned by the pontiff or by an ecumenical council and a person who pertinaciously rejects non-definitive doctrine is to be punished with just penalties: however, these cannot be imposed if after warning by the Apostolic See or by the ordinary the person retracts.[110]

---

[105] C. 218: 'Those who are engaged in the sacred disciplines enjoy a lawful freedom of inquiry and of prudently expressing their opinions on matters in which they have expertise, while observing a due respect for the *magisterium* of the Church'. Unlike the other rights, this is not described or treated as a 'human right': it is merely treated as a kind of concession, a 'lawful freedom'. *CCL: TC*, 152, J. Provost's view of the canon is that 'At the very least, the ecclesiastical *magisterium* must be acknowledged and taken into serious consideration in expressing theological opinions'. But, he says, 'This does not rule out dissent', when this is based on respect: 151–2. See also P. Huizing and K. Walf, 'What does the "right to dissent" mean in the Church?', *Concilium*, 158 (1982), 3; H. Haring, 'The rights and limits of dissent', ibid., 95; J. Provost, 'The Catholic Church and dissent', ibid., 13.

[106] *Theses on the relationship between the ecclesastical magisterium and theology* (1975). The official Latin text of the *Theses*, with a commentary by O. Semmelroth and K. Lehmann, is published in *Gregorianum*, 57 (1976), 549–63. An English translation is found in C. E. Curran and R. A. McCormick (eds.), *Readings in Moral Theology No. 3: The Magisterium and Morality* (New York, 1982) 151–70. See also R. M. Gula, 'The right to private and public dissent from specific pronouncements of the ordinary magisterium', *Église et Théologie*, 9 (1978), 319.

[107] *CIC*, c. 751.

[108] C. 1364; for general defences see cc. 1323–4; baptized persons who have fallen into heresy, apostasy, or schism as a matter of conscience do not incur these censures: *COCLA*, 497.

[109] *CIC*, c. 1369.   [110] C. 1371.

THE PRACTICE OF FAITH: RELIGIOUS LIBERTY IN SECULAR SOCIETY

Rights which Roman Catholic canon law recognizes as deriving from the inherent dignity and equality of the human person are fundamental not only to life within the church but also to life in civil society.[111] The law of the Church of England neither claims nor presents a compendium of fundamental human rights to practise the faith in secular society, although rights deriving from the canons, as rights under the law of the land, may be operative in the civil context as well as the ecclesiastical.[112] Broadly, for both churches the extent to which rights protecting the faith are enforceable in civil law depends on their recognition by and incorporation in that law.

Religious freedom is protected by both domestic and European law. In the absence of a separate body of secular law dealing with this subject, religious liberty exists in domestic civil law either by virtue of the silence of the law (when the law does not prohibit religious conduct) or by virtue of a right expressly or implicitly conferred by law.[113] In this context, the faithful of both the Church of England and the Roman Catholic Church share and enjoy a freedom to practise their faith within secular society, based on a principle of neutrality, equal to that of members of any other religious community.[114] These include the right to settle property for the advancement of religion, the right to enjoy church services free from disturbance, rights of access to computerized personal information containing material about religious belief, and rights of those in prison to the ministrations of a chaplain.[115] The practice of faith cannot, however, excuse or justify violations of the state's criminal law.[116]

The United Kingdom is a signatory to the European Convention of Human Rights (1950) which prescribes that '[e]veryone has the right to freedom of . . . religion [which] ... includes freedom . . . either alone or in community with others and in public or private, to manifest his religion or belief, in worship,

[111] For the relationship between civil law, canon law, and civil liberties, see *supra* Ch. 1; for Roman Catholic teaching concerning religious liberty and for Pope John XXIII's approval of the ECHR see *Pacem in Terris* (1963) and *DH* (1965) I: 'This right of the human person to religious freedom must be given such recognition in the constitutional order of society as will make it a civil right'; see also J. Langan, 'Human rights in Catholicism', *Journal of Ecumenical Studies*, 19 (1982), 25; K. Walf, 'Gospel, church law and human rights: foundations and deficiencies', *Concilium* (1990) 32; D. Hollenbach, *Claims in Conflict: Retrieving and renewing the Catholic Human Rights Tradition* (New York, 1979) Ch. 1.   [112] See *supra* Chs. 1 and 8.

[113] See *supra* Ch. 1.

[114] *Re Carroll* [1931] 1 KB 317 (CA) at 336 *per* Scrutton LJ: '[i]is, I hope, unnecessary to say that the Court is perfectly impartial in matters of religion'; *Neville Estates v Madden* [1961] 3 All ER 769 at 781 *per* Cross J: '[a]s between different religions the law stands neutral'.

[115] See Chs. 4,8,16; St J. A. Robilliard, 'Should parliament enact a religious dscrimination act?', *PL* (1978), 379; T. Lorenzen, 'The theological basis for religious liberty: a Christian perspective', *Journal of Church and State*, 20 (1979), 425.

[116] *Blake v DPP* (1993), Hill, *EL*, 13; *R v Senior* [1899] 1 QB 283; see St J. A. Robilliard, *Religion and the Law* (Manchester, 1984), Ch. 7.

teaching, practice and observance'. Freedom 'to manifest one's religion or beliefs shall be subject only to such limitations as are prescribed by law'. These limitations must be 'necessary in a democratic society in the interests of public safety, for the promotion of public order, health or morals, or for the protection of the rights and freedoms of others'.[117] Whilst it has not been incorporated into domestic law (rights enunciated in the Convention are not directly enforceable in municipal courts) the Convention is of strong persuasive authority and is often appealed to in the resolution of disputes by the civil courts.[118] Violations of the Convention may result in a petition to and enquiry by the European Commission of Human Rights and in proceedings in the European Court of Human Rights which, as we shall see in the following sections, have dealt in recent years with a small number of cases concerning religious liberty in the United Kingdom.[119] Generally, the domestic and European rules discussed in the following sections are applicable to the practice of faith by Christians belonging either to the Church of England or to the Roman Catholic Church.

The Offence of Blasphemy

Public statements offensive to the Christian faith are regulated by the two common law offences of blasphemy.[120] The offence of *blasphemous libel* is committed if a person publishes in a permanent form any matter attacking the

[117] Art. 9; Art. 14 (the enjoyment of the rights and freedoms set forth in this Convention shall be secured without discrimination on any ground such as . . . religion'; see also the United Nations' Universal Declaration of Human Rights (1948) Art. 18; see J. E. S. Fawcett, *The Application of the European Convention on Human Rights* (Oxford, 1987) 235–250 and M. G. Belgiorno de Stefano, 'Religious freedom in the decisions of the European Court of Human Rights', University of Rome Department of Public Law *Yearbook* (Rome, 1989) 239–243.

[118] Usually as an aid to the interpretation of legislation, the courts will presume that e.g. parliament would not intend to legislate contrary to it; accordingly the courts will favour an interpretation of domestic law which is consistent with the convention: *R v Chief Immigration Officer, ex p Salamat Bibi* [1976] 1 WLR 979; *AG v Guardian Newspapers* [1987] 3 All ER 316, [1988] 3 All ER 545 (HL); more boldly, Lord Denning had stated in *Birdi v Secretary of State for Home Affairs* (unreported but referred to in *R v Secretary of State for Home Affairs, ex p Bhajan Singh* [1979] QB 198) that if a parliamentary statute conflicted with the convention, 'I might be inclined to hold it invalid'—in the *Bhajan Singh* case, however, he explained: '[i]if an Act of Parliament contained any provision contrary to the Convention, the Act of Parliament must prevail'.

[119] In 1966 the UK made (and has since renewed periodically) the necessary declaration under ECHR, Arts. 25 and 46, accepting the compulsory jurisdiction of both the Commission and Court; Art. 50: the court 'shall, if necessary, afford just satisfaction to the injured party.' Decisions of the European Court of Justice are binding: European Communities Act 1972, s. 3; *Re Thomas Tyler*, European Commission of Human Rights, April 1994, 3 *ELJ* (1995) 348: the Commission accepted jurisdiction but declined to impugn the Church of England's Con. Ct. decision; the Commission seems to have suggested that clear evidence of actual bias may be redressed.

[120] C. Kenny, 'The evolution of the law of blasphemy', *CLJ*, 1 (1922), 127; N. Walter, *Blasphemy: Ancient and Modern* (London, 1990); R. Webster, *A Brief History of Blasphemy* (Southwold, 1990); A. Bradney, *Religions, Rights and Laws* (Leicester, 1993), ch. 5.

Christian religion, God, Christ or other sacred persons, the Bible, or the doctrine of the Church of England. Liability arises if the matter is calculated to outrage and insult a Christian's religious feelings.[121] The attack must be such as to give rise to a tendency to cause a breach of the peace.[122] The crime of blasphemous libel is an offence of strict liability. Whilst publication must be intentional, liability arises regardless of whether the defendant intended to blaspheme. In *Lemon* the House of Lords held, by a majority, that intention to outrage and insult Christian believers is not required: the minority held that intent to blaspheme was required.[123] It may be that the offence of *blasphemy*, which is committed by speaking matter offensive to the Christian religion, is also one of strict liability.[124] Judicial statements expressing justifications for the offences, based on the protection of Christianity as fundamental to society and the safeguarding of public morals and public order, and its confinement to statements offensive only to the Christian religion,[125] have been criticized in recent years and there have been calls for abolition of its present form.[126]

Employment

The law of the Church of England contains no equivalent to the fundamental rights of employment contained in Roman Catholic canon law: these include freedom to promote the ministry of the church, immunity from coercion in choosing a state in life,[127] the right to give witness to Christ in conducting secular business and functions, and the right to 'freedom in secular affairs which is common to all citizens'.[128] Indeed, Vatican II considered the secular realm as the ordinary focus of lay apostolic activity.[129] Yet under secular law

---

[121] *Bowman v Secular Society Ltd* [1917] AC 406 (HL).

[122] *R v Gott* (1922) 16 Cr App R 87; *R v Wicks* (1936) 25 Cr App R 168; see also *R v Ramsay and Foote* (1883) 15 Cox CC 231.

[123] *Whitehouse v Lemon and Gay News Ltd* [1979] AC 617, [1979] 1 All ER 898 (HL); J. R. Spencer, 'Blasphemy: the Law Commission's Working Paper', *Criminal Law Review* (1981) 810.

[124] Stephen's *Digest of the Criminal Law* (9th edn., 1950), Art. 214.

[125] Its confinement to Christianity was upheld as not offensive to the ECHR by the European Court of Human Rights in *Gay News Ltd and Lemon v United Kingdom* (Application 8710/79) (1982) 5 EHRR 123; in *Lemon* [1979] AC 517 at 658, Lord Scarman considered that it ought to be extended to insults to other religions, but that the judges could not affect this); in *R v Chief Metropolitan Stipendiary Magistrate, ex p Choudhury* [1991] 1 QB 429 at 452 (concerning Salman Rushdie's *Satanic Verses*) the Divisional Court agreed but stated that an extension would 'encourage intolerance, divisiveness and unreasonable interference with freedom of expression'.

[126] Law Commission Working Paper No. 79. 'Offences against religion and public worship' (1981); Law Commission Report No. 145 (18 June 1985); for discussion of these and other reports see K. G. Routledge, 'Blasphemy: the report of the Archbishop of Canterbury's Working Party on offences against religion and public worship: a personal view', *ELJ*, 1(4) (1989), 27; D. W. Elliott, 'Blasphemy and other expressions of offensive opinion', *ELJ*, 3 (1993), 70; see also M. Grieve, 'Blasphemy laws: first rights or last rites?', *Counsel* (Jan/Feb 1995) 10.

[127] *CIC*, cc. 209–23.

[128] Cc. 224–31. For the right to join trades unions see J. Jukes, 'Regolamento for employment by Roman Curia', Canon Law Society *Newsletter*, No. 91 (1992) 30.

[129] S. E. Euart, 'Council, code and laity: implications for lay ministry', *The Jurist*, 47 (1987) 492.

there is no specific protection against discrimination on grounds of religion concerning admission to and dismissal from employment.[130] The Race Relations Act 1976 covers only discrimination on grounds of colour, race, nationality, or ethnicity: the omission of religion was deliberate.[131] However, the Employment Protection (Consolidation) Act 1978 gives to every employee a right not to be unfairly dismissed. Dismissal because of an employee's religious convictions is *prima facie* unlawful unless the employer has made reasonable efforts to accommodate these.[132] Similarly, refusal to employ and dismissal from employment of a person who does not wish to join or remain in any trade union are unlawful if the employee 'genuinely objects on grounds of conscience or other deeply held personal conviction'.[133] There is no specific provision for involvement in industrial action although religious conscientious objection enables an employee to avoid dismissal in a closed shop workplace.[134] More detailed rules apply to the employment of teachers. Under the Education Act 1944 no person shall be disqualified from being a teacher (in a county school or in any voluntary school) by virtue of religious opinions or by reason of attending or failing to attend religious worship; similar protection is given to teachers employed in state-maintained special agreement schools.[135] Religion may, however, be a criterion of employment in voluntary-aided schools.[136] It has been decided judicially that if a person fails to take advantage of reasonable accommodation provided by the school authorities this will bar a complaint.[137]

[130] Cf. Fair Employment (Northern Ireland) Act 1989 which seeks to promote equality of opportunity between persons of different religious belief: s. 20: the principle of equality, ss. 7–9: code of practice, and ss. 1–6: the Fair Employment Commission, the tribunal and complaints system.

[131] S. 3(1); see A. Bradney, *Religions, Rights and Laws* (1993) 109; J. Bowers, *Employment Law* (London, 1990) 106–7; only when 'race' is coincident with 'religion' does the statute apply; for Sikhs see *Mandla v Dowell Lee* [1983] 2 AC 548 (HL), for Jews, *Seide v Gillette Industries Ltd* [1980] IRLR 427.

[132] S. 54(1)-(3); see *George v Plant Breeding International, Times*, 7 Oct. 1991: dismissal of an employee required during harvest to work 12 hours a day for 7 days a week who wished to attend church was held unfair; but no mention was made of the desire to attend church; *Lindhorst-Jones v Aber Building Suppliers, Times*, 19 Nov. 1986: dismissal for refusal to work on Sundays due to bell-ringing commitments was unfair; as to whether the employer has acted reasonably in accommodating religious convictions see *Ahmad v ILEA* [1975] 1 All ER 574 (CA).

[133] Employment Protection (Consolidation) Act 1978, s. 58(1), (4)-(8), as amended 1980; Employment Act 1990, s. 1(1).

[134] *Young, James and Webster v UK* [1981] IRLR 408; *Goodbody v British Railways Board* [1977] IRLR 84; *Saggers v British Railways Board* [1978] IRLR 435.

[135] Education Act 1944, s. 30; for state-maintained special agreement schools see Education (Approval of Special Schools) Regs. 1983, Sched. 2, para. 14; see also Education Reform Act 1988, s. 84(13).

[136] Teachers in voluntary-aided schools and reserved teachers in voluntary-controlled schools have protection only against being paid less or being deprived of promotion or other advantage due to religious opinion or because they give religious education or attend religious worship: Education Act 1944, s. 30.

[137] *Ahmad v ILEA* [1975] 1 All ER 574 (CA); *Lal v Board of Governors, Sacred Heart Comprehensive School, Dagenham* (unreported, 7 Nov. 1990).

Special provisions exist in relation to employment and abortions. Whereas according to Roman Catholic teaching and canon law there is a general prohibition against abortion,[138] Church of England statements oppose 'any form of victimisation or discrimination against surgeons, doctors, nurses and medical, health or social workers who cannot, in conscience, assist in or recommend abortion'.[139] Under the Abortion Act 1967 'no person shall be under any duty, whether by contract or by statutory or other legal requirement, to participate in any treatment authorized by this Act to which he has a conscientious objection'; in any legal proceedings the burden of proof of conscientious objection rests on the person claiming to rely on it.[140] The rule applies only to those participating in an abortion and does not apply to those communicating in a clerical capacity details about abortions.[141] Similarly, under the Human Fertilisation and Embryology Act 1990, no person who has a conscientious objection to participating in any activity governed by the statute (including scientific experiments on human feotal tissue) shall be under a duty to do so; the burden of proof of conscientious objection rests on the person relying on it.[142]

As in the Roman Catholic Church, the canon law of the Church of England requires observance of Sunday ('particularly by attendance at divine service'), of the principal feasts, and of other days.[143] Undertaking work on a Sunday is governed principally by a person's contract of employment. If this does not require work on a Sunday the person is protected; however, the employee may give written notice to the employer 'opting-in' to do Sunday work by express agreement. If a contract of employment requires Sunday work, a shop worker may at any time give the employer written notice that he objects to Sunday working: 'opting-out' notice may be revoked by 'opting-in' notice and by express agreement to work on Sundays generally or on a particular Sunday. The employer must provide a written statement explaining the employee's statutory opting-out right. Both dismissal and selection for redundancy of a protected or opted-out shop worker are unfair if the reason for this was a

---

[138] *Quaestio de abortu* (1974); *CIC*, c. 220: the right to privacy; c. 1397: homicide; c. 1398: a person who actually procures an abortion incurs a *latae sententiae* excommunication; c. 1331: excommunication; c. 1328: attempted abortion; c. 1329: complicity; for specific sanctions see cc. 695, 1041; J. McAreavey, 'Abortion and the sacrament of penance', *The Furrow* (1993), 230.

[139] General Synod Resolution, July 1975: for this and other statements see *Abortion and the Church*, A Report by the Board for Social Responsibility (London, 1993) 23 f.; encyclical *Veritatis Splendor* (1993).   [140] S. 4.

[141] *Janaway v Salford Health Authority* [1989] 1 AC 537, concerning a medical secretary who refused to type letters of referral to the hospital; D. Poole, 'Janaway: a comment', *Law and Justice* (1988), 82; for nurses see *Royal College of Nurses v DHSS* [1981] AC 800; a father has no general right to be consulted: *Paton v British Pregnancy Advisory Service* [1979] QB 276; *C v S* [1987] All ER 1230.   [142] S. 38.

[143] Canon B6: Sundays and other days of special observance; see also *Acts of Convocation*, 99–102 for resolutions concerning the obligations of Sunday observance: 'the Church of England adheres to the ancient rule that members should fulfil this obligation of worship at least by attendance at the Lord's Service'; *CIC*, c.1244–53.

refusal (or proposed refusal) to do shop work on Sundays (or on a particular Sunday) or because the employee gave or proposed to give opting-out notice. Dismissal is also unfair if the reason for it was that the employee brought proceedings against the employer to enforce these statutory rights. A protected or opted-out shop worker may not be subjected to any detriment, through any act or any deliberate failure to act, by his employer on the ground that the shop worker refused or proposed to refuse to work on Sunday, or that he gave or proposed to give an opting-out notice. Remedies may be sought by way of a complaint to an industrial tribunal.[144]

Education

The European Convention on Human Rights requires member states, in the exercise of any functions which they assume in relation to education, to respect the right of parents to ensure for their children education conforming with their own religious convictions.[145] There is no equivalent law in the Church of England to the fundamental right to a Christian education of the faithful under Roman Catholic canon law.[146] However, the Education Reform Act 1988 requires religious education (though not denominational) to be part of the basic curriculum in all maintained schools; syllabuses must reflect the 'fact' that religious traditions of Britain are in the main Christian, though syllabuses must also take into account the other principal religions.[147] A central role is played by the local Standing Advisory Council on Religious Education (SACRE), which must be constituted by the local education authority. It must be comprised of a collection of representative groups: one must represent the Church of England and the others must represent 'such Christian and other religious denominations as, in the opinion of the authority, will appropriately reflect the principal religious traditions in the area'.[148] The provision of religious education is dependent, broadly, on the status of the school in question. Religious education in a county school must be in accordance with an agreed syllabus drawn up by a local 'conference'[149] convened by the local

---

[144] Sunday Trading Act 1994, s. 4, Sched. 4.   [145] Art. 2, First Protocol.

[146] *CIC*, cc. 217, 229, 793; unlike the Church of England, the Roman Catholic Church has a body of canon law dealing specifically with schools: cc. 796–806.

[147] Education Reform Act 1988, ss. 2(1), 8(3); see J. M. Hull, 'Religious education and Christian values in the 1988 Education Reform Act', *ELJ*, 2 (1990–92), 69.

[148] Education Reform Act 1988, s. 11. SACRE must also have a representative of the governing bodies of grant-maintained schools which were formerly county or voluntary controlled schools, and each representative group has one vote for the purposes of decision-making: s.11(6); for a critical study see S. Poulter, 'The religious education provisions of the Education Act 1988', *Education and the Law*, 2 (1990) 1; the number of members appointed to represent a group must broadly reflect 'the proportionate strength of that denomination or religion in the area': Education Act 1993, s. 255.

[149] Education Act 1944, s. 26(1) and Sched. 5. The conference consists of the same representative groups as the SACRE; if no agreement is reached the Secretary of State appoints a body to prepare a syllabus: see N. Harris, *Law and Education: Regulation, Consumerism and the Education System* (London, 1993) 207.

education authority. Parents have a right of free access to information pertaining to the teaching of religion (including the agreed syllabus and schemes followed by teachers) as well as a right to complain about religious education.[150] Parents of children in maintained schools have the right to withdraw their children from such classes and the right to send them elsewhere if the type of religious education which they desire is not available and if the child cannot reasonably be sent to a maintained school providing the religious education sought.[151] Parents of boarding pupils in maintained schools have a right to seek a particular religious education in the school itself provided this does not involve any additional expense to the local education authority.[152]

Provisions for worship also vary between different types of school. In county schools the act of worship must be 'wholly or mainly of a broadly Christian character'.[153] In all maintained schools, whilst no condition of entry may be imposed requiring a child to attend, or refrain from attending, any Sunday school or place of worship,[154] pupils must take part in a collective act of worship, but parents have the right to withdraw a child.[155] Parents of boarding pupils in maintained schools have a right to withdraw their children to attend worship on religious days set aside by their religious body.[156] The right has also been recognized at common law: a member of the Church of England has a religious liberty to observe days of obligation by attendance at church.[157] Responsibility for arranging collective worship lies with the head teacher in a county school (in consultation with the school's governing body) and with the governing body (after consultation with the head teacher) in a grant-maintained or voluntary school; it must normally be conducted on school premises and may take place in age or class groups.[158]

Although parliamentary statute lays down general rules about choice of and admission to church schools, these have a right to select children on the basis

[150] For the right to information see Education Act 1988, s. 22; SI 1989/954, ss. 5(5), 6; DES Circular, 14/89, para. 24; for complaints concerning, *inter alia*, timetabling, content of religious education, and LEA policy see s. 23; see also the *Bell Case* (1990) *Times*, 7 Dec. 1990. SACRE may advise on the agreed syllabus for the area, including advice on teaching methods, choice of materials, and provision of teachers: s. 11(1), (2).

[151] Education Reform Act 1988, s. 9(3), (4)(b); maintained schools are county or voluntary schools and any grant-maintained school: ss. 6(7), 25(1).

[152] Education Reform Act 1988, s. 9(7); see also DES Circular, 3/89, para. 42: Secretary of State's suggestion that religious leaders be allowed to lead religious education.

[153] Education Reform Act 1988, s. 7(1). This will be the case if 'it reflects the broad traditions of Christian belief without being distinctive of any particular Christian denomination' (s. 7(2); SACRE may direct whether it is appropriate for the requirement of collective worship to apply to a school: ss. 7(6), 12(1). For SACRE determinations see DES Circular 3/89, s. 6(3)(a).

[154] Education Reform Act 1988, s. 9(1).

[155] Education Reform Act 1988, ss. 6(1), 9(2); s. 10(1)(a): it is for the head teacher to secure attendance. [156] Education Reform Act 1988, s. 9(7).

[157] *Marshall v Graham* [1907] 2 KB 112, concerning non-attendance at school under the Elementary Education Act 1870 to observe Ascension Day.

[158] Education Reform Act 1988, s. 6(2)-(6).

of religious affiliation in order to preserve the school's character.[159] Religious education in voluntary church schools (aided or controlled) must be in accordance with either the agreed syllabus or the practice which applied before the school acquired its voluntary status or with the trust deeds establishing the school.[160] Grant-maintained church schools have special representation on the local Standing Advisory Council for Religious Education and must be consulted when changes to agreed syllabuses are proposed. The governing body of such a school has those powers enjoyed by schools of the same description immediately before it became grant-maintained. The Secretary of State's approval must be obtained before a governing body can change the character of the school.[161] Whereas ordinarily school inspections are carried out by the state,[162] special provision exists in connection with inspections of voluntary schools: the governing body selects the inspector and inspections must be conducted at prescribed intervals; the inspection report must be made available to the public and a summary must be supplied to the parents of each registered pupil.[163]

The Diocesan Boards of Education Measure 1991 makes provision for the involvement of the Church of England in religious education in secular society.[164] For every diocese there must be established a Diocesan Board of

[159] Education Act 1944, ss. 27(1),(6), 28(1); if a school acquires grant-maintained status, arrangements for religious education are the same as those operating before acquisition of this status: Education Act 1993, ss. 139–41. See also Education Reform Act 1980, s. 6, enabling the LEA to make admission arrangements; s. 102; such schools also have a right to establish religious criteria to avoid overcrowding: *Choudhury v Governors of Bishop Challenor Roman Catholic Comprehensive School* [1992] 3 All ER 227 (HL); see generally R. Green, *Church of England Church Schools: A Matter of Opinion* (London and Southwark Diocesan Board of Education, Schools Division, 1982). For funding see J. M. Hull, 'Church-related schools and religious education in the publicly-funded education system of England', in *Church and State in Europe: State Financial Support, Religion and the School*, Proceedings of the European Consortium for Church-State Research (Milan, 1992) 181.

[160] *R v Trustees of the Roman Catholic Diocese of Westminster, ex p Andrews* (1990) 2 Admin LR 142,151 (CA): the trust deed provided that the religious doctrines and practices of the school 'shall in all respects be according to the principles and subject to the regulations and discipline of the Roman Catholic Church'; see also M. Cruickshank, *Church and State in English Education* (London, 1963); J. Murphy, *Church, State and Schools in Britain* (London, 1971); Church Schools (Assistance by Church Commissioners) Measure 1958.

[161] Education Act 1944, ss. 28(1), 104; Education Reform Act 1988, ss. 11(3), 57, 79, 84(8) (which provides that '[t]hat syllabus shall not provide for religious education to be given to pupils at such a school by means of any catechism or formulary which is distinctive of any particular religious denomination, but this provision is not to be taken as prohibiting provision in the syllabus for the study of such catechisms or formularies), 88–9.

[162] Education (Schools) Act 1992, s. 9.

[163] Ibid., s. 13; this extends to collective worship and empowers inspectors to report on the 'spiritual, moral, social and cultural development of pupils'; for the purposes of the statute, denominational education means 'religious education which is required . . . to be included in the school's basic curriculum, but is not required to be given in accordance with an agreed syllabus': s. 13(3A).

[164] It repeals the Diocesan Education Committees Measure 1955; in s. 5(5) of the Parochial Church Councils (Powers) Measure 1956, 'diocesan board of education for the diocese' replaces 'diocesan education committee for the diocese'.

Education, a body responsible to the diocesan synod and composed of the bishop, two persons nominated by the bishop (being either a suffragan bishop, a full-time assistant bishop, or an archdeacon), not less than fourteen nor more than eighteen members elected by the diocesan synod, and not less than four nor more than eight co-opted members.[165] The bishop, after consultation with the board, must appoint a director of education for the diocese to act as secretary of the board, which itself may be a body corporate or unincorporate.[166] The board's function is to promote in the diocese education 'consistent with the faith and practice of the Church of England', in particular religious education and religious worship. It must also promote church schools in the diocese and advise the governors of such schools and trustees of church educational endowments (and any other body or person concerned) on any matter affecting church schools in the diocese. It is under a specific duty to promote co-operation between the board and bodies or persons concerned with any aspect of education in the diocese. Generally, the board must perform such functions as are assigned to it by the Measure and such other functions (not contrary to the Measure) as are assigned by the diocesan synod, other than functions relating to church schools or church educational endowments.[167]

The Measure requires the board's advice and consent in relation to specific transactions. The governing body of a church school (and the trustees of any church educational endowment held wholly or partly in connection with any church school) must obtain the advice of the board (and have regard to it) before applying or entering into any agreement or arrangement for or in connection with the discontinuance or any change in the status, size, or character of the school.[168] Nor may proposals under the Education Reform Act 1988 be published to make a significant change in the religious character of a church school unless the board consents in writing.[169] Similarly, proposals

---

[165] S. 1(1), (2), Sched., Pt. I, 1, 2: the elected members must include 2 ordained clerks, at least 6 lay persons, and at least 6 members of the diocesan synod; co-opted members must have experience of church schools in the diocese and experience of other areas of the board's work; s. 1(2): the diocesan synod may resolve that the board be otherwise constituted with the consent of the bishop and the Secretary of State.   [166] S. 1(4), (5).

[167] S. 2(1); s. 2(2): the board has power to do anything incidental or conducive to the discharge of its functions; s. 2(3): it must report annually to the diocesan synod on the exercise of its functions; for proceedings see Sched., Pt. II.

[168] S. 3; s. 10(2): any reference to a change in the character of a school means 'a change in the religious character of the school'.

[169] S. 3; s. 10: 'church educational endowment' means 'an educational endowment which includes among the purposes for which it may be applied religious education according to the faith and practice of the Church of England'; 'church school' means 'a Church of England voluntary school or a grant-maintained school which was such a voluntary school immediately before it became a grant-maintained school'; 'Church of England voluntary school' means 'a voluntary school in respect of which any trust deed or other instrument requires provision to be made at the school for religious education according to the faith and practice of the Church of England or in which, in the absence of any such instrument, such provision has been made by custom and practice'.

for acquisition of grant-maintained status must include an account of the advice given by the board.[170] The board must also be consulted by a local education authority before appointing a person to represent the Church of England as a member of a Standing Advisory Council on Religious Education. Moreover, before modifying a trust deed or other instrument relating to a church school, the Secretary of State must consult the board.[171] The board is empowered to give directions to governing bodies of aided church schools with regard to their functions concerning status, continuance, size, or character of those schools as well as to trustees of any church educational endowment held wholly for a church school in the diocese.[172]

CONCLUSIONS

The law of the Church of England dealing with faith and doctrine aims to strike a balance between safeguarding received faith and formulating it afresh to accommodate the changing needs of contemporary society. Whereas in Roman Catholic canon law all the faithful have a canonical duty to present the faith to the world, in the Church of England legal duties to teach are confined to ordained ministers, readers, and lay workers. As in Roman Catholic canon law, there is a range of rights to instruction, and the deanery synod and parochial church council have specific duties to evangelize: moreover, extensive evangelization structures are provided by norms operating at both national and diocesan levels. Doctrinal development is in the keeping of General Synod, and elaborate procedural rules exist to preserve the received faith and to facilitate thorough consideration of proposed innovations: diocesan synods and parochial church councils are forbidden to develop or make doctrinal statements as, formally, are the church's courts. Unlike in the Roman Catholic Church, where canon law requires intellectual assent on the part of all the faithful to both definitive and non-definitive doctrine, in the Church of England only the ordained clergy and some lay officers must declare their belief in the faith of the church, though the precise meaning of 'assent' remains unclear. Enforcing doctrinal standards is in the keeping of the bishop and, whilst guidelines from the House of Bishops permit reasonable questioning of the faith, in serious cases provision exists to penalize ministerial dissent in the church courts; however, doctrinal offences are not as clearly defined as their counterparts in Roman Catholic canon law, nor is there an explicit right of dissent. The civil law forbids offensive attacks on the faith of either church,

---

[170] S. 5.   [171] S. 6(1) (under s. 11 of the 1988 Act); s. 6(2) (under s. 102 of the 1988 Act).
[172] Ss. 7, 8; for Boards of Education in diocesan norms see e.g. *ODYB: IF*, 265; *WDHI*, Ch. 4, 207; *SDH*, VII, C.6; *RBG*, B.10.

though it is undeveloped in relation to the practice of faith in the context of employment. Finally, secular law seeks to entitle the faithful of both churches to a Christian education in civil society, an entitlement treated in Roman Catholic canon law as a fundamental human right.

10

Liturgy: Creation and Control

Worship is central to the life and action of the believing community. The Church of England has chosen to conduct its public worship in a formal manner; liturgy is the principal method by which worship is expressed and organized. Liturgical law both orders and facilitates public worship: it enables the enjoyment of the spiritual benefits of worship but at the same time it obliges members to worship in accordance with the prescribed forms. The liturgical revolution of the last twenty years has heralded the end of uniformity; today the law of the Church of England allows the use of a multiplicity of liturgies. This chapter examines the terms of the new facilitative law, the extent to which it employs a principle of subsidiarity (distributing rights of liturgical innovation to all levels of the church), and the ways in which the General Synod enjoys an overriding power of liturgical authorization. As in Roman Catholic canon law, executive control of liturgy is vested in the bishop. In this context, the study covers the episcopal *jus liturgicum* which retains prominence particularly in the ecumenical context. At the same time, however, as with the Roman Catholic system, flexibility surfaces as a central value: the law allows a considerable degree of liturgical freedom to ministers and laity at the parochial level.

LITURGY AND LITURGICAL LAW

Both legally and theologically, liturgy is the formal expression or mode of worship. In civil law 'worship' has been defined judicially as 'a form of ceremony' involving 'submission to the object worshipped, veneration of that object, praise, thanksgiving, prayer or intercession'; a religious service bearing these characteristics is 'an act of worship'. Unless accompanied by these, the recital of a creed or 'a ceremony of instruction in the tenets' of a religious community does not constitute worship.[1] Theologically, 'liturgy'

---

[1] *R v Registrar General, ex p Segerdal* [1970] 3 All ER 886 at 892 *per* Buckley LJ: the case concerned the Church of Scientology and whether one of its 'chapels' was to be registered as a 'place of meeting for religious worship' under the Places of Worship Registration Act 1855, s. 3. CA held that 'worship' did not take place at the building; approved in *Re South Place Ethical Society, Barralet v AG* [1980] 3 All ER 918 *per* Winn LJ: worship is an occasion upon which people 'humble themselves in reverence and recognition of the dominant power and control of any entity or being outside their own body and life.'

may signify the whole of Christian life as worship and service as well as corporate worship conducted in accordance with the church's services.[2] In the Church of England liturgy is understood both as a means by which God speaks to the church and as a means by which the church responds to God in worship.[3] The essential elements of worship are adoration, confession, thanksgiving, and supplication. Liturgical order is justified on a number of grounds: to enhance corporate identity, to prevent sloppiness, disjointedness, and disproportion.[4] There is no legal definition of 'liturgy' as such—the legal signification for liturgy is a 'form of service'. According to the Church of England (Worship and Doctrine) Measure 1974, 'form of service' means 'any order, service, prayer, rite or ceremony whatsoever'.[5]

In modern canonical jurisprudence the purpose of liturgical law is to enable and order the fulfilment of the theological objectives of worship. Historically, however, liturgical law was not seen in these terms. The sixteenth-century reformers had feared two kinds of liturgical anarchy: the anarchy of numerous forms and the anarchy of no form at all. The Act of Uniformity 1549, designed to protect 'one convenient and meet order . . . of common and open prayer and administration of the sacraments . . . and none other or otherwise', was the first of a series of statutes commanding a single liturgical form, culminating in the Act of Uniformity 1662 and the introduction of the Book of Common Prayer.[6] As Sir John Nicholl said in *Kemp v Wickes*, 'those acts of uniformity established a particular liturgy to be used throughout the realm'.[7] The 1662 Act was fundamentally coercive: the clergy were bound to 'say and use' the 'Order or Liturgy' of the Book of Common Prayer: it was enacted, as its Preamble states, to effect a 'universal agreement in the worship of Almighty

---

[2] Rom. 15: 15–16 (*leitourgia* as the 'people's work'); Phil. 2: 30.

[3] Doctrine Commission, *Believing in the Church* (1981) 80–106; D. E. W. Harrison and M. C. Sansom, *Worship in the Church of England* (London, 1982) ch. 1.

[4] Ibid.; see also *The Worship of the Church*, Report of the Liturgical Commission on its work 1986–91 (GS 364) para. 19: 'the worship of the Church is the point of integration between God, theology and life . . . worship provides not only the right place for theological reflection but also is the right milieu for sharpening up pastoral theology and for Christian formation. Worship is where people learn the faith, express it and grow as Christians: it provides both the agenda and the experience.'

[5] S. 5(2): this includes 'the services for the ordination of priests and deacons and the consecration of bishops and the catechism or form of instruction before confirmation'; see also Canon B1(3): 'form of service shall include the collects, the lessons (designated in any Table of Lessons), 'any other matter to be used as part of a service', any 'Table of rules for regulating a service', and any Table of Holy Days including a Table of all the feasts in the *BCP* and any other Table approved by General Synod.

[6] G. R. Elton, *The Tudor Constitution* (2nd edn., Cambridge, 1982) 397–8: the 1549 Statutory Prayer Book survived until 1552; a new model introduced by the Act of Uniformity 1558 was the more Protestant one of 1552 but with modifications taken from the 1549 book. The 1662 statute led to the resignation of about 2,000 clergy: see J. T. Wilkinson, *1662 and After: Three Centuries of English Nonconformity* (London, 1962), ch. 4.

[7] (1809) 3 Phillim 264; 161 ER 1320 at 1332 (Arches Ct.).

God'.[8] The judges stressed its coercive nature: 'the object of the Act of Uniformity of 1662 was to prevent divergences of ceremonies.'[9]

Movements for liturgical reform led, through the Royal Commission in 1904 and the abortive attempt to introduce the Prayer Book of 1928, to proposed reforms in the 1960s and 1970s, and resulted in the introduction in 1980 of the *Alternative Service Book*.[10] Liturgies may be viewed as facilities. In 1985 the Archbishop of Canterbury expressed the general dissatisfaction of the church with what was perceived to be too restrictive a body of law, a body of law from which there were commonly 'considerable departures', both major and minor.[11] The new view of the church on liturgical law proposes flexibility and participation: as the Archbishop of Canterbury said in the 1974 debate, the objective of the law is to help people 'in a more lively participation in worship without loss of reverence or mystery'.[12] In the Church of England liturgy is governed directly, and in considerable detail, by legal rules, though as a general rule these do not specify the purposes and nature of liturgy and liturgical law. The position is rather different in the Roman Catholic Church.

According to Roman Catholic doctrine and canon law, liturgy is an expression by the people in terms of their relationship to Christ and the church: it is a response to God's initiative, a dialogue between the word and actions of God and his people.[13] Liturgy exists to enable sanctification of the faithful through worship.[14] The whole church, clergy and laity, shares in the exercise of the

---

[8] The 1662 Prayer Book incorporates amendments effected by the Calender (New Styles) Act 1750 and the Prayer Book (Table of Lessons) Act 1871. The Worship and Doctrine Measure 1974 repealed alterations made by the Clergy (Ordination and Miscellaneous Provisions) Measure 1964 and the Prayer Book (Further Provisions) Measure 1968.

[9] *Gore-Booth v Bishop of Manchester* [1920] 2 KB 412 *per* Lord Coleridge.

[10] The archbishops issued an abridged version of the 1662 Prayer Book in 1947 incorporating elements of the 1928 Prayer Book. In 1955 a Liturgical Commission was set up and in 1965 the Prayer Book (Alternative and Other Services) Measure was enacted *inter alia* to 'authorise the use by way of experiment of alternative forms of service deviating from the Book of Common Prayer'. The 1947 versions appeared as Series 1 in 1966, with the Liturgical Commission 1967 work leading to Series 2, 1973–8, now gathered together in *ASB*.

[11] HL Deb, Vol. 263, 18 Feb. 1965, 651 at 653: he spoke of 'small deviations from the text and the rubrics of the Prayer Book' and of 'considerable use of whole forms of service which are illegal and yet familiar and widely welcomed'; ibid., 656: 'The rigidity of the law means that it is as culpable to alter the psalms or the lessons to meet some urgent circumstances, or to change some archaic phrase in a prayer to meet the needs of a particular congregation . . . as it is to alter the whole structure of a service. It is the laity who have made it clear that they do not desire this rigidity'; see also the Liturgical Commission Report, *Patterns of Worship* (London, 1990).

[12] HL Deb, Vol. 354, 14 Nov. 1974, 867 at 870 (commenting on Series II). Nevertheless, the role of law in the regulation of liturgy remains problematic. Given the theological meaning of worship, and its stress on the intimate exchanges betwen God and the people of the church, it may be felt by some difficult to justify the legal regulation of a fundamentally spiritual 'transaction'. For the charismatic there is a basic antithesis between law and liturgical freedom. See generally D. E. W. Harrison and M. C. Sansom, *Worship in the Church of England* (London, 1982), ch. 1; for the Roman Catholic approach see below.

[13] Constitution on the Sacred Liturgy, *Sacrosanctum Concilium* (1963), ch. 1.

[14] *CIC*, c. 834, derived from *SC*, 7.

office of sanctifying, and liturgical actions themselves are not private actions but celebrations of the church itself with the presence and active participation of the faithful.[15] The faithful have the right (*ius*) to worship God according to the prescriptions of their own rites approved by the legitimate pastors of the church.[16] In contrast to the Church of England, the detailed liturgical law is to be found outside the 1983 Code, in apostolic constitutions, papal letters, particular law, and in the ritual books (*ordines*) and their preambles (*praenotanda*) and rubrics. The Code contains only the general framework underlying these: 'for the most part the Code does not define the rites which are to be observed in celebrating liturgical actions'; 'current liturgical norms retain their force unless . . . contrary to the canons of the Code'.[17] There has been much discussion in recent years about the nature and authority of liturgical norms reflecting the movement since Vatican II towards greater flexibility and adaptability of the law to the needs of the worshipping community. The liturgical rules are 'juridical norms that govern the actual celebration of the sacraments and other services'.[18] Though the principles of promulgation and interpretation apply, liturgical law is not a disciplinary law, but operates to allow celebration of the mysteries of the sacraments.

THE AUTHORIZED LITURGIES

The Roman Catholic code of canon law does not expressly specify the church's authorized liturgies. The many authorized Roman Catholic liturgies were prepared by the Consilium for the Implementation of the Constitution on the Liturgy (1964) and promulgated by Paul VI, in the decrees of the Congregation of Sacred Rites (until 1969), subsequently by the Sacred Congregation for Divine Worship (1969–75), and latterly by the Sacred Congregation for Sacraments and Divine Worship. The principal liturgies are to be found in the Roman Missal (1969), the Roman Ritual (1969–84),[19] and the Roman Pontifical (1968–84).[20]

By the Church of England (Worship and Doctrine) Measure 1974, General

---

[15] *CIC*, cc. 835–7 (*SC*, 26); for other offices of sanctification (e.g. prayers, works of penance) see c. 839.

[16] *CIC*, c. 214; each person by baptism belongs to a specific ritual church (c. 111).

[17] *CIC*, c. 2.

[18] *CCL: TC*, 593; F. R. McManus, 'Liturgical law and difficult cases', *Worship*, 48 (1974), 347; W. Kelley, 'The authority of liturgical laws', *The Jurist*, 28 (1968), 397; J. Huels, 'The interpretation of liturgical law', *Worship*, 55 (1981), 218.

[19] Rite of Marriage (1969), Rite of Baptism for Children (1969), for Adults (1972), Rite of Funerals (1969), Rite of Religious Profession (1970), Rite of Anointing and Pastoral Care of the Sick (1972), Holy Communion and Worship of the Eucharist Outside Mass (1973), and Rite of Penance (1973).

[20] Including the Ordination of Deacons, Priests and Bishops (1968), Rite of Institution of Readers and Acolytes etc (1972), Ceremonial of the Bishops (1984); see *CCL: TC*, 596.

Synod repealed the Act of Uniformity 1662.[21] The Book of Common Prayer is not, today, the only authorized liturgy, though the law protects its continued use as one of the several liturgies which are legally approved.[22] The principle of uniformity has been abandoned. The operative principle today is that of conformity of worship. There are four specifically authorized forms of service under Canon B1: the forms of service contained in the Book of Common Prayer 1662; the shortened forms of Morning and Evening Prayer set out in the Schedule to the Act of Uniformity Amendment Act 1872; the form of service authorized by Royal Warrant for use upon the anniversary of the day of the accession of the reigning monarch; and any forms of service approved under Canon B2 or Canon B4, to which we shall turn presently.

According to guidance issued by the authority of the Standing Committee of the General Synod, the new legal regime is designed to maintain a balance between the use of old and new forms of service. Though the distinction is not expressly made in law, the document distinguishes between 'statutory' forms of service (Holy Communion, Morning Prayer, and Evening Prayer) and 'non-statutory' forms of service.[23] The general scheme of the church's liturgical law rests on the concept that the law 'defines' or 'specifies' the permissible liturgies. Within the broad categorization of statutory and non-statutory forms of service, the law envisages two classes of permitted liturgy, distinguished in part by the procedures employed in their formation: authorized and approved liturgies. Canons B1 to B4 employ different notions to classify the lawful liturgies (and here there is something of a confusion of terminology): broadly the classes are the 'authorized' liturgies (B1): those forms of service author-ized directly by law, including those which are authorized 'alternatives' (B3), and the 'approved' liturgies, approved by General Synod (B2). The 'approved' liturgies are also classified as 'authorized' services: Canon B1(1)(d). Under Canon B4 services may also be 'approved' liturgies when approved (as we shall see later) by convocation, the archbishops, or the ordinary for use on special occasions; again, these 'approved' services are also 'authorized': B1(1)(e). The same applies to services authorized for experimental use under Canon B5A: these too are 'authorized' services (B1(1)(f)).

A full list of the liturgies authorized for use is found in the guidance issued on the authority of the Standing Committee of General Synod.[24] The liturgical books containing both the statutory and non-statutory services are (a) the Book of Common Prayer (1662), which is authorized without time limit; (b) the

---

[21] Sched 2., with the exception of s. 10 (concerning non-ordained persons administering the sacrament) and s. 15 (concerning lecturers' assent to the Thirty-Nine Articles).

[22] See below.

[23] *Public Worship in the Church of England: A Guide to the Law Governing Worship and Doctrine in the Church of England,* Issued by the authority of the Standing Committee of the General Synod (London,1986) 2, 3–5; the distinction is commonly employed in diocesan norms: see e.g. *CAD*, 37; *CF*, C.1, *WDHI*, ch. 2. [24] *Public Worship*, 12–13.

Alternative Service Book (1980); (c) the Ministry of the Sick (1983); and (d) Series 1 (Solemnization of Matrimony and Burial Services) and Series 2 (Baptism and Confirmation). The services in (b) to (d) are authorized for use until 31 December 2000. As in Catholic canon law, the canons themselves do not generally specify rites for particular services: only occasionally are these mentioned. For instance, if an infant is privately baptized, he/she is to be subsequently received into the church's congregation 'according to the form and manner prescribed in and by the office for Private Baptism authorized by Canon B1'.[25] Again, a baptized person (but not episcopally confirmed) wishing to be formally admitted into the Church of England, must be received by the rite of confirmation, and any person episcopally confirmed received 'according to the Form of Reception approved by the General Synod'.[26] If persons have contracted a civil marriage, and desire to add thereto a service of solemnization of matrimony, a minister may if he sees fit use such form of service as may be approved by synod under Canon B2.[27]

THE PROCESS OF LITURGICAL FORMATION

In addition to the modern church's received liturgies, Roman Catholic canon law provides for the formation of liturgical books; liturgical formation is ultimately vested in the Roman pontiff. As a result of Vatican II, particular liturgical books are prepared by the respective territorial authority.[28] The local ordinary must attest that reprinting of liturgical books and their translation correspond with the approved edition (c. 826). According to Canon 838(2), it is for the Apostolic See to order the sacred liturgy of the universal church. It is the function of the pontiff 'to publish the liturgical books [and] to review their translations into vernacular languages'. The conference of bishops is competent to prepare both translations and particular rituals adopted to the needs of their territories and to publish them with the prior review (*recognitio*) of the Holy See.[29] In the opinion of commentators, however, the canon does not seem to give to the conference of bishops a role 'in the development of a new rite'.[30] Similar arrangements for centralized liturgical authorization operate in the Church of England.

---

[25] Canon B22(8); see also B27 for conditional baptism in accordance with the form of service authorized by Canon B1.   [26] Canon B28.

[27] Canon B36: no record of any such service shall be entered in the register books of marriage; see *Public Worship*, 13 for 'commended services', e.g. prayer and dedication after civil marriage.

[28] *SC*, 63; for liturgical commissions see *CIC*, c. 360 and *COCLA*, 284, for the curial Sacred Congregation for Sacraments and Divine Worship and the preparation of liturgical texts for papal approval.

[29] *CIC*, c. 838(3); see also c. 455(2); 'In virtue of power conceded by the law, the regulation of the liturgy within certain defined limits belongs also to various kinds of competent territorial bodies of bishops lawfully established': c. 22(2).   [30] *CCL: TC*, 604; *SC*, 4.

The Power to Formulate and Authorize Liturgy

With regard to the Church of England a distinction must be made between the *formulation* and the *authorization* (and approval) of liturgies. An implicit concept of subsidiarity seems to operate. In accordance with Convocation Resolutions passed in 1954, the Archbishops appointed a standing Liturgical Commission. Reconstituted by General Synod under the Synodical Government Measure 1969,[31] in 1971 the Commission became a permanent subordinate body of the General Synod. Regulated by Synod's standing orders and an internal constitution, its functions are 'to prepare forms of service at the request of the House of Bishops for submission to that House in the first instance', to advise on the experimental use of forms of service authorized by the Synod, and to exchange information and advice on liturgical matters with other churches within and outside the Anglican Communion.[32] It is the General Synod which authorizes liturgies; the power is given by the Church of England (Worship and Doctrine) Measure 1974: 'It shall be lawful for the General Synod . . . to make provision by Canon with respect to worship . . . including provision for empowering the General Synod to approve, amend, continue or discontinue forms of service.'[33] There had been fears that the Measure would weaken establishment and the control of parliament over liturgical matters; its enactment simply put on a legal footing the principle that a church ought to be autonomous in the regulation of its own worship.[34]

Under the 1974 Measure Synod has empowered itself, subject to the limitations considered below, to create *any* form of service.[35] By Canon B2[36] it is lawful for Synod 'to approve forms of service for use . . . and to amend any form of service approved by the General Synod under this canon'. Synod may 'approve the use of any form of service for a limited period, or without limit of period'. It may also extend the period and discontinue 'any such form of service'. According to the Measure, new legal provisions for liturgy effected by canon or regulation 'shall have effect notwithstanding anything inconsistent therewith contained in any of the rubrics of the Book of Common Prayer'.[37]

It is not only Synod, however, which possesses the legal power to authorize liturgies. Unlike Roman Catholic canon law which requires papal authorization,

---

[31] Sched. 2, Art. 10(2).

[32] See *CBC*, 29–30 for its constitution, membership, term of office, business and procedure, and *GSSO*, SO 119 (see *supra* Ch. 4).

[33] S. 1(1); see also s. 1(1)(b): Synod may make provision by canon or regulations under canon 'for any matter', including those concerning worship, 'to which any of the rubrics contained in the Book of Common Prayer relate'.

[34] HL Deb, Vol. 354, 14 Nov. 1974, 867 at 868–9; 871 *per* Archbishop of Canterbury: the Measure 'gives to the General Synod . . . considerably more power in the control of worship'.

[35] Compare *CF*, C.1: General Synod 'has no power of itself' to alter or vary the services in the *BCP*.   [36] CE(WD)M 1974, s. 1(1)(a).

[37] Ibid., s. 1(2).

the law of the Church of England operates a principle of liturgical subsidiarity. Rights to authorize the use of services (by means of approval) are distributed throughout the church down to the ministerial level. The 1974 Measure enables Synod to allow (by canon) Convocation, the archbishops, and diocesan bishops to approve forms of service for use on occasions for which no provision is made by forms of service contained in the Book of Common Prayer or the authorized liturgies (s.1(5)).[38] The law also allows experimental use of draft forms of service. Under the 1974 Measure, when a form of service is in the course of preparation for submission to Synod for approval by canon, Synod may by canon allow the archbishops to 'authorize' (not 'approve') the use of that draft service (s.1(6)). Such practice has now been authorized in general terms by Canon B5A, without the need for synodical approval for each draft service. In exercising this liturgical right the archbishops (presumably they must act jointly) must first consult with Synod's House of Bishops.[39] No equivalent right is conferred by Canon B5A on Convocation or on diocesan bishops.

Pursuant to the 1974 Measure,[40] Canon B5(2) confers on a minister the right to use forms of service considered suitable by him for those occasions for which no provision is made by an existing form of service (authorized or approved under Canons B2 and B4). The minister may also permit another minister to use the said forms of service. This is an important new provision but, strictly, does not enable the creation of new services at this ministerial level. According to the guidance issued on the authority of the General Synod's Standing Committee, a minister may design (for example) a 'family service', being a statutory service (Holy Communion, Morning Prayer, or Evening Prayer) 'in a simplified form'. The service must, however, be within 'the limits of lawful authority' and a minister enjoys no right to 'abbreviate or adapt such services beyond the limit of the alternatives provided within the authorised texts even to make it more convenient for a congregation which includes a good many young people'.[41] The guidance recognizes, however,

---

[38] See now Canon B4; for the archiepiscopally authorized service for Remembrance Sunday see *Public Worship* (1986) 13. In the 1928 Prayer Book controversy, Convocation Resolutions recognized an inherent power in the bishops to authorize the use of forms of service: *Acts of Convocation*, 61 at 63: 'the bishops, in the exercise of that legal or administrative discretion, which belongs to each bishop in his own diocese, will be guided by the proposals set forth in the Book of 1928, and will endeavour to secure that practices which are consistent with neither the Book of 1662 nor the Book of 1928 shall cease'. For episcopal authorization of deviation see below.

[39] S. 1(6) confers a right on General Synod to provide by canon that 'the archbishops may authorise that service in draft form to be conducted by a minister in the presence of a congregation consisting of such persons as the archbishops may designate'; Canon B5A(1) is worded rather differently: it enables the archbishops to 'authorise such form of service for experimental use for a period specified by them on such terms and in such places or parishes as they may designate'.

[40] S. 1(5)(b).

[41] *Public Worship*, 5: 'Only the options permitted within the Prayer Book or the ASB may be used'.

that '"Family Services" take a form largely unrelated to any of the permitted forms for the Holy Communion or Morning Prayer or Evening Prayer'. In these cases, '[p]rovided that opportunity is given each Sunday for parishioners to attend the "statutory services" . . . the parish priest may also use such forms as he considers suitable and this discretion covers "Family Services" and "Guest Services"'.[42] Some diocesan regulations have been developed to supplement this guidance, but this is by no means a uniform practice. These prescribe, variously, that the formulation of family services is permissible and occasionally norms require the agreement of both the incumbent and the parochial church council, though norms generally repeat the prohibition that these must not become a substitute for the statutory services.[43] Some diocesan norms specify that only the authorized options are permitted for use,[44] whilst others require, with regard to adaptations, that the incumbent and parochial church council 'bear in mind' the values of worship, welcome, nourishment, and fellowship and, if the same order is regularly used, to send it to the bishop and to keep in touch with the diocesan worship committee.[45]

Guidance has now also been issued for parishes to design liturgical texts for local use enabling, indeed, parishes 'to introduce material from other sources into local texts'; the creation of these 'parish editions' is subject to the law of copyright.[46] In any case, where the parish wishes to vary existing forms of service, in creating a parish edition, or wishes to use other forms of service for which no authorized service is provided, these matters may be referred to the bishop for pastoral advice and guidance.[47] In many dioceses there is a liturgical committee to which the bishop may himself turn for guidance and to which he may delegate responsibility in this area; alternatively the bishop may issue general guidance regulating these questions.[48] Sometimes diocesan norms expressly permit parishes to produce 'parish editions', repeating the duty to obtain copyright permission.[49]

Limits and Controls

Whilst for the purposes of theological debate during the deliberative stage of the legislative process the principle that the Church of England 'belongs to the true and apostolic Church of Christ' is undoubtedly of central importance, three sets of formal rules limit the formulation and authorization of liturgy by

---

[42] Ibid., 5–6. [43] *BDM*, D5; *SDH*, A7. [44] *WDHI*, ch. 2, 19–21.
[45] *DG: BOP*, 3.2.
[46] *Liturgical Texts for Local Use: Guidelines and Copyright Information* (published by the Central Board of Finance) (London, 1988) (see ibid., 3 for the material which must be contained in the parish edition). [47] Ibid., 2, based on Canon B5(2), (4).
[48] *Liturgical Texts* (1988), 2; see e.g. *LBGCP*, 26: Liturgical Group to advice on liturgical matters and to help with 'scrutinising and developing new forms of liturgy'; unlike in Roman Catholic canon law, the question of translating liturgical texts has not been the subject of legal treatment (see *supra* n. 29). [49] *BDM*, D.3; *WDHI*, ch. 2, 38; *GDBOP*, 3.

General Synod. They impose both procedural and substantive limitations. Section 3 of the 1974 Measure forbids Synod to make canons authorizing a form of service 'unless it has been approved by the General Synod with a majority in each House thereof of not less than two-thirds of those present and voting'. No regulation can be made under a canon approving, amending, continuing, or discontinuing a form of service without the same majorities. Moreover, a form of service must be such as is in the opinion of the synod 'neither contrary to, nor indicative of a departure from, the doctrine of the Church of England in any essential matter' (s.4(1)). The synod itself shall determine conclusively whether there is a departure from the church's doctrine (s.4(2)).[50] A parallel provision is contained in Canon B2(1) in relation to 'approved' liturgies. General Synod's constitution, appended to the Synodical Government Measure 1969, centralizes episcopal control in the synodical process of formulation. Under Article 7, a provision 'touching . . . the services or ceremonies of the Church of England or the administration of the Sacraments or sacred rites' must be referred to the House of Bishops before final approval by Synod. Synod's approval may then only be in the form proposed by the bishops. There is also provision for the Convocations to review liturgical provisions, but ultimately they have no power of veto.[51] A measure or canon providing for permanent changes in the services of baptism or holy communion or in the Ordinal must not be finally approved by General Synod unless the measure or canon (or the substance of their proposals) has been approved by a majority of the dioceses at meetings of their diocesan synods. The same applies to schemes for constitutional union or a permanent and substantial change of a relationship between the Church of England and another Christian body whose members reside in Great Britain.[52]

There are special provisions for the continued use and protection of the Book of Common Prayer 1662. Synod must exercise its powers to provide for worship to ensure that the forms of service contained in the 1662 Book remain available for use in the church.[53] However, Synod and parliament both possess the power to abolish or to discontinue the use of the 1662 Book.[54]

[50] See *supra* Ch. 3 for the possibility of challenge by means of judicial review in the civil courts to the use of General Synod's legislative power to create liturgy.

[51] The procedures are the same as those for doctrinal revision: see Chs. 3 and 9; see also *GSSO*, SO 72–80, 81–94; the participation of the laity in the process of revision accords with the concept of authority underlying the principle of synodical government: see generally D. Gray, 'The revision of canon law and its application to liturgical revision in the recent history of the Church of England', *The Jurist*, 48 (1988), 638.

[52] SGM 1969, Sched. 2, Art. 8. The stage at which this is done is to be determined by the archbishops.

[53] CE(WD)M 1974, s. 1(1): 'the powers of the General Synod under this subsection shall be so exercised as to ensure that the forms of service contained in the Book of Common Prayer continue to be available for use in the Church of England.'

[54] For this claim (though without explanation) see *HLE*, para. 936, n. 3; this view is clearly tenable in the light of the terms of the principle of parliamentary and General Synod legislative supremacy: see *supra* Ch. 3.

Parliamentary statutes have indeed altered some of its provisions.[55] Synod expressly repealed the Act of Uniformity in the 1974 Measure,[56] it has amended the Prayer Book by means of measure,[57] and it may alter the Prayer Book by canon under the authority of a parent measure.[58] As Synod has repealed the parent, so to speak, of the 1662 Prayer Book (that is, the Act of Uniformity), so it has power to destroy the child of that statute, the Prayer Book itself. However, given the principle of continued use, contained in the 1974 Measure, Synod could not use is powers under that Measure to abolish the Prayer Book: a fresh measure would have to be enacted.[59]

Similar controls exist when liturgies are authorized or approved at lower ecclesiastical levels pursuant to the operative principle of subsidiarity. On occasions for which no provision is made in the Book of Common Prayer or by the General Synod (under Canon B2), forms of service to be authorized by Convocation, the archbishops, and diocesan bishops must not be contrary to or indicative of a departure from the church's doctrine.[60] These bodies must decide whether 'in their opinion' a liturgy is consistent with ecclesiastical doctrine. They must also be satisfied that the liturgies are reverent and seemly.[61] The same requirement applies to forms of service approved and used by ministers, though these may authorize forms of service for which there is no existing provision '[s]ubject to any regulation made from time to time by the Convocation of the province'.[62] In short, the law of the Church of England has moved away from the principle of a single uniform liturgy—and now enables the making, authorization, approval, and use of a multiplicity of liturgies. The principal characteristics of the legal regime are facility and subsidiarity.[63]

---

[55] See *supra* n. 8.   [56] Sched. 2. The whole Act is repealed except ss. 10, 15.

[57] See e.g. Admission to Holy Communion Measure 1972 s. 1: the *BCP* rubric shall not prevent Synod providing by canon or regulation for admission to communion of other baptized persons. For amendments by the Church Assembly see Ordination (Miscellaneous Provisions) Measure 1964 and Prayer Book (Further Provisions) Measure 1968.

[58] CE(WD)M 1974, s.1 (2). However, under s. 1(1)(b) Synod may not *under the 1974 Measure* alter the *BCP* rubrics about publication of banns of matrimony. It could, of course, create a measure repealing this prohibition.   [59] I.e. repeal s. 1(1) which secures continued use.

[60] CE(WD)M 1974, s. 4(3); Canon B4(1)–(3).

[61] Canon B4; these terms are not defined and therefore a subjective test presumably applies.

[62] Canon B5(2).

[63] How far subsidiarity may be pushed is in part an ecclesiological question; the following model is unlikely to be the subject of legislative reform: the minister and parochial church council ought to be empowered by law to design liturgies, with limits built into the system (e.g.: they must be seemly and reverent, conform to the church's doctrine, and they must be submitted for approval to the bishop); this raises questions of ecclesiology—the requirement of episcopal approval might meet the claim that a parochially created liturgy would still be the act of the church and not the merely the liturgical act of the congregation; see *The Worship of the Church*, para. 68.

THE ADMINISTRATION OF LITURGY: ORDER AND CONTROL

Technically in Roman Catholic canon law, in order to be considered as liturgy, worship takes place when it is carried out in the name of the church by persons lawfully deputed and through acts approved by the authority of the church.[64] According to *Lumen Gentium*, 'the faithful are deputed by the baptismal character to the worship of the Christian religion': liturgy is carried out by the baptized of the community under the presidency of the ordained ministers.[65] The supervision of the sacred liturgy depends solely on the authority of the church: liturgical supervision resides in the pontiff and, in accord with the law, the diocesan bishop.[66] The liturgical books approved by the competent authority are to be faithfully observed in the celebration of the sacraments; therefore no one on personal authority may add, remove, or change anything in them.[67] This does not, it seems, absolutely forbid deviations from the liturgical books and law. As we have seen, in Catholic thought liturgical law exists to facilitate worship. Consequently it must be applied flexibly, offering choices and options. Liturgical norms are treated as 'aesthetic norms' which can be relaxed in order to allow an accurate expression of worship according to the community's needs.[68] The diocesan bishop has the responsibility to supervise liturgical discipline and may dispense with the requirements of universal and particular liturgical law.[69] A minister cannot unilaterally dispense from liturgical laws,[70] though some writers stress that a governing principle is the *de minimis* rule and the directory rather than mandatory nature of liturgical law.[71]

Similar arrangements operate in the Church of England, in which the law has recognized a right to worship vested in parishioners.[72] As a general

---

[64] *CIC*, c. 834(2).

[65] *LG*, 11; see *post* Ch. 11 for the Code's general principles on sacramental law.

[66] *CIC*, c. 838; *SC*, 22; the presumption is that the bishop has all the power of governance over liturgy; the diocesan has power to issue liturgical norms by which all are bound: c. 838(4); see also c. 375: bishops as priests of sacred worship; *COCLA*, 1335, bishops' conference of England and Wales legislation, *Briefing* 85, 1: permanent deacons are obliged to recite daily morning and evening prayer.   [67] *CIC*, c. 846.

[68] *CCL: TC*, 595: 'liturgical celebrations . . . are matters of the most intimate faith and piety, which are articulated communally. . . . The norms that govern them are more aesthetic and artistic than juridic or canonical. . . . The renewed tone and spirit that infuse them . . . and the relative weight of their demands in the face of conflicting pastoral expectations have led to a legitimate openness, a recognition of the religious value of diversity, and an invitation to cultural and other adaptation.'   [69] *CIC*, c. 87–8; (see also c. 392(2).
[70] *CIC*, c. 89.

[71] D. J. Ward, 'Liturgy and law', *Readings*, 396 at 402; see also R. K. Seasoltz, *New Liturgy, New Laws* (Collegeville, Mn., 1980).

[72] Pastoral Measure 1983, s. 27(5)(a): concerning provisions as to parish churches and pastoral schemes, 'the parishioners of the parish shall have the same rights of worship in each of the parish churches'; see also Canon B15(1) for the 'duty' of all who have been confirmed to receive Holy Communion regularly and esp. at the festivals of Christmas, Easter, and Whitsun or Pentecost; for extra-canonical duties (arising from Convocation Resolutions and diocesan regulations) placed on the laity to attend services see *supra* Ch. 8.

principle (subject to the rules in Canons B43 and B44 considered below dealing with liturgical ecumenism) ministers are under a canonical duty only to use authorized or approved services, though some diocesan regulations present the duty in terms that 'clergy are expected' to use only the authorized liturgies.[73] By Canon B1(2) the minister's duty is to have a good understanding of the forms of service and 'he shall endeavour to ensure that the worship offered glorifies God and edifies the people'; '[e]very minister shall use only the forms of service authorised by this Canon', the authorized (and approved) services being of course: those listed in Canon B1; those approved by Convocation, the archbishops, or diocesan bishops; those authorized for experimental use archiepiscopally (draft forms of service); and those which the minister himself 'authorizes' under Canon B5.[74] Perhaps unnecessarily (given its status as a promise to fulfil a pre-existing canonical duty), the obligation is also imposed by the ministerial declaration of assent under Canon C15.[75] Judicial decisions that a minister is under a duty to use only the 1662 Prayer Book are not now good law.[76]

The Duty to Provide Services

The law imposes on ministers a duty to provide the facility of some liturgies, the 'statutory services'; obliquely it confers upon the laity a corresponding right to such services similar to that in Catholic canon law.[77] However, the duty may be relaxed in prescribed circumstances by dispensation. Under Canon C24(2) '[e]very priest having a cure of souls shall . . . celebrate, or cause to be celebrated, the Holy Communion on all Sundays and other greater Feast Days and on Ash Wednesday, and shall diligently administer the sacraments and other rites of the Church'.[78] The priest may relax this duty 'for some reasonable cause approved by the bishop of the diocese' (C24(3)). Similar provisions apply to the statutory services of Morning and Evening Prayer. According to Canon B11, 'Morning and Evening Prayer shall be said or sung in every parish church at least on all Sundays and other principal Feast Days, and also on Ash Wednesday and Good Friday'.[79] Similarly, under Canon C24(1) it is the duty of '[e]very priest having a cure of souls . . . in the absence of reasonable hindrance . . . [to] provide that . . . Morning and Evening Prayer daily and on the appointed days the Litany shall be said in the church, or one of the churches, of which he is the minister'.

---

[73] *TBF*, 3.1.   [74] Canon B1(2).

[75] Canon C15(1): 'I will use only the forms of service which are authorised or allowed by Canon'. The declaration under the Act of Uniformity 1662, s. 9 was 'I will conform to the liturgy of the Church of England as it is now by law established'.

[76] *Colefatt v Newcomb* (1705) 2 Ld Raym 1205; *Bennett v Bonaker* (1828) 2 Hag Ecc 25; *Martin v Machonockie* (1868) LR 2 A&E 116; *Newbery v Goodwin* (1911) 1 Phillim 282.

[77] *CIC*, c. 843. For the right to the sacraments see *post* Ch. 11.   [78] See also B14(1).

[79] B11(1).

The canons allow a degree of delegation. Under Canon B11(1) '[r]eaders, such other lay persons as may be authorized by the bishop of the diocese, or some other suitable lay person, may . . . say or sing Morning and Evening Prayer (save for the Absolution)'. This may be done 'at the invitation of the minister of the parish or, where the cure is vacant or the minister is incapacitated, at the invitation of the churchwardens'.[80] Indeed, on all other days the minister of the parish, together with other ministers licensed to serve in the parish, 'shall make provision for Morning and Evening Prayer to be said or sung either in the parish church or, after consultation with the parochial church council, elsewhere as may best serve to sustain the corporate spiritual life of the parish'.[81] The laity have a right to know about these services: public notice must be given in the parish, by tolling the bell or other appropriate means, of the time and place where prayers are to be said or sung.[82] The laity can request the bishop to enforce the canonical duty to provide these liturgical facilities, either by judicial proceedings or by means of episcopal executive action.[83]

More extensive relaxation by dispensation of the duty to provide services is legally allowed with regard to Morning and Evening Prayer. The general principle is that the 'reading of Morning and Evening Prayer in any parish church . . . may *only* be dispensed with in accordance with the provisions of Canon B14A' (promulgated in 1994).[84] This also applies to the statutory service of Holy Communion.[85] The reading of Morning and Evening Prayer in any parish church as required by Canon B11, or the celebration of Holy Communion in any parish church as required by Canon B14 'may be dispensed with' in certain circumstances. First, these services may be dispensed with on an occasional basis 'as authorised by the minister and the parochial church council acting jointly'. There is no express provision in the canon for disagreements between the minister and the council over occasional dispensation: implicitly, of course, as their joint action is required, if the minister and council disagree no dispensation is possible.[86] Secondly, these statutory services may be dispensed with on a regular basis 'as authorised by the bishop

---

[80] B11(2).

[81] B11(3); also, 'so that the pattern of life enjoined upon ministers by Canon C26' is served; see Ch. 7.

[82] B11(3); see also B7: the minister having the cure of souls 'shall give adequate public notice, in any way which is locally convenient, of the feast days and fast days to be observed and of the time and place of services on those days'.

[83] *Rugg v Bishop of Winchester* (1868) LR 2 PC 223; *Parnell v Roughton* (1874) LR 6 PC 46 at 53.

[84] B11(3). Presumably 'reading' includes 'singing', as required under B11(1). See also Extra-Parochial Ministry Measure 1967: a minister may perform offices and services at the home of resident parishioners and of anyone whose name is on the electoral roll but who is not resident in the parish (s. 1).   [85] B14(2).

[86] Canon C18(4) appears to create an informal right of appeal to the bishop, but (unlike in relation to disagreement over variation of services, discussed below) this is not explicitly stated in the Canon.

on the request of the minister and the parochial church council acting jointly'. It would seem that, on an occasional basis, joint ministerial and conciliar agreement is permissible in addition to relaxation allowed by the 'reasonable cause' rule under Canon C24(2) with regard to Holy Communion. Morning and Evening Prayer may only be dispensed with in accordance with Canon B14A (B11(3)), save for 'reasonable hindrance' under C 24(1).

The canon further regulates the use of these provisions by way of limitation. In exercising these powers, the minister and the parochial church council or the bishop, as the case may be, 'must be satisfied that there is a good reason for doing so'. All three parties 'shall have regard to the frequency of services of Morning and Evening Prayer or the celebration of Holy Communion . . . in other parish churches or places of worship in the diocese'. Similarly, they must 'ensure that no church ceases altogether to be used for public worship'. The canon also regulates cases in which there is more than one parish church or place of worship in a benefice (and where the minister holds benefices in plurality with more than one parish church or place of worship). In these circumstances the minister and the council acting jointly 'shall make proposals to the bishop as to what [statutory services] are to be held in each of the parishes churches or places of worship . . . [and] if the bishop is satisfied with the proposals he shall authorise them accordingly'. However, in default of the minister and council making satisfactory proposals, 'the bishop shall make such direction as he considers appropriate'. Again, in exercising these powers 'the bishop shall ensure that no church ceases altogether to be used for public worship'.[87]

Ministerial Control and Choice of Liturgy

As a general principle, in the Church of England (as in Roman Catholic canon law), liturgical matters come under the oversight of the bishop. By Canon C18(4), to every bishop belongs 'the right . . . of conducting, ordering, controlling, and authorising all services in churches'.[88] However, the incumbent directly controls the performance of divine service throughout his benefice.[89] No cleric can conduct divine service publicly in whole or in part within the benefice without the consent of the resident incumbent.[90] Consent is not

---

[87] B14A(1)-(2); under para. (3) these powers extend to any parish centre of worship designated under the Pastoral Measure 1983, s. 29(2). [88] See Ch. 6.

[89] *Wood v Headingley-cum-Burley Burial Board* (1892) 1 QB 713 at 729; for the conducting of services in unconsecrated buildings see Pastoral Measure 1983, s. 29; see also *Moysey v Hillcoat* (1828) 2 Hag Ecc 30; *Bishop of Down v Miller* (1861) 11 I Ch R App 1; *Kitson v Drury* (1865) 29 JP 643; *Richards v Fincher* (1874) LR 4 A&E 255.

[90] C8(4) (this and exceptions to it are discussed in Ch. 7); sometimes the principle appears in relation to a specific matter: see e.g. Canon B29(4), concerning absolution; for judicial recognition of the basic rule see *Carr v Marsh* (1814) 2 Phillim 198 at 206; *Farnworth v Bishop of Chester* (1825) 4 B&C 555 at 568; *Nesbitt v Wallace* [1901] P 354.

necessary if abrogated by law or forfeited by some default on his part.[91] In addition to canonical provision enabling lay people to assist in liturgical action,[92] many diocesan norms deal directly with the problem of non-availability of ordained ministers for services (not only because of vacancy) which may then be conducted by lay persons.[93]

With regard to choice of liturgy, the Church of England is regulated by a large body of instruments provided by the central legal system as well as by diocesan regulations and guidance. The legal right to choose a particular liturgy lies in the first instance with the minister and the parochial church council jointly (Canon B3(1)). If these disagree, and so long as the disagreement continues, by operation of law the forms of service to be used are those contained in the 1662 Prayer Book. However, this need not be used if other forms of service were in regular use during at least two of the four years preceding the disagreement; in these circumstances 'the parochial church council . . . resolves that those other forms of service shall be used either to the exclusion of, or in addition to, the forms of service contained in the [1662] book'. If the council does not so resolve, the 1662 Prayer Book presumably is to be used.[94] There is no specific provision for the matter to be settled by the bishop. Nor are there specific provisions to determine what is to happen if several non-1662 Prayer Book services have been in use during this period. Although it prescribes that the council shall resolve that these other services are to be used, the canon does not prescribe what is to happen if there is disagreement as to which of these is/are to be used.[95]

Diocesan norms have gone some way to increase regulation for the problem of choice and disagreement, some stressing the concept of 'partnership' as the

[91] *MacAllister v Bishop of Rochester* (1880) 5 CPD 194 at 203; under C17(6) the archbishop may give permission to priests or deacons ordained overseas (within the meaning of the Overseas and Other Clergy (Ministry and Ordination) Measure 1967) or to a bishop in a church not in communion with the Church of England (whose orders are recognized or accepted by the Church of England) to officiate within his province: 'such minister shall possess all such rights and advantages and be subject to all such duties and liabilities as he would have possessed and been subject to if he had been ordained by the bishop of a diocese in the province of Canterbury or York.' [92] See *post* Part V.

[93] *TDH*, A.11. When no minister is available for Morning or Evening Prayer, 'the churchwardens are to arrange for "some suitable lay person" to officiate'); *SDDH*, B.28: when a lay person, other than a reader, is asked to conduct a family service on an occasional basis, written approval should first be sought from the area bishop; before giving permission the area bishop will wish to satisfy himself that the person has received suitable training, that the incumbent will ensure that adequate and on-going support is given, and that the proposal has the formal approval of the churchwardens and the parochial church council. When conducted on a regular basis a cleric or reader ought to attend.

[94] Canon B3(2), declaratory of CE(WD)M 1974, s. 1(3); for exceptions see B3(3), cathedrals.

[95] The canon does not state that 'all' services which were in regular use are to continue to be used, though this may have been the intention; if therefore the canon allows a discretion to choose between non-1662 Prayer Book services in use, and the incumbent and council cannot agree, it seems that the council must decide, subject to the Canon C24(7) duty to consult together on matters of general concern; see generally *supra* Ch. 4.

basis for joint agreement between the incumbent and the parochial church council.[96] Sometimes, however, with regard to alternative services and options within these (even when these are agreed), '[t]he decision as to which of these options will be used rests with the minister conducting the service and, strictly speaking, forms no part of the joint agreement between the incumbent and the PCC'; however, in such cases it is 'hoped that an incumbent will always discuss with the Council the way he proposes to conduct services and the options he proposes to use'.[97] Indeed, some diocesan regulations prescribe that if there is disagreement over the operation of Canon B3 (concerning choice) '[d]isputes shall be referred to the Bishop for guidance'.[98]

According to the Wakefield diocesan regulations, which generally incorporate the 1986 Guidance issued on the authority of General Synod's Standing Committee,[99] the council and incumbent ought in choosing to give 'particular attention to the views and preferences of those who come to church regularly, but the needs of those who attend occasionally require to be considered too'. With regard to these 'minority needs', there should, if possible be a solution which goes some way to meeting these which may be met satisfactorily if some provision is made for them at Sunday services. Parishes ought also to devise systems enabling periodical review of parish worship.[100] Any continuing disagreements should be referred to the rural dean and lay chairman of the deanery synod or to the archdeacon.[101] The Wakefield norms, again incorporating the 1986 Guidance, recommend a procedure for complaint. If members of a congregation who are not also members of the council are not content with the choice of services, and the use of alternative services in particular, they should inquire of the council secretary about the agreement reached in council and its liturgical policy and ask (or persuade) members of the council to raise the issue; if unsuccessful they should ask the secretary to table the matter for formal consideration by the council.[102]

The choice of liturgies for occasional offices (such as marriages, funerals, and perhaps baptisms) is governed by Canon B3(4).[103] When more than one form of any of the services known as occasional services (other than the order of confirmation) is authorized by Canon B1 for use on any occasion, 'the decision as to which form of service is to be used shall be made by the minister who is to conduct the service'. However, 'if any of the persons concerned objects beforehand to the use of the service selected by the minister, and he

---

[96] *TDH*, A.3; *SDDH*, B.2.　　[97] Ibid.　　[98] *BRDSEI*, Ai.

[99] *Public Worship*, 3–5.　　[100] *WDHI*, ch. 2, 11–18.

[101] Ibid., ch. 2, 32; 27–32 generally on disagreement.

[102] Ibid., ch. 2, 31: the matter may be raised directly at the annual parochial church meeting.

[103] See generally *OLAC*, 234 (for choice); the advice is silent as to whether, if there is no incumbent or priest-in-charge, a reader (if there is one) may act as 'minister'; 'occasional offices' do not seem to have been defined legally (*HLE*, para. 936, n. 6); they are commonly understood to include churching of women, ministry to the sick, and the ministry of absolution: see *HLE*, paras. 1045–7.

and the minister cannot agree as to which form is to be used, the matter shall be referred to the bishop of the diocese for his decision'.[104] The provision is badly constructed: it places no clear duty on the minister to consult the 'person concerned' (undefined) before making his decision and before their right to object arises, though this is arguably what was intended; nor does it clarify the binding (or otherwise) nature of the bishop's direction. Again, some diocesan norms treat the problem: '[i]n the case of the Occasional Offices (Baptism, Marriage, Funeral) the choice of service lies with the officiating minister', although any lay persons who are particularly involved are entitled to express their preference beforehand and, whenever possible, such preference should be respected by the officiating minister; if there is disagreement the matter 'should be referred to the Bishop, whose decision shall be final'.[105]

Liturgical Deviation and Variation

In its theological setting, viewing liturgical texts as 'living texts', there is a direct problem here for the legal system and its regulation of liturgical action—the legal regime seems to express a movement away from maximal regulation to minimal regulation, but not so far as deregulation.[106] The basic principle at work last century was summed up in *Martin v Mackonochie*: 'It is not open to a minister to the Church to draw a distinction in acts which are a departure from or violation of the rubric [of the 1662 Prayer Book], between those which are important and those which appear to be minor.'[107] Yet the courts had earlier introduced the possibility of deviation. In *Kemp v Wickes*, Sir John Nicholl explained in the Arches Court that '[i]t is by a lenient and liberal interpretation of the laws of disability and exclusion, and not by a captious and vexatious construction and application of them, that the true interests and the true dignity of the church establishment are best supported'.[108] Today, a minister may have a right to deviate from liturgies under the judicial principle that some liturgical rubrics might be classified as merely directory and not mandatory; rubrics are not to be interpreted in the same way

---

[104] A similar provision exists with regard to forms of service for ordination and resolution of the question by the bishop or archbishop; the minister of the church where the service is to be held has a right to be consulted: B3(5).

[105] *RBG*, A.1; see also *WDHI*, ch. 2, 22 (on the guidance contained in *Public Worship*, 6) for unilateral discretion as to special or occasional services.

[106] The creation and choice of liturgies may clearly be the subject of regulation, being concerned with visible and material decisions; the regulation of liturgical acts and postures, however, remains problematic. The liturgical jurisprudence of the Church of England has not developed concepts similar to those in Roman Catholic canon law presenting liturgical norms as aesthetic norms (see *supra* n. 68). The use of rules expressed in terms of *words* is, it is submitted, one major cause of the problem of regulation. The creation of instruction to enable a degree of flexibility, analogous to musical or choreographic instruction by *symbols*, has apparently not been explored as an alternative to regulation by word-norms.   [107] (1868) LR 2 A&E 116.

[108] (1809) 161 ER 1320 at 1333.

as a statute.[109] The classification has not been developed fully with the consequence that it is by no means clear when a rubrical requirement is obligatory and when directory.[110]

More importantly, an explicit right of unilateral ministerial deviation is conferred by Canon B5(1): '[t]he minister may in his discretion make and use variations which are not of substantial importance in any form of service authorised by Canon B1 according to particular circumstances'; he may vary both the authorized and the allowed liturgies.[111] The Canon forbids variations which are contrary to or indicate a departure from the church's doctrine in any essential matter; they must also be reverent and seemly (B5(3)). The minister must decide these matters in the first instance, but if there is any doubt a right exists to refer the matter to the bishop. The Canon does not specify who enjoys this right.[112] In any event there is no *duty* to refer the matter.[113] If referred, the bishop has a discretion: 'he may give such pastoral guidance, advice or directions as he may think fit'.[114] These provisions probably also apply to variations of occasional offices when these are authorized (or approved).[115] In any event, according to the opinion of the Legal Advisory Commission, '[i]n principle, each of the forms of service authorised by Canon B1 must be regarded as separate and distinct from the others'. As a general rule, therefore, 'an incumbent is not entitled to use—albeit with the approval of the [parochial church council]—a form of service which is in effect an amalgam of two or more of them'. As such, 'the BCP and the two ASB rites may all be available for use but on any given occasion one particular rite must be used, not a form of service combining elements from two or more'. There are two qualifications: a combination may be used (a) under the power to effect minor variations, and (b) where express provision is made in one form of service for borrowing material from another (but there is no such provision in the 1662 Prayer Book rite). The officiating minister, in the opinion of the

---

[109] *Bishopwearmouth (Rector and Churchwardens) v Adey* [1958] 3 All ER 441: strictly the *dictum* only applies directly to *judicial* interpretation of rubrics, and by inference to *ministerial* interpretation.

[110] Interestingly, CE(WD)M 1974 refers to the 1662 rubrics as 'directions' and 'instructions' (s. 5(2)).

[111] B5(1); the provision is declaratory of CE(WD)M 1974, s. 1(5); see for its predecessor the Prayer Book (Alternative and Other Services) Measure 1965 s. 5.

[112] B5(4): 'If any question is raised . . . it may be referred to the bishop'. Such a reference 'shall be without prejudice to the matter in question being made the subject-matter of proceedings under the Ecclesiastical Jurisdiction Measure 1963'.

[113] B5(4): 'it may be referred'. Compare the provision in the *BCP*, ix (discussed below), *requiring* questions of doubt with regard to the *BCP* to be referred to the bishop.   [114] B5(4).

[115] Oddly, however, Canon B5(1) includes reference only to forms of service 'authorised' under Canon B1. Occasional offices are not mentioned in B1, although B3(4) refers to 'occasional offices . . . authorised by Canon B1'; variation of services would seem to be possible when no provision is made in the authorized services under B5(2), as under B5(3) 'All *variations* in forms of service and all forms of service under this Canon' must be seemly, reverent, and not contrary to the church's doctrine.

Commission, 'may decide between any options authorised within any form of service and may make appropriate minor variations, but if the officiant is not the incumbent, the incumbent can give him directions'. Moreover, the parochial church council 'has the right to comment upon the choice of such options and the incumbent will presumably endeavour as far as possible to meet its views and those of the congregation, if they are made known'.[116]

The problem of variation has been treated in diocesan norms. These commonly repeat the principle that there is 'no lawful authority to abbreviate or adapt . . . services beyond the limit of the alternatives provided with the authorised text', not even to make it more convenient for the young.[117] Though legally the canons assign to the minister the function of determining whether a variation is seemly, reverent, not contrary to church doctrine, and not of substantial importance, diocesan norms exist which require that doubt about the 'definition' of such matters 'must' be referred to the bishop.[118]

Bishops and Liturgical Variation and Deviation

With regard to episcopal involvement in deviation and variation, a distinction must be made between authorizing deviation from an existing form of service and authorizing the use of a form of service when no provision exists. At the time of the prayer book controversy of 1928, convocation assumed (in its resolutions) a corporate and individual episcopal power to authorize deviations from the single liturgical use of the 1662 Prayer Book.[119] The bishop's *ius liturgicum* has enjoyed limited judicial recognition in relation to the authorization of liturgical actions when there is no legal provision on a matter.[120] A bishop may permit the use of a service when there is no existing provision;

---

[116] *OLAC*, 234; 235: to accommodate the 'realities of current practice' the Commission advises that with regard to the *BCP* rite of Holy Communion it would be lawful to substitute the summary of the law for the Ten Commandments, and to omit the exhortation and perhaps use a revised prayer for the church; these 'might therefore be regarded as not being of substantial importance'. The Collects are more difficult and with regard to the Epistles and Gospels, translations of these authorized under the Prayer Book (Versions of the Bible) Measure 1965 may be permitted with the agreement of the parochial church council; however, using passages from scripture or prayers instead of Collects 'wholly different from those appointed could not be regarded as within the scope of the officiant's discretion' under B5(1).   [117] *CAD*, 37.

[118] *RBG*, A.1: 'If there is any doubt about [whether the variation is reverent, seemly, or contrary to church doctrine] or if there is any question of the definition of the words "substantial importance" the matter must be referred to the Bishop'; *SDDH*, B.4; see also *TDH*, A.3, for reference to the bishop when a service may 'in any way' be considered 'unsound or questionable'; *WDHI*, ch. 2, 15: 'should' be referred for his 'pastoral guidance'.

[119] *Acts of Convocation*, 61 at 63.

[120] *Re Lapford (Devon) Parish Church* [1954] 3 All ER 484, concerning the reservation of the sacrament, Chancellor Wigglesworth recognized that '[w]hen the bishop considers that something not provided for is needed, it is for the bishop to make provision in the exercise of that authority which he has in his diocese'. See *post* Ch. 12.

intersticial liturgy-provision by bishops is lawful but limited. As we have seen, the ordinary has a general power under Canon B4(3) to 'approve forms of service for use in any cathedral or church or elsewhere in the diocese on occasion for which no provision is made'; he must, once more, be satisfied that 'in both words and order' the forms of service are 'reverent and seemly' and are neither contrary to nor indicative of a departure from the doctrine of the Church of England in any essential matter.[121] A bishop may not authorize the use of a service departing from the church's doctrine. Today, the episcopal power to authorize the use of services has been incorporated so extensively into the revised canons that a claim to employ a distinct and autonomous *ius liturgicum* would for practical purposes be unnecessary.[122] This is also acknowledged in diocesan norms, which sometimes recognize the bishop's power to authorize forms of service 'within his jurisdiction' for occasional use not found in the Prayer Book.[123] In addition, some general regulation exists at diocesan level concerning the role of a bishop present at actual services; sometimes these prescribe that a draft form of the service to be used must be sent to the bishop in advance of the service.[124]

The *ius liturgicum* and deviation from existing forms of service is rather different, however. When a bishop conducts a service himself, he may vary, subject to the same limitations, as may any minister under Canon B5.[125] However, the bishop has *no* liturgical right under the Canon to authorize ministers to deviate from or vary forms of service under the canons. As we have seen, under Canon B5(4) the minister may now vary unilaterally and there is no ministerial duty to refer the matter to the bishop. The bishop simply has a right to give guidance, advice, or directions if requested.[126] To this extent, any episcopal *ius liturgicum* that may have previously existed has in these circumstances been abrogated by the revised canons. However, if a question of deviation from the 1662 Book arises, 'to appease all such diversity . . . and for the resolution of all doubts . . . the parties that so doubt . . . shall resort to the Bishop of the Diocese, who by his discretion shall take order for

---

[121] B4(3), when no provision is made in the *BCP* or by General Synod under B2 or by Convocation or archbishops under B4; the Canon is worded subjectively and no express provision is made for an appeal against the bishop's decision.

[122] See *RACCL* (1947), memorandum on 'lawful authority' by Vaisey J, 215 *et seq.*; *HLE*, para. 934, n. 10: 'the "lawful authority" controversy may be said to be over'.

[123] *PDH*, H.1.2; *WDHI*, ch. 2, 23.   [124] *DSBN*, Ad clera notices, 1989/9.

[125] Interestingly, unlike the case of a non-episcopal minister, where a reference to an ecclesiastical superior—the bishop—is possible (B5(4)), if there is doubt as to whether a bishop's variation is (e.g.) contrary to the doctrine of the church, no express provision exists for a reference to (e.g.) the archbishop.

[126] For a challenge in the secular field to a Minister's 'direction' see *R v Secretary of State for Transport, ex p Greater London Council* [1986] QB 556; for a challenge to 'guidance' for want of rationailty, *R v Secretary of State for the Environment, ex p Nottinghamshire County Council* [1986] AC 240; for a general discussion as to whether there is a duty to follow episcopal 'guidance' see Chs. 1 and 7.

the quieting and appeasing of the same'.[127] This accords with the general provision in Canon C 18 that bishops have the power of ordering, controlling, and authorizing all services. As we have seen, the bishop also has extensive powers under Canon B 14A to dispense with the celebration of the statutory forms of service on a regular basis, subject to the limitations described above; this is only indirectly a use of liturgical power, more directly it is the use of an executive power to dispense with the application of liturgical canon law.[128]

LITURGICAL ECUMENISM

The bishop's *ius liturgicum* is built extensively into the new law on liturgical ecumenism. The diocesan bishop has the power (which if employed must be exercised in conjunction with the diocesan board of finance and the pastoral committee) to authorize the entering of church-sharing agreements enabling Church of England churches to be used for 'worship in accordance with the forms of service and practice of the sharing Churches'. The agreement may provide for joint services and 'may dispense, to such extent as may be necessary, with the requirement to hold certain services of the Church of England on Sundays and other days'.[129] Canons B43 and B44, promulged under the Church of England (Ecumenical Relations) Measure 1988, allow a bishop to authorize rites of other churches, non-internally authorized services, to be used in worship in Church of England churches.[130] In addition, he has power to authorize non-Anglicans to perform liturgical acts in Church of England services and to authorize Church of England clerics to perform liturgical services according to the rites of other churches.[131] The operative legal schemes are interesting in so far as they regulate the action of and confer conditional rights upon those who are not members of the Church of

---

[127] *BCP*, ix, 'Concerning the Services of the Church'; see *MIECL*, 57. There appears here, with respect to doubt about the *BCP*, to be a contradiction betwen the *BCP*, ix requirement and the permissive right in Canon B5(4).

[128] For the judicial enforcement of consultation procedures see *Re Union of Benefices of Whippingham and East Cowes, St James, Derham v Church Commissioners for England* [1954] 2 All ER 22 (PC); for a similar provision concerning funeral rites see Canon B38(2) and (6): 'If any doubts shall arise whether any person deceased may be buried according to the rites of the Church of England, the minister shall refer the matter to the bishop and obey his order and direction.'

[129] Sharing of Church Buildings Act 1969, s. 4.

[130] S. 1(c); for a Roman Catholic perspective see A. Tuché, 'The Code of Canon Law of 1983 and ecumenical relations', M. Thériault and J. Thorn (eds.), *The New Code of Canon Law*, Proceedings of the 5th International Congress of Canon Law (Ottawa, 1986) Vol. I, 401 at 408–10.

[131] Church of England (Ecumenical Relations) Measure 1988, s. 1(a) and (b). Under s. 3 the General Synod must ensure that no person, unless an episcopally ordained priest in a church whose orders are recognized and accepted by the Church of England, shall preside at the Holy Communion celebrated according to the rites of the Church of England; nor may any person (unless he is a Church of England clerk in holy orders) solemnize a marriage according to the Church of England's rites.

England.[132] The precise rules vary depending on the service involved. We shall deal with these in the following chapters. The general principles, however, are as follows.[133]

The Regulation of Invitations

Canon B43 enables baptized ministers and lay persons who are members of (and in good standing in) other churches to be invited in writing by the incumbent to perform certain liturgical acts in Church of England services.[134] The incumbent must obtain the approval of the bishop and the parochial church council to invite others to assist in the distribution of the sacrament at Holy Communion or if, on a regular basis, he wishes to invite a non-Anglican to say or sing Morning or Evening Prayer. An incumbent may only invite a non-Anglican to assist on a regular basis at baptisms, marriages, or funerals if requested by the parties involved and with episcopal approval. For confirmations and ordinations within the parish, the invitation may be given only by the bishop and with the approval of the incumbent and council. Those invited must also be authorized to perform similar liturgical functions in their own church. The bishop may authorize non-Anglican services to be used in Church of England churches. An incumbent with the approval of the bishop and the parochial church council may invite members of another church to take part 'in joint worship with the Church of England or to use a church . . . for worship in accordance with the forms of service and practice of that other church'.[135] Similar provisions exist with regard to cathedrals.[136]

Furthermore, Canon B43 enables clerics of the Church of England to perform acts in non-Anglican liturgies which they are able to perform in the Church of England. Bishops may accept invitations with the approval of the incumbent of the parish in which the service is to take place. If the service is being conducted in another diocese, the bishop must obtain the approval of the host diocesan bishop. A bishop wishing to take part in ordinations, confirmations, or to preside at Communion in another church must obtain the approval of the archbishop. Priests and deacons enjoy similar rights. Episcopal approval

---

[132] For discussion about the enforceability of rights of third parties see Ch. 16.

[133] Diocesan norms have been devised (1) to commend informal ecumenical gatherings or gatherings under the auspices of the council of churches (*CDH*, 64, with proper election to these by the parochial church council or the annual parochial meeting); (2) on setting up a bishop's adviser on ecumenism (*CF*, C.1 concerning new religious movements: 'Any attempts to use physical or psychological force . . . run counter to the principles of religious liberty and such practices are fundamentally unacceptable to the churches').

[134] Canon B43(1)(1); see the 'Stanwick Declaration' (1987) for concepts of 'co-operation to commitment'.

[135] Canon B43(9); see also the norms contained in *Multi-Faith Worship?*, 'Guidance on the situations which arise', published on behalf of the House of Bishops by the Inter-Faith Consultative Group of General Synod's Board of Mission (1993, GS Misc. 411).

[136] B43(10): the dean and chapter may invite with episcopal approval.

and the approval of the parochial church council is required before accepting an invitation to participate in any non-Church of England service on a regular basis. If the Anglican cleric (bishop or priest) is invited to preside at Holy Communion in another church the archbishop or the bishop (as the case may be) must not approve unless satisfied that there are special circumstances which justify acceptance of the invitation and that the rite and elements are not contrary to Church of England doctrine in any essential matter. Similarly, a bishop or priest participating in the ordination or consecration of a minister in another church may not (by laying on of hands or otherwise) 'do any act which is a sign of the conferring of Holy Orders, unless that Church is an episcopal Church with which the Church of England has established intercommunion'.[137] A deaconess, lay worker, or reader must obtain the incumbent's approval for occasional invitations; for participation on a regular basis, the bishop, the incumbent, and the parochial church council must all approve. When an incumbent withholds approval an invitee may appeal to the bishop who, if he considers the approval to have been withheld unreasonably, may authorize the applicant to take part in the other church's service. The bishop is under a duty to inform the incumbent 'of the reasons for his determination'.[138]

General executive guidance concerning the implementation of these provisions in the form of a Code of Practice is published under the authority of General Synod.[139] In some dioceses the terms of the Code have been incorporated into diocesan regulations some of which prescribe, for instance, that a use of B43 ought to be preceded by an application through the bishop's ecumenical officer though, in the case of occasional joint services, the bishop's approval 'should be taken as read'; if frequent and regular, and in all cases of doubt, the parties should consult the bishop's ecumenical officer.[140]

Local Ecumenical Projects

Under Canon B44 the diocesan bishop has a right to enter a Local Ecumenical Project agreement,[141] designed to enable the establishment of provisions about shared buildings, shared ministry, and shared liturgy.[142] A bishop has a right to

---

[137] B43(5).

[138] B43(7). There seems to be no right of appeal if an incumbent refuses a bishop.

[139] *Ecumenical Relations: Ecumenical Canons B43 and B44 Code of Practice* (1989), 10–12.

[140] *CF*, D.1; see also for ecumenical officers *DDBF*, A8 and A9 for special notice.

[141] Church of England (Ecumenical Relations) Measure 1988, s. 6(1): LEP means 'a scheme under which Churches of more than one denomination agree, in relation to an area or institution specified in the scheme, to co-operate in accordance with the provisions of the scheme in matters affecting the ministry, congregational life or buildings of the Churches which are participating in the scheme'.

[142] Church of England (Ecumenical Relations) Measure 1988, s. 2(1); *Code of Practice*, 31 (App. i); see also the British Council of Churches document *Local Church Unity* (1985); in Nov.

enter a local ecumenical project only with churches designated by the arch-bishops.[143] Before entering an agreement, the bishop must obtain the approval of the incumbent and parochial church council involved and the diocesan pastoral committee (after consultation with the deanery synod).[144] The agreement may last for not more than seven years and must be in writing. The bishop has the right to revoke any agreement unilaterally, thereby withdrawing the Church of England, but he is under a duty to consult with the appropriate authority of each participating church, each parochial church council, and the diocesan pastoral committee. The canon provides no specific right of appeal against the bishop's decision.

Once a bishop has entered a local ecumenical project he is no longer free to authorize *any* liturgical arrangements. The canon imposes upon the bishop the duty to make an instrument in writing before authorizing the performance of liturgical acts. Before making an instrument the bishop must consult the parochial church council involved. The episcopal instrument may dispense in part with the required regular services,[145] and it may authorize ministers of participating churches to baptize in Church of England churches in accordance with a rite authorized by the participating church. The episcopal instrument may also authorize a priest of the Church of England or a non-Anglican minister to preside at a service of Holy Communion in accordance with a rite authorized by a participating church and it may authorize joint services including baptism and confirmation. The bishop must be satisfied that the participating church's rites do not depart from the doctrine of the Church of England.[146] The bishop has a right to revoke or amend an instrument by making a subsequent instrument only after consultation with the parochial church council concerned. There is an overriding requirement: the bishop shall so exercise his powers 'as to ensure that public worship according to

1988 there were 550 LEPs and the Church of England is a full partner in about 75% of these. The leaders in an LEP form the Sponsoring Body. LEP churches make a formal agreement, to which the Church of England bishop may be party; this is a local covenant registered with the Sponsoring Body; the LEP may have a constitution spelling out in detail the terms of the agreement: *Code of Practice*, 1–9.

[143] Church of England (Ecumenical Relations) Measure 1988, s. 5(1); the archbishops cannot designate a church which does not subscribe to the doctrine of the Holy Trinity or does not administer the sacraments of baptism and Holy Communion; the Sharing of Church Buildings Act 1969 must also apply to the designated church. *Code of Practice*, App. I (including, *inter alia*, the Roman Catholic Church, the Baptist Union, the Greek Orthodox Church, the Methodist Church, and the Moravian Church). The matter has been the subject of regulation at diocesan level: *CF*, D.2 (the parish contemplating an LEP must consult the bishop's ecumenical officer); *PDH*, App. 12; *RBG*, A.12–13 (obligation to follow the Code of Practice; A13 lists churches in communion with CE); for distinction between 'local covenant' (based on the notion of a solemn agreement/pledge before God, B43) and LEP (B44) see *BRDSEI*, Ji.   [144] Canon B44(1).

[145] I.e. those services under para. 2 of B11, para. 1 of B11A, paras. 1 and 2 of B14, B40. He may also regulate invitations under B43.

[146] Under B44(1)(e) the bishop can make provision 'for the holding of joint services with any other participating church'.

the rites of the Church of England is maintained with reasonable frequency in a parish'.[147]

LITURGICAL OFFENCES: JUDICIAL CONTROL

A further function of the law is to protect the free enjoyment of liturgical action: this is secured by both church-made and state-made law. Broadly, the former regulates the performance of liturgical acts by the clergy by means of rules creating ecclesiastical offences. The latter regulates disturbance of liturgy through disorder by means of criminal offences. As a general principle, the dominant secular law operative in this area is applicable equally to the Church of England and the Roman Catholic Church.

In the first instance, rules imposing ministerial duties to provide services, those requiring the use of legally approved liturgies, and those forbidding substantial deviations are enforceable by executive episcopal action.[148] Their violation may also be treated in the church courts. To this extent, the law of the Church of England allows for judicial control of liturgical action. Illegal liturgical action may constitute an ecclesiastical offence. Under the Ecclesiastical Jurisdiction Measure 1963, proceedings may be instituted charging an offence against the laws ecclesiastical involving matters of ritual and ceremony.[149] Though a substantial deviation could in theory result in judicial proceedings, the effects of the nineteenth-century ritualist cases would render a prosecution unlikely today.[150] Indeed, in so far as the 1963 Measure was enacted when the dominant principle was that of uniformity, the extent to which a ritual offence might be committed, in the light of the considerable flexibility afforded by the new authorized liturgies, has not been settled or clarified.

Ministerial failure to perform liturgical duties may constitute neglect of duty if serious, persistent, or continuous.[151] Though the Ecclesiastical Jurisdiction Measure 1963 does not specify the mental elements of liturgy-related offences, on the authority of several nineteenth-century judicial dicta it seems likely that a cleric would technically have a defence if his action was neither intended nor wilful.[152] If neglect of duty is only occasional or accidental then, needless to say, a defence is available, but a mistaken notion of a minister's rights would

---

[147] B44(5).   [148] See *supra* Ch. 7.

[149] S. 14(1)(a); in *Heywood v Bishop of Manchester* (1884) 12 QBD 404 non-observance of the *BCP* was classified as an offence 'against ritual'; for ecclesiastical offences see *supra* Chs. 5, 7.

[150] *Gore-Booth v Bishop of Manchester* [1920] 2 KB 412; *Heywood v Bishop of Manchester* (1884) 12 QBD 404; *Elphinstone v Purchas* [1870] LR 3 A&E 66 (no deviation); *Newbery v Goodwin* (1811) 1 Phillim 282; it was decided in *Hutchins v Denziloe and Loveland* (1792) that if a minister introduces any irregularity into a service, the churchwardens cannot interfere but must refer the matter to the bishop.   [151] EJM 1963, s.14(1)(b)(ii).

[152] *Rugg v Bishop of Winchester* (1868) LR 2 A&E 247.

not excuse.[153] The courts may also enjoy a degree of liturgical control under the faculty jurisdiction.[154]

With regard to protection against disturbance, under the Ecclesiastical Courts Jurisdiction Act 1860 it is a criminal offence to commit 'riotous, violent or indecent behaviour' in the course of lawful liturgical action.[155] Protection is afforded equally to Church of England and Roman Catholic liturgy. The offence may be committed in any cathedral, church, or chapel of the Church of England, in any chapel of any religious denomination, or in any certified place of religious worship.[156] This applies not only when those acts are committed during the celebration of 'divine service' but at any time, including in any churchyard or burial ground.[157] Moreover, it is a criminal offence to molest, disturb, vex, or trouble (or by any other unlawful means to disquiet or misuse) any preacher duly authorized to preach or any clergyman in holy orders ministering or celebrating any sacrament or any divine service, rite, or office.[158] The offence may be committed by a clergyman acting in an indecent or violent way in his own church or churchyard.[159] Trial is summary, with appeal against conviction lying to the crown court.[160]

Under the Offences Against the Person Act 1861 it is also an offence to obstruct (or attempt to obstruct) by threats or force any clergyman or other minister in or from celebrating divine service or otherwise officiating in any church, chapel, meeting house, or other place of divine worship. The same applies with respect to the performance of a duty in the lawful burial of the dead in any churchyard or other burial place. Similarly, it is an offence to strike or offer any violence to (or to arrest pursuant to any civil process) any clergyman or other minister who is engaged in (or is, in the knowledge of the offender, about to engage in) any of these rites or duties (or is in the offender's knowledge going to or returning from their performance).[161] Disruption of lawful liturgical action may lawfully be dealt with not only by the police but

---

[153] *Bennett v Bonaker* (1828) 2 Hag Ecc 25.   [154] See *post* Ch. 16.

[155] S. 2; for 'indecency' see *Worth v Terrington* (1845) 13 M&W 761 at 795; indecency need not simply signify that which tends to deprave or corrupt, nor need it have sexual connotation: it simply means creating a disturbance: *Abrahams v Cavey* [1968] 1 QB 479 ('Oh you hypocrites, how can you use the word of God to justify your policies', shouted after the Foreign Secretary had read a passage from Micah 4 at a service arranged and televized for a Labour Party conference in a Methodist church, was an offence); in *Jones v Catterrall* (1902) 18 TLR 367 'idolatory' called out during the service was held to be 'indecent'.   [156] Places of Worship Registration Act 1855.

[157] See also Burial Laws Amendment Act 1880, ss. 7, 8.

[158] Ecclesiastical Courts Jurisdiction Act 1860, s. 2; *Cope v Barber* (1872) LR 7 CP 393; for a wide understanding of 'sacrament' and 'divine service' see *Matthews v King* [1934] 1 KB 505; 'clergyman in holy orders' normally excludes a minister not episcopally ordained: *Glasgow College v AG* (1848) 1 HL Cas 800 at 819, 823. For the possibility of proceedings under the 1860 Act in the diocese of Blackburn with respect to intrusion during a baptism service see *Times* 18 Nov. 1994.   [159] *Vallancey v Fletcher* [1897] 1 QB 265.

[160] Ss. 2, 4; Criminal Justice Act 1967, s. 92(1), Sched. 3, Part 1; Courts Act 1971, ss. 8, 56(2), Scheds. 1, 9, Pt. 1.

[161] Offences Against the Person Act 1861, s. 36; Criminal Law Act 1967, s. 1.

also by church authorities.[162] One of the duties of churchwardens is to maintain order at the time of divine service but, according to the Legal Advisory Commission, their power to apprehend or eject must be exercised 'without unnecessary violence [to] any person creating a disturbance'.[163] A person may be removed for disturbing the congregation at the time of divine service even though no part of that service is actually proceeding at the time.[164]

CONCLUSIONS

Liturgical law in the Church of England has undergone radical reform in the last twenty years. Though much of the large body of operative law retains the traditions of the past, the principle of uniformity has been replaced by that of conformity. The Book of Common Prayer 1662 is now only one of a multiplicity of liturgical forms permitted for use by the General Synod which, like the pontiff in Roman Catholic canon law, possesses the ultimate legal power of liturgical authorization. Significantly, however, the law distributes rights to authorize liturgies throughout the church: to Convocation, the archbishops, bishops, and to ministers. There is at work a principle of liturgical subsidiarity enabling partnership between clergy and laity, but the new allowed liturgies must not depart from the church's doctrine. A new feature of the modern legal framework of the Church of England, and of structures operating within that framework, is the introduction of regulation not only by the central legal system itself but also by central executive guidance and by norms operating at diocesan level. The control of liturgical law and order rests principally with the bishop (though collectively the House of Bishops is increasingly issuing statements in this area). He occupies a key administrative position: his *ius liturgicum* now has a firm legal basis and is incorporated extensively into the law; it has enjoyed a new lease of life particularly in the episcopal right to regulate liturgy in its ecumenical setting. As in Roman Catholic canon law, flexibility is the essential mark of liturgical law: ministers and the parochial laity enjoy rights of liturgical choice and ministers have an express right of liturgical variation without episcopal approval.

[162] Ecclesiastical Courts Jurisdiction Act 1860, s. 3.
[163] Ibid.; Canon F15(3); *OLAC*, 48.
[164] *Williams v Glenister* (1824) 2 B&C 699

PART V

The Rites of the Church

11

Baptism and Confirmation

Whether the Church of England ought to employ liberal or restrictive approaches to the admission of candidates for baptism has been the subject of much debate recently.[1] In contrast with the Roman Catholic Church,[2] the use of canonical regulation in the Church of England is limited. Canon law, which governs preparation and admission, imposes a general duty on ordained clergy not to refuse baptism: it confers a ministerial right only to delay, and norms have been devised at diocesan level to regulate the use of this discretion. Celebration of baptism is governed principally by liturgical rubrics and after-care by canon law and, in more detail, by diocesan norms. In this Chapter we shall examine these arrangements and the canonical regulation of preparation for and admission to the twin initiation rite of confirmation, which has similarly been extensively supplemented by diocesan norms.

PREPARATION FOR BAPTISM

The doctrine of the Church of England treats baptism and the Eucharist together as a dominical sacrament.[3] Baptism is 'a sign of profession, and mark of difference, whereby Christian men are discerned from others that be not christened' as well as a 'sign of Regeneration or new Birth, whereby, as by any instrument, they that receive baptism rightly are grafted into the Church'. By baptism 'the promises of forgiveness of sin, and of our adoption to be the sons of God by the Holy Ghost, are visibly signed and sealed; Faith is confirmed, and Grace increased by virtue of prayer unto God'.[4] These

---

[1] M. Reardon, *Christian Initiation: A Policy for the Church of England*, A Discussion Paper, GS Misc 365 (London, 1991) 48–9 (at 5: in 1970 there were 466 baptisms in the Church of England for every 1,000 live births; by 1987 there were 289); *Baptism, Thanksgiving and Blessing*, A Report of the Doctrine Commission, GS 56 (London, 1971); *Baptism, Eucharist and Ministry 1982–1990: Report on the Process and Responses*, World Council of Churches (Geneva, 1990).

[2] *CIC*, c. 840: sacraments as instituted by Christ are actions of the church and of Christ, and participation in them contributes to the process of sanctification; c. 841: the power to determine what constitutes validity rests with the supreme authority; cc. 213, 843: a right to the sacraments exists if the candidate seeks them at the appropriate time, with the proper disposition, and is not prohibited by law; c. 842: the initiatory sacraments are baptism, confirmation, and Eucharist; c. 844: sharing of sacraments; c. 845: general prohibition as to repetition; c. 846: sacramental laws are to be observed strictly; c. 848: prohibits payment for the sacraments; see T. Tierney, 'The right of the faithful to the sacraments', *Catholic Lawyer*, 23 (1977), 57.　　　　[3] *AR*, Art. 25.

[4] Ibid., Art. 27; diocesan policies often describe baptism as both a gift from God and a human response. See e.g. Sheffield diocesan synod's *Infant Baptism* (1984), a resource leaflet containing

doctrinal ideas concerning the nature and effect of baptism are reflected in the liturgies: in baptism, commanded by Christ, the baptized becomes a member of the fellowship of the church, receiving forgiveness of sins and being brought by the Holy Spirit to new birth and made one with Christ in his death and resurrection.[5] Baptism has not been defined canonically beyond the statement that by it the newly baptized are received 'into Christ's Church'.[6] The same understanding appears in judicial decisions.[7] Baptism has additional legal effects: it is a pre-condition for admission to holy communion, ordination, and to various ecclesiastical offices and institutions.[8] Similarly, Roman Catholic canon law presents baptism as the gate to the sacraments, necessary for salvation in fact or at least in intention, freeing individuals from their sins and effecting for them a rebirth as children of God configured to Christ; by it they are incorporated into the church.[9] Both churches forbid the repetition of baptism.[10]

In common with Roman Catholic canon law,[11] rules concerning preparation vary depending on whether the candidate is an infant or adult. In relation to infant baptism, as a preliminary '[d]ue notice, normally of at least a week, shall be given before a child is brought to the church to be baptised'.[12] The

the policy agreed by the diocesan synod, Sheffield Diocesan Education Committee: 'Baptism is an occasion for the experience of pardoning, conversion, cleansing' by which a person gains 'admission to the family of the Church'.   [5] *ASB*, 243 ff.

[6] Canon B21; in so far as liturgical definitions have been approved by canon (B1), these may be said in a loose sense to enjoy canonical authority.

[7] *Kemp v Wickes* (1809) 3 Phillim 264; ER 1320 at 1322 *per* Dean of Arches; for the idea that baptism effects regeneration see *Escott v Mastin* (1842) 13 ER 241 at 249 and *Gorham v Bishop of Exeter* (1850) Moore's Special Reports 462; *Williams v Bishop of Salisbury* (1864) 2 Moore PCCNS 375; *Re St Barnabas, Kensington* [1990] 1 All ER 169 at 171, for the orthodoxy of the doctrine of 'one baptism for the remission of sins'.

[8] Canons B15A, C4(1), D2(1), E4(1); for lay admission to institutions see *supra* Ch. 8.

[9] *CIC*, cc. 204, 849; see *LG*, 16 for baptism by desire; c. 205: the baptized are fully in communion with the Catholic church who are joined with Christ in its visible structure by the bonds of profession of faith, of the sacraments, and of ecclesiastical government; *COCLA*, 157; see also A. Tuché, 'The code of canon law of 1983 and ecumenical relations', M. Thériault and J. Thorn (eds.), *The New Code of Canon Law*, Proceedings of the Fifth International Congress of Canon Law (Ottawa, 1986) I, 401 at 402.

[10] *AR*, Art. 27: 'The baptism of young Children is in any wise to be retained in the Church, as most agreeable with the institution of Christ'; M. Reardon, *Christian Initiation*, 21; G. W. Kuhrt, *Believing in Baptism* (Mowbrays, 1987) 74: the idea is proposed that infant and adult/believer baptism are not 2 different entities but should be expounded in the same theology; see below for repetition.

[11] *CIC*, c. 851: 'it is necessary that the celebration of baptism be properly prepared': parents and sponsors must be suitably instructed so that they 'understand the meaning of this sacrament and the obligations which attach to it'; c. 852: the provisions of the canons on adult baptism apply to all who, having ceased to be infants, have reached the use of reason; c. 11: the use of reason is presumed on completion of the 7th year; c. 97: adulthood is attained on completion of the 18th year.

[12] Canon B22(1); the provision does not specify upon whom the duty to give notice is cast, presumably on parents or guardians seeking baptism, but not on godparents; for diocesan norms requiring notice of 1 month see e.g. *SDDH*, C.2, *CDH*, 91, *PDH*, H.3.2; for notice longer than 1 week, see *TBF*, 3.16.

minister is under a canonical duty to instruct 'the parents or guardians of an infant to be admitted to Holy Baptism that the same responsibilities rest on them as are in the service of Holy Baptism required of the godparents'.[13] Whilst parents or guardians have, therefore, a canonical right to instruction, the canons are silent as to the standard and the subject-matter of instruction: in Roman Catholic canon law instruction must include teaching about the meaning of the sacrament.[14] The duty to instruct does not apply to baptism administered in emergencies.[15]

Provision for preparation and instruction is often made in the Church of England by norms operating outside the canons: these are designed to ensure that the parents or guardians are aware of the significance of baptism and serve a function broadly comparable to norms issued by the conference of bishops in the Roman Catholic Church.[16] By Act of Convocation, clerics are recommended to visit the homes of godparents to enquire 'as to [their] spiritual fitness' and to explain the meaning of the sacrament and their responsibilities.[17] Diocesan synods frequently issue baptismal 'policies' requiring each parish to have a scheme of preparation for parents, and where possible godparents, before baptism takes place.[18] Parochial policy expressed in a scheme should be agreed by the parochial church council and the incumbent. Forms of preparation vary and sometimes state that the scheme should not be so harsh as to alienate the people from the life of the church nor so lax as to give the impression that baptism is a mere formality.[19] Diocesan norms occasionally encourage the involvement in preparation of an 'outside consultant' who has experience in this particular pastoral area.[20] The catechumenate (comprising

[13] Canon B22(3); interestingly, the liturgical rubrics do not require that the minister be satisfied before celebration that the parents or guardians have been instructed; for godparents' responsibilities see below. [14] *CIC*, c. 851(2).

[15] If a person survives and a service is subsequently conducted in church there is no express duty to instruct (*ASB*, 280); baptism has occurred and C22(3) applies only before its celebration; cf. the Roman Catholic position under *CIC*, c. 865(2): in danger of death the person must have 'some knowledge of the principal truths of the faith'. [16] *CIC*, c. 455.

[17] *Acts of Convocation*, 66–7 (adoption of recommendations by Canterbury convocation, 1939); ibid. 155 (1957): 'the Minister should see the parents and proposed godparents in order to explain to them their part in the Service, the obligations which they assume, and their responsibilities in the after-care of the child'; this seems wider than the duty under Canon C8(4) which empowers ministers to visit the homes of those on the electoral roll.

[18] E.g. *SDH*, I, B.2(a) and 3; as to the legality of these doctrinal statements under the terms of SGM 1969, s. 4(1) see *supra* Ch. 9.

[19] *SDH*, I, B.2(a); the requirement of agreement envisaged here is very different from (and perhaps contrary to) the principle that the incumbent must only consult and co-operate with the council under Canon C24(7) and PCC(P)M 1956, s. 2(1), (2)(a): these suggest that all such decisions belong to the incumbent alone: see *supra* Ch. 9 for legality of doctrinal statements under ibid. s. 2(2)(b).

[20] Sheffield Diocese, *Infant Baptism* (1984); see also *BRDSEI* , Bi: the incumbent with the assistance of the council should formulate a positive approach to the education of parents; *LDR*, 15: regular review of preparation programme; *PDH*, H.3.1, App. 8; *DSBN*, Ad clerum notice, 1989/14: visits; *TBF*, 3.16: 'The minister should be satisfied that the parents are aware of the significance of the promises they will make in the service and can make these promises in good faith.'

the body of candidates for baptism) is not an institution known to the Church of England's contemporary law as it is in Roman Catholic canon law, though there have recently been calls for its reinstatement and for the formation of a register of those preparing for baptism.[21]

With regard to adult baptism, the minister has a canonical duty to instruct, or cause to be instructed, a candidate 'of riper years and able to answer for himself . . . in the principles of the Christian religion'; the minister must also 'exhort' the candidate to 'prepare himself with prayers and fasting that he may receive this holy sacrament with repentance and faith'.[22] As these duties to prepare and instruct apply only to a candidate 'able to answer for himself' *and* 'of riper years'[23] it seems unlikely that they apply also to infants (not being of riper years) who are able to answer for themselves; the expression 'riper years' is not defined and the use of the word 'and' in the canon suggests that the duties do not apply.[24] The canonical provision governing those who are to be received into the Church of England by baptism simply states that these 'shall be instructed'; it does not spell out the terms of the ministerial duty nor the standard and subject matter of instruction.[25]

INFANT BAPTISM

In common with the Roman Catholic Church, Church of England clergy are under no canonical duty to seek out candidates for baptism.[26] In the Roman Catholic Church parents have a canonical duty to bring children to be baptized; in the Church of England this duty is imposed not by the canons but by liturgical rubrics; it also appears in an Act of Convocation.[27] There is no

---

[21] M. Reardon, *Christian Initiation*, 9–10, 35–9; see also the Board of Education working party's *A New Revised Catechism* (London, 1990); for the catechumenate in the Roman Catholic Church see *CIC*, cc. 205–6 and *supra* Ch. 9; for episcopal regulation, cc. 455, 788, 863.

[22] Canon B24(1); *BCP*, 279, Ministration of Baptism to Such as are of Riper Years.

[23] Canon B24(1); in cases where the candidate is mentally handicapped, for example, this requirement would apparently not apply.

[24] However, see below for their role in the liturgy under *ASB*, 241 (n. 2).

[25] Canon B28(1); the provisions of B24(1) presumably apply.

[26] See, however, *BCP*, 573 and the duty under the Ordinal charge 'to seek for Christ's sheep . . . that they may be saved through Christ for ever'; see also *post* n. 140.

[27] *CIC*, c. 867, normally within 'the first few weeks' of birth, or if in danger of death 'without delay'. Whilst it is still understood that the *BCP* requires clergy to admonish the people that they do not defer baptism of infants any longer than 2 Sundays after the birth of the child (Hill, *EL*, 297, n. 19), no such requirement is found in the current edition of the *BCP* (nor does such a provision appear in the *ASB*); for a reference (without discussion) to the possibility that parents are under such a duty, see *Christian Inititation*, 15–16; the duty to admonish had been recognized by Act of Convocation: *Acts of Convocation*, 69. The statute 3 Jac 1, c. 5, s. 14 (repealed) obliged 'all popish recusants' to bring their children to be baptized in the parish church. For this, and the view of Dr. Lawrence (1806) that—given the duty extends to 'any infant' ('any child' under Canon 68 of the 1603 Canons)—'[t]here is no distinction of parishioners who frequent the church or any other place of worship': R. Phillimore, *Ecclesiastical Law*, Vol. 1, 494–5.

express equivalent in English canon law to the Roman Catholic rule that parental consent (or that of guardians) must be given to make the celebration of infant baptism licit.[28]

Admission and Exclusion

Whereas in Roman Catholic canon law there is a general right to baptism,[29] in the Church of England the right of a parent to have a child baptized arises indirectly from the ministerial duty to baptize. As a basic principle, the minister is under a canonical duty to baptize all infants from the parish who are presented as candidates: no minister 'shall refuse or . . . delay to baptise any infant within his cure that is brought to the church to be baptised'.[30]

Canon B22(4) allows considerable ministerial discretion to delay baptism and even to refuse it, but its terms are far from clear. First, a ministerial delay is lawful 'for the purpose of preparing or instructing the parents or guardians or godparents'.[31] The canon does not clarify whether lack of understanding, genuine intent, right reasons for seeking baptism, fitness, or willingness to practise the faith constitute lack of preparation and instruction and therefore grounds for delay.[32] Secondly, though strictly the canonical duty to give notice is not binding on the laity,[33] no minister may refuse or delay baptism 'provided that due notice has been given'.[34] In other words, if parents or guardians fail to notify as prescribed, a ministerial refusal or delay will be lawful, presumably until notice is duly given.[35] Thirdly, no minister may refuse or delay baptism 'provided that . . . the provisions relating to godparents in these canons are observed': if the canonical requirements concerning godparents are not met then ministerial refusal or delay will, it seems, be lawful.[36] In all three sets of circumstances it is not clear whether the minister *must* refuse or delay or

---

[28] *CIC*, c. 868(1).

[29] *CIC*, cc. 213, 843: '[t]he sacred ministers cannot refuse the sacraments to those who ask for them at appropriate times, are properly disposed and are not prohibited by law from receiving them'; see M. R. Quinlan, 'Parental rights and admission of children to the sacraments of initiation', *Studia Canonica*, 25 (1991), 385.

[30] Canon B22(4); *BCP*, 263 (rubric); Canon 68 of the 1603 Canons contained no limitation of the duty to those 'within his cure'.   [31] Ibid.

[32] M. Reardon, *Christian Initiation*, 27 identifies 3 possible situations: (i) the parents genuinely want their children to be baptized and brought up as Christians, and are genuinely open to becoming practising Christians themselves; (ii) the parents genuinely want their children to be baptized and, so far as they understand it, want them brought up as Christians, but do not appear to be ready to become practising Christians themselves; (iii) the parents want their children to be baptized apparently for wrong and quite inadequate reasons, and are most unlikely ever to want to become practising Christians themselves; 'those in category (i) should be allowed baptism, those in category (iii) should normally not, and those in category (ii) would still be treated differently by different parishes and clergy'.   [33] See *supra* Ch. 8.

[34] B22(4).

[35] Ibid.: the Canon does not specify whether the minister may or must delay in the absence of notice.   [36] See below for the qualifications and fitness of godparents.

whether he mostly has a *discretion* to do so.[37] The position in Roman Catholic law is clearer: if the hope that the infant will be brought up in the Catholic religion is 'altogether lacking, the baptism is to be put off according to the prescriptions of particular law'; the parents must be informed of the reason.[38]

These difficulties have prompted the suggestion in the Church of England that the terms of the canon law be altered to extend to the minister a right to exclude if the sponsors are not 'willing and able' to fulfil their promises or if there is no evidence of a 'sincere desire' on the part of parents or guardians that the child shall grow up as part of the Christian community.[39] Whilst the modern liturgy requires parents, guardians, and godparents to declare publicly that they are 'willing' to assist in the building up of the candidate's faith,[40] there has been no debate as to whether a genuine and honest belief on the part of the minister that such a declaration would be offensive both to the consciences of the minister administering it and the parties making it would give rise to a legal right to objection.[41] Indeed, diocesan norms concerning the terms of Canon B22(4) vary. Whilst many repeat the basic prohibition against refusal,[42] others aim to impose the obligation that the minister 'should seek' an assurance that baptismal responsibilities will be faithfully observed.[43] When a

[37] M. Reardon, *Christian Initiation*, 32; the draft canon proposed by the *RACCL* (1947) prescribed that refusal and delay would be lawful in the absence of notice and in the absence of candidates for godparent satisfying the canonical qualifying requirements (for draft Canons 30 and 31, see ibid., 122–3).

[38] *CIC*, cc. 867, 868(1), (2); the Sacred Congregation for the Doctrine of the Faith in 1970 decreed that delay should occur in relation to those parents 'who are polygamous, unmarried, married lawfully but lapsed altogether from the regular practice of the faith, or those who request their child's baptism as a purely social convention'.

[39] M. Reardon, *Christian Initiation*, 7, 10–11, 32 for the history of these proposals; the Ely Commission Report, *Christian Initiation: Birth and Growth in the Christian Society*, GS 30 (London, 1971): 'We believe . . . that the rite of Infant baptism may properly be administered to children whose parents show real and positive evidence that initiation into the church will be accompanied by instruction for life in the faith'; however, 'We are, indeed, unanimously of the opinion that the Church must never refuse Baptism if sincerely desired for their child by its parents or guardians'. The Doctrine Commission Report, appended to the Ely Report, concluded: 'if the parents are clear that Baptism is what they are seeking, and are prepared to make the promises, they ought not to be refused' (para. 10).

[40] *ASB*, 243; *BCP* makes no reference to parental promises.

[41] It is arguable that the minister has a duty to protect the consciences of parishioners under the ministry of cure of souls; see also ECHR, Art. 9(1): the right to freedom of conscience; see below for conscientious objection in *Bland v Archdeacon of Cheltenham* [1972].

[42] *SDDH*, C.4; *PDH*, H.3.2.

[43] *RDL*, BP.3; *RBG*, A.4: 'Occasions may arise when an incumbent may feel that it is right to refuse or to postone baptism. When a parish has a "baptismal policy" the understanding and goodwill of neighbouring parishes should be sought, the policy must be that of the parish and not simply of the incumbent, and the policy, so far as is humanly possible, should be administered so sensitively as to eliminate as far as possible a feeling of rejection by the parents. Ideally the decision not to proceed should be the parents' decision. In every case the Service of Thanksgiving for the Birth of a child . . . should be offered and it should also be offered to those parents who are conscientiously unable to take part in a baptism Service'; for similar provision see also *BDM*, E.2. The thanksgiving service (*ASB*, 213) is a normative precursor to baptism.

baptismal policy operates, within the general framework of a diocesan synod policy, some norms state that 'where the right dispositions appear . . . to be lacking, the parish priest might rightly urge the parents to postpone'; avoiding any suggestion of rejection, 'ideally the decision not to proceed should be the parents' decision.[44]

Enforcement

In the Church of England, refusal or delay may be the subject of executive or judicial regulation. If the minister 'shall refuse or unduly delay to baptise any such infant', the parents or guardians (but not the proposed godparents) have a right to apply to the diocesan bishop; the bishop is under a canonical duty to consult with the minister and must give such directions as he thinks fit.[45] If the bishop directs the minister to proceed with baptism, ordinarily the minister must obey the episcopal direction.[46] If the bishop directs not to proceed there is no express right of recourse to (for example) the provincial archbishop; in the absence of a right of appeal, the matter may be the subject of judicial review.[47] The matter may also be the subject of an application to the European Commission on Human Rights.[48]

An unlawful refusal may also constitute a judicially actionable ecclesiastical offence of ministerial neglect of duty.[49] The Arches Court in *Bland v Archdeacon of Cheltenham* concerned neglect of duty to admit to baptism under

---

[44] *LDR*, 15; *LDHI*, III, 1; *ODYB* 234: if there is a decision to delay, the period for postponement should be fixed. [45] B22(2).

[46] See *supra* Ch. 7; arguably the bishop has no power to refuse, as this would amount to complicity in the minister's violation of Canon B22(4); there is no express episcopal power to dispense with the duty imposed by B22(4).

[47] This may be the case in so far as the matter involves a public law right: see *supra* Ch. 5. Canon Law Society *Newsletter*, No. 96 (1993) 17, 'Exercise of parental role of Muslim father over Christian baptism of daughter', extract from *Independent* 24 July 1993, concerning a Muslim father who sought an injunction under the Children Act 1989 to prevent the mother (to whom he was not married) from having their child (in the mother's custody) baptized in the Church of England: Swindon County Court remitted the matter to the High Court. I have not been able to trace any further information relating to this case.

[48] It has been decided by the European Commission on Human Rights that a minister of an established church may not impose conditions for baptism contrary to lawful directives of superior church authorities: J. E. S. Fawcett, *The Application of the European Convention on Human Rights* (2nd edn., Oxford, 1987) 249, 250: the applicant, a minister in the state church of Denmark and incumbent of a parish, made it a condition for baptism that the parents attend 5 periods of religious instruction; the church authorities were of the opinion that he had no such right and advised him to abandon the practice. He refused to do so: a consistory court postponed its treatment of action against him pending the Commission's decision on the admissibility of his application under ECHR, Art. 9(1). The Commission decided that 'Art. 9(1) does not include the right of a clergyman in his capacity of a civil servant in a State church system to set up conditions for baptising, which are contrary to the directives of the highest administrative authority within that church': 7373/76 (Denmark) 5 DR 157.

[49] EJM 1963, s. 14, neglect must be serious, persistent, and continuous; s. 16: a single act or omission of neglect suffices.

Canon 68 of the 1603 Canons.[50] The minister explained in the consistory court that 'he demurred at baptizing the child on grounds of doctrine and conscience' — 'neither of the parents were regular communicants', '[t]he father was not a believer and declined to attend church', there was 'no reasonable prospect that the child would be given a Christian upbringing or instruction, or any encouragement in the Christian faith' and to have baptized would have been 'an instance of indiscriminate infant baptism' which the minister held to be 'contrary to the true doctrine of the Christian faith and to Holy Scripture'.[51] The minister's appeal against conviction was allowed because, *inter alia*, the chancellor had misdirected the assessors on the meaning of neglect of duty. It was held that 'the act of refusal to baptize a child is not a doctrinal offence . . . [but] is concerned with pastoral work and activity'. A refusal must be intended: if at interview with the parent the minister expresses 'a clear and final intention not to baptize the child if and when brought to the church for baptism, it would constitute a refusal'. A refusal would not in general be lawful because based on a conscientious objection, though exclusion because of adherence to a particular doctrinal view of baptism derived from Anglican theology must be put to and taken into account by the assessors in trying the case.[52] A delay would not constitute an offence: '[i]n his evidence [the appellant] maintained that he was thinking of delay rather than complete refusal, and if that had been accepted, the alleged offence could not be sustained.' It would be lawful to delay to 'instruct the parents further and consider with them all that is involved in the solemn rite of baptism, for the child, for the parents and the godparents, and for the church community'. The Deputy Dean did not elaborate on the reasonableness of a delay: in any event a delay, it is submitted, would be regulated by episcopal direction.[53]

Special Cases

As in Roman Catholic canon law,[54] a minister ordinarily baptizes only those children whose parents reside within his territorial cure of souls. When a minister 'intends to baptise any infant whose parents are residing outside the boundaries of his cure . . . [he] shall not proceed to the baptism without having sought the goodwill of the minister of the parish in which such parents

---

[50] [1972] 1 All ER 1012; the charges related to events in 1966.   [51] Ibid., 1016.

[52] Ibid., 1017–18 (absence of a general right to conscientious objection was based on a decision of the provincial court in *Watkins-Grubb v Hilder* (1965) (unreported); see *supra* Ch. 7.

[53] Reliance on Acts of Convocation in this regard may have justified a delay; if the appellant had been 'influenced by the high ideals of the importance of baptism, which are generally consistent with those expressed in several official reports and decisions of the Convocations and in the report and resolutions of the Anglican bishops at the 1948 Lambeth Conference', this 'would have been highly relevant on the issue whether the neglect of duty (if any) was serious': ibid., 1018.   [54] *CIC*, c. 862.

reside'.[55] The structure of this Canon imposes only a duty to seek the goodwill of the other minister, there is no canonical duty to obtain the goodwill (or consent) of that minister, nor does the latter enjoy a canonical right of veto.[56] Whilst many diocesan norms simply repeat this principle[57] some impose a duty to *obtain* the other minister's goodwill and consent.[58] Whether such norms are contrary to the Canon or merely impose a requirement additional to that in the Canon depends on whether the Canon is construed widely or restrictively. Furthermore, diocesan norms sometimes prescribe that ministers should agree on the date and place of baptism as well as a programme for preparation and follow-up: if agreement cannot be reached the matter should be referred to the bishop 'whose decision is final'.[59] By canon, however, a minister must baptize if the names of the parents or of one of them are on the electoral roll of the minister's cure.[60] Some diocesan norms expressly extend these general procedures to baptism before and after adoption.[61]

Baptism in time of emergency poses different problems. As a general principle, the minister of every parish 'shall warn the people that without grave cause and necessity they should not have their children baptized privately in their houses'.[62] When proposing to baptize a child in a hospital or nursing home (and presumably other places *sui generis*) whose parents do not reside in his cure (or whose names are not on the electoral roll) the minister shall send their names and addresses to the minister of the parish in which they reside.[63] In extreme cases, no minister 'being informed of the weakness or danger of death of any infant within his cure and therefore desired to go to baptise the same shall either refuse or delay to do so'; a ministerial failure may constitute neglect of duty.[64] The same rule applies in the Roman Catholic

[55] B22(5). The use of the word 'intends' merely covers cases where delay or refusal would be otherwise justified: see above; the 1947 draft Canon 30(2) simply imposed the duty 'to send the Minister . . . the name and address of the infant': *RACCL*, 122; see also *Acts of Convocation*, 68: 'Inasmuch as the jurisdiction of a parish priest in the cure of souls does not extend beyond the borders of his parish', baptism 'ought not to be administered to the children of persons beyond the priest's jurisdiction *without the knowledge* of the incumbent of the parish in which those persons reside' (emphasis added).

[56] Cf. the terms of Canon B44(4)(1)(c): celebration of baptism according to another church's rite 'with the goodwill of the persons concerned'.

[57] *PDH*, H.3.2; *ODYB: IF*, 234; *RBG*, A.4; *BDM*, E.1; *LDR*, 15; *SDDH*, C.5.

[58] For the duty to obtain goodwill or consent see *TBF*, 3.16; *BRDSEI*, Bi; *LDHI*, III, 1; *CDH*, 92; *CF*, C.2; *DSBN*, Ad clerum notice 1989/14: If the minister is unwilling to give his consent on grounds thought to be unreasonable the matter should be referred to the Bishop for his decision'; *SDH*, I, B.7, 5: 'The goodwill of the incumbent of the parish where they live should be obtained'; *NDIB*, I, 2.1: approval if possible.

[59] *SDH*, I, B.7. Beyond the diocesan bishop's powers as 'principal minister' (C18(1) and (4)), there seems to be no clear legal basis for provisions of this type. [60] B22(5).

[61] *SDH*, I, B.9.

[62] B22(9); the norm is for full liturgical public celebration: see below for Canon B21.

[63] B22(7).

[64] B22(6). In other words, the minister cannot be compelled to travel beyond the boundary of his cure; the draft Canons of 1947 (Canon 30(4) had prescribed that the minister must not refuse or delay 'lest it die through his default unbaptized': *RACCL*, 122; for neglect of duty in extreme cases see *HLE*, para. 1357, n. 8 (no authority given).

Church.[65] A special modern liturgy has been designed for emergency baptism. Its terms place the responsibility for requesting emergency baptism on parents (there is no reference to guardians) and the minister is under a duty to assure them that questions of 'ultimate salvation' or questions concerning a Christian funeral do not depend upon whether or not the child has been baptized.[66] A minister has a canonical duty to bring a child baptized in emergency who survives to church to be received into the congregation according to the form and manner prescribed by the office for private baptism authorized by canon.[67] In Roman Catholic canon law the infant of Catholic parents or of non-Catholic parents who is in danger of death is validly and licitly baptized 'even against the will of the parents'.[68]

ADULT BAPTISM

Canonical regulation of baptism of those of riper years is less detailed, and in some key respects radically different from that regarding infant baptism. In Roman Catholic canon law, though all unbaptized people are able to be baptized, '[t]o be baptised, it is required that an adult have manifested the will to receive baptism'.[69] In the Church of England, at least a week before the baptism is to take place, by canon 'the minister shall give notice to the bishop of the diocese or whomsoever he shall appoint for that purpose'. Moreover, '[e]very person thus baptised shall be confirmed by the bishop so soon after his baptism as conveniently may be; that so he may be admitted to the holy Communion'.[70] There is no canonical provision concerning ministerial refusal or delay in baptizing adults.[71] This silence may suggest a greater degree of ministerial discretion here than for infant baptism, but whether it generates a legal liberty to exclude (in the absence of wish or undertaking to be confirmed or of commitment which the candidate must profess liturgically at baptism) has not been settled by the formal law. The matter is, however, frequently regulated by diocesan norms. Sometimes these prescribe that baptism should take place only where there is an expectation that the candidate will be confirmed as soon as possible afterwards.[72] Some norms allow adult baptism only at a confirma-

---

[65] *CIC*, c. 867(2): 'An infant in danger of death is to be baptised without any delay'.

[66] *ASB*, 280–1; the right to the normal burial service is not unconditional: for Canon B38(2) and *BCP*, 326 see *post* Ch. 14.

[67] B22(8); *ASB*, 280. Although not specified, the duty is presumably cast on the parents or guardians.

[68] *CIC*, c. 868(2); the rule has been the subject of much criticism: see J. W. Robertson, 'Canons 867 and 868 and baptizing infants against the will of parents', *The Jurist*, 45 (1985), 631; c. 870: a foundling or abandoned child is to be baptized unless upon diligent investigation proof of baptism is established; c.871: if aborted feotuses are alive, they are to be baptized if possible.

[69] *CIC*, cc. 864–5.   [70] Canon B24(2), (3).

[71] Canon B22 is headed simply 'Of the Baptism of Infants'.

[72] *SDH*, I, B.10; *BRDSEI*, Bi; *CF*, C.2.

tion service unless 'pastoral or practical needs' require otherwise.[73] Whereas the Church of England seems to have no explicit provision for baptism of adults in danger of death, the Roman Catholic Church operates the rule that an adult in danger of death may be baptized if 'the person has in any way manifested an intention of receiving baptism and promises to observe the commandments of the Christian religion' in the event of survival.[74]

CELEBRATION OF BAPTISM: VALIDITY AND REGULARITY

Roman Catholic canon law presents the minimal criteria for a valid baptism; requirements in the Code regulate its full liturgical celebration. Baptism should be administered in accord with the order prescribed in the approved liturgical books, except for the case of urgent necessity when only what is required for the validity of the sacrament must be observed,[75] that is 'washing with true water together with the required form of words'.[76] In the Church of England the criteria for valid baptism are defined not in the canons but by liturgical formulae and judicial decisions. Emergency baptism, in which the minimal requirements must be satisfied, may be taken as the paradigm. Baptism may be celebrated outside a full liturgical context only when 'grave cause and necessity' require.[77] Baptism is administered validly with the application of water and with the recital of the words 'I baptize you in the name of the Father, of the Son, and of the Holy Spirit'.[78] The decision in *Kemp v Wickes*[79] clarified some basic principles. First, 'the use of water with the invocation of the name of the Father, of the Son, and of the Holy Ghost, [is] held to be the essence of baptism'. Secondly, 'baptism, so administered, even by a layman or a woman, was valid'. Thirdly, 'a person, who had been so baptized was not to be baptized again'. Fourthly, 'provided the essence of baptism, according to what has generally been received among Christians as the essence of baptism, had taken place', baptisms administered in other churches will be recognized as valid for the purposes of the Church of England.[80] Fifthly, baptisms adminis-

---

[73] *ODYB: IF*, 234; *TBF*, 3.16.   [74] *CIC*, c. 865(2).   [75] C. 850.   [76] C. 849.

[77] B22(9): the minister of every parish 'shall warn the people that without grave cause and necessity they should not have their children baptised privately in their houses'.

[78] *BCP*, 278, rubric towards the end of the Ministration of Private Baptism of Children; *ASB*, 280.

[79] (1809) 3 Phill 264 at 269; ER at 1322, 1324 *per* Dean of Arches, Sir John Nicholl: this had been the case 'from the earliest times'. The case concerned exclusion from burial of a person who had been baptized by a dissenter); *AR*, Art. 27, which speaks of the 'wholesome effect' of baptism; *ASB*, 224: 'a second birth, new creation and life in union with [God]'; for *BCP* and survival of idea as part of pre-Reformation canon law see *Escott v Mastin* (1842) 13 ER 214 at 249.

[80] *Kemp v Wickes* 270–1: the Dean of Arches listed baptisms in the Roman Catholic Church, the Greek Church, the Presbyterian Church, and those by the Calvinistic Independents; 'it could not be said of any of these persons that they were unbaptized; each had been admitted into the Christian Church in a particular form'.

tered privately are valid.[81] These principles have been applied in a series of subsequent cases.[82] They do not, however, specify whether the baptizer must have a right intention to effect valid baptism, whether the baptizer must be a baptized person,[83] or whether the candidate must have a right intention.[84] In Roman Catholic canon law, similarly, a lay person can baptize validly in cases of necessity though it is unclear whether the baptizer's right intention is a criterion of validity; baptism is not to be conferred in a private house outside the case of necessity.[85]

In the Church of England other requirements regulate the full liturgical celebration of baptism, violation of which will render the baptism not invalid but irregular. By canon '[i]t is desirable that every minister having a cure of souls shall normally administer' baptism on Sundays at public worship when the most number of people come together, so that 'the congregation there present may witness the receiving of them that be newly baptised into Christ's Church'.[86] The service is to be conducted in accordance with the authorized or approved baptismal liturgies found in the Book of Common Prayer 1662, in the Alternative Service Book, and the Series II services.[87] The same approach is employed by the Roman Catholic Church.[88]

In common with the Roman Catholic Church,[89] the law provides no single method for the application of water in baptism. Though canonically '[i]n every church and chapel where baptism is to be administered, there shall be provided a decent font with a cover for the keeping thereof',[90] there is no legal

---

[81] Ibid. 285: 'baptism in a house . . . performed by a layman . . . [even] without necessity . . . was not an invalid baptism, and the party could not be re-baptized'.

[82] The decision was followed concerning the same subject by the Arches Court in *Escott v Mastin* (1842) 4 Moo PCC 104; 13 ER 241; *Nurse v Henslowe* (1844) 3 Notes of Cases 272; *Titchmarsh v Chapman* (1844) 3 Notes of Cases 370; *Cope v Barber* (1872) LR 7 CP 393 at 402 per Willes J; *Re St Barnabas, Kensington* [1990] 1 All ER 169 at 171: 'Baptism can be received only once'.

[83] See *Escott v Mastin* (*supra* n. 82) 253–4 for the suggestion that a baptizer need not have been baptized in order to administer baptism validly.

[84] However, for adult baptism (esp. for repentance) a right intention is envisaged in the liturgy but no rule requires it: *ASB*, 231–2, *BCP*, 283–5.

[85] *CIC*, cc. 861, 863: reservation to the bishop; c. 860: private homes and hospitals.

[86] Canon B21; diocesan norms invariably repeat this and often recommend that, if the baptism is to be private, some regular members of the congregation ought to be present: *TBF*, 3.16; *PDH*, H.3.2; *SDDH*, C.9.

[87] The administration of these is governed by the principles described in Ch. 10.

[88] *CIC*, c. 850: in accordance with the approved liturgies; c. 856: on Sunday, cc. 857, 859: in the parish church, unless just cause suggests otherwise.

[89] *CIC*, c. 854: 'baptism is to be conferred either by immersion or by pouring, the prescriptions of the conference of bishops being observed'; c. 853: outside necessity cases, water should be blessed.

[90] F1(1); it 'shall stand as near to the principal entrance as conveniently may be, except there be a custom to the contrary or the Ordinary otherwise direct; and shall be set in as spacious and well-ordered surroundings as possible': para. (2); the font bowl 'shall only be used for the water at the administration of Holy Baptism and for no other purpose whatsoever': para. (3); for House of Bishops' resolutions 1987 see *Re St Barnabas, Kensington* [1991] Fam 1: a baptismal pool is lawful; for incorporation of these resolutions in diocesan norms see e.g. *PDH*, App. 14; *Re St George's, Deal* [1991] Fam 6; cf. *Re St Nicholas, Gosforth*, ELJ, 1(5) (1988), 4; for the Roman Catholic requirement that there be a font see *CIC*, c. 858.

requirement that baptism must take place at the font.[91] Indeed, immersion, affusion, submersion, and sprinkling are all lawful methods of administration.[92] However, according to liturgical norms, a 'threefold administration of water (whether by dipping or pouring) is a very ancient practice of the Church, and is commended as testifying to the faith of the Trinity in which candidates are baptized. Nevertheless, a single administration is also lawful and valid.'[93] Canonically, signing with the cross is 'no part of the substance of the sacrament' but its use is lawful,[94] and by liturgical norms the sign of the cross may be made in oil blessed for this purpose.[95]

At the service the parties to the baptism, including the congregation, are under a canonical duty to perform those acts and responses required by the authorized baptismal liturgies.[96] Baptisms may be lawfully administered (as in Roman Catholic law) by an ordained minister, normally a priest, or in the absence of a priest or when required to do so a deacon.[97] Baptisms administered by readers or lay workers are valid but, it seems, irregular.[98] In the case of infant baptism, by liturgical norms the parents and godparents present the candidate and must make declarations promising to bring up the child in the Christian faith.[99] The members of the congregation are not required to do likewise though they are under a duty to welcome the newly baptized.[100] When a child is old enough to understand, the parents and godparents answer the questions put and 'at the discretion of the priest the children may also answer them'.[101] With regard to baptism of a person of riper years, by liturgical norms the candidate must declare to uphold and live the Christian faith; again, the congregation must welcome the newly baptized but there is no declaration to support them, although provision exists for the renewal of the congregation's baptismal vows.[102] No specific canonical provision has been made with respect to the baptism of the mentally handicapped.[103] Members of other churches

---

[91] *ASB*, 247, permitting dipping or pouring.

[92] D. Stancliffe, 'Baptism and fonts', *ELJ*, 3 (1994), 141; G. K. Brandwood, 'Immersion baptistries in Anglican churches', *Archeological Journal*, 147 (1990), 420.

[93] *ASB*, 242 (n. 9).   [94] Canon B25.   [95] *ASB*, 241 (n. 3).

[96] B9(1), (2). For the non-binding effect of the canons on the laity see *supra* Ch. 8; for Roman Catholic canon law see *supra* n. 89.

[97] B21; *ASB*, 241 (n. 1); *BCP* (Ordinal) 553 at 565; whilst Canon C18(4) deals with the bishop administering ordination and confirmation, it does not expressly empower the bishop personally to administer baptism in the parish.

[98] See *supra* Ch. 8; arguably, any other lay person could lawfully administer baptism in a full liturgical setting—*ASB*, 241 (n. 1): 'Holy Baptism is normally administered by the parish priest . . . and he may delegate its administration to other lawful ministers. Where rubrics indicate that a passage is to be said by "the priest", this must be understood to include any other minister authorized to administer Holy Baptism.'   [99] *ASB*, 243.

[100] Ibid., 242 (n. 7); 226 (n. 12), for baptism, confirmation, and Holy Communion); 248: the welcome.   [101] *ASB*, 241 (notes); *BRDSEI*, Bi.

[102] *ASB*, 234; see *CIC*, c. 866 for confirmation immediately following baptism of adults.

[103] *Baptism, Eucharist and Ministry 1982–1990*, Report on the Process and Responses (1990) 47: 'the church today should be able, on sound theological and psychological grounds, to provide the blessing of baptism and life in the community for persons who are physically or mentally impaired'; for Roman Catholic approaches see J. Huels, '"Use of reason" and the reception of the sacraments by the mentally handicapped', *The Jurist*, 44 (1984), 209.

(including lay persons) may upon invitation assist in the baptism (but not baptize) if they are authorized to perform a similar duty in their own church.[104] A Church of England bishop may authorize ministers of other churches participating in a local ecumenical project, with the goodwill of the persons concerned, to baptize in a place of worship of the Church of England in accordance with a baptismal rite authorized by any participating church; he may also make provision for the holding of joint services of baptism.[105] Though video-recording of baptisms has not been the subject of specific legislation, permission to do so must, in the opinion of the Legal Advisory Commission, be sought from the incumbent.[106]

CONDITIONAL BAPTISM AND REBAPTISM

Conditional baptism is permitted in Roman Catholic canon law.[107] In the Church of England, when 'the validity of a former baptism can be held in question' any person 'desiring to be received into the Church of England . . . shall be instructed and . . . conditionally baptised'.[108] Though conditional baptism of infants is not specifically addressed by the canons, liturgical provision is made for this.[109] Whilst the Church of England recognizes forms of baptism celebrated in other churches,[110] there have been calls to regulate more explicitly the case of those baptized in infancy in the Church of England who seek 'rebaptism'.[111] Occasionally diocesan norms prescribe that if a

---

[104] B43(1)(1)(e); *Ecumenical Relations: Code of Practice* (1989) 26; for procedures and consents see *supra* Ch. 10

[105] B44(4)(1)(c),(e); for this and a common baptismal certificate see *Ecumenical Relations: Code of Practice* (1989), 26.

[106] *OLAC*, 80–2, 92–4; 80: parochial fees orders made under the Ecclesiastical Fees Measure 1986 do not prescribe a fee for granting permission to record a baptism; it is for the parochial church council to determine whether a fee should be charged for using audio- or video-recording equipment inside the church; but the incumbent retains the right to refuse to allow a baptism service to be recorded; any fees paid either by the parents or the recordist are payable to the council and not to the incumbent. [107] *CIC*, c. 869.

[108] Canon B28(1); the ministerial duty is mandatory, presumably if a genuine desire is present.

[109] *BCP*, 273, rubric for the Ministration of Private Baptism of Children; *ASB*, 279: the minister is under a rubrical duty to administer baptism in the form, 'N, if you have not already been baptized, I baptize you . . . '; see also *Escott v Mastin* (1842) 13 ER 241 at 253–4.

[110] See *Kemp v Wickes* (1809) ER 1320 at 1322, 1324; *Ecumenical Relations: Code of Practice* (1989) 27 (para. 104): in an local ecumenical project that includes those who think that infants are not proper candidates for baptism, 'the consciences of individuals and of the ministers of other Churches should be respected in this matter': 'At the same time no practice should be agreed that repeats, or appears to repeat, baptism once given'; para. 105: some local ecumenical projects (in which the Baptist Church participates) provide that where a baptized individual is baptized again they are deemed to be members of the Baptist church alone and not of any other participating church; para. 106: 'In an LEP the issue of who may be admitted to baptism, and what preparation is to be required, should be discussed with representatives of other participating Churches in the Sponsoring Body.'

[111] M. Reardon, *Christian Initiation*, 43–7, without contradicting the church's teaching on the indelibility of baptism; see also *Kemp v Wickes supra* n. 110 at 1329.

candidate expresses commitment and questions the validity of a first baptism (usually as an infant), because it is seen to have lacked any genuine response to faith, such requests 'should always be refused'; refusal must be accompanied by an explanation; if immersion is appropriate, the minister must explain that this is not itself baptism.[112]

AFTER-CARE OF THE BAPTIZED

Canon law of the Church of England makes provision for the care of the newly baptized but only in relation to infants. Whilst priests also owe a general and continuing duty to those baptized within their cure of souls, this responsibility is assigned principally to the parents and godparents, an arrangement similar to that of sponsors in the Roman Catholic Church.[113] Though a right to nominate a person as godparent vests in the parent or guardian,[114] admission to the office of godparent is in the keeping of the minister responsible for the baptism. An infant candidate must have no fewer than three godparents, of whom at least two shall be of the same sex as the child and at least one shall be of the opposite sex, 'save that, when three cannot conveniently be had, one godfather and godmother shall suffice'.[115] Parents may be godparents for their own children 'provided that the child have at least one other godparent'.[116] To qualify as a godparent a candidate must be baptized and confirmed, though the minister may 'dispense with the requirement of confirmation in any case in which in his judgment need so requires'; if the minister chooses not to dispense with the requirement, no express right of appeal to the bishop is provided.[117]

The responsibilities of godparents are fixed by canon. A godparent shall be a person 'who will faithfully fulfil their responsibilities both in their care for the children committed to their charge and by the example of their own godly living'.[118] At the service of baptism both parents and godparents assume the obligation to give the child the help and encouragement it needs, by prayer, example, and teaching.[119] A candidate of riper years shall choose three, or at

---

[112] See e.g. *RBG*, A.4.

[113] *CIC*, c. 872, assigned to both infant and adult candidates; c. 873, only one male or one female sponsor or one of each sex is to be employed; c. 874, they must: have completed their 16th year, be confirmed Catholic and have received the Eucharist, and not be the parent of the candidate; the canons do not spell out their responsibilities beyond that of helping the baptized 'to lead a Christian life in harmony with baptism'.

[114] This is not given by canon but seems to be assumed: *Acts of Convocation*, 66: 'to induce and assist parents to obtain suitable sponsors'.

[115] B23(1); these provisions are not strictly binding on the laity (see Ch. 8).

[116] B23(1); *Acts of Convocation*, 67: 'It may be pointed out that the child's parents may often be the best godparents.'

[117] B23(4); in the absence of a right of appeal, judicial review may lie: *supra* n. 47.

[118] B23(2).

[119] *ASB*, 243; *BCP*, 266 ff.

least two, sponsors 'who shall be ready to present him at the font and afterwards put him in mind of his Christian profession and duties'; the same qualification and power of dispensation applies to sponsors as to godparents.[120] Failure to discharge responsibilities imposed by canon may be addressed by executive direction but cannot be the subject of judicial proceedings.[121] The Legal Advisory Commission has suggested that godparents 'have no obligation in substantive law and there is no legal significance in a particular person being a godparent'.[122] It has also been pointed out by the Commission that though there is no procedure to enable parents of a child to remove one godparent and substitute another, there is no reason why 'parents should not make an informal arrangement with other persons to act as additional "godparents"'.[123] Nor is canonical provision made for the appointment of substitutes upon the death of a godparent.[124]

The spiritual significance of baptism, the generality of these provisions, and perhaps the problem of enforcement, have stimulated the development of norms at diocesan level. These frequently prescribe continuing care of the newly baptized and of the family if there is one. Surprisingly, however, no provision is usually made for the continuing care of godparents or sponsors. Diocesan norms go some way towards the principle of delegation of functions and responsibilities. Acknowledging that care of the newly baptized is the responsibility of the whole church, norms commonly prescribe that parochial church councils should design schemes for post-baptismal follow-up and nurture, for the training of lay people to carry out this work, for regular review of follow-up arrangements, and for the duty to inform families concerned about the possible involvement of lay people in after-care.[125] Diocesan arrangements of this sort are supported by the moral authority of Act of Convocation. Visitation of baptized children should be undertaken with a view to their enrolment in the parish Sunday school or to their being otherwise instructed; where possible baptized children should be commended to the clergy when they move from one parish to another; and attendance at public worship should be encouraged from the earliest years: Sunday School should not be regarded as a substitute for taking part in public worship.[126] When a minister baptizes a child whose parents reside in another parish, 'a

---

[120] B23(3). This duty does not seem to be mentioned in the liturgies; as to the applicability of godparents' qualifications to sponsors, see ibid., para. (4).   [121] See *supra* Ch. 8.
[122] *OLAC*, 137.   [123] *Ibid.*

[124] The popular idea that godparents become legal guardians *ex officio* in the event of the death of parents seems to be without foundation; see generally *OLAC*, 137.

[125] *SDH*, I, B.2(c); Sheffield Diocese, *Infant Baptism*; *PDH*, H.3.9; *LDR*, 15; *CDH*, 92–3; *SDDH*, C.10, 11; *LDHI*, III, 2; *NDIB*, I, 2.1; *CF*, C.2; this is wider than the legal duty on the incumbent and council to consult and co-operate: *supra* n. 19.

[126] *Acts of Convocation*, 156 (1957 Recommendations).

certificate of baptism should be sent to the parish priest who is responsible for the pastoral care' of the baptized infant.[127]

To assist the process of follow-up, and to enable verification that baptism has been administered, as in Roman Catholic canon law,[128] a record of baptisms must be kept. In all matters pertaining to the registration of baptisms, every minister must observe the law from time to time relating thereto.[129] By canon in every parish church where baptism is to be administered there must be provided a register book which must be maintained and kept in accordance with statutes and measures and the rules and regulations made under them from time to time in force.[130] The duty to provide a register lies with the parochial church council.[131] By synodical measure ministers have a duty to register all public and private baptisms administered in the parish; the baptism must be registered as soon as possible after its celebration.[132] When the ceremony of baptism is performed in any place in a parish other than a parish church by a person who is not a minister of the parish, the person by whom it is performed must as soon as possible after its performance send to the incumbent or priest-in-charge a certificate signed by him certifying when and where the ceremony was performed.[133]

CONFIRMATION

As with baptism, the administration of confirmation is governed not only by rules of the central legal system of the Church of England but also by norms

[127] Ibid., 68; for baptismal certificates see *post* n. 132.   [128] *SDH*, I, B.8, 9.
[129] Canon B39(1); *CIC*, cc. 875–8.
[130] Canon F11(1),(2); Parochial Registers and Records Measure 1978, s. 1(1); *Acts of Convocation*, 155: the names of godparents should whenever possible be recorded in the baptismal register and on certificates of baptism (a Recommendation of 1957).
[131] Parochial Registers and Records Measure 1978, s. 1(2); under s. 6 custody of the register belongs to the incumbent and in a vacancy to the churchwardens.
[132] Ibid., s. 2(1); Baptismal Registers Measure 1961, s. 2 governs certificates (see Sched., Pt. II for the form of the certificate including the 'Christian name of the baptised person'); a fee is payable: Parochial Fees Order 1995, Sched., Pt. 1; parish registers are public books: *Dormer v Ekyns* 2 Barn 269; a parish baptismal register stating the date of birth is not sufficient evidence of this: *R v Clapham* 4 C&P 29. For diocesan norms and the baptism of adopted children see *LDHI*, III, 2; *BDM*, E.3; *PBR*, III.1; *NDIB*, I, 3.
[133] Parochial Registers and Records Measure 1978, s. 2(2); s. 2(3) (as amended by the Church of England (Miscellaneous Provisions) Measure 1992, s. 4, Sched. 1, para. 2): when the ceremony is performed in an extra-parochial place or an institution to which a cleric is licensed under the Extra-Parochial Ministry Measure 1967, s. 2, then (unless the ceremony if performed in a church, chapel or institution for which a register is provided), the person who performed the ceremony must as soon as possible send a certificate signed by him to the incumbent or priest-in-charge of, in the case of a ceremony performed in an extra-parochial place, such of the adjoining parishes as the diocesan bishop may direct, or, in the case of an institution, the parish in which the institution is situated. Correction of errors is governed by s. 4. The general provisions are applicable also *inter alia* to cathedrals, collegiate churches, and any other church not belonging to a parish: s. 5.

operating at diocesan level. In contrast with Roman Catholic canon law,[134] the Church of England's law contains no definition of confirmation.[135] According to the Thirty-Nine Articles, confirmation is 'not to be counted for [a sacrament] of the Gospel' for it has 'not any visible sign or ceremony ordained of God'.[136] Nevertheless, confirmation is treated today as an integral part of the initiation process, its celebration separated chronologically from baptism by the development of the practice of infant baptism.[137] In theological terms, broadly, whereas in baptism the Holy Spirit visits to cleanse, to effect forgiveness, regeneration, or new birth, and to admit to Christ's church, in confirmation by the laying on of hands the Holy Spirit is represented as confirming or sealing baptism, as entering to dwell, and as conferring the gifts of the Spirit to strengthen the candidate for life in the Christian faith, the candidate also ratifying or confirming baptism.[138]

Preparation and Admission

In the Roman Catholic Church the principal responsibility to ensure that confirmation is conferred on those who 'properly and reasonably request it' rests with the diocesan bishop.[139] Parents and pastors are to see that the faithful are properly instructed to receive it and that it is approached at the appropriate time.[140] Church of England canon law requires every minister who has a cure of souls to seek out diligently children and other persons 'whom he shall think meet to be confirmed'. The minister is under a canonical duty to 'use his best endeavour to instruct them in the Christian faith and life as set forth in the Holy Scriptures, the Book of Common Prayer, and the Church Catechism'.[141]

[134] *CIC*, c. 879: 'The sacrament of confirmation impresses a character and by it the baptized, continuing on the path of Christian inititation, are enriched by the gift of the Holy Spirit'; it binds the individual 'more perfectly to the church; it strengthens them and obliges them more firmly to be witnesses to Christ by word and deed and to spread and defend the faith'.

[135] Cf. Canon 60 of the 1603 Canons: 'all bishops should lay their hands upon children baptized and instructed in the catechism of Christian religion, praying over them, and blessing them, which we commonly call confirmation'; for episcopal laying-on of hands as confirmation see Canon B27(1): no fuller canonical definition is given than this.   [136] *AR*, Art. 25.

[137] For the historical background see G. Dix, *The Theology of Confirmation in Relation to Baptism* (London, 1946, Reprint, 1948); O. C. Quick, *The Christian Sacraments* (London, 1927, Reprint, 1955) 190 ff.; J. Martos, *Doors to the Sacred* (London, 1981). For the idea (used in Orthodox theology) of baptism and confirmation as a single rite, confirmation being the second of the two baptismal acts, see A. J. Mason, *The Relation of Confirmation to Baptism* (London, 1891); cf. for the development of the view that the Holy Spirit is conferred at baptism G. W. H. Lampe, *The Seal of the Spirit* (London, 1951); for three schools of thought on the relation of baptism to confirmation in the Church of England see *Ecumenical Relations: Code of Practice* (1989) 28.

[138] *ASB*, 246, 256, 258; *BCP*, 297 ff.; Ecumenical and Report of the Joint Committee of the Convocations of Canterbury and York, *Baptism and Confirmation Today* (1954) for 'water-baptism' and 'spirit-baptism'.   [139] *CIC*, cc. 885, 899.

[140] C. 890.

[141] Canon B27(2); this duty may embrace the duty to seek out the unbaptized: *supra* n. 26; for the catechism (hardly used today), *BCP*, 289: 'An instruction to be learned of every person before he be brought to be confirmed by the bishop'.

Diocesan norms prescribe that before candidates are presented for confirmation the minister must verify baptism and that there should be a full course of instruction which each candidate has attended regularly. These norms graft onto the canonical duty the requirement that instruction should cover the teaching of the church and the responsibilities of church membership.[142] Though neither canon law nor (usually) diocesan norms require the godparents (or indeed the whole church community) to prepare a candidate specifically for confirmation, a duty is assumed by the liturgical promise at baptism for parents and godparents to bring baptized infants to confirmation.[143] Whilst canon law places the primary responsibility to instruct on ministers, there is no legal obstacle to this function being performed by any member of the laity reasonably qualified to do so: often diocesan norms encourage the full participation of the congregation in the preparation process.[144] If a candidate (usually an adult) seeking confirmation is unable to accommodate parochial arrangements concerning instruction, there seems to exist no provision by which a person might satisfy the need for instruction any other way.

In Roman Catholic canon law the faithful are obliged to receive confirmation at the appropriate time, being at 'about the age of discretion'; all baptized persons are capable of receiving confirmation. Outside the danger of death, to be licitly confirmed it is required that, for any person with the use of reason, candidates be suitably instructed, properly disposed, and able to renew their baptismal promises.[145] A person cannot, it seems, at any time demand confirmation in the Church of England as of right.[146] The church employs a system of qualifications for candidature; if these are not met a minister is *prima facie* under a duty to refuse to present (and the bishop is impeded from confirming). First, confirmation candidates must be baptized persons.[147] The incumbent having cure of souls must be satisfied that confirmation candidates have

---

[142] *NDIB*, I, 3; *RBG*, A.5; *LDR*, 20; *TBF*, 3.17; *SDH*, I, C.4.

[143] *ASB*, 243; *BCP*, 270: exhortation at the end of the ministration of public baptism: they are to take care that the newly baptized infant is brought to the bishop to be confirmed as soon as he/she can recite the Apostles' Creed, the Lord's Prayer, and the Ten Commandments.

[144] *CDH*, 76; *PDH*, H.3.3; *BDM*, E.4; *CF*, C.2.

[145] *CIC*, cc. 889–91: the conference of bishops may specify an age; c. 97(2): children who have reached age 7 are presumed to have the use of reason; see M. J. Balhoff, 'Age for confirmation: canonical evidence', *The Jurist*, 45 (1985), 549; for different approaches of episcopal conferences see *COCLA*, App. III.

[146] See however Canon B24(3): 'every person thus baptised shall be confirmed by the bishop so soon after his baptism as conveniently may be; that so he may be admitted to the Holy Communion'; *BCP*, 288, rubric at end of the office of baptism for those of riper years: '[i]t is expedient that every person thus baptized, should be confirmed by the bishop, so soon after his baptism as conveniently may be', and 296; see also *RACCL* (1947), draft Canon 35(2): 'every Minister . . . shall remind his people that all persons who have been baptized and are come to a competent age, and have not been confirmed, are to be brought to the Bishop for Confirmation'; *Acts of Convocation*, 156 (Recommendations of 1957): 'The prospect and duty of Confirmation should be kept before children in Sunday Schol and in their religious instruction.'

[147] Canon B27(1); *ASB*, 252.

been validly baptized and must ascertain the date and place of baptism; before
or at the time assigned for the confirmation the minister shall give to the bishop
the names of candidates together with their age and the date of their baptism.[148] This requirement cannot be dispensed with; as we have seen, '[i]f the
minister is doubtful about the baptism of a candidate for confirmation he shall
conditionally baptise him . . . before presenting him to the bishop to be
confirmed'.[149]

Secondly, '[t]he minister shall present none to the bishop but such as . . .
can say the Creed, the Lord's Prayer, and the Ten Commandments, and can
also render an account of their faith according to the [church's] Catechism'.[150]
Whilst in practice this is no longer required, the canons provide no express
exceptions to this rule, nor for ministerial or episcopal dispensation from the
requirement. Strictly, beyond being able to recite these, wider instruction is
apparently not a prerequisite to the valid or lawful celebration of confirmation.
Though the minister is under a duty to instruct candidates to the best of his
ability, and ordinarily the bishop confirms by 'laying his hands upon children
and other persons *who have been instructed* in the Christian faith', there is no
specific requirement that *only* those who have received this wider instruction
may be admitted to confirmation. Indeed, the minister appears to be under no
canonical duty to assure the bishop that they have been properly instructed in
the Christian faith. If a minister refuses to present a person for lack of
instruction a bishop, as principal minister of the diocese, presumably has the
right to override the incumbent's refusal, provided the bishop is satisfied that
the candidate is sufficiently instructed and able to render an account of the
Christian faith; there is no specific guidance on this point.[151]

Thirdly, as with Roman Catholic canon law, the Church of England fixes no
particular age for confirmation. However, '[t]he minister shall present *none* to
the bishop but such as are come to years of discretion'.[152] This expression is
not defined and there is no express canonical requirement that the candidate
actually *understands* the meaning of confirmation for admission to it or for its

---

[148] B27(4).   [149] B27(5).

[150] B27(3); no provision is made to test this, nor is there apparently any position as to whether
these must be said from memory or may merely be read.

[151] On the other hand, if presenting candidates is seen not as a delegated function but one
inherent in the incumbency (C24(5)), the bishop may not be lawfully empowered to override the
incumbent's refusal. In practice a candidate would be asked to present himself at another parish
church. If an incumbent wishes to present a non-qualifying candidate, in so far as (in practice) the
bishop's role may be conceived as merely ministerial or executive, it is difficult to envisage an
opportunity for or a circumstance in which the bishop might object.

[152] B27(3); *CIC*, c. 891: 'The sacrament of confirmation is to be conferred on the faithful at
about the age of discretion unless the conference of bishops determines another age or there is a
danger of death or in the judgment of the minister a grave cause urges otherwise.'

valid celebration.[153] Liturgically, candidates must simply declare publicly to 'accept the Christian faith' and profess belief in the Trinity.[154] This arrangement of course affords a considerable degree of latitude and in practice, particularly in the case of the physically or mentally disabled, evidence of a general assent may be sufficient to satisfy this requirement.[155] The matter has been the subject of considerable debate but this has as yet not led to a change in the law.[156] Dioceses vary as to the minimum age for confirmation and many norms state that candidates below a specified age cannot be presented without episcopal consent.[157]

The Celebration of Confirmation

In the Church of England to the bishop 'belongs the right . . . of celebrating the [rite] . . . of confirmation';[158] the diocesan bishop is the ordinary minister of confirmation: '[t]he bishop of the diocese shall himself minister (or cause to be ministered by some other bishop lawfully deputed in his stead) the rite of confirmation throughout his diocese as often and in as many places as shall be convenient'.[159] The same applies in Roman Catholic canon law though a presbyter may also confer confirmation validly.[160] The Church of England has three liturgies for the celebration of confirmation: it is the bishop's right to choose which is to be used though he is under a canonical duty to consult the minister of the church where the service is to be held.[161] Diocesan norms often indicate that the bishop is willing to accept the choice of the incumbent on most occasions though often they prescribe that two weeks' notice be given.[162]

---

[153] See, however, diocesan directives: e.g. *SDH*, I, C.3: the bishop expects the presenting incumbent to ensure that all candidates are old enough to understand the meaning of their confirmation and baptismal promises and to have an active commitment to Jesus Christ.

[154] *ASB*, 232; there is no equivalent in the *BCP*, 297 ff.

[155] *BCP*, 288, rubric for baptism of those of riper years; 296, rubric at end of the Catechism: 'So soon as children are come to a competent age, and can say in their mother tongue the Creed, the Lord's Prayer and the Ten Commandments, and also can answer the other questions of the short Catechism, they shall be brought to the Bishop.' For the mentally handicapped see generally M. Bayley, *The Local Church and Mentally Handicapped People*, (London, 1984), approved by General Synod, July 1984. [156] *Acts of Convocation*, 69–72; *Confirmation Today* (1954).

[157] E.g. for the age fixed at 7, see *ODYB: IF*, 235; for below 11, see *SDDH*, App. B to Pt I; for 11: *LDHI*, III, 4; *BDM*, E.4; *TBF*, 3.17; for 12: *CDH*, 76; *DSBN*, Ad clerum notice 1989/2; some norms do not fix an age: *LDR*, 20, area bishop's regulations; for the discretion of the incumbent: *CF*, C.2.: *NDIB*, I, 3.1. [158] C18(4).

[159] B27(1).

[160] *CIC*, c. 882: presbyters may do so under a faculty given by universal law or a special concession of a competent authority; c. 883: a presbyter equivalent in law to a bishop, who has the mandate of the bishop, or in danger of death any pastor, has the faculty to confirm automatically by universal law; see also c. 884). [161] B3(4), (5).

[162] *SDHB*, I, C.5. Directives of this sort may give rise to a morally binding estoppel but cannot block the bishop's use of his canonical right; *PDH*, App. 8; *RBG*, A.5; *GDM*, L.1; *CF*, C.2; *CDH*, 78 (reception); *TBF*, 3.18.

By liturgical norms the minister presents the candidates to the bishop who, laying his hands on the head of each, says 'Confirm, O Lord, this your servant N with your Holy Spirit'. Where the liturgy prescribes that anything is to be said or done by the bishop, he may delegate these functions to other ministers, but only the bishop is to confirm. At his discretion, the bishop may also anoint candidates with oil which he has previously blessed.[163] If it is desired for a sufficient reason that a Christian name be changed, 'the bishop may, under the laws of this realm, confirm a person by a new Christian name, which shall be thereafter deemed the lawful Christian name of such person'.[164] Diocesan norms often prescribe that it is appropriate for unbaptized candidates to be baptized by the bishop at the service of confirmation.[165] Moreover, by liturgical norms, when candidates for confirmation are presented at the same service as candidates for both baptism and confirmation, the precise ordering of the service and the place of baptism should be determined by consultation between the bishop and the parish priest.[166] Provision is made for candidates (as well as members of the congregation at the discretion of the bishop) to renew their baptismal vows.[167] The canons allow a minister or lay member of another church to be invited to participate in elements of the confirmation service (with the exception of confirming itself) with the consent of the bishop, the incumbent, and the parochial church council.[168] A Church of England bishop may accept an invitation to take part in a confirmation service in a church other than the Church of England only with the approval of his archbishop.[169] When party to a local ecumenical project, a bishop may make provision by written instrument and after consultation with the parochial church council for the holding of joint confirmation services with any participating church.[170]

After-Care and the Effects of Confirmation

There is an imbalance in the legal framework of the Church of England between post-baptismal care and post-confirmation care. The canons make no express provision for the after-care of those newly confirmed,[171] nor usually do diocesan directives.[172] The rubrical requirement (affirmed by Act of Convocation) that 'every one shall have a godfather or godmother as a

---

[163] *ASB*, 226 (n. 7).

[164] B27(6); *Re Parrott, Cox v Parrott* [1946] Ch 183; [1946] 1 All ER 321; no accidental change of name is possible as the intention of both the bishop and the candidate is required before a change of name can occur; the baptismal register may not be altered but a marginal note should be made: *OLAC*, 182.   [165] *SDHB*, I, C.2; *supra* n. 162.

[166] *ASB*, 226 (n. 10).   [167] E.g. *ASB*, 255; *BCP*, 297.

[168] Canon B43,1(3); *supra* Ch. 10.   [169] B43(2)(b)(iii).

[170] B44(4)(1)(e); *Ecumenical Relations: Code of Practice*, 27–9: (care should be taken 'not to overshadow the dignity and primacy of baptism, nor to polarise baptism and confirmation'.

[171] They come ordinarily under the care of the minister having cure of souls: see *supra* Ch. 7.

[172] See exceptionally *CF*, C.2 (sponsors).

witness of their confirmation' seems to have fallen into desuetude and the earlier canonical requirement that confirmation candidates have sponsors has not been re-enacted in the modern canons.[173] In Roman Catholic canon law a register of confirmations must be kept and confirmation candidates must have a sponsor who performs those functions carried out by baptismal sponsors.[174]

As in Roman Catholic canon law,[175] the legal effects of confirmation can be simply stated: only those baptized and confirmed may be admitted as deacons and priests, readers, and lay workers;[176] those confirmed or desirous of being confirmed may be admitted to Holy Communion, received into the church, and may be admiited as an ecclesiastical judge or registrar, and have their name entered on the electoral roll.[177] As we have seen, a minister may dispense with the requirement that a godparent must be confirmed.[178] To this end, a register of all confirmations must be kept in the parish,[179] and diocesan directives sometimes require that this be completed and signed by the bishop at the time of confirmation.[180] Though there seems to be no rule to this effect, the common opinion is that confirmation (like baptism) cannot be repeated.[181]

CONCLUSIONS

In the Roman Catholic Church parents and sponsors of candidates for infant baptism must be instructed in the meaning of the sacrament and the obligations

---

[173] *BCP*, 296, catechism rubric; *Acts of Convocation*, 156; Canon 29 of the 1603 Canons; *On the Way: Towards an Integrated Approach to Christian Initiation* (London, 1995) GS Misc 44, para. 4.34. This accepts after-care as the responsibility of the church community and accords with the view expressed in the Ely Report, *Christian Inititation: Birth and Growth in the Christian Society*, GS 30 (London, 1971) para. 109.

[174] *CIC*, cc. 892–3: sponsors; c. 895: register; *COCLA*, 1335: register is to be kept in the parish rather than at the diocesan curia; a certificate of confirmation is normally given: *CCL: TC*, 491.

[175] Confirmation is required for admission to several offices, institutions, and rites: *CIC*, c. 1033: orders; c. 645: religious institute; c. 241: to a seminary; c. 1065: marriage.

[176] Canons C4, E4, E7; the same applies to sponsors and godparents (subject to a dispensation under Canon B23); confirmed status is not required for entry on the electoral roll: *CRR*, r. 1(2); actual communicant status or the desire for confirmation are prerequisites for admission to the various assemblies of the church: *supra* Chs. 4 and 8.

[177] *Supra* Ch. 8; Canon B28: confirmation generates reception into the church; for Canons B15A, B24(3) *post* Ch. 12; see M. Reardon, *Christian Initiation*, 39 ff. for infant baptism, confirmation at 7 years of age, and communion to follow, plus a public profession of faith at 17; see also Ely Report, 46: communion before confirmation: to encourage candidates to maintain membership; *Communion before Confirmation* (1985), report of General Synod's Board of Education working party on Christian Initiation and Participation in the Eucharist.

[178] B23(4).

[179] Canons B39(2), F11(3); Parochial Registers and Records Measure 1978, s. 6(1): the duty to enter and record the confirmation (together with any change of name) is placed on the minister presenting the candidates: B39(2); this does not, however, specifically impose a duty to keep and maintain the register; for Roman Catholic law see *CIC*, cc. 894–6.

[180] *SDH*, I, C.12; *LDHI*, III, 2.2; *RBG*, A.5; *LDR*, 20.

[181] R. Phillimore, *Ecclesiastical Law*, I, 516.

attaching to it. In the Church of England, whilst canon law confers a general ministerial duty to instruct, it does not spell out standards for instruction: these are provided by diocesan norms which seek to ensure that adult candidates and parents, guardians, and godparents of infant candidates are made aware of the significance of baptism and responsibilities flowing from it. In the same way that Roman Catholic canon law recognizes a right to baptism, the canons of the Church of England forbid refusal; delay of baptism is permitted and diocesan norms often allow what may amount to indefinite postponement in the absence of proper preparation and commitment. Recourse against refusal or delay may be made to the diocesan bishop and an intentional and final refusal may constitute the ecclesiastical offence of neglect of duty. In the Church of England the duty not to refuse is applicable technically only to infant baptism and not to adult baptism. Both churches set minimal criteria for validity (most rules exist simply to regulate its full liturgical celebration), both allow in exceptional cases baptism by the laity and conditional baptism, and both forbid a repetition of the sacrament. Whilst in both churches a basic responsibility is assigned canonically to godparents, in the Church of England provision for after-care or follow-up is made by norms varying between dioceses. Whereas Roman Catholic canon law contains a definition of confirmation, the law of the Church of England does not: this task is performed by doctrinal and liturgical texts. In both churches candidates for confirmation have a canonical right to instruction and the Church of England's minimal canonical structures are supplemented by schemes devised at diocesan and parochial level; age requirements for confirmation vary as between the dioceses. Unlike Roman Catholic canon law, in the Church of England neither canon law nor diocesan norms make formal provision for follow-up.

12

Eucharist, Confession, and Penance

The Eucharist is the principal liturgical act in both the Church of England and the Roman Catholic Church. The latter possesses a large body of canon law dealing with the celebration of Eucharist and of penance, treated as a sacrament of reconciliation, and also rights of admission to them. Whilst in the Church of England the basic legal framework concerning celebration of and admission to the Eucharist is found in the canons and judicial decisions, many extra-legal norms have been devised, particularly with regard to its administration by the laity in the absence of a presiding priest and its reception by a baptized person who has not yet been confirmed. Whereas the Church of England possesses little modern law on private confession, the precise terms and status of the ministerial duty not to disclose information given in confession, a duty presented in absolute terms in Roman Catholic canon law, remain unclear, as do the terms of the considerable body of secular law which exists to regulate disclosure of this information in judicial proceedings.

THE EUCHARIST

The formal doctrine of the Church of England treats the Eucharist (Holy Communion or the Lord's Supper) as a sacrament instituted by Christ.[1] It is a 'remembrance of the sacrifice of the death of Christ and of the benefits which we receive thereby' and a memorial of the Last Supper.[2] In the Eucharist the people of the church draw near to God, offering themselves as a sacrifice of thanks and praise.[3] The church has rejected the doctrine of the Eucharist as an actual sacrifice, an understanding of the Eucharistic sacrifice which asserts that Jesus is immolated, as well as the doctrine of transubstantiation.[4] These doctrines, including that of memorial, have been preserved in the Roman Catholic Church (which still adheres formally to the language of transubstantiation) and its canon law, under which the Eucharistic celebration is seen as sanctifying the people of God: the Eucharist is the summit and source of all

---

[1] *AR*, Arts. 25, 28; *BCP*, 236, Order for the Administration of the Lord's Supper or Holy Communion. [2] *BCP*, 294: Catechism; *ASB*, Rite A (113), Rite B (175).
[3] *Believing in the Church* (1981) 101; *Patterns for Worship* (1990) 11 ff.
[4] *AR*, Arts. 31, 36.

Christian worship and life,[5] it is the action of Christ himself and of the church, and in it Christ offers himself to God and gives himself as spiritual food to the faithful who participate actively and together in their own way in its celebration.[6] The faithful have a duty to celebrate and receive the sacrament devoutly and frequently;[7] they are recommended to receive Holy Communion during the Eucharist and must receive Communion at least once a year.[8]

Celebration: Roles, Rights, and Duties

In Roman Catholic canon law a valid and licit celebration of the Eucharist is confected only under the presidency of an ordained priest acting in the person of Christ.[9] A non-ordained person who attempts to confect a Eucharist incurs automatic excommunication.[10] To be a valid celebration the elements must be bread and wine.[11] It is sinful (*nefas est*) to consecrate either one element without the other or both outside the celebration of the Eucharist.[12] Other rules go to liceity rather than to validity.[13] The priest must receive the Eucharist frequently and is recommended to receive it daily.[14] It is not lawful for a priest to celebrate more than once a day unless permitted in exceptional cases by the law or, if priests are lacking, by the bishop for a just cause.[15] The priest may not celebrate without the participation of at least some member of the faithful except for a just and reasonable cause.[16] The saying of the Eucharistic prayer is reserved to the priest: it is not lawful for deacons or lay persons to say this or to perform any action proper to the celebrating priest.[17] Whilst the ordinary minister of Holy Communion is a bishop, priest, or deacon,[18] and these ordinarily distribute the elements, other lay members of the faithful may administer the elements if this function is expressly assigned

---

[5] *CIC*, c. 897: the sacrifice of the cross is perpetuated; c. 899: Christ is 'substantially present under the forms of bread and wine'; *SC*, II and *EM*, Instruction on the Worship of the Eucharistic Mystery (1967).   [6] *CIC*, c. 899.

[7] C. 898: the pastors must clarify the doctrine of the sacrament to the faithful; *EM*, I.

[8] *CIC*, cc. 918, 920; the duty to receive must be fulfilled during the Easter season unless fulfilled for a just cause at some other time.   [9] C. 900.

[10] C. 1378(2).

[11] C. 924: 'The Most Sacred Eucharistic sacrifice must be offered with bread and wine, with which a small quantity of water is to be added'; the bread must be recently made of wheat alone (and unleavened: c. 926); the wine must be natural wine of the grape and not corrupt; see however Sacred Congregation Instruction (1929): bread made of any substance other than wheat is invalid matter; if it contains other matter this will not affect the validity of the celebration if it can be considered still to be 'substantially' made of wheat: *CCL: TC*, 657.   [12] *CIC*, c. 927.

[13] C. 900(2): 'A priest who is not canonically impeded celebrates the Eucharist licitly observing the prescriptions of the following canons'.   [14] Cc. 904, 276(2).

[15] *CIC*, c. 905; see also *PO*, 13; *EM*, 44; *CCL: TC*, 646 (such as Christmas).

[16] *CIC*, c. 906; *SC*, I, 2; the Roman Missal now provides for a 'Rite of mass without a congregation'; formerly the presence of a server was mandatory: *CCL: TC*, 647–8.

[17] *CIC*, c. 907.   [18] C. 910.

or in cases of necessity.[19] Provision is made for concelebration, usually optional but sometimes mandatory, but priests are forbidden to concelebrate the Eucharist with priests or ministers of churches not in full communion with the Roman Catholic Church.[20]

The law of the Church of England is similar in some essentials. Only an episcopally ordained priest, male or female, has the right to preside at the Lord's Supper.[21] When the bishop is present it is appropriate but not mandatory that he should act as president.[22] A parochial church council is empowered to pass a resolution preventing a female priest from presiding at or celebrating Holy Communion in the parish.[23] The bishop has no right to veto the making of such a resolution.[24] The administrative body of a cathedral enjoys similar powers.[25] The resolution may be rescinded but whilst it is in force a person discharging any function in relation to the parish must not act in contravention of it.[26] It is an offence against the laws ecclesiastical for a bishop, priest, or deacon to act in contravention of a parochial resolution.[27]

In contrast to Roman Catholic canon law, the bread may be leavened or unleavened; it must be made 'of the best and purest wheat flour' and the wine is to be 'fermented juice of the grape, good and wholesome'.[28] The sacrament must be administered in both kinds, bread and wine, except in cases of

---

[19] C. 230(3); *SC*, 29; *LG*, 35; episcopal approval is not required, but usually deputation is by the diocesan bishop; under c. 1248(2), the bishop sets out general regulations on Sunday celebrations without a priest, but he is not obliged to specify which lay persons may distribute Communion.

[20] *CIC*, cc. 902, 908; *UR*, 8, 14, 22; a 1972 secretariat instruction affirmed the basic principle that: 'of its very nature, the celebration of the Eucharist signifies the fullness of the profession of faith and ecclesial communion': see *CCL: TC*, 649, n. 40. See also *supra* Ch. 7.

[21] Canon B12; this includes women (Canon C4B); see *supra* Ch. 7.

[22] *ASB*, 115 (n. 2); such a right is not listed in C18; indeed, *BCP* seems to assume that a bishop present will not preside (256, rubric): 'Then shall the Minister first receive the Communion in both kinds himself, and then proceed to deliver the same to the Bishops . . . (if any be present)'.

[23] Priests (Ordination of Women) Measure 1993, s. 3(1), Sched. 1, Resolution A.

[24] S. 3(5): a council has no power to consider a motion for a resoluton if the incumbent or priest-in-charge of the benefice concerned, or any team vicar or assistant curate for that benefice, is a woman ordained to the office of priest (s. 3(3); 4 weeks' notice of the motion must be given by the council secretary and the meeting considering the motion must be attended by at least one half of the members of the council entitled to attend (s. 3(4)); a copy must be sent to, *inter alia*, the diocesan bishop and the diocesan registrar (s. 3(5)).

[25] S. 4; s. 8: 'administrative body' has the same meaning as in the Cathedrals Measure 1963.

[26] S. 3(2), (6); it is unclear whether the principle that PCC resolutions are not directly enforceable in the courts is also applicable to these resolutions (see *supra* Ch. 3); for the possible applicability of s. 19 of the Sex Discrimination Act 1975, see *supra* Ch. 7.

[27] S. 5: proceedings may be taken under the EJM 1963; the Measure does not specify the elements of the offence.

[28] Canon B17(2); *Williams v Bishop of Salisbury* (1862) 2 Moo PCCNS 375; it is the responsibility of the churchwardens, with the advice and direction of the minister, to provide a sufficient quantity of bread and wine for the number of communicants to receive (17(1)); the bread and wine 'shall' be brought to the Communion table in a patten or convenient box and the wine in a convenient cruet or flagon. For the meaning of Communion 'table' see *Re St Stephen's, Walbrook* [1987] 2 All ER 578 (*supra* Ch. 9); *Faulkner v Litchfield* (1845) 1 Rob Ecc 185 (Arches Ct.)

necessity.[29] Intinction is lawful when there are concerns about infection; the question of hygiene is sometimes addressed by diocesan norms.[30] Whilst ordinarily no person may distribute elements unless ordained, lay people may do so if authorized by the bishop.[31] Under synodical regulations the incumbent or priest-in-charge must apply in writing to the bishop, the application must be supported by the churchwardens and must specify the name and relevant particulars of the proposed person. The bishop may only authorize a baptized and confirmed person to distribute the elements.[32] The bishop's power to permit or refuse is discretionary, as is his power to specify the circumstances or conditions of the authorization.[33] Whilst a deacon is forbidden to preside at the Eucharist a right exists to assist the celebrant in the distribution of the elements and in reading the Holy Scriptures.[34] Moreover, the minister has a right to invite a lay person to read the epistle and Gospel but the bishop may direct otherwise.[35] Liturgical rubrics forbid the laity to make the greeting, say the Collect, give the absolution, the peace, and the blessing: these (as well as taking the bread and cup, saying the Eucharistic prayer, and breaking the bread) are reserved to the president. Where necessary, however, the president may delegate the remaining parts of the service to others.[36] Lay distribution of the elements has been the subject of extensive regulation by diocesan norms. Sometimes these require the person proposed to

---

[29] Sacrament Act 1547, s. 8; *BCP*, 261, rubric: 'it shall suffice that the Bread be such as is usual to be eaten', 'the best and purest Wheat Bread that conveniently may be goten'. For the ritualist controversies over posture and ceremonies connected with consecration see *Read v Bishop of Lincoln* [1892] AC 644 (PC), in which *Hebbert v Purchas* (1871) LR 3 PC 605 and *Ridsdale v Clifton* (1877) 2 PD 276 (PC) were considered; and *Martin v Machonockie* (1868) LR 2 A&E 116; among the practices held to be illegal were the mixing of wine and water and the priest prostrating himself during the prayer of consecration. See now *OLAC*, 138–41.

[30] Intinction is lawful in cases of necessity when e.g. a 'communicant or the congregation as a whole is fearful of contracting or communicating a contagious disease', but it seems that the use by each communicant of an individual cup into which the wine is poured from a common chalice or flagon would be a departure from liturgical custom (see Matt. 26: 27; Mark 14: 23; Luke 22: 17; I Cor. 11: 26–9); *OLAC*, 138, 141; for intinction and hygiene under diocesan norms see e.g. *DGBOP*, 3.6; *WH*, 27; *RBG*, A.3; *DSBN*, Ad Clerum Notice 1989/5.   [31] Canon B12(1), (3).

[32] Regulations made by the Church Assembly in 1969; these seem to enjoy a continuing authority under Canon B12, though the Canon does not specifically say that they continue in force: it simply refers to synodical regulations which General Synod 'may make from time to time'; the 1969 Regulations were made under the Prayer Book (Further Provisions) Measure 1968, s. 2(1), repealed by the Worship and Doctrine Measure 1974; under reg. 1(2), where the cure is vacant and no priest-in-charge is appointed, an application may be made by the rural dean and must be supported by the churchwardens.

[33] Reg. 2; 'bishop' for the purposes of the regulation means a diocesan or a person appointed by him, being a suffragan, assistant bishop, or archdeacon of the diocese.

[34] *BCP*, 555 at 565 (Form and Manner of Making Deacons). See *supra* Ch. 7 for the terms of a deacon's licence.   [35] Canon B12(4).

[36] *ASB*, 115; 'The sermon is an integral part of the Ministry of the Word. A sermon should normally be preached at all celebrations on Sundays and other Holy Days' (ibid., 116, n. 12); the sermon is not part of the administration of Holy Communion under a 1662 BCP celebration: *Re Robinson, Wright v Tugwell* [1897] 1 Ch 85 at 96 (CA); for consideration of lay participation in reading (including the reading of the Gospel) see e.g. *CDH*, 96.

be at least seventeen years of age,[37] and most require the parochial church council to consent to nomination.[38] Often the permission is given for a fixed term (usually three years); although renewable on the expiration of the period, permission normally lapses automatically on a vacancy.[39]

Holy Communion must be celebrated on all Sundays (and other specified days) in the parish church distinctly, reverently, and in an audible voice. It need not be celebrated if some good reason not to do so is approved by the diocesan bishop; in churches and chapels dependent on a parish church, it is to be celebrated as regularly and frequently as may be convenient, subject to the direction of the ordinary.[40] Similar provisions exist for cathedrals.[41] As in Roman Catholic canon law,[42] a minister must normally celebrate the Eucharist only in a consecrated building or a building licensed for worship; the diocesan bishop has power to dispense with this requirement.[43] Ordinarily, the laity have no direct right to receive Communion at home. However, the minister 'may celebrate . . . in any private house wherein there is any sick, dying, or so impotent that he cannot go to church';[44] '[w]hen any person sick or in danger or so impotent that he cannot go to church is desirous of receiving the most comfortable sacrament of the Body and Blood of Christ, the priest, having knowledge thereof, shall as soon as may be visit him, and unless there be any grave reason to the contrary, shall reverently minister the same to the said person at such place and time as may be convenient'.[45] The position is similar in Roman Catholic canon law.[46] In the Church of England, reservation of the sacraments for distribution to the sick is lawful if episcopally approved.[47] Extended Holy Communion, the administration of already consecrated elements, is treated at length by diocesan norms. Many expressly authorize the

---

[37] *RBG*, A.3; *CDH*, 95; *WH*, BP.8 for the distinction between, on one hand, presiding, consecrating, and celebrating (which may be carried out only by a priest) and, on the other distributing the elements (which may be carried out by lay people).

[38] *GDM*, J.1; *LDHI*, III.16; *PDH*, H.2.1; *WH*, BP.8; *BRDSEI*, D(iv): unanimous agreement of the PCC required. [39] *CDH*, 95; *SDDH*, B.14.

[40] Canon B14; it must be celebrated on principal feast days and on Ash Wednesday.

[41] Canon B13; see also *BCP*, 236, rubric.

[42] *CIC*, c. 932; under c. 933 'For a just cause and with the express permission of the ordinary it is licit for a priest to celebrate the Eucharist in a sacred edifice of another church or ecclesial community that does *not* have full communion with the Catholic Church, scandal being avoided'.

[43] Canon B40; see *Jones v Jelf* (1863) 8 LT 399 (Arches Ct.) [44] B40, proviso.

[45] B37(2); para. 1 imposes a duty on ministers to keep themselves informed when any person is sick or in danger of death and to exhort, instruct, and comfort that person 'in such manner as he shall think most needful and convenient'; para. 3: the priest may lay hands on the person and anoint with oil on the forehead with the sign of the Cross; *BCP*, 312: Order for the Visitation of the Sick; 323: Communion of the Sick. [46] *CIC*, cc. 911, 921–2: the viaticum.

[47] For reservation and the 1662 *BCP* see *Re Lapford (Devon) Parish Church* [1954] 3 All ER 484; for Series 2 Holy Communion, rubric 40 (for consumption of bread and wine 'which is not required for the purposes of Communion') which was held in *Re St Peter and St Paul, Leckhampton* [1967] 3 All ER 1057 to make reservation lawful; *St John the Evangelist, Bierley* [1989] 3 All ER 214; for Series 3, see rubric 36; see also *CPR*, regulations for reservation, which speak of the 'right of every priest to reserve' the sacrament; see also *SDDH*, B.15, B.17.

distribution of the elements, including by lay people, to the housebound provided this is approved by the bishop and agreed by the incumbent and the parochial church council.[48] Some norms authorize distribution of the elements by priests (but not readers) at house group meetings, again with episcopal approval and the agreement of the incumbent and parochial church council.[49] With regard to the distribution of the elements at a service in church in the absence of a priest (the elements being either reserved in the church or brought to it from another), diocesan norms similarly require episcopal approval and the agreement of the incumbent and parochial church council. Usually the norms set out the circumstances in which this is permissible, principally when a priest is not available; sometimes authorization is general, sometimes norms require specific episcopal approval for each occasion of an extended Communion.[50] Some norms completely forbid extended Communion at a service in church.[51]

Whenever Communion is administered, every minister celebrating must receive the sacrament himself,[52] and the dean, provost, canons residentiary, and other ministers of a cathedral church must receive Communion every Sunday unless 'they have a reasonable cause to the contrary'.[53] Confirmed members of the church have a canonical duty to receive Communion regularly and especially at the festivals of Christmas, Easter, and Whitsun.[54] Liturgical rubrics recommend communicants to prepare carefully before receiving Communion.[55] The minister is under a canonical duty to teach the people so that they come to Communion prepared.[56]

In contrast to the Roman Catholic Church, there is in the Church of England no canonical duty on a minister to celebrate Communion only in the presence of the faithful. By liturgical rubrics, however, a priest must not celebrate in church according to the Book of Common Prayer 1662 without a convenient number present to communicate; indeed, even if there there are not more than twenty qualified communicants in the parish, the minister must not celebrate Communion unless at least three communicate with him.[57] Moreover, apart from home Communion, it seems from judicial decisions from last century that an ecclesiastical offence may be committed if a minister celebrates without at least three present.[58] Although the communion services contained in the Alternative Service Book contain no rubrical requirements concerning the

---

[48] See e.g. *NDIB*, I, 6; *GDM*, J.6; *LDR*, 125; *WH*, BP.8; *LDHI*, III, 18.

[49] *WH*, BP.8; *GDM*, J.7; *TBF*, 3.15, 3.16.

[50] *BRDSEI*, Diii; *WH*, BP.8; *GDM*, J.8; *BDM*, D.4; *PDH*, H.2.2 (awaiting regulations from the House of Bishops).   [51] *DSBN*, Ad clerum notice, 1989/3; *CF*, C.3; *LDHI*, III,17.

[52] Canon B12(2); the law seems to be silent as to what happens when the minister is a notorious offender; see below.   [53] Canon B13(2).

[54] Canon B15(1); though largely unenforceable, a failure to communicate may have legal consequences: see *supra* Ch. 8.

[55] *ASB*, 115, n. 1: 'Careful devotional preparation . . . is recommended'; *BCP*, 247 f. (rubrics and exhortation)   [56] Canon B15(2): 'as is required by the Book of Common Prayer'.

[57] *BCP*, 262, rubrics at the end of the Order.

[58] *Parnell v Roughton* (1874) LR 6 PC 46; *Ridsdale v Clifton* (1876) 1 PD 316.

presence of the laity, the assumption underlying the rubrics and the liturgical language is that others will be present.[59]

Unlike Roman Catholic canon law, limited forms of inter-denominational Eucharist are possible in the Church of England. A baptized minister of, or lay person of good standing in, a designated church may be invited to lead the intercessions at the Holy Communion and to assist in the distribution of the elements.[60] The invited person must be authorized to perform these functions in his or her own church.[61] A person from another church is not able *by invitation* to preside at Holy Communion in a Church of England service according to that church's rites.[62] However, the incumbent of a parish may (with the approval of the bishop and the parochial church council) invite members of other designated churches to take part in a joint Eucharist according to the rites of that other church.[63] A Church of England priest may lawfully accept an invitation to preside at Holy Communion in another church only with episcopal approval and, if on a regular basis, with the approval of the incumbent and parochial church council of the parish in which the Eucharist is to take place.[64] A bishop may accept an invitation to preside with archiepiscopal approval.[65] The archbishop or bishop giving approval must be satisfied of special circumstances which justify acceptance of the invitation and that the Eucharistic rite and the elements are not contrary to or indicative of a departure from the Church of England's doctrine in any essential manner.[66]

If a Local Ecumenical Project is operative, a bishop may authorize by instrument a Church of England priest to preside at a service of Holy Communion in accordance with a rite authorized by any other participating church.[67] A bishop may also authorize the holding in a Church of England place of worship of services of Holy Communion presided over by a minister of another participating church.[68] Finally, a bishop may by instrument author-

---

[59] Their presence is in line with the view that the Eucharist is an action of the church in which the community participates: *supra* n. 3.

[60] For basic principles of liturgical ecumenism see *supra* Ch. 10.   [61] Canon B43(1)(1).

[62] In any event the parent Measure (the Church of England (Ecumenical Relations) Measure 1988) forbids anyone to preside at Communion unless episcopally ordained in a church whose orders are recognized and accepted by the Church of England (s. 3); *Ecumenical Relations: Code of Practice* (1989) 20.   [63] Canon B43(9); *Code of Practice* (1989) 24: joint celebrations.

[64] B43(3); the bishop must be satisfied that there are special circumstances which justify acceptance of the invitation and that the rite and elements used are not contrary to or indicative of any departure from the doctrine of the Church of England: B43(4); *Code of Practice* (1989) 20–3 regulates *inter alia* the Eucharistic elements, the form of the Eucharist, and disposal of consecrated elements.   [65] B43(2).

[66] B43(4).

[67] Canon B44(4)(1)(d); (4)(2): the bishop must be satisfied that the rite and elements used are not contrary to (nor depart from) the Church of England's doctrines in any essential matter.

[68] Canon B44(4)(1)(f); para.(4)(3)(b) makes it clear that where a minister of another church uses a rite similar or identical to an authorized Eucharistic rite of the Church of England it must not be 'held out or taken to be a celebration of the Holy Communion according to the use of the Church of England'; *Code of Practice* (1989) 20, 23–4.

ize the holding of a joint service of Holy Communion in a place of worship of the Church of England presided over by an episcopally ordained minister of any other participating church whose orders are recognized and accepted by the Church of England.[69]

Eucharistic Discipline: Admission and Exclusion

In Roman Catholic canon law, everyone has a right to the sacraments if requested at the appropriate time, with the correct disposition, and if not prohibited by law.[70] A specific right to admission to the Eucharist is recognized by Canon 912; baptism is a pre-condition: 'Any baptized person who is not prohibited by law can and must be admitted to Holy Communion'.[71] The sick and those in danger of death enjoy a special right.[72] The Code excludes excommunicates (by operation of law),[73] and an excommunicated minister is forbidden any 'ministerial participation in celebrating the Eucharistic sacrifice'.[74] It also excludes those who are subject to an interdict after the imposition or declaration of a medicinal penalty.[75] An excommunication or interdict is lifted automatically when the person is repentant or withdraws from the sin giving rise to the sanction.[76] A person who obstinately persists in manifest sin is also denied admission.[77] The elements which must previously be satisfied are not easily defined.[78] In these instances, as a general principle a pastor has no right or discretion to admit but must administer the exclusion.[79] However, a confessor may remit an automatic excommunication or interdict if it would be hard on the penitent to remain in a state of serious sin, and thereby be barred from holy communion; the penitent must then have recourse to the minister's ecclesiastical superior.[80]

Persons who are *conscious* of grave sin are forbidden by operation of law to celebrate mass and to receive Communion; the minister must exclude them.[81]

---

[69] Canon B44(4)(1)(f), (5).   [70] *CIC*, cc. 210, 920, 213, 843; *supra* Ch. 11.

[71] C. 842: one who has not received baptism cannot be validly admitted to the other sacraments; celebration of Eucharist, along with baptism and confirmation, are required for full Christian initiation.

[72] *CIC*, c. 921; cc. 530, 911, 922; the sacrament is to be reserved for such cases (c. 925).

[73] C. 915, 1331.   [74] C. 1331.   [75] C. 915.   [76] Cc. 1347, 1358.

[77] C. 915; the person may not be said to be 'properly disposed' under cc. 843, 898.

[78] *CCL: TC*, 653: a manifest sin is one which is publicly known; obstinacy exists where a person has not heeded the warnings of church authorities, but no specific procedures are set down in the Code in this regard; cf. c. 1347 for warnings as to censures.

[79] See, however, cc. 921–2 for the viaticum. According to J. Huels 'The minister cannot assume, for example, that the sin of public concubinage arising from divorce and remarriage is always grave in the internal forum. Any prudent doubt about either the gravity or the public nature of the sin should be resolved by the minister in favor of the person who approaches the sacrament': *CCL: TC*, 653.

[80] *CIC*, c. 1357; for the application of procedures to abortion cases see J. McAreavey, 'Abortion and the sacrament of penance', *The Furrow* (1993), 230; see *post* Ch. 13 for the position of divorcees.   [81] *CIC*, c. 916.

The common opinion is that persons are 'conscious' when they are morally 'certain' of having committed a grave sin.[82] However, a person who makes sacramental confession cannot be excluded by the minister. If there has been no sacramental confession, such a person has a right to admission if there was a grave reason for not having confessed and has had no opportunity to do so. In such circumstances the individual is exhorted 'to be mindful of the obligation to make an act of perfect contrition, including the intention of confessing as soon as possible'.[83]

In the Church of England, by contrast with baptism or marriage, not every person resident in a parish has a right of admission to Holy Communion. As a general principle, the right to admission is enjoyed only by those who are members of the Church of England: '[t]here shall be admitted to the Holy Communion . . . members of the Church of England who have been confirmed' and 'members of the Church of England who . . . are ready or desirous to be so confirmed' according to the church rites; the duty to admit applies equally to members who have been 'otherwise episcopally confirmed with unction or with the laying on of hands'.[84] As Fletcher Moulton LJ explained in *R v Dibdin*, '[t]he particular rights which we have here to consider are the rights of the members of the Established Church to receive the Holy Communion in the church of their own parish. That they have an absolute right so to receive it in the absence of lawful cause to the contrary is not denied. It is a right expressly given by statute'.[85] Under the Sacrament Act 1547, with regard to communion 'in both kinds', the 'minister shall not without a lawful cause deny the same to any person that will devoutly and humbly desire it, any law, statute, ordinance or custom contrary thereunto in any way notwithstanding'; the person seeking communion is under a statutory duty to 'try and examine his own conscience before he shall receive the same'.[86] The right is enforceable in the civil courts at common law.[87] A clerical refusal to admit may constitute an ecclesiastical offence and the cleric would have 'to allege and prove a "lawful" cause to justify his refusal'.[88] Any baptized person in danger of death has an automatic right to admission.[89]

Canon B16 deals with 'notorious offenders not to be admitted to Holy Communion'.[90] Its provisions apply when the minister is persuaded that

---

[82] *CCL: TC*, 653.

[83] *CIC*, c. 916 is based on Tridentine doctrine (based on I Cor. 11: 28–9); a 1967 instruction of the worship of the Eucharistic mystery adds that private confessions should not be heard during the celebration of the mass: *EM*, 35. [84] B15A(1)(a).

[85] [1910] P 57 at 120 (CA).

[86] 1 Ed. 6, c.1, s.8: in relation to examination of conscience the word actually used in the statute is 'maye'.

[87] [1910] P 57 at 107 *per* Cozens-Hardy MR (by an action on the case); *Harris v Hicks* 2 Salk 548.

[88] [1910] P 57 at 107; *Jenkins v Cook* (1876) 1 PD 80. [89] Canon B15A(1)(d).

[90] *MIECL*, 69: 'wrongful repulsion by the minister could involve him in serious litigation in the temporal courts, amongst other things for defamation'.

'anyone of his cure' is in malicious and open contention with his neighbours or has committed 'other grave and open sin'. The latter has been classified judicially as a course of life (as opposed to some particular action or isolated act), which is in conflict with Christian morality and causes offence to the public conscience;[91] the sin is not open if known only to the minister.[92] Two processes are possible under Canon B16. First, ordinarily, if the minister is satisfied that there is no public sin, or if there is that the person is repentant, he must admit without further process. If not so satisfied the minister is under a duty to give an account to the diocesan bishop or ordinary.[93] The minister is forbidden 'to refuse the sacrament to any' until he has received the superior's order and direction. The minister must obey the ordinary's order and direction, and admit or refuse admission accordingly.[94] However, if the order is a refusal, before implementing it the minister must 'call' the person who shall be 'advertised . . . that in any wise he presume not to come to the Lord's Table'. The Canon is unclear as to the effect of the order if the minister does not call and advertise to the person excluded—if no order is received from the ordinary, a ministerial exclusion may, it seems, be lawful.[95] In short, the minister has no right to exclude unless and until in receipt of the ordinary's direction.

Secondly, and extraordinarily, if the minister is satisfied that admission will cause a 'grave and immediate scandal to the congregation' he has a duty not to ('shall not') admit. This is the only circumstance in which the minister must summarily exclude.[96] The minister must refer the matter to the ordinary within seven days of the exclusion and obey the resulting order and direction. In both cases, before issuing the order and direction, the ordinary is under a canonical duty to afford the person an opportunity for interview. There is no specific episcopal or ministerial duty to give reasons. The canons contain no rules equivalent to the Catholic principle about a prior or intended confession. It is submitted that when a person, as part of the congregation, makes a general confession in which he/she publicly repents of all sins and which is followed by absolution effecting deliverance from all sins (in accordance with the terms of the Eucharistic liturgy), that person must be admitted to Communion: the

---

[91] *Banister v Thompson* [1908] 365 at 385 *per* Dean of the Arches: 'moral code of Christendom'; ibid., 387.   [92] *R v Dibdin* [1910] P 57 at 137 *per* Farwell LJ.

[93] If the see is vacant, and the ordinary is the diocesan bishop, the minister must refer to the provincial archbishop; if the archbishopric is vacant, to the archbishop of the other province: B16(2).

[94] *R v Dibdin* [1910] P 57 at 137 *per* Farwell LJ: 'It is both the duty and the privilege of the priest to administer the sacrament; it can never be his privilege, although it may in some cases be his duty, to refuse to administer it, for privilege is that which he claims as due to himself; duty is that which he owes to others.'

[95] *Jenkins v Cook* (1875) LR 4 A&E 463 (Arches Ct.); reversed on appeal by PC (I PD 80); PC decisions are not now binding: *supra* Ch. 5.

[96] *HLE*, para. 978: sometimes referred to as 'lesser excommunication'. It is the minister's 'duty' to exclude: *R v Dibdin* [1910] P 57 at 123 *per* Fletcher Moulton (CA).

Canon cannot be invoked as that person is no longer 'without repentance'.[97] Whilst exclusion was justified by the Sacrament Act 1547 to protect the conscience of the person seeking admission,[98] the civil judges have considered that the scheme exists to protect the community.[99]

It has been decided judicially (probably *obiter*) that a minister must exclude '[p]ersons cohabiting under a void marriage [who] are living in open sin',[100] but a minister cannot exclude from Holy Communion a man married to his deceased wife's sister when that marriage is valid under civil law.[101] In the York province, by Act of Convocation (1938), a minister may exclude from Holy Communion a divorced person who has remarried within the lifetime of a former spouse. The minister must refer the matter to the bishop: if satisfied that admission 'ought not to give grave offence to the Church nor would be to the hurt of their souls', the bishop 'shall direct that they be not excluded therefrom by reason of the marriage so contracted'; such persons are to be admitted if they have resided in the parish 'through the preceding six months'. The direction, which must be communicated in writing to the minister and the parties, 'shall be accepted as final both in the particular province and in all other dioceses of the province'.[102] A similar provision was revoked for the Canterbury Province by General Synod in 1982.[103] Diocesan norms occasionally prescribe that an incumbent may admit divorcees 'unless the incumbent considers this will cause grave offence to the congregation in which case the Bishop should be consulted'.[104]

In Roman Catholic canon law special rules apply in relation to children who, as a basic rule, are to be admitted if they have the proper disposition.[105] Confirmation is not a prerequisite to admission to the Eucharist: according to ecclesiastical practice, a baptized child receives first Communion at around

---

[97] Both the 1662 BCP and the ASB Communion services contain a general confession and absolution. The Dean of the Arches in *Banister v Thompson* [1908] P 365 at 385, suggested that the person ought to have 'openly declared himself to have truly repented and amended his naughty life so that the congregation may be satisfied'; that there be evidence of 'actual amendment of life' is not, after all, required by the modern Canon; see Canons 26, 27, 109 of the 1603 Canons; see also *Atherton v Wood* (1983) (unreported, Chichester diocese): the bishop has a discretion not to proceed in the consistory against a cleric who acted without episcopal approval.

[98] To avoid 'the danger and indignation of God threatened to them which presume to receive the same unworthily'.

[99] For the purpose of the scheme see *Banister v Thompson* [1908] P 362 at 385 *per* Dean of the Arches: the rules are 'intended to prevent some public mischief. The clergyman in repelling any one is not simply, or even chiefly, exercising godly discipline on the person repelled, but he is acting as a public officer for the protection of the whole community.'

[100] *R v Dibdin* [1910] P 57 at 123 *per* Fletcher Moulton (CA).

[101] Ibid. (CA) and [1912] AC 533 (HL).   [102] *Acts of Concocation*, 90–1.

[103] Canons, 182; as to the continuing effect of the York Province regulations see *post* Ch. 13.

[104] *BRDSEI*, Dii; see also *BDM*, D.4: the incumbent may admit; there is no need for the bishop's consent.

[105] *CIC*, c. 98: a person of 18 or over is an adult; those below 18 are minors; before completion of the 7th year a minor is called an infant and is held to be incompetent (*non sui compos*); once the 7th year is complete the minor is presumed to have the use of reason.

the age of seven, before confirmation but after the child's first confession.[106] Children must have a sufficient knowledge and careful preparation so as to understand the mystery of the sacrament 'according to their capacity'; they can then receive the Host if able to do so with faith and devotion.[107] The Eucharist may be given to children who are in danger of death even if they do not have sufficient knowledge or preparation; in such circumstances they must nevertheless be able to distinguish the Body of Christ, which they must receive reverently, from ordinary food.[108] The Code seems to give a broad discretion to pastors to determine these matters; given the right to the sacraments, any doubt must be resolved in favour of the child.[109] The law of the Church of England makes no special provision for children and the Eucharist, though there are legally authorized services designed to cater for their presence.[110] However, it has been observed that whilst many in the Church of England want to retain the traditional order of infant baptism, confirmation, and Holy Communion, others feel that children ought to be admitted to the Eucharist before confirmation.[111] As we have seen, canonically, any member of the church ready or desirous to be confirmed may be admitted.[112] Consequently, many diocesan norms permit admission of children who have reached puberty but are under eighteen to the Eucharist before confirmation provided they are ready and desirous to be confirmed. Arrangements vary: in the first instance a request should be made to the bishop (or his suffragan) with the full endorsement of both the incumbent and the parochial church council after a full debate of the subject; a preliminary code of practice should also be submitted and the bishop must review the situation every three years.[113]

Under Roman Catholic canon law an adult lacking the use of reason is to be

---

[106] *CCL: TC*, 608; see *supra* Ch. 11.

[107] C. 913(1); see the Sacred Congregation for Divine Worship's *Directory on Children's Masses* (1973) 10.   [108] *CIC*, c. 913(2).

[109] *CCL: TC*, 652–3.

[110] *ASB*, 117, in addition to the prescribed blessings, 'the president may at his discretion use others'; according to ecclesiastical convention, the president blesses children at communion; ibid., 212 ff.: services of thanksgiving for the birth and adoption of a child may be conducted in Holy Communion: by the rubrics these may be used either at the beginning of Holy Communion or after the sermon; if used, the prayers of intercession may be omitted; the services may also be used on their own; they should normally be used in church but the priest has a discretion to use them at a home or hospital; for 'family services' see *Patterns for Worship* (1989) 2–5.

[111] M. Reardon, *Christian Initiation*, paras. 113 ff.; see also *Communion before Confirmation*, report of the General Synod Board of Education Working Party on Christian Initiation and Participation in the Eucharist (London, 1985).

[112] Canon B15(1); *BCP*, 300, rubric at the end of the Order of Confirmation.

[113] For this arrangement see *ODYB: IF*, 235; *BRDSEI*, D(i) authorizes either confirmation at 7 or admission to Holy Communion before confirmation, provided the parochial church council and incumbent consent and the bishop is consulted; *CF*, C.3: admission before confirmation is permissible provided the minister is committed to the parish for at least 3 years to manage the scheme, he is satisfied about continuing education for the child concerning the Eucharist, and the parents are happy to support the child; *TBF*, 3.15; cf. *SDDH*, C.21 which forbids Communion before confirmation.

regarded as an infant.[114] Whilst the Code does not treat expressly the mentally handicapped, given the principle of equal dignity and the general right to the sacraments,[115] it is commonly understood that handicapped persons may be admitted to the Eucharist if, in the absence of evidence of cognitive faith, they enjoy an intuitive faith and can appreciate the sacredness of the Eucharist.[116] The parish pastor is under a canonical duty to ensure that, as far as their condition allows, catechetical formation is to be given to them.[117] Their admission to the sacraments today is usually permitted by norms issued by dioceses and episcopal conferences.[118] In the Church of England there seems to be no formal body of law on the mentally handicapped; once confirmed, or if ready and desirous of confirmation, their admission to Communion arises as a matter of right. A recent report of a General Synod Committee states that the mentally handicapped 'should be encouraged to be confirmed, [to] become communicant members of the church'.[119]

Admission of Members of Other Churches

Members of other churches enjoy conditional rights of admission to Holy Communion under the canons of the Church of England.[120] Four classes are contemplated. A person who has been episcopally confirmed, with unction or with the laying on of hands, otherwise than by the Church of England's rites enjoys the right.[121] The same applies to a baptized person who is a communicant member of another church which subscribes to the doctrine of the Holy Trinity provided that person is in good standing in that church.[122] If these conditions are satisfied, in the opinion of the Legal Advisory Commission the person is 'free to receive Holy Communion according to the rites of the Church of England without the prior invitation of the incumbent', nor can the incumbent prevent the exercise of this right.[123] The minister is under a duty to set before such a person who regularly receives Communion over a long

---

[114] *CIC*, c. 44.   [115] Cc. 208, 213.

[116] The Code does not define 'use of reason'; see J. A. Griffiths, 'Cognitive faith and the problem of mental handicap in canon law', in N. Doe (ed.), *Essays in Canon Law* (Cardiff, 1992) 89.   [117] *CIC*, c. 777(4).

[118] See J. Huels, '"Use of reason" and reception of the sacraments by the mentally handicapped', *The Jurist*, 44 (1984), 209; see e.g. the pastoral statement of the Roman Catholic Bishops of England and Wales, *All People Together* (London, 1981); D. Wilson, 'Symbols and readings — reflections from celebrating mass with mentally handicapped people', *Liturgy*, 9(5) (1985) 181.

[119] M. Bayley, *The Local Church and Mentally Handicapped People* (London, 1984) 5–6; *Re Holy Innocents, Fallowfield* [1982] 3 WLR 666 at 671: Ch. Spafford observed in a faculty case that recent enactments and codes of practice on access to buildings 'all embody the necessity for bearing in mind the likely needs of the disabled'.

[120] In this respect the law of the Church of England confers rights outside the church; for the degree to which these are enforceable see Ch. 1 *supra*.   [121] Canon B15A(1)(a).

[122] Canon B15A(1)(b).

[123] *OLAC*, 5.1: 'Paragraph 1 [of Canon B15A] is governed by the word "shall" and not by the word "may"; this therefore leaves no option to the incumbent.'

period, which appears likely to continue indefinitely, the normal requirements for communicant status in the church.[124] A baptized person may be admitted if authorized under synodical regulations.[125] Any baptized person in immediate danger of death must be admitted.[126] If a minister is in doubt as to whether to admit he is under a canonical duty to refer the matter to the diocesan bishop, and to follow the bishop's guidance.[127] Usually diocesan norms simply repeat the terms of the governing canon.[128]

The Roman Catholic Church's stance on the reception of the Eucharist by non-Catholics is more restrictive.[129] Broadly, the Roman Catholic Church does not usually admit to Holy Communion those who have been baptized or baptized and confirmed in another church (including the Church of England) unless they have been received into the Roman Catholic Church.[130] They may be admitted, however, in exceptional circumstances. According to Canon 844, a Catholic minister may licitly administer Eucharist to members of other churches which in the judgment of the Apostolic See are in the same position as oriental churches not in full communion with the Catholic Church; the non-Catholic must initiate a request for the sacrament and be properly disposed.[131] When a non-Catholic is in danger of death or in other cases of grave necessity, a Catholic minister may licitly administer the Eucharist to those not in full communion with the Catholic Church. In these circumstances the approval of the bishop or conference of bishops must be obtained, the non-Catholic must be unable to approach a minister of his/her own church, must on their own ask for it, be properly disposed, and manifest catholic faith in the Eucharist.[132] It remains unclear which churches are meant to be covered by these rules. The Secretariat for Promoting Christian Unity has stressed that other churches must

---

[124] Canon B15A(2); once the incumbent has done so, the decision to comply with those requirements rests with the individual concerned: *OLAC*, 5.

[125] Canon B15A(1)(c); see also Admission to Holy Communion Measure 1972, s. 1 (Synod may make provision by canon or regulation for admission to Communion of 'other baptized persons').

[126] B15A(1)(d).   [127] B15A(3).

[128] *CDH*, 95; *BF*, 3.15; *DSBN*, Ad clerum notice 1993/2: ministers should be circumspect in requiring a person who regularly attends Holy Communion to be confirmed: 'serious consideration should be given to the significance and value of acts of adult commitment made in other Christian traditions.'

[129] *UR*, 8: sharing 'may not be regarded as a means to be used indiscriminately toward restoring Christian unity. . . . Unless the conference of bishops . . . or the Holy See has ruled otherwise, the local bishop is the authority competent to decide with prudence what the right course of action should be in view of all the circumstances of time, place, and people.'

[130] For the purposes of members of the Church of England see its *Ecumenical Relations: Code of Practice* (1989) 38 (App. IV): 'It must be noted that the sharing in prayer and worship which Roman Catholics are urged to undertake with their fellow Christians does not include sacramental sharing. The RC bishops . . . point out that occasional exceptions are made in the form of individual admissions to holy communion, but the general laws remain in force'; for statements of Roman Catholic bishops expressing this position, see ibid., 37.

[131] *CIC*, c. 844(3); *UR*, 13.

[132] c. 844(4); A. Tuché, 'The code of canon law of 1983 and ecumenical relations', 401 at 408–409.

'have kept the substance of Eucharistic teaching'.[133] Vatican II's *Decree on Ecumenism* singled out the Anglican Church as an ecclesial community occupying 'a special place among those communions in which Catholic traditions and institutions in part continue to exist' but there has been no formal papal judgment specifying that Anglicans come within the terms of these norms.[134] The bishops and episcopal conferences have power to enact general norms on this subject; before so doing they must consult with the local competent authority of the non-Catholic church involved.[135] A member of the Catholic faithful has a right to celebrate the Eucharist according to the rites of a non-Catholic church in cases of necessity or when genuine spiritual advantage suggests, when it is physically or morally impossible to approach a Catholic minister. The other church must treat the Eucharist as a valid sacrament.[136]

CONFESSION AND PENANCE

Whereas the Roman Catholic Church possesses a large body of law on confession and penance, the Church of England does not. In the former penance is treated as a sacrament, in the latter the matter is the subject of debate.[137] The following outlines the rules governing the administration of confession and the duty of confidentiality imposed upon clerics not to disclose information given in confession.

The Celebration of Confession and Penance

The law of the Church of England provides for both public and private confession. Baptized persons have a canonical duty to make general confession in the liturgical services of the church, followed by absolution which can be pronounced only by a priest.[138] The services of Holy Communion require both confession and absolution in mandatory terms: the congregation must confess and the priest must absolve.[139] At Morning and Evening Prayer confession is discretionary.[140] Apart from confession in the ordinary or regular round of liturgical services, an individual may make private confession to God

---

[133] Communication, 17 Oct. 1973 (*CCL: TC*, 610).   [134] *UR*, 13.   [135] *CIC*, c. 844(5).
[136] c. 844(2).

[137] *AR*, Art. 23; see e.g. E. J. Bicknell, *A Theological Introduction to the Thirty-Nine Articles of the Church of England* (2nd edn., London, 1925) 359; see also *Patterns for Worship*, 122 (for proposed new form of 'reconciliation'), 278–9.   [138] Canon B29.

[139] *BCP*, Order for the Administration of Holy Communion; *ASB*, 32, Rite A, 120, 127, Rite B, 187.

[140] *BCP*, the general confession, followed by what is described in the rubric as 'The Absolution or Remission of sins to be pronounced by the Priest alone, standing; the people still kneeling'; *ASB*, 48–9, 61 ('The minister may say').

in two ways, either alone or in the presence of a priest in auricular confession. Canon B29 imposes on baptized persons a duty to examine at all times their lives and conversations by the rule of God's Commandments. Whenever baptized persons perceive themselves to have offended 'by will, act or omission', they must confess to God with the full purpose of amendment of life, so that they may receive the forgiveness of their sins—this God has promised to all who turn to Him with 'hearty repentance and true faith'.[141]

Any baptized person who cannot quiet his own conscience by public general confession or by personal confession to God may seek private auricular confession with a priest; this is not enjoined but must occur voluntarily.[142] Whereas the priest is under a duty to receive general confession and to absolve in the liturgical setting of Holy Communion, no canonical duty is placed on the priest either to hear the confession or to absolve with regard to auricular confession;[143] the penitent's entitlement is merely to make a request, and a priest seems to have a lawful discretion not only to refuse to hear the confession but also, if confession is heard, to refuse absolution on the ground that the penitent has no intention to amend his life. When a baptized person cannot quiet his own conscience, 'but requires further comfort or counsel, let him come to some discreet and learned minister . . . that . . . he *may* receive the benefit of absolution, together with ghostly counsel and advice'.[144] Different rules apply to those who are sick or in danger of death. By canon law 'a priest *may* exercise the ministry of absolution anywhere in respect of any person who is in danger of death or if there is some urgent or weighty cause'.[145] A sick person whose 'conscience is troubled in any weighty matter, *should* make a special confession of his sins, that the priest *may* absolve him if he humbly and heartily desire it'.[146] There is no requirement in the canons that a person must perform a penance.[147] On the other hand, in these circumstances, according to liturgical rubrics '[h]ere *shall* the sick person be moved to make a special confession of his sins, if he feel his conscience troubled with any weighty matter. After which confession, the Priest *shall* absolve him (if he

---

[141] Canon B29(1).

[142] *Rector and Churchwardens of Capel St Mary, Suffolk v Packard* [1927] P 289: at 301: compulsory confession is illegal and habitual confession lawful; in this case the Dean of the Arches considered that 'the Church of England expressly allows persons . . . to make confession to a minister *and directs ministers to hear confessions*'.

[143] B29(2): the penitent 'may receive the benefit of absolution'; for the pre-Reformation duty to confess see R. H. Helmholz, *Roman Canon Law in Reformation England* (Cambridge, 1990) 113–14; see generally M. Dudley and G. Rowell, *Confession and Absolution* (London, 1990).

[144] Canon B29(2): 'to the quieting of his conscience and avoiding of all scruple and doubtfulness.'

[145] Canon B29(2): 'If there be any who by these means', i.e. the means for baptized persons to fulfil their duty to confess as mentioned in B29(1); for danger of death 'or if there is some urgent or weighty cause' see ibid., para. (4).					[146] Canon B29(3).

[147] R. Phillimore, *Ecclesiastical Law*, I, 538.

humbly and heartily desire it)'.[148] There appears to be a dissonance between the priest's canonical discretion and his rubrical duty. It has been advised that the service entitled 'A Form for the Reconciliation of a Penitent' is provided not only for sick persons.[149]

These arrangements are very different from those in Roman Catholic canon law. In the sacrament of penance, the faithful confess their sins, proposing to reform, and thereby obtain from God forgiveness of sins committed after baptism through absolution; the wound caused by sin to God, to the person, and to the church is healed by the sacrament as a process of healing and reconciliation.[150] All the faithful have a canonical duty to celebrate the sacrament, confessing serious sins, at least once each year.[151] To be validly celebrated, the penitent must be properly disposed and have the intention to amend.[152] The penitent has a right to choose a confessor.[153] Individual confession and absolution is the ordinary method of reconciliation and only moral or physical impossibility relieves (for a limited time) a person of the duty to confess individually.[154] General absolution may be given to a group if those in it have confessed individually beforehand. A priest can absolve generally without prior individual confession if the penitent is in danger of death or in cases of serious necessity, when there are insufficient confessors.[155] A Roman Catholic may lawfully receive the sacrament when necessity requires or there is a genuine spiritual advantage, and when it is morally and physically impossible to approach a Roman Catholic priest, from a non-Catholic minister in whose church penance is treated as a sacrament.[156]

In Roman Catholic canon law absolution may be given only by a validly ordained priest.[157] The minister has some discretion in arranging times for

---

[148] *BCP*, 317, rubric in the Order for the Visitation of the Sick; when Holy Communion is celebrated for a person sick or in danger of death, confession and absolution are mandatory: *supra* n. 139.

[149] GS Misc 169. B. J. T. Hanson, *Legal Aspects Concerning ' A Form for the Reconciliation of a Penitent'*, GS Misc 169, 1983: this is a service within the meaning of CE(WD)M 1974, s. 5(2) and needs authorization by General Synod.

[150] *CIC*, c. 959; *LG*, II, 11; see *GDBOP*, 6.1 for norms concerning child protection and confidentiality.

[151] *CIC*, cc. 988–9; those wishing to celebrate the Eucharist must confess individually beforehand if they are conscious of grave sin: c. 916; c. 988(2) recommends that the faithful confess venial sins; for the distinction between these see the guidance of the International Theological Commission 1983, *Origins*, 13 (1984), 523; J. H. Provost, 'First penance and first Eucharist', *The Jurist*, 43 (1983), 450. [152] *CIC*, c. 987.

[153] C. 991; and to employ an interpreter, c. 990; for indulgence, see cc. 992–7.

[154] C. 960; the proper place for its celebration is in churches, or elsewhere for just cause: c. 964.

[155] C. 961; the bishop has a right to lay down norms with the agreement of the episcopal conference; the penitent must be properly disposed and intend to confess individually as soon as possible thereafter; he is under a further duty to confess actually: c. 962; *CCL: TC*, 677–80.

[156] *CIC*, c. 844(2).

[157] C. 965; 979: the priest in posing questions is to proceed with prudence and discretion, with attention to the age and condition of the penitent; he is to refrain from asking the name of an accomplice; c. 1387: soliciting penitent to commit sexual sin; for prohibition against asking 'disgusting questions' in confessions in the Church of England see *Poole v Bishop of London* (1859) 5 Jur NS 522 at 524, on appeal: (1861) 14 Moo PCC 262.

individual confession[158] but as a general rule 'if the confessor has no doubt about the disposition of a penitent who asks for absolution, absolution is not to be refused or delayed'.[159] In danger of death cases, every priest has a duty to absolve.[160] This applies both to the Catholic faithful and to non-Catholics.[161] A Roman Catholic priest may lawfully administer penance to members of non-Catholic churches not in full communion with Rome which subscribe to penance as a sacrament, if they ask on their own and are properly disposed.[162] Though an act of penance is not strictly within the terms of the canonical definition of the sacrament, liturgically an act of penance is treated as consummating the sacrament.[163] In the administration of the sacrament the minister acts as a judge and is under a duty to enjoin a salutary and suitable penance in keeping with the quality and number of sins.[164] The penitent is obliged to perform the penance personally, and if a person intends to perform no penance this may be a ground upon which a minister may lawfully refuse to absolve.[165] A statement of the conference of bishops of England and Wales repeats the general duty to do penance by setting aside days for prayer, denial, and works of charity; Friday is a special penitential day and abstinence from meat and alcohol is recommended.[166]

By contrast with Roman Catholic canon law,[167] a Church of England priest does not require a faculty to hear confessions and to absolve. However, no Church of England priest may exercise the ministry of absolution in any place without the permission of the minister who has cure of souls. This applies 'unless he is authorised by law to exercise his ministry in that place without being subject to the control of the minister having the general cure of souls'. A priest is authorized by law to exercise the ministry when the penitent is in danger of death or in other cases of urgent or weighty cause.[168] In the Church

---

[158] *CIC*, c. 986(1).

[159] C. 980; if a person is excommunicate or subject to an interdict, there is no right to penance (cc. 1331–2); the right returns when these are lifted (c. 1347); under c. 1357 a confessor has a right to remit in the internal forum an automatic censure of excommunication or interdict if it would be hard for the penitent to remain in a state of serious sin; the penitent must then have recourse to the ordinary; for a discussion of the procedures see J. McAreavey, 'Abortion and the sacrament of penance', *The Furrow* (1993), 230; A. Stenson, 'Penalties in the new Code: the role of the confessor', *The Jurist*, 43 (1983), 406.   [160] *CIC*, c. 986(2).

[161] For these and other cases of grave necessity concerning non-Catholics, members of churches not in full, see *CIC*, c. 844(4): the person must be properly disposed, be unable to approach for penance a minister of their own community, and manifest a faith in the sacrament of penance.

[162] C. 844(3); as the Church of England does not hold penance to be a sacrament, it seems unlikely that a Roman Catholic priest could validly absolve one of its members.

[163] C. 959, the definitional Canon, contains no reference to an act of penance; the doctrine that 'True conversion is completed by expiation for the sins committed, by amendment of life', is contained in the Rite of Penance of the Roman Ritual: see *CCL: TC*, 690.

[164] *CIC*, cc. 978, 981.   [165] C. 981; *CCL: TC*, 689.

[166] *COCLA*, 1339–1341 (there is no duty to eat fish, nor has there ever been).

[167] A priest must have a faculty by law, office, or concession to exercise the ministry: see *CIC*, cc. 965–9; in danger of death cases no faculty is required: c. 976.

[168] Canon B29(4).

of England, a faculty must be obtained in order to authorize the use of a confessional table and chair when these are intended for the hearing of voluntary confessions.[169] A faculty may also issue to authorize the placement of a confessional box.[170] Diocesan norms generally do not deal with private auricular confession though sometimes they recommend it as a preliminary to the ministry of healing; occasionally norms prohibit priests from exercising the ministry of private absolution until they have been in holy orders for at least two or three years and have received instruction.[171]

The Seal of the Confessional: The Duty of Confidentiality

Roman Catholic canon law forbids the disclosure of information given in the sacrament of reconciliation: '[t]he sacramental seal is inviolable; therefore, it is a crime for a confessor in any way to betray a penitent by word or in any other manner or for any reason'; the duty of confidentiality is also imposed on interpreters and any third-party recipient of information revealed.[172] However, some commentators suggest that the duty attaches only to information revealed 'in order to receive absolution'.[173] It seems a priest could not disclose even with the consent of the penitent.[174] Further, the confessor is absolutely forbidden to use knowledge acquired from confession when this might harm the penitent.[175] A confessor who directly violates the seal of confession incurs an automatic excommunication reserved to the pontiff, and indirect disclosure may be punished with a penalty in accord with the seriousness of the offence.[176]

In contrast, the law of the Church of England merely *recommends* that a minister should not disclose information received in the exercise of the ministry of absolution. The subject is not dealt with in the revised Canons. The unrepealed proviso of 1603 Canon 113 states that if any man confesses his

---

[169] *Re St Mary, Tyne Dock* [1954] 2 All ER 339 at 345.

[170] In *Roffe-Silvester v King* [1938] 4 All ER 147, the consistory court's order to remove a confessional box was set aside by the Arches Ct.

[171] *RBG*, A.8 (3 years); *LDR*, 6 (2 years); see *LDHI*, III, 20.10 for confession and the ministry of healing.

[172] *CIC*, c. 983; the Rite of Penance uses similar language: 'Conscious that he has come to know the secret of another's conscience only because he is God's minister, the confessor is bound by the obligation of preserving the seal of confession absolutely unbroken.'

[173] J. A. Coriden, *Introduction*, 127; F. R. McManus argues that 'No distinction is made among the matters confessed, whether the sinful action itself or attendant circumstances, or the acts of satisfaction or penances imposed': *CCL: TC*, 691.

[174] The code is silent on this point; cf. the decision of the High Court in the Irish decision of *Cook v Carroll* [1945] IR 515 at 524 *per* Gavan Duffy J: non-disclosure could not be waived by one or either party without the priests consent. [175] *CIC*, c. 984.

[176] C. 1388; for the position in the United States see R. S. Stake, 'Professionalism and confidentiality in the practice of spiritual direction', *The Jurist*, 43 (1983), 214; W. H. Tiemann and J. C. Bush, *The Right to Silence: Privileged Clergy Communication and the Law* (2nd edn., Nashville, 1983).

secret and hidden sins to the minister, for the unburdening of his conscience and to receive spiritual consolation, 'we do not in any way bind the said Minister by this our Constitution, but do straitly charge and admonish him, that he do not at any time reveal and make known to any person whatsoever any crime or offence so committed to his trust and secrecy (except they be such crimes as by the laws of this realm his own life may be called into question for concealing the same), under pain of irregularity'.[177] The Doctrine Commission has suggested that the 'rule' binds only in conscience.[178]

The absence of a binding canonical duty not to disclose was assumed in 1959 when Convocations passed a resolution reaffirming '*as an essential principle of Church doctrine* that if any person confess his secret and hidden sin to a priest for the unburdening of his conscience, and to receive spiritual consolation *and absolution* from him, such priest is strictly charged that he do not at any time reveal or make known to any person whatsoever *any sin* so committed to his trust and secrecy'.[179] The ministerial duty not to disclose applies only to information disclosed in order to obtain absolution: in this respect the rule is narrower in scope than the prohibition in Canon 113. In another respect, however, it is wider: the prohibition in the resolution applies to 'any sin', as opposed to 'any crime'. Given the absence of a clear and binding canonical prohibition against disclosure, and the non-enforceability of the Act of Convocation, *prima facie* the suggestion that a cleric would be in grave danger of censure by the ecclesiastical courts in the event of violating the seal is questionable.[180]

The internal rules of these two churches must be set in their wider legal environment. Whether a court in civil or in criminal proceedings would either admit evidence given in auricular confession or indeed compel its disclosure by a priest is not clear. Some judicial dicta suggest that a secular judge may admit evidence given in auricular confession.[181] The admission of confession evidence is discretionary and some dicta have suggested that the courts would

---

[177] For argument that the pre-Reformation prohibition against disclosure (*inter alia* contained in Canon 21 of the Fourth Lateran Council 1215) may continue see R. Bursell, 'The seal of the confessional', *ELJ*, 1(7) (1990), 84 at 87–8. The origin of the exception is unclear.

[178] *Doctrine in the Church of England* (London, 1938) 192: 'The confession is heard under the "seal" of absolute secrecy. This rule is necessary in order that freedom of confession may be secured. It is essential to the due discharge of the confessor's office that this rule should be held to be so binding on the priest's conscience that he cannot consider himself released therefrom by the authority of the civil or other power.'

[179] *Acts of Convocation*, 165; *RACCL* (1947) 157, recommended the creation of a new canon (no. 66) forbidding a priest 'by word, writing sign, directly or indirectly, openly or covertly, or in any way whatsoever, at any time to reveal . . . any sin, crime, or offence', or to make use of such information; the rule would have applied to information given to obtain absolution.

[180] R. Bursell, 'The seal of the confessional', at 105 ff., for the possibility of proceedings under the EJM 1963 s. 14(1)(b).

[181] *R v Gilham* (1828) 1 Mood. CCR 452 (not a sacramental confession); *Broad v Pitt* (1828) 3 C&P 518.

not compel disclosure.[182] Other judicial statements, however, suggest that a judge might order a priest to disclose information; he would be in contempt of court if he refused.[183] In any event, communications passing in confession are not privileged.[184] With regard to the Church of England, as we have seen, the prohibition against disclosure is not strictly and clearly binding and could not therefore be presented as a duty arising under the law of the land; in relation to the Roman Catholic Church, the terms of the canon law forbidding disclosure, which may be classified under civil law as terms of a contract, are inferior to those of the common law.[185]

In the civil context, it is arguable that both the Catholic canonical duty and the English exhortation may be protected to a limited degree by the equitable doctrine of confidentiality. A person, either a confidant or a third party, who receives information given in confidence may be restrained by injunction from disclosing that information; the duty is applicable in both the public and the private sphere.[186] Confidential communications are protected as a matter of public policy.[187] Disclosure may not be restrained, however, if the information is trivial, if it has already entered the public domain, or if it is required in the interests of the administration of justice.[188] In short, it is arguable that a minister who has been given information in confession might be under an equitable, but not an absolute, duty not to disclose.

CONCLUSIONS

Both canonical systems contain elaborate rules about the celebration of the Eucharist, which both churches treat as a dominical sacrament. The faithful

---

[182] *AG v Briant* (1846) 15 LJ Ex 265 at 271 *per* Alderson B; *R v Griffin* (1853) 6 Cox 219 *per* Alderson B (non sacramental); *Ruthven v De Bour* (1901) 45 SJ 272; for a discussion of these cases see R. Bursell, 'The seal of the confessional'. For the admissibility in evidence of confessions see Police and Criminal Evidence Act 1984, s. 76: excluded if the result of oppression or if unreliable; confession is defined in s. 82 as including any statement wholly or partly adverse to the party who made it, whether made to a person in authority or not and whether made in words or not'; s. 82(3): the court may exclude evidence at its discretion.

[183] *R v Hay* (1860) 2 F&F 4: it was unclear whether the communication was a Roman Catholic sacramental confession; *R v Kent* (1865) cited in Hansard's Parliamentary Debates, Series 3, Vol. 179 (HL) 12 May 1865 (Church of England cleric).

[184] For an excellent discussion which includes comparative material (esp. setting the problem in the context of the European Convention on Human Rights) and suggestions for reform see D. W. Elliott, 'An evidential privilege for priest–penitent communications', *ELJ*, 3 (1995), 272; *Wheeler v La Merchant* (1861) 17 Ch D 675 at 681; *Normanshaw v Normanshaw* (1893) 69 LT 468; *AG v Mulholland* [1963] 1 All ER 767 at 771 *per* Denning MR (*obiter*); *D v NSPCC* [1978] AC 11; G. D. Nokes, 'Professional privilege', *LQR*, 66 (1950), 88; J. Noel Lyon, 'Privileged communications—penitent and priest', *Criminal Law Quarterly* (Toronto), 7 (1964–5), 327.

[185] See *supra* Ch. 1.

[186] *Argyll v Argyll* [1967] Ch. 302: marital communications; *AG v Jonathan Cape Ltd* [1976] QB 752 (HL): cabinet secrets.   [187] *Rumpyng v DPP* [1964] AC 814 (HL).

[188] Ibid.; *AG v Guardian Newspaper* [1988] 3 All ER 545; ECHR, Art. 8

have a duty to celebrate the Eucharist frequently and its celebration must take place in accordance with liturgical law. In both systems a valid celebration occurs under the presidency of an ordained priest, as a norm in the presence of the worshipping community, though in addition each system allows for the distribution of the elements by lay people. Many diocesan norms in the Church of England enable extended Communion to be celebrated with the administration of reserved elements in a service in church conducted in the absence of a priest. Some diocesan norms prohibit this. The Church of England's law concerning admission and exclusion is, by and large, more liberal than that of the Roman Catholic Church. Whereas Roman Catholic canon law imposes a duty on the faithful to celebrate the sacrament of penance, the law of the Church of England imposes this duty only in relation to general confessions in the setting of the Holy Communion. In Roman Catholic canon law a minister has a duty to hear confessions and to absolve; in the Church of England the minister has a discretion to exercise the ministry of absolution. Each church shuns disclosure of information given in confession: in the Church of England non-disclosure is recommended, in the Roman Catholic Church it is commanded.

13

Marriage and Divorce

For the Church of England, the right to marry in the parish church is treated as one of the package, so to speak, of rights enjoyed by parishioners. This Chapter explores the basis and terms of this right, procedural matters relating to solemnization, and the canonical requirements for a valid marriage operating within the context of the civil law. These subjects are addressed directly by the church's central legal system though, unlike in the Roman Catholic Church in which tribunals are most active in the field of matrimonial canon law, the jurisdiction of the Church of England's courts to regulate marriages no longer exists. The Church of England's law remains largely undeveloped with regard to divorce and remarriage, about which there has been considerable debate recently, and the legal position of mixed marriages. With respect to these matters, the practice of the church diverging fundamentally from that of the Roman Catholic Church, the dominant system of regulation in the Church of England is to be found in executively formulated norms issued centrally and episcopally at diocesan level.

THE RIGHT TO MARRY

In Roman Catholic canon law '[a]ll persons who are not prohibited by law have a right to marriage' (c.1058). This is a broad principle of freedom. The individual's right to marry in church cannot be exercised, however, if it is not the appropriate time or if the person is not properly disposed. In these circumstances, and if the person is prohibited by law, the minister may refuse marriage.[1] Moreover, the bishop has the power to prohibit marriage temporarily not only if there is a suspicion of an impediment but also if in his opinion the union would cause harm to the parties themselves or to the community: 'the ordinary can prohibit the marriage of his own subjects . . . but only for a serious cause and as long as that cause exists'.[2] It is commonly understood that the position in the Church of England is very different: every resident of a parish has a right to be married in the parish church. The principle has been

---

[1] *CIC*, c. 843: these represent the general limits on the right to the sacraments (see also c. 213). It is the duty of the minister to see that those who seek the sacraments, including marriage, are 'prepared' to receive them.

[2] Ibid., c. 1077; J. Waterhouse, *The Power of the Local Ordinary to Impose a Matrimonial Ban* (Washington, 1952); R. W. Guiry, 'Immaturity, maturity and Christian marriage', *Studia Canonica*, 25 (1991), 93.

enunciated in many official reports, in guidance, and by the commentators.[3]
Even if the parties have 'never set foot in the church before'[4] the minister has a
duty to solemnize the marriage of his parishioners on request 'and is guilty of
neglect if he refuses (for which disciplinary proceedings may be taken in the
ecclesiastical courts)'.[5] The minister enjoys no general legal right of conscientious objection. This basic understanding does not clearly represent the law.

The Ministerial Duty to Solemnize

Marriage in the Church of England may take place after the publication of
banns in the parish church (the most common method), by means of an
ordinary's common licence (dispensing with the need for banns), by special
licence granted in the name of the Archbishop of Canterbury, or following the
grant of a civil superintendent registrar's certificate.[6] According to the report
An Honourable Estate (1988), '[i]t is widely accepted that, by providing that
virtually all marriages should be solemnized in the Church of England, Lord
Hardwicke's Act [1753] gave everyone the legal right to be married in his or
her parish church'.[7] In its attempt to prevent the celebration of clandestine

---

[3] *Anglican Marriage in England and Wales: A Guide to the Law for Clergy*, produced by the
Faculty Office of the Archbishop of Canterbury, (London, 1992) para. 6.1; *MIECL*, 76: 'It seems
that every parishioner is entitled to marriage in church after banns, whether the parties are
members of the Church of England or not'; Dale, *LPC*, 60–1; St. J. A. Robilliard, *Religion and
the Law* (Manchester, 1984) 200–1; D. McClean, 'Marriage in England', in *Marriage and Religion
in Europe*, Proceedings of the European Consortium for Church–State Research (Milan, 1993) 187
at 192–3.   [4] *Solemnization of Marriage* (1971), Law Commission Working Paper No. 35.
[5] Faculty Office *Guide*, para. 6.1; sometimes the right is expressly recognized in diocesan
regulations: *CAD*, 32; *OLAC*, 161: when a parish has more than one parish church, the bishop
may direct under the Pastoral Measure 1983, Sched. 3, para. 14(4) as to publication of banns or
where solemnization is to take place; if the bishop does not so direct the parties may specify; if
they do not, the incumbent has a discretion to choose; *OLAC*, 166: if a building is designated a
parish centre of worship under the Pastoral Measure 1983, s. 29(1), this is deemed to be a parish
church for the purposes of the Marriage Acts; the effect of s. 29(3) is that persons residing in a
parish having a parish centre of worship (but not a parish church) may be married either in the
centre of worship or, if they so elect, in the parish church of the adjoining parish; see *OLAC*, 170
for marriages in dean and chapter cathedrals (being extra-parochial places) which may be
authorized by the bishop as an authorized church or chapel (Marriage Act 1949, s. 21).
[6] Marriage Act 1949, s. 5.
[7] The report of a Working Party established by the Standing Committee of the General Synod
(London, 1988) para. 97; cf. Bishop of Guildford 16(1) *GSRP* (1985) at 208: 'the right of every
parishioner to be married in his church derives from ecclesiastical law, not from State law, from
pre-Reformation Canons. In 1754 Lord Hardwicke's Act of Parliament regulated the existence of
an already existing right'; T. Coningsby, 'An honourable estate—a personal view of the report of
the working party of General Synod', *ELJ*, 1(3) (1988), 10: this proposes the idea that 'the right of
parishioner to be married in his parish church may be a common law right'; as such the right exists
as no more than a corollary of the duty under the Act of Uniformity 1551, s. 1 to attend the parish
church (see *Cole v Police Constable 443A* [1937] 1 KB 316 in which Lord Goodard suggested that
the right to attend for public worship existed now at common law and was not dependent on the
(now repealed) 1551 statute). Cf. Serjt. Talfourd and Sir W. Follett *arguendo* in *Davis v Black*
(1841) 113 ER 1376 at 1379: 'but at common law the party desiring to be married could have no
right to call on any particular clergyman to perform the duty.'

marriages this statute imposed the duty upon all individuals (except Quakers and Jews) to be married in the parish church. No marriage was valid unless solemnized according to the rites of the Church of England in the church of the parish in which one or both of the parties resided in the presence of a clergyman and two other witnesses.[8] The proposition that this statute is to be understood as giving a right to the parishioner is questionable. The statute was not about conferring rights on parishioners. It sought simply to eradicate clandestine marriages by imposing a *duty* on residents to marry only in the parish church.[9] For the parishioner there was no choice—there was no right to choose. The only right that existed was to exercise the statutory duty. The notion of a class, residents of a parish, becomes crucial. Before the 1753 Act, a minister if requested had a duty to marry *only from* the class of residents in his parish; he could not solemnize the marriage of those who were not resident: this was an ecclesiastical obligation arising from canon law.[10] The 1753 Act imposed on the minister a duty, if requested, to marry *all from* the class of residents (except Jews and Quakers); this was a secular obligation arising from public law. These duties must be distinguished.

The statutory duty was repeated in the Marriage Act 1823 (which repealed the 1753 Act).[11] The duty was destroyed, however, by the Marriage Act 1836.[12] This statute created the right to be married elsewhere 'according to such form of ceremony as they may wish to adopt' and introduced marriage by registrar's certificate. Parishioners no longer had to marry only in the parish church, they now had a choice.[13] The modern proposition about an autonomous parishioner's right, based in part on a misunderstanding of the structure of the 1753 statute, has survived as an assumption or legal fiction. It has survived not least because it has met with judicial approval. However, judicial statements of the proposition have simply been *obiter*—though of high authority—and some of them are not clear.[14]

The most commonly cited decision is *Argar v Holdsworth*. It concerned the failure of a clergyman to marry a couple in accordance with an episcopal licence. In the consistory court the cleric was found guilty of neglect of duty. The Arches Court overturned the decision because the articles of prosecution were defective. In the Arches Court Sir George Lee accepted that a clergyman

---

[8] S. 1: in relation to marriage by banns, 'The Marriage shall be solemnized in one of the Parish Churches or chapels where . . . Banns have been published, and in no other Place Whatsoever'. The duty is similarly expressed in relation to marriage by licence (s. 4).

[9] See A. H. Manchester, *Modern Legal History* (London, 1980) 360–6; L. Stone, *The Family, Sex and Marriage in England: 1500–1800* (London, 1977) 33–5.

[10] For Lyndwood's statement of the rule see R. Phillimore, *Ecclesiastical Law*, I, 600–1; G. Jacob, *New Law Dictionary* (5th edn., London, 1744) 'Marriage'. [11] 4 Geo. IV, c. 76.

[12] 6 & 7 Will. IV, c. 85.

[13] P. M. Bromley and N. V. Lowe (eds.), *Bromley's Family Law* (8th edn., London, 1992) 40–1; the whole of the 1823 statute and the whole of the 1836 Act (with the exception of ss. 3,17, 45) were repealed by the Marriage Act 1949, Sched. 5, Part I.

[14] E.g. *HLE*, para. 1357; *MIECL*, 74, *Honourable Estate*, 82.

'might be prosecuted by any one for neglect of his clerical duty' if he refused to carry out the terms of a licence authorizing marriage: 'a licence was a legal authority for marriage, and . . . a minister was guilty of breach of his duty who should refuse to marry pursuant to a proper licence from his ordinary'.[15] It is difficult to determine precisely the *ratio* of the case but it seems simply to be that in considering articles for the prosecution of a cleric for neglect of duty a consistory court must not reject those 'articles which alone pleaded the facts relative to [the] cause'. Though the litigation occurred only five years after the 1753 Act, it is unclear whether the case was decided on this statute; there is no reference to it. In any event the case cannot be understood as authority for the proposition that a minister is under a duty to marry parishioners even against his wishes when the proposed form of marriage is by banns: it related only to marriage by licence. Moreover, the principle that 'anyone' might prosecute is not now good law; nor is the case binding authority for both provinces, having been decided by the Arches Court of Canterbury.[16] If the case was decided on the 1753 Act, it may also have lost its authority since that statute is now repealed.[17] The proposition was repeated in the secular courts *obiter* in *Davis v Black* (1841)[18] and *R v James* (1850),[19] which, similarly, decided questions relating to licences. In *Tuckniss v Alexander*,[20] Kindersley VC suggested two legal reasons for the ministerial duty: 'If a licence is produced to a clergyman from his ordinary, from his diocesan, directing him, or in terms authorizing him, to marry two persons in his church or chapel, his canonical obedience requires him, as well as the rights of the parties require him, to perform the marriage according to that licence.' In short, in these cases the 'right to marry' was recognized as arising by virtue of the terms of a licence and not, it is

---

[15] (1758) 2 Lee 515; 161 ER 424 *per* Sir George Lee;

[16] For authorized complainants under Ecclesiastical Jurisdiction Measure 1963, s. 19 and for doctrines of precedent see *supra* Ch. 5.

[17] F. Bennion, *Statutory Interpretation* (London, 1984) 430; *Farrell v Alexander* [1977] AC 59, [1976] 2 All ER 721; *R v Heron* [1982] 1 All ER 993; *Eton College v Minister of Agriculture* [1964] Ch 274.

[18] (1841) 1 QB 900; 113 ER 1376: for failure to carry out a licence, the complainant must declare *inter alia* that a request to marry was made by both parties and that the clergyman was able but not willing to carry it out (*per* C. J. Denman, ibid.1380); 'it may perhaps be said that the duty is cast on [the cleric]' (*per* J. Pattison ibid. 1381) the case concerned the possibility of an action for damages; 'The duty is charged as arising upon notice of the proper licence to the clergyman. I much doubt whether such a duty does necessarily so arise. He might be engaged in some previous duty before he had knowledge of the licence and that would surely constitute a good justification in an Ecclesiastical Court' (*per* J. Williams); 'The duty should appear to grow from the facts stated in the declaration; and there is no duty, unless both parties be willing to be married' (*per* J. Coleridge).

[19] (1850) 3 Car & Kir 167; 175 ER 506; the parties obtained a registrar's certificate under the Marriage Act 1836 and the minister refused to marry because they were not confirmed; convicted at first instance (Liverpool Assizes), reversed by Court for Crown Causes Reserved; at 510 *per* Alderson B: 'The parties had a right to be married at any time when they presented themselves in canonical hours'; the cleric was found to have acted reasonably; see also *R v Ellis* (1888) 16 Cox CC 469.   [20] (1863) 32 Ch 794 at 806.

submitted, by virtue of an autonomous right to which, in any event, no judicial reference was made.

The litigation in *Banister v Thompson* and *R v Dibdin* resulted in the House of Lords deciding that a cleric could not, by virtue of the provisions of the Deceased Wife's Sister's Marriage Act 1907, lawfully bar from Holy Communion a man married to his deceased wife's sister.[21] This is the *ratio* of the decisions. In the Divisional Court, the Court of Appeal, and the House of Lords the judges commented *obiter* on whether a cleric could refuse to solemnize the marriages of such people. Generally, they based their comments on a very wide understanding of *Argar v Holdsworth*. No detailed analysis of the case is to be found in any of the judgments. A proviso to s.1 protected a cleric who refused to marry such persons from ecclesiastical censure. In the Divisional Court, Lawrence J stated 'Before the Act the vicar, as part of the duties of his office, was bound to perform the marriage service upon all persons dwelling in the parish who lawfully presented themselves'; though he dissented on the issue at hand, Bray J stated: 'persons so marrying are *not* entitled *as of right* to be married in their parish church *as are other parishioners*'.[22] For Fletcher Moulton LJ, in the Court of Appeal, 'One of the duties of the clergyman within this realm is to perform the ceremony of marriage, and parishioners have the right to have that ceremony performed in their parish church'.[23] It is submitted that not only were these statements *obiter* but they were based on a general proposition which *Argar* had not decided—*Argar* had decided a much narrower point in relation to marriage by licence.

The assumption has also been made by Parliament. The Matrimonial Causes Act 1965 supposes the right when it states that the minister cannot be compelled to marry a divorced person whose former spouse is still living.[24] In summary, it is suggested that the 1753 Act never conferred a right on the parishioner, but rather imposed a duty. If the 1753 statute is (as is commonly understood) the origin of the parishioner's 'right' (and the ministerial duty), it existed only until 1836. At that date parliament abolished the duty, and it has survived since as a powerful legal fiction. The source of the right has not been

---

[21] *Bannister v Thompson* [1908] P 362 for the decision by the Dean of the Arches; at 393: 'But for the proviso a clergyman would be under a legal obligation to proclaim the banns of marriage, and to register it in the parish church: *Argar v Holdsworth*'; *R v Dibdin* [1910] P 57 (Dv. Ct,CA); [1912] AC 533 (HL).   [22] [1910] P 57 at 88, 99.

[23] [1910] P 57 at 129; for Cozens-Hardy MR, ibid., 88;

[24] S.8; see also the Marriage Act 1836, s. 31: 'Provided always, and be it enacted, that notwithstanding any such Licence as aforesaid to solemnize Marriage in any such Chapel, the Parties may, if they think fit, have their Marriage solemnized in the Parish Church . . . in which heretofore the Marriage of such Parties or either of them might have been legally solemnized'; Marriage Act 1949, s. 23: 'Provided that nothing in this section shall deprive a person of the right to be married in any church in which he would otherwise have been entitled to be married'. See also the Welsh Church Act 1914, s. 23: 'including any law conferring any right to be married in such a church', repealed by the Welsh Church (Temporalities) Act 1919, s. 6.

identified—certainly, there existed the right to 'ask' for marriage.[25] These cases decided matters arising in relation to marriage by licence, not marriage by banns. They do not, in strict law, stand for the proposition that a minister must not refuse parishioners proposing marriage by banns. In any event, the present view is that, unlike the Roman Catholic priest, the Church of England minister has no *general* legal right to a conscientious objection. Nevertheless, as in Roman Catholic canon law, though a minister may not refuse arbitrarily, he may lawfully refuse in certain circumstances.

Lawful Refusal

The basic principle described above is subject to the qualification that ministers, in some circumstances, may lawfully refuse to solemnize the marriage of a parishioner. As Lord Fletcher Moulton said in *R v Dibdin*, the minister must not refuse 'unless there be a lawful cause for refusing'.[26] Indeed, the minister is under a *duty* to refuse when the parties lack the legal capacity to marry.[27] Similarly, if neither of the parties is resident the minister must refuse, though he cannot use non-residence as a cloak for a general conscientious objection.[28] Lack of residence will not, however, invalidate the marriage.[29] The minister may also delay in order to fulfil his canonical duty to make enquiries about impediments and residence.[30] The minister seems to have a limited discretion to refuse, if for example the parties unreasonably demand marriage by licence when the minister may be engaged in the performance of another lawful duty.[31] In relation to marriage by banns, the cleric is entitled to

[25] *Supra* n. 7 (Bishop of Guildford); see the statute 3 Jac 1, c. 5: obligation on recusant Roman Catholics to marry according to the rites of the Church of England; G. Jacob, *New Law Dictionary* (1744) 'Marriage': 'marriages that are made in the ordinary course are to be *by asking* in the church'. See also 5&6 Ed 6, c. 12: priests allowed to marry 'Provided alway, that this Act nor any thing therein contained shall extend to give liberty to any person without *asking* in the church'. See also Jacob, *New Law Dictionary*, 'Marriage', for the principle that 'Where a mutual contract of marriage . . . can be proved, the Ecclesiastical Courts will compel the parties to solemnise their marriage'. [26] [1910] P 57 at 129.

[27] E.g. the Canon B32 rule that no minister shall solemnize matrimony between 2 persons either of whom (not being a widow or widower) is under 18 (unless the consent of a parent or guardian is given). See, for validity, below.

[28] For marriage after publication of banns, by archiepiscopal special licence, and by common licence, see Canon B34; for residence see Marriage Act 1949, s. 6; a person living in one parish, but who habitually worships in another, may marry in the latter if their name is on the electoral roll (s. 72); for the residence requirements as to marriage by banns where one of the parties resides in the parish see s. 6(1); for common licence (where one of the parties has his 'usual place of residence' in the parish immediately before the grant of the licence) see s. 15(1)(a); for registrar's certificate (where residence is in a registration district), s. 34; for licence for problem cases see *OLAC*, 167–9. The minister must enquire into residence and may be subject to ecclesiastical censure for failing to do so: *Priestly v Lamb* (1801) 6 Ves 421; *Diddear v Faucit* (1821) 161 ER 1421; *Wynn v Davies and Weaver* (1835) 1 Curt 69.

[29] Marriage Act 1949, s. 24; *Nicholson v Squire* (1809) 16 Ves 259 *per* Lord Eldon.
[30] Canons B33, B35(2).
[31] *Davis v Black* (1841) 113 ER 1376 at 1378; *R v James* (1850) 175 ER 506 at 512.

receive one week's notice and may refuse to publish banns if the notice is not given.[32] Furthermore, under Canon B30(3) the minister has a duty 'to explain to the two persons . . . the Church's doctrine of marriage . . . in order that they may discharge aright their obligations as married persons'. It is unclear when a ministerial delay to fulfil this duty amounts to a refusal.

The law provides for conscientious objections in limited circumstances. A minister cannot be compelled to marry divorcees whose former spouses are still living (this is discussed more fully below).[33] The minister may refuse where there is a relationship of affinity between the parties not amounting to a prohibited relationship.[34] These arrangements have been designed, as was said in *R v Dibdin*, 'to protect the clergyman's conscience from being offended in the performance of any of the duties of his office'.[35] The minister may also refuse to give his consent to the solemnization of a marriage under a superintendent registrar's certificate.[36] Furthermore, the law affords the right of an objection to those present at the marriage service. If a person alleges and declares an impediment, that the parties may not lawfully marry, then the minister is under a duty to defer solemnization until such time as the truth be determined.[37]

Baptism is not, it seems, a legal pre-condition of marriage. The modern understanding is that a minister could not refuse to marry on the grounds that one or other of the parties has not been baptized.[38] In the light of the terms of the legal fiction, that *any* resident is entitled to marry on request, this is logical.[39] The rubrics of the Book of Common Prayer 1662 do not appear to require parties to be baptized; they simply state that '[i]t is *convenient* that the new-married persons should receive the Holy Communion at the time of their

[32] Marriage Act 1949, s. 8; see also *Voysey v Martin* cited in Phillimore, *Ecclesiastical Law*, (undated) I, 603, n. (c): 'In all such cases the law would require the clergyman to exercise due enquiry, and would warrant him in delaying or, as the case may be, finally refusing to publish banns.' Once notice is given the minister must publish the banns: Faculty Office *Guide* para. 7.12; see also *R v Dibdin* [1910] P 57 at 126; s. 6(1) of the Marriage Act 1949 does not itself impose a duty to publish banns but simply relates to the venue of publication; see also *OLAC*, 162.

[33] See below.

[34] Deceased Wife's Sisters Act 1907; Deceased Brother's Widow's Marriage Act 1921; Marriage (Prohibited Degrees of Relationship) Act 1986, s. 3, inserting into the Marriage Act 1949 a new s. 5A.

[35] [1910] P 57 at 93 *per* J. Bray, construing the proviso to s. 1 of the 1907 statute.

[36] Marriage Act 1949, s. 17 proviso.

[37] *BCP*, 303, rubrics: against God's law and the law of the realm; see also *Beamish v Beamish* (1861) 9 HL Cas 274 at 327, 331, 333, 347; *ASB*, 289: may not 'lawfully marry'.

[38] House of Bishops' *Guidelines for the Celebration of Mixed-Faith Marriages in Church* (1992) para. 2; *Honourable Estate*, App. I; *No Just Cause: The Law of Affinity in England and Wales* (London, 1984) 10; in the 2nd edn. (1985) of *MIECL*, at 91, Garth Moore was of the opinion that a minister may be able to refuse if 'neither party has been baptized'; this does not appear in the latest edition.

[39] See, however, Convocation Resolution of 1938: 'the clergy should not be bound by the law of England to celebrate the marriage in church of two persons of whom neither has been or is willing to be baptized': *Acts of Convocation*, 93.

marriage, or at the first opportunity afterwards'.[40] Whether 'convenient' imports a duty has not been decided judicially.[41] In *Jenkins v Barrett* Sir John Nicholls stated in the Arches Court: 'As to the question whether a clergyman is bound to marry a dissenter, baptized or unbaptized', 'to the merits of [this] question . . . I shall not avert in any way'.[42] Indeed, according to the report *Church and State*: '(in theory) a minister could probably be compelled to celebrate the marriage of two unbaptized persons'.[43] There is no judicial authority to support this. Nor has it been decided whether a minister could rely on his right under section 8 of the Marriage Act 1949 to insist before publication of banns that the parties give notice 'stating the *christian* name . . . of each of them'.[44] The matter is given some consideration in diocesan regulations many of which state that baptism is not a legal requirement.[45] However, some diocesan norms prescribe that where both parties are unbaptized 'they should not be married, nor seek to be married, with the Church's service'; but when one is unbaptized and 'can with a good conscience and with sufficient understanding take . . . part in the Marriage Service, the marriage may take place in church, with the permission of the bishop, which must be obtained before the banns are published'.[46] Other diocesan regulations prescribe that an incumbent cannot refuse to marry the unbaptized but should seek the bishop's advice.[47] According to recent guidelines issued centrally by General Synod's House of Bishops, marriage by licence can be refused if one of the parties is not baptized; this has been incorporated into some diocesan regulations, though these sometimes allow the granting of a common licence where one is unbaptized if the priest is satisfied that the unbaptized party can with 'good conscience and right understanding' take part in the service; the priest should provide a letter to this effect which will be handed in with the application for a common licence; a priest may suggest baptism and confirmation but not simply as a means to qualify.[48]

There have been attempts to make baptism a canonical requirement.[49] The

---

[40] *BCP*, 311.

[41] *R v Moorhouse James* (1850) 19 LJMC 179: *arguendo* it was suggested that 'it is convenient' ought to be construed as words of obligation.

[42] (1827) 1 Hag Ecc 12; see also *HLE*, para. 1003, n. 1: 'it is thought that even where both parties were unbaptised such a claim could not lawfully be refused, at any rate in the case of marriage after . . . banns.'   [43] *Church and State* (1970) paras. 200–10.

[44] The statute does not state that 'christian name' is the baptismal name; however, Lord Stowell stated in *Pouget v Tomkins* (1812) 2 Hag Con 236: 'In strictness, I conceive that all parts of a baptismal name should be set forth . . . in proclamation of banns, it is also highly proper that they be enumerated'; cf. *HLE*, para. 1017, n. 1; though he did not define 'Christian name' as the baptismal name, see J. Ormerod's distinction between 'the name of baptism' and other 'true names' in *Dancer v Dancer* [1949] P 147.   [45] *CAD*, 34.

[46] *CDH*, 100–1.   [47] *ODYB: IF*, 236; see also *LDHI*, III.12.

[48] House of Bishops' *Guidelines for Mixed-Faith Marriages* (1992) para. 4; *CAD*, 34.

[49] Michael Saward's 1988 proposal to allow a minister to refuse unbaptized couples or where one party was a practising member of a non-Christian religion was rejected, although it was not without considerable support: 1(3) *ELJ*, 1(3) (1988), 10.

Archbishops' Commission of 1947 introduced a draft canon forbidding the marriage in church of two unbaptized persons and reserving to the bishop discretion to permit marriage where one of the parties was baptized.[50] The canon was not enacted—nor has the recommendation of the 1988 Report that 'the best way to deal with the matter would be to place the solemnisation of such marriages at the discretion of the minister guided by such regulations as may be made from time to time by the General Synod'.[51] In short, if a minister refused to marry because of lack of baptism, he may technically be acting lawfully; the point is unclear and the silence of the law may confer a residualist right of conscientious objection. In any event, diocesan regulations often make express provision for pre-nuptial preparation, some prescribing that the minister 'should endeavour to secure baptism of the persons concerned before the marriage takes place' and that, '[i]f this proves impossible, the Bishop should be consulted'.[52] In contrast, in Roman Catholic canon law as a general rule baptism is a prerequisite to sacramental marriage in church: '[o]ne who has not received baptism cannot be validly admitted to the other sacraments'.[53] In certain limited cases, however, canon law allows marriage when one of the parties is not baptized.[54] The conference of bishops of England and Wales has recently promulgated legislation requiring enquiries to avoid invalidity and 'injudicious marriages'.[55]

Sanctions and Remedies

There is considerable uncertainty as to whether unlawful refusal by a minister constitutes an ecclesiastical offence, as well as uncertainty as to what remedies, if any, might be available to parties refused marriage. It has not been decided judicially whether a refusal is an indictable criminal offence.[56] The Marriage Acts 1949 to 1986 create a series of criminal offences in relation to the solemnization and registration of marriages. These include solemnizing a marriage outside prescribed hours and places, and solemnizing according to the rites of the Church of England without banns having been duly published. Acts giving rise to liability must be 'wilfully and knowingly' performed. These are punishable by imprisonment 'for a term not exceeding fourteen years'. The are no specific statutory defences.[57]

---

[50] *RACCL* (1947) 126, draft Canon 37: 'No minister shall allow Matrimony to be celebrated in his Church between two persons neither of whom has been baptized'.

[51] *Honourable Estate*, App. I, para. 204.   [52] *PBR*, III.26; *CDH*, 97; *BRDSEI*, E(i).

[53] *CIC*, c. 842.   [54] Ibid., cc. 1143–4; see *post* for mixed marriages.

[55] *COCLA*, 1337; *Briefing* 86, 158,

[56] *R v James* (1850) 3 Car & Kir 167; 175 ER 506: the judges refused to answer the question; for Alderson B 'this is an ecclesiastical matter altogether'; Patteson J: 'Suppose a case of publication of banns in the church, and the clergyman would not marry the parties because they did not wish to be confirmed, and we were to hold that that was wrong, it clearly would not be indictable.'

[57] Marriage Act 1949, s. 75 (and see s. 76); Marriage Act 1983, Sched. 1.

It is commonly said that refusal to marry by banns constitutes an ecclesiastical offence of neglect of duty.[58] The proposition is based, as with the general ministerial duty, on judicial statements which are *obiter*. In relation to marriage by licence, however, this may have been the assumption underlying *Argar v Holdsworth*, though Sir George Lee in the Arches Court would put it no higher than that a clergyman '*might* be prosecuted by anyone for neglect of his clerical duty; that the suit for such neglect might be brought in order to his being admonished or suspended in the Archdeacon's Court'.[59] Proceedings would be instituted under the Ecclesiastical Jurisdiction Measure 1963, which allows prosecution only if neglect is 'serious, persistent or continuous' (s.14). Though this formula seems to contemplate prosecution only if there is a series of refusals, section 16 suggests that a single refusal would be sufficient: no proceedings under the measure can be brought 'unless the act or omission constituting the offence' occurred within three years ending with the day on which proceedings are instituted. Sir George Lee stated in *Argar* that 'anyone' might complain in the Archdeacon's Court: this no longer exists, and under the 1963 Measure parties could not 'as of right' proceed against a refusing cleric: they must be authorised complainants (s.19).[60] In any event defences based on reasonable excuse or justification may be available, but the law provides no systematic account of these.[61] According to *Argar*, 'if [the minister] had reason to believe the licence was obtained fraudulently, and only delayed to gain time for inquiry, that would be proper matter for his defence'.[62] In *Davis v Black*, Williams J assumed that failure to carry out the terms of a licence would be actionable but if the cleric was otherwise engaged 'that would surely constitute a good justification in an Ecclesiastical Court'.[63] Failure to carry out the terms of a licence may amount to violation of the oath of canonical obedience.[64]

An ecclesiastical offence might be committed if a minister fails to make due inquiry concerning the parties' residence.[65] According to judicial principles, the test seems to be objective. The minister must employ due diligence but if he uses all 'reasonable means' in the inquiry he will not be liable.[66] Insistence on notice under section 8 of the Marriage Act 1949 would probably satisfy the

---

[58] Faculty Office *Guide*, para. 6.1; *HLE*, para. 1357.   [59] (1758) 2 Lee 515 at 516.
[60] See *supra* Ch. 5.
[61] See also *Bland v Archdeacon of Cheltenham* [1972] 1 All ER 1012 for the concept of reasonableness in relation to refusal to baptize; see generally *supra* Ch. 7.   [62] 161 ER 424.
[63] (1841) 113 ER 1376 at 1381.   [64] *Tuckniss v Alexander* (1863) 32 Ch 794 at 806.
[65] For this view see *HLE*, para. 1007, n. 2. However, the duty is not expressly imposed by the canons. For marriage by banns it may be implicit in a joint reading of the Marriage Act 1949, s. 75(1)(b): banns must be 'duly published' and of Canon B35: duty 'to observe the law relating thereto'.
[66] *Nicholson v Squire* (1809) 16 Ves 259 *per* Lord Eldon: 'If a clergyman, not using due diligence, marries persons, neither of whom is resident in the parish, he is liable at least to ecclesiastical censure'; see also Phillimore, *Ecclesiastical Law*, I, 601 for reasonable means.

due diligence requirement.[67] Though Canon B32 forbids a minister to marry minors under eighteen (without the consent of parents or guardians), under section 3(4) of the Marriage Act 1949, unless he 'had notice of dissent', '[a] clergyman shall not be liable to ecclesiastical censure for solemnizing the marriage of an infant after the publication of banns without the consent of the parents or guardians'.

Although it has not been decided whether an action for damages could be brought for ministerial refusal, judicial dicta have suggested that this might be possible.[68] In *Davis v Black*, concerning marriage by licence (not by banns), counsel argued that an action on the case lay for a refusal so that the parties be 'repaired in damages'. Lord Denman stated: 'I am by no means prepared to say that such an action as that might not be maintained, upon the declaration raising a proper complaint of a public officer neglecting his public duty to the temporal, and it might be to the very great damage of an individual. Such a neglect of a duty of a clergyman may be actionable, if it be malicious and without probable cause.'[69] However, it is difficult to identify precisely not only the actual loss but also the basis of liability. The principle that a failure to fulfil a public statutory duty is actionable would probably not be applicable,[70] though 'misfeasance in a public office', when an official has been guilty of oppressive or arbitrary conduct, may possibly give rise to an action for damages.[71] A similar uncertainty surrounds the discretionary prerogative order of *mandamus* issued by the High Court. Though this has not been judicially considered in relation to a refusing cleric, *mandamus* is often used to compel performance of public duties by public bodies.[72] As a general rule,

---

[67] *Nicholson v Squire* (1809) 16 Ves 259 *per* Lord Eldon, concerning the right to notice rule in s. 2 of the 1753 statute: 'If he has used the means, given to him, and was misled, he is excusable; but he can never excuse himself if no inquiry was made'; see also *Wynn v Davies* (1835) 1 Curt 69 *per* Sir Herbert Jenner Fust: 'if he chooses to dispense with the notice which he is entitled to require, and if it should turn out that the parties are not entitled to have the banns published in his parish, he must take upon himself the consequences of his own neglect to do that which the law has provided for his security'; there was some debate as to whether the ecclesiastical offence existed: for Jenner Fust 'the law may exist, though it may have been suffered to sleep'. For statutory exceptions see Marriage Act 1949, ss. 6(4), 15(1)(b), 35(3), 72 and City of London (Guild Churches) Act 1952, s. 22(2).

[68] *Argar v Holdsworth* (1758) 161 ER 424 *per* Sir George Lee: 'I said that possibly Argar might have an action for damages.'

[69] (1841) 113 ER 1376 at 1381. If a minister and the parties entered an express or implied contract to use the parish church for marriage an action for breach of contract may possibly lie: if e.g. the parties paid fees in advance a contract may be implied from conduct: *The Amazonia* [1990] 1 Lloyd's Rep 238 at 242.

[70] See W. V. H. Rogers (ed.), *Winfield and Jolowicz on Tort* (14th edn., London, 1994), ch. 7: the ministerial duty is not, for the reasons outlined above, a statutory duty.

[71] For this embryonic tort see K. M. Stanton, *The Modern Law of Tort* (London, 1994) 469 and *Jones v Swansea City Council* [1989] 3 All ER 162, [1990] 3 All ER 737; *Dunlop v Woollahra Municipal Corporation* [1982] AC 158 (PC); *Rookes v Barnard* [1964] AC 129; *Bradford City MC v Arora* [1991] 2 QB 507.

[72] *R v Metropolitan Police Commissioner, ex p Blackburn* (1968) 2 QB 150: CA accepted that *mandamus* may lie to compel police to carry out legal duty to enforce criminal law; for *mandamus* generally see *supra* Ch. 4.

however, *mandamus* lies only when no other form of redress is available.[73] Because hierarchical recourse to the minister's bishop may lie to a refused party, and because civil marriage exists as an alternative, it is unlikely that *mandamus* would issue.

In conclusion, though the criminal offences specified under the Marriage Acts are reasonably clear, the definitional elements of ecclesiastical offences are not.[74] The possible offence of refusal is ancient, poorly defined, and (not least because of the lack of clarity surrounding the exact terms of the duty and the available defences) in practical terms it would be adventurous to contemplate a prosecution today.[75] Whatever its basis in strict law, whether it exists as a legal fiction rather than as a right flowing from formal law, the proposition concerning the right to marriage in the parish church has in practice acquired the force of law: today it is doubtful whether it could be challenged successfully. In any event, rather than being judicially enforced, the right would be more appropriately enforced by means of executive direction from the bishop to the refusing minister. Ideally, canonical provision should be made to clarify the matter.

CRITERIA OF VALIDITY AND SOLEMNIZATION

Theologically, holy matrimony is treated in the Church of England not as a sacrament but as sacramental in nature. It is 'an honourable estate, instituted of God in the time of man's innocency, signifying unto us the mystical union that is betwixt Christ and his Church'.[76] Canon law approves this understanding:[77] 'The Church of England affirms, according to our Lord's teaching, that marriage is in its nature a union permanent and lifelong, for better for worse, till death do them part, of one man with one woman, to the exlcusion of all others on either side, for the procreation and nurture of children, for the hallowing and right direction of the natural instincts and affections, and for the mutual society, help and comfort which the one ought to have of the other,

---

[73] The same idea has been applied to refusals to publish banns: *OLAC*, 164.

[74] For the lack of clarity of terms of many ecclesiastical offences, and for the possible applicability of ECHR, Art. 7 in this regard, see *supra* Ch. 7.

[75] As mentioned in relation to refusals on the ground of lack of baptism, *An Honourable Estate* (1988) 78 concluded: 'We certainly cannot imagine two persons . . . suing a minister because he felt himself unable to marry them.'

[76] *BCP*, 301, The Form of Solemnization of Matrimony; *AR*, Art. 25: 'Matrimony . . . [is] not to be counted for [one of the] Sacraments of the Gospel', for it has not 'any visible sign or ceremony ordained of God' but is partly one of the 'states of life allowed in the Scriptures'; *ASB*, 288: 'Scriptures teach us that marriage is a gift of God in creation and a means of his grace, a holy mystery in which man and woman become one flesh.'

[77] Canon B30(2): 'The teaching of our Lord affirmed by the Church of England is expressed and maintained in the Form of Solemnisation of Matrimony in the Book of Common Prayer.'

both in prosperity and adversity'.[78] Matrimony is treated as more than a contract but it springs from a contract,[79] from the free exchange of consents of those party to it, a state in which both parties are 'joined together by God', in which they have 'consented together'.[80]

As a general principle, the ecclesiastical requirements necessary to create a valid marriage contract are the same as those of civil law. A marriage is void *ab initio* (treated as never having existed) if the parties lacked legal capacity or if the formalities were not satisfied. In civil law parties lack legal capacity if they are within the prohibited degrees, under age, if either party is already lawfully married at the time, or if they are not male and female respectively.[81] Similarly, in canon law the parties must not be within the prohibited degrees of kindred and affinity: 'all marriages purported to be made within the said degrees are void' (Canon B31).[82] To this end there is a canonical duty on the minister to enquire about impediments when application is made for matrimony to be solemnized in the church or chapel of which he is the minister (Canon B33). No person under sixteen years of age shall marry 'and all marriages purported to be made between persons either of whom is under sixteen years of age are void' (Canon B31(1)). No minister shall solemnize matrimony between two persons either of whom (not being a widow or widower) is under eighteen years of age unless the parents or guardians consent (Canon B32). Marriage is a union 'of one man and one woman' (Canon B30).[83]

The formal requirements vary between marriage by banns, licence, and

---

[78] Canon B30(1); para. (3): it is the duty of the minister to whom application is made for marriage to be solemnized in the church of which he is minister 'to explain to the two persons who desire to be married the Church's doctrine of marriage as herein set forth, and the need of God's grace in order that they may discharge aright their obligations as married persons'.

[79] *MIECL*, 72; *BCP*, 305.

[80] *BCP*, 303, 305; see also *Marriage, Divorce and the Church*, The Root Report (London, 1971); *Marriage and the Church's Task* (London, 1978); *An Honourable Estate* (1988), ch. 1 .

[81] Matrimonial Causes Act 1973, s. 11; Poulter, 'The definition of marriage in English law', *MLR*, 42 409; the minister must inquire as to impediments (Canon B31); according to Marriage Act 1949, s. 25 if any persons knowingly and wilfully intermarry according to the rites of the Church of England (otherwise than by special licence) in any place other than a church or other building in which banns may be published, without banns, common licence, or registrar's certificate, or if these are void, or if they knowingly and wilfully consent to or acquiesce in the solemnization of the marriage by any person who is not in holy orders, the marriage will be void.

[82] Canon B31(2): subject to the provisions of the Marriage (Prohibited Degrees of Relationship) Act 1986, no person shall marry within the degrees listed in the table of kindred and affinity contained in the Canon; '[t]he Table shall be in every church publicly set up and fixed at the charge of the parish'.

[83] See also Matrimonial Causes Act 1973, s. 11(c), requiring parties to be respectively male and female; in civil law, for 'marriages' of those who have had operations effecting a 'sex change' as being void, see *Corbett v Corbett* [1971] P 83 (applied in *R v Tan* [1983] QB 1053): persons born one sex remain that sex for the purposes of marriage law; the principle has been upheld by the European Court of Human Rights: *Cossey v UK* [1991] 2 FLR 492; see below n. 102 for the Roman Catholic Church's approach to this question.

registrar's certificate.[84] Marriage by banns is the most common form and failure to ensure that the banns are 'duly published' in the prescribed form and in accordance with rubrical requirements of the liturgical books will invalidate.[85] It seems that in all cases in which the courts have held banns not to have been duly published, there has been a fraudulent intention to conceal identity; the reason for concealment is immaterial.[86] In relation to all forms of marriage carried out according to the rites of the Church of England, solemnization must be effected by a clerk in holy orders in the presence of at least two other witnesses.[87] If there is only one additional witness this will not invalidate the marriage.[88] Under Canon B35 a marriage 'may not be solemnized at any unreasonable hours but only between the hours of eight in the forenoon and six in the afternoon'; a marriage contracted outside these hours would not be void.[89] It is a criminal offence to solemnize

[84] Canon B35(2): 'In all matters pertaining to the publication of banns and the solemnization of matrimony every minister shall observe the law relating thereto, including, so far as they are applicable, the rules prescribed by the rubric prefixed to the office of Solemnization of Matrimony in the Book of Common Prayer'; *BCP*, 301; see also rubrics in *ASB*, 285. For licences see B35(1) and Marriage Act 1949, s. 16; for certificates see ibid., s. 17—ministerial consent is needed; a marriage in the Church of England may not be authorized on the authority of a registrar's certificate by licence (s. 26(1)); *OLAC*, 164: 'a licence [from the ordinary] is . . . a dispensation from the necessity of publishing banns'; see Marriage Act 1949, ss. 15–16, and for special licence s. 79(6)).

[85] Marriage Act 1949, ss. 6–14: in limited circumstances an authorized lay person may publish (s. 9)—see also *OLAC*, 163; for circumstances in which the clergyman 'shall not solemnize' without certification of publication of banns see s. 11. The rubrics are to take effect 'so far as they are consistent with the provisions' of the Act (s. 7(2)). The time for publication is during the morning service but if there is none during the evening service (s. 7(1)); certificates of publication must be produced to the incumbent of the church where the marriage is to be solemnized (s. 11); see *OLAC*, 163 for publication of banns in churches subject to sharing agreements under the Sharing of Church Buildings Act 1969. See generally M. G. Smith and Others, 'Report of the Working Party on the legal preliminaries to marriage', *ELJ*, 3 (1995), 323 and for the origins of banns, R. Hanford, 'The medieval foundations of the banns of marriage', University of Wales LL M. Dissertation (Cardiff, 1995).

[86] *Chipchase v Chipchase* [1939] 3 All ER 895 at 899–900; the parties must give the name by which they are generally known: see *Dancer v Dancer* [1949] P 147.

[87] Marriage Act 1949 (as amended by Marriage Act 1983, Sched. 1), ss. 22, 25; *Culling v Culling* [1896] P 116. For impersonation as a criminal offence see Marriage Act 1949, s. 75(1)(d); *R v Ellis* (1888) 16 Cox CC 469. The clergyman must be a different person than the bridegroom: *Beamish v Beamish* (1861) 9 HL Cas 274. Solemnization by a deacon is irregular but valid: *R v Millis* (1844) 10 Cl & Fin 534 at 656, 748, 859–60; *Cope v Barber* (1872) LR 7 CP 393; see now guidelines issued by the archbishops in 1992 (Canons of the Church of England, 187): 'a deacon may officiate at a marriage only if the consent of the incumbent and/or minister is first given.' In the appended note 'In the first year following ordination as deacon . . . a deacon should rarely, if ever, solemnize a marriage and should only do so for exceptional reasons'.

[88] *Wing v Taylor* (1861) 2 Sw & Tr 278 at 286.

[89] *Catterall v Sweetman* (1845) 1 Rob Ecc 304 at 317 *per* Dr Lushington; see also Church of England (Legal Aid and Miscellaneous Provisions) Measure 1988, s. 5 for marriage of the housebound. *OLAC*, 172: the law makes no provisions for solemnization in Church of England churches according to the rites of the Roman Catholic Church or other non-Anglican churches except under the Sharing of Church Buildings Act 1969; a non-Anglican minister (or authorized lay person) may assist in the solemnization under Canons B43 and B44 but by the Church of

outside these times.[90] Marriage may be solemnized only in authorized buildings and within three months of the completion of the publication of banns, the grant of licence, or entry of notice in the superintendent registrar's marriage notice book.[91] Lack of residence will not invalidate.[92]

In its liturgical setting the marriage is probably constituted as soon as there has been a reciprocal agreement of both parties to take each other as husband and wife, at the joining together of their hands and the minister's pronouncement that they are man and wife.[93] The precise language of the marriage service is not a criterion of validity nor need the words of the ceremony be spoken by the parties; consent may be communicated otherwise.[94] The opening address, the statement by the parties that there is no lawful impediment, the placing of rings, and the benediction are not essential for validity, they are merely symbolic.[95] The choice of liturgy lies with the minister though the parties have a right to object in which case the matter must be referred to the diocesan bishop.[96] According to guidelines issued jointly by the two archbishops in 1992, '[t]he authorised services should be used without variation whether the officiating minister is a bishop, priest or deacon'.[97] Strictly, however, the minister has a canonical right to make minor variations and there is no duty to refer the matter to the diocesan bishop.[98] Regulation of video-recording of the service is now usually subject to diocesan norms which recommend the making of agreements enabling the imposition of conditions to prevent disruption of the service.[99]

In civil law a marriage is voidable (taken to have existed unless and until

England (Ecumenical Relations) Measure 1988, s. 3(b) there is a ban on a non-Anglican 'solemnizing a marriage according to the rites of the Church of England'.

[90] Marriage Act 1949, s. 75.

[91] Ibid., ss. 12, 15, 16(3), 25, 33; the clergyman must register the marriage in duplicate: ss. 53–5.   [92] *Pouget v Tomkins* (1812) 2 Hag Con 142.

[93] *Quick v Quick* [1953] VLR 224.

[94] *Harrod v Harrod* (1854) 1 K & J 4; *OLAC*, 171: limited provision is made for services conducted in a foreign language; however, 'a regular marriage would not be solemnized if the whole service were to be conducted in a foreign language only', it must be in English (Canon B42). Understanding the service would, it is submitted, be a criterion of validity; according to the Commission the charge, promises, and vows must be translated by an interpreter chosen by the minister (and ought not to be a friend or relative of the couple) and the interpreter should sign the register as one of the witnesses; the only exceptions seem to be under the Registration of Marriages (Welsh Language) Reg. 1986, SI 1986/1445, and under Canon B42 where in college chapels etc. Latin may be used.

[95] *Beamish v Beamish, supra* n. 87, 329–31 *per* Willes J and 339 *per* Lord Campbell: for civil purposes joining of hands is not required.

[96] Canon B3(4); this operates on the assumption, often made in diocesan regulations, that solemnization of marriage is an 'occasional office': see *supra* Ch. 10.

[97] Canons of the Church of England, 187; a service of solemnization may take place after a civil ceremony if the minister is satisfied that the civil marriage has been contracted (Canon B36).

[98] Canon B5(1)–(3); see *supra* Ch. 10.

[99] E.g. *BDM*, G.11, which includes direction for charges payable; *DDBF*, A.7; *GDM*, K.1–4; *RDL*, BP.15, for 'code of practice'; see also *OLAC*, 80–2, 92–4.

declared void by a competent court) and may be annulled subsequently on several grounds: if it is unconsummated (through inability or refusal); if there was a lack of consent (through unsoundness of mind, duress, fraud, or mistake); if at the time of the marriage either party was suffering from mental disorder; if at the time of the ceremony the respondent was suffering from venereal disease in a communicable form; or, if at the time of the ceremony, the respondent wife was pregnant by someone other than the petitioner.[100] The canon law of the Church of England does not contain a doctrine of voidable marriages. However, in 1938 the Convocations passed a resolution approving 'as valid reasons for declaring a marriage null and void the . . . grounds . . . contained in the Matrimonial Causes Act 1937', namely that 'the marriage has not been consummated owing to the wilful refusal of one party to consummate the marriage'; that 'either party . . . was at the time of the marriage and unknown to the other of unsound mind or a mental defective or subject to recurrent fits of insanity or epilepsy'; that 'either party was at the time . . . and unknown to the other suffering from venereal disease in a communicable form'; and that 'the woman was at the time . . . and unknown to the man pregnant by some other man'.[101]

The Church of England's criteria of validity are considerably less detailed than those appearing in Roman Catholic canon law. Under Canon 1055 the matrimonial covenant is entered by a man and a woman and cannot validly exist between baptized persons unless it is also a sacrament. By Canon 1134 a valid marriage is by its very nature perpetual and exclusive.[102] The 'diriment impediments' prevent a person from validly contracting marriage,[103] and find a direct parallel in Church of England law: lack of age, physical impotence, prior marriage bond (cc.1083–5), and consanguinity and affinity (cc.1091–2).[104] A

---

[100] Matrimonial Causes Act 1973, s. 12; s. 13 for bars to relief: petitioner's conduct, lapse of time, and petitioner's knowledge. For the limited applicability of the doctrine of frustration to the marriage contract see *Kenward v Kenward* [1951] P 124.

[101] *Acts of the Convocations*, 92. For Garth Moore refusal to consummate was not a ground for nullity in canon law. A void marriage is one which has never existed — refusal to consummate can only occur after the ceremony. If the theological idea that a marriage is completed on consummation is used, refusal may be a ground and the civil and canon law are reconciled; there is no reference to the convocation resolution: *MIECL*, 75–6; in support of Moore's thesis see *Napier v Napier* [1915] P 184 CA; see also the Report of the Archbishops' Commission, *The Church and the Law of Nullity of Marriage* (1949).

[102] See T. P. Doyle, 'The theology of marriage: where are we today?', *Studia Canonica*, 19 (1985), 357; I. Gramunt, 'The essence of marriage and the code of canon law', *Studia Canonica*, 25 (1991), 365; P. K. Thomas, 'Marriage annulments for gay men and lesbian women: new canonical and psychological insights', *The Jurist*, 43 (1983), 318; Canon Law Society *Newsletter*, No. 94 (1993) 60 Document IX, 'Sentence on nullity of marriage involving sex change therapy'.

[103] *CIC*, c. 1073; W. H. Woestman, 'Too many invalid marriages', *Studia Canonica*, 24 (1990), 193; I. Gramunt and A. Wauck, 'Capacity and incapacity to contract marriage', *Studia Canonica*, 22 (1988), 147; W. H. Woestman, 'Dissolution of a ratified non-consummated marriage: a procedure sinking into oblivion', *Studia Canonica*, 21 (1987), 195.

[104] *COCLA*, 1337, for the Roman Catholic conference of bishops of England and Wales legislation, *Briefing* 85, 114: on c. 1083(2), the civil law requirement as to age (16) must be observed.

marriage occurs through the consent of the parties: people who lack sufficient reason therefore do not contract a valid marriage.[105] Persons not capable of assuming the essential matrimonial rights and duties which are to be usually given and accepted are incapable of contracting a valid marriage; this provision forms the basis of most nullity proceedings.[106] Other grounds vitiating consent include ignorance, error about the identity of the partner, fraud, simple error (cc.1096–9), simulation of consent, fear, and force.[107] As a general rule, '[o]nly those marriages are valid which are contracted in the presence of the local ordinary or pastor or a priest or deacon delegated by either of them, who assist, in the presence of two witnesses'.[108] As to liturgy, Roman Catholic canon law seems to be more liberal than that of the Church of England, marriage may be celebrated by liturgies customarily employed;[109] the essential element of the ritual is the exchange of consent.[110]

Some criteria of validity, notably the bar of sacred orders, find no direct parallel in Anglican canon law.[111] A competent ecclesiastical authority may dispense with these (c.1078).[112] As in English law,[113] when there is doubt about the validity of a marriage there is a presumption that it is valid until the contrary is proven (c.1060). Unlike in the Church of England, the annulment of marriages is the function of the church's courts.[114]

DIVORCE AND REMARRIAGE

In recent years marriage discipline, the theological principles underlying it, divorce, and remarriage have been the subject of considerable debate in both

[105] *CIC*, cc. 1057, 1095; L. Örsy, 'Matrimonial consent in the new code', *The Jurist*, 43 (1983), 29; G. J. Roche, 'Consent is a union of wills: a study of the bilateral dimension of matrimonial consent', *Studia Canonica*, 18 (1984) 415.

[106] *CIC*, c. 1095(3); A. Mendoca, 'Effects of personality disorders on matrimonial consent', *Studia Canonica*, 21 (1987), 66; A. McGrath, 'On the gravity of causes of a psychological nature in the proof of inability to assume the essential obligations of marriage', *Studia Canonica*, 22 (1988), 67.   [107] *CIC*, cc. 1101–3.

[108] C. 1108: an authorized lay person may assist: c. 1112. For place of marriage see c. 1115, for extraordinary marriage (in danger of death) c. 1116.

[109] By *CIC*, c. 1119 'Outside a case of necessity, the rites prescribed in the liturgical books approved by the Church or received through legitimate customs are to be observed in the celebration of marriage'. Local rites may be approved by the conference of bishops (c. 1120).

[110] T. P. Doyle, *CCL: TC*, 798.

[111] *CIC*, c. 1087; see J. A. Coriden, 'Celibacy, canon law and synod 1971', *Concilium*, 8(8) (1972), 109; see also disparity of cult (c. 1086); subject to a public vow of chastity (c. 1088); and conditional marriage (c. 1102).

[112] *CIC*, c. 1078: bishops can dispense with all diriment impediments except those reserved to the pontiff (sacred orders, crime (c. 1090)) and consanguinity; see *COCLA*, 1285, for the authentic interpretation (1985) prescribing that a bishop cannot dispense (under c. 87) outside danger of death from canonical forms for the marriage of two Catholics.

[113] *Re Bradshaw* [1938] 4 All ER 143.

[114] H. F. Doogan (ed.), *Catholic Tribunals: Marriage Annulment and Dissolution* (Newtown, Australia, 1990); see also *supra*, Ch. 5, n. 30.

the Church of England and the Roman Catholic Church.[115] In Roman Catholic canon law the essential properties of marriage are 'unity and indissolubility';[116] 'from a valid marriage arises a bond between the spouses which by its very nature is perpetual and exclusive'.[117] As we have seen, a marriage may be annulled in Roman Catholic canon law when the criteria of validity have not been satisfied. In these circumstances the parties are free to (re)marry. Convalidation validates a marriage which was canonically invalid *ab initio*.[118] If the union is terminated by a civil divorce, the canonical bond continues to exist. According to Canon 1141 a ratified and consummated marriage (one between two baptized persons) cannot be dissolved by any human power or for any reason other than death.[119] Canon 1142 enables the pontiff to dissolve an unconsummated, ratified marriage for a just cause at the request of both parties, or one of them if the other is unwilling.[120] A marriage between two non-baptized persons is dissolved by means of the Pauline Privilege when one party becomes baptized as a convert and the other no longer wishes to cohabit; the first marriage is dissolved by the second.[121] Whilst both the church's official teaching and canon law prescribe indissolubility and forbid remarriage, an internal forum solution has recently been proposed, through an examination of each case on its merits, by which divorced and remarried Roman Catholics may receive Holy Communion: it is for those involved to judge their own position in conscience before God.[122]

As a basic principle, the Church of England's *canon law* does *not*

---

[115] For a survey of the issues and literature concerning the Church of England see A. Clarkson, S. Pix, J. Rees, and D. Sherwood, 'Marriage in church after divorce: a working party report', *ELJ*, 2 (1992), 359 at 360: 1 in every 20 weddings in Anglican churches in England and Wales now involves at least one person who has been divorced, compared with 1 in 250 in 1976.

[116] *CIC*, c. 1056; c. 1055.   [117] Ibid., c. 1134.

[118] Ibid., cc. 1157, 1159, 1160: these allow for the curing of (1) impediments; (2) defects of consent; (3) lack of form; J. J. O'Rourke, 'Considerations on the convalidation of marriage', *The Jurist*, 43 (1983), 387; L. A. Bogdan, 'Simple convalidation of marriage in the 1983 code of canon law', *The Jurist*, 46 (1986), 511.

[119] W. J. S. Wamboldt, 'Canon law on the indissolubility of marriage in the Roman Catholic Church', *Studia Canonica*, 21 (1987), 265.

[120] The canon also allows dissolution of non-ratified marriages (between a baptized and a non-baptised person); see W. H. Woestman, 'Dissolution of a ratified non-consummated marriage: a procedure sinking into oblivion', *Studia Canonica*, 21 (1987), 195; for the pre–1983 position see W. O'Connor, 'The indissolubility of a ratified, consummated marriage', *Ephemerides Theologiae Louvaniensis*, 13 (1936), 692.

[121] *CIC*, c. 1143; the non-baptized party must be questioned to determine whether he/she wishes also to receive baptism and to cohabit (c. 1144); for the right to a second marriage see c. 1146.

[122] For the official restrictive position see Canon Law Society *Newsletter*, No. 101 (1995) 38, 'Letter of Cardinal Ratzinger to the bishops of the Catholic Church concerning reception of Holy Communion by divorced and remarried members of the faithful' (given at Rome with papal approval from the offices of the Sacred Congregation for the Doctrine of the Faith, 14 Sep. 1994): 'the Church affirms that a new union cannot be recognised as valid if the preceding marriage was valid'; see also for the proposed solution J. Jukes, 'A comment on the divorced and remarried within the Christian community', ibid., No. 93 (1994) 27; M. G. Lawler, 'Indissolubility, divorce and holy communion', *New Blackfriars*, 76 (1995), 229.

unequivocally forbid the remarriage of divorcees. In civil law a marriage may be ended by dissolution or by annulment (or death). Dissolution terminates an otherwise valid marriage. The Matrimonial Causes Act 1973 provides that there is only one ground for divorce: the irretrievable breakdown of marriage (s. 1(1)). This must be evidenced by proof of one of five facts, namely: adultery, unreasonable behaviour, desertion, two years' separation, or five years' separation (s. 1(2)). Each of these has been the subject of extensive consideration by the civil courts.[123] The law encourages spouses to attempt reconciliation.[124] As we have seen, the Church of England follows the law of the land as regards nullity and a cleric is free to marry those whose former marriage has been annulled.[125] The problem lies with those whose former marriage has been dissolved. In the opinion of the Legal Advisory Commission, '[t]he publication of banns may not be refused on the grounds that one or both of the parties are divorced and have former partners living'. If the incumbent or minister in charge refuses to publish, the aggrieved party could apply to the High Court for an order to publish banns but, as it lies in the discretion of the judge and as an alternative remedy (application to the superintendent registrar) is available 'it would be unlikely that an order would, in the exercise of the discretion, be granted'.[126]

At the obvious expense of vulgarizing a set of complex theological issues and ideas, in the Church of England one basic understanding is that, short of annulment, a remarriage is contrary to scripture.[127] The so-called 'Matthean exception' forbids divorce except on grounds of unchastity.[128] The Pauline Privilege allows the separation of believers married to unbelievers.[129] In line with the terms of the church's liturgical books,[130] various reports have stressed

---

[123] Bromley and Lowe, *Family Law*, 187 ff.   [124] Ibid., 221; see s. 6 of the 1973 Act.

[125] Faculty Office *Guide*, para. 11.1; the idea surfaces occasionally in diocesan regulations: *CDH*, 101: a certificate of nullity from a civil court 'may' be accepted as evidence of nullity; *WBRG*, F.1(f).

[126] *OLAC*, 164: a cleric should require the production of the original sealed decree absolute before proceeding to publish; ibid., 165 for the House of Bishops' Guidelines' prohibition against issuing a common licence if one of the parties is divorced. See also the Church Assembly debate (Jan–Sept 1950) for the distinction between permanance and dissolubility.

[127] For the theological context of these ideas see *Honourable Estate*, ch. 1; Mark 10: 11–12, whoever divorces his wife and marries another commits adultery against her; and if she divorces her husband and marries another she commits adultery); Luke 16: 18, everyone who divorces his wife and marries another commits adultery, and he who marries a woman divorced from her husband commits adultery; Mark 10: 8, 'the two shall become one flesh'; see also Gen. 2: 24; Eph. 5: 31.

[128] Matt. 5: 32; Matt. 19: 9 'whoever divorces his wife, except for unchastity, and marries another, commits adultery'. For the prohibited degrees see Matt. 19: 3.

[129] 1 Cor. 7: 15: 'If the unbelieving partner desires to separate, let it be so; in such a case the brother or sister is not bound'; see also I Cor. 7: 8–9.

[130] *BCP*, 301 ff.; *ASB*, 288: 'It is God's purpose that . . . [a] husband and wife give themselves to each other in love throughout their lives.'

the indissolubility or permanence of marriage,[131] though there has been a movement towards the idea that indissolubility is evolutionary.[132] The church's canon law reflects the basic theological stance defining marriage as a 'union permanent and life-long . . . till death do them part . . . [and] to the exclusion of all others on either side' (Canon B30(1)). However, this Canon does not expressly forbid divorce by dissolution—the prohibition is implicit. Express prohibitions are to be found not in the canon law but, *inter alia*, in Resolutions passed by Convocation. Moreover, the ban does not appear to be uniform throughout the two provinces. In 1957 the Canterbury Convocation affirmed four Resolutions which it had passed in 1937–8.

Convocation Resolutions

First, marriage is indissoluble: 'according to God's will, declared by Our Lord, marriage is in its true principle a personal union, for better or for worse, of one man and one woman, exclusive of all others on either side, and indissoluble save by death.' Secondly, in consequence, 'remarriage after divorce during the lifetime of a former partner always involves a departure from the true principle of marriage as declared by Our Lord'. Thirdly, in order 'to maintain the principle of lifelong obligation which is inherent in every legally contracted marriage and is expressed in the plainest terms in the Marriage service, the Church should not allow the use of that service *in the case of anyone* who has a former partner still living'. Lastly, while 'affirming its adherence to Our Lord's principle and standard of marriage', it was recognized that 'the actual discipline of particular Christian Communions in this matter has varied widely from time to time and place to place'; it was decided that the Church of England is competent to enact such a discipline of its own in regard to marriage as may from time to time appear 'most salutary and efficacious'.[133]

In the York province, Convocation Resolutions passed in 1938 still seem to be operative; they have not since been expressly re-affirmed or altered. These are basically the same as the Canterbury Resolutions but with the following differences. First, the York Resolution affirmed that 'both divorce itself and re-marriage' involved a departure from Christ's teaching. Second, the lifelong obligation was inherent in every 'marriage contract between Christians (however solemnized)'—the Canterbury Resolution contained no such limitation. Thirdly, when two persons have contracted a legal marriage during the lifetime of a former partner of either of them, and either or both of them desire to be baptized or to partake of Holy Communion, the minister must refer the

---

[131] *Putting Asunder* (London, 1966); the Lichfield Report, *Marriage and the Church's Task* (London, 1978); *An Honourable Estate* (1988) 8; 12(2) *GSRP* (1981) 798 at 845.

[132] Root Report, *Marriage, Divorce and the Church* (London, 1971) 17, n. 33: rather than existing *ab initio*, indissolubility is something into which partners grow (36, n. 70); Lichfield Report, 18, 10.   [133] *Acts of Convocation*, 90–1.

case to the bishop. The bishop must have regard to the church's standard of marriage and to the pastoral care of the parties. If he is satisfied that their admission 'ought not to give grave offence to the Church nor would be to the hurt of their souls', 'he shall direct that they be not excluded therefrom by reason of the marriage so contracted'. Such persons are to be admitted if they have resided in the diocese 'through the preceding six months'. The bishop must communicate this direction in writing to the minister and the parties; the direction 'shall be accepted as final both in the particular diocese and in all other dioceses of the province'.[134]

A similar pastoral regulation, relating to the reception of the sacraments by persons, was adopted by the Canterbury Convocation in 1937.[135] This was modified in 1957 and revoked by General Synod in 1982.[136] The equivalent Resolutions made by the York Convocation may still be operative in the York province as the General Synod did not expressly revoke these.[137] Strictly, as a general point, these convocation norms impose no legal obligations on either the bishop or the minister concerned. They are not canon law but resolutions contained in an Act of Convocation and, having been classified as such by General Synod, are not judicially enforceable.[138]

House of Bishops' Guidelines 1985

In 1985 General Synod's House of Bishops issued guidelines dealing with divorce and remarriage (and a draft resolution which was not presented to or accepted by General Synod). In the light of General Synod's statement in 1981 that there are circumstances in which a divorced person may be married in church during the lifetime of a former spouse, the House of Bishops considered that provision ought to be made for clergy (holding the view that a 'second' marriage is possible) to be free in some cases to solemnize.[139] The guidelines

---

[134] Ibid.   [135] Ibid., 93–4; this Reolution (5) was rejected by the Lower House.
[136] Canons of the Church of England, p.182 (Nov. 1982); the 1957 Canterbury Resolution 2(A) set down the following procedure: for those who had contracted a marriage in civil law during the lifetime of a former partner, and either/both desired baptism, confirmation, or Communion, the incumbent had to refer to matter to the bishop; if the parties were acting in good faith and it was not to cause offence to the church, the bishop was under a duty to approve in writing. By Res. 2(B) no church service was to be available (revoked by General Synod, July 1985 (Canons, p.182)). See *Public Worship* (1986), 13 for a service of prayer and dedication after civil marriage commended by the House of Bishops.
[137] See, however, Canon H1(2): Convocation may make provision by instrument but this power 'shall be exercised consistently with the exercise of functions by the General Synod and, in the event of any inconsistency, the provision made by the General Synod shall prevail': in view of this it is arguable that General Synod's Resolutions (1982–5), revoking the Canterbury Convocation Reslutions 2A–B of 1957, prevail over the York Convocation Resolutions of 1938.
[138] It is unclear whether the doctrine of canonical obedience extends to a corporate resolution enacted by the bishops; as the Resolutions were lawful it may be that they represent a 'lawful command of the bishop': see *supra* Ch. 7
[139] House of Bishops' Report, *Marriage Discipline*, GS 669, 13 Feb. 1985.

deal with three matters. First, in relation to the past marriage, people will be free to marry in church if the dissolved relationship was one which, either in original intention or as it developed, clearly failed to acquire the nature and purpose of marriage as taught by Christ (for example: if there was no free consent, if the union had not been consummated, if there had been persistent infidelity, or a unilateral decision not to have children). They would likewise be free to marry if the prime reason for the breakdown was arbitrary action by the other party or the applicant was divorced against his/her will; again, they would be free to marry if the applicant had turned to Christ and this had caused incompatability of spirit which love could not overcome.

Secondly, with regard to the present attitude and approach of the applicants, they would be free to marry in church when the applicants' relationship was not a direct cause of the breakdown and when they demonstrate a mature view of the circumstances of divorce; if a party accepts no responsibility for the breakdown, this may be evidence of a lack of maturity. Similarly, where the applicant appears to be free from personal conflict with the divorced partner, has faced the requirement to forgive, acknowledges that divorce is a breach of God's will, is repentant, and has ensured reasonable provision for dependents (and shows a continuing concern for their well-being), they also may be free to marry. Thirdly, with respect to the proposed marriage, the applicants will be free to marry if the couple shows they are growing in a Christian understanding of marriage in accordance with the teaching of Christ and accept Christian doctrine and practice in such a way that they sincerely intend to seek God's help in making and sustaining their proposed marriage.

Diocesan Norms

The practice of the Church of England today varies from diocese to diocese. According to a recent study one in five dioceses adheres strictly to the Convocation Resolutions.[140] Most diocesan bishops have created norms dealing with the problem of remarriage broadly in line with the freedom proposed in the Guidance issued by the House of Bishops. Indeed, the draft resolution of the House of Bishops is often expressly incorporated into diocesan regulations.[141] These norms usually impose a duty to consult the bishop for his guidance and advice whilst leaving the final decision to the discretion of the minister.[142] Some stress the idea that it is the couple, not the cleric, who are 'the ministers of the sacrament of marriage'.[143] Very rarely do norms prescribe

---

[140] A. Clarkson, S. Pix, J. Rees, and D. Sherwood, 'Marriage in church after divorce', *ELJ*, 2 (1990–2), 359.   [141] *EDH*, B.4.7–9; *RBG*, A.6; *WBRG*, F.1; *DGBOP*, 4.7–9; *GDM*, I.9.
[142] *DSBN*, Ad clerum 1989/4; *BRDSEI*, Eii; *WBRG* (1993) F.1(d), (f): write with information to the suffragan; occasionally manuals are produced: *SMD* (compiling a handbook), *Anglican Marriage in the Isle of Man: A Guide to the Law for Clergy* (1993).   [143] *CAD*, 33.

that the bishop will give 'directions'.[144] Rather, the decision is that of the priest alone, and not of the bishop, many explaining that the bishop can neither approve nor disapprove: episcopal permission is not required and cannot be given.[145] Consultation is often justified expressly 'in order to achieve the maximum amount of pastoral consistency and fairness throughout the diocese', sometimes expressed as 'uniformity of practice'.[146] The norms become operative when ministers 'in good conscience believe that they can conduct a "second" marriage',[147] usually recommending that, though banns must be read, no reference ought to be made to marital status.[148] Some provision is also made for continuing pastoral care subsequent to a remarriage.[149]

By way of contrast, some diocesan norms prescribe that remarriage is not the normal practice, the Convocation Resolutions remaining in force.[150] These forbid the celebration of such marriages when there is an interregnum and sometimes provide that a minister's decision to remarry in an instant case will lapse on vacancy;[151] though some state that during a vacancy the rural dean must consult the bishop.[152] Many prescribe that remarriage ought to be by banns, with common licence of the ordinary being used only in exceptional circumstances, whilst others forbid remarriage by licence in stronger terms.[153] Indeed, occasionally regulations forbid a service or blessing if one of the parties has been involved in the breakdown of the previous marriage or if remarriage will produce a 'public' or 'open scandal' or if there may be 'scandal for recognisable and public reasons'.[154] Some regulations recommend that the incumbent, parochial church council, and the area bishop create a code of principles for conducting second marriages. Typically, the agreed practice may refuse both a service in church and a service of prayer and dedication (a) if the situation causes 'open scandal or is likely to do so' and (b) when the proposed second marriage has been 'in some direct and unmistakable sense a reason for the breakdown of the earlier marriage'.[155] Some norms recommend that team ministries create similar principles.[156]

The Matrimonial Causes Act 1965

Ministerial freedom to solemnize a 'second' marriage is also conferred, it is submitted, by civil law regardless of the terms of Acts of Convocation and

---

[144] *SDH*, D.18: only in extremely unusual circumstances is the bishop willing to give directions and 'he is not able to adjudicate in appeals against a decision not to proceed with such a marriage'.
[145] Guildford Diocese (bishop's occasional paper 1); episcopal regulations permitting a relaxation of Convocation Rules may be conceived in one sense as expressions of the power of dispensation (for dispensation, discusssed by the Root Report, App. 5, p. 133, see *supra* Chs. 2, 6.
[146] *TBF*, 320–21; *WBRG*, F.1(f).   [147] *BDM*, G.9.   [148] Ibid.
[149] Ibid.; *TBF*, 320–1.   [150] *CAD*, 33.   [151] *RDL*, BP. 26.
[152] *PDH*, App. 1, *Bishop's Notice* 4; *WBRG*, F.1.
[153] *CDH*, 101; *DDBF*, A.6; *DGBOP*, 4.7–9.   [154] *TDH*, A.20–2; *DDBF*, A.6.
[155] *CF*, C.4.2.
[156] *PDH*, App. 1, *Bishop's Notice* 4: these should agree a uniform practice'; *GDM*, I.11–19: deanery chapters ought to discuss the matter.

regardless of the terms and conditions given by executive central episcopal guidance or by diocesan regulations. Under section 8 of the Matrimonial Causes Act 1965, where a decree of divorce has been made absolute 'either party to the former marriage may marry again'. Moreover, 'No clergyman of the Church of England . . . shall be compelled (a) to solemnize the marriage of any person whose former marriage has been dissolved and whose former spouse is still living; or (b) to permit the marriage of such a person to be solemnized in the church or chapel of which he is the minister'.

Two interpretations of this provision are possible. First, the provision may be read in the light of the legal fiction that a cleric is under a duty to marry all parishioners. On a strict interpretation, section 8 creates a legal *privilege* to refuse. It is a ministerial privilege, enjoyed by no other, to exercise a conscientious objection. The minister enjoys a similar privilege to refuse permission to use the church for solemnization. The civil law prohibits interference with this privilege. The prohibition applies equally to the Church of England: an episcopal command to a minister to solemnize a marriage, for example, would be unlawful, as would disciplinary proceedings. Divorced parishioners have no unconditional right to marry in the parish church. Secondly, on a wider interpretation, section 8 creates a ministerial *discretion*; this understanding has surfaced in several diocesan regulations.[157] Implicit in the words 'no clergyman shall be compelled to solemnize' are the propositions 'a minister may refuse' and 'a minister may solemnize'.[158] By its ban on compulsion, it confers upon the minister a public law *right* to choose refusal or solemnization. The section must be read as a whole. Choice is contemplated in so far as the minister may, after all, permit the use of the church; if he consents another minister may solemnize; indirectly it confers a right on a willing minister to celebrate such marriages.

---

[157] *CDH*, 101: 'Every clergyman has full legal liberty to refuse to solemnise such a marriage or to permit the marriage of such services to be solemnised . . . [and] the decision whether to exercise his *statutory discretion* to marry in church a person who is divorced during the lifetime of that person's former spouse now rests entirely with the incumbent concerned.' The arrangement is also conceived simply as conferring a right: *BDM*, G.9: civil law 'gives every clergyman the right for conscience sake to refuse to conduct such a service himself or to allow his church to be so used'; *CAD*, 34: 'civil rights' of clergy; *DDBF*, A.6: the cleric is entitled to permit/refuse 'after he has duly examined his conscience and the case'; *CF*, C.4.2; for this as conferring a clerical freedom see *WBRG*, F.1(d); *DSPR*, Ad clerum 1992/2: if the incumbent refuses another minister may solemnize only with the consent of incumbent *and* the parochial church council; see also ibid. for the statement that Canon C8(4) 'stipulates that the Diocesan Bishop has no right to authorise another minister to officiate in that Incumbent's church, if consent is refused'.

[158] Judicial comments in *R v Dibdin* [1910] P 57 do not clarify the terms of a similar provision in Matrimonial Causes Act 1857, s. 57: dissolution on the ground of adultery and the proviso that 'no clergyman . . . shall be compelled to solemnize'; Cozens-Hardy MR: 'in the Act of 1857, which authorised the remarriage in this country . . . of divorced persons in the churches of the Established Church, a limited protection is given to a clergyman who conscientiously objects to perform a marriage ceremony, which otherwise would have been obligatory upon him' (ibid., 108): J. Bray: 'In the [1857] Act the clergyman was bound to allow the marriage to be solemnized in his church' (ibid., 94).

This second interpretation raises an important question about the relationship between the civil law and the church's internal norms. As we have seen, non-legal resolutions (Acts of Convocation) forbid remarriage, many diocesan norms are designed to ensure consistency, and some encourage parishes to formulate principles regulating remarriage. Yet, on a wider reading of section 8, the civil law allows remarriage. The church's internal regulations effectively fetter the use of this statutory discretion if they seek either to limit remarriage or to permit it in every case of a request. However, as a general principle of civil law, statutory discretions cannot be fettered. Each case must be examined on its own merits and any policies or rules developed, which anticipate decisions and which render the holder of the discretion unable to exercise that discretion, are illegal.[159] Convocation resolutions deny the minister any choice and some diocesan regulations expressly see these as a fetter.[160] Moreover, for the future, a synodical canon could not command such marriages—if it did it may be void as repugnant to section 8. Any new canonical provision would have to harmonize with the terms of section 8 (if this is conceived as conferring a statutory discretion)—and only a synodical measure (or parliamentary statute) could destroy the section.[161]

MIXED MARRIAGES

In the Roman Catholic Church mixed marriages are governed directly by the 1983 Code and by new legislation promulgated by the episcopal conference of England and Wales. In the Church of England, on the other hand, the subject is treated most extensively not by the church's central legal system but by executive guidance. In substance, the approaches of the two churches are similar.

---

[159] If the resolutions are to be applied without regard to individual cases, do not allow a change of direction, or admit anyone with something new to say, they may be classified as 'rules' rather than 'policies' and would, as such, be illegal: *British Oxygen Co Ltd v Minister of Technology* [1971] AC 610; *R v Port of London Authority, ex p Kynoch Ltd* [1919] 1 KB 176; *Re Findlay* [1985] AC 318.

[160] *DDBF*, A.6: civil law is 'not in accordance with the Acts of Convocation'; *WBRG* (1993), F.1(f): a cleric permitting a second marriage 'has effectively made a *permanent decision* on the principle of re-marriage'; *PDH*, App. 1, *Bishop's Notice*, advises that a team ministry 'should agree a uniform practice'.

[161] For the view that a measure would be required see House of Bishop's *Guidelines for the Celebration of Mixed-Faith Marriages in Church* (1992) para. 1. If the section is construed as a discretion, it is arguable that the civil law confers a right on the church to solemnize such marriages. Resolution 9 of the 1938 Convocation rules stated: 'the Church should be free (1) to forbid the use of its buildings for any marriage when one of the parties has a former partner in marriage still living; and (2) to make its own regulations concerning the admission of such persons to the Sacraments and other privileges of the Church'. For the legal consequences of divorce on candidacy for ordination under the Clergy (Ordination) Measure 1990 and Canon C4 see *supra* Ch. 7.

According to Roman Catholic canon law, a marriage between two baptized Roman Catholics is a sacramental marriage. Mixed marriages are not: of these there are two species. A marriage between a Roman Catholic and a baptized member of another church not in full communion with the Roman Catholic Church is a mixed marriage and is *prima facie* forbidden.[162] A marriage between a Roman Catholic and a baptized Anglican is also a mixed marriage. Moreover, a 'disparity of cult' marriage is invalid: this is a marriage between a Roman Catholic, baptized and received into the church (being a person who has not defected by a formal act) and a unbaptized person.[163] With both types of marriage, however, the bishop may grant permission if there is a just and reasonable cause; he is not to grant it unless three conditions precedent are satisfied: the Roman Catholic party must declare preparedness to remove dangers of falling away from the faith and promise to do all in his/her power to have the children of the marriage baptized and brought up in the Roman Catholic church; the other party must be informed of the promise and obligation; and both parties must be instructed on the essential nature and purpose of marriage.[164] It is for the episcopal conference to prescribe the manner in which the Roman Catholic party's declarations and promises (which are always required) are to be made and how the non-Roman Catholic party is to be informed.[165] Legislation designed to give effect to this has recently been promulgated by the episcopal conference of England and Wales.[166]

The Roman Catholic Church's rules about liturgical form apply also to mixed marriages, though the bishop has the right to dispense from the form in individual cases whilst preserving the necessary element of the exchange of consent required for validity.[167] When canonical form is dispensed, a non-Roman Catholic minister or civil servant may receive the exchange of consents.[168] Thus, according to legislation promulgated by the national episcopal conference, for serious reasons the church is willing 'to waive the requirement [under c.1127] that her members marry before a Roman Catholic bishop, priest or deacon'. Reasons for granting dispensations from canonical form should

---

[162] *CIC*, c. 1124; E. de Bhaldraithe, 'Mixed marriages in the new code: can we now implement the Anglican-Roman Catholic recommendations?', *The Jurist*, 46 (1986), 419.

[163] *CIC*, c. 1086; L. Örsy, 'Ecumenism and marriage', in M. Thériault and J. Thorn (eds.), *The New Code of Canon Law* (Ottawa, 1986) II, 1041.

[164] Ibid., c. 1125; see also *COCLA*, 1295, authentic interpretation (1987) of c. 1103: defect of consent is applicable to marriages of non-Catholics.   [165] *CIC*, c. 1126.

[166] *COCLA*, 1337–8; *Briefing* 90, 139.

[167] *CIC*, c. 1127: there must be only one consent in ecumenical celebrations; the promulgation of *Matrimonia mixta* (1970) and the instruction *Matrimonii sacramentum* (1966) have resulted in both bishops conferences and curial decisions clarifying the terms of these rules; see J. Lynch, 'Mixed marriages in the aftermath of *Matrimonia mixta*', *Journal of Ecumenical Studies*, 11 (1974), 643; *CCL: TC*, 803, n. 177; ibid., 805 for the *Mixed Marriages: Particular Norms for South Africa*, South African Bishops' Conference, 9 Jan. 1970.

[168] *CCL: TC*, 803: this is the opinion of T. P. Doyle (but if a catholic priest or deacon is present, he may assist but cannot ask for or receive assent).

concern the spiritual well-being of the parties (especially if the non-Roman Catholic party is attached to the familial faith), the tranquility and peace of their personal or family relationships, or the special relationship that the non-Roman Catholic party has to a minister or non-Roman Catholic place of worship.[169]

With the obvious exception of royal marriages which are subject to additional and special rules under civil law,[170] the little formal law that exists on marriage in the Church of England is basically more liberal in terms of general principle. With respect to marriage by banns, the common understanding is that any parties, Christian or non-Christian, may marry in the parish church. There is no legal bar to mixed marriages provided the union is not prohibited by law and the requirements of validity and form are satisfied.[171] This basic legal position is qualified, however, by a more restrictive approach, similar to that of episcopal approval in the Roman Cathoic Church, set by both Guidance of General Synod's House of Bishops and diocesan regulations. According to the House of Bishops' Guidelines with regard to marriage by common licence, the issuing of the licence is a matter 'entirely at the discretion of the diocesan bishops'; the policy of the House of Bishops, though, is 'to refuse marriage by licence where neither party is baptized'. Where only one party is baptized a statement is required 'that the other party does not reject the Christian faith and desires marriage in church'.[172] A similar scheme operates for special licences.[173] The crucial test is 'whether [the parties] are prepared to move towards a vision of marriage compatible with Christian understanding'. Therefore, in making the pastoral judgment the minister should look for acceptance of marriage as exclusive, lifelong, and involving commitment; 'the minister should err, if at all, on the side of generosity'.[174]

The guidance also deals with liturgical considerations: there ought to be no omissions from the marriage service though additions 'might be appropriately made in the form of a reference to the faith of the non-Christian partner'.[175] As we saw in Chapter 10, provision is made under Canons B43 and 44 for Church of England clergy to participate in liturgical celebrations of marriage according to the rites of other churches.[176] Though he may assist in elements of a

---

[169] *COCLA*, 1338–9; *Briefing* 90, 140: the priest must inform the parties of the possibility of dispensation from form; the power to dispense from form lies with the ordinary and 'care must be taken that the requirements of both canon law and civil law be fulfilled'.

[170] Act of Settlement 1700, s. 2: marriage to a Roman Catholic will result in loss of a right of succession; Royal Marriages Act 1772: until age 25 the consent of the monarch is required; see generally C. d'O. Farran, *MLR*, 15 (1951), 53; C. Parry, *International and Comparative Law Quarterly*, 5 (1956) 61.

[171] See *supra*; *Guidelines for the Celebration of Mixed-Faith Marriages in Church* (1992) para. 2; *The Marriage of Adherents of Other Faiths in Anglican Churches*, Report of the Inter-Faith Consultative Group of the Board of Mission to the House of Bishops, Board of Mission Occasional Paper No. 1 (1992).

[172] *Guidelines* (1992), para. 4.   [173] Faculty Office *Guide*, paras. 9.4, 10.3.

[174] *Guidelines for Mixed-Faith Marriages*, paras. 11–14.   [175] Ibid., para. 19.

[176] See *supra* Ch. 10.

Church of England marriage rite, a non-Anglican minister cannot solemnize a marriage according to a Church of England rite.[177] As with remarriage, diocesan norms have been designed to regulate mixed marriages, many incorporating the House of Bishops' Guidelines.[178] Some norms impose a requirement to consult the bishop,[179] and some advise the Christian party to make no written undertaking as to the education of children of a mixed marriage.[180]

CONCLUSIONS

The law of the Church of England with respect to marriage and divorce is untidy. The right to marry in the parish church is founded on a legal fiction rather that on a positive law, and its origins cannot easily be identified: the degree of certainty with which the basic principle is presented cannot be justified. Its existence, recognized in judicial dicta of persuasive but not binding authority, is based on an assumption which seems to have been acted on even by Parliament. Ministerial rights to refuse solemnization may be exercised only when there is a failure to satisfy requirements as to validity and regularity. As under Roman Catholic canon law, a minister may lawfully refuse marriage if the criteria for validity and form are not satisfied. Legally, in both churches (as in civil law) the basic liturgical criterion is the exchange of consent. Unlike in the Roman Catholic Church, the Church of England's formal canon law does not clearly forbid the marriage of divorcees. Prohibitions which exist are to be found only in non-legal pastoral regulations made by Convocation: these remain the only general church provision on the matter. Often incorporating Guidance issued centrally by General Synod's House of Bishops, guidance not of course having full synodical authority, diocesan regulations vary. Commonly these recognize a ministerial discretion to solemnize 'second' marriages whilst requiring ministers to consult the bishop before doing so. The ministerial right to refuse rests ultimately on civil law. In Roman Catholic canon law there is a general prohibition against mixed marriages though these may be solemnized non-sacramentally with episcopal approval. In contrast, though permissible, mixed marriages are regulated principally not by the formal law of the Church of England but by means of executive guidance issued centrally and at diocesan level; lack of baptism is neither a ground for refusal nor a criterion of validity.

---

[177] Church of England (Ecumenical Relations) Measure 1988, s. 3(b).
[178] *DGBOP*, 4.3; *LDHI*, III.12.
[179] *TBF*, 3.20; *DSPR*, Ad clerum 1992/3: if clergy are requested then application should be made to the bishop who will make the 1992 House of Bishops' Guidelines available; for a norm requiring consultation with the rural dean or a surrogate see *LDHI*, III, 12; for norms as to preparation (to uncover difficulties) see e.g. *BDM*, G.8.
[180] *ODYB: IF*, 238, which also makes provision, after marriage according to a Roman Catholic rite, for episcopal permission to use a service of prayer and thanksgiving.

14

Funerals and the Disposal of Human Remains

The disposal of human remains is regulated by a complicated tangle of state-made and church-made law. The law of the Church of England generally treats the disposal of corpses and cremated remains in the same way. The right to burial in the churchyard, which now extends to the disposal of cremated remains, is one of the package of rights enjoyed by parishioners. The law regulates both the exercise of burial rights and, as does Roman Catholic canon law, rights concerning the use and choice of funeral services. In contrast, exhumation, reservation of grave spaces, erection of memorials, and the disposal of remains in closed churchyards arise by way of privilege and not as general rights—these matters fall within the jurisdiction of the consistory courts. The law of the Church of England does not deal specifically with the pastoral care of the bereaved, this task is left to the discretion of the minister subject to regulation by diocesan and other extra-legal norms. In this Chapter we shall also examine the growing body of diocesan norms dealing with the ministry of deliverance.

THE BURIAL OF BODIES

Whilst the law of the Church of England does not expressly require that a corpse should be buried in ground consecrated according to the rites of the church,[1] there is a presumption that an area used for burials in a churchyard or other burial ground of a parish should be consecrated; where no documentary evidence is available it is presumed that the ground has been consecrated.[2]

---

[1] For consecration see *post* Ch. 15; see *R v Tiverton Burial Board* (1858) 31 LTOS 233; 22 JP 529; 6 WR 662 for a dispute between a burial board and a bishop concerning the introduction of markers between the consecrated and unconsecrated portions of a burial ground (the case concerned the terms of the Metropolitan Burials Act 1852, s. 30 and Burials (Beyond the Metropolis) Act 1853, s. 7).

[2] *OLAC*, 25–6: with regard to a local authority or private cemetery company burial ground, there is no obligation to provide a consecrated area; whilst an officiating minister who conducts a burial according to the rites of the Church of England in unconsecrated ground is not subject to proceedings for a breach of ecclesiastical law (Burial Laws Amendement Act 1880, s. 12), Canon B38(5) makes express provision for burial in unconsecrated ground: the 'officiating minister, on coming to the grave, shall first bless the same'.

The Right to Burial in Consecrated Ground

It is commonly understood that a living person has a right to burial in the parish.[3] The right is said to 'crystallise . . . when the person in question dies'.[4] Strictly, however, the right is vested in those who by law have the responsibility for disposing of the body and arranging a funeral.[5] It is 'not competent to an executor or administrator, or to any other person on whom the law imposes the duty of burying the deceased . . . to deprive him of that right'.[6] These are forbidden to keep the body unburied or to do anything which prevents burial or offends or endangers the health of the community.[7] Nevertheless, enactments commonly treat the right as though it were vested in the deceased person.[8] A person who has died within the parish, even if a complete stranger to the parish until the moment of death, has a common law right to burial in the parish burial ground, whether a churchyard or cemetery.[9] The common law does not distinguish between members of the church or non-members, Christians or

---

[3] *Maidman v Malpas* (1794) 1 Hag Con 205; *R v Coleridge* (1819) 2 B & Ald 806; *Kemp v Wickes* (1809) 3 Phillim 264, 161 ER 1320 at 1333; *Re Kerr* [1894] P 284 at 293 *per* Tristram Ch: 'The Court should further observe, that . . . by the Common Law as well as by Ecclesiastical Law any person (subject to certain exceptions) dying in England is entitled to Christian burial in the accustomed form in a consecrated burial-ground belonging to his own parish.'

[4] *Re West Pennard Churchyard* [1991] 4 All ER 124 at 126 *per* Newsom Ch (Bath and Wells Con. Ct.).

[5] Persons possessing the right are ranked in a hierarchy, from executors to local authorities: *Holtham v Arnold* (1986) 2 BMLR 123; *Grandison v Nembhard* (1989) 4 BMLR 140; see Public Health (Control of Disease) Act 1984, s. 46(1).

[6] *Re Kerr* [1894] 284 at 293.

[7] *Williams v Williams* [1882] 20 Ch D 659; *R v Stewart* (1840) 12 A&E 773; burial where no other arrangements can be made is regulated by the Public Health (Control of Diseases) Act 1984, s. 46: *OLAC*, 24. Anatomy Act 1984, s. 4: the Secretary of State may grant a licence to carry out anatomical examinations if a person, either in writing or orally in the presence of 2 or more witnesses during his last illness, has expressed a request that his body be used after his death for anatomical examination; if the person lawfully in possession of the body after death has no reason to believe that the request was withdrawn, he may authorize the use of the body in accordance with the request; no authority may be given in respect of a body by a person entrusted with the body for the purposes only of its interment or cremation. See also Human Tissue Act 1961.

[8] Burial Acts 1852–1906; Pastoral Measure 1983, Sched. 3, para. 15; Church of England (Miscellaneous Provisions) Measure 1976, s. 6, as amended 1992, s. 3.

[9] *Re Kerr* [1894] 284 at 293; *Winstanley v Manchester Overseers* [1910] AC 7 at 15; *AG v Strong* (1868) 1 Seton's Judgments, 5th edn., 485 suggests that the churchwardens and incumbent must consent to the burial of those dying out of the parish (except in the case of travellers having a family burial place); for admonishing a churchwarden for allowing strangers to be buried in the churchyard to the detriment of parishioners (improbable action today) see *The Case of the Harrow Churchwardens*, Burn, *Ecclesiastical Law*, I, 258, and *Littlewood v Williams* (1815) 6 Taunt 277; *Re Atkins* [1989] 1 All ER 14 at 16 *per* Edwards Ch: 'The parish priest who buries a parishioner has the right at common law to open the soil of the churchyard for that purpose'; *Re St Mary Magdalene, Lyminster* [1990] 2 *ELJ* (1991) 127 *per curiam*: an incumbent has no right to derogate from the parishioners' rights in the soil of the churchyard by burying a body or ashes of a non-parishioner in the churchyard unless he obtains the consent of the parishioners signified by the parochial church council.

non-Christians.[10] The right to bury, vested in those responsible for disposal, is enforceable in the civil courts by *mandamus*.[11]

Under the terms of the internal law of the Church of England, which is declaratory of the common law, the right to burial flows from a clerical duty to bury. Every minister has a canonical duty 'to observe the law' in relation to burial of the dead.[12] It is 'the duty of every minister to bury . . . the corpse . . . of any person deceased within his cure' and corpses 'of any parishioners or persons whose names are entered on the church electoral roll of his parish whether deceased within his cure or elsewhere'.[13] Personal representatives are entitled to remove a body to the parish of residence and demand its burial there.[14] Due notice of the burial must be given,[15] and before burial takes place the incumbent must be satisfied that a certificate of disposal of the body has been issued by the registrar of births and deaths.[16] When a person is not a parishioner, is not on the electoral roll or does not die in the parish, an incumbent has a discretionary right to consent to burial in the churchyard— in deciding whether to give consent the incumbent must have regard to any general guidance issued by the parochial church council.[17] In such cases, if the incumbent refuses consent the consistory court has no jurisdiction to grant a faculty to authorize such a burial against the incumbent's veto.[18] Diocesan norms commonly repeat these provisions.[19] Whilst special provisions apply to the choice of rite at the burial service, the unbaptized,[20] including those baptized validly by a layperson,[21] suicides or excommunicates may be buried in consecrated ground.[22] On a union of parishes under a pastoral scheme, those resident in the united parish have the rights of parishioners in respect of burials

---

[10] The assumption is made in the Welsh Church (Temporalities) Act 1945, s. 4(1); but see *Kemp v Wickes* (1809) 3 Phillim 264 at 274 *per* Sir John Nicholl: 'It is the duty of the parish minister to bury all persons dying within his parish, all Christians . . . It does not limit the duty to the burial of persons who are of the Church of England'; see also *Vann* (1851) 2 Den 325 for 'Christian burial'; *Price* (1884) 15 Cox CC 389: it seems unlikely that Lord Campbell could have meant that 'Jews, Mohammedans and Hindoos' were entitled to Christian burial.

[11] *R v Coleridge* (1819) 2 B & Ald 806.　　　[12] Canon B38(1).

[13] Canon B38(2); Church of England (Miscellaneous Provisions) Measure 1976, s. 6(1); under the 1603 Canons, Canon 68 no minister could refuse or delay burial of any corpse, convenient warning having been given.　　　[14] *OLAC*, 24.

[15] B38(2); For notice see *Titchmarsh v Chapman* (1844) 1 Rob Ecc 175; and *Ex p Titchmarsh* (1845) 9 Jur 159.　　　[16] For the procedures see *OLAC*, 26.

[17] Church of England (Miscellaneous Provisions) Measure 1976, s. 6(2); s. 6(3): 'minister' means the incumbent of the benefice to which the parish belongs or, if the benefice is vacant, the minister acting as priest-in-charge or the curate licensed to the charge of the parish or, if there is no such minister or curate, the rural dean; see also *Neville v Bridger* (1874) 30 LTR 690.

[18] *Re St Nicholas's, Baddesley Ensor* (1983) Fam 1.

[19] E.g. *RBG*, A.7; *NDIB*, IV, 46; *CDH*, 52.

[20] Nor the baptized child of a Nonconformist: *Kemp v Wickes* (1809) 3 Phillim. 264; *Nurse v Henslowe* (1844) 3 NC 272.

[21] *Mastin v Escott* (1841) 6 Jur 765; the minister seems to have a discretion as to whether to bring the body into church: Burn, *Ecclesiastical Law*, I, 267.

[22] *OLAC*, 224: suicides; *LDR*, 30: suicides may be buried in consecrated ground; see below.

in that parish.[23] Residents of a new parish created otherwise than by a union of parishes retain their original rights of burial until they obtain rights of burial as parishioners of the new parish.[24]

In the opinion of the Legal Advisory Commission the responsibility for digging a grave falls upon those charged with making the funeral arrangements; the incumbent's duty is merely to indicate the place at which the grave is to be dug and its depth, he is not responsible to provide a grave-digger.[25] It has been decided judicially that a minister cannot be compelled to bury the body in a particular vault or part of the churchyard: he has a 'right to prescribe the position where a burial is to take place'.[26] On old authority a parishioner cannot insist that a body be buried as near as possible to ancestors in a particular part of the burial ground.[27] Nor do the personal representatives have a right to insist on an unusual mode of burial.[28] There is no common law or canonical right to burial in the church itself; if this is desired a faculty must be obtained.[29] Similar rules apply in the Roman Catholic Church: the funeral must take place in the church of the parish of which the deceased was a parishioner (though there is a right to choose another church with the consent of its pastor and after the deceased's pastor is informed) or in the church of the parish in which the person died.[30] If the parish has its own cemetery, the faithful are to be interred there unless another burial ground has been chosen by the deceased or by those responsible for arranging the interment;[31] special permission must be obtained for burial in a church.[32]

Burial in Closed Churchyards

A minister has no right to allow an interment when a burial ground is closed. Closure of a parish churchyard or other burial ground destroys all right of

---

[23] Pastoral Measure 1983, Sched. 3, para. 15(1) provides that any parishioner who, before the union, had any rights of burial in a churchyard in the parish shall (so long as the churchyard remains open) continue to have those rights and shall not become entitled by virtue of the union to rights of burial in any other churchyard.

[24] Pastoral Measure, 1983, Sched. 3 para. 15(2): 'On the creation . . . of a new parish by a pastoral scheme, the persons residing within . . . the limits of the new parish shall continue to have the same rights and privileges in respect of burials which they enjoyed before the creation of the new parish, but such rights shall cease when they obtain rights of burial as parishioners of the new parish'; *OLAC*, 24; *Hughes v Lloyd* (1888) 22 QBD 157.   [25] *OLAC*, 25.

[26] *Re West Pennard Churchyard* [1991] 4 All ER 124 at 127; see also *Ex p Blackmore* (1830) 1 B & Ald 122; *In re Marks (deceased)*, *Times* 28 Oct. 1994; *OLAC*, 25.

[27] *Fryer v Johnson* (1755) 2 Wils. 28.

[28] *R v Coleridge* (1819) 2 B & Ald 806 (iron coffin).

[29] *Gilbert v Buzzard* (1820) 3 Phillim. 348 *per* Lord Stowell: 'In our country the practice of burying in churches is said to be anterior to that of burying in what are now called churchyards, but was reserved for persons of pre-eminent sanctity of life'; see E. L. Thomas (ed.), *Baker's Law Relating to Burials* (6th edn., London, 1901) 1–2.

[30] *CIC*, c. 1177; see generally R. Rutherford, *The Death of a Christian: the Rite of Funerals* (New York, 1980).

[31] *CIC*, c. 1180; everyone, unless prohibited, is entitled to choose a cemetery for burial.

[32] Ibid, c. 1242, unless it is the pontiff, a cardinal, or a diocesan bishop.

burial in it.[33] A churchyard which is also a burial ground may be closed for further burials by Orders in Council made on the representation of the Secretary of State for the Environment under the Burial Act 1853 and the Local Government Act 1972; the Order in Council simply empowers the Secretary of State to stop burials and impose restrictions additional to those imposed by statute or common law.[34] As a general rule, once closed a burial ground cannot be used for further burials of corpses: 'it is unlawful . . . to bury the dead in any church, chapel, churchyard or burial place, within the limits to which the order extends'.[35] The Legal Advisory Commission of the Church of England, however, is of the opinion that 'the fact that a churchyard is a closed churchyard does not necessarily mean that no burials may legally take place there as this will depend upon the exact terms of the Order (or Orders) in Council applicable to it'.[36] Special rules apply to disused burial grounds. Under the Open Spaces Act 1887 a 'disused burial ground' is 'any burial ground which is no longer used for interments, whether or not such ground shall have been partially or wholly closed for burials under the provisions of any statute or Order in Council'.[37] If land in a disused burial ground has been consecrated according to the rites and ceremonies of the Church of England it seems that a faculty may be granted to authorize burial.[38] Under the Pastoral Measure 1983 where any human remains are believed to be buried in or beneath a redundant building or in any land to which a redundancy scheme applies, the body or person in whom the property is vested (or to whom it is leased or licensed) must not demolish, sell, lease, or otherwise dispose of it or any part of it unless the human remains have been removed and reinterred or cremated.[39]

[33] *Re West Pennard Churchyard* [1991] 4 All ER 124 at 126 *per* Newsom Ch (Bath and Wells Con. Ct.): 'At common law, every parishioner has a right of burial in the churchyard of the parish (unless it is closed by due legal process)'; 'until closure, all legal burial rights continue' (ibid., 128).

[34] Burial Act 1853, s. 1; Local Government Act 1972, s. 272, Scheds. 26 (para. 15) and 30.

[35] Burial Act 1853, s. 3. It is an offence to bury remains in a closed churchyard or burial ground contrary to the terms of an Order in Council: Burial Act 1855, s. 2, as amended by Criminal Law Act 1977, s. 31 and the Criminal Justice Act 1982, ss. 38, 46.

[36] *OLAC*, 61: the burial of relatives may take place; for procedures for tracing an Order in Council, see ibid. 61–2; the Order in Council may allow for exceptions to its terms: the most usual exceptions and qualifications refer to burials in vaults or in family graves or to permit the burial of a named person with a close relative: see e.g. Burial Grounds (Manchester) Order 1948, SI 1948 No. 2352; Halsbury, *Laws of England* (4th edn., London, 1975) Vol. 10, para. 1207, n. 2.

[37] Open Spaces Act 1887 s. 4, amending the Disused Burial Grounds Act 1884. It was the same meaning as that appearing in the Metropolitan Open Spaces Act 1881. E.g. the Disused Burial Grounds Act 1884, as amended by the Disused Burial Grounds (Amendment) Act 1981, forbids (subject to certain exceptions) the erection of buildings on closed burial grounds (ss. 3, 4).

[38] Disused Burial Grounds (Amendment) Act 1981, s. 5: this statute 'shall not apply to any consecrated land and shall not affect the jurisdiction of the Consistory Court' (s. 5); s. 9: '"consecrated land" means land which has been consecrated according to the rites and ceremonies of the Church of England'.   [39] Pastoral Measure 1983, s. 65, Sched. 6.

The Burial Service

In Roman Catholic canon law the Christian faithful are to be given a church funeral according to the norm of law; church funerals are to be celebrated according to the norms of the liturgical books and at the service the church prays for the spiritual support of the dead, it honours their bodies, and it brings to the living the comfort of hope.[40] In the Church of England only those dying in the parish, those whose names are entered on the electoral roll, and non-parishioners whose burial is permitted by the incumbent have a legal right to a funeral conducted according to the rites of the Church of England as prescribed by canon.[41] When the burial is in consecrated ground, only authorized persons can perform the funeral service of the Church of England. Ordinarily this is the incumbent of the benefice in which the burial is to take place, or if there is a vacancy the priest-in-charge or a curate licensed to the parish. With respect to persons who are parishioners or who die in the parish or whose names are entered on the electoral roll, the minister of a parish situated wholly or partly in an area which is chargeable with the expenses of a cemetery (or for the use of which a cemetery or crematorium has been designated by the diocesan bishop) shall, where he is requested to do so, 'be under the same obligation to perform or arrange the performance of funeral services in the crematorium or cemetery as he has to perform or arrange the performance of funeral services in any churchyard of his parish'.[42] In some cases the performance of a funeral sevice does not require the consent, nor is subject to the control of the minister of the parish in which it is performed. The minister of a parish may perform a funeral service in any cemetery (or crematorium) situated in another parish if the deceased person dies or was resident immediately before death in, or had his name entered on the electoral roll of, the other parish.[43] Similarly, a person licensed to perform funeral services on premises forming part of or belonging to a university, college, school, hospital, or public or charitable institution may perform a funeral service in any cemetery (or crematorium) if the deceased person was resident in such premises or was employed by or enrolled as a student at the institution in question immediately before death.[44] Many diocesan norms prescribe that if those concerned request the funeral to be conducted by a minister other than a minister of the parish, ordinarily the

---

[40] *CIC*, c. 1176: through the rites the Church asks spiritual assistance for the departed.

[41] B38(2).

[42] Church of England (Miscellaneous Provisions) Measure 1992, s. 2(4); *OLAC*, 27: in these circumstances 'the incumbent is required to take or arrange for the funeral service (and does not merely have the right to do so)'.

[43] Church of England (Miscellaneous Provisions) Measure 1992, s. 2(1), (2), (4); s. 2(6): the minister includes the incumbent, team vicar, and priest-in-charge; Canon C8(2)(d); for statements of the general principle see *Johnson v Friend and Ballard* [1860] 6 Jur NS 280; *Wood v Burial Board of Headingley-cum-Burley* [1892] 1 QB 713.

[44] Church of England (Miscellaneous Provisions) Measure 1992, s. 2(3), without prejudice to the Extra-Parochial Ministry Measure 1967, s. 2.

permission of the parish minister must be obtained as a matter of courtesy: if this is not possible, whilst he may officiate without permission the requested minister must inform the parish minister before or as soon as practicable after the funeral service.[45]

It is the minister's right to choose which of the prescribed forms of service is to be used but if the parties concerned object the matter must be referred to the bishop.[46] Generally the minister must read the whole service though minor variations may be made.[47] Ministers and members of non-Anglican churches may be invited to assist in the conducting of a funeral service.[48] Unordained persons may conduct funerals in churchyards or in the consecrated part of a cemetery provided notice is given at such time and to such persons as the burial authority directs.[49] If the unordained person is to read a Church of England funeral service he must be authorized to do so by the incumbent of the parish.[50] As soon as possible after, the minister must register the burial in the prescribed form.[51] Ministers have a legal right to demand the payment of legally prescribed burial fees.[52] Whilst canon law does not make specific provision for pastoral care of the bereaved,[53] guidelines have been issued regulating visits, the conducting of funeral services, and the organization at parochial level of groups of lay people employed to undertake ministry to the bereaved.[54]

Both churches deny funeral rites to specified classes, but the denial is not absolute. In Roman Catholic canon law unless they have given a sign of repentance before death, notorious apostates, heretics and schismatics, and other manifest sinners (for whom rites cannot be performed without public scandal to the faithful) are deprived of funeral rites; if doubt arises the local ordinary is to be consulted and his decision is to be followed.[55] The local ordinary may permit the use of funeral rites for unbaptized children (if their

---

[45] *PDH*, H.6; *SDH*, I, G.5; *BRDSEI*, AB; *TBF*, 3.22; cf. the baptism rule under Canon B22(5).

[46] Canon B3(4); *BCP*, 326; *ASB*, 305.

[47] *Re Todd* (1844) 3 NC Suppl. ii; *OLAC*, 24; for the range of authorized funeral services outside *BCP* 1662 see *ASB*, 305 f.; for variations not of substantial importance see Canon B5.

[48] Canon B43(1)(1)(e); there is no specific provision for so doing, but the bishop may it seems authorize by instrument under a local ecumenical project non-Anglicans to participate in funeral services according to Church of England rites, or in joint funeral services, as he might authorize a Church of England minister to perform funeral services according to the rites of another church (Canon B44); see also Ch. 10 *supra*.   [49] Burial Laws Amendment Act 1880, ss. 1, 6.

[50] *OLAC*, 28.

[51] Canon F11; Parochial Registers and Records Measure 1978, s. 3, as amended by the Church of England (Miscellaneous Provisions) Measure 1992, s. 4, Sched. 1, para. 3.

[52] See *post* Ch. 17.   [53] Cf. *CIC*, c. 529(1).

[54] *Funerals and Ministry to the Bereaved*, A Handbook of Funeral Practices and Procedures (London, 1989) and *The Role of the Minister in Bereavement: Guidelines and Training Suggestions* (Church House Publishing, London, 1989), both issued by the Churches' Group on Funeral Services; also e.g. *LDR*, 30–1, *CF*, C.6 (lay assistance); *BRDSEI*, AB.

[55] *CIC*, c. 1184; under a 1973 letter of the Sacred Congregation for the Doctrine of the Faith, the pastor must explain the circumstances to those involved: *CCL*: TC, 840; see also D. Power, 'The funeral rites for a suicide and liturgical developments', *Concilium*, 179 (1985), 75.

parents intended baptism) and for baptized members of some non-Catholic churches unless this is contrary to the wishes of the deceased and a non-Catholic minister is available.[56] In the Church of England burial may not ordinarily be conducted according to the rites of the Church of England as of right with respect to those who have died unbaptized,[57] those who 'being of unsound mind' have committed suicide[58] (as to the propriety of the coroner's verdict, the minister has no right to inquire)[59] and those who have been declared excommunicate for some grievous and notorious crime: the prohibition does not apply if a person testifies the deceased's repentance.[60]

When the deceased is unbaptized, excommunicate, or a suicide, or 'in any other case', a relative, friend, or legal representative having charge of or being responsible for the burial has a right to request that the funeral be conducted according to rites other than those normally prescribed.[61] On such a request the minister 'shall use' such service as may be prescribed or approved by the ordinary. The service must not be contrary to or depart from the doctrine of the Church of England. Forms of funeral service approved by the General Synod for the burial of suicides must be used where applicable instead of those services prescribed or approved by the ordinary, unless the person responsible for the burial requests otherwise.[62] If any doubt arises as to whether any deceased person is to be buried according to the church's funeral rites, the minister is under a canonical duty to refer the matter to the bishop; the minister must then 'obey his order and direction'.[63] A person responsible for the burial also has a right to request a service not according to any of the rites of the Church of England.[64] Prayers for the dead, so long as they conform to the doctrine of the church, are not illegal.[65] There is no legal impediment to

---

[56] *CIC*, c. 1183.

[57] *Kemp v Wickes* (1809) 3 Phillim 264 at 269 *per* Sir John Nicholl: 'Now that law in the rubric forbids the burial service to be used for persons who die unbaptized. It is not a matter of option; it is not matter of expediency or benevolence . . . whether a clergyman shall administer the burial service, or shall refuse it . . . for the rubric, thus confirmed by the statute, expressly enjoins him not to perform the office.' Cf. the marriage of the unbaptized: *supra* Ch. 13.

[58] A person must have put an end to his own life ('laid violent hands upon himself') being, at the time, of years of discretion and in his senses: *Clift v Schwabe* (1846) 3 CB 437 at 472–6 *per* Pollock CB; *Dufour v Professional Life Assurance Co* (1858) 25 Beav 599 at 602; see also Church of England Board for Social Responsibility, *Ought Suicide to be a Crime?* (London, 1959).

[59] *Cooper v Dodd* (1850) 2 Rob Ecc 270; but the coroner must direct that remains are to be interred in the churchyard or other parish burial ground and the interment may be carried out in any of the ways authorized by the Burial Laws Amendment Act 1880.

[60] Canon B38(2); *Kemp v Wickes* (1809) 3 Phillim. 264 at 271–2.   [61] B38(2).

[62] Ibid.; for suicides and murder victims see *SDDH*, B.23; *WH*, BP.29; *TBF*, 3.22; *LDR*, 30: suicides may be buried in consecrated ground; *OLAC*, 224 (no special form of service for suicides has as yet been approved by General Synod).   [63] B38(6).

[64] Burial Laws Amendment Act 1880, s. 13; this may occur at the option of the responsible person, with or without a religious service at the grave as he thinks fit (s. 6).

[65] For faculty cases on the subject see *Rector and Churchwardens of Capel St Mary, Suffolk v Packard* [1927] P 289; if the prayers involve the doctrine of purgatory they are unlawful: *AR*, Art.

the reading of the burial service, for those not falling in the special three classes, on unconsecrated ground.[66]

Disinterment

Though the personal representatives are entitled to the possession of the body for the purposes of burial, after burial the body comes under the protection of public authorities.[67] There is no right to disinterment.[68] Ordinarily, under the Burial Act 1857, a body cannot be removed from a 'place of burial' without the Secretary of State's licence: as a general principle, a licence is required in all cases where the remains are disinterred from unconsecrated land and re-buried in unconsecrated land.[69] However, if the corpse is buried in consecrated ground it comes under the protection and control of the consistory court. If disinterment is from consecrated ground and reinterment is in consecrated ground a faculty is needed but there is no need to obtain a licence.[70] If disinterment is from unconsecrated ground and reinterment in consecrated ground a licence is required for disinterment and a faculty for reinterment; it is not clear whether, in relation to disinterment from consecrated ground and reinterment in unconsecrated ground, a faculty is required for disinterment and a licence for re-interment.[71] In these cases, the consistory court enjoys a discretion and must exercise this sparingly and only in special circumstances: a faculty would not be given simply for the sake of rendering visits more convenient: the underlying assumption is that the court must protect the remains of a deceased person interred in consecrated ground in accordance with the rites of the Church of England when it was the express or presumed intention of all those taking part that the earthly remains of the deceased were to be finally laid at rest once and for all.[72] If the application is made on private grounds, the court will in practice be guided by the wishes of the deceased, or of their relatives and friends.[73] A faculty may be authorized for the removal of

---

22; see also *Breeks v Woolfrey* (1838) 1 Curt 880; *Re Parish of South Creake* [1959] 1 All ER 197; *Re St Mary the Virgin, Ilmington* [1962] 1 All ER 560; [1962] P 147; for the Roman Catholic canon law on funeral masses see *CIC*, c. 1185.

[66] *Kingsmill v Rugg* [1868] 18 LTNS 94; LR 2 PC 59.

[67] *Foster v Dodd* [1867] LR 3 QB 67, *per* J. Byles J.

[68] *Re Atkins* [1989] 1 All ER 14 at 16.   [69] S. 25.

[70] Ibid; *Re Pope* [1857] 15 Jur 614: disinterment allowed for the purposes of identification; see also *Druce v Young* [1899] P 84; *OLAC*, 28–29: this interpretation was agreed by the Home Office in 1985.   [71] *Holy Trinity, Freckleton* [1995] 3 *ELJ* (1995) 429.

[72] *Re Smith (deceased)* [1994] 1 All ER 90, following *Re Atkins* [1989] 1 All ER 14 and *Re St Luke's Holbeach Hurn, Watson v Howard* [1990] 2 All ER 749; see also *CF*, F.6.4: exhumation is permitted if e.g. a move is proposed from a public to a private grave, or if there has been a mistake; *ODYB*, 251.

[73] *In re Dixon* [1892] P 386; *Holy Trinity, Freckleton* [1995] 3 ELJ (1995) 429, 350; see also *St Luke's, Whaley Thorn* [1994], ibid.: petition by parents for exhumation of a husband stabbed to death by his wife who was convicted of manslaughter: the deceased had expressed no wishes as to place of burial.

a corpse for public purposes, for example on sanitary grounds; in such cases the wishes of the deceased's relatives will be consulted and considered as to the place to which the remains are to be moved.[74] Unauthorized disinterment is a criminal offence and may also constitute an ecclesiastical offence.[75]

Exclusive Burial Rights, Reservation, and Memorials

Parishioners have no right to the exclusive property in a grave nor can a minister give any person such a right.[76] The consistory court has a discretionary power to grant a faculty conferring an exclusive right of burial in a particular vault or part of a churchyard.[77] Under the Faculty Jurisdiction Measure 1964 all exclusive rights of burial in churchyards will cease in the year 2064 unless granted, enlarged, or continued by a faculty issued after 1964.[78] An exclusive right of burial may be granted to a non-parishioner[79] and may be assigned but the courts are reluctant to allow a freehold estate to pass. The precise nature of an exclusive burial right is unclear: it is similar to but not the same as an easement.[80] Such grants may be limited to a certain family so long as they continue parishioners or inhabitants, or to a person and his heirs and family.[81] The grant must be made by deed and not orally.[82] The minister has no independent power to confer an exclusive right, the title must be confirmed by faculty.[83] The incumbent's request does not fetter the discretionary power of the consistory court to grant or refuse the exclusive right.[84] It seems that if an exclusive burial right is violated by an unauthorized infringing burial in the exclusive plot the ecclesiastical courts may be able to provide relief.[85]

A person has a right to petition the consistory court for a faculty permitting the reservation of a gravespace. The authorization is discretionary, though if 'there is plenty of room in the churchyard it is freely granted to a petitioner

---

[74] *Rector of St Helen's, Bishopsgate v Parishioners* [1892] P 259; see also *Vicar et al. of St Mary Abbot's v Parishioners* [1873] Tristram's Reports 17; *Vicar et al of St Botolph v Parishioners* [1892] P 161; *In re St Nicholas Cole Abbey* [1893] P 58 compare *In re Plumstead Burial Ground* [1895] P 225.   [75] For ecclesiastical offences see *Adlam v Coulthurst* [1867] LR 2 A&E 30.
[76] *OLAC*, 25.
[77] *Rugg v Kingsmill* (1868) LR 2 PC 59; for diocesan norms see *SDDH*, N.28; *NDIB*, IV.46; for governance of cemeteries in Roman Catholic canon law see *CIC*, cc. 1240–3 (under c. 1243, particular law is to regulate cemetery discipline).   [78] S. 8(1).
[79] *Re Sargent* [1890] 15 PD 168; *Kellett v St John's, Burscough Bridge* (1916) 32; TLR 571.
[80] *Re Hendon Churchyard* (1910) 27 TLR 1; see P. Sparkes, 'Exclusive burial rights', *ELJ*, 2 (1991), 133 at 132; for a right of burial by prescription see *Crisp v Martin* (1876) 2 PD 15 (removal by statute).
[81] *Magnay v Rector, Churchwardens and Parishioners of the United Parishes of St Michael, Paternoster Royal and of St Martin, Vintry* (1827) 1 Hag Ecc 48.
[82] *Bryan v Whistler* (1828) 8 B&C 288.   [83] *De Romana v Roberts* [1906] P 332.
[84] *Rich v Bushnell* (1827) 4 Hag Ecc 164.
[85] *Re St Luke's Holbeach Hurn, Watson v Howard* [1990] 2 All ER 749 (Lincoln Con. Ct.: exhumation was ordered) distinguishing *Reed v Madon* [1989] 2 All ER 431 (exclusive right not enforced); for the possibility of damages see P. Sparkes, 'Exclusive burial rights', 133 at 147.

who has a legal right of burial'.[86] The faculty requires whoever is incumbent when the petitioner dies to allow the remains to be buried in the position defined in the faculty; the faculty deprives the incumbent of his right to choose location.[87] The court may take into account a variety of factors including, *inter alia*, an incumbent's refusal to consent, the views of the parochial church council, the association of the petitioner with the church or parish, and the presence of the remains of relatives in the churchyard.[88] An incumbent's promise or assurance that a plot will be reserved is unenforceable.[89] A parochial church council has a right to give 'general guidance' to an incumbent concerning reservations, and it may adopt an internal practice by which petitions for reservations will always be opposed; however, resolutions of this sort will not be binding on the consistory court.[90]

The right to burial does not entitle the deceased's relatives or personal representatives to erect any memorial over the grave.[91] Monuments must not be erected in a churchyard without faculty authorization, though as a matter of diocesan practice chancellors may delegate to the incumbent the power to permit their erection.[92] If the incumbent refuses or the matter is outside the scope of his delegated power, a petition may be made to the consistory court.[93] The basic principles governing the granting of faculties apply in the exercise of the court's discretion.[94] The church courts are reluctant to allow memorial tablets to be placed in churches; their placement is a privilege, not a right, and can be done only by faculty which will be granted in exceptional circumstances.[95]

THE DISPOSAL OF CREMATED REMAINS

Under secular law after the cremation of the remains of a deceased person the ashes must if he so desires be given into the charge of the person who applies

[86] *Re West Pennard Churchyard* [1991] 4 All ER 124 at 126–7; for diocesan norms concerning reservation see e.g. *NDIB*, IV, 47, *CF*, F.6.1–2; for the requirement to approach the DAC see *SDDH*, O.53–4, *WH*, BP.37.
[87] *Re West Pennard Churchyard* [1991] *supra*, n. 86, 127; such a faculty can be applied for 'with the concurrence of the incumbent, by a person who does not have a legal right of burial'.
[88] *Re St Nicholas's, Baddesley Ensor* [1983] Fam 1; *Re West Pennard Churchyard supra*, n. 86.
[89] *Re St Luke's, Holbeach Hurn supra*, n. 85.
[90] *Re West Pennard Churchyard supra*, n. 86.   [91] *OLAC*, 54.
[92] *Re Woolmington Churchyard* [1957] 2 All ER 323; *RBG*, D.6; *LDHI*, V.7.7; *SDDH*, O.45.
[93] *Re Little Gaddesden Churchyard, ex p Cuthbertson* [1933] P 150 (Arches Court).
[94] Ibid.: marble monuments were allowed; cf. *Re Peter Kineton* [1967] 1 WLR 347; *Re St Paul, Hanging Heaton* [1968] 1 WLR 1210: marble refused; faculty for photographs on headstone refused (*Re St Mary's, Fawkham* [1981] 1 WLR 1171 (Arches Ct.); *Re St Mark's Haydock* [1981] 1 WLR 1164: photographs ordered to be removed; *Re St James, Heywood* [1982] 1 WLR 1289; for epitaphs: *Re St Mark's, Heydock (No. 2)* [1981] 1 WLR 1167: Liverpool Con. Ct. held that a woman with whom the deceased had associated was not to be named on the headstone, though the phrase 'he loved those who loved him' was permissible.
[95] *Dupuis v Ogbourn St George Parishioners* [1941] P 119; *Re St Nicholas, Brockenhurst* [1978] Fam 157; *Re St Margaret, Eartham* [1981] 1 WLR 1129.

for the cremation. If not they are to be retained by the cremation authority and, in the absence of any special arrangement for their burial or preservation, they must either be decently interred in a burial ground or in land adjoining the crematorium reserved for the burial of ashes or else shall be scattered there.[96] According to Roman Catholic canon law, a person choosing cremation for reasons opposed to the Christian religion has no right to ecclesiastical funeral rites; this alters the position under the 1917 Code which forbade funeral rites to be used for those cremated.[97] For others wishing to be cremated, though burial of the body is recommended, cremation is not forbidden if it is desired for reasons consistent with Christian teaching;[98] but funeral rites are not to be performed at the place of cremation.[99]

With regard to the Church of England the position is rather different—no enquiry into the deceased's motive is necessary. In *Re Atkins* it was said that 'the Church makes no distinction in canon law between a corpse and the ashes of a cremated body; both should be treated with the same reverence and decency and accorded the same dignity in interment'.[100] By canon, '[c]remation of a dead body is lawful in connection with Christian burial'.[101] By synodical measure, '[a] person who has the right of burial in the churchyard or other burial ground of a parish shall have a right of burial therein of his cremated remains'.[102] As with bodies, it is 'the duty of every minister to bury the . . . ashes of any person deceased within his cure'; the right belongs to those resident in the parish, those dying in it, and those whose names are on the electoral roll; the ashes of non-parishioners may be buried with the permission of the incumbent having regard to the general guidance of the parochial church council.[103] The rules as to authorized ministers and the choice of rites for burial of a body also apply to disposal of cremated remains; however, a funeral service at a crematorium may be performed only in

---

[96] Cremation Regs. 1930, as amended 1952–85 (SI 1985, No 153); *The Disposal of Cremated Remains* (London, 1965), Ch. 8.　　　　[97] *CIC*, c. 1184; for the 1917 position see *CCL: TC*, 840.
[98] *CIC*, c. 1176(3).
[99] Holy Office, Instrument on Cremation of Corpses, 8 May 1963, *CCL: TC*, 837, n. 26.
[100] [1989] 1 All ER 14 at 16 *per* Quentin Edwards Ch.
[101] Canon B38(3); Convocation had been satisfied that 'The Church's doctrine of the resurrection does not preclude the practice of cremation': *Acts of Convocation* 87.
[102] Church of England (Miscellaneous Provisions) Measure 1992, s. 3; D. A. Smale (ed.), M. R. R. Davies, *Law of Burial, Cremation and Exhumation* (6th edn., Crayford, 1993) 185. However, it is possible that the right to disposal of cremated remains in a parish burial ground is one of common law. In *Price* (1884) 15 Cox CC 389; (1884) 12 QBD 247 Stephen J recognized that 'burial' was a synonym for 'disposal': the common law right was to 'disposal of human remains', including cremated remains; cf. *Williams v Williams* (1882) 20 Ch D 659 *per* Kay J. For a decision of the Commissary Court and the question of granting a faculty for interment in a church see *Re St Peter's Folkstone* [1982] 1 WLR 1283.
[103] Canon B38(2); for non-parishioners, as the right to burial of bodies embraces thr right to burial of cremated remains, the provisions of the Church of England (MIscellaneous Provisions) Measure 1976, s. 6(2) seem to apply.

accordance with directions given by the bishop.[104] When a body is to be cremated the burial service may precede, accompany, or follow the cremation and may be held either in the church or at the crematorium.[105]

Disposal in Open Churchyards

The ashes of a cremated body 'should be reverently disposed of by a minister in a churchyard or other burial ground . . . or on an area of land designated by the bishop . . . or at sea'.[106] With the exception of disposal at sea, this rule does not clarify the precise mode of disposal: whether it must be only by burial or whether it may be by some other means. Two modes of disposal of cremated remains have been approved. First, burial has been treated judicially as the ordinary mode of disposal of cremated remains. In *Re Dixon* (1892) Chancellor Dr. Tristram in the London Consistory Court stated: 'where a body has been consumed in a fire, it has been customary to collect the ashes and to bury them in a churchyard, accompanied with the use of the Order for the Burial of the Dead, and there does not appear to the Court to be any legal objection to the same course being followed where there has been a previous cremation in pursuance of directions left by the deceased.'[107] In *Re Kerr* (1894) Tristram presented burial of ashes as a common law right.[108] Parishioners entitled to the burial of ashes in the churchyard have no right to burial within the church, although this may be authorized by faculty.[109] A faculty is needed for the exhumation and reinterment of cremated remains; the consistory courts' jurisdiction must, as with exhumation of bodies, be exercised sparingly.[110]

Secondly, by Act of Convocation (operative in the York province) the ashes

[104] See *supra* and Canon B38(7); Church of England (Miscellaneous Provisions) Measure 1992, s. 2(5) repeals Cremation Act 1902, which provided that the incumbent was not obliged to perform the burial service. [105] B38(4)(a).
[106] B38(4)(b); 1992 Measure, s. 3(1): the bishop may consecrate land in the diocese for the sole purpose of burying cremated remains.
[107] (1892) P 386: the case concerned a faculty petition to disinter a corpse intended to be cremated; the faculty was refused. For consideration of the case see *Re Atkins* [1989] 1 All ER 14 at 18. See also *Williams v Williams* (1882) 20 Ch D 659 for the Secretary of State not objecting to burial of cremated remains in a consecrated Welsh churchyard. [108] [1894] P 284 and below.
[109] *Re St Peter's, Folkestone* [1982] 1 WLR 1283: in relation to the burial of cremated remains in churches, not churchyards, the practice may have been permitted only restrictively: *per* Newey Ch. at 1286: 'In our Canterbury Diocese it would seem that since the 1939–45 war only on four occasions have faculties been granted for the burial of cremated remains in churches and no faculties have been granted for the burial of bodies in churches.' For faculties and the burial of bodies in churches see *HLE*, para. 1312, esp. n. 10 and the cases mentioned therein, Halsbury, *Laws of England*, Vol. 10 para. 1118, *Rugg v Kingsmill* (1868) LR 2 PC 59, and generally P. Sparkes, 'Exclusive burial rights'.
[110] *Re Atkins* [1989] 1 All ER 14 at 16; *Re St Mary Magdalene, Lyminster* [1990] *ELJ*, 2 (1991), 127: difficulty in visiting through illness was an insufficient ground; *Re Knowle Churchyard* [1994] *ELJ*, 3 (1994), 259: leave to remove a father's ashes from a consecrated churchyard to rebury them with the mother's was refused; *Re Edward William Knight, Deceased* [1993] *ELJ*, 3 (1994), 257; *Re Sidney Wilson Marks, Deceased* [1994] *ELJ*, 3 (1995), 352; see also Pastoral Measure 1983, s. 65.

of a cremated body should be disposed of in consecrated or dedicated ground 'by burial' or 'by strewing them reverently on the surface of the ground and covering them lightly with earth'; '[t]o scatter ashes broadcast on either consecrated or unconsecrated ground without covering them is a method which may be unseemly or irreverent and cannot be recommended'.[111] When disposed of in a churchyard, this may be done in or upon an existing grave, or alternatively suitable provision should be made in a special plot of ground.[112] Many diocesan regulations provide that ashes may be put in existing graves without the authority of a faculty and that either interment or strewing is permissible; some regulations prohibit scattering whilst others do not recommend it;[113] a faculty must be obtained to set aside in a churchyard an area for the burial of cremated remains.[114]

Disposal in Closed Churchyards: Privileges

By a synodical measure of 1992 'a person shall *not* have a right of burial of his cremated remains . . . in a churchyard or burial ground which has been *closed* by an Order in Council'. However, burial may be authorized by faculty: the prohibition does not apply if burial takes place 'in accordance with a faculty authorising the burial or in an area which has been set aside by a faculty for the burial of cremated remains generally'.[115] The underlying assumption seems to be that, having been closed for further burials, burial would not 'lawfully be effected';[116] if authorized by faculty burial is permitted as a privilege and not as a right.[117] The faculty may be general or particular.[118]

---

[111] *Acts of Convocation*, 158.   [112] Ibid.

[113] *ODYB: IF*, 250; *SDDH*, B.21, O.51–2; *WH*, BP.30; *RBG*, A.7; *LDHI*, V, 7; *CF*, F.6.3; *PDH*, U.4; *SDH*, I, G: scattering is not recommended.

[114] *HLE*, para. 1315; *MIECL*, 115. Reservation of an area for cremated remains may however, still require a faculty. Newsom states: 'Another class of faculty is for the reservation of an area for the burial of cremated remains. This arrangement is now very common and may be made in respect of an open churchyard or a closed one': *FJCE*, 170; *OLAC*, 25: 'Faculties are often granted to permit part of the churchyard (including a closed churchyard) to be set aside for the interment of cremated remains'; *Re St Edmund, West Kingsdown* [1989] *ELJ*, 1(5) (1989), 5.

[115] Church of England (Miscellaneous Provisions) Measure 1992, s. 3(1) proviso; *OLAC*, 25: 'Although a parishioner has a right to have his ashes buried in a churchyard, this is not so when the churchyard has been closed by Order in Council except pursuant to a faculty'.

[116] B38(2); one presumes that a faculty cannot be granted for such a burial if this is contrary to the terms of an Order in Council. In England the synodical measure of 1992 seems to be silent on this point.

[117] *HLE*, para. 1306; para. 1273, n. 6: 'The word "faculty" signifies a privilege or special dispensation granted to a person by favour and indulgence to do that which by the law he cannot do; *Termes de la Ley* 324'. See *Re St John's, Chelsea* [1962] 1 WLR 706 and *Nickalls v Briscoe* [1892] P 269. *HLE*, para. 1311: 'A faculty . . . renders liberty on a person to do something; it does not command him to do anything'. The question of whether a faculty must be obtained to authorize lawful acts on consecrated ground is of course related to the chancellor's jurisdiction: in *Vicar and One of the Churchwardens of St. Botolph without Aldgate v Parishioners of the Same* [1892] P 161 at 167, Dr. Tristram stated: 'The final control of the church and churchyard is vested in the chancellor, as ordinary for that purpose.'   [118] Parochial Fees Order 1995, Pt. II, 4.

The scope of this rule is not entirely clear. As the synodical measure simply denies a person's 'right of burial' in a closed churchyard or other burial ground, it is submitted that the incumbent has a discretion without faculty to permit disposal of cremated remains in closed churchyards or other burial grounds in limited circumstances. First, the synodical measure does not expressly forbid the strewing of ashes in a closed churchyard or other burial ground.[119] Secondly, burial of cremated remains may be authorized expressly by the terms of the Order in Council closing the churchyard or burial ground.[120] Thirdly, the synodical measure does not state that the burial of cremated remains in closed churchyards is unlawful except when authorized by faculty. It simply prescribes that no right of burial exists when the churchyard or burial ground is closed 'except in accordance with a faculty authorizing the burial'. Indeed, as cremation was put on a statutory footing in 1902, it might be assumed that pre–1902 Orders in Council closing churchyards do not prohibit expressly the burial of cremated remains in closed burial grounds.[121] If the Order in Council does not forbid the burial of cremated remains, it is submitted that no faculty is needed for a minister to permit burial: as a matter of general principle there is no requirement to obtain a faculty for the doing of lawful acts on consecrated ground.[122] Since there is no prohibition against it (neither in the Order in Council nor in the synodical measure) a legal freedom exists to permit burial. This legal freedom had been recognized long before 1992 in the leading case of *Kerr*,[123] but in that case the London Consistory Court imposed the additional requirement of obtaining a faculty; this requirement was unnecessary as, once more, there was no need for a faculty to authorize the performance (by a cleric) of a lawful act. Whilst pre–1992 commentaries explain that a faculty was required to authorize burial of cremated remains in a closed *churchyard* and under the floor of a closed *church*,[124] the principle in *Kerr* was far narrower.

In *Kerr* a faculty was sought in the Consistory Court to place the cremated

---

[119] The 1992 Measure does not classify strewing as burial; cf. Parochial Fees Order 1995, r. 3: 'In . . . this Order . . . "burial" includes . . . the interment or deposit of cremated remains.'

[120] Smale, *Law of Burial*, 76, 229; indeed, Newsom observes: 'This arrangement is now very common and may be made either in respect of an open or a closed [churchyard]': *FJCE*, 170.

[121] Smale, *Law of Burial*, 76, 229, suggesting that the burial of cremated remains may have been permitted pursuant to a faculty under the Burial Act 1853, s. 1; an Order in Council could of course prescribe this.

[122] *Re St Mary's Tyne Dock No. 2* [1958] 1 All ER 1 at 6 (Durham Con. Ct.: a faculty 'confers liberty on a person to do something'). However, in this case Wigglesworth also referred to a decision of Ch. Kempe in *St Luke's, Newcastle* (1912) (unreported) in which Kempe seemed to assume that a faculty may be granted for the introduction of something in the church 'which can be lawfully introduced into it'. This too, it is submitted, is illogical, since a faculty is only required for something which would otherwise be unlawful.   [123] [1894] P 284.

[124] Halsbury, *Laws of England*, Vol. 10, paras. 1121, 1211; *HLE*, para. 1312 (nn. 9, 10); the authorities given to support this are the Standard Table of Fees made by the Church Commissioners under the Ecclesiastical Fees Measure 1962, s. 2; Parochial Fees Order 1972, SI 1972 No. 177.

remains of a parishioner behind a memorial tablet inside the wall of a closed parish church. Four statutes prohibited 'burial' within the church.[125] Chancellor Tristram granted a faculty for interment under the floor of the closed church: neither the immurement nor the interment under the floor was a 'burial' within the meaning of the statutes; nor was the interment forbidden by the Orders in Council closing the church. The provisions in those instruments applied only to burial of an (uncremated) corpse: 'in none of these sections does there occur a single expression which indicates that they were intended to apply to cases of cremation . . . the prohibitions therein contained refer only to the burial of a dead body.'[126] Tristram was also persuaded to grant the faculty as this was the wish of the parishioners; however, he would have been prepared to refuse the faculty '[i]f the interment of cremated ashes in an urn in the church is objectionable on sanitary grounds, such interment might well be held, but not otherwise, as falling within the mischief aimed at by the statutes'.[127] Indeed, for Tristram 'by Common Law as well as by Ecclesiastical Law any person . . . dying in England is entitled to Christian burial in the accustomed form in a consecrated burial-ground belonging to his own parish, or in the parish in which he may have died, it is not competent to an executor or administrator, or to any other person on whom the law imposes the duty of burying the deceased, *by cremation* to deprive him of that right, unless he has left written directions or expressed in his life a wish to be cremated'.[128] Whilst *Kerr* established as part of London diocesan law that 'cremated remains could not be lawfully interred in *any church* except under the authority of a faculty',[129] the decision is not direct authority for the general proposition that a faculty is needed to authorize the burial of cremated remains in a closed *churchyard*. What *Kerr* does represent is that burial of cremated remains is not unlawful if not prohibited by the closing Order in Council. In this respect the new 1992 legislation appears to be more restrictive than preexisting arrangements. Yet it remains unclear whether it represents the abrogation of a common law freedom to dispose of cremated remains in a closed churchyard when this is not forbidden by the closing Order in Council.

Finally, as the purpose of the law on closure of burial grounds is primarily that of public health, by adopting a purposive approach to its interpretation (even when an Order in Council forbids burial of cremated remains) it is arguable that, if there is no objection on sanitary grounds to the burial of cremated remains in a closed churchyard or other burial ground, then application of these rules does not serve the purpose for which they were created.[130] It

---

[125] Church Buildings Act 1818, s. 80; Public Health Act 1848, s. 83; Burials (Beyond the Metropolis) Act 1853, s. 3; Burials Act 1855, s. 2.　　　　　　　　　[126] [1894] P 284.
[127] Ibid., 291, 294.　　　　[128] Ibid., 293.　　　[129] Ibid., 295.
[130] See P. Sparkes, 'Exclusive burial rights', 133 at 145; for Tristram's use of the purposive approach, see *Kerr supra* n. 123, 290. The only justification is that there is no distinction between burial of bodies and ashes.

is untenable to argue that a faculty is required simply to give expression to the principle that the consistory courts have control over consecrated ground. By contrast with the disposal of bodies, it is superfluous to prohibit or control burial of ashes on grounds of hygiene, since they are sterile, anywhere (including in a closed churchyard).

EXORCISM: THE MINISTRY OF DELIVERANCE

In Roman Catholic canon law exorcism is the invocation of the name of God with the aim of removing evil from some person, animal, place, or thing. Public exorcism must be carried out in accordance with established rites.[131] Under the 1983 Code no one may lawfully exorcise the possessed without the special and express permission of the local ordinary. The ordinary may grant permission to exorcise only to a priest endowed with piety, knowledge, prudence, and integrity of life.[132] In the Church of England, whilst the Canons of 1603 provided that ministers were not to attempt exorcism without the licence and permission of the bishop, modern canon law does not deal with exorcism.[133] According to a statement of the Archbishop of Canterbury, exorcism may be performed only by an experienced person authorized by the diocesan bishop, and should be followed by continuing pastoral care.[134] The subject is treated at length by diocesan norms. Ordinarily, any priest may deal directly with exorcism by means of prayer and sacrament; special care must be taken to avoid denying or reinforcing the claimed experience of affected persons. No exorcism of a person may be made or attempted without informing and consulting the bishop or his advisers especially appointed for this purpose. The involvement of medical experts is usually required. With regard to deliverance from evil in a building, a blessing, counselling, or the celebration of Holy Communion may be appropriate in the first intsance. The ministry of deliverance should always be treated as a strictly private matter and many norms forbid communication of any kind with the media.[135]

CONCLUSIONS

The law of the Church of England on disposal of bodies and cremated remains seeks to strike a balance between, on one hand, the safeguarding of ecclesiastical discipline and ministerial and episcopal control, and on the other hand the

---

[131] *COCLA*, 736.   [132] *CIC*, c. 1172.   [133] Canon 72 (repealed).
[134] Statement to the General Synod 30 June 1975; for prayers for the dead see *supra* n. 65.
[135] *CDH*, 89; *BRDSEI*, Hi; *ODYB: IF*, 240; *WH*, BP.26; *LDHI*, III, 23; *TBF*, 3.24; *LDR*, 50; *RBG*, A.11; *PDH*, H.7; *BDM*, D.6; *DSBN*, Ad Clerum Notice, 1989/10, duty to consult the archdeacon acting on bishop's authority; *EDH*, B.17; *WDHI*, ch. 2, 75; *SDH*, I, F

wishes of the deceased, their family, and personal representatives. It has many direct points of contact with Roman Catholic canon law. In both canonical systems a person has a right to burial in the parish according to the prescribed funeral rites; both churches deny funeral rites to specified classes: in the Church of England special forms of service may be employed for the unbaptized, suicides, and excommunicates. In Church of England law, the right to burial of a body in the churchyard or other burial ground is declaratory of the common law. Burial of non-parishioners may be permitted by an incumbent who must have regard to general guidance issued by the parochial church council. There is no right to burial in a church, to exhumation, to property in a reserved grave, or to the erection of a memorial; these may be permitted by faculty granted under the discretion of the consistory court. Whilst in Roman Catholic canon law funeral rites may be denied those who have sought cremation for reasons incompatible with the Christian religion, in the Church of England a minister cannot refuse burial of a body or of cremated remains in the parish churchyard or other burial ground. The right to burial of bodies and cremated remains is lost, however, when the churchyard or burial ground is closed by Order in Council; in these circumstances a faculty must be obtained. Yet the extent of a minister's discretion without faculty to permit disposal of cremated remains in a closed churchyard or other burial ground by strewing or by burial, if not forbidden by the Order in Council, is unclear. The law of the Church of England does not deal specifically with pastoral care of the bereaved or of those seeking the ministry of deliverance; these matters are dealt with by extra-legal norms.

PART VI

The Management of Church Property

15

The Acquisition and Disposal of Property

Like the Roman Catholic Church, the acquisition and disposal of property in the Church of England is governed by both internal and state-made law. However, many rules created by the Church of England and contained in synodical measures operate instead of or in addition to rules of civil law. There follows an examination of the powers of institutions and persons, those ecclesiastical corporations capable of ownership of property in the Church of England, to acquire and dispose of property, and the structures which exist to control the exercise of these powers. Two particular themes are pursued: the centrality of episcopal oversight and the rights of the wider church to participate in decisions concerning acquisition and disposal of property. The Chapter concentrates mainly on realty but concludes with a short section on ecclesiastical chattels. Whereas decisions of consistory courts commonly regulate acquisition and disposal of movables, diocesan quasi-legislation is not extensively employed in relation to the subjects dealt with in this Chapter.

REAL PROPERTY

The complexity of the Church of England's property law has been the subject of criticism and proposals have recently been made for its overall simplification.[1] Whilst there are some fundamental similarities between the two systems, Roman Catholic canon law is by and large far simpler. In Roman Catholic canon law only prescribed juridic persons are capable of owning property;[2] so

---

[1] Hill, *EL*, x; for a proposed draft Church Property Measure prepared by an Ecclesiastical Law Society Working Party under the chairmanship of Chancellor George Spafford see *ELJ*, 2 (1992), 305, 388 (hereafter *DCPM*). As we shall see in this Chapter, the Church Commissioners are closely involved with the acquisition and disposal of different types of church property: *WAOB* (8.39) recommends transference to the proposed National Council of the commissioners' functions with respect to grants towards cathedrals, clergy housing, approval of the acquisition, disposal and improvement of parsonage houses (many of the functions in relation to which are to be transferred ultimately to the dioceses), approval of glebe sales (and the consideration of representations against proposed sales), casework arising under the Pastoral Measure 1983 (including issuing draft schemes and the consideration of representations), and functions under the Cathedrals Measure 1963.

[2] *CIC*, c. 1255: the universal church, the apostolic see, particular churches, and other juridic persons, whether public or private, are capable of acquiring, retaining, administering, and alienating temporal goods in accord with the norm of law; c. 1256: right of ownership under the pontiff belongs to that juridic person which has lawfully acquired the temporal goods; c. 1257: all temporal goods so belonging are governed by cc. 1258–1310; for property owned by a juridic person see c. 116; see also Liberty of Religious Worship Act 1855, s. 2, extending the Roman Catholic Charities Act 1832, s. 1.

too in the Church of England ownership is vested in different ecclesiastical institutions enjoying corporate legal personality. In Roman Catholic canon law, which claims for the church an innate right to acquire, retain, administer, and alienate property independent of civil power, temporal goods (including realty) may be properly acquired, used, and disposed of for the purposes of ordering divine worship, for providing decent support for ministers, and for performing the works of the apostolate and of charity especially towards the needy.[3] Similarly, for the Church of England, it is an operative legal assumption that much ecclesiastical property is held by church bodies as representatives of or on behalf of the members of (and others associated with) the church.[4] This is based on theological doctrines of stewardship and trusteeship.[5]

The two ecclesiastical systems differ most radically as to the basis upon which rules are organized to regulate acquisition and disposal. Whereas for the Church of England forms of regulation depend on the *type* of the property in question, under Roman Catholic canon law they depend on its *value*. Moreover, for the Church of England the extent to which church-made law enables the participation of the church generally in decisions to acquire and to dispose also depends on the type of property in question. With most of the models discussed below the law reserves to the Church Commissioners and the diocesan bishop central positions of oversight.[6] Only rarely do diocesan

---

[3] *CIC*, c. 1254; J. Hite, 'The administration of church property', *Readings*, 408; for 'temporal goods' as including real property see *CCL: TC*, 859, n. 9; for the general problem of conflict between civil law and Roman Catholic canon law see *supra* Ch. 1; the operative doctrinal documents are set out in *COCLA*, 775.

[4] This is merely a general and sometimes troublesome legal assumption; strictly, each piece of property is held for different purposes: for example, the church and churchyard are held for the benefit of parishioners; the parsonage and pre–1976 glebe are held for the benefit of the parson; post–1976 glebe is held for the benefit of the diocesan stipends fund; and the corporate property of the diocesan finance board is held for the benefit of that board. Under the Local Government Act 1894, s. 75(2) 'ecclesiastical property' includes property held for spiritual purposes, for the benefit either of a person holding an ecclesiastical office or of church members; for the purpose of giving notice to owners, lessees, and occupiers, under the Acquisition of Land Act 1981, s. 12(3) 'ecclesiastical property' means 'land belonging to any ecclesiastical benefice, or being or forming part of a church subject to the jurisdiction of the bishop of any diocese or the site of such a church, or being or forming part of a burial ground subject to such jurisdiction'. See also *Rector and Churchwardens of St George's Hanover Square v Westminster Corporation* [1910] AC 225 (HL). Ecclesiastical property may also be understood as property held for an 'ecclesiastical purpose' the meaning of which varies according to its context (see e.g. *OLAC*, 1–3 on the meaning of 'ecclesiastical purpose' under the Parochial Church Councils (Powers) Measure 1956, s. 5). As a basic principle, ecclesiastical property enjoys charitable status: whilst much church property is subject to s.36 of the Charities Act 1993, the consent of the Charity Commissioners is often not required for the disposal of church property, specific exemption arising under s. 36(2); Sched. 2: the Church Commissioners and any institution administered by them are exempt charities for the purposes of this Act.

[5] Lambeth Conference, 1908, Resolution 48: *AT: HS*, 379; *AR*, Art. 38: 'The riches and goods of Christians are not common, as touching the right, title and possession of the same'; for the concepts in diocesan norms see *post* Ch. 16.

[6] C18(4): to the bishop belongs the rights 'of granting a faculty or licence for all . . . additions [and] removals' from churches, chapels, churchyards, and consecrated burial grounds and 'of

norms express policies forbidding acquisition from or disposal to secular and religious bodies whose objectives and doctrines are inconsistent with those of the church.[7] Under Roman Catholic canon law, whilst civil contract law must be observed (unless contrary to divine law or canon law),[8] the conference of bishops sets the minimum and maximum values of property constituting the church's 'stable patrimony'.[9] Arrangements for disposal are organized accordingly. Property over the maximum value can be alienated only with the permission of the competent authority; if the goods are of special artistic or historical interest the permission of the Holy See must be obtained.[10] Disposals of stable patrimony between the minimium and maximum values can be alienated only with the permission of the bishop who must obtain the consent of the finance council, the college of consultors, and interested parties; in relation to parishes, when the property is below the minimum fixed by the conference of bishops, the competent authority would be the pastor.[11] There must be 'a just cause such as urgent necessity, evident usefulness, charity or some other serious reason' for the alienation; particular written evaluations of the property must be obtained from experts to determine a suitable price.[12] Property must not be sold for less than its estimated value and the proceeds are to be applied as the competent authority directs.[13] If permission has not been

consecrating new churches, churchyards, and burial grounds'; beyond this the Canon makes no provision for episcopal oversight of acquisition or disposal of realty. However, once a diocesan chancellor is appointed by the diocesan bishop, for the purposes of faculties the latter has no control: this passes to the chancellor as ordinary: for this and reservation (by letters patent) of matters to the bishop see *supra* Ch. 5.

[7] See below for disposal of movables and *post* Ch. 17 for the investment policies of the Church Commissioners.

[8] *CIC*, c. 1290; in the event of conflict, of course, for secular purposes civil law prevails: *supra* Ch. 1. See generally A. J. Maida, 'The Code of Canon Law of 1983 and the property of the local church', in M. Thériault and J. Thorn (eds.), *The New Code of Canon Law* (Ottawa, 1986) II, 743.

[9] *CIC*, cc. 1291–2; J. Hite, 'Church law on property and contracts', *The Jurist*, 44 (1984), 117; V. de Paolis, 'Temporal goods of the church in the new code: with particular reference to institutes of religious consecrated life', *The Jurist*, 43 (1983), 343; F. G. Morrisey, 'The conveyance of ecclesiastical property', *Proceedings of the Canon Law Society of America* (Washington, 1976), 123.

[10] *CIC*, c. 1292(2); those who must take part in the process of alienation through their advice or consent are not to give their advice or consent 'unless they have first been thoroughly informed concerning the economic situation of the juridic persons whose goods are proposed for alienation and concerning previous alienations': c. 1292(4).

[11] C. 1292(1); the diocesan bishop needs the same consents to alienate goods belonging to the diocese itself; for property owned by juridic persons not subject to the diocesan bishop, permission must be obtained from the competent authority fixed by that juridic person's statutes; see *COCLA*, 802 for examples of these provisions in practice, particularly as to whom is the competent authority: e.g. for alienation by the diocesan bishop of goods of the diocese, the consent of the 2 councils is required as well as the permission of the Holy See when the value exceeds the maximum amount.

[12] *CIC*, c. 1293; other safeguards prescribed by legitimate authority are to be observed to prevent harm to the church.

[13] C. 1294: money is to be either invested carefully for the advantage of the church or wisely expended in accord with the purposes of the alienation.

obtained the disposal is canonically invalid.[14] Stable patrimony whose value falls below the minimum may be alienated by its owner without permission of a higher authority.[15]

Cathedral Property

Whilst ownership of cathedral property vests in the cathedral's corporate capitular body,[16] a capitular body, dean, provost, or canon has the power to acquire land by gift *inter vivos* or by will, to acquire land to provide access to land owned by the capitular body, dean, provost, or canon as the case may be, or for improving the amenities of any such land. The capitular body is empowered to acquire land for improving the amenities of the cathedral church, for any such ecclesiastical, educational or other charitable purpose connected with the cathedral church, or any parish church of which the cathedral church is the parish church, and for the provision of houses to be occupied by persons engaged or to be engaged in duties connected with the cathedral church. The capitular body, dean, provost, or canon also has the power to sell, grant a lease of, exchange, mortgage, or charge land and to dedicate land for the purposes of a highway. Before exercising these powers the capitular body, dean, provost, or canon must obtain the consent of the Church Commissioners and, when exercising the power of disposal, leasing, mortgaging, or charging of a house or residence, the consent of the bishop and of the dean, provost, or canon normally occupying the house; where the house is allocated for the use of a holder of a dignity the right of presentation to which is vested in Her Majesty, the consent of Her Majesty must be obtained.[17] These consents are not required for the grant of a lease to a clerk in holy orders holding office in the cathedral church or to any person employed in connection

---

[14] C. 1296; a person who alienates without the necessary consents and counsels incurs a just penalty: c. 1377.

[15] C. 1285: donations from movable goods are not part of the stable patrimony; diocesan norms supplement these general provisions: e.g. Diocese of Westminister, *Parish Administration Manual* (1993) Ch. 9: for purchases the permission of the Finance Board is required; the Property Services Office must be consulted to give advice; for disposals the Westminister Roman Catholic Diocesan Trustee must be satisfied that the terms of the proposed disposal are the best reasonably obtainable.

[16] Cathedrals Measure 1963, ss. 15, 16; for discharge of functions delegated to the administrative body see *supra* Ch. 4; *DCPM*, cl. 9(1) repeats these provisions. With regard to Roman Catholic canon law, transaction by the cathedral's capitular body must be carried out in accordance with its statutes: *CIC*, c. 506.

[17] Cathedrals Measure 1963, s. 20 (as amended by Charities Act 1993, Sched. 6, para. 6); the purchaser's solicitor is not required to be satisfied that the necessary consents have been given as the Church Commissioners will be a party to the conveyance and by the Cathedrals Measure 1963, s. 20(5) their sealing of the conveyance is conclusive evidence that the Measure's provisions have been met.

with the cathedral church or to the acquisition of land by gift *inter vivos* or will.[18] The consent of the Charity Commissioners is not required.[19]

Special provisions apply to the transfer of property. The Church Commissioners may prepare and submit to Her Majesty in Council for confirmation a scheme transferring property of a capitular body to the Church Commissioners for such consideration and on such terms as the commissioners think fair and reasonable. The transfer cannot include the cathedral church or buildings belonging to it. A scheme may also be submitted to transfer to a capitular body property owned by the commissioners. In preparing and submitting such schemes the commissioners must obtain the consent of the administrative body of the cathedral church concerned as well as the consent of the dean, provost, or canon if the scheme transfers property vested in these.[20]

New Churches

In Roman Catholic canon law no church is to be built without the express written consent of the diocesan bishop, who may not consent unless satisfied that it is necessary for the good of souls; before consenting he must consult the presbyteral council and the rectors of neighbouring churches.[21] With regard to the Church of England, the acquisition of land for the building of a new church is governed principally by synodical measure. The Church Commissioners are empowered to make grants or loans (*inter alia* to diocesan boards of finance) for the provision of church buildings in any area where they are of the opinion that, having regard to recent housing developments, that area is not sufficiently provided with suitable church buildings of any description. This power is exercisable only at the written request of the diocesan pastoral committee and with the consent of the bishop.[22] Although anyone may convey land to the Church of England,[23] a special power of acquisition of land by way of gift, devise, or purchase for a new church is vested in the Church Commissioners.

---

[18] S. 20; *DCPM*, cl. 9(2): a capitular body must not sell or otherwise dispose of land vested in it without first consulting the dean, provost, or canon in whom it would have been vested; cl. 11 repeats the provisions of s. 20.

[19] This is because by virtue of Charities Act 1993, s. 96(2)(a) ecclesiastical corporations are not charities within the meaning of the statute and are therefore not subject to the prohibitions in s. 36(1). [20] Cathedrals Measure 1963, s. 19(1); *DCPM*, cl. 10 repeats these provisions.

[21] *CIC*, c. 1215; c. 1216: the principles and norms of liturgy and sacred art must be observed in the building of a church and the advice of experts must be used.

[22] New Housing Areas (Church Buildings) Measure 1954, s. 1: payments made out of their general fund shall be on such terms and conditions as the Commissioners think proper having regard to the circumstances in which the payment is made; payments may be made for projects connected to a church-sharing agreement: Sharing of Church Buildings Measure 1970, s. 2.

[23] New Parishes Measure 1943, s. 14: power of corporations to give land for sites of churches, as amended by Charities Act 1993, Sched. 6, para. 3; see also Gifts for Churches Acts 1803 and 1811, of which *DCPM* proposes the repeal; Pastoral Measure 1983, s. 76: an incumbent may grant land, with the consent of the diocesan parsonages board, under s. 14 of the New Parishes Measure 1943.

The power may be used only (1) to acquire a church or part of a church or any other building fit to be used as or converted into a church; (2) to acquire any land as a site for a new church or for a church to be substituted for an existing church or for enlarging the site of an existing church; (3) to acquire any building to be used as a church hall (or as both a church or other place of worship and a church hall) or any land for the site of a building to be so used (or for enlarging the site of an existing building so used); and (4) to acquire any land for providing access to or for improving the amenities of any such property. The Commissioners may acquire land for the purpose of providing or extending churchyards and burial grounds. They may also receive gifts of money for the purchase of land to be held for these purposes.[24] Once acquired by the Church Commissioners, the land vests in the incumbent for the time being of the parish in which the land or building is situated.[25] These powers of acquisition also apply to church buildings subject to a sharing agreement when the ownership is to vest in the Church of England or jointly with another church.[26]

Church planting, the establishment of a new congregation or worship centre, has not been the subject of canonical provision but is regulated by guidance endorsed recently by General Synod's House of Bishops. The guidance recognizes that planting by one church, even within its own boundaries, can clearly have an effect on the ministry of other parish churches and churches of other denominations. Church planting should normally be accompanied by careful long-term planning in partnership with the deanery concerned, some form of mission audit, and an examination of the areas of possible growth. The reasons for planting a new church should be clearly identified by those proposing it and may include the fact that a congregation is too large for a building or that an area of a parish has little or no contact with the existing church. At the earliest stage there should be full consultation, where appropriate, with the archdeacon and rural or area dean who must refer the matter to their respective pastoral committees, the archdeaconry ecumenical officer, and the diocesan adviser on mission and evangelism, the leaders of other denominations, other local congregations and civic, local, and community leaders and groups. The possibilities for using existing buildings should be explored at an early stage and where a new congregation is fully established (and its financial

[24] New Parishes Measure 1943, s. 13; Pastoral Measure 1983, s. 76: the diocesan board of finance holding land may grant it to the Church Commissioners for the purposes mentioned in s. 13; for acquisition of land by the Church Commissioners and grants of land to these and incumbents see *DCPM*, cls.1–3; see cl.8 for dealings with surplus land.

[25] New Parishes Measure 1943, s. 16, as amended by Church of England (Miscellaneous Provisions) Measure 1992, s. 8. The Consecration of Churchyards Act 1867 enables land for extension of a churchyard to be conveyed directly to an incumbent.

[26] Sharing of Church Buildings Measure 1970, s. 2(2), (3); 'sharing agreement' and 'church building' have the same meaning as under the Sharing of Church Buildings Act 1969, ss. 1(1), 12(1); by s. 3 of the 1970 Measure ownership is to be construed as under the 1969 Act.

situation is clear) it may be appropriate at this stage to examine the possibilities for new church buildings. Advice should be sought from the bishop as to whether the building to be used for worship should be designated as a 'centre for worship'. Joint oversight and responsibility should be agreed, whether or not the leader is in priest's orders: '[l]ocal oversight is the ultimate responsibility of the person who shares the cure of souls within the boundaries concerned with the bishop, even if this is temporarily delegated by agreement.' Similarly, the parochial church council remains responsible for all legal and financial matters. The church planting team should be carefully selected, trained, authorized, and supported and should have 'a mixed membership according to class, gender, age and ethnicity as appropriate'. Whilst the guidance does not prescribe a standard constitution, agreements should be drawn up between planting and planted churches and between the diocese and the planting church: agreements should deal with buildings, leadership, administration, financial obligations of the diocese, decision-making, appraisal and review, ecumenical involvement, liturgy, and worship.[27]

When the land in question is unconsecrated[28] the owner of any land or building acquired by the commissioners has various powers of disposal. The owner may sell, exchange, appropriate, transfer, or reconvey that land or building or any part of it. If the Church Commissioners are the owners, the consent of the bishop and incumbent must be obtained. If the owner is the incumbent the consent of the Church Commissioners and the bishop must be obtained. None of them may consent unless satisfied that the land or building (or part of these) is no longer required for the purpose for which it was acquired.[29] The proceeds of sale must be paid to the Church Commissioners and applied for such purposes for the benefit of the benefice (or ecclesiastical district) in which they are situated or for charitable purposes as agreed between the Commissioners and the bishop after consultation with the owner.[30] Where the land or buildings were acquired for valuable consideration and have been held for less than twenty years the owner must, before offering it for sale, offer to resell it to the person from whom it was acquired at such price as failing agreement may be determined by arbitration.[31]

---

[27] *Breaking New Ground: Church Planting in the Church of England* (1994), A Report Commissioned by the House of Bishops, GS 1099, Part 8 (Guidance) (App. I contains guidance on development). For similar provisions in diocesan norms see e.g. *SDDH*, R.17–18.

[28] These provisions do not affect the disposal of consecrated land: New Parishes Measure 1943, s. 17(5).   [29] New Parishes Measure 1943, s. 17.

[30] Ibid.; for the meaning of consultation see *Re Union of Whippingham and East Cowes, St James Benefices, Derham v Church Commmmisssioners* [1954] 2 All ER 22; *Parochial Church Council of St Martin, Lincoln v Church Commissioners* (1968) *Times* 13 Nov. 1968; *Elphick v Church Commissioners* [1974] AC 562.

[31] New Parishes Measure 1943, s. 17(2), provided that if the person to whom it is offered refuses the offer or does not accept it within 6 weeks the right of pre-emption ceases.

Consecrated Land: Redundancy and Disposal

In Roman Catholic canon law a new church must be dedicated or at least blessed as soon as possible. If a church cannot be employed for divine worship it may be relegated to profane (but not sordid) use and disposed of by its owners with the consent of the diocesan bishop, who must consult the presbyteral council.[32] With respect to the Church of England, when land is acquired for the building of a church, a building upon it does not become a parish 'church' unless and until consecrated for the purpose of public worship according to the rites and ceremonies of the Church of England.[33] This occurs when an act or sentence of consecration is signed by a diocesan bishop (or his commissary) by which 'he separates and sets apart the building from all profane and common uses whatsoever, dedicates the same to the service of Almighty God for the performance therein of divine offices and consecrates the same for the celebration of such offices'.[34] It is commonly understood that a bishop has an absolute right to give or withhold consent to the foundation and consecration of a church; the right to consecrate also belongs to the bishop.[35] Though there is no strict requirement for churchyards to be consecrated, they are as a matter of ecclesiastical practice; it depends on the terms of the bishop's consecrating sentence.[36] As consecration confers an indelible mark, its effects can be removed only by parliamentary statute, by synodical measure, or by episcopal action pursuant to these.[37] For this reason dedication, rather than consecration, may be preferrable.[38] It has been commonly

[32] *CIC*, cc. 1217, 1222; see *post* Ch. 16 for dedication and its effects.

[33] 'Church' means 'any church or chapel which has been consecrated for the purpose of public worship according to the rites and ceremonies of the Church of England' and includes 'a building used or intended to be used partly for the purpose of such public worship and partly for the purpose of a church hall, whether the whole building is consecrated or only such part thereof as is used or intended to be used for the purpose of such public worship': Pastoral Measure 1983, s. 87(1); for a narrower definition see Interpretation Measure 1925, s. 5; see also CCEJM 1991, s. 19: '"church" includes any building which is licensed for public worship according to the rites and ceremonies of the Church of England and is subject to the faculty jurisdiction'; for unconsecrated buildings and their licensing as a worship centre see Canon B40.

[34] *Re St John's, Chelsea* [1962] 1 WLR 706 at 708; Canon C18(4): the right to consecrate; see *DCPM*, cl. 5 for procedures on the petition of the freehold owner for consecration of churches and burial grounds.

[35] *Segwick v Bourne* [1920] 2 KB 267 at 275 (even if the incumbent objects: *Rugg v Bishop of Winchester* (1868) LR 2 A & E 247; LR 2 PC 223).

[36] Newsom, *FJCE*, 147; Consecration of Churchyards Acts 1867,1868; see also *Re Coleford Cemetery* [1984] 1 WLR 1369; under the Church of England (Miscellaneous Provisions) Measure 1992, s. 3(2) a burial ground may be consecrated for the purpose of burying cremated remains.

[37] *Re St Martin-le-Grand, York* [1989] 2 All ER 711; CCEJM, s. 22: for episcopal removal, the bishop must be satisfied that the building or land is not held or controlled by any ecclesiastical corporation or by the diocesan finance board and that no purpose would be served by its remaining consecrated.

[38] *Re Tonbridge School Chapel (No. 2)* [1993] 2 All ER 338 (Rochester Con. Ct.) at 345: faculty jurisdiction was assumed over consecrated land owned by a non-church body, as was control over leasing.

accepted that ownership of a consecrated church and churchyard vests in the incumbent of the benefice as a corporation sole for the time being; the incumbent holds it to the use of the parishioners (the fee being in abeyance as a consequence of consecration); a right of succession vests in the next incumbent.[39]

Once consecrated the land comes within the jurisdiction of the diocesan ordinary and the consistory court, but this does not extend to disposal of consecrated land.[40] Disposal of consecrated land is governed by three basic principles.[41] First, it is not possible to dispose of consecrated land for secular purposes without the authority of parliamentary statute or synodical measure.[42] Secondly, it is not lawful to sell, lease, or otherwise dispose of any church or part of a church or the site or part of the site of any church or any consecrated land belonging or annexed to a church except in pursuance of powers conferred by the Pastoral Measure 1983.[43] Thirdly, disposal in these ways may take place only when the church is declared redundant: it is not lawful to make any order or give any direction to close a church on the ground that it is no longer required for use as a church: 'the only procedure for closing a church on that ground shall be by way of a declaration of redundancy'.[44] A declaration of redundancy and subsequent disposal may be effected under either a pastoral scheme or a redundancy scheme.

[39] *Re St Luke's, Holbeach Hurn* [1990] 2 All ER 749 (Lincoln Con. Ct.); *St Botolph Without Aldgate (Vicar and One of the Churchwardens) v Parishioners* [1892] P 161; *St Gabriel, Fenchurch Street (Rector and Churchwardens) v City of London Real Property Co Ltd* [1896] P 95; the position of the incumbent is analogous to that of a life tenant: *Ecclesiastical Commissioners for England and Wales v Rowe* (1880) 5 App Cas 736 at 744; see *post* Ch. 16 for defects in this idea and the limitations on the use of the 'freehold'.

[40] EJM, s. 6; CCEJM, s. 11(1); 'curtilage' was understood in *Re St George's Oakdale* [1976] Fam 210 as a small area of the churchyard physically adjoining the church building and required to serve some purpose of the church building in a necessary or useful way; if consecrated, the statutory principles apply for the purposes of alienation; if unconsecrated, curtilage falls within the faculty jurisdiction (Faculty Jurisdiction Measure 1964, s. 7) and the incumbent's power to alienate is subject to faculty approval: *Re St Mary Magdalene, Paddington* [1980] 1 All ER 279; see also New Parishes Measure 1943, s. 17(5).

[41] For the European setting of this problem see D. McClean's review of *Redundant Religious Buildings*, A Report of the Committee on Culture and Education, Doc. 6032, Council of Europe (Strasbourg, 1989), *ELJ*, 2 (1990–2), 181–2.

[42] *St Gabriel, Fenchurch Street (Rector and Churchwardens) v City of London Real Property Co Ltd* [1896] P 95; *Re St Peter's, Bushey Heath* [1971] 2 All ER 704 at 706: 'It is impossible to create a legal estate in consecrated land, save under the authority of an Act of Parliament or a Measure'; see, however, *Re Tonbridge School Chapel (No. 2)* [1993] 2 All ER 338 at 346 *per* Goodman Ch: this is 'a generalisation and is not justified by the authorities taken as a whole.'

[43] Pastoral Measure 1983, s. 56(2); s. 30(1): a pastoral scheme may include provision for the disposal of the whole or any part of a churchyard or other land annexed to or belonging to a church or any burial ground vested in the incumbent of the benefice but not annexed or belonging to a church; a chapel consecrated to 'divine worship' is not covered by s. 56, see *Re Tonbridge School Chapel (No. 2)* [1993] 2 All ER 338: Rochester Con. Ct.: nothing at common law prevents the leasing of consecrated chapels in private houses, schools, hospitals, or similar institutions; for licensing secular use of consecrated land see *post* Ch. 16.

[44] Pastoral Measure 1983, s. 56(1).

Pastoral Schemes: if the diocesan pastoral committee and the bishop decide that it is no longer justifiable to keep a particular church open as a place of worship, they may make a proposal, which may be put into effect by a pastoral scheme,[45] to declare the church redundant: the effect of a declaration of redundancy is to close a church for regular worship. A pastoral scheme may make a declaration of redundancy in respect of a church or any part of it which is not required as a parish church (or chapel of ease) or which will cease to be so required as a result of the scheme.[46] The scheme may also provide for the appropriation of a churchyard or other land annexed or belonging to a church or any burial ground vested in the incumbent of the benefice (but not annexed or belonging to a church) to such use as may be specified in the scheme and for the disposal of any such property.[47] When it is the intention to provide a new church or other place of worship to replace the church to be declared redundant, special provisions apply. The Church Commissioners must be satisfied that a new church or place of worship in the area of a benefice is to take the place of an existing church. The scheme must declare the existing church redundant and may provide for payment to the commissioners of the proceeds of any sale or exchange of the building (or part of it).[48] A scheme may be made only if one of four conditions is satisfied: (1) the Commissioners must have been advised by the Advisory Board for Redundant Churches that it is satisfied that the church to be declared redundant is of such small interest or requires such extensive structural repair that demolition would not be objectionable; (2) the Commissioners must be advised by the Advisory Board that it is satisfied with a proposal to preserve features of interest by incorporating them in the new church or some other building; (3) notwithstanding the Advisory Board's advice, the Commissioners must be satisfied that for reasons regarded by them as sufficient the demolition of the church to be declared redundant should be authorized; or (4) the Commissioners must be satisfied that a suitable use will be available for the church when the declaration takes effect. If under a pastoral scheme the church is to be disposed of or demolished with the intention of providing a replacement, the Commissioners must also be satisfied that a suitable building will be available (but not necessarily in the same parish) for use in the interim period.[49]

When a church is declared redundant and it is not proposed to sell or demolish, the Diocesan Redundant Churches Uses Committee must make

---

[45] Diocesan norms usually simply repeat the following rules e.g. *SDDH*, R.7: it is the policy of the pastoral committee only to issue proposals for redundancy at the request of the parochial church council; *GDM*, B.6; see also ibid. B.12 and *BDM*, K.6 on temporary closure of buildings with episcopal licence. For pastoral schemes and the participation of the local church in their preparation see *supra* Ch. 3.   [46] Pastoral Measure 1983, s. 28(1).
[47] S. 30.
[48] S. 46(1); demolition by the diocesan finance board may be provided for (s. 46(2); see *PMCP*, 59 for non-statutory public inquiries when the church is listed.
[49] S. 46(3)-(7); see s.46(8) for church-sharing agreements and redundant churches.

every endeavour to find suitable alternative uses for it. When it has found a suitable use it must report to the Church Commissioners.[50] Where a pastoral scheme makes a declaration of redundancy and the Commissioners are satisfied that a suitable use will be available, the scheme may authorize appropriation for that purpose. If satisfied that no suitable alternative use is available, the Commissioners must decide whether to preserve or demolish the church. The Advisory Board for Redundant Churches is to advise the Commissioners about *inter alia* the historic and archeological interest of the church with a view to whether or not the church ought to be preserved or demolished. The Board must report its proceedings to the archbishops, and copies must be sent to the Church Commissioners and laid before General Synod.[51] The ownership of redundant churches is vested in the Churches Conservation Trust: this has as its object the preservation, in the interests of the nation and of the Church of England, of churches and parts of churches of historic or archeological interest, or architectural quality.[52]

Redundancy Schemes: closure and disposal may also be effected under a redundancy scheme. When a declaration of redundancy is to be made under a pastoral scheme ownership of the building (and its contents) vests automatically in the Diocesan Board of Finance. A redundancy scheme may not be prepared until at least six months later.[53] The diocesan board of finance is not, however, at this stage permitted to dispose of the church.[54] The Commissioners may after the expiration of this period make the redundancy scheme and in so doing must consult the bishop and, if it is proposed to demolish, the Advisory Board. They must serve a draft scheme on *inter alia* the diocesan finance board, the Advisory Board, and the local planning authority; although under a duty to give public notice of the scheme, there is no express right vested in a parochial church council to object. The diocesan Redundant Churches Uses Committee must make every effort to find a suitable use for the redundant building and if a suitable use is found the scheme may provide for the appropriation of the building to such use as specified in the scheme.[55]

If an alternative use cannot be found the redundancy scheme may provide for the appropriation of the property 'empowering the Commissioners, subject to any conditions prescribed by the scheme, to sell, give or exchange the

---

[50] S. 42; for the Committee's constitution and composition see Sched. 5, paras. 5–12.

[51] S. 41; for the Board's constitution and composition see s. 41(1) and Sched. 5, paras. 1–4; s. 43.

[52] S. 44: it has power *inter alia* to permit occasional worship; Pastoral (Amendment) Measure 1994, s. 13; *PMCP*, 55–6: 'Each case would have to be considered on its merits but it may be said that in the normal course the Commissioners would be unlikely to overrule the [Advisory Board].'

[53] S. 49(1): they may make a redundancy scheme, however, if the church is of small interest, repair would prove too expensive, and a suitable use is available.

[54] S. 49(2): its powers deal with maintenance and use.

[55] Ss. 50, 51(1); *PMCP*, 69: prospective purchasers or lessees should be informed that negotiations will have to be conditional on the statutory procedures being satisfied.

property concerned or any part of it' for such uses as appear to the Commissioners to be suitable.[56] When a redundancy scheme provides that the property is to remain vested in the diocesan board of finance, the scheme may also enable appropriation and empower the Commissioners, subject to conditions prescribed by the scheme, to sell, give, or exchange the land for the approved uses.[57] Similarly, when a redundancy scheme provides for demolition, it may provide for the sale, gift, exchange, or lease by the Commissioners of the site or part of it, for the disposal of materials arising from demolition and they may either specify the use for which land is disposed of or allow it to be used without limitation; they may also appropriate the land for ecclesiastical purposes of the parish. Proceeds of sale must be paid to the Commissioners, two-thirds of the net proceeds and premiums going to the diocesan pastoral account.[58] Where a bishop certifies that a church has not been used for divine service since 1 April 1964, and provided that the incumbent, patron, and parochial church council consent, the Commissioners may make a redundancy declaration and scheme in the same way and proceeds of sale shall be applied similarly.[59]

Provision exists for the amendment of redundancy schemes permitting disposal and demolition. When a church is vested in the Churches Conservation Trust or in the diocesan board of finance a pastoral scheme may provide for its restoration to use as a church.[60] A redundant church is not subject to the legal effects of consecration.[61] Provision also exists for the transfer of a redundant church to the Secretary of State who can acquire and preserve it; in these cases redundancy schemes cease to apply.[62] Whilst ordinarily the church courts are expressly excluded from the arrangements concerning disposal of churches, except in an emergency no demolition or partial demolition of a church may take place without the authority of a faculty.[63]

Parsonage Property

Parsonage land includes a parsonage house and any building or land vested in or acquired by the incumbent of a benefice as a parsonage house, or as the site for such a house.[64] A parsonage house means the official residence of the incumbent of a benefice, in whom ownership vests; a team vicar's house, the designated residence of a vicar in a team ministry, is normally vested in the

---

[56] S. 51(1), (2).   [57] S. 51(3).

[58] S. 51(5); for church-sharing agreements s. 51(8); s. 52: part of the remaining one-third goes to the Churches Conservation Trust; see also s. 53 for orders of Commissioners determining or varying payments to redundant churches fund.   [59] S. 54; *PMCP*, 40.

[60] S. 58, and to revoke the declaration and scheme; see s. 59 for vesting of property.

[61] S. 61(1).   [62] S. 66.

[63] CCEJM, ss. 17–18; *Re St Barnabas' Church, Dulwich* [1994] Fam 124.

[64] Endowments and Glebe Measure 1976, s. 45(1); historically 'parsonage land' was synonymous with 'benefice' and included the church: *Re Alms Corn Charity, Charity Commissioners v Bode* [1901] 2 Ch 750 at 758.

diocesan board of finance.[65] In any benefice where such action is thought desirable (and whether or not the existing residence has been disposed of) the incumbent, or during a vacancy the diocesan bishop, has various powers of acquisition. Either may purchase or erect a house or purchase land for the site of a house (not exceeding six acres) suitable for the residence and occupation of the incumbent. In exercising these powers, the consent of the Church Commissioners, the Diocesan Parsonages Board, and where the incumbent acts the diocesan bishop, must be obtained. The Church Commissioners have a discretionary power to lend moneys to the incumbent or bishop for the purpose of acquisition and building. Any house purchased becomes the residence of an incumbent of a benefice when the bishop issues a certificate to this effect.[66]

Where the residence house and appurtenances are inconveniently situated or too large, or where 'for other good and sufficient reasons it shall be thought advisable to sell or dispose of the same or of any part thereof', the incumbent has three basic powers of disposal: during a vacancy the powers are vested in the bishop. The incumbent may sell the residence house and appurtenances, or any part of them (with any land contiguous thereto belonging to the benefice) either together or in parcels. The incumbent may pull down the residence house and outbuildings or any of them and sell the materials and the site. The incumbent may exchange the house and appurtenances for any other house suitable for his residence and occupation and pay and receive money in respect of equality of exchange.[67] These powers may be exercised only with the consent of the Church Commissioners, the Diocesan Parsonages Board, and (in cases where the power is exercised by the incumbent) the bishop: the consent of the Charity Commissioners is not required.[68] The patron and the parochial church council have rights to be notified of and to object to (but not to veto) the sale or demolition of a residence belonging to the benefice and to the erection of a new one. Representations are communicated to the Church Commissioners who before consenting to the exercise of the power in question must consider any objection; the Commissioners must inform the patron and council of the reasons for their conclusion.[69]

[65] Repair of Benefice Buildings Measure 1972, s. 31(1); *DCPM*, cl. 14 suggests the basic retention of these rules; new parsonages may be acquired by the Church Commissioners and property vests automatically in the incumbent: New Parishes Measure 1943, ss. 13, 16. For the housing of unbeneficed clergy see D. Faull and J. Rees, 'The church and housing', *ELJ*, 3 (1995), 313 at 316.

[66] Parsonages Measure 1938, ss. 2, 11; for an overview of the Diocesan Parsonages Board under the Repair of Benefice Buildings Measure 1972 see *supra* Ch. 4. For the Roman Catholic position, which permits leasing arrangements to be made by the conference of bishops, see *CIC*, cc. 1297–8.

[67] Parsonages Measure 1938, s. 1; Endowments and Glebe Measure 1976, s. 34: this applies also to an excluded part of the parsonage house (see *post* nn. 76, 78); diocesan norms usually repeat the following rules: see e.g. *LDHI*, V, 16; *GDM*, E.8, 11; *RBG*, E.3; *ODYB: IF*, 259.

[68] Charities Act 1993, s. 96(2); *supra* n. 19.

[69] Parsonages Measure 1938, as amended by the Church Property (Miscellaneous Provisions) Measure 1960, s. 3; *DCPM*, cl. 15 suggests the basic retention of these rules.

Where it appears to a diocesan parsonages board that any of the powers of disposal should be exercised, the board must report to the bishop. If the bishop and incumbent (or simply the bishop in a vacancy) request the board to do so, the board may frame proposals for the exercise of such power. The board's proposals and recommendations must be communicated to the bishop and (except in a vacancy) to the incumbent. The Church Commissioners may make recommendations as may be deemed fit as to the costs, charges, and expenses which may be incurred in connection with the exercise of the power; any recommendations made are, if the diocesan parsonages board concurs, binding on the person exercising the power.[70] The patron has no right of pre-emption over any property belonging to a benefice in respect of which it is proposed to exercise a power of sale.[71] Disposals of parsonages must be registered, and certified as such by the Church Commissioners, under the Land Registration Act 1925.[72]

All moneys received from any sale or exchange must be paid to the Church Commissioners.[73] The Commissioners must in their discretion apply and dispose of any moneys arising from the sale or exchange of a parsonage but only for limit purposes. They may use the proceeds for the payment of costs, charges, and expenses of such disposal, for the purchase of a new parsonage, for the repayment of any money spent with the previous consent of the Church Commissioners and the diocesan parsonages board for the purpose of rendering the property more readily saleable, for removal expenses of the incumbent, and for the repayment of grants made by them for the purchase of a residence house. If moneys are not applied in these ways, the Commissioners must hold the same for the benefit of the particular benefice by way of investment and augmentation. The Commissioners have a duty to notify the patron of the benefice and the parochial church council of any proposed application and disposition of moneys, and must consider any representations made.[74] When a pastoral scheme designates a house as a parsonage, or under it a house is transferred to an incumbent of a team ministry, this shall be without prejudice

---

[70] Parsonages Measure 1938, s. 3(2), (3); *DCPM*, cl. 17; for the incumbent's power to make restrictive covenants and easements see Church Property (Miscellaneous Provisions) Measure 1960, ss. 8, 9.

[71] Patronage (Benefices) Measure 1986, s. 34(1): previously a right existed under the Parsonages Measure 1938, s. 4.

[72] S. 99; Repair of Benefice Buildings Measure 1972, s. 14: when the parsonage board is notified by the Commissioners that they have consented to the sale, exchange, or demolition of a parsonage house, or have agreed that it should be sold, exchanged, or demolished, the board must keep insurance on foot until the sale, exchange, or demolition and, where it is to be sold or exchanged, it must carry out such repairs as it thinks necessary or desirable to facilitate sale or exchange; if the house remains in occupation the board must also carry out such repairs as it thinks necessary for such occupation.   [73] Parsonages Measure 1938, s. 1(5).

[74] Ibid., ss. 5, 7; under s. 6 interim income shall be added to the capital by way of accumulation unless the Church Commissioners think it fit to pay this to the incumbent or to apply it as income of the benefice; *DCPM*, cls. 18–20; diocesan norms usually prescribe for removal and resettlement expenses: see e.g. *CDH*, 85–7; *SDDH*, K.20, 33–4; *GDM*, E.8, 11.

to any power to dispose of the house or to the subsequent power of the bishop to give directions as to the place where the incumbent or vicar is to reside.[75]

The incumbent has a limited power to lease parsonage property. This may be done for a period not exceeding the duration of his incumbency, and the lease must contain a condition that the agreement will be avoided if the bishop by order requires the incumbent to reside in the parsonage.[76] During a vacancy the bishop can authorize sequestrators to grant a lease for such period as the bishop may determine, but he must obtain the consent of the Church Commissioners.[77] Where the Commissioners are satisfied that any parsonage land (including the house) is not necessary for the convenient occupation of the incumbent, or is not required as the residence house of the incumbent, they may provide for its transfer to the diocesan board of finance. In so doing they must consult the board and the incumbent (or any sequestrators concerned). The diocesan board of finance then holds the property as glebe land (See below).[78]

Diocesan and Parochial Trust Property

The diocesan board of finance (a company) is empowered to acquire, hold, and dispose of real and personal property for purposes connected with the Church of England.[79] In exercising its powers the board must comply with such directions as may from time to time be given by the diocesan synod.[80] Property held on trust for the benefit of diocesan parishes is vested in the 'diocesan authority' as 'holding' or 'custodian' trustee (usually the board of finance)[81] with a representative body from the parish acting as 'managing trustee'. The representatives are usually the incumbent alone, the parochial church council, the churchwardens, or combinations of these, all of which must inform the diocesan authority of the holding, acquisition, and administration.[82] The trust

---

[75] Pastoral Measure 1983, s. 31; Sched. 3, para. 9.

[76] Pluralities Act 1838, s. 59; see also Endowments and Glebe Measure 1976, s. 29: letting an 'excluded part' of parsonage house is forbidden (see also n. 78); s. 30: incumbent in receipt of rent for excluded part must pay the sum to the diocesan board of finance; *DCPM*, cl. 29.

[77] Endowments and Glebe Measure 1976, s. 38(2); leasing of parsonages is excluded from the Rent Acts: *Bishop of Gloucester v Cunnington* [1943] 1 All ER 61 (CA); *Brandon v Grundy* [1943] 2 All ER 208 (CA); this has recently been questioned: *Hobbs and Bishop of Chichester v Naiff* (1992) (unreported, Haywards Heath County Court).

[78] 1976 Measure, s. 32; by s. 34 the power of the incumbent to sell the residence house applies to any excluded part of it, being 'any part of the parsonage house which by reason of a certificate of the bishop under section 11 of the Parsonages Measure 1938 is to be deemed not to form part of that house': s. 45(1); the question of whether a house is a parsonage house 'shall be conclusively determined by the Commissioners': s. 45(2); *DCPM*, cl. 31.

[79] Diocesan Boards of Finance Measure 1925, s. 1(2)(a)(b); *DCPM*, Part V codifies the following rules dealing with parochial church property.

[80] Diocesan Boards of Finance Measure 1925, s. 3; under the Charities Act 1993, s. 36(1) the consent of the Charity Commissioners must ordinarily be obtained, unless exempt under s. 36(2).

[81] Incumbents and Churchwardens (Trusts) Measure 1964, s. 1; PCC(P)M, s. 6(2).

[82] Incumbents and Churchwardens (Trusts) Measure 1964, s. 3.

instrument itself sometimes contains a special power of sale; in any event, as a general principle under civil law, charitable trustees possess the powers of a tenant for life, including the power of sale.[83]

The Incumbents and Churchwardens (Trusts) Measure 1964 applies to any interest (being an estate or interest in land or an interest in personal property) which is acquired or held on charitable trusts established for ecclesiastical purposes of the Church of England.[84] Neither the churchwardens nor the incumbent may acquire any interest in realty or personalty to which the Measure applies (being an interest in personalty held or to be held on permanent trusts), except an interest in personal property by gift or under a will, without the consent of the diocesan authority.[85] Similarly, no managing trustees may sell, lease, exchange, charge, or take any legal proceedings relating thereto without the consent of the diocesan authority (or, in the case of legal proceedings its agent) in addition to any other consents or orders required by law either from the Charity Commissioners or otherwise.[86]

The parochial church council, a body corporate, has power to acquire (by way of gift or otherwise) any property real or personal for any ecclesiastical purpose affecting the parish or any part of it.[87] The council is also empowered to acquire property for any purpose in connection with educational schemes to provide facilities for the spiritual, moral, and physical training of persons residing in or near the parish. Subject to the general law and to the provisions of any trusts affecting any such property, the council has the power to manage, administer, and dispose of any property acquired. With regard to the acquisition and disposal of property for educational schemes, the council must not exercise its power without the consent of the diocesan education board which may consent upon such terms and conditions as it considers appropriate in all the circumstances. A council cannot acquire any interest in land (other than a short lease) or in any personal property to be held on permanent trusts without the consent of the appropriate diocesan authority in which legal title vests as custodian trustee.[88] With regard to the acquisition and disposal of trust property, the council acting as a managing trustee must obtain the consent of the diocesan authority and any other consents required by law.[89]

The disposal of property held for a church school is regulated by the

---

[83] Settled Land Act 1925, s. 29. In practice, however, the Charity Commissioners take the view that if there is no express power of sale in the trust instrument and if the land is functional land (in that trusts require it to be used for the purposes of the charity), a sale would be in breach of trust, and therefore the implied power of sale under s. 29 does not apply.

[84] 1964 Measure, s. 2(1): some estates and interests are excluded including those in any church, churchyard, burial ground, parsonage houses, and those vested in the Official Custodian for Charities.   [85] S. 4, by virtue of s. 2(2).

[86] S. 5.

[87] Diocesan norms usually simply repeat the following rules: e.g. *CDH*, 143; *SDDH*, O.62; *CF*, F.7; *LDR*, 160; *GDM*, B.14; *BDM*, K.7.   [88] PCC(P)M, ss. 5–6.

[89] Ibid., s. 6(3); Incumbents and Churchwardens (Trust) Measure 1964, s. 5; s. 3(1): if a council has property to which this measure applies, it must inform the diocesan authority which must, if the

Diocesan Boards of Education Measure 1991. The governing body of any church school, and the trustees of any church educational endowment held wholly or partly for any church school, must obtain the advice of the diocesan education board and must have regard to that advice before making any application or entering into any agreement or arrangement with any body or person for or in connection with 'any disposal (whether by sale or otherwise) of the premises of the school or any part thereof'.[90] Whereas the legislation governing disposal of property managed by incumbents, churchwardens, and parochial church councils limits their legal powers so that if they agree a sale without the requisite consent the custodian trustee may refuse to convey, the 1991 Measure merely imposes a duty to consult; however, a failure to do so may not affect a purchaser.

Glebe Property

Before 1976 glebe was property, other than the parsonage house, vested in the incumbent as part of the endowment of the benefice.[91] Today glebe property may be classified as diocesan land—usually residential or agricultural—vested under the Endowments and Glebe Measure 1976 in the diocesan board of finance;[92] it is property held, managed, and dealt with by the board for the benefit of the diocesan stipends fund.[93] The diocesan board of finance has a general power to acquire property to be held as diocesan glebe land only with the consent of the Church Commissioners. The board may appropriate diocesan lands already vested in it for use as diocesan glebe with the consent of both the Church Commissioners and the Charity Commissioners. When the proposal is to appropriate land vested in the board but managed by a parochial church council or churchwardens, the board may appropriate such property as glebe only with the consent of the council or managing trustees as the case may be.[94]

Measure applies, vest it in itself and make a scheme for its management by the incumbent and churchwardens under para. 6 of the Schedule. I.e. the acquisition and disposal of parochial church council trust property should always be dealt with under the 1956 Measure.

[90] Diocesan Boards of Education Measure 1991, s. 3(1).

[91] Endowments and Glebe Measure 1976, s. 45(1); Repair of Benefice Buildings Measure 1972, s. 31(1): '"glebe building" means any building, wall, fence or work which the incumbent of a benefice is bound by virtue of his office to maintain in repair, not being a parsonage house or comprised in a parsonage house'; diocesan norms usually simply repeat these and the following rules: *LDHI*, VIII, 1; *CDH*, 114; *SDDH*, M.25–6; *ODYB: IF*, 254.

[92] Endowments and Glebe Measure 1976 s. 15. Disputes as to rights to glebe are to be settled by the Church Commissioners: s. 15(4); the diocesan finance board can require the incumbent to provide information concerning glebe land: s.16; the board is under a duty to list diocesan glebe lands and send the list to the Commissioners: s. 17. Transference to the board may also be effected under a pastoral scheme: Pastoral Measure 1983, s. 31.

[93] S. 19(1); schemes for the management of the fund must be made by the diocesan finance board with approval of the Commissioners.

[94] S. 18; *DCPM*, Part IV codifies these provisions.

The board is empowered to sell, lease, exchange, mortgage, or otherwise deal with diocesan glebe land upon such terms as the Church Commissioners may approve in writing.[95] When it proposes to sell glebe property, and before it applies to the Commissioners for approval, the board is under a duty to notify the incumbent of the benefice in the parish where the land is situated of the proposed disposal and the incumbent has twenty-one days to make written representations; in a vacancy, the churchwardens must be notified. The Charity Commissioners have no power of control over the sale of glebe.[96] A contract of sale must include prescribed terms.[97] Proceeds of sale must be paid to the Church Commissioners and the sum shall be allocated by the Commissioners to the capital account of the diocesan stipends fund of that diocese.[98] All rents or other periodical payments in the nature of income received by the diocesan finance board in respect of glebe must be paid to the Commissioners and allocated to the income account of the diocesan stipends fund of that diocese.[99] The board has the power to grant to the Commissioners *inter alia* any building on any diocesan glebe land which is a church or part of a church or is fit to be converted into a church, as well as land as the site for a new church.[100]

MOVABLES

As we have seen, many of the powers conferred upon ecclesiastical corporations to acquire and dispose of realty expressly include the power to acquire and dispose of personalty.[101] The law of the Church of England seeks to strike a balance between, on one hand, the worshipping and financial needs of the church and, on the other hand, the value of conservation. Whilst conferring a general freedom to acquire and dispose of movables used for ecclesiastical purposes, church legislation effects regulation chiefly through the faculty jurisdiction.

---

[95] S. 20; s. 22: where the board has sold, exchanged, or leased any glebe and the document effecting the transaction contains a restricitve covenant imposed for the benefit of any church land or parsonage land, that covenant is enforceable by the board as if it were the owner of the land.

[96] Charities Act 1993, s. 96(2)(b); *supra* n. 19.

[97] E.g. the sale will be subject to any tenancies, covenants, easements, and other rights, as well as rights in the nature of easements necessary for the reasonable enjoyment of any parsonage or church land: Endowments and Glebe Measure 1976, s. 15(1)(a),(b); Law of Property Act 1925, s. 56(1): covenants may be imposed for the benefit of church property vested in other ecclesiastical bodies.   [98] Endowments and Glebe Measure 1976, s. 25(1).

[99] Ibid., s. 25(4).   [100] Ibid., s. 23(1).

[101] When used for spiritual purposes chattels are known usually as 'ornaments': *Westerton v Liddell* (1857) Moore's Special Reports 133 at 156, cited with approval in *Re St Michael and All Angels, Great Torrington* [1985] Fam 81 at 89. For acquisition of sacred and other objects in Roman Catholic canon law see *CIC*, cc. 1269–70.

Freedom of Acquisition

Acquisition of some items is required by law. In every church or chapel there must be a font, a holy table, communion plate, communion linen, ministerial surplices, reading desks and a pulpit, seats for the congregation, at least one bell, a Bible and a Book of Common Prayer, an alms box, and register books of baptisms, confirmations, marriages, and burials.[102] The duties to provide these and to meet the necessary expenses are imposed canonically on the parochial church council.[103] The council's power to discharge these duties derives from synodical measure and any disagreement must be dealt with or determined in such manner as the diocesan bishop may direct.[104] A record of all additions to parochial churches and chapels must be kept in a book provided for that purpose by the council.[105] Ownership of items lawfully acquired is vested in the churchwardens on trust for the use of the parishioners.[106]

Freedom of acquisition is limited by the rules governing the introduction of items into the church; rules apply both to these chattels which must be provided and to those for which there is no duty but a liberty to make provision.[107] If any addition is proposed to be made in the ornaments or furniture of the church it is the duty of the minister and churchwardens to obtain a faculty.[108] Whether or not an item may be introduced into a church is to be determined by the ordinary.[109] This applies to the proposed introduction of any article in any church, its churchyard, or other consecrated buildings and land which form or are within the curtilage of a church covered by the faculty jurisdiction, as well as any buildings not consecrated but licensed for public worship.[110] The chancellor must give written guidance concerning those items which may be introduced without faculty,[111] and provision exists specifying which introductions may be dealt with by general and specific faculties issued

---

[102] Canons F1–12; for baptismal and burial registers: Parochial Registers and Record Measure 1978, ss. 1–5.   [103] Canon F14.

[104] PCC(P)M, ss. 5(1), 9(3).   [105] F13(4).

[106] Canon E1(5): in the churchwardens is vested property in the plate, ornaments, and other movable goods of the church; *Re Consecrated Land in Camomile Street* [1990] 3 All ER 229 at 233; *OLAC*, 143: 'Whatever expression is used, whether it be "property in", "the vesting of the property in", "possession of" or "legal title to" the contents, the right so described is not an absolute right of ownership, but is held and to be exercised for and on behalf of the parishioners'; *St Mary Northolt (Vicar and Churchwardens) v Parishioners* [1920] P 97; see also Incumbents and Churchwardens (Trusts) Measure 1964, s. 2(2)(f): an interest in personalty held on permanent trusts is exempted in relation to personalty 'vested in churchwardens in the goods, ornaments, and movables of the church of which they are churchwardens and in an incumbent or churchwardens in any other chattel'.

[107] *Re St Michael and All Angels, Great Torrington* [1985] Fam 81 at 89 (Court of Ecclesiastical Causes Reserved).   [108] Canon F13(3).

[109] EJM, s. 6(1)(b); CCEJM, s. 14 (archdeacon); see *supra* Ch. 5.

[110] CCEJM, s. 11, Sched. 7, para. 2.

[111] s. 11(8); *CCEJMCP*, 62: these may include cruets, vases, altar linen, authorized service books, hymn books, fire extinguishers, movable hymn boards, display stands, kneelers, carpets and curtains, decorative banners, and furniture in church halls.

by the archdeacon.[112] The consistory court in exercising its discretion to permit or forbid introduction must have regard to the legality of its introduction (including whether it conflicts with the ecclesiastical doctrine) and may have regard to the nature and aesthetic quality of the item and the wishes of the parishioners.[113] A tabernacle, a sanctuary bell, a confessional box, and other items used for superstitious reverence cannot be introduced into the church; an aumbry, hanging pyx, or 'sacrament house' may be introduced.[114] Whilst the parochial church council has a general power to acquire personalty for any ecclesiastical purposes affecting the parish, it may only acquire personalty to be held on permanent trust with the consent of the diocesan authority.[115] Freedom of acquisition is also limited by the rules concerning the re-ordering of the interior of a church.[116]

The introduction of chattels into a cathedral, falling outside the faculty jurisdiction, is governed by the Care of Cathedrals Measure 1990.[117] Objects may be introduced only by the administrative body in furtherance of its duties under the cathedral's constitution and statutes with respect to the ordering of services or otherwise in furtherance of the mission of the cathedral church. However, there is a general prohibition against permanent addition to a cathedral of any object which would affect its architectural, archeological, artistic, or historic character.[118] Applications to make a permanent addition are reviewed in the first instance by the Cathedral Fabric Advisory Committee and determined by the Cathedrals Fabric Commission whose decision, if a refusal, may be examined by a Commission of Review.[119] A threatened addition may, if *prima facie* illegal, be the subject of an episcopal order which the administrative body is under a duty to obey; the bishop may if he considers it necessary and expedient seek an injunction to prevent its introduction.[120]

---

[112] Faculty Jurisdiction Rules 1992, App. A. Many Diocesan norms repeat these provisions: for carpets, remembrance book, altar frontals, paintings, pews see e.g. *SDDH*, Pt. II, Annex E.3; *CF*, F.3, 6 (the parochial church council cannot accept a gift without a faculty), *RBG*, D.3, E.1; *LDR*, 115–6; *ODYB: IF*, 246.

[113] *Re St Mary, Burley in Wharfedale* [1990] *ELJ*, 2 (1991), 130 (steel altar candlesticks); *Re St Mary, Tenbury Wells* [1990] *ELJ*, 2 (1991), 130 (comfortable chairs); *Re Wadworth Parish Church* [1993] *ELJ*, 3 (1994), 259 (carpet); *Re St Richard of Chichester, Peel Hall* [1993] *ELJ*, 3 (1994), 259 (crosses permissible: no multiplicity); *Re St George with St Anne and St Mark, Brighton* [1994] *ELJ*, 3 (1995), 353 (introduction of a work of art permissible if aesthetically pleasing and congruous with the character of the church, if not inconsistent with church doctrine, not affecting the structure of the church, and not adversely affecting the finances of the parish); *Re St Mary the Virgin, Cottingham* [1994] *ELJ*, 3 (1995), 347 (statue of Virgin Mary and Child: controversial item and insufficient support).

[114] *Re St Mary, Tyne Dock* [1954] P 369; [1958] P 156; for the problematic stations of the cross see *Re St Peter, St Helier, Morden* [1951] P 303; *Re St Anselm, Belmont* [1990] *ELJ*, 2 (1990), 65 (aumbry).   [115] PCC(P)M, ss. 5(1), 6(1).

[116] For FJR, r. 8, *Re St Luke the Evangelist, Maidstone* [1994] 3 WLR 1165 and *Re Holy Innocents, Fallowfield* [1982] Fam 135 see *post* Ch. 16.

[117] S. 18: parish church cathedrals may in certain circumstances elect to be subject to the faculty jurisdiction; the 1990 Measure does not then apply: see *post* Ch. 16.   [118] S. 2(1)(c).

[119] For a detailed discussion of the powers and procedures see *post* Ch. 16.

[120] Care of Cathedrals (Supplementary Provisions) Measure 1994, ss. 1, 3–6; see *supra* Ch. 4.

Freedom of Disposal

Whilst Roman Catholic canon law forbids absolutely the disposal of certain sacred objects,[121] the law of the Church of England contains no general prohibitions against the disposal of movables. Falling outside the faculty jurisdiction, disposal of cathedral movables is governed by the Care of Cathedrals Measure 1990.[122] There is a general prohibition against the sale, loan, or other disposal of any object vested in the capitular body which is of architectural, archeological, artistic, or historic interest.[123] If the application for approval to dispose relates to objects in the possession of the chapter it must be made directly to the Cathedrals Fabric Commission; a refusal may be examined by a Commission of Review.[124] As with acquisitions, the bishop may make an order against disposal and seek an injunction preventing it or, if disposal has already occurred, a restoration order.[125]

The parochial church council may dispose of personalty vested in the diocesan authority (it will be so vested if held on permanent trust) only with the consent of that authority.[126] Similarly, when incumbents, churchwardens, or councils hold as managing trustees, disposal must be consented to by the custodian trustees.[127] If it is proposed to remove from a church an ornament or furniture, the minister and churchwardens must obtain a faculty.[128] A chancellor may direct which items may be disposed of without faculty authorization.[129] Ordinarily, a consistory court would not grant a faculty for the disposal of contents of a church without a parochial church council resolution

---

[121] *CIC*, c. 1190: '[i]t is absolutely forbidden to sell sacred relics'; for sacred objects see c. 1186; goods of religious institutes are governed by c. 634 and those of societies by c. 741; a person who alienates unlawfully shall be subject to a just penalty: c. 1377.

[122] Care of Cathedrals Measure 1990, s. 18: a parish church cathedral may opt to come within the faculty jurisdiction in which case the Measure does not apply.

[123] S. 2(1)(b); for procedure and enforcement see *post* Ch. 16.   [124] Ss. 6(1)(a)(iv), 13.

[125] Ss. 1, 3–6 (of the 1994 measure). For an injunction or restoration order application must be made to the court of the Vicar-General of the province.

[126] PCC(P)M, s. 5(2): subject to the terms of any trust, the council can dispose of any property acquired under this section; see also s. 6(2), (3): personalty held on permanent trust vests in the diocesan authority; the council cannot sell, lease, or exchange without the consent of the diocesan authority; *OLAC*, 144: a resolution must be passed by a majority of those present at its meeting under *CRR*.   [127] Incumbents and Churchwardens (Trusts) Measure 1964, s. 5.

[128] F13(3); Pastoral Measure 1983, s. 56(2): the prohibition against sale, lease, or other disposal applies only to the church or 'any . . . part of a church'; this includes, therefore, fixtures (such as the font); the following rules govern movables and not fixtures which are treated as part of the realty: *OLAC*, 145.

[129] CCEJM, s. 11(8); *GDM*, D.9: items of a sacramental or devotional nature—e.g. altars, fonts, lecterns, pulpits—may be disposed of by gift or sale to another church; items made or dedicated for ecclesiastical purposes, but not especially sacramental or devotional—e.g. pews, Glastonbury chairs, vestry furniture, ironwork—may be disposed of by gift or sale to another church; sale for secular purposes could also be allowed if difficulty is experienced in finding a genuine church buyer; items of a domestic nature—plain chairs, cupboards, pianos, chests, tables—may be disposed of by sale or gift at the discretion of the parochial church council; *CDH*, 23; *CF*, F.6; *RBG*, D.8.

supporting the petition.[130] Any disposals by sale designed to effect financial advantage to the parish must be scrutinized by the court with special care.[131]

The Court of Arches in *Re St Gregory's, Tredington* laid down guiding principles for cases of disposal by sale and disposal by gift.[132] The church-wardens may sell goods, the ownership of which is vested in them, only with the consent of the parochial church council under the authority of a faculty; sales executed without these are void. There must be an acceptable reason for the sale—such as the goods are now redundant or there is a financial emergency—and in assessing this the court must take into account the particular ministry of the community in question. Whether the sale is to be authorized lies in the discretion of the consistory court which must take into account any advice given to it by the Diocesan Advisory Committee. By synodical measure, a faculty may impose a condition requiring a specified period to elapse before disposal takes place, in order to allow museums and the like to bid.[133] Adequate provision must be made for the application of proceeds of a sale with the money being settled so that income is paid either to the parochial church council or accumulated for a period.[134]

For a disposal by gift, the court must be satisfied that sufficient goods remain for the purposes of the donating church; it may not approve the giving of items having a long historical association with the church but should recommend instead the giving of another item which would not affect the historical link. If an item is given in memory of a person, the court should ensure that the person will be remembered adequately by some other means and that the donor's family is consulted before the execution of the gift.[135]

Special rules apply to the disposal of libraries. The consistory court may authorize the sale of books from a parochial library in the diocese and the proceeds of sale shall be applied for such ecclesiastical purposes of the parish as the faculty may direct. In exercising its control over sales, the court must obtain and consider the advice of the Diocesan Advisory Committee and may impose such conditions on the disposal as it thinks fit. Whether the library falls within the terms of the legislation is to be determined conclusively by the

---

[130] F13(3): concerning 'removals', the churchwardens and incumbent must obtain a faculty; *OLAC*, 144.

[131] For the adoption of these principles see *Re St Helen's, Brant Broughton* [1974] Fam 16; *Re St Mary's, Broadwater* [1976] Fam 222; *Re St Mary's, Bow* [1984] 1 WLR 1363; *Re St Agnes, Toxteth Park* [1985] 1 WLR 641; for refused disposal see *Re St Mary's, Barton-upon-Humber* [1987] Fam 41 and *Re St Mary of Charity, Faversham* [1986] Fam 143; *Re St Hallows, South Cerney* [1994] *ELJ*, 3 (1995), 347: sale to ensure survival rather than to increase funds is permissible; *Re Middleton with Cropton* [1990] *ELJ*, 2 (1990–2), 319: sale of a 1493 cup.

[132] [1972] Fam 236, adopting *Re St Mary's, Gilston* [1967] P 125, *Re St Mary's, Westwell* [1968] 1 WLR 513 and overruling *Re Vicar and Churchwardens of St Mary, Northolt v Parishioners of St Mary, Northolt* [1920] P 97.   [133] CCEJM, s. 12(1)(b).

[134] *Re St Mary's, Gilston* [1967] P 125.

[135] *Re St Gregory's, Tredington* [1972] Fam 236 at 244, 246.

Charity Commissioners.[136] The disposal of cathedral libraries is governed by the Care of Cathedrals Measure 1990 and the procedures described above with respect to disposal of objects apply.[137] Special rules also apply to the disposal of chattels on the closing or demolition of a church. Before any church is demolished in pursuance of a redundancy or pastoral scheme, or is appropriated for a use specified in such a scheme, the font, communion table, and plate must be transferred to some other church in the area of the benefice. If these are not needed, they may be transferred to any church or chapel in the diocese as directed by the bishop; no faculty is required.[138]

Disposal of goods without the necessary formalities and consents is unlawful.[139] If improperly removed goods are sold in market overt the buyer will acquire good title if, *inter alia*, he has acted in good faith (regardless of any negligence) and if he had no notice of any defect or want of title in the seller.[140] In the Legal Advisory Commission's view the proper plaintiffs in an action of conversion to recover chattels are the churchwardens and perhaps the parochial church council.[141] When a sale has not been authorized by the consenting authorities and by faculty, it is arguable that the churchwardens or council would not be estopped by a claim that they had good title to sell: as a general principle, a corporate body cannot be estopped from denying that it has entered a contract which was *ultra vires*; it cannot be bound by estoppel to do something beyond its powers or to refrain from carrying out its duty.[142] After the expiration of six years from the date of conversion the right to recover is

---

[136] Parochial Libraries Act 1708; EJM, s. 6(1)(b)(ii); Faculty Jurisdiction Measure 1964, s. 4(1) as amended by CCEJM, Sched. 7, para. 1; see also *Re St Mary's, Warwick* [1981] Fam 170: sale authorized to a university which had housed the library for 20 years; a faculty was granted subject to the conditions that the university was not to sell it for at least 100 years and that it should be made available for consultation by 'anyone with a genuine interest', including particularly officers and parishioners of St Mary's, Warwick; the proceeds were made available for the repair of fabric, glass, and ancient ornaments of the church.   [137] Care of Cathedrals Measure 1990, s. 3.

[138] Pastoral Measure 1983, s. 64(2); the scheme may also make provision for 'the disposal of any other contents of the church, not being tombstones, monuments or memorials commemmorating deceased persons buried in the church or in any land belonging or annexed thereto': s.64(3); s.64(4) provides that there is no need for a faculty; *Re The Church of the Ascension, Hulme* [1991] *ELJ*, 3 (1993), 60: on redundancy title vested in the diocesan board of finance and the parish had no title to sell.

[139] The churchwardens may be liable for theft under the Theft Act 1968, s. 1(1); by s. 5(3): 'Where a person received property from or on account of another, and is under an obligation to the other to retain and deal with that property or its proceeds in a particular way, the property or proceeds shall be regarded (as against him) as belonging to the other.'

[140] *OLAC*, 147; Sale of Goods Act 1979, s. 22(1); however, the churchwardens have a 'special property' in the goods (holding them as they do for the use of the parishioners) and not a 'general property' (*Nyberg v Handelaar* [1892] 2 QB 202) and the 1979 Act applies only to contracts entered into by those having 'general property': *OLAC*, 146 does not seem to address this.

[141] *OLAC*, 148, not the incumbent.

[142] *OLAC*, 149; *Den Norske Creditbank v The Sarawak Economic Development Corporation* [1988] Lloyd's Rep. 616.

lost.[143] It has not been settled whether churchwardens refusing to proceed may be compelled in the civil courts to do so by way of *mandamus*.[144]

CONCLUSIONS

In contrast with the Roman Catholic Church, the Church of England's regulation of acquisition and disposal of property is based on the type rather than the value of property. Under Roman Catholic canon law the church has an inherent right to acquire property for the ordering of divine worship, for the decent support of ministers, and for the works of the apostolate and of charity; the conference of bishops sets the maximum and minimum values of property and disposal may occur only with the consent of a competent authority designated according to the value of the property in question. Whilst the Church of England confers a general freedom of acquisition and disposal, procedural law contains an elaborate system of consents applicable to all forms of real and personal property. Only exceptionally can property be acquired or disposed of without the concurrence of the Church Commissioners, the diocesan board of finance, and the diocesan bishop. However, procedural law distributes extensive rights for incumbents and parochial church councils to be consulted over (but not to veto) proposals to acquire and to dispose of property. With regard to realty, control is effected by institutional executive consents; for personalty, by contrast, judicial consent in the form of a faculty is needed. The law on disposal has burgeoned in recent years with the declining need for plant and this has given rise to a much more sophisticated complex of rules than operates in other areas of ecclesiastical life.

[143] Limitation Act 1980, s. 2, in cases other than theft.
[144] *OLAC*, 149; for corporations not enforcing *ultra vires* contracts see G. H. Treitel, *The Law of Contract* (8th edn., London, 1991) 510–11.

16

The Use and Maintenance of Property

The legal framework of the Church of England regulating the use and maintenance of property is designed to give effect to the principle that in a general sense property does not belong to any one generation but is a heritage to be enjoyed by successive generations. In common with the Roman Catholic Church, the law of the Church of England imposes a wide range of duties to ensure the proper use and care of property and it prescribes procedures enabling oversight of the discharging of these duties to standards set by those charged with the responsibility of oversight.[1] Elaborate rules govern the use of consecrated and unconsecrated property, the sharing of church buildings, the use of property held on religious charitable trusts, and the care, maintenance, and development of the many forms of church property. These matters have been the subject of large-scale reforms in recent years, particularly the faculty jurisdiction which, it is increasingly thought, ought to be exercised in order to fulfil the pastoral needs of the worshipping community.[2]

THE USE OF PROPERTY

The use of consecrated and that of unconsecrated church property are governed by different rules. As may be expected, the legal regime governing the use of consecrated property is rather more rigorous than that dealing with unconsecrated property.

[1] As we shall see in this Chapter, the Church Commissioners have certain functions with respect to care and maintenance, notably making grants towards the cost of cathedral repairs and liabilities and approving improvements to parsonage houses: *WAOB* recommends that these functions be transferred to the proposed National Council and its departments (8.39); it also recommends the establishment by the Council of a Church Heritage Board charged *inter alia* with devising policies to make the best use of buildings and negotiating with state bodies on heritage matters (App. C.14). The Commission also recommends that the Council, with regard to its holding property as a corporate body, be an exempt charity for the purposes of the Charities Act 1993 (5.27).

[2] Ecclesiastical buildings used for ecclesiastical purposes (except residential buildings from which ministerial duties of office are performed) are exempted from the provisions of the Planning (Listed Buildings and Conservation) Act 1990 (s. 60(1), (3)); nor do they constitute monuments for the purposes of control under the Ancient Monuments and Archeological Areas Act 1979.

Consecrated Property

The freehold of a church and churchyard, vesting in the incumbent, is held for the use of the parishioners,[3] its management on their behalf being the responsibility of the incumbent, the churchwardens, and the parochial church council.[4] Whilst the keys of a church belong to the incumbent,[5] churchwardens have a right of access to the church and churchyard to carry out their lawful ecclesiastical functions.[6] Parishioners are entitled to a right of way to the church,[7] and enjoy a right of access to it (and to remain there) for the purpose of attendance at divine worship so long as there is sufficient space.[8] Due to problems of security diocesan norms have been devised to restrict access at times other than for attendance at divine worship.[9] Objects within the church (such as bells and organs) may be used only for those purposes prescribed by law and permitted by the incumbent, churchwardens, and parochial church council.[10] Similarly, in Roman Catholic canon law 'the faithful have a right of access for divine worship', and during the time of 'sacred celebrations' admission to a church building must be free.[11]

---

[3] *Winstanley v North Manchester Overseers* [1910] AC 7; *Vicar and One of the Churchwardens of St Botolph Without Aldgate v Parishioners of the Same* [1892] P 161 (but the control of the church and churchyard vests in the consistory court); *St Gabriel, Fenchurch Street (Rector and Churchwardens) v London Real Property Co Ltd* [1896] P 95 at 101; Church of England (Miscellaneous Provisions) Measure 1978, s. 8 (*supra* Ch. 15).   [4] PCC(P)M, s. 4(1)(ii)(c).

[5] *Daunt v Crocker* (1867) LR 2 A&E 41; *Ritchings v Cordingley* (1868) LR 3 A&E 113.

[6] *OLAC*, 48; this advice has surfaced as a rule in some diocesan norms: e.g. *GDM*, F3.

[7] *OLAC*, 53: a private right of way may be granted in the nature of an easement by faculty; *St Edmundsbury and Ipswich Diocesan Board of Finance v Clark (No. 2)* [1973] 3 All ER 902, [1975] 1 All ER 772; *OLAC*, 53: some footpaths through churchyards have been recorded by local authorities as rights of way under the National Parks and Access to the Countryside Act 1949, ss. 32–3 (now replaced by the Wildlife and Countryside Act 1981).

[8] *Griffin v Dighton* (1864) 5 B & S 92; *Cole v Police Constable 443A* [1937] 1 KB 316; *supra* Ch. 10

[9] *SDH*, II, C; for security generally *SDDH*, O.20; *CDH*, 177; *BDM*, K.10; *WDHI*, ch. 4, 221.

[10] The churchwardens and parochial church council must allow goods and ornaments to be used in connection with divine service under the direction of the incumbent: e.g. *Harrison v Forbes and Sisson* (1860) 6 Jur NS 1353; *Redhead v Wait* (1862) 6 LT 580. Bells are not to be rung contrary to the direction of the incumbent or minister (F8(2), F15(1)) and if their ringing is an unlawful interference with a person's use and enjoyment this may constitute a nuisance at common law (*OLAC*, 17–19 for *Soltau v De Held* (1851) 2 Sim NS 133, *Martin v Nutkin* (1724) 2 P Wms 266) and an injunction may be granted imposing conditions on use: see the Australian case of *Haddon v Lynch* [1911] VLR 5 and *Hardman v Holbertson* [1866] WN 379; see also the Environmental Protection Act 1990, s. 79(1)(g): 'noise emitted from premises so as to be prejudicial to health or a nuisance' is a statutory nuisance; for recent cases see R. H. Bloor, 'Clocks, bells and cockerels', *ELJ*, 3 (1995), 393. Elaborate rules exist for the use of registers and records (*supra* Ch. 4). The Legal Advisory Commission has advised, in draconian terms, that the organ should not ordinarily be used by anybody except the organist, or his deputy (undefined) in cases of holiday or illness, except by joint permission of the incumbent, the parochial church council, and the organist: *OLAC*, 190.

[11] *CIC*, cc. 1214, 1221; for the right of assembly see c. 215; cc. 1205–7; dedications and blessings must be certified: c. 1209; as soon as it is completed, a new church must be dedicated or

According to Roman Catholic canon law a sacred place may be used only for purposes consistent with the promotion of divine worship, piety, and religion. Whilst any use not in accord with the holiness of the place is forbidden, exceptionally the ordinary 'can permit other uses which are not contrary to the holiness of the place in individual instances'.[12] In the Church of England, unless lawfully authorized, consecrated property cannot be used for purposes inconsistent with the object of consecration, the property having been set aside through consecration exclusively for sacred uses.[13] The primary responsibility for ensuring that property is not used for purposes inconsistent with consecration lies not with the incumbent or the council but with the churchwardens. By canon, the churchwardens and their assistants must not suffer the church or chapel to be profaned by any meeting therein for temporal objects inconsistent with the sanctity of the place.[14] They enjoy powers of expulsion; instances of public disorder may constitute a variety of civil and ecclesiastical offences.[15] However, in some cases it is the minister who must regulate use. When any church or chapel is to be used for a play, concert, or exhibition of films or pictures the minister must take care that the words, music, and pictures are such as befit the House of God, are consonant with sound doctrine, and make for the edifying of the people. In exercising this discretion, the minister must consult the local or other authorities concerned with precautions against fire and other dangers required by law to be taken in the case of performances or exhibitions. The minister is obliged to obey any general directions relating to such use of a church or chapel issued from time to time by the bishop or other ordinary, and if any doubt arises as to the observance of these provisions the minister must refer the matter to the bishop or other ordinary and obey his directions.[16] Indeed, in Roman Catholic canon law sacred places are 'violated through seriously harmful actions posited in them which scandalize the faithful and are so serious and contrary to the holiness of the place, in the judgment of the ordinary, that it is not licit to perform acts of worship in them until the harm has been repaired through a penitential rite in accord with the norm of the liturgical books'.[17]

Outside these cases, whether consecrated churches and churchyards may be put to secular uses is regulated by the faculty jurisdiction which, as a general rule, cannot authorize a fundamental frustration of the property's sacred use.[18]

---

at least blessed, and cathedral and parish churches must be dedicated with a solemn rite: c. 1217. Loss of dedication occurs if the building suffers major destruction, is permanently given over for profane uses, or through a decree of the competent ordinary: c. 1212.

[12] *CIC*, c. 1210.   [13] For consecration see *supra* Ch. 15.   [14] F15(1).

[15] F15(2), (3); *supra* Ch. 8; *HLE*, paras. 1048, 1361.

[16] F16; the public performance of a play requires a licence: Theatres Act 1968, s. 12, Local Government Act 1972, s. 204(6); diocesan norms rarely deal with the subject: see exceptionally *PDH*, H.4, App. 1: in cases of doubt the matter should be referred to the bishop; for recommendations to seek advice from designated diocesan officers see *BDM*, 1.5, *WDHI*, ch. 1, 36.

[17] *CIC*, c. 1211.   [18] *Re St John's, Chelsea* [1962] 2 All ER 850 at 852.

The granting of faculties is discretionary and the ecclesiastical courts permit controlled relaxation of this principle in limited circumstances only.[19] The courts sometimes authorize by faculty the use of a portion of consecrated property for purposes which are of benefit to those using the church, to the parishioners, and to the public.[20] A faculty may authorize use of part of a church by a third party in order to generate revenue to assist in the maintenance of the church; however, no legal estate can be created in consecrated land, so no lease can be made of it, and third-party users are therefore licensees.[21] A licence may be granted either by the court or by the incumbent as holder of the freehold.[22] The licensing arrangement should be the subject of a covenant between the third party and the parochial church council (and the incumbent, if the licensor) under which the secular third-party user is obliged to pay a user fee to the council.[23] Similarly, the consistory court must determine whether a prescriptive right of way (or to lights) by way of licence arises incidentally to the issue of a faculty.[24] As an overriding principle, these arrangements must ensure that the whole of the church continues to be a church for sacred purposes, that the licence is not of a part regularly needed for sacred purposes, and that satisfactory provision is made to ensure that the third-party secular user does nothing to prevent or disturb its general use as a church.[25] The same basic principles apply to consecrated churchyards. A faculty is required, for example, to authorize setting aside part of a consecrated churchyard for widening a public highway, for making and fencing a pathway across a churchyard as a private way to adjoining premises, for the erection of buildings to be used for secular purposes, and for the construction of electricity installations;[26] similar authorization is required in the case of

---

[19] *Sutton v Bowden* [1913] 1 Ch 518 at 551 *per* Farwell LJ.

[20] *Vicar of St Nicholas, Leicester v Langton* [1899] P 19; *Lee v Hawtrey* [1898] P 63; for cases involving conversion of parts of churches for use as lavatories, kitchens, meeting rooms etc., and the construction of church halls in churchyards see e.g. *Re St Thomas, Lymington* [1980] 2 All ER 84; *Re All Saints, Melbourn* [1992] 2 All ER 786.

[21] Pastoral Measure 1983, s. 56(2), (3): these prohibit a lease or other disposition but allow a faculty to authorize 'suitable use'; for general principles as to how the power may be exercised see *Re St Mary's, Aldermary* [1985] Fam 101; see *Re Tonbridge School Chapel No.2* [1993] Fam 281 for a lease of a consecrated chapel by a non-church body: s.56(2) held not to apply to the chapel as it was consecrated for 'divine' worship as opposed to 'public' worship (it was not a 'church' under s. 87(1)).

[22] *Re St Paul's, Covent Garden* [1974] Fam 1; see also *Re St Mary's Aldermary* [1985] Fam 101.   [23] The leading case is *Re All Saints', Harborough Magna* [1992] WLR 1235.

[24] *Re St Martin le Grand, York* [1989] 2 All ER 711; see also *Re St Clement's, Leigh-on-Sea* [1988] 1 WLR 720 on an alleged right of way arising under the Law of Property Act 1925, s. 62; for rights of way and redundant churches see Pastoral Measure 1983, s. 60; for faculty approving a right of way over an unconsecrated churchyard see *Re St George's Church, Oakdale* [1975] 2 All ER 870; see also D. Harte, 'Churchyards and coffin ways', *Rights of Way Law Review* (1993) 17; for rights to light see Newsom, *FJCE*, 151.   [25] *Re St Peter, Vere Street* (1992) (unreported).

[26] *Re Bideford Parish, ex parte Rector etc. of Bideford* [1900] P 314; *St Gabriel, Fenchurch Street (Rector and Churchwardens) v City of London Real Property Co Ltd* [1869] P 95; *Re St Mary's, Luton* [1966] 3 All ER 638; for faculties and rights of way see *Walter v Montague and Lamprell* (1836) 1 Curt 253; *Morley Borough Council v Vicar and Churchwardens of St Mary the Virgin, Woodkirk* [1969] 3 All ER 952.

closed or disused consecrated churchyards.[27] Unauthorized interference with the churchyard by an incumbent may constitute an ecclesiastical offence and may therefore be restrained by injunction.[28]

Faculty jurisdiction to effect control over use of property also exists by way of legal fiction. In some cases unconsecrated property is treated as if it were consecrated: a building episcopally licensed (after 1 March 1993) for public worship, as well as all articles within it, are subject to the faculty jurisdiction as if the building were consecrated. However, the bishop may after consultation with the Diocesan Advisory Committee direct that this provision does not apply. The bishop removing such a building from faculty jurisdiction may direct that any article appertaining to it shall remain under that jurisdiction. These orders may be varied or revoked.[29] With regard to buildings licensed before that date, the bishop may make a revocable order to direct that any building episcopally licensed for public worship, and its contents, shall be subject to the faculty jurisdiction as if it were consecrated.[30] It has been suggested that although licensed buildings are subject to faculty jurisdiction as if consecrated (because in the absence of consecration the freehold is not in abeyance), transactions concerning licensed buildings may be authorized by the consistory court 'as comparatively freely as if [the court] were dealing with unconsecrated' property.[31]

Unconsecrated Property

In the Church of England the effects of consecration may be lifted by parliamentary statute, by synodical measure, or by episcopal order.[32] As in Roman Catholic canon law,[33] the bishop's removal order may contain such conditions and requirements as the bishop thinks fit including 'the maintenance of orderly behaviour in or on the building or land so affected'.[34] Special rules apply to the use and enjoyment of unconsecrated property. Being property used for the purposes for which it was acquired, rules vary depending on the

---

[27] *Vicar of St John the Baptist, Cardiff v Parishioners of St John the Baptist, Cardiff* [1898] P 155; *Re St Peter the Great, Chichester* [1961] 2 All ER 513; but the court seems not to have jurisdiction to authorize the use of a closed churchyard as part of a public highway where it has been dedicated for use as an open space under the Open Spaces Act 1906: *Ex parte West Riding County Council* (1935) 52 TLR 111.

[28] *Bennett v Bonaker* (1830) 3 Hag Ecc 17; *Batten v Gedye* (1889) 41 ChD 507; *Marriott v Tarpley* (1838) 9 Sim 279 for civil injunction; injunctions may be granted at the instance of the parochial church council under PCC(P)M, s. 4(1)(ii)(c); see also *St Edmundsbury and Ipswich Diocesan Board of Finance v Clark* (No. 2) [1973] 3 All ER 902, [1975] 1 All ER 772 (CA); for trespass see *Jones v Ellis* (1828) 2 Y & J 265. [29] CCEJM, s. 11.

[30] Faculty Jurisdiction Measure 1964, s. 6. [31] Newsom, *FJCE*, 184.

[32] *Supra*, Ch. 15.

[33] *CIC*, c. 1222: a church which cannot be employed for divine worship and is impossible to repair can be relegated by the diocesan bishop to profane (but not sordid) use with the consent of those 'who legitimately claim rights regarding the church' and as long as the good of souls is not thereby impaired. [34] CCEJM, s. 22(1), (2)(b).

property in question. With respect to parsonage houses neither the incumbent nor any sequestrators may grant a lease of any excluded part of a parsonage house belonging to the benefice; such leases are void.[35] In relation to other parsonage land the diocesan board of finance may require the incumbent to supply particulars of a lease and its terms.[36] The diocesan board of finance may lease its property with the approval of the Church Commissioners.[37] No incumbents or churchwardens acting as managing trustees may lease trust property without the consent of the board of finance.[38] The same applies to leases made by a parochial church councils.[39]

Control of unconsecrated land under the faculty jurisdiction is minimal. However, where unconsecrated land forms or is part of the curtilage of a church, the ordinary has the same jurisdiction over such land as over the church.[40] Since the fee simple usually vests in the incumbent, the fee not being in abeyance, legal estates may be made in the land.[41] Judicial decisions give rise to a number of rudimentary principles: the consistory court must proceed by way of analogy with cases about consecrated churchyards; it must ensure that the church building itself will not be injured and services held in it not disturbed; the interests of the church may require the imposition of restrictive covenants; and a legal estate may be created and buildings developed on the curtilage which has the effect of conveying the land outside the faculty jurisdiction.[42]

CHURCH-SHARING AGREEMENTS

Recent years have seen the development of a large body of law regulating the extent to which buildings belonging to the Church of England may be made the subject of sharing agreements with other churches. The Sharing of Church Buildings Act 1969, applicable to both the Church of England and the Roman Catholic Church,[43] and the Sharing of Church Buildings Measure 1970 present the basic legal framework. The subject has given rise to a number of issues, not least the degree of freedom which churches enjoy in designing agreements regulating the sharing of church buildings. The Sharing of Church Buildings Act 1969 applies to church buildings used or proposed to be used as a place of

---

[35] Endowments and Glebe Measure 1976, s. 29; *supra* Ch. 15.   [36] S. 31.
[37] Ss. 20(1).   [38] Incumbents and Churchwardens (Trusts) Measure 1964, s. 5.
[39] PCC(P)M, s. 6.
[40] Faculty Jurisdiction Measure 1964, s. 7(1); for 'church' see Interpretation Measure 1925, s. 3; curtilage is such unconsecrated part of a churchyard which physically adjoins the church as is required for the purpose of the church: *Re St George's, Oakdale* [1975] 2 All ER 870; *Re St John's Bishop's Hatfield* [1967] 2 All ER 403.
[41] *Re St Mary Magdalene, Paddington* [1980] Fam 99.
[42] *Re St Peter's, Bushey Heath* [1971] 1 WLR 357; *Re Christ Church, Chislehurst* [1973] 1 WLR 1317.   [43] 1969 Act, Sched. 2.

worship, church hall, youth club, or residence for ordained ministers or lay workers.[44] Nothing in the statute affects 'any practice' by the churches to which it applies of 'lending church buildings temporarily for particular occasions to other religious bodies'.[45]

The Agreement: Form and Parties

The 1969 Act sets out terms which must be incorporated into a church-sharing agreement, terms which may be incorporated, and the parties legally empowered to make it. It is lawful for any two or more churches to which the statute applies[46] to make agreements for the sharing of church buildings and to carry such agreements into effect.[47] The agreement may apply to a single or to two or more existing or proposed church buildings in the same locality.[48] Whilst the parties may generally provide in the agreement for ownership of the shared buildings to be vested solely or jointly in all or any of the parties,[49] in relation to agreements dealing with consecrated churches and residence houses of the Church of England ownership must remain in the Church of England.[50] No sharing agreement may be made concerning a cathedral church belonging to the Church of England.[51]

As for the parties to the agreement, with regard to the Church of England the diocesan board of finance, the incumbent, and the parochial church council (all corporations) are required to enter the agreement together 'on behalf' of the church.[52] However, these cannot enter an agreement without the consent of the

---

[44] S. 12(1); for parliamentary debate see Hansard (HL) 30 Jan. 1969, 1285; see also D. W. Faull, 'Shared churches', *Research Bulletin* (Institute for the Study of Worship and Religious Architecture) (1973), 77. [45] S. 13.

[46] Sched. 2; HL Deb, Vol. 298, 30 Jan. 1969, 1279 at 1282 (hitherto, of course, the main difficulty had been that church buildings could be used only for the purposes of the church to which they belonged). [47] S. 1(1).

[48] S. 2(2); 'locality' is not defined.

[49] S. 1(2); s. 2(1): when the agreement relates to an existing or proposed building the ownership of which is vested (or continues to be vested) in only one of the sharing churches, the trusts for which the building is held must include the purposes and provisions of the agreement; s. 2(2): when the building is to be owned jointly ownership is to be vested in trustees representing the churches; it must be ensured that the purposes of the agreement incorporated into a trust retain their charitable status: s. 2(5).

[50] S. 5(1)(a); an unconsecrated church being the subject of an agreement must not be consecrated unless the Church of England is sole owner; a church subject to an agreement may remain or become a parish church provided it is in the sole ownership of the Church of England: otherwise, it may be designated as a parish centre of worship: s. 5. As a basic rule, residence houses owned by the Church of England cannot be the subject of a sharing agreement: s. 7(3).

[51] S. 10; however, the dean and chapter may authorize a chapel or other part of the cathedral to be used for the purposes of public worship according to the rites of another church to which the statute applies: see also *supra* Ch. 10.

[52] S. 1(3)(a); if the benefice is vacant or suspended the reference to the incumbent shall be substituted by the minister-in-charge 'but otherwise a sharing agreement shall not be made on behalf of the Church of England during a vacancy in the benefice concerned': s. 1(6). No provision seems to be made for the patron as party (or as consenting party) to the agreement.

diocesan bishop and the diocesan pastoral committee.[53] With respect to other churches, the statute prescribes as parties 'such persons as may be determined by the appropriate authority of the Church' (for the Roman Catholic Church the appropriate authority is the diocesan bishop) which may themselves require the consent of any body or person specified by that authority.[54] The person in whom the building is vested and any managing trustees must also be parties.[55] The agreement is binding on the successors of the parties to it.[56]

The sharing agreement must be made under seal and registered with the required consents signified in writing and registered with the deed.[57] It may be amended only by the agreement of the parties to it, and with the consents required for its formation,[58] and must contain provision for its own termination;[59] it may provide for the withdrawal of any church if the withdrawing church is not the sole or previous owner of the building.[60]

The Substance of the Agreement: Terms

A sharing agreement must make provision for the finances, improvement, and management of the shared building. As a basic principle the primary responsibility for management rests with the owning church or (in the case of jointly owned churches) with the managing trustees. The legal powers of any person or body to apply money to provide, improve, or manage (including repair and furnishing) the building continue to be applicable.[61] The obligation to manage the building and its contents when owned solely by one of the churches remains with the authorities of or the trustees representing that church; when jointly owned the trustees are responsible for its management.[62] Both sets of duties must be discharged in accordance with the provisions of the agreement and any arrangements made under it. Accordingly, the agreement may include provision for consultation, for payment of contributions towards management expenses, and that any movables required for worship of a sharing agreeing church are to be the responsibility of the authorities of that church.[63] Where a

---

[53] S. 1(4): if the bishop is ill or absent, or the see is vacant, the archbishop may authorize a suffragan or assistant bishop or archdeacon to act; if the archbishop is unable to authorize the other provincial archbishop may do so: s. 1(7)); if the building is to be held on trust for educational purposes the diocesan education board (instead of the pastoral committee) must consent as well as the Secretary of State: s. 1(5).   [54] S. 1(3)(b), (4); Sched. 2.

[55] S. 1(3).   [56] S. 1(9).   [57] S. 1(8).   [58] S. 1(10).

[59] S. 9(1)(a); if the agreement relates to 2 or more buildings it must provide for terminating the sharing of each building so that sharing among other buildings can continue on the termination of sharing of the first.

[60] S. 9(1)(b); it may provide for financial readjustments as between the churches on termination or withdrawal.

[61] S. 3(1), (3), (6); for the powers of the Church Commissioners see Sharing of Church Buildings Measure 1970, s. 2.

[62] S. 3(2): the parochial church council has the responsibility to maintain, see below; for the Roman Catholic Church, the Roman Catholic Trustees, incorporated under the Charitable Trustees Incorporation Act 1872, are the trustees for the purposes of the 1969 statute.

[63] S. 3(4), (5).

sharing agreement relates to a consecrated building the faculty jurisdiction does not apply in respect of movables required for the worship of any sharing church other than the Church of England.[64]

A sharing agreement must 'make provision, in the case of a building used as a place of worship, for determining the extent to which it is available for worship'. These terms may only allow for worship 'in accordance with those forms of service and practice of the sharing churches respectively'. The agreement may provide for the holding of joint services on such occasions as are approved by the sharing churches and, with respect to the Church of England, the agreement may dispense with the holding of statutory services 'to such extent as may be necessary'. If invited by a minister, reader, or lay preacher of another church, a minister, reader, or lay preacher of sharing churches 'may . . . take part in conducting worship in that building in accordance with the forms of service of that other church . . . [n]otwithstanding any statutory or other legal provision'. The right is not absolute but is to be 'exercised in accordance with any rules or directions given by either Church and to any limitation imposed by or under the sharing agreement'. Similarly, 'the participation of the communities of the sharing Churches in each other's worship shall be governed by the practice and disciplines of those churches in like manner as if they worshipped in separate buildings'.[65] With respect to both the Church of England and the Roman Catholic Church, therefore, the terms of a sharing agreement concerning worship are subject to the rules of those churches designed to regulate ecumenical arrangements concerning shared liturgy.[66] Marriages may be solemnized in a shared church building if it is registered for this purpose and the legal requirements as to publication of banns apply to a shared church building.[67] In the opinion of the Legal Advisory Commission of the Church of England banns should, if possible, be published by a clergyman and their publication will be lawful only if effected at a service performed according to the rites of the Church of England or authorized by canon. If banns are published by a lay person, the Commission's view is that 'this may only be in the course of a service of Morning or Evening Prayer according to the rites of the Church of England'.[68]

Sharing Agreement Constitutions

As a matter of ecclesiastical practice[69] sharing agreements incorporate constitutional structures. These seek to ensure that sharing churches are treated,

---

[64] S. 5(3).   [65] S. 4(1)–(3).

[66] See *supra* Ch. 10 for Canons B43 and B44.

[67] S. 6; hitherto under the Marriage Act 1949, Part III, a Church of England church could be registered or used for the solemnization of non-Anglican marriages.   [68] *OLAC*, 163.

[69] The following paragraph is built on a sample survey of sharing agreements from the dioceses of Ely and Bath and Wells. Models were devised by participating churches and circulated by the Churches Main Committee, Circular No. 1970/4/P; see also British Council of Churches, *Guidelines to the Sharing of Church Buildings Act 1969*.

typically, 'in principle as having equal rights to the use of the church building and as being equally responsible for meeting the cost of management'. Often a joint council is established to administer the agreement consisting of an equal number of members representing the sharing churches; for the Church of England these usually include the incumbent or minister-in-charge, the church-wardens, and members selected from the parochial church council. Constitutional rules provide for chairmanship by the incumbent (or in his absence by the vice-chairman), quorum and voting (matters are usually to be determined by majority vote, the chairman having a casting vote) and procedure (the regulation of which lies with the council itself) at meetings. When the church building is owned by the Roman Catholic Church, chairmanship vests in the Roman Catholic priest or his deputy.

Functions of the joint council naturally vary: often, however, it is conferred with powers to settle disputes, to agree details of work to be carried out, to advise those responsible for repair and maintenance, to agree changes in furnishings, and generally to facilitate joint action and the settlement of questions of detail which arise from the implementation of the sharing agreement. Some agreements allow the solemnization of marriages according to the rites of a sharing church only with the express approval of the Church of England incumbent or minister-in-charge, and agreements often require notice before termination. Many prescribe expressly for the continuing operation of the faculty jurisdiction in relation to matters falling within this with regard to the Church of England.

An Assessment

The provisions of the 1969 Act constitute a state-made ecumenical covenant under seal; its basic object is to facilitate a common use of ecclesiastical plant to effect a wider and more economical distribution of financial responsibilities. However, the statutory model and the contractual terms arising from it are not without their practical defects. Three may be mentioned. First, the evolution of a sharing agreement to accommodate local needs is difficult; effectively the procedures require the creation of a new agreement. Secondly, it may be seen as weighted in favour of the Church of England; unlike other churches, continued ownership of consecrated Church of England buildings is mandatory and the statute prohibits both the consecration of jointly owned buildings and their designation as parish churches.[70] Thirdly, whilst the beneficiaries (congregation members) by virtue of constitutions under the agreement (but not by virtue of the statute) may directly participate in the administration of the agreement, they cannot enforce its terms. As a general principle, the statutory agreement is enforceable (and its violation actionable) only by those privy to the agreement as a matter of the civil law of contract; for the Church of

[70] *Supra* n. 50.

England only the diocesan board of finance, the incumbent, and the parochial church council acting jointly have rights to enforce the agreement on behalf of its direct beneficiaries, the congregation.[71]

RELIGIOUS AND ECCLESIASTICAL CHARITABLE TRUSTS

Trust schemes, an important source of property for the Church of England, are regulated by a tangle of church-made and state-made law. Ordinarily, church-made law requires one authority to act as custodian or holding trustee and another to act as managing trustee; state-made law governs validity and the rights of beneficiaries; both state-made and church-made law govern the rights and duties of trustees over the use of trust property.

Validity

The charitable status of a trust is dependent on the proposed use of the trust property. A gift for the 'advancement of religion' will enjoy charitable status provided that an element of public benefit arises from the use of the trust property.[72] The concept of use is central and the gift is charitable only in so far as its objects serve that purpose.[73] The advancement of religion may be defined as the pastoral or missionary promotion of spiritual teaching in a wide sense, the maintenance of the doctrine upon which that teaching rests, and the maintenance of the observances, structures, and property necessary for its promotion.[74] An 'ecclesiastical charity' includes an endowment held for any lawful spiritual purpose, for the benefit of any spiritual person or ecclesiastical office, or for use by any church or denomination of a building as a church, chapel, mission room, Sunday school, or otherwise. It also includes property held for the maintenance, repair, or improvement of any such building or for the maintenance of divine service in it, or otherwise for the benefit of any particular church or denomination or any of its members.[75]

The element of public benefit is essential and is determined as a question of fact.[76] If subsidiary activities are not themselves religious the gift may never-

---

[71] Dealing as they do with a matter of property, the contract would be enforceable under the principle enunciated in *Forbes v Eden* (1867) LR 1 Sc & Div 568 (HL) as applied in *Buckley v Cahal Daly* (1991); whether the terms of an agreement would be enforceable by a third party beneficiary not privy to the agreement (e.g. a congregation member) is unclear.

[72] *Commissioners of Income Tax v Pemsel* [1891] AC 531.

[73] *Re White, White v White* [1893] 2 Ch 41 (CA); *Re Ward, Public Trustee v Berry* [1941] 2 All ER 125 (CA) (RC trust).

[74] *Keren Kayemouth Le Jisroel Ltd v IRC* [1931] 2 KB 465 at 477 (CA); *United Grand Lodge of Ancient Free and Accepted Masons of England v Holborn Borough Council* [1957] 3 All ER 281 at 285; see *supra* Ch. 9 for the meaning of 'religion'.

[75] Local Government Act 1894, s. 75(2); Charities Act 1993, s. 96.

[76] *Gilmour v Coats* [1949] 1 All ER 848; the case has been the subject of criticism: see H. Picarda, 'New religions as charities', *NLJ*, 131 (1983), 436.

theless retain its charitable status.[77] Furthermore, the courts have tended to the view that if the trust could be administered in a way which would benefit the public, but the trust property, under the terms of the trust, could be used in a way which would not benefit the public, then only charitable elements of the trust take effect.[78] A scheme which has as its object the propagation of a religion or religious practice which is subversive to morality may not be permitted as a matter of public policy.[79] A trust for superstitious purposes will not ordinarily enjoy charitable status, though judicial decisions applying this principle have usually concerned religion other than that promoted by the Church of England and the Roman Catholic Church.[80] Exceptionally, gifts associated with the veneration of relics or saints or miracles may enjoy charitable status; however, even if the superstition is legally acceptable the gift may not enjoy charitable status if public benefit cannot be established.[81] A gift for the celebration of masses for the dead, it seems, will not be void when the masses are celebrated in public.[82]

Consequently, gifts to 'the Church of England' or the 'Church of Rome' are charitable,[83] as are gifts to establish a bishopric, to provide for clergy, to increase their stipends, to preach a commemorative sermon, and to pay expenses of clergy societies.[84] The same applies to gifts to be used for the education of ordination candidates, for the relief of sick and aged clergy in a particular diocese, to a parish church for such objects connected with it as the minister shall think fit, for church expenses generally, and to provide an

[77] *Re Warre's Will Trusts, Wort v Salisbury Diocesan Board of Finance* [1953] 2 All ER 99: gift to create a retreat house for 'religious contemplation and the cleansing of the soul' of members of the Church of England did not have a sufficent public benefit; ancillary uses were not sufficiently subsidiary.

[78] *Re Hetherington* [1990] Ch. 1: saying of masses in public is charitable; the following have been held to be religious charities: gifts for the 'worship of God': *AG v Pearson* (1817) 3 Mer 353; for the distribution of Bibles: *AG v Stepney* (1804) 10 Ves 22; for organized pilgrimages: *Re McCarthy* [1958] IR 311; for the Church Missionary Society: *Re Clergy Society* (1856) 2 K & J 615; for the conversion of Roman Catholics to Protestantism: *AG v Becher* [1910] 2 IR 251; for the defence of the doctrines of the reformation: *Re Delmar Charitable Trust* [1897] 2 Ch 163; for the Sunday School Association: *R v Income Tax Special Commrs, ex p Essex Hall* [1911] 2 KB 434.

[79] *Bourne v Keane* [1919] AC 815 at 845 (HL).

[80] *Thornton v Howe* (1862) 31 Beav 14: a gift for the publishing and propagation of the sacred writings of Joanna Southcote, a 'patently demented visionary', held to be a religious charity.

[81] *Bourne v Keane* [1919] AC 815 at 855; *Gilmour v Coats* [1949] AC 426.

[82] *Re Caus, Lindeboom v Camille* [1934] Ch 162; followed in *Re Hetherington* [1990] Ch 1 (despite doubts expressed in *Gilmour v Coats* [1949] AC 426).

[83] *Re Barnes, Simpson v Barnes* [1930] 2 Ch 80; *Re Schoales, Schoales v Schoales* [1930] 2 Ch 75; see the Roman Catholic Diocese of Westminister *Parish Administration Manual* (1993), 8.5 for a model form of bequest for charitable purposes of a parish.

[84] *AG v Bishop of Chester* (1785) 1 Bro CC 444; *Pennington v Buckley* (1848) 6 Hare 451: gift for the benefit of unbeneficed curates; *Gibson v Representative Church Body* (1881) 9 LR Ir 1 and *Re Macnamara, Hewitt v Jones* (1911) 104 LT 771; *Re Parker's Charity* (1863) 32 Beav 654; *Re Charlesworth, Robinson v Archdeacon of Cleveland* (1910) 101 LT 908; *Re Randell* (1888) 38 Ch. D 213: clergy education; *Re Strickland* [1936] 3 All ER 1027: prizes for Sunday school.

organist or choristers.[85] However, gifts for 'parish work' are not charitable as may not be those for 'diocesan purposes' not being restricted to the advancement of religion.[86] When a gift is expressed to be made to the holder of a religious (or ecclesiastical) office it must be established that the property is not to be used as a gift only to the person currently holding the office but is to be held by that person and his successors in office as trustees.[87] Therefore, gifts to a minister and his successor, to a vicar and churchwardens 'for the time being', to the vicar of a named church for the use of his work in the parish, and to an archbishop to be used for such purposes as he should think fit are charitable.[88] On the other hand, where the holder of the charitable office is not given sole control over the use of the property, the presumption that its purposes are charitable is inoperative.[89] Gifts for the use of providing, maintaining, or decorating a place of religious worship are *prima facie* charitable as are gifts for the maintenance of churchyards, burial grounds, and parsonage houses.[90]

Administration: Duties and Accountability

The fundamental administrative duty of trustees is to give effect to the settlor's intentions as expressed in the trust instrument[91] (in so far as these are capable

[85] *Re Williams, Public Trustee v Williams* [1927] 2 Ch 283; *Re Forster, Gellatly v Palmer* [1939] Ch 22; *Re Bain, Public Trustee v Ross* [1930] 1 Ch 224, *Re Martley, Simpson v Cardinal Bourne* (1931) 47 TLR 392: for the benefit of the work of a cathedral, and *Re Eastes, Pain v Paxon* [1948] Ch 257: gift to the vicar and churchwardens of a particular church for any purposes in connection with it; *Re Scowcroft, Ormrod v Wilkinson* [1898] 2 Ch 638; *Re Royce, Turner v Wormold* [1940] 2 All ER 291.

[86] *Re Stratton, Knapman v AG* [1931] 1 Ch 197: gift to vicar 'for parochial institutions or purposes'; *Farley v Westminster Bank Ltd* [1939] AC 430; *Trustees of Cookstown Roman Catholic Church v IRC* [1953] 34 TC 350; *Re Rumball, Sherlock v Allan* [1956] Ch 105; cf. *Re Macgregor, Thompson v Ashton* (1932) 32 SR NSW 483: a gift for diocesan purposes was charitable.

[87] For the operation of the so-called 'O'Hagan clause' see *Re Meehan, Tobin and Tobin v Gohalan and Meehan* [1960] IR 82: a gift to a bishop for the time being; *Re Flinn, Public Trustee v Flinn* [1948] Ch 241.

[88] *Thornber v Wilson* (1855) 3 Drew 245: gift to the Roman Catholic minister of a particular chapel for a term of years; *Re Garrard, Gordon v Craigie* [1907] 1 Ch 382; *Re Simson, Fowler v Tinley* [1946] 2 All ER 220, distinguishing *Farley v Westminsiter Bank Ltd* [1939] AC 430; *Re Flinn, Public Trustee v Flinn* [1948] Ch 241: gift to a Roman Catholic archbishop, distinguishing *Re Davidson, Minty v Bourne* [1909] 1 Ch 567: gift to a Roman Catholic archbishop for the time being to be distributed between charitable, religious, or other societies in connection with the Roman Catholic faith in England.

[89] *Re Spensley's Will Trusts, Barclay's Bank Ltd v Staughton* [1954] 1 All ER 178 (CA); see also *Dunne v Byrne* [1912] AC 407: gift to a Roman Catholic archbishop and his successors to be used wholly or partly as he might judge appropriate to religion in his diocese was held not to be charitable.

[90] *Re Robertson, Colin v Chamberlin* [1930] 2 Ch 71; *Re Church Estate Charity, Wandsworth* (1871) 6 Ch App 296; *Re Barker, Sherrington v Dean and Chapter of St Paul's Cathedral* (1909) 25 TLR 753; *Re Vaughan, Vaughan v Thomas* (1886) 33 Ch D 187; *Re Manser, AG v Lucas* [1905] 2 Ch 184: Quaker burial ground; *AG v Bishop of Chester* (1785) 1 Bro CC 444; for gifts to provide flowers as charitable see *Elphinstone v Purchas* (1870) LR 3 A & E 66; *OLAC*, 44.

[91] Although trusts are usually created by written instrument, it is not essential for a religious charitable trust to be in writing to be enforced by the courts: Halsbury, *Laws of England*, Vol. 5(2), para. 65; Roman Catholic Charities Act 1860, s. 5.

of being carried out and not contrary to law).[92] Under civil law, when the original purposes of the trust have become redundant or are frustrated by initial or subsequent failure, an application may be made by the trustees to the Charity Commissioners or the High Court to establish a *cy près* scheme, provided there is evidence that the settlor had a paramount charitable intent,[93] to substitute purposes as near as possible to the purposes originally specified.[94] Some diocesan norms instruct trustees to consult the General Synod office before making an application.[95] By synodical measure, when a pastoral scheme unites one parish with another or alters the area of a parish, the purposes of a charity designed to benefit the original parish must be applied to the new parish.[96] Similarly, if the trust contains a condition as to the performance of divine service or any other act at a church, and the church ceases to be used for divine service, the condition is to be taken as referring to the parish church of the parish in which the specified church was situated.[97]

The civil law imposes a general duty on charity trustees to fulfil their responsibilities honestly and efficiently.[98] Whilst the trust instrument itself may provide for visitation by the settlor or some other designated person, general policing powers over religious charitable trustees are exercisable by the Charity Commissioners.[99] When trust property is vested in and managed by ecclesiastical authorities, oversight may also be effected through schemes operating under the internal law of the Church of England. Parochial trust property vested in diocesan authorities and administered by incumbents, churchwardens, or parochial church councils acting as managing trustees cannot be held on permanent trust, disposed of, or let without the consent of the custodian trustee; where the managing trustee administers a trust the diocesan authority has a right to be informed.[100] However, custodian trustees

---

[92] *AG v Calvert* (1857) 23 Beav 248; *Re Malling Abbey Trusts, Beaumont v Dale* [1915] 31 TLR 397: even when the settlor prescribes that only persons adhering to particular religious doctrine are to benefit.   [93] *Re Lysaght* [1966] Ch 191.

[94] E.g. *Re Robinson* [1923] 2 Ch 332: requirement that the preacher wear a black gown during services; *Re Rymer* [1895] 1 Ch 19: legacy to a Roman Catholic seminary in the diocese of Westminster closed before the death of testator; Charities Act 1993, s. 13: subsequent failure.

[95] *GDM*, C.2.   [96] Pastoral Measure 1983, Sched. 3, para. 11(5).

[97] Ibid., para. 11(9).

[98] G. Moffat and M. Chesterman, *Trusts Law: Texts and Materials* (London, 1988) 708 ff.

[99] Charities Act 1993, ss. 6–12; for the purposes of parochial trusts under *CRR*, r. 10(3)(c) no person may serve on a parochial church council if disqualified from being a charity trustee under the Charities Act 1993, s. 72.

[100] PCC(P)M, s. 6(1); Incumbents and Churchwardens (Trusts) Measure 1964, s. 2(3): any question as to whether personal property is held or to be held on permanent trust shall be determined by a person appointed by the bishop or during a vacancy by the guardian of spiritualities; the Charity Commissioners are not bound by any such determination; s. 3(1): where an incumbent, churchwarden, an ecclesiastical corporation, or a parochial church council hold, acquire, or administer any interest to which this measure applies, they must inform the diocesan authority thereof in writing; s. 3(6): the exercise by the diocesan authority of powers given under s. 3 shall not affect or prejudice the jurisdiction or powers of the High Court or the Charity Commissioners to establish a scheme for the administration of any charity to which this Measure

do not seem to possess specific powers to investigate how or whether managing trustees are fulfilling the terms of a trust; nor can the custodian trustee forbid a proposed investment.[101] Nevertheless, there seems to be no legal obstacle to the ordinary visitor of an ecclesiastical corporation policing the administration of a trust managed by that corporation,[102] and supervision may be effected by inspection of the terrier containing details of parochial trusts.[103] Indeed, diocesan norms are being developed which instruct managing trustees to 'pay careful regard to the terms under which the trust was established' and not 'to interpret the usage for trust funds as widely as possible'.[104] Whereas the Charity Commissioners may be directly involved in supervising parochial trusts, their supervisory powers are excluded in relation to ecclesiastical charities administered by the Church Commissioners and 'any institution which is administered by them'.[105]

Roman Catholic canon law also provides a system of supervision in relation to *inter vivos* charitable gifts and pious wills through the director of charities, an office of particular law, and under universal law through the diocesan bishop. The formalities of civil law must be met, otherwise the canonical obligation falls on 'the heirs [who] must be advised of the obligation by which they are bound to fulfil the will of the [donor]'. The legitimately accepted wills of the faithful who give or leave their resources to pious causes, through an act which becomes effective either during life or at death, are 'to be fulfilled with the greatest diligence even as regards the

applies or otherwise; s. 4: an incumbent or churchwarden may not acquire any interest in land or personal property to which the Measure applies 'except an interest in personal property by gift or under a will without the consent of the diocesan authority'.

[101] The problem is addressed in some diocesan norms: e.g. *BDM*, J.5: holding permanent trusts is a breach of ecclesiastical law and whilst the custodian trustee makes the investment the wishes of the managing trustee are paramount; see Chs. 15 and 17 for acquisition, disposal, investment, and accounting.

[102] See *post* for the terrier; also P. Smith, 'Points of law and practice concerning ecclesiastical visitations', *ELJ*, 2 (1990–2), 189 at 203; Pastoral Measure 1983, Sched. 3, para. 11 on pastoral schemes and re-vesting of trust property: 'Any question arising as to the application of any such property or the income thereof shall be referred to the bishop of the diocese, whose decision shall be final and conclusive.' Cathedrals Measure 1963, s. 11(e): cathedral constitutions may provide for 'the administration of . . . any trust fund applicable to any special purpose connected with the cathedral church'.

[103] Canon F17: every bishop must procure so far as he is able a full note and terrier of all lands, goods, and other possessions of the parochial churches and chapels therein, to be compiled and kept by the minister and churchwardens in accordance with instructions and forms prescribed from time to time by General Synod; the archdeacon must at least once in 3 years, either in person or by the rural dean, satisfy himself that this has been carried out in all parishes within his jurisdiction.

[104] *GDM*, C.2; *BDM*, J.5; *LDHI*, VIII, 8: responsibility for trust policy is placed on the diocesan secretary; *SDDH*, O.62: advice is available from the Diocesan Board of Finance Trusts Officer; see also *ODYB: IF*, 25. It has been proposed that *CRR* be amended to reflect the requirement in the Charities Act 1993 that every charity must report annually on its activities and that there must be financial statements, to be examined by the parochial church council, which have been independently audited: see draft Church Representation Rules (Amendment) Resolution 1995, GS 1174X.

[105] Charities Act 1993, Sched. 2.

manner of administration and distribution of the goods'. The ordinary is the executor of all pious wills whether they are made during life or on the occasion of death; the ordinary 'can and must exercise vigilance, even through visitation, so that pious wills are fulfilled' and other executors must render him an account concerning the performance of their duty. Moreover, a person who accepts the role of trustee must inform the ordinary of this trust and indicate all trust goods (movables and immovables) along with the obligations attached to them; if the donor expressly prohibits this, the person must not accept trusteeship. The ordinary must demand that goods held in trust be safeguarded and must exercise vigilance on behalf of the execution of the pious will. If, through no fault of the administrator, the fulfilment of the obligations becomes impossible (due to diminished income or some other reason) the ordinary can diminish them equitably after consultation with the interested parties and his finance council.[106]

Rights of Beneficiaries and Breach of Trust

Under civil law, the right to nominate a beneficiary belongs primarily to the settlor.[107] In order for a person to enforce the terms of the trust he must have *locus standi* as a beneficiary. Whether he does depends upon the intention of the settlor as expressed in the trust instrument. Various schemes have been devised to ascertain the settlor's intent. Under these the Church of England enjoys a considerable degree of privilege. First: when the settlor has not expressly named a particular religion, a trust created for the purpose of maintaining a church or for promoting the worship of God is presumed to be a trust for the advancement of the established religion of the Church of England.[108] Secondly, where the settlor establishes a trust for religious purposes generally it is presumed that he intended to benefit a religion to which he himself practised adherence; determining his intention is a question of fact.[109] Thirdly, where there is no expressed intention, or when the terms of the trust instrument are ambiguous, the settlor's intent must be ascertained by examination of extrinsic evidence.[110] When parishioners are the intended beneficiaries, 'parishioner' has been taken to mean a person occupying premises in the parish liable to be rated.[111] This rating system, of course, has been

---

[106] *CIC*, cc. 1299–1302,1310; D. J. Ward, 'Trust management under the new code of canon law', *The Jurist*, 44 (1984), 134; P. Zielinski, 'Pious wills and mass stipends in relation to canons 1299–1310', *Studia Canonica*, 19 (1985), 115.   [107] *AG v Leigh* (1721) 3 P Wins 145.

[108] *AG v Pearson* (1817) 3 Mer 353 at 409; *AG v Calvert* (1857) 23 Beav 248 at 258; when, however, the religious charity is eleemosynary (where a named college is to benefit, for example) then the presumption is that the settlor intended to benefit persons of all religious persuasions: *AG v St John's Hospital, Bath* (1876) 2 Ch D 554.   [109] *Shore v Wilson* (1842) 9 Cl & Fin 355.

[110] *Drummond v AG for Ireland* (1849) 2 HL Cas 837.

[111] *Etherington v Wilson* (1875) 1 Ch D 160; *Kensit v Rector of St Ethelburga, Bishopsgate Within* [1900] P 80.

replaced and the effect upon this of the council tax, introduced in 1993, is now unclear.[112] Indeed, where a charitable intention is clearly identified but the objects are uncertain, the gift will not automatically fail.[113] With the exception of charities administered by the Church Commissioners and any institution administered by them, prospective beneficiaries normally have a right of access to documents describing the trust, including, with regard to parochial trusts, access to the terrier.[114]

Failure to fulfil the duties of trusteeship may constitute a breach of trust under civil law; sanctions depend on the nature and gravity of the breach.[115] Ordinarily the sanctions arising under the Charities Act 1993 apply to trustees of any religious charity.[116] With regard to breaches of trusts by incumbents, churchwardens, and parochial church councils, as managing trustees they must keep the custodian trustee indemnified in respect of all costs, proceedings, and demands.[117] When the trustee is an ordained person, it is unclear whether a breach of trust would be neglect of duty sufficient to constitute an ecclesiastical offence; whilst general duties of trusteeship are imposed not by ecclesiastical law but by civil law, neglect of duties specially imposed by synodical measure may be subject to proceedings in the church courts.[118] The provisions of the Charities Act 1993 do not apply to ecclesiastical charities of the Church of England administered by the Church Commissioners 'and any institution which is administered by them'.[119]

CARE AND MAINTENANCE: REPAIRS

Roman Catholic canon law states that '[a]ll whose concern it is are to take care that such cleanliness and propriety is preserved in churches as befits the house of God and that anything which is out of keeping with the sanctity of the place is precluded'; in the repair of churches the principles and norms of the liturgy and of sacred art are to be observed with the advice of experts; beyond these requirements, internally maintenance is a matter for particular law designed to retain ecclesiastical exemption.[120] The Church of England's rules dealing with

---

[112] Local Government Act 1992.   [113] Charities Act 1993, s. 16.

[114] They may consult the register of charities: Charities Act 1993, s. 2.

[115] Charities Act 1993, s. 75; for charity accounts, ss. 19–27; s. 73: removal on grounds of criminal conviction, bankruptcy, mental incapacity, failure or unwillingness to act, and absence; s. 24: giving advice.

[116] See generally H. Picarda, *The Law and Practice Relating to Charities* (London, 1977).

[117] PCC(P)M, s. 6(4)(d).

[118] See *supra* Ch. 7 for neglect of duty; Pastoral Measure 1983, s. 74: with respect to suspended or vacant benefices, property is to be managed by the minister-in-charge.

[119] Charities Act 1993, Sched. 2.

[120] *CIC*, cc. 1218, 1220; the vicar forane must ensure that 'the good appearance and condition of the churches and of sacred furnishings are carefully maintained especially in the celebration of the Eucharist and the custody of the Blessed Sacrament, that the parish books are correctly inscribed

care and maintenance are best analysed according to types of property. The law has undergone radical reform in recent years and is supplemented by a series of codes of practice and diocesan norms. Though one of the achievements of the legislators has been the meticulous distribution of duties of care, remarkably it makes no systematic provision for the standard of care which must be attained beyond the unspecified (and therefore arguably subjective) standards sought by those bodies entrusted with the function of supervision.

Cathedrals

Any body charged with the care and maintenance of a cathedral 'shall in exercising those functions have due regard to the fact that the cathedral church is the seat of the bishop and a centre of worship and mission'.[121] The cathedral statutes and constitution must provide that all the functions of the capitular body in relation to property shall be delegated to the administrative body.[122] The statutes and constitution must make provision for the appointment of a cathedral architect and the administrative body must appoint an archeological consultant.[123] The administrative body must ensure that the architect (in consultation with the consultant) prepare every five years a written report dealing with works which are considered necessary to be executed as soon as possible; the administrative body must keep a record of all works executed on the cathedral church and its precincts.[124] The administrative body is also required to provide for periodic inspection of all buildings, other than the cathedral church or ancillary buildings, which the capitular body is required to repair, being buildings situated within the cathedral close or allocated as residences for those holding office in the cathedral church.[125]

The administrative body of a cathedral church must not carry out works on,

and cared for, that ecclesiastical goods are carefully administered, and finally that the rectory is maintained with proper care': c. 555(3). The Diocese of Westminster *Parish Administration Manual* (1993), ch. 5 makes provision for log books, and ch. 10 for the role of a Property Service Office and quinquennial surveys and reports; 10. 3 prescribes the role of the Diocesan Liturgical Commission which must be consulted when re-ordering of a church is proposed; for the Historic Churches Committee see 10.4.

[121] Care of Cathedrals Measure 1990, s. 1; for a short study of the background to the Measure see the Chichester Report, *Care of Churches and Cathedrals* (1984) and J. W. Bullimore, 'Where now the draft Care of Cathedrals measure?', *ELJ*, 1(3) (1988), 24; for recent recommendations concerning the governing legislation see the Report of the Archbishops' Commission on Cathedrals, *Heritage and Renewal* (London, 1994) 115 at 127.

[122] Cathedrals Measure 1963, s. 10(1)(h).

[123] Ibid., s. 10(1)(k); if the Cathedrals Fabric Commission notifies that the archeological significance of the cathedral does not warrant the appointment of an archeological consultant, one need not be appointed: Care of Cathedrals Measure 1990, s. 14(1).

[124] Care of Cathedrals Measure 1990, s. 14(1), (2); for the meaning of 'precincts' see *OLAC*, 30–6: 'precinct' is that area indicated on the plan by the Cathedrals Fabric Commission pursuant to s. 13(4) of the Care of Cathedrals Measure 1990 and refers to 'land in the immediate environs of the cathedral and of which the cathedral is the focus'.   [125] Cathedrals Measure 1963, s. 27.

above, or below land vested in the capitular body which would materially affect the architectural, archeological, artistic, or historic character of the cathedral church (or any building within its precinct which for the time being is used for ecclesiastical purposes). Nor must it carry out such work affecting the immediate setting of the cathedral or any archeological remains within the precinct.[126] It may, however, carry out works in furtherance of its duties under ths statutes and constitution with respect to the ordering of services and in furtherance of the mission of the cathedral, works of a temporary nature, and works which do not affect the fabric of the cathedral.[127] The process of authorizing work proposed by the administrative body involves the participation of the cathedral's own Fabric Advisory Committee, which must be established by the administrative body, and a central authority, the Cathedrals Fabric Commission.[128] It is the duty of the Fabric Advisory Committee to advise the administrative body on the care, conservation, repair, and development of the cathedral church and to consider and determine any application to it by that body.[129] The duties of the Cathedrals Fabric Commission are: to advise the administrative body and the Fabric Advisory Committee on the care, conservation, repair, and development of the cathedral church; to consider and determine any application made to it by the administrative body; and to promote co-operation between the Commission and organizations concerned with the care and study of buildings of architectural, archeological, artistic, or historic interest in England. The Commission is also under a duty to assist administrative bodies by participating in educational and research projects to promote the care, conservation, repair, or development of cathedral churches and their ancillary buildings and to maintain jointly with the Council for the Care of Churches a library of books, plans, drawings, photographs, and other material relating to cathedral churches and the objects in them.[130]

In the first instance proposals must be submitted to the Fabric Advisory Committee for approval. The Committee has power, after consultation with the administrative body and subject to the agreement of the Commission, to

---

[126] Care of Cathedrals Measure 1990, s. 2(1); s. 16: General Synod's Standing Committee must appoint a Cathedral (Rules) Committee which may make such rules as it considers necessary or desirable to give effect to the Measure and these may make provision for any matter of procedure arising under the Measure; see Care of Cathedral Rules 1990 (SI 1990 No. 2335).

[127] Care of Cathedrals Measure 1990, s. 2(2).

[128] S. 3(1); a parish church cathedral may opt to come within the faculty jurisdiction, in which case the following procedures do not apply (s. 18); for composition of the Commission see Sched. 1; the Commission may also give advice to the Council for the Care of Churches: s. 11; s. 4(1); for the administrative body's duty to keep an inventory see s. 13.

[129] S. 4(2); it is composed of between 3 and 5 members appointed by the administrative body (being either clerks in holy orders or persons employed by the body) and between 3 and 5 members appointed by the Cathedrals Fabric Commission (which must consult the body before appointment) with special knowledge of the care and maintenance of buildings of outstanding architectural or historic interest and a particular interest in the cathedral concerned: Sched. 2, para. 1; the dean, provost, and residentiary canons may attend and speak but not vote: ibid., para. 3.

[130] S. 3(2).

determine that approval for proposals need not be given and to vary or revoke any such determination.[131] If the administrative body wishes to have it determined whether the proposal is one for which approval must be obtained, the Fabric Advisory Committee is empowered to determine that question.[132] When an application is made the chapter clerk must display a notice stating that details of the proposal are available for inspection and that written representations may be made to the Fabric Advisory Committee; the chapter clerk is under a further duty to notify the Commission; where the proposals involve works on, above, or below land the fee simple in which is vested in the chapter of the cathedral church, and when those works will materially affect the architectural, archeological, artistic, or historic character of the cathedral church (or any building within the precinct) the chapter clerk must also notify the local planning authority.[133] The Fabric Advisory Committee is under a duty to consider written representations in determining whether to approve (unconditionally or conditionally) or to reject the application.[134] In the event of a refusal, or if the committee approves subject to conditions, the administrative body may appeal to the Cathedrals Fabric Commission which can confirm, reverse, or vary the Committee's determination; if the Commission refuses to approve, or refuses to reverse the determination of the Committee, or refuses to vary conditions imposed by the Committee, the administrative body has a right to request that the Commission's decision be reviewed; it may be reversed, varied, or confirmed by a Commission of Review.[135]

When the proposal involves permanent alterations to the fabric of the cathedral or precinct buildings, the demolition of any part of these, the disturbance or destruction of any archeological remains, or the sale, loan, or other disposal of any object (of outstanding architectural, archeological, artistic, or historic interest), an application for approval must be made to the Cathedrals Fabric Commission; an application for approval of any other proposal is made to the Committee.[136] There are similar provisions for publication of the proposal and written representations to the Commission, which it must consider.[137] The Commission must determine whether to approve (unconditionally or conditionally) or reject the application.[138] The

---

[131] S. 5(1).   [132] S. 5(2).

[133] S. 7(1); i.e. the local planning authority must be notified of works listed in s. 2(1).

[134] S. 7(2); the Committee secretary must send notice of its decision to the administrative body and if appropriate to the local planning authority: s. 7(3).

[135] Ss. 9, 10(1)(b); for the constitution of the Commission of Review see s. 10(2), (4)–(7).

[136] S. 6(1); if the administrative body or the Committee wishes to have determined to which body an application is to be made, the Commission 'shall have power to determine that question': s. 6(2); for notices required in each application procedure see ss. 7, 8.

[137] S. 8: the chapter clerk must display the proposals and send notice of the proposals to the cathedral's Fabric Advisory Committee, English Heritage, and the national amenity societies.

[138] S. 8(2); it must notify the administrative body, the Fabric Advisory Committee, English Heritage, the national amenities societies, and the Royal Commission on the Historical Monuments of England: s. 8(3).

administrative body has a right of appeal against a refusal (or against conditions imposed on approval) to a Commission of Review which may reverse, confirm, or vary the decision or any part thereof.[139]

Any actual or threatened contravention by an administrative body of these procedures may be dealt with in the first instance at interview by the bishop who may then order a special visitation; the administrative body is under a duty to obey an episcopal direction made either before the bishop conducts the interview or after he has ordered a special visitation (but before the actual hearing) or after a special visitation. The bishop may also seek from the Vicar-General an injunction or a restoration order, if he considers it necessary or expedient, which the administrative body is obliged to obey.[140]

Parochial Church Buildings

Responsibility for the care and maintenance of parochial church buildings is shared by the diocese and the parish. Any body or person carrying out functions of care and maintenance must have 'due regard to the role of the church as a local centre of worship and mission'.[141] Care and maintenance are organized and regulated by arrangements which ensure the availability of expert advice, by duties to maintain imposed directly upon the parish, by oversight through the diocesan ordinary, and by systems of regular inspection.

First, the law provides that expert advice about care and maintenance is to be supplied by a diocesan advisory committee for the care of churches established in each diocese.[142] The committee has a duty when requested to give advice to the diocesan bishop, chancellor, archdeacons, parochial church councils, intending faculty applicants, the diocesan pastoral committee, persons engaged in planning, designing, or building new places of public worship (not being buildings within the jurisdiction of the consistory court), and 'such other persons as the committee may consider appropriate'.[143] It must act in this

---

[139] Ss. 9, 10. For the composition of the Commission of Review see s. 10(3).

[140] Care of Cathedrals (Supplementary Provisions) Measure 1994, ss. 1–8; *supra* Ch. 4.

[141] CCEJM, s. 1; for the idea in diocesan norms that the church 'belongs' to successive generations see e.g. *TBF*, 6.3; *SDH*, II, A.1; *GDM*, D.1, though this role is not the paramount consideration: *Re St Luke the Evangelist, Maidstone* [1994] 3 WLR 1165.

[142] CCEJM, s. 2(1); Sched. 1 sets out its written constitution: a chairman (appointed by the bishop), the diocesan archdeacons, and not less than 12 other members, 2 appointed from the bishop's council from among the elected members of the diocesan synod, and not less than 10 others appointed by the bishop's council having *inter alia* knowledge of the history, development, and use of church buildings, of the church's liturgy and worship, of architecture, archeology, art, and history, and experience of the care of historic buildings and their contents; s. 15 requires the chancellor to consult the DAC. For judicial discussion of the DAC's duty to give good advice see *Re St Mary, Sullington* [1991] *ELJ*, 3 (1993), 117, and for the committee's relationship to the consistory court, *Re St Andrew, Cheadle Hulme* [1993] *ELJ*, 3 (1994), 255.

[143] CCEJM, Sched. 2, para. 2; for its model code of business and procedure see *CCEJM: CP*, para. 120 and App. 5; a chancellor should normally follow the advice of the DAC in aesthetic matters: *Re St Mary, Sullington* [1991] *ELJ*, 3 (1993), 117.

advisory capacity in relation to grants of faculties; the architecture, archeology, art, and history of places of worship; the use, care, planning, design, and redundancy of these; the use and care of their contents; and the use and care of churchyards and burial grounds.[144] It must also review and assess the degree of risk to materials arising from any proposals relating to the conservation, repair, or alteration of places of worship, churchyards and burial grounds, and their contents, and keep records relating to its work.[145]

Secondly, by canon 'churches and chapels in every parish shall be decently kept and from time to time, as occasion may require, shall be well and sufficiently repaired and all things therein shall be maintained in such an orderly and decent fashion as best becomes the House of God'.[146] By synodical measure the care and maintenance of a church still in use is the responsibility of the parochial church council.[147] Fulfilment of this duty is supervised by the ordinary: it is the duty of the minister and churchwardens, if any repairs are proposed, to obtain a faculty or licence of the ordinary before proceeding to execute the repair.[148] The diocesan chancellor is under a duty to give written guidance to all parochial church councils, ministers, and churchwardens in the diocese 'as to those matters within the jurisdiction of the consistory court which he for the time being considers, after consultation with the diocesan advisory committee, to be of such a minor nature that they may be undertaken without a faculty'.[149] The diocesan chancellor is empowered to confer on an archdeacon the jurisdiction of the consistory court in faculty matters relating to the archdeaconry to such extent and in such manner as may be prescribed; the archdeacon by delegation, therefore, 'shall have power to grant a faculty in any cause of faculty falling to be considered by him which is unopposed'; if he refuses to grant, or considers that the matter should be dealt with as a matter of urgency without reference to the advisory

---

[144] CCEJM, Sched. 2, para. 1(a).   [145] Ibid., para. 1(b), (c).

[146] F13(1); Endowments and Glebe Measure 1976, s. 39: liability to repair, or pay a contribution towards the cost of repairing, a chancel falls on the parochial church council; for the duty to maintain the font, the holy table, communion plate and linen, and surplices see Canons F1–5; F14: the cost of repairs is to be borne by the parochial church council; the number of cases in which a lay rector continues to be liable for chancel repairs has diminished by virtue of the Ecclesiastical Dilapidations Measure 1923, s. 52 and by the Tithe Act 1936. For cases when a lay rector is still liable see *OLAC*, 39.

[147] PCC(P)M, s. 4(1)(ii)(b): its powers, duties, and liabilities attach to the 'care maintenance preservation and insurance of the fabric of the church and the goods and ornaments thereof'; the council is liable only to the extent of funds available for repairs: *Veley v Pertwee* (1870) LR 5 QB 573; for insurance see *post* Ch. 17. For the archdeacon's power to execute repairs and charge the parish see below.

[148] F13(3): archdeacons no longer have power to grant certificates for minor works (Faculty Jurisdiction Measure 1964, s. 12 repealed; all faculties granted under this power remain in force as if they were faculties granted under CCEJM, s. 14); see *Re St Thomas à Becket, Framfield* [1989] 1 All ER 170 at 173 for churchwardens' liability to ensure faculty is obtained.

[149] CCEJM, s.11(8); diocesan norms commonly contain lists of repairs not requiring faculty: e.g. *SDDH*, N.2; *ODYB: IF*, 241; *BDM*, K.1; *SDH* II, A.2.

committee, or if the grant is opposed, the archdeacon must refer the matter to the diocesan chancellor.[150] By canon, a record of all repairs executed must be kept[151] and by synodical measure the churchwardens must compile and maintain a terrier appertaining to the church, an inventory of all articles appertaining to the church, and a log-book with full notes of all alterations, additions, and repairs to the church, lands, and articles appertaining to it.[152]

Thirdly, the obligation of sufficient maintenance is policed by two systems of inspection.[153] A primary duty of inspection is imposed on the churchwardens. They must, at least once in every year, inspect or cause an inspection to be made of the fabric of the church and all articles appertaining to it. Each year they must deliver to the parochial church council (and on behalf of the council to the annual parochial church meeting) an annual fabric report and an account of all actions taken or proposed during the previous year for the protection and maintenance of property. In carrying out these duties the churchwardens must act in consultation with the minister.[154] Moreover, under the Inspection of Churches Measure 1955 the diocesan synod must establish a scheme to provide for the inspection of every church in the diocese at least once every five years.[155] Every scheme must provide for the establishment of a fund (by means of contributions from parochial, diocesan, and other sources) to be used for the cost of inspection. Schemes must also provide for the appointment of a qualified architect or surveyor approved by the diocesan advisory committee to inspect the churches and to report on every church inspected; copies of the report must be sent to the archdeacon, the incumbent, the parochial church council, and the secretary of the advisory committee.[156] If an inspection has not been made for over five years, or is in his opinion unsatisfactory, the archdeacon can arrange another with the consent of the bishop.[157] The archdeacon is also under a duty at the annual visitation to survey in person or by deputy all church chancels within the archdeaconry.[158]

If a parochial church council fails to fulfil its duties of care and maintenance, a variety of powers is available to the consistory court and the archdeacon. The chancellor may issue an injunction to restrain unlawful acts, make a restoration order, and he may order a party to faculty proceedings to pay resulting costs

---

[150] S. 14. The archdeacon cannot, however, make an order for costs or expenses, nor issue an injunction or make a restoration order.

[151] F13(3): the record must indicate where specifications and plans may be inspected if not deposited with the book.   [152] CCEJM, s. 4.

[153] Diocesan norms commonly repeat these provisions: *LDHI*, V, 5; *SDH*, II, A.5; *TBF*, 6.1; *SDDH*, O.36–9; *CDH*, 11; *BDM*, K.1; *GDM*, D.2–4.   [154] CCEJM, s. 5.

[155] Inspection of Churches Measure 1955, s. 1 (as amended by CCEJM, s. 3, Sched. 3; where no scheme has been made it is the responsibility of the bishop to establish a scheme: ibid., para. 3; the inspection must include notable 'movable articles').   [156] S. 1(1), (2).

[157] S. 2; s. 3: the cost of the archdeacon's inspection is covered by the diocesan synod's fund; where a parish has no council, the appropriate authority is the churchwarden: s. 4.

[158] C22(5).

and expenses.[159] The archdeacon has a duty to direct 'the amendment of all defects in the walls, fabric, ornaments and furniture'.[160] If the direction is disobeyed, the archdeacon may apply for a faculty to carry out the repairs himself, or for a faculty in default, in which case an order can be made to cover expenses; failure to obey the order may constitute contempt of court.[161] The archdeacon is also empowered to summon an extraordinary meeting of the parochial church council to discuss defaults.[162] Special rules apply to the maintenance of redundant churches.[163]

Churchyards

Similar provisions for advice, oversight by the ordinary (through the faculty jurisdiction), keeping records of repairs, and inspection apply to churchyards.[164] Consecrated churchyards must be maintained in 'such an orderly and decent manner as becomes consecrated ground'.[165] The primary responsibility for the maintenance of a churchyard, open or closed, falls on the parochial church council.[166] Under the Local Government Act 1972 maintenance may be made the subject of an agreement with a local authority which will contribute towards the cost of maintenance.[167] In the case of closed churchyards, the parochial church council has a right to transfer the responsibility for maintenance to the local civil authorities.[168] As it comes within the jurisdiction of the ordinary a faculty must be obtained to authorize substantial repairs.[169]

The parochial church council is under a canonical duty to fence churchyards; the maintenance of fences is 'at the charge of those in whom by law or custom liability belongs'.[170] Similarly, under synodical measure the parochial council has a duty to maintain trees in a churchyard including those proposed to be planted.[171] The duty to keep the churchyard in decent order does not

---

[159] S. 13; see also Faculty Jurisdiction Rules 1992 and Faculty Jurisdiction (Injunctions and Restoration Orders) Rules 1992 (SI 1992 Nos. 2882, 2884).   [160] C22(5).
[161] CCEJM, ss. 12, 13, 16.   [162] S. 20.   [163] *Supra* Ch. 15.
[164] The rules applicable depend on the status of the churchyard in question: consecrated churchyards adjacent to a church designated for burial may be open or closed (Burial Act 1853, s. 1 as amended by Local Government Act 1972, s. 272; see *supra* Ch. 14) or used or disused (Open Spaces Acts 1887, s. 4, and 1906, s. 29); for unconsecrated churchyards see *Re St Peter's, Bushey Heath* [1971] 1 WLR 357. The consistory court enjoys faculty jurisdiction over both: Faculty Jurisdiction Measure 1964, s. 7 (unconsecrated land forming part of the curtilage falls within the jurisdiction); see also CCEJM, s. 11: faculty jurisdiction covers all parish churches 'and the churchyards and articles appertaining thereto'.   [165] Canon F13(1), (2); *OLAC*, 52.
[166] PCC(P)M, s. 4(1)(ii)(c).   [167] S. 214(6), (8); *OLAC*, 51.
[168] Local Government Act 1972, ss. 215, 272; *OLAC*, 63–5: faculty jurisdiction continues; 66–9: local authorities' responsibilities.   [169] F13(3).
[170] F13(2).
[171] CCEJM, s. 6(1); when a tree maintainable by the council is felled, lopped, or topped the council may sell or otherwise dispose of the timber and the net proceeds of sale must be paid to the council and applied for the maintenance of the church: s. 6(2); the chancellor may issue guidance: s. 6(3); *CCEJM: CP*, paras. 83–9, recommends that the diocesan advisory committee issue guidance on the subject.

extend to the ordinary maintenance of monuments: the primary responsibility for their repair falls on their owner.[172] Diocesan norms often instruct councils to create rules encouraging next-of-kin to maintain the graves of relatives.[173] If the parochial church council wishes to remove a monument the owner's permission must be obtained; if this is withheld, or the owner cannot be traced, a faculty may be granted authorizing the repair, removal, or demolition of a monument.[174] In the opinion of the Legal Advisory Commission, the parochial church council has no duty nor any general power to cut grass; however, if the owner of herbage allows it to become an obstruction to parishioners making proper use of the churchyard, the churchwardens and the parochial church council should apply to the ordinary for permission to put the churchyard in order by cutting the herbage.[175] A Code of Practice applicable to the two provinces encourages parochial church councils to formulate 'a proper plan' for the maintenance of churchyards to be reviewed annually. The code of practice recommends the creation of a churchyard committee or a churchyard officer 'to carry forward the plan on a day-to-day basis, in collaboration with the minister' with a duty to report to the council and 'be subject to its directions'.[176]

Parsonages (and Other Benefice Property)

The Repair of Benefice Buildings Measure 1972 provides for the repair of parsonage houses held by the diocesan parsonages board, and other buildings belonging to a benefice. As a general principle, the responsibility for the care and maintenance of a parsonage house is shared by the incumbent and the diocese. For the purposes of the Measure 'repairs' is defined as such works of repair or replacement as are needed 'to keep in repair the structure and exterior of the buildings of the parsonage house' and to keep in repair and proper

---

[172] *OLAC*, 54. If the owners cannot be traced the responsibility to keep the churchyard in a safe state means that the parochial church council 'must bear the responsibility for dangerous monuments'.

[173] *SDH*, II, B.6; *GDM*, D.13 for the diocesan chancellor's regulations. *CCEJM: CP*, para. 75: with regard to tombstones and memorials, 'The primary responsibility for their condition rests with the person who erected [them]'; 'after that person's death . . . with the heirs of the person commemorated . . . there is no way of compelling them to maintain [them], except possibly where it is a danger to the public. For this reason it may be appropriate to require a donation to the upkeep . . . as a condition for a faculty' authorizing its erection. The council may be liable if injury is suffered as a result of lack of maintenance: *OLAC*, 56 ff.

[174] Faculty Jurisdiction Measure 1964, ss. 3, 4.

[175] *OLAC*, 50, 51; the rector of an ancient parish church had originally the right to the herbage but this right has generally devolved to the vicar; in either case the right is absolute subject to the user of the churchyard as a burial ground (*Greenslade v Darby* (1868) LR 3 QB 421 at 429) and the jurisdiction of the ordinary.

[176] *CCEJM: CP*, para.75; see generally P. Burman and H. Stapleton, *The Churchyards Handbook* (3rd edn., London, 1988); the advice is often repeated in diocesan norms: e.g. *SDH*, II, B.7; *SDDH*, N.2, M.24; *BDM*, K.8.

working order installations and fixtures, fittings, and appliances, including 'works of interior decoration necessitated in consequence of such works'.[177] Unusually, the Measure speaks of the 'standard of care'; however, it does not elucidate the concept beyond the requirement that '[i]n determining . . . the standard of care appropriate to any building of a benefice, regard shall be had to the age, character and prospective life of the building, and . . . the special architectural or historic interest of the building'.[178]

A scheme similar to that for church buildings is to be instituted. Every diocesan synod must provide by scheme either for the appointment of a parsonages board or for designating the diocesan board of finance to discharge the functions of a parsonage board; every scheme must also provide for the appointment of fit persons to be surveyors and determine their remuneration.[179] The parsonages board, a body corporate composed of all archdeacons and clerics elected by beneficed and licensed diocesan clergy and lay persons, has power to hold property, borrow money, execute works, and such other ancillary powers as are provided by the diocesan synod's scheme. The board must present an annual report and accounts to the diocesan synod and send a copy to the Church Commissioners, and it is under a duty to 'comply with any such directions as may be given to [it] by resolution of the diocesan synod'.[180]

It is the duty of the board to cause an inspection to be made by a diocesan surveyor of all the buildings of each diocesan benefice every five years; a report of the inspection must be sent by the surveyor to the board stating *inter alia* what repairs are required, the cost and urgency of repairs (including interior decoration), whether improvements are expedient, and whether the house should be replaced; a copy of the report must be sent by the board to the incumbent stating his right to make representations. The board is under a duty to consider any representations duly made by the incumbent and must, if he so desires, give him an opportunity of meeting the board (or a committee or representative of it).[181] It is the duty of the board to carry out repairs specified in the report; work on repairs 'immediately necessary' must be commenced within a year of confirmation of the report and must be completed 'as soon as possible'; other works must be executed within such period as is recommended by the report or, if no period is recommended, as the board thinks expedient.[182]

---

[177] S. 2(1).

[178] S. 2(2): the latter provision is included 'in the case of a building included in a list under s. 54 of the Town and Country Planning Act 1971'.   [179] S. 1(1), (2).

[180] S. 1(4), (5), (7), (8): under s. 1(9) if the diocesan board of finance is the designated board, its functions may be delegated to a committee reflecting 'adequate representation of the clergy and laity'.   [181] S. 4.

[182] S. 5(1): the incumbent has a right to make representations. The board must notify him of its decision and he may appeal to the Church Commissioners: s. 5(2), (3).

Provision exists for interim inspection and repairs, as well as powers of entry to carry out inspections and repairs.[183]

The incumbent has a duty 'to take proper care of a parsonage house, being a duty equivalent to that of a tenant to use premises in a tenant-like manner'.[184] The incumbent must notify the board of any repairs appearing necessary to him and, with respect to urgent repairs needed for reasons of safety or to prevent further damage or deterioration, or to meet a liability to other persons, he must notify without delay.[185] The incumbent may as agent of the board carry out such repairs as the board may generally or specifically authorize.[186] Ordinarily, the cost of repairs is to be met by the board from the parsonages fund.[187] However, where the surveyor's report (periodic or interim) reveals that any repairs are necessary 'by reason of damage caused or aggravated by any deliberate act of the incumbent or a previous incumbent or any default of his duties [to take proper care]' the board may on completion of the repairs by notice require the incumbent or his personal representative to pay all or part of the cost of repair attributable to the incumbent's act or default; the board may take proceedings to enforce it.[188] During a vacancy the general responsibility for care and maintenance rests with the bishop but the duty to take proper care of the house rests, by diocesan norms, with the churchwardens.[189] The liability of incumbents to make payments towards to cost of repairing glebe buildings has been abolished; the responsibility for repairs now lies with the board.[190]

Objects, Records, and Registers

Whilst ownership is vested in the churchwardens, the responsibility for the care and maintenance of the 'goods and ornaments' of a church is by synodical measure placed on the parochial church council.[191] The parochial church council's duty to maintain movables decently applies to fonts, holy tables,

---

[183] Ss. 8, 11; for the board's duty to obtain insurance see s. 12.

[184] S. 13(1); the duties of the board do not affect any liability of the incumbent as owner, tenant, or occupier to persons other than the board; but the board must indemnify him in respect of any claim by such a person or any expense incurred by reason of such liability if the claim or expenses arise out of the execution of or failure to execute repairs; liability to his successor is excluded: s. 13(2).   [185] S. 13(3).

[186] S. 13(5).

[187] S. 17; for the board's power to pay rates and other outgoings see s. 16; see also *post* Ch. 17 for contributions to the fund made, *inter alia*, by the parochial church council.

[188] S. 13(4).

[189] S. 26: during vacancy these functions vest in the sequestrators or, if not under sequestration, with the bishop; s. 13(1) and (4) duties vest in the churchwardens: *SDH*, III, V.4; for managing trustees' duty to maintain trust property see *OLAC*, 207.

[190] Endowments and Glebe Measure 1976, s. 28.

[191] PCC(P)M, s. 4(1)(ii)(b); for ownership see *supra* Ch. 15.

communion linen, surplices, pulpits, and seats.[192] The same regime for advice concerning maintenance and repair, oversight, inspection, and enforcement as applies to the church applies also to its contents.[193] On vacating office churchwardens are under a duty to 'deliver to their successors any goods of the church remaining in their hands together with the . . . inventory, which shall be checked by their successors'.[194]

Archdeacons have power to order the removal of valuable articles to places of safe keeping. If it appears to an archdeacon that any article appertaining to a church in his archdeaconry which he considers to be of architectural, artistic, historical, or archeological value is exposed to danger of loss or damage and ought to be removed to a place of safety, he may order that the article in question shall be removed from the church and deposited in such place as may be specified in the order.[195] Unless the archdeacon is of the opinion that the article should be removed immediately, he is under a duty to notify the churchwardens, any other person having custody of it, the parochial church council, and the diocesan advisory committee of the facts as they appear to him, and inform them that he will consider any written representations made by them (before a date specified in the notice). When he makes an order without such notice he is under a duty to notify the committee of the removal as soon as practicable thereafter. If a person upon whom notice is served refuses or fails to comply with the order the archdeacon may apply to the consistory court for an order for delivery to a safe place. After removal the archdeacon must apply for a faculty authorizing retention in the place of safety. These provisions do not apply to records or registers.[196]

Both the Roman Catholic Church and the Church of England operate a complex system for the keeping and maintenance of records. Under Roman Catholic canon law each parish must possess parish books including baptismal, marriage, and death registers as well as registers prescribed by the conference of bishops or the diocesan bishop: it is for the pastor to ensure that these are adequately inscribed and carefully preserved in a registry or archive.[197] In the

---

[192] Canon F1: provide a 'decent font with a cover for the keeping clean thereof'; F2: the holy table 'shall be kept in a sufficient and seemly manner, and from time to time repaired'; F3: communion plate must be 'kept washed and clean'; F4: communion linen must be 'maintained'; F5: surplices 'shall be . . . maintained in a clean condition'; F6: unless it is not required, 'a decent pulpit'; F7 does not mention maintenance of seats but only their provision; if a person has a right to a pew, responsibility for repair falls on that person: *Crisp v Martin* (1876) LR 2 Eq 643; for diocesan norms regulating repairs to organs (and occasional provision for the position of diocesan organ adviser) see e.g. *TBF*, 6.3; *WDHI*, ch. 4, 223; *SDDH*, O.31–3.; for repairs to bells see e.g. *WDDH*, ch. 4, 223, *SDDH*, O.21.   [193] See above.

[194] Canon E1(5).

[195] CCEJM, s. 21(1); *CCEJM: CP*, para. 64 recommends that valuable items be deposited in cathedral repositories; for diocesan norms concerning security see above.

[196] CCEJM, s. 21(2)–(7).

[197] *CIC*, c. 535; see also cc. 877, 895, 1054 (baptisms), c. 788 (catechumens), c. 895 (confirmations), cc. 1121, 1133 (marriages), c. 1053 (ordinations), cc. 955, 958 (mass offerings), c. 1182 (deaths), c. 1082 (dispensations); for curial documents see cc. 490–1, 1284, 1339, and for diocesan documents cc. 474–491; see also *supra* Ch. 4.

Church of England the subject is governed by the Parochial Registers and Records Measure 1978, as amended by the Church of England (Miscellaneous Provisions) Measure 1992.[198] As a basic principle, by canon register books must be maintained 'in accordance with the Statutes and Measures relating thereto, and the rules and regulations made thereunder and from time to time in force'.[199] Ownership of baptism and burial register books is deemed to be vested in the parochial church council; ownership of register books of marriages, confirmations, and services vests in the incumbent.[200] The custody of register books of baptisms, confirmations, banns of marriage, marriages, burials, or services vests in the incumbent or, during a vacancy, in the churchwardens.[201] The duty to take care of these is placed on the custodian: '[e]very person having the custody of any register books or records in parochial custody shall be responsible for their safe-keeping, care and pre-servation'.[202] The standard of care is carefully prescribed.[203] The bishop may from time to time issue such directions with respect to the safe-keeping, care, and preservation of records and registers in parochial custody and all persons concerned must comply with these directions; the expense of complying with these is to be met by the parochial church council.[204] The bishop may establish a diocesan record office in which the minister may deposit any register books of baptisms, marriages, and burials not in use or any documents of value; some documents must be deposited there.[205] The chief officer of the diocesan records office has custody of registers and records deposited there and is responsible for their safe-keeping, care, and preservation.[206]

If the standard of care, the episcopal directions, or the mandatory depositing rules have not been complied with the bishop is under a duty to notify the custodians and the parochial church council of the facts as they appear to him and to inform them that he will consider any written representations before a specified date. If after considering representations the bishop is of the opinion that the matter is urgent he may order the records and registers to be deposited in the diocesan record office; otherwise, he may make an order requiring compliance. If any person refuses or fails to comply with the episcopal order

---

[198] Church of England (Miscellaneous Provisions) Measure 1992, s. 4 and Sched. 1; *A Guide to the Parochial Registers and Records Measure 1978* (London, 1992); these rules are repeated in diocesan norms: e.g. *WDHI*, ch. 4, 215–16; *PDH*, Q.2; *CDH*, 29 f.; *BDM*, K.9; *SDH*, II, E; *GDM*, D.14–18; *SDDH*, Q.2–5. [199] F11(2).

[200] Parochial Registers and Records Measure 1978, s. 1(2); s. 25: 'records' means materials in written or other form setting out facts or events or otherwise recording information; 'register books' means register books of baptisms, confirmations, banns of marriage, marriages, burials, and services of public worship. [201] S. 6(1), (2).

[202] S. 11.

[203] Sched. 2, as amended by the Church of England (Miscellaneous Provisions) Measure 1992, Sched. 1, para. 12: every register must be kept in a wood-lined, rust-proof, vented steel cabinet, the door of which is fitted with a multi-lever lock or in a fire-proofed muniment room. The rules also contain details about temperature and humidity.

[204] Parochial Registers and Records Measure 1978, s. 11. [205] S. 7, 10. [206] S. 14.

the bishop may apply to the county court for an order that the registers or records be delivered to the diocesan records office.[207] This is an interesting example of a bishop's ability to invoke the assistance of a secular court to strengthen his visitatorial authority in the diocese.

In addition to these duties of care, as with church buildings and contents and churchyards, the law imposes a system of mandatory inspection. Though it is unclear whether this relates to all registers, the diocesan bishop must cause register books and records in parochial custody to be inspected and reported on periodically (by such persons(s) as he may appoint) every six years; the report, containing a list of registers 'and a list describing the records' inspected, must be made to the bishop or a person designated by him and copies sent (by the inspector) to the chief officer of the diocesan record office, the minister concerned, and the parochial church council. The custodian must give access at any reasonable time and give the person inspecting such facilities as he may reasonably require; expenses must be paid by the parochial church council.[208] Similar, though more ancient and slightly less well developed, arrangements exist for the care and maintenance of ecclesiastical libraries.[209]

REGULATING DEVELOPMENTS: RE-ORDERING

The work and mission of a worshipping community, and the liturgical needs of that community, naturally generate the need for change. In Roman Catholic canon law alteration of buildings is permitted only with episcopal approval.[210] With regard to the Church of England,[211] any proposed development of a consecrated church or churchyard, by means of re-ordering, must be authorized by faculty or licence,[212] the ordinary seen as providing 'an independent element which may be ideal in balancing the more immediate demands of local church members with the public interest in conserving church buildings'.[213] The archdeacon is empowered to grant a licence in writing for a re-ordering scheme for a temporary period not exceeding twelve months. In exercising this power the archdeacon must be satisfied that the scheme does not involve any interference with the fabric of the church, fixing any item to the fabric, or the disposal of any item.[214]

---

[207] S. 12. See s.13 for return of registers and records to parochial custody.   [208] S. 9.

[209] Parochial Libraries Act 1708, ss. 2, 3. See s. 9 for the bishop's power to make rules for preservation; for cathedrals see Cathedrals Measure 1963, s. 11(1)(d) and Care of Cathedrals Measure 1990, s. 13 (inventories).   [210] *CIC*, c. 1215.

[211] For cathedrals see above.

[212] Canon F13(3); alterations made without faculty may constitute an ecclesiastical offence: *St Pancras Vestry v Vicar and Churchwardens of St Martin's-in-the-Fields* (1860) 6 Jur NS; *Lee v Vicar and Churchwardens of Herne* (1892) Trist 217; for enforcement against defaulters see above.

[213] For criticisms generally see D. Harte, 'Church *v.* state in listed building control', *Journal of Planning Law* (1985), 611, 690.   [214] FJR, r. 8.

Permanent re-ordering schemes must be authorized by faculty.[215] The discretion of the diocesan chancellor is to be exercised in accordance with a growing body of general principles enunciated recently by the Arches Court in *Re St Luke the Evangelist, Maidstone*.[216] 'In deciding upon alterations to a church a Chancellor should have in mind that': (1) 'the persons most concerned with worship in a church are those who worship there regularly, although other members of the Church who are not such regular worshippers may also be concerned';[217] (2) 'where a church is listed there is a strong presumption against change which would adversely affect its character as a building of special architectural or historic interest',[218] and 'to rebut that presumption there must be evidence of a sufficient weight to show a necessity for such a change for some compelling reason, which would include the pastoral well-being of the church';[219] (3) 'whether a church is listed or not a Chancellor should always have in mind not only the religious interests but also the aesthetic, architectural and communal interests relevant to the church in question';[220] and (4) 'although the present and future needs of worshippers must be given proper weight a change which is permanent and cannot be reversed is to be avoided wherever possible'.[221] To these may be added the consideration of proprietory rights, the costs involved,[222] and whether there has been a procedural irregularity on the part of the parish or a failure to consult interested persons.[223] Faculty control also extends to the erection of

[215] Canon F13(3); CCEJM, s. 11(8): chancellor's directions; diocesan norms list major alterations and extensions requiring a faculty and the prescribed procedure: e.g. *TBF*, 6.2; *SDDH*, O.34; *EDH*, A.16; *CDH*, 52; *PDH*, App. 1; *GDM*, E.1–3; *SDH*, II, A.   [216] [1994] 3 WLR 1165.

[217] *Nickalls v Briscoe* [1892] P 269 at 283 *per* Lord Penzance, Dean of the Arches: 'the sacred edifice has a future as well as a past. It belongs not to any one generation, nor are its interests and condition the exclusive care of those who inhabit the parish at any one period of time. It is in entire conformity with this aspect of the parish church that the law has forbidden any structural alterations to be made in it, save for those which are approved by a disinterested authority in the person of the Ordinary, whose deputed discretion and judgment we are here to exercise today.'

[218] *Re St Mary, Beddington* [1987] *ELJ*, 1 (1987), 36, decision in favour of a conservation argument.

[219] Whether 'well-being' is the same as 'need' or 'wishes' of parishioners is unclear. For reordering to accommodate liturgical fashion and for a reluctance to refuse a faculty on grounds of doctrine see *Re St Peter, St Helier, Morden, Re St Olave, Mitcham* [1951] P 303; *Re St Augustine's, Brinksway* [1963] P 364; cf. *Re St Mary the Virgin, West Moors* [1963] P 390; *Re St Edward the Confessor, Nottingham* [1980] 126 SJ 835: aesthetically acceptable but doctrinally unsound, faculty refused.

[220] *Re St Mary the Virgin, Selling* [1980] 1 WLR 1545; *Re St Stephen's, Walbrook* [1986] 2 All ER 603 *per* Sir Anthony Lloyd: 'there are hardly ever any rights or wrongs in matters of aesthetics. There are differences of opinion.'; see also D. Harte, 'Doctrine, conservation and aesthetic judgments in the Court of Ecclesiastical Causes Reserved', *ELJ*, 1(2) (1987), 22.

[221] *Re All Saints Melbourn* [1990] 1 WLR 833.

[222] *Re Holy Innocents, Fallowfield* [1982] Fam 135; *Re St Martin's, Ashton-upon-Mersey* [1981] 1 WLR 1288; *Re St Mary's, Lancaster* [1980] 124 SJ 428.

[223] *Re St Michael's, Great Torrington* [1985] 2 All ER 993; for relaxation see *Re St Cuthbert's, Doveridge* [1983] 1 WLR 845: failure to post the citation notifying interested parties on or near the principal door of the church under FJR 1967, r. 3(1) as amended by FJR 1975, r. 4(1).

new buildings on unconsecrated property,[224] as well as the conversion or re-ordering of a consecrated churchyard.[225] When re-ordering involves a major extension the court must be satisfied by undertakings from the parochial authorities that the extension will not be used for unsuitable purposes.[226] When new buildings encroach on the churchyard the court must be satisfied about and sanction any disturbance to graves, including removal and exhumation.[227]

It is arguable today that chief amongst these guiding ideas is that of the pastoral need and wishes of the parishioners, present and future. Those charged with oversight of re-ordering 'should have due regard to the role of a church as a local centre of worship and mission'.[228] The principle is an old one[229] which has been applied time and time again in faculty cases.[230] It may not impose a legal duty on the judges to apply it (and several judgments recognize that it is not *the* determinant),[231] but it is nevertheless a principle of strong persuasive authority: recent decisions clearly indicate a judicial willingness, when all other considerations are equal, to facilitate and realize the wishes of the parishioners.[232]

CONCLUSIONS

The law relating to the use and maintenance of church property seeks to effect a balance between the various needs for sensible supervision, to protect the values of conservation and heritage, and to act upon legitimate ecclesiastical development. The use and development of consecrated parochial property falls within a system of judicial control and recent legislation has instituted an elaborate system for protection against arbitrary use and development, particularly with respect to cathedrals. Whilst the law provides ample duties to

---

[224] For deconsecrated land see Pastoral Measure 1983, s. 30.

[225] *Re St Peter, Roydon* [1969] 1 WLR 1849; *Re St James, Heywood* [1982] 1 WLR 1289.

[226] *Corke v Rainger* [1912] P 69; *Re St John's, Chelsea* [1962] 1 WLR 706; *Re St Ann's, Kew* [1977] Fam 12; *Re All Saints', Melbourn* [1990] 1 WLR 633.

[227] *Re St Thomas, Lymington* [1980] Fam 89; Faculty Jurisdiction Measure 1964, s. 3: in cases of removal by faculty the owners have rights of consultation and consent, though the latter may be overriden in prescribed instances of refusal; for extensions on disused burial grounds see the Disused Burial Grounds Act 1884, as amended by the Open Spaces Act 1887; *Re St Mary's, Luton* [1968] P 47; *Re St Luke's, Chelsea* [1977] Fam 12.   [228] CCEJM, s. 1.

[229] *Groves and Wright v Rector, Parishioners and Inhabitants of Hornsey* (1793) 1 Hag Con 188, 161 ER 521 (I am grateful to The Rev. P. L. S. Barrett for drawing my attention to this decision); *Vicar and Churchwardens of Tottenham v Venn* (1874) 4 A & E 221; *Peek v Trower* (1881) P 21; *Re Kerr* [1894] P 284.

[230] E.g. *Re St Stephen Walbrook* [1987] 2 All ER 578 at 597–8.

[231] *Nickalls v Briscoe* [1892] P 269.

[232] *Re St Michael and All Angels, Great Torrington* [1985] 1 All ER 993; *Re All Saints', Melbourn* [1990] 1 WLR 833 (Arches Ct.); cf. *Re St Mary's, Banbury* (1987) Fam 136 *per* Sir John Owen, Dean of Arches: the matter should not be decided solely according to the wishes of the parishioners.

maintain and structures for oversight, with the exception of objects, it does not specify standards to be attained. Whilst state-made law regulates the use of shared churches, a mixture of state-made and church-made law regulates the administration of charitable trusts. Diocesan norms add little to the general legal framework of the Church of England in the area of use and maintenance of property.

17

The Administration and Control of Finance

The legal organization of finance in the Church of England, like that of the Roman Catholic Church, serves four basic functions. First, the law requires the existence of prescribed funds for specified ecclesiastical objects. Secondly, it assigns to authorities at national, diocesan, and parochial levels the functions of holding, administering, investing, and applying these funds. Thirdly, it imposes structures enabling control over and accountability for financial management. Fourthly, when the law requires expenditure it confers upon bodies and persons rights to make claims upon the church's funds. Whilst there are structural principles common to all bodies involved in financial management, the precise terms of these arrangements vary as between the bodies in question. Regulation of funds, fund-holders, expenditure (on stipends, clergy compensation, and pensions), ecclesiastical fees, legal aid, and costs in judicial proceedings is effected mainly by the church's central legal system. Acquisition, investment, and insurance are regulated by both internal church law and civil law. In contrast with Roman Catholic canon law, the redistribution of funds within the Church of England to meet expenditure (the quota system) and payment of expenses of ministers are regulated almost entirely by extra-legal norms rather than by the church's central legal system.

THE HOLDING OF FUNDS: EXECUTIVE BODIES

The law of the Church of England requires the existence of several prescribed funds to be used for the work of the church. As with Roman Catholic canon law (in which financial management is devolved),[1] the law in the Church of England assigns fund-holding and management responsibilities both to central

---

[1] For administrative services dealing with the finances of the Holy See see *PB* (1988): the Administration of the Patrimony of the Apostolic See is 'to administer the properties owned by the Holy See in order to underwrite the expenses needed for the Roman Curia' (Arts. 172–5); the Prefecture for the Economic Affairs of the Holy See supervises and governs temporal goods of those administrations dependent on the Holy See or of which the Holy See has charge (Arts. 176–9), *COCLA*, 1167; see generally C. Ritty, 'Changing economy and the new code of canon law', *The Jurist*, 26 (1966), 469.

or national and to local ecclesiastical authorities in the dioceses and parishes.[2]

The Central Board of Finance

Whilst not a direct creation of synodical measure, General Synod's Central Board of Finance, a company and registered charity, is governed by secular company and charity law, by its memorandum and articles of association, and by Standing Orders of General Synod.[3] The Board is 'responsible as the financial executive of the Synod for the management of the financial business of the Synod'.[4] The Board may at any time submit such reports 'as it thinks fit' to General Synod on the financial business of the General Synod, of Synod's subordinate bodies, and of any body in receipt of moneys voted by General Synod, as well as on the financial implications of any item of business included on General Synod's agenda.[5] Bodies spending money voted by General Synod must lay before the Board (not later than 1 March in each year) estimates of the expenditure required in the forthcoming calendar year and, after consultation with synod's Standing Committee, the Board must include in the annual budget 'such estimate or so much of it as in its judgment is financially expedient'.[6] Not later than 31 July each year the Board must present to General Synod the accounts of the Synod for the preceding year, the budget for the following year, and motions for the authorization of expenditure required under the various heads of the estimates. When General Synod has approved the budget and such recommendations relating to it as it thinks fit, the amounts so approved 'shall be held to be votes of the Synod and may be applied by the Board to the objects specified'.[7]

The Board has a discretionary power (not a duty) to call upon any body in

[2] *WAOB* recommends radical changes in the church's structures for financial management. It suggests that the proposed National Council should have the following specific tasks: financial planning and assessment of the overall financial resource needs of the church; determination (within a framework agreed by the House of Bishops and General Synod and after discussion with the dioceses) of the allocation of income from the Church Commissioners' assets; management of redistributing resources within the church (in discussion with the dioceses); submission for approval by General Synod of the budgets for ministry training and national church responsibilities (5.6); the Council's finance department would direct (under the Council's oversight) the national financial policies of the church (5.19, App. C.19); for audit and reports see App. B, draft Measure clauses 5, 6. For proposals concerning the Church Commissioners and the Pensions Board see below.

[3] Whilst set up under the power conferred on General Synod by the SGM 1969, Sched. 2, Art. 10(2), the CBF is not classified as a 'subordinate body' of General Synod (see GS 1136, 3); it is not listed as exempt from the provisions of the Charities Act 1993. This Chapter does not explore the Corporation of the Church House, a charity incorporated by royal charter to own, provide, and run Church House Westminster. The Corporation is separate from the Central Board of Finance.

[4] *GSSO*, SO 97; WAOB recommends that the Board's functions be transferred to the proposed National Council which would, in turn, delegate many of these to the Council's Finance Committee (on which the dioceses would be represented) (5.38). [5] *GSSO*, SO 98.

[6] SO 99.   [7] SO 100.

receipt of voted moneys to account to the Board for the monies so voted and the Board may conduct such audit of the accounts of that body as the Board deems desirable.[8] In presenting the yearly accounts the Board must report to General Synod any expenditure in excess of money voted and must lay before Synod 'the explanation of the body concerned, together with the observations of the Board and its recommendations as to the conditions, if any, upon which the excess expenditure shall be condoned and now sanctioned'.[9] A body to whom money is voted may submit to the Board a supplementary estimate of additional expenditure if the original vote is inadequate; in turn, the Board may submit to Synod a supplementary estimate upon which General Synod may make a supplementary vote.[10] No motion or recommendation shall have effect in authorizing expenditure from synodical funds unless General Synod gives the authorization in express words.[11] The two principal funds which the Board administers are the General Synod Fund and the Central Church Fund.[12]

The Church Commissioners

The Church Commissioners form a body corporate, established under the Church Commissioners Measure 1947 from a merger of the Ecclesiastical Commissioners (established in 1836) and the Governors of Queen Anne's Bounty (established in 1704 for 'the Augmentation of the Poor Clergy'). All property hitherto held by those bodies is now held on trust by the Church Commissioners for the purposes of the Church of England.[13] The Commissioners are the two archbishops, all the diocesan bishops, the three Church Estates Commissioners (two of whom are appointed by the Crown and the third by the Archbishop of Canterbury), the Lord Chancellor, the Lord President of the Council, the Home Secretary, the First Lord of the Treasury, the Chancellor of the Exchequer, the Speaker of the House of Commons, the Lord Chief Justice, the Master of the Rolls, the Attorney-General, the Solicitor-General, the Lords Mayor of London and York, the Vice-Chancellors of the Universities of Oxford and Cambridge, and thirty-five others appointed and nominated by, *inter alia*, General Synod and the two archbishops.[14] The

---

[8] SO 101.   [9] SO 102.   [10] SO 103.

[11] SO 104: 'That the Synod authorize the Central Board of Finance to expend a sum not exceeding [a named sum]'.

[12] The General Synod Fund, spent on the work of Synod's subordinate bodies (see Ch. 4), is formed by contributions from the dioceses and parochial church councils: see below for practices relating to acquisition; the Central Church Fund (established in 1915) is used for the general purposes of the Board: *WAOB* recommends that this be overseen and administered by the proposed National Council (5.38).

[13] Church Commissioners Measure 1947 (as amended in 1964 and 1970), ss. 1, 2.

[14] Ibid., Sched. 1. The others are: 5 deans, 10 other clerics and 10 laypersons appointed by General Synod, 4 lay persons nominated by Her Majesty and 4 by the Archbishop of Canterbury (of whom 2 must be or must have been Queen's Counsel) and 2 aldermen of the city of London appointed by the Court of the City of London.

recent Turnbull Commission has proposed radical reforms of the structures described in the following paragraphs.[15]

The Church Commissioners Measure 1947 does not define their functions beyond the general principle that they enjoy 'all functions, rights and privileges' hitherto enjoyed by the Ecclesiastical Commissioners and the Governors of Queen Anne's Bounty.[16] The Commissioners must hold and administer a General Fund consisting of all income received in respect of property and funds held by them. From it they must discharge all trusts and commitments to which that income is subject and any expenses and obligations falling on them in discharge of their functions. The balance remaining in the fund must be available for any purpose for which any surplus of the common fund of the Ecclesiastical Commissioners or the corporate fund of Queen Anne's Bounty would have been available.[17] The General Fund is used to make grants for stipends, pensions, church building, and parsonages, and loans to theological colleges.[18]

The Church Commissioners transact their business either through general meetings or through their Board of Governors. An annual general meeting (ordinarily chaired by the Archbishop of Canterbury) must be held in every financial year for the purpose of considering, and if necessary passing resolutions concerning, the annual report and accounts of the Commissioners and any other matters which may be brought before the meeting by the Board of Governors or by the chairman. At the AGM the Commissoners appoint members of the Board of Governors, consider and (if thought fit) adopt the recommendations of the Board as to the allocation of such moneys as the

---

[15] *WAOB*: accepting that '[t]he Church Commissioners should remain as an important body which links Church and State' (8.14), the Commission recommends that they continue as trustees of the church's historic assets but would be 'ring-fenced, so that neither the Commissioners nor any other body in the church could spend the capital from them unless authorised by legislation to do so' (8.15). Along with composition changes (8.21), the Commissioners would carry out the functions of the present Assets Committee and some of the trustee functions of the Board of Governors (8.20); a new Assets Committee would oversee day-to-day management of the Commissioners' portfolio but it would not—unlike the present Assets Committee—have exclusive power in all matters relating to the management of assets (8.22); an Audit Committee (with the existing external auditors) would scrutinize all aspects of the work of the Commissioners and the Assets Committee and report to the Commissioners; the Commissioners would (as now) have to report annually to General Synod and parliament (8.22, 23). The Commissioners would continue to determine and monitor asset policy and retain the power to sell, purchase, exchange, or let land (8.38), but allocation of income provided by the Commissioners would be transferred to the proposed National Council (8.39).

[16] S. 2.

[17] S. 10(4)-(6).

[18] For stipends and pensions see below; for the involvement of the Commissioners in transactions concerning glebe, parsonage houses, and redundant churches, *supra* chs. 15, 16; see also the Church Commissioners (Loans for Theological Colleges and Training Houses) Measure 1964, although as a matter of policy no loans are now made, the income for theological colleges being now derived from 'fees' paid by the Advisory Board for Ministry; New Housing Areas (Church Building) Measure 1954; Church Schools (Assistance by Church Commissioners) Measure 1958; Church Commissioners (Assistance for Priority Areas) Measure 1988.

Board may report to be available. Notice of the general meeting must be given to every member.[19]

With the exception of business transacted at a general meeting, the functions and business of the Church Commissioners must be exercised and transacted in accordance with the provisions of the Church Commissioners Measure 1947 (as amended) by a Board of Governors.[20] The Board is composed of the archbishops, the three Estates Commissioners and twenty-two other Commissioners appointed by the Commissioners, and such other Commissioners as the Board may co-opt.[21] The Board is empowered to refer for consideration and report any matter within its jurisdiction to the General Purposes Committee or the Assets Committee or to any other committee of Commissioners which the board may appoint. The Board may authorize these committees by way of delegation to do and complete any matter on its behalf. Moreover, the Board is empowered to make general rules for the direction and guidance of these committees including 'the general principles upon which that committee shall act in carrying out such functions as may from time to time be delegated to them by the Board'.[22] Notice of the business to be considered at a meeting of the Board must be given to its members and to those diocesan bishops who are not members.[23]

The General Purposes Committee comprises the three Estates Commissioners and not less than eight nor more than ten other Commissioners appointed by the Board of Governors; at least two must be diocesan bishops, at least three clerks in holy orders, and at least three lay persons. The Assets Committee comprises the First Church Estates Commissioner, one Commissioner being a clerk in holy orders appointed for three years by the Board, and not less than three and no more than five lay Commissioners appointed for three years by the Archbishop of Canterbury. The First Church Estates Commissioner is chairman of each committee and a deputy chairman is elected annually by each committee. The functions of the General Purposes Committee are to consider, recommend, and report to the Board on how to apply or distribute such sums as the Board determines to be available for application or distribution and to act on behalf of the Commissioners in any matters which the Committee considers urgent. The Assets Committee has, subject to any general rules made by the Board, 'an exclusive power and duty' to act on behalf of and in the name of the Commissioners in all matters relating to the management of those assets of the Commissioners the income of which is carried into their General Fund. This includes the power to purchase, sell, or let land and to make, realize, and change investments. The Committee is under a duty to recommend to the Board, from time to time, what sums are available

---

[19] S. 4(1).   [20] Ss. 3,5(1).

[21] S. 5(1), Sched. 2; the Estates Commissioners are royal appointments and the Second Estates Commissioner a junior minister and (by custom) a member of the House of Commons.

[22] S. 5(4).   [23] S. 5(5).

for application or distribution by the Commissioners and what sums should be appropriated to reserve and for reinvestment.[24] The basic procedures to be employed by the Commissioners, by the Board, and by the two Committees are laid down in the 1947 Measure, though as a general principle each body has the power to regulate its own procedure.[25]

The 1947 Measure lays down a simple system for audit: the accounts of the Commissioners 'shall in every year be audited in such manner and by such person as the Treasury may direct'.[26] The Board of Governors must prepare a report each year on the work and proceedings of the Commissioners and must present the report and accounts for that year to the Commissioners at the annual general meeting. Within thirty days of the meeting the secretary must transmit the report and accounts, together with a copy of any resolution passed by the Commissioners, to the Home Secretary who must lay these before both Houses of Parliament. Copies of these documents must also be sent to the Secretary of General Synod who must put them before Synod.[27] There seems to be no specific duty on Synod to scrutinize these documents though in practice the report and accounts are debated every other year.[28] Not being a subordinate body of General Synod, the Church Commissioners are under no legal duties to consult General Synod, its Standing Committee, or its financial executive (the Central Board of Finance) prior to the exercise of their functions.[29]

The Pensions Board

The Church of England Pensions Board, established under the Clergy Pensions Measure 1926 and now governed in the main by a synodical measure of 1961, is directly accountable to General Synod. The Board, a body corporate, consists of a chairman and not less than twenty-one or more than twenty-three other members appointed or elected by General Synod and the Church Commissioners.[30] The Board is empowered to appoint central committees (consisting of board members) to which, subject to the provisions of the Measure, it may delegate any of its functions; it may appoint other local committees (consisting of persons whether board members or not) for any areas, whether dioceses or not, to which it may delegate any of the Board's functions.[31] The duty of the Board, or its delegatees, is to 'control and administer the system of pensions' established by the Measure, as amended.[32] The Board has power to enter into agreements for the receipt and

---

[24] S. 6. [25] S. 7, Sched. 4. [26] S. 11; see also s. 10. [27] S. 12.
[28] *GSSO*, SO 95–6 impose a duty to note.
[29] For criticism of its structures concerning investment see below.
[30] Clergy Pensions Measure 1961, s. 21: 1 appointee must be a diocesan bishop: s. 21(3)(b)); *WAOB* recommends the reconstituting of the Board, the formulation of pensions policy by the proposed National Council (in discussion with the dioceses) with the new Board acting as trustee of a new clergy pensions scheme (9.5 ff.) [31] S. 23.
[32] S. 24.

payment of actuarial equivalents of any contributions or pensions made under the Measure and to borrow money for the purposes of pensions for clergy widows and dependants.[33] The Pensions Board is subordinate to the Church Commissioners who may give to it 'directions of a general character as to the exercise and performance' by the Board of its functions. The directions must be such as appear to the Commissioners 'requisite or expedient for securing a due balance between the amounts respectively of the liability imposed on [the Commissioners'] general fund . . . and the resources of that fund available for meeting the liability'. The Pensions Board must give effect to the Commissioners' directions.[34]

All payments by the Church Commissioners to the Pensions Board for clergy pensions must be paid out of the Commissioners' General Fund. With respect to pensions for widows and dependants, the Commissioners must pay out of the General Fund to the Board sums required by the Board for these purposes.[35] Contributions payable with respect to widows and dependants and sums received from the General Fund must be paid by the Board into the Clergy (Widows and Dependants) Pensions Fund which is administered by the Board.[36] Similarly, the Board administers the Clergy Pensions Augmentation Fund into which it must pay any testamentary or other gift to the Board for the relief of poverty of retired clergy or for the provision of homes of residence for retired clergy and their wives and for the widows and dependants of deceased clergy; subject to any conditions imposed by the testators or donors, the Board has a discretion to apply the fund or any part of it for these purposes.[37] The Board also administers a Church Workers Pension Fund for these, their widows, and dependants,[38] and may make loans to retired clergy and church workers (or their wives or widows) to assist them to purchase, build, rebuild, or improve dwelling houses.[39] The Treasury must from time to time appoint an auditor to audit the accounts of any fund or trust administered by the Board. The auditor must carry out the audit at such times as the Treasury directs and must report to General Synod; the Board too must present annually to the Synod a report with respect to any such fund.[40]

Diocesan Financial Executives and Funds

Although the matter is not treated expressly by synodical measure, normally under their Standing Orders the standing committee of the diocesan synod is responsible for advising the president and the synod on the determination of priorities in the allocation of any funds at the disposal of the synod.[41] The

---

[33] S. 24.   [34] S. 25.   [35] S. 17(1), (2).   [36] S. 18(1), (2).   [37] S. 19.
[38] Ss. 27–8; see also Church of England (Pensions) Measure 1988, s. 17.
[39] S. 26(1)(e), added by Clergy Pensions (Amendment) Measure 1967, s. 4(1).
[40] S. 34.
[41] *MSODS*, SO 106. In practice, of course, Standing Orders may vary as between dioceses.

diocesan board of finance is the financial executive of the diocesan synod and is responsible for the custody and management of the synod's funds.[42] Under the Diocesan Boards of Finance Measure 1925, the diocesan board of finance, a registered company, is constituted by the diocesan synod and its activities are regulated both by civil company law and by synodical measure. Its memorandum and articles of association must empower the board to hold property and transact business for purposes connected with the Church of England. The diocesan synod may augment the board's powers if this is necessary or expedient in view of the requirements of the diocese. The board is composed of the diocesan bishop and not less than three-quarters of the other members must be elected by the diocesan synod or, if allowed by the memorandum and articles, wholly or partly by the diocesan deanery synods; the remainder must be elected, nominated, or co-opted as prescribed by the company's memorandum and articles ensuring that not less than two-thirds of those elected are members of the diocesan synod and that a majority are laypersons.[43] The diocesan board of finance is subject to the direct control of the diocesan synod: it 'shall in the exercise of its powers and duties comply with such directions as may from time to time by given to the board by the Diocesan Synod'.[44] Whilst particular functions are assigned by a variety of synodical measures, the board's general functions are as prescribed by its constitution.[45]

In addition to the audit procedures applicable to it under the Companies Act 1985,[46] by Standing Orders of the diocesan synod, normally the diocesan finance board must in each year submit to the synod's standing committee a report and accounts for the preceding financial year and a draft budget for the following year: the standing committee may make to the board and to synod such recommendations thereon as it thinks fit.[47] The diocesan board of finance must also present to the synod the accounts for the preceding year and the budget for the following year as approved by the board. The budget must provide for the expenditure required by every committee and other body responsible to the synod, subject to any reductions made by the board on grounds of priority or financial expediency after consultation with the synod's standing committee.[48] In presenting the accounts for the preceding year the board must report any expenditure in excess of the funds voted for that year and give the explanation of the body responsible, together with the board's own comments and recommendations as to how the excess expenditure shall be sanctioned.[49] Before a proposal involving expenditure is put to the diocesan synod, the prescribed notices must be given.[50] The diocesan board of finance is

---

[42] Ibid., SO 107.   [43] Diocesan Boards of Finance Measure 1925, s. 1.

[44] Ibid., ss. 1(2)(b), 3 (words substituted by the Synodical Government Measure 1969, s. 4(7)).

[45] As contained in its memorandum and articles of association: its involvement in the acquisition, use, and disposal of property is discussed in Chs. 15 and 16.

[46] Companies Act 1985, ss. 384–94.   [47] *MSODS*, SO 108.

[48] SO 109; SO 110 provides for the submission of supplementary budgets.   [49] SO 111.

[50] SO 112: 35 days' notice must be given to the standing committee 'to give opportunity for their views on the proposal to be formulated and expressed during the debate'.

forbidden to expend or engage to expend any of the synod's funds for which it is responsible without the authority of a money resolution.[51]

By synodical measure, the Church Commissioners must for each diocese open and keep two accounts: a stipends fund[52] and a pastoral account.[53] Over these the diocese itself has some legal control. With regard to the *diocesan stipends fund*, two accounts must be opened and kept: a capital account and an income account to which the Commissioners must allocate all moneys and other property held by them on behalf of that fund in such proportions as they shall determine. In so doing the Commissioners must consult the diocesan bishop and the diocesan board of finance.[54] The Commissioners must allocate between the accounts of each diocesan stipends fund payments, legacies, donations, contributions, and other money or property received for the credit of the fund.[55] Money allocated to either account is not credited direct to that account, but is taken over and held as part of the Commissioners' General Fund, and in lieu the accounts are credited with a sum charged upon the General Fund of an amount equal in value to the money taken over.[56] Subject to such charges as are imposed on the capital of the stipends fund, money standing to the credit of the capital account of the stipends fund may, at the discretion of the Commissioners (and on the special request of the bishop made with the concurrence of the diocesan finance board) be appropriated as an endowment fund held by the Commissioners for any benefice within the diocese or as an augmentation of any such endowment fund; in default of and subject to any such appropriation, it shall be kept standing to the credit of the capital account.[57] Moreover, again subject to overriding charges, money standing to the credit of the income account must be applied in providing or augmenting the stipends or other emoluments of incumbents or licensed assistant curates or other persons who are declared by the bishop to be engaged in the cure of souls within the diocese. Such applications must be made with directions from time to time given by the bishop (or a person duly authorized by him) with the concurrence of the diocesan board of finance.[58] The diocesan board of finance has a right to be furnished with both accounts annually.[59]

With regard to the *diocesan pastoral account*, under the Pastoral Measure 1983 the Church Commissioners must transfer into this any moneys payable under a pastoral scheme and such other moneys as the bishop and the diocesan board of finance, after consultation with the Commissioners, direct the Commissioners to accept (not being moneys for the disposal of which provision is

---

[51] SO 113: the resolution must be in the prescribed form; SO 114: no money motion may be moved otherwise than by a member authorized by the board.

[52] Diocesan Stipends Funds Measure 1953, s. 1(1).   [53] Pastoral Measure 1983, s. 77(1).

[54] Diocesan Stipends Funds Measure, 1953, s. 1; *WAOB* proposes that the Commissioners continue to hold the dioceses' stipends and pastoral funds (8.38) but that the maintenance of diocesan stipends funds income accounts be transferred to the proposed National Council (8.39).

[55] S. 2.   [56] S. 3.   [57] S. 4.   [58] S. 5.   [59] S. 7.

made under any other enactment). Every diocesan finance board must as soon as is practicable after the end of each financial year prepare an account of the moneys paid into or out of the diocesan pastoral account during that year. This must include a statement of the amount by which the pastoral account was in debit or credit at the beginning and end of that year. Moreover, the finance board must send to the Commissioners annually a copy of the account prepared by the board duly audited as well as a copy to the diocesan synod.[60] Expenses incurred by or on behalf of (or under the authority or direction of) the bishop, any pastoral committee, any diocesan redundant churches uses committee, or by the Commissioners in implementing the Pastoral Measure 1983 may be paid out of the moneys standing to the credit of the diocesan pastoral account as the Commissioners may determine.[61] Where, after consultation with the diocesan board of finance, the Church Commissioners are satisfied that any moneys standing to the credit of a diocesan pastoral account are not required (or likely to be required) for meeting these expenses, then at the request of the board they may apply those moneys by way of grant or loan. Application may include the provision, restoration, improvement, or repair of diocesan churches and parsonage houses or to other purposes of the diocese or any benefice or parish therein. They may also apply those moneys for the benefit of the diocese for general or specified purposes or transfer those moneys to the capital or income account of the diocesan stipends fund. Before making a request for applications, the board must consult the Commissioners about the purposes for which the board wishes the moneys to be used. Only with the agreement of the Commissioners is the board entitled to request that the moneys be transferred to a fund, held on behalf of the diocese or any benefice or parish, not being a fund held and administered by the Commissioners. If at any time there is not a sufficient amount standing to the credit of the pastoral account to meet such expenditure the Commissioners may, if they think fit, make an advance out of the General Fund towards this and transfer from the diocesan pastoral account into their General Fund the amount of the advance.[62]

Parochial Financial Executives

Whilst the central legal system of the Church of England confers upon parishes a basic financial autonomy, in some cases regulation provides for direct control

---

[60] Pastoral Measure 1983, s. 77. For some of the sums subscribed to the pastoral account see Ch. 15.

[61] S. 78, but this does not include salaries or wages of persons in the regular employment of the bishop, any board or committee of the diocese, or the Commissioners.

[62] S. 78; with regard to funds held by the capitular body of a cathedral accounts must be audited annually, submitted to the Church Commissioners, and published: Cathedrals Measure 1963, s. 38; the capitular body may lend and borrow money subject to the limitations imposed by s. 35; for cathedral finances generally see *Heritage and Renewal*, The Report of the Archbishops' Commission on Cathedrals (1994) Ch. 13.

of financial management by diocesan authorities.[63] To provide assistance for financial management, many dioceses have a stewardship adviser.[64] One function of the parochial church council is 'the collection and administration of all moneys raised for church purposes and the keeping of accounts in relation to such affairs and moneys'.[65] To this end, the council is empowered 'to frame an annual budget of moneys required for the maintenance of the work of the Church in the parish and otherwise and to take such steps as they think necessary for the raising collecting and allocating of such moneys'. The parochial church council enjoys a specific power 'jointly with the minister to determine the objects to which all moneys to be given or collected in church shall be allocated subject to the directions contained in the Book of Common Prayer as to the disposal of money given at the offertory'.[66] In the event of disagreement, the matter is to be referred to the diocesan bishop whose directions are final.[67] The incumbent has a right, recognized judicially, to dispose of money collected from services held elsewhere than in church as he thinks fit.[68] The council also seems to have a power to borrow money,[69] as well as the power to receive money from land put to secular uses.[70] Practices vary as between councils, but funds and accounts will be established to cover both recurring and occasional expenses.[71]

Every parochial church council must furnish to the annual parochial church meeting the audited accounts of the council for the year ending on 31 December immediately preceding the meeting and an audited statement of the funds and property, if any, remaining in the hands of the council at that date. The accounts and statement must be submitted to the meeting for approval. If approved, they must be signed by the chairman of the meeting who must in turn deliver them to the council by which they must be published.[72] The accounts of all trusts administered by the council must be laid before the

---

[63] See below for the role of the deanery synod in relation to the quota system; under *Model Rules for Deanery Synods* (1990), r. 69, the standing committee must in each year submit to the deanery synod a report and audited accounts for the preceding year, a statement showing the estimated expenditure of the synod during the next financial year, and proposals for raising the income required to meet such expenditure.

[64] E.g. *ODYB: IF*, 262; *BDM*, J.7; *SDDH*, T.9, V.44–5; *SDH*, VI, C.2; *CDH*, 138; *TBF*, 8.1; *PDH*, M.2; *GDM*, B.4; *LDHI*, VI, 1.   [65] PCC(P)M, s. 4(1)(ii)(a).

[66] S. 7(i), (iv); diocesan norms commonly recognize the duty on the incumbent and the council to agree: *BDM*, M.3; for application of collections from confirmation services to be determined by the bishop see e.g. *LDHI*, III.24.   [67] S. 9(3); see Ch. 8 for the parish treasurer.

[68] *Marson v Unmack* [1923] P 163; the incumbent and churchwardens, acting jointly, may dispose of alms collected at the offertory in a parochial chapel: *Moysey v Hillcoat* (1828) 2 Hag Ecc 30 at 56; *Dowdall v Hewitt* (1864) 10 LT 823; for Easter offerings as belonging of right to the incumbent, see e.g. *CDH*, 171; *PDH*, C.7.

[69] *Re St Peter, Roydon* [1969] 2 All ER 1233; this does not include the power to give security: ibid., 1237–8.   [70] *Supra* Ch. 16.

[71] P. Carter and M. Perry, *A Handbook of Parish Finance* (3rd edn., London, 1992), ch. 7.

[72] *CRR*, r. 9(1)-(3). The rules for audit are at present under review to conform to the Charities Act 1993.

diocesan authority annually.[73] It is for the annual parochial meeting to appoint auditors to the council.[74] Incumbents, churchwardens, and parochial church councils must obtain the consent of the appropriate diocesan authority before acquiring funds to be held on permanent trust; as managing trustees, they must then inform the diocesan authority as custodian trustee of the administration of the fund in question.[75]

Roman Catholic Organization

Meaningful comparisons with the organization of finances in the Roman Catholic Church under the 1983 Code might be made with respect to the lower ecclesiastical levels.[76] According to Canon 1274, unless other provisions have been made for the support of the clergy, each diocese is to have a special institute which collects and manages funds acquired for the support of clergy. The conference of bishops must ensure that an institute exists which provides sufficiently for their financial needs. Moreover, each diocese is required to establish a 'common fund' through which the bishops may satisfy obligations towards other persons who serve the church, to meet the needs of the diocese, and to aid poorer dioceses. Provision exists to create a federation of institutes to fulfil these functions. It falls to the bishop to assist in procuring 'those means whereby the Apostolic See can properly provide for its service of the universal church according to the conditions of the times'.[77]

The ordinary must supervise the administration of church funds with the assistance of the diocesan finance council.[78] Administrators of temporal goods must present to the local ordinary an annual report which in turn he is to present to the finance council for its consideration (c.1287(1)). The council is composed of at least three members of the faithful ('truly skilled in financial affairs as well as in civil law and of outstanding integrity') appointed by the diocesan bishop; appointees, who cannot be 'related to the bishop', hold office for a term of five years (cc.228, 492). The council must prepare each year, according to the directions of the diocesan bishop, a budget of the income and expenditure foreseen for the governance of the diocese in the coming year; at the end of the year it must examine a report of receipts and expenditure (c. 493).

---

[73] PCC(P)M, s. 8; see *OLAC*, 195–6 for changes under regulations made pursuant to Part VI Charities Act 1993.

[74] *CRR*, r. 9(4)(d), App. II, para. 1(g); *BDM*, J.8 forbids appointment of a council member as auditor. [75] *Supra* Ch. 15.

[76] *Supra* n. 1 for the Holy See.

[77] *CIC*, c. 1271; c. 1272: where benefices still exist, the conference of bishops must supervise their management by norms approved by the Apostolic See. Diocese of Westminster, *Parochial Administration Manual* (1993) 1: for the purposes of civil law property is vested in and financial management is carried out by the Westminster Roman Catholic Diocese Trustee, a limited company and registered charity; major policy is determined by the Finance Board and the Diocesan Finance Committee approves budgets and monitors performance.

[78] *CIC*, cc. 1276–7.

In each diocese, after consultation with the college of consultors and the council, the bishop must appoint a finance officer, for a renewable five-year term, who may not be dismissed except for grave cause (to be assessed by the bishop after consulting the college of consultors). It is the duty of the finance officer to administer the goods of the diocese under the authority of the bishop in accordance with the budget determined by the council. From the income of the diocese the finance officer is to meet the expenditure which the bishop (or others deputized by him) legitimately authorizes. The finance officer must report receipts and expenditure at the end of the year to the council (c. 494). Each parish must have its own finance council obliged to act in accordance with universal law and episcopal norms (c. 537).[79]

THE ACQUISITION OF FUNDS

The cost of running the Church of England falls broadly upon the faithful; there is no general provision for state financial support.[80] The central legal system of the church provides only a minimal framework regulating the acquisition of funds, though advisory structures exist at diocesan level to enable effective fund-raising.[81] Ordinarily, arrangements in the Church of England confer powers or rights rather than duties to acquire funds. The legal framework is not coercive and only exceptionally are duties imposed on bodies and persons to contribute to funds. The position in the Roman Catholic Church is different.

Compellable Payments to the Church: Fees

Any sum due to a corporation of the Church of England under the terms of a valid contract is recoverable as a debt under civil law. Consequently, sums owed under disposal or leasing agreements, interest on investments, insurance returns, and covenanted gifts, for example, may be recovered in legal proceedings.[82] In addition to these, funds are acquired by means of fees lawfully chargeable by

[79] Every juridic person must also have a finance council (c. 1280) which must act in accordance with cc. 1281–8; see also A. Farrelly, 'The diocesan finance council: functions and duties according to the code of canon law', *Studia Canonica*, 23 (1989), 149; *CIC*, c. 531: parish accounts and stole fees. Diocese of Westminster, *Parochial Administration Manual* (1993) 1.5: the parish is not a juridic person in civil law and parish trusts are held by the Westminster Roman Catholic Diocese Trustee; ibid., ch. 4 describes the provisions of the Charities Acts applicable to accounting.

[80] For the basic position and exceptions see D. McClean, 'State financial support for the church: the United Kingdom', *Church and State in Europe: State Financial Support, Religion and the School*, Proceedings of the European Consortium of Church and State Research (Milan, 1992) 77 at 79.

[81] One of the functions of the Central Board of Finance is to give encouragement to develop Christian stewardship. [82] *OLAC*, 199.

ecclesiastical authorities on the occurrence of particular ministrations. The Ecclesiatical Fees Measure 1986 empowers the Church Commissioners to prepare a draft Parochial Fees Order, prescribing amounts payable to those specified in the Order. These must be laid before General Synod for approval. Whilst the draft order need not be debated by Synod, if its Standing Committee so determines, by giving notice a Synod member may insist on debate. If approved by Synod without amendment the Church Commissioners must then make the order. If approved with amendments the Commissioners may make the order as amended or withdraw it for further consideration. A parochial fees order does not come into force until it has been approved by Parliament and sealed by the Church Commissioners as a Statutory Instrument.[83]

The Parochial Fees Order 1995 sets out the table of fees.[84] One part of each fee is payable to the incumbent and the other to the parochial church council. Whilst fees must ordinarily be paid to the incumbent of the benefice, the incumbent has a right to sign a deed of assignment in favour of the diocesan board of finance; alternatively, the incumbent may direct either generally or in particular cases that all or part of any fee which would otherwise be payable to him shall be payable to the minister performing the service or duty.[85] During a vacancy in a benefice, fees otherwise payable to the incumbent are payable to the diocesan board of finance or to such other person as the board, after consultation with the bishop, may direct.[86] The 1995 Order states that the fees listed in the table 'are to be payable to the persons named therein'. This does not, it seems, impose a duty to demand the full fee prescribed but confers a discretion to demand a fee below the fixed maximum or indeed to waive the payment of any fee. Many diocesan norms, on the basis of guidance issued by the Church Commissioners, recognize a right to waive a fee if there is an acceptable pastoral reason; some dioceses discourage the practice.[87] In any event, if a demand is made fees payable by order are recoverable as a debt.[88]

Under the 1995 Order, in respect of baptisms, though a fee may not be demanded for the baptism itself,[89] a fee may be imposed for the issue of the baptismal certificate and of a short certificate of baptism.[90] With respect to marriages, fees are payable for the publication of banns, for the certificate issued at the time of their publication, and for the service.[91] Fees are payable

---

[83] Ecclesiastical Fees Measure 1986, ss.1, 2. See also *GSSO*, SO 46.
[84] SI 1994 (GS 1163).   [85] 1995 Order, Part II, para. 7.
[86] Ecclesiastical Fees Measure 1986, s. 3(1).
[87] Church Commissioners, *A Guide to Church of England Fees* (London, 1986) 6,7: fees are 'legally payable' and 'Any departure, as a general rule, from the practice of collecting fees would be undesirable'; for diocesan norms discouraging waiver see e.g. *GDM*, A.2; *BDM*, B.11; for assigning see *PDH*, C.4, 19, 20; *ODYB: IF*, 255; *BRDSEI*, AA; *CDH*, 103, 127; *TBF*, 4.6.
[88] S. 7: an incumbent who retains a fee must declare this to the diocese, the Commissioners, and the Inland Revenue; see e.g. *GDM*, A2.   [89] Baptismal Fees Abolition Act 1872, s. 1.
[90] Baptismal Registers Measure 1961, s. 2.
[91] See also Ecclesiastical Fees Measure 1986, s. 3(2): a fee for solemnization of marriage in a licensed chapel is the amount fixed by order, but any provision in the licence as to whom it is payable continues to apply.

for a funeral service conducted in church, for burial in a churchyard (in a new or existing grave) or cemetery, or for cremation following a service in church, for the burial of a body in a churchyard on a separate occasion, for burial of cremated remains in a churchyard on a separate occasion, or for burial in a cemetery on a separate occasion. They are also payable when there is no service in church, for a service in a crematorium or cemetery, for burial of a body or cremated remains in a churchyard, and for the issue of a certificate issued at the time of burial. The fee for a burial in a churchyard 'on a separate occasion' means on any occasion other than immediately following a service in church (for example the interment of cremated remains). No fee is payable in respect of the burial of a still-born infant, or for the funeral or burial of an infant dying within the period of one year after birth. If a full service is held at the graveside the incumbent's fee is increased to that payable where the service is held in church. Fees are also payable for the erection of monuments and for searches in registers.[92]

The ecclesiastical courts are empowered to make provision for costs, fees, and expenses incurred in ecclesiastical legal proceedings.[93] With regard to faculty proceedings, costs and fees are governed by a series of synodical measures and the power to order (subject to certain fixed fees and scales) is vested exclusively in the diocesan chancellor.[94] The person in whose favour the order is made may recover costs in the county court.[95] At any point in faculty proceedings the chancellor may order any party to give security for costs and expenses of any other party and for the court fees (including those of the chancellor and registrar).[96] Consistory court fees are fixed from time to time by fees orders, the drafts of which must be laid before General Synod, made by the Fees Advisory Commission.[97] In uncontested petitions all court fees are payable by the petitioner though in some dioceses arrangements exist by which these are paid by the diocesan board of finance.[98] Provision exists for the chancellor to issue a special citation adding as a party to proceedings a person alleged to be responsible (wholly or in part) for an act or default in consequence of which proceedings were instituted. That person may be ordered to pay the whole or part of the costs of (and consequential upon) the proceedings; this may include expenses incurred in carrying out work authorized by faculty.[99] Ordinarily, the responsibility for meeting a party's costs and expenses lies with that party and no order issues in respect of them;

---

[92] Sched. Pts. I and II.

[93] *CIC*, c. 1464 (determination); c. 1595 (absent parties); c. 1580 (expert witnesses); c. 1611 (sentence to determine); c. 1469 (liability, imposition, and waiver); c. 1571 (witnesses reimbursed).

[94] CCEJM, s. 14: the archdeacon has no power to award costs and must refer to the chancellor any petition for a faculty where he considers that any question of costs or expenses arises.

[95] EJM, s. 61; see also Faculty Jurisdiction Measure 1964, s. 11. [96] EJM, s. 60.

[97] Ecclesiastical Fees Measure 1986, ss. 4–6. [98] Newsom, *FJCE*, 203; Hill, *EL*, 401.

[99] CCEJM, s. 13. S. 12 deals with archdeacons' expenses).

in contested petitions the costs 'follow the event'.[100] Extraordinarily, however, depending on the circumstances of the case, the court may order one party to pay the costs of the other party or parties.[101] As a general principle, costs in appeals follow the event though in special cases no order for costs is made.[102] Costs of disciplinary proceedings, covering those of the bishop and promoter, the recovery and payment of expenses and fees, are regulated by the Ecclesiastical Jurisdiction Measure 1963.[103]

Voluntary Payments

Whilst parish funds may be derived from a variety of voluntary sources,[104] legal regulation of fund-raising in the Church of England is minimal. The parochial church council, empowered to take steps by raising and collecting moneys to meet its annual budget, has a specific power 'to make, levy and collect a voluntary church rate for any purpose connected with the affairs of the church including the administrative expenses of the council and the costs of any legal proceedings'.[105] Though there is a general prohibition imposed by parliamentary statute against enforcing or compelling payment of the rate,[106] its levying could be made the subject of a contract.[107] Money acquired and collected at Holy Communion forms (by operation of law) part of the general funds of the parochial church council and must be disposed of jointly by the council and the minister.[108] The Legal Advisory Commission is of the view that '[t]he bishop has the right to say whether or not there shall be a collection at any service he conducts' (such as an institution, induction, confirmation, or ordination) but if there is a collection 'strictly its destination rests with the incumbent and [council]'.[109] It is the responsibility of the churchwardens, with the assistance of a sidesperson if required, to collect alms.[110] Money deposited

---

[100] *Re St Peter and St Paul, Scrayingham* [1992] 1 WLR 193; if the parties have acted reasonably and honestly costs will lie where they fall: *Re St Mark's, Heydock* [1981] 1 WLR 1164.

[101] *Re St John, Chelsea* [1962] 1 WLR 706: a petition and cross-petition failed and the petitioners were ordered to pay a third of the costs of the opposing parties; *Re West Camel Church* [1979] Fam 79: court fees were split between the parties; *Re St Mary's, Luton* [1968] P 47: an unsuccessful opponent was ordered to pay most of the costs of the petitioner.

[102] *Re St. Helen, Brant Broughton* [1974] Fam 16; *Re St Michael and All Angels, Torrington* [1985] Fam 81.   [103] Ss. 58–63 (as amended).

[104] See *supra* Ch. 16 for charitable trusts.   [105] PCC(P)M, s. 7(ii).

[106] Compulsory Church Rate Abolition Act 1868, s. 1. For exceptions see ss. 3–5 and *Watson v All Saints, Poplar, Vestry* (1882) 46 LT 201; *R v Churchwardens of St Matthew, Bethnal Green* (1883) 50 LT 65 (CA), (1885) 53 LT 634 (HL); *London County Council v Churchwardens of St Botolph, Bishopsgate* [1914] 2 KB 660.

[107] *R v St Marylebone Vestry* [1895] 1 QB 771 (CA).

[108] Church of England (Legal Aid and Miscellaneous Provisions) Measure 1988, s. 13, Canon B17A; in the event of disagreement the matter must be determined by the bishop: PCC(P)M, ss. 7(iv), 9(3).

[109] *OLAC*, 69; the bishop's power to authorize a collection presumably arises under C18(4).

[110] *Marson v Unmack* [1923] P 163; fit persons are appointed by the priest: *Cope v Barber* (1872) LR 7 CP 393 at 403; for assistance by a sidesperson see Canon E2(3).

in an alms box, which by canon must be provided in every parochial church and chapel, must be applied 'to such uses as the minister and parochial church council shall think fit'; if they disagree, the ordinary must determine disposal.[111] Covenants today form a substantial source of income and are subject to regulation by civil law enabling the donee to recover tax at standard rate and the donor to recover higher rate tax.[112] Dioceses often provide for 'giving initiatives' sometimes prescribing that a person (other than the treasurer) be appointed as parish 'giving director' and provision is made for special training and oversight by a diocesan 'Christian giving adviser'.[113] If the parochial church council opens a missionary or charitable purposes fund, and the purpose for which it was established has been fulfilled (or has lapsed) there may be an obligation to return moneys given by donors or if this is not possible to apply the fund to a related object.[114] A parish may acquire funds through the letting of parish property and the sale of realty and personalty.[115]

The Quota System

The quota system organizes the acquisition of funds, accumulated at diocesan or parochial level, by bodies within the church for application to prescribed ecclesiastical objects. The dioceses transfer to the Central Board of Finance, the Church Commissioners, and the Pensions Board funds determined in accordance with a table of apportionment (based on actual and potential income) approved by General Synod. The diocese's contribution is derived, in turn, from contributions made by the parishes.[116] The quota (or 'parish share') has been described as 'a system of voluntary taxation' whereby 'each parish church is assessed for an annual contribution to diocesan funds'.[117] It

---

[111] Canon F10; for charging for admission to concerts and exhibitions and for copyright issues see *OLAC*, 72–97; for the practice of admission charges to cathedrals see *Heritage and Renewal*, 147 ff.

[112] Finance Act 1990, s. 25; see generally P. Carter and M. Perry, *Handbook of Parish Finance* (3rd edn., London, 1992) 70.   [113] *SDHB*, 64.

[114] Fund-raising appeals are governed by the Charities Act 1993, ss. 59–63. See *OLAC*, 43: the House of Bishops in 1946 made recommendations to diocesan bishops about appeals: the archdeacon should be informed at least a month before a public appeal is made by any parochial authority to persons outside the parish or congregation, 'and he may make regulations and request that the conditions set out in the Bishop's report be observed' (see Church Assembly, *House of Bishops Report on Charitable Appeals*, CA 824B). For the *cy-près* doctrine see G. Moffat and M. Chesterman, *Trusts Law: Text and Materials* (London, 1988) 637–42; *Chichester Diocesan Fund and Board of Finance v Simpson* [1944] AC 341; *Re North Devon and Somerset Relief Fund* [1953] 1 WLR 1260; *Re Gillingham Bus Disaster Fund* [1958] Ch 300, [1959] Ch 62 (CA).

[115] *Supra* Chs. 15, 16.

[116] See Carter and Perry, *Parish Finance*, 26; some dioceses operate a 'parish ministry contribution' scheme separate from the quota which, like the quota, is based on a request (*SDH*, VI, C).

[117] *MIECL*, 92; in 1994 the quota contributed £151,780,000, as compared with 1992 £125,254,000: Central Statistical Unit, 3 Feb. 1994.

has been defined by synodical measure as 'an amount to be subscribed to the expenditure authorised by diocesan synods'.[118]

The request for payment is made either by the diocesan synod or by the deanery synod. The diocesan synod directs the diocesan board of finance, by virtue of a power conferred by measure,[119] to frame a draft budget which (as we have seen) the board submits to the synod's standing committee, which in turn 'may make to the board and the synod any recommendation thereon as it thinks fit'.[120] The synod then by resolution either apportions the expenditure among the parishes or delegates that function to the deanery synods (on which the parishes are actually represented).[121] By measure, '[i]f the diocesan synod delegate to deanery synods functions in relation to the parishes of their deaneries, and in particular the determination of parochial shares in quotas allocated to the deaneries, the deanery synod shall exercise those functions'.[122] There is no legal framework for the determination of the quota. The process of assessment is not governed by synodical measure and each diocese develops its own norms to regulate the assessment, which, broadly, are made according to the social and economic characteristics of each parish: some are based on potential income, some on actual income and ability to pay, some on average adult attendance at services, some on the size of the electoral roll, others on the number of clergy in a parish, and many on combinations of these.[123] Whilst no synodical measure imposes any express responsibility on the parochial church council to find and provide funds which will constitute the quota, it is the council which makes the contribution; this is paid to the diocesan board of finance which distributes the fund to the appropriate authorities for the payment of *inter alia* stipends, pensions, and ministry and training costs.

Whilst it may not be a tax in the strict legal sense the quota bears some of the characteristics of a tax or charge. Ordinarily, a tax or charge is understood to be a contribution levied on persons, property, income, or transactions, the contribution being assessed proportionately to fixed criteria (such as the value or amount of the object taxed or ability to pay), for the purpose of financing public services.[124] A key element in the concept of a tax or charge is that of a

---

[118] SGM 1969, s. 5(4).   [119] Diocesan Boards of Finance Measure 1925, ss. 1, 3.
[120] *MSODS*, SO 108, 109.   [121] *CRR*, r. 24(6).
[122] SGM 1969, s. 5(4); *WAOB* recommends that the proposed National Council be assigned the task of managing arrangements for the redistribution of resources within the church and for the apportionment of national costs among the diocese (5.6).
[123] E.g. *TBF*, 4.4; *WDHI*, ch. 4, 209; *LDHI*, V, 1–2; *NDIB*, I, 8; for a general survey see *The Political Economy of the Church*, Portsmouth Diocese (1981) 3; missionary and charitable donations are often exempted from the assessment: see Carter and Perry, *Parish Finance*, 85.
[124] C. Whitehouse and E. Stuart-Buttle, *Revenue Law: Principles and Practice* (8th edn., London, 1990), ch. 1; *Pryce v Monmouthshire Canal and Railway Co* [1879] 4 App Cas 197; *Metal Industries Ltd v Owners of the S.T. Harle* (1962) SLT 114; *Daymond v SW Water Authority* [1976] 1 All ER 39.

demand which if not met may lead to the imposition of a sanction.[125] Often the quota system is described in diocesan norms as giving rise to an 'obligation', a 'liability', a 'responsibility', or a 'commitment' to pay; some dioceses classify the quota as a 'request' to contribute, or 'encourage' its payment.[126] Whilst describing it as a 'voluntary payment', exceptionally norms prescribe that the quota should be seen 'as a matter of the greatest obligation . . . the first charge on a parochial budget'; sometimes they prescribe that 'making good the shortfall (for whatever cause) in payment of its Share by a parish is the responsibility of the other parishes in the Deanery concerned as determined by the Deanery Standing Committee' and that '[a] poor record in paying its Share is always taken into account when loans for diocesan funds are requested'; and an appeal procedure is laid down when an assessment is questioned.[127] If, as a matter of fact, the exchanges between the diocesan synod or deanery synod and the parish are in the nature of a demand, and if consequences flow from its non-payment, then an element of compulsion may be present. Whether the parochial council is under a legal obligation to pay a demand for the quota is a matter of debate. Two lines of argument suggest that no obligation arises. First, one of the 'functions' of a parochial church council is 'putting into effect any provision made by the diocesan synod or the deanery synod, but without prejudice to the powers of the council on any particular matter'.[128] However, in framing an annual budget required for the maintenance of the work of the church in the parish 'and otherwise', the council has a 'power' 'to take such steps as they think necessary for the raising collecting and allocating of such moneys'; crucially the council has a 'power' jointly with the minister 'to *determine* the objects to which *all moneys* to be given or collected in church shall be allocated'.[129] Secondly, if the matter were tested judicially, a demand for payment would in all probability be unlawful: such demands can be made only upon the clearest express authority of a parliamentary statute which, as a matter of judicial construction, would be interpreted strictly.[130] As synodical measures enjoy the same authority as parliamentary statutes, General Synod could in theory enact a measure imposing an obligation to pay the quota.[131]

---

[125] *Congreve v Home Office* [1976] QB 629 (CA); see also *Leake v Commissioners of Taxation* [1934] 36 WALR 66 (Aust).

[126] *PDH*, M.2: 'christian duty to give financially'; *GDM*, C.1:payment is 'encouraged'; *BDM*, F: 'commitment'; *NDIB*, I, 8: 'request'; *SDH*, VI, C.1: 'ask'.

[127] *BDM*, J.1–2: the appeal may be made only on the ground that since the parochial weighting was determined there has been a marked change in the mix of the actual congregation or in the numbers of potential givers.   [128] PCC(P)M, s. 2(2)(c).

[129] (Emphasis added), ibid., s. 7(i), (iv).

[130] Bill of Rights 1689, Art. 4: 'the levying of money for or to the use of the crown by pretence of prerogative without grant of parliament . . . is or shall be illegal'; *Bowles v Bank of England* [1913] 1 Ch 57; *AG v Wiltshire Dairies* [1921] 37 TLR 884; *Commissioners for Customs and Excise v Cure and Deeley Ltd* [1962] 1 QB 340; *Sheffield City Council v Grainger Wines* [1978] 2 All ER 70; *Vestey v IRC* [1980] AC 1148.   [131] *Supra* Ch. 3.

On the other hand, a legal obligation to pay the quota might arise by way of a multipartite contract. Key parties to the quota arrangement possess contractual capacity: the diocesan board of finance, the diocesan parsonage board, the central board of finance, the Church Commissioners, and the parochial church council are all corporations. The quota is used to meet the services provided by these bodies. The basic question is whether the parochial church council has implicitly entered into an agreement with these corporations, with the diocesan or deanery synods as statutory bodies mediating between the corporations and the council, to pay the quota. A multipartite contract to supply and enjoy services rendered (the provision of stipends, housing, pensions, and so on) may generate an obligation to contribute to the cost of those services. Whether there is a contract depends on the intentions and conduct of the parties involved: for an orthodox contract to arise an offer and acceptance may be implied from the conduct of the parties (such as the actual provision and enjoyment of services),[132] consideration may be supplied by the existence and distribution of benefits and burdens as between the parties.[133] Above all there must be an intent to create legal relations and to treat the agreement as binding.[134] A contract may also arise by way of an estoppel: if the parish represents that the quota will be paid, and this representation is relied upon by church authorities, it may be held to be inequitable to avoid payment;[135] if by convention the parties have acted upon the agreed assumption that the quota is to be paid,

---

[132] *The Amazonia* [1990] 1 Lloyd's Rep 238 at 242; *Re Charge Card Services* [1989] Ch 497; *Hart v Mills* (1846) 15 LJ Ex 200: an offer to supply goods by sending them may be accepted by using them; *Smith v Hughes* (1871) LR 6 QB 597 *per* Blackburn J: 'If, whatever a man's real intentions may be, he so conducts himself that a reasonable man would believe that he was assenting to the terms proposed by the other party, and that other party upon that belief enters into a contract with him, the man thus conducting himself would be equally bound as if he had intended to agree to the other party's terms'; see also Supply of Goods and Services Act 1982, s. 12 (s. 15 imports an implied term that a 'reasonable charge' will be paid).

[133] *Midland Bank Trust Co Ltd v Green* [1981] AC 513: consideration is a benefit to the promisor and a detriment to the promisee and vice versa; a promise, express or implied, may constitute consideration: *Thorensen Car Ferries v Weymouth Portland BC* [1977] 2 Lloyd's Rep 614. However, past consideration will not as a general rule be good consideration unless it is part of a 'continuing transaction'—if the understanding was that the act to be paid for is made in advance and there is a subsequent promise to pay for it, this will be good consideration: *Re Casey's Patents* [1892] 1 Ch 104.

[134] *Rose and Frank Co v JR Crompton & Bros Ltd* [1925] AC 445: promises based on 'honour clauses' not binding; cf. *Home Insurance Co v Administratia Asigurarilor* [1983] 2 Lloyd's Rep 674: contractual intention may not be negatived by honour clause; *Edwards v Skyways Ltd* [1964] 1 WLR 349: promise of an *ex gratia* payment created an obligation to pay; for acceptance by silence see *Western Electric Ltd v Welsh Development Agency* [1983] QB 796.

[135] *Robertson v Minister of Pensions* [1949] 1 KB 227 *per* Lord Denning: 'if a man gives a promise or assurance which he intends to be binding on him, and to be acted on by the person to whom it is given, then, once it is acted upon, he is bound by it'; if a person by conduct or words creates an expectation of payment, this may give rise to an estoppel: *Inwards v Baker* [1965] 2 KB 507.

the parish may be estopped from refusing payment.[136] A quasi-contractual obligation to pay may also arise from customary practice.[137]

Whilst in a critical case of withholding the quota it is wholly unclear whether either of these approaches might apply, they may be used by General Synod to form the basis of legal regulation of the quota system. First, it has been assumed that General Synod is legally competent to create by measure a compulsory contribution scheme: models for such a scheme already exist.[138] Secondly, a contractual model may be employed by General Synod in the enactment of a measure to render an agreed scheme for payment legally enforceable: a model exists in the form of statutory agreements to share church buildings and to contribute to the maintenance of shared buildings.[139]

Roman Catholic Canon Law

Arrangements in the Church of England are rather different from those in the Roman Catholic Church. Roman Catholic canon law recognizes for the church an innate right to require from the faithful whatever is necessary for the ends proper to it (c.1260). Whilst the faithful have the right to give freely to the church, the diocesan bishop is bound (under c.1261) to admonish them concerning the obligation (under c. 222) to assist with the needs of the church so that the church has what is necessary for divine worship, for apostolic works, for works of charity, and for the sustenance of ministers. The faithful have a specific canonical duty 'to contribute to the support of the church by collections . . . according to the norms laid down by the conference of bishops' (c.1262). 'Offerings' are subject to special regulation. As a general principle,

---

[136] *Amalgamated Investment and Property Co v Texas Commerce International Bank* [1982] QB 84.

[137] *Bryant v Foot* [1867]; for moral obligations to pay as enforceable see *J Evans and Co v Heathcote* [1918] 1 KB 418; promises to pay for services rendered under a legal duty to do so may not be enforceable, however, as being against public policy: *Morgan v Palmer* (1824), unless the party has acted beyond its duty: *Glasbrook Bros v Glamorgan County Council* [1925] AC 270; such a promise will be enforceable if there are no grounds in public policy against its enforcement: *Ward v Byham* [1956] 2 All ER 318. In providing services provincial and diocesan authorities are sometimes acting under a legal duty—a promise to pay for these may therefore be enforceable if there is no reason in public policy to prevent enforcement.

[138] Repair of Benefice Buildings Measure 1972, s. 19; the diocesan synod by scheme provides for the parsonages board to make an annual estimate of expenditure of the board and proposals for meeting it; the scheme may provide 'for the payment' by the parochial church council 'of such annual contributions towards the estimated expenditure of the Board as may be determined in accordance with the scheme'; it must not be in excess of the sum approved by the diocesan synod and sums not needed are refunded; see also Endowments and Glebe Measure 1976, s. 39: liability for chancel repair is imposed on the parochial church council.

[139] One possible solution may be a multipartite contract, created under and regulated by synodical measure, between the parochial church council and the diocesan board of finance (acting as agent of the diocesan or deanery synod) entered into in consideration of services provided on their (or the church's) behalf by the Central Board of Finance and/or the Church Commissioners.

the minister may ask nothing for the administration of the sacraments beyond the offerings defined by the competent authority, always being careful that the needy are not deprived of the sacraments through poverty (c. 848). Offerings must be determined by the meetings of bishops of each ecclesiastical province (c. 1263). In accordance with the approved custom of the church, any priest who celebrates a mass may accept an offering to apply the mass for a specific intention (cc. 945–6). Any appearance of 'trafficking or commerce' is forbidden (c. 947) and it is for the provincial council to determine by decree the amount of the offering (cc. 952, 1264(3)).[140] The local ordinary may prescribe the taking up of a special collection for specific parochial, diocesan, national, or universal projects which must thereafter be transmitted to the diocesan curia (c. 1266). These moneys are then put into, *inter alia*, the diocesan common fund. Canon law governs directly the Roman Catholic Church's equivalent to quota in the Church of England. The diocesan bishop has a right 'to impose a moderate tax on public juridic persons subject to his authority'. *Taxa* should be proportionate to income and may be imposed only after hearing the diocesan finance council and the presbyteral council. The bishop may also impose an extraordinary (but moderate) tax on other physical and juridic persons 'only in cases of grave necessity' and with due regard for particular laws and customs.[141]

THE DEVELOPMENT OF FUNDS: INVESTMENTS

Roman Catholic canon law provides a minimal structure for the regulation of investment and assigns to the diocesan ordinary a central position of oversight. Money realized from alienation of property is either to be expended in accord with the purposes of the alienation or it may be invested carefully for the benefit of the church (c. 1294). With the consent of the ordinary, administrators of temporal goods may invest only money which is left over after expenses have been met; a report on investments must be made to the ordinary at the end of each year (c. 1284(2)). The finance council may invest only with the approval of the ordinary.[142] Moneys assigned to a particular endowment

---

[140] See also *CIC*, cc. 953–6: satisfaction and transferral of mass offerings; cc. 957–8: duties of ecclesiastical officers to oversee administration; for pious wills see cc. 1299–310, and for stole fees c. 531.

[141] *CIC*, c. 1263; see also c. 264 for episcopally imposed tax to provide for the needs of seminaries; G. L. Broussard, 'Ecclesiastical taxation: an historical synopsis', Catholic University of America JCL Dissertation (Washington, 1966). Diocese of Westminster, *Parochial Administration Manual* (1993), ch. 2.6: the assessment is based on the income of the parish which, if unable to pay, must complete a form requesting reduction: 'The assessment must be paid by cheque in advance, or by standing order on a monthly or quarterly basis throughout the year. There must be no variation in this without prior consultation with the Finance Office'; see ibid., ch. 6 for covenanting.

[142] *CIC*, c. 1281 (for penalties for failure see c. 1377); the parish finance council has no express canonical power to invest: c. 537; for clerics investing see cc. 282, 286 and T. Smiddy, 'Negotiatio', *The Jurist*, 11 (1951), 486.

are to be invested cautiously and profitably, for the benefit of the foundation, with the approval of the ordinary who must consult interested parties and the diocesan finance council (c. 1305). In addition to these canonical provisions, civil law is applicable to Roman Catholic charitable trustees exercising powers of investment.[143]

The position in the Church of England is different: direct episcopal control is minimal. Generally, the distribution, scope, and control of powers to invest depend on the investing body or fund in question. The subject is regulated principally by the Church Funds Investment Measure 1958. This legislation applies to the corporate funds of the Central Board of Finance, the corporate funds of any diocesan authority, and the funds of any church educational endowment; it also applies to any funds held on trust by the Central Board of Finance, any diocesan authority, or any other persons or bodies for exclusively charitable purposes connected with the Church of England.[144] The trustees may invest such fund (or part of it) by contributing the same to an Investment Fund or by depositing moneys belonging to such fund in a Deposit Fund. The contribution or deposit must be for an 'authorized investment'. The trustees may invest notwithstanding anything contained in any trust instrument,[145] and such investments are exempted from the jurisdiction of the Charity Commissioners.[146]

The Investment Fund of the Central Board of Finance is held and administered as a common fund for the benefit of the funds contributed to it. Any moneys comprised in an Investment Fund 'shall from time to time be invested at the discretion of the [Board] in the purchase of any investments or property of any sort either real or personal' (whether or not they are investments 'authorized by the general law for the investment of trust funds') or upon loan on the security of any property of any description or without security. This may be done provided the Board by instrument in writing declares that the power of investment shall be restricted in the manner declared in the instrument. Church bodies do not have an entitlement to contribute to the fund as of right but must obtain the consent of the Board which has a discretion to refuse. When the contribution is made from an existing trust fund, consents must also be obtained as required by the trust instrument. The Board must keep accounts of the assets and liabilities of each investment, income, and expenditure and the accounts must be audited.[147] Moneys which the Board does not think fit to

---

[143] Diocese of Westminster, *Parochial Administration Manual* (1993), ch. 2 (see below for civil law); chs. 9.9, 10.7: Catholic National Mutual Ltd is the dedicated insurance company.

[144] S. 2; Pastoral Measure 1983, s. 44(6) confers the same power on the Churches Conservation Trust.

[145] S. 3(1); s. 8: 'trust instrument' means *inter alia* any statute, measure, or trust deed affecting the administration of a fund to which the Measure applies.   [146] S. 4.

[147] Sched., paras. 2–18, as amended by Church of England (Miscellaneous Provisions) Measure 1995, S. 7, Sched.; *WAOB* recommends that the Board's investment functions be transferred to the proposed National Council (5.39, 39).

invest immediately may be placed in the Deposit Fund, the power to deposit being subject to any consents required by a trust instrument. The Board has a discretionary power to determine the terms upon which money might be deposited (including the rate of interest and the length of notice required for withdrawals). Sums deposited may be invested *inter alia* in shares or securities of any registered building society and in any investments for the time being authorized by law for the investment of trust funds. The Board must keep accounts which are to be audited.[148]

The Pensions Board may invest any moneys available for investment in any investment falling within Schedule 1, the Trustee Investments Act 1961 (in which case control of investment is effected by the terms of that statute), in the acquisition of freehold or leasehold land in England and Wales, or in any investment fund or deposit constituted under the Church Funds Investment Measure 1958 (in which case control is effected by the terms of that Measure).[149] The exercise of investment powers by a diocesan board of finance is regulated by the Church Funds Investment Measure 1958,[150] and subject to directions given by the diocesan synod for which it acts as financial executive.[151] With regard to the Diocesan Parsonages Fund a diocesan parsonage board has the same powers of investment as trustees of trust funds. However, the diocesan synod may provide by scheme that the powers of the board in respect of the management of the Parsonages Fund and the receipt of moneys payable into that Fund shall be exercisable by the diocesan board of finance on behalf of the parsonages board.[152] The parochial church council has a limited power of investment of trusts funds held by it for charitable purposes.[153] Whilst ordinarily the council can act only with the consent of the diocesan authority,[154] with respect to investments, where the diocesan authority acts as the custodian trustee, the Public Trustee Act 1906 applies and the decision lies wholly with the council: the diocesan authority must concur in carrying out the investment unless this involves a breach of trust.[155]

The Church Funds Investment Measure 1958 does not apply to the Church Commissioners. Under the Church Commissioners Measure 1947, the Assets Committee may (subject to any general rules made by the Board of Governors) make, realize, and change investments of assets of the Commissioners the

---

[148] Ibid., paras. 19–26.

[149] Church of England (Pensions) Measure 1988, s. 14; Clergy Pensions Measure 1961, s. 33.

[150] S. 2(b).   [151] Diocesan Boards of Finance Measure 1925, s. 3.

[152] Repair of Benefice Buildings Measure 1972, s. 17(1).

[153] Church Funds Investment Measure 1958, s. 2(d) ('any persons or bodies'); the same power would, it seems, vest in incumbents and churchwardens. For investments by cathedral bodies see Cathedrals Measure 1963, s. 21: the consent of Church Commissioners is required; see ss. 34–5 for loans and borrowing powers.   [154] PCC(P)M, s. 6(3).

[155] Public Trustee Act 1906, s. 4(2); *OLAC*, 203; diocesan norms often recognize the power of parochial managing trustees to invest independently of the holding trustee: e.g. *BDM*, J.5; *LDHI*, V.9.

income of which is carried into their General Fund. The Committee must recommend to the Board from time to time what sums are available for reinvestment.[156] The exercise of the Commissioners' investment powers has been the subject of criticism in recent years,[157] and it has been recognized judicially that choice of investments is, broadly, a matter for the Commissioners. In *Harries (Bishop of Oxford) and Others v Church Commissioners*, Sir Donald Nicholls in the High Court considered affidavit evidence concerning the manner in which the Commissioners formulated and implemented their investment policies. It was argued that the Commisioners ignored ethical considerations in choosing *inter alia* to invest in South African companies and in arms manufacturing. The Vice-Chancellor concluded that the Commissioners, when investing funds of which they were trustees, may take into account non-financial ethical considerations only in so far as this would not jeopardize the profitability of their investments; their investment policy (for 1989) could not to be challenged because the Church of England held a specific view on the ethical question at issue. However, the Commissioners may not make a financially disadvantageous investment on ethical grounds, for example, (1) if the nature of the investment was in direct opposition to the purpose of the charity in question, and (2) if implementing an investment policy would alienate supporters of the charity so as to produce a significant reduction in the charity's income. In the instant case, the Vice-Chancellor was satisfied that the Commissioners had considered the matter prior to investment and had discharged their duty to fulfill their *raison d' être*, 'generating money'.[158]

THE APPLICATION OF FUNDS: MANDATORY EXPENDITURE

As we have seen, the law of the Church of England commonly confers discretionary powers on ecclesiastical authorities to dispose of funds as they think fit for purposes connected with the church.[159] Sometimes, however, the law imposes duties on authorities to apply funds for specified purposes. In so

---

[156] S. 6(3)(a), (b).

[157] Addressing specifically the investment policies of the Church Commissioners, the Lambeth Report, a report to the Archbishop of Canterbury by the Lambeth Group and Coopers and Lybrand, 19 July 1993, concluded that many of the problems which have been encountered 'stem from the structure of the Commissioners' organisation which is not well suited to present-day requirements'. For criticism by the House of Commons Social Security Committee see *Church Times*, 21 Apr. 1995; *WAOB* recommends that the Commissioners retain their investment powers: draft measure App. B, cl. 9(1)(a), including powers over ethical policy (8.38).

[158] [1992] 1 WLR 1241: there was 'no identifiable yardstick which can be applied to a set of facts so as to yield one answer which can be seen as "right" and the other "wrong"'.

[159] See also *supra*, Ch. 15.

doing it indirectly confers rights entitling bodies and persons to make claims upon funds held.

Insurance of Property

Insurance of ecclesiastical property is governed by both church-made and state-made law. In the Roman Catholic Church, administrators of goods are under a canonical duty to take care that no property entrusted to them is lost or damaged, to 'take out insurance policies for this purpose, insofar as such is necessary' and to ensure that the prescriptions of civil law in this regard are met.[160] With respect to the Church of England, one duty (arising from synodical measure) of the parochial church council is to arrange 'insurance of the fabric of the church and the goods and ornaments thereof'.[161] Where any property is vested in the diocesan authority, the council must keep the authority indemnified with regard to all insurance premiums payable in respect of the property and all costs, charges, and expenses incurred by the authority in relation to the insurance of the property in question.[162] The duty to insure is not, however, unqualified. The terms of the insurance arrangement and the nature and extent of contractual obligations to pay premiums, needless to say, will be limited by the funds available. The Legal Advisory Commission has recently formulated norms of good practice. Advice should be sought of an insurance company 'experienced in the insurance of ecclesiastical buildings'. The ideal is to insure the building against the costs of restoring it, in the event of its destruction, to its earlier condition together with ancillary expenses such as professional fees and hiring a substitute building for use during reconstruction. With more ancient or larger buildings this may be an unattainable ideal and the premium may prove too costly. In such cases 'the insurance principle of average must be borne in mind . . . the rule that if a property is insured for only a proportion of its value and damage occurs to a part of the property insurers will be liable to pay only the same proportion in respect of the loss that the sum insured bears to the full restoration cost'. In relation to church treasures, the Commission advises that 'there is no legal requirement for insurance to cover the full market value and that a practical compromise may be the insurance of any such objects for a sum which would cover the cost of a good modern replacement'.[163] In addition, many diocesan regulations require insurance cover to be updated regularly.[164] The adequacy of insurance cover is usually policed by visitation.[165] Many dioceses operate a group scheme (organized by the diocesan board of finance) in co-operation with

---

[160] *CIC*, c. 1284(2).   [161] PCC(P)M, s. 4(1)(ii)(b).   [162] Ibid., s. 6(4)(b), (c).
[163] *OLAC*, 152 ff.
[164] For diocesan norms and the Ecclesiastical Insurance Group see e.g. *BRDSEI*, AC; *BDM*, J.6; *TBF*, 4.7; *GDM*, C.3; *SDDH*, M.11–12; for parsonage house *TBF*, 7.3; *PDH*, D.7.
[165] *SDH*, II, D.2.

the Ecclesiastical Insurance Group, and diocesan norms often direct parishes to join the scheme.[166] Insurance arrangements and terms have given rise to a number of diocesan norms requiring greater security measures to be taken by parochial church councils.[167]

Third-party (or public liability) insurance, covering accidents or injuries involving members of the public, poses a special problem. With regard to the Church of England it has been suggested that 'under the law of tort, if a member of the [parochial church council] is aware of the dangerous condition of a church building and takes no steps to prevent injury to third parties, he could be liable in the tort of negligence'.[168] The view of the Legal Advisory Commission is that the council should treat this insurance 'as of the highest priority'.[169] No obligation to insure against public liability, however, is imposed at present by internal church law. The stimulus to arrange third-party insurance flows from civil law duties. For the purposes of the Occupiers' Liability Act 1957, under which occupiers of property to which members of the public are admitted owe a duty of care to those persons and are liable to pay damages for breach of that duty, the Legal Advisory Commission has advised that 'occupier' includes the parochial church council and the incumbent. In relation to a particular gravestone the responsible party is the person who erected it, and in relation to a closed churchyard (where liability for maintenance has passed to it), the local authority. During a vacancy, and where there is a priest-in-charge, responsibility may belong to the bishop.[170] The duty applies to visitors and other persons lawfully on the property,[171] but not generally to trespassers.[172] The duty is to take such care as in all the circumstances of the case is reasonable to see that the visitors will be reasonably safe in using the property for the purposes for which they are permitted to be there.[173] To this end the duties imposed by church law and civil law to maintain the property to the required standards may be treated as designed to satisfy the standard required by the general civil law duty of care.[174]

Moreover, under the Employers' Liability (Compulsory Insurance) Act 1969, when an ecclesiastical body acts as an employer it must insure against its liability if an employee suffers injury or disease arising out of and in the course of employment.[175] Consequently, the Legal Advisory Commission advises that parochial church councils 'should insure against liability to claims by persons using the church, churchyard or any parochial building or land and if they are employers against liability to compensate their employees,

---

[166] *GDM*, C.3.   [167] *SDHB*, II, C; *GDM*, D.11.
[168] Carter and Perry, *Parish Finance*, 49.   [169] *OLAC*, 153.
[170] *OLAC*, 56 (cf. Occupiers' Liability Act 1984).
[171] Wildlife and Countryside Act 1981 (persons using private rights of way). ·
[172] *OLAC*, 56.
[173] Occupiers' Liability Act 1957, s. 2(1), (2).
[174] *OLAC*, 57 for paths, fences etc. and *supra*, Ch. 16.   [175] S. 1.

whether full or part-time, for injury or disease suffered through their employment'.[176] Under the Repair of Benefice Buildings Measure 1972 the diocesan parsonage board must insure all parsonage houses and glebe buildings in the diocese. It has a duty to pursue all insurance claims in respect of this property.[177]

Remuneration and Stipends

According to Roman Catholic canon law when ordained clergy dedicate themselves to the ecclesiastical ministry 'they deserve a remuneration which is consistent with their condition in accord with the nature of their responsibilities and with the conditions of time and place'; remuneration 'should enable them to provide for the needs of their own life and for the equitable payment of those whose services they need'.[178] However, clergy are canonically bound 'to cultivate a simple style of life and are to avoid whatever has a semblance of vanity'; income surplus to needs should be used for the good of the church and for works of charity.[179] The conference of bishops is under a duty to manage a clergy fund and to establish norms for the provision of proper living for clerics.[180] Lay people engaged in the service of the church have a right to worthy remuneration befitting their condition whereby, with due regard to the provisions of the civil law, they may provide for their own needs and the needs of their families.[181]

In the Church of England rights to remuneration for work are distributed according to the position held. Ordinarily rights to remuneration are statutory though in some cases they may be contractual. Parish clerks and sextons are entitled to such salaries as are determined by the incumbent and parochial church council.[182] Remuneration (if any) for organists is governed by the terms of the contract entered on appointment by an incumbent with the

[176] *OLAC*, 154: 'the limit of indemnity should not be less than £2 million'; questions may arise as to who precisely is the owner/occupier or employer, and therefore 'any policy should insure the whole "church interest" ', i.e. the interests of bishop, incumbent, priest-in-charge, council, and churchwardens; *Re St Helen's, Brant Broughton* [1973] 3 All ER 386.

[177] S. 12; for presentation of basic rules concerning exemption of all places of public religious worship and church halls from the payment of rates under civil law (though parsonage property is rateable) see e.g. *GDM*, E.10.

[178] *CIC*, c. 281(1); see para. (3) for remuneration of married deacons to provide for their own support and that of their families.

[179] C. 282; see also cc. 531, 551, stole fees for remuneration of clerics.

[180] Cc. 1272, 1274; *PO*, 20.

[181] *CIC*, c. 231(2); c. 1286: administrators of temporal goods in making contracts of employment must observe, according to the principles taught by the church, the civil laws relating to labour and social life; they are to pay those who work for them under contract 'a just and honest wage which would fittingly provide for their needs and those of their dependents'.

[182] PCC(P)M, s. 7(iii), *OLAC*, 194: 'These officers are the subject of a contract of service between the parish clerk or sexton on the one hand and the PCC and the incumbent on the other, and the ordinary law as to contracts of service applies'.

agreement of the parochial church council.[183] The same applies to lay and ordained persons employed in sector ministry.[184] Readers and lay workers usually receive no remuneration but when they are paid 'it may be possible to infer that they are working under a contract of employment' in which case they are entitled to remuneration as prescribed by that contract.[185] Ordinarily written particulars of employment will contain terms as to the scale or rate of remuneration.[186] However, if a contract of employment is silent, under secular law a reasonable remuneration is payable, assessed by way of *quantum meruit*.[187] Persons may not be licensed as stipendiary readers or lay workers unless the bishop is satisfied that adequate provision has been made for the stipend and for insurance against sickness or accident.[188] The position of ordained clergy may be summarized as follows. Full-time stipendiary ministers in parochial appointments (as incumbents, priests-in-charge, team vicars, and assistant curates) are paid (and housed) through the Church Commissioners from the appropriate diocesan stipends fund. Part-time stipendiary ministers in parochial appointments holding an additional appointment in the sector ministry are paid by the Church Commissioners with income from additional appointments forming part of the stipend. Part-time priests-in-charge and assistant curates are paid by the Church Commissioners.[189] Indeed, a bishop cannot admit a person into holy orders unless satisfied that 'he is provided of some ecclesiastical office' within the diocese to which, with the exception of non-stipendiary ministers, remuneration ordinarily attaches.[190]

The Church Commissioners act as the Central Stipends Authority, a body established by and responsible to General Synod, and stipends to incumbents and most assistant ministers are paid from the diocesan stipends funds administered by the Commissioners. However, though the Commissioners as a matter of ecclesiastical practice recommend national maxima and minima

---

[183] *OLAC*, 188.

[184] Ibid., 123: ordained persons engaged in the sector ministry may also hold an office in which case the rules discussed below concerning stipends will apply.   [185] Ibid., 124.

[186] Ibid., 126, including hours of work and provision for sick pay.

[187] See e.g. *Way v Latilla* [1937] 3 All ER 759, *Powell v Braun* [1954] 1 WLR 401; the same applies to sick pay: *Mears v Safecar Security Ltd* [1981] IRLR 99; this implied term is, however, excluded if there is any contractual term on the subject, even if simply in the form 'such amount as X may determine': see *Re Richmond Gate Property Co Ltd* [1965] 1 WLR 335.

[188] Canon E6(4); E8(3).

[189] The general scheme is often described in diocesan norms: e.g. *NDIB*, III.33; with regard to cathedral staff, the dean, provost, and 2 residentiary canons engaged exclusively in cathedral duties are paid by the Church Commissioners such stipends as the Commissioners may from time to time determine; the capitular body may pay additional stipends with the consent of the Commissioners: Cathedral Measure 1963, s. 28; remuneration for other ordained clergy or lay persons connected with the cathedral is paid by the Commissioners: ibid., s. 31; see ss. 30, 32 for removal expenses and grants for the acquisition, erection, improvement, or repair of houses of clergy holding office in the cathedral.   [190] Canon C5(1); *supra* Ch. 7.

each year, it is the diocese which calculates the stipend payable.[191] The Commissioners must apply moneys standing to the credit of the income account of the diocesan stipends fund 'in providing or augmenting the stipends or other emoluments of incumbents, assistant curates licensed under seal and other persons who are declared by the bishop to be engaged in the cure of souls within the diocese'. Once the stipend is determined, a right to it arises: the moneys 'shall be so applied in accordance with directions from time to time given, with the concurrence of the Diocesan Board of Finance, by the bishop or a person duly authorised for that purpose by him'. These directions, in turn, must be 'consistent with any directions given by the Commissioners, in the exercise of their functions as the Central Stipends Authority, with respect to the forms and levels of the pay of those persons'. Moreover, the bishop (or a person authorized by him) must, in determining the directions to be given, 'have regard to any advice given by the Commissioners' with respect to the application of the money.[192] The diocesan pastoral committee has a special responsibility for 'the provision of appropriate spheres of work and conditions of service for all persons engaged in the cure of souls and the provision of reasonable remuneration for such persons'.[193]

Ordained clergy and persons in lay ministry may also receive income from a variety of other sources. Incumbents have a right to any endowments generated by the particular benefice. The Church Commissioners must pay from the diocesan stipends fund a 'guaranteed annuity' comprising the net annual endowment income of the benefice or £1,000 (whichever be the less) towards the incumbent's stipend.[194] Where the guaranteed annuity is £1,000, if the net annual benefice income exceeds that sum, the incumbent is entitled to receive an annual personal grant of a sum equal to the amount of the excess.[195] Both the guaranteed annuity and the personal grant are payable by such instalments and on such days as the Commissioners may determine.[196] The Commissioners have a special power to pay out of their General Fund such sums as they think fit towards the stipend of archdeacons who also have a right to an annual grant of not less than that payable as endowment income of the archdeaconry.[197] The income account of the diocesan stipends fund is charged with the payments towards the stipend or other emoluments of any assistant curate or clerical or

---

[191] E.g. Ordination of Women (Financial Provisions) Measure 1993, s. 11: ' "national minimum stipend" . . . means the national minimum stipend of clergymen of incumbent status for that year in the Annual Report of the Commissioners as the Central Stipends Authority'; the Authority's general regulations are contained in an Act of Synod, Nov. 1982; *WAOB* recommends that the Authority's functions, including decisions about stipend levels, be transferred to the proposed National Council (8.39).

[192] Diocesan Stipends Funds Measure 1953, s. 5. [193] Pastoral Measure 1983, s. 2(3)(a).

[194] Endowments and Glebe Measure 1976, s. 1; for pastoral schemes see s. 1(3).

[195] S. 2; for pastoral schemes see s. 2(2) and for benefices held in plurality, s. 3.

[196] S. 5; what constitutes an endowment is to be determined conclusively by the Commissioners: s. 7; for quarterly payments see Ecclesiastical Commissioners (Powers) Measure 1938, s. 7.

[197] S. 6.

lay assistant engaged in the cure of souls in any parish of an annual sum of the same amount as that which would be applicable by the Commissioners for augmenting these. Any question of the amount to be allocated must be determined conclusively by the Commissioners.[198] In all these schemes, there is no explicit right of appeal against an allocation.[199] The incumbent of a benefice has a right to Easter offerings.[200] Other income may be derived from direct parochial giving, parochial fees (discussed above), and income from local trusts. In calculating the stipend, these are taken into account.

There is no formal internal law dealing with expenses of ordained and lay people engaged in parochial ministry. Whilst the parochial church council is strictly under no legal duty to pay expenses,[201] on the basis of guidance issued by the Church Commissioners as the Central Stipends Authority[202] diocesan norms commonly assume a responsibility on the parochial church council to do so. Typically, norms prescribe that the parochial church council and the minister involved must agree on a policy about the scale and timing of reimbursement and the items which it covers; sometimes they require an annual review and provide that any advice needed is to be sought from the archdeacon.[203] For national insurance and taxation purposes clergy are classified as employed persons in receipt of emoluments and pay national insurance contributions. Consequently, they are eligible for maternity, sickness, and industrial injury benefits. The Church Commissioners, treated as the employer for these purposes, are obliged to pay the national insurance contribution and are also responsible for the deduction of income tax.[204] Many diocesan norms contain guidance about sickness benefits.[205]

Special provisions apply to the remuneration of archbishops and bishops. An annual stipend is payable to them together with such greater sum as the Church Commissioners may from time to time determine and various allowances. Sums payable are fixed periodically by schemes confirmed by Order in

---

[198] S. 8(3); see also Ecclesiastical Commisioners (Curate Grants) Measure 1946.

[199] When a draft pastoral scheme deals with endowment income (Pastoral Measure 1983, s. 33) a right of appeal exists: *supra*, Ch. 5.

[200] *BCP*, 262; *Cooper v Blakiston* [1907] 2 KB 688 at 700 (CA); [1909] AC 104 (HL); these are taxable: *Slaney v Starkey* [1931] 2 KB 148.　　　[201] PCC(P)M, s. 7 does not mention the duty.

[202] The Central Stipends Authority, *The Parochial Expenses of the Clergy: A Guide to their Reimbursement* (1986).

[203] For diocesan norms recognizing a right to expenses enjoyable by incumbents, priests-in-charge, assistant curates, team vicars, deaconesses, readers, and lay workers see *NDIB*, III.34; *BDM*, B.12; *PDH*, C.8; *GDM*, A.3; *BF*, 4.4, 4.6; *SDDH*, K.39–40; *WH*, BP.17; *LDHI*, V.17; *CDH*, 167; *SDH*, V, C.3: these include postage, telephone, stationery, maintenance of robes, hospitality, and travelling expenses; ibid., II, B.5: 'Every PCC should undertake to pay in full the expenses incurred by assistant staff in the course of their duties. The assistant staff member should submit a regular claim for these expenses, suitably itemised, to the treasurer of the PCC.'

[204] See Churches Main Committee, *The Taxation of Ministers of Religion*, Guidance Notes Revised 1991, Circular No. 1991/15.

[205] *BDM*, B.9; *SDDH*, K.32; *NDIB*, I, 7; for grants, loans, and help on occasions of debt see e.g. *ODYB: IF*, 256; *NDIB*, III, 40; *PDH*, C.9, G.1; *TBF*, 4.5; *SDDH*, K.33.

Council. In making the scheme the Commissioners must consult the diocesan bishop and board of finance. If the bishop in whose favour the scheme is to be made remains in occupation of the see, the scheme must be made at his request and only with his approval. A scheme may be amended with the approval of the Standing Committee of the General Synod.[206] Provision also exists for the payment of stipends, augmentations, grants, and expenses to cathedral staff.[207]

Compensation

The implementation of rules, both on discipline and on administrative reorganization, may result in loss of office or other ecclesiastical post. Legislators in the Church of England have dealt with this problem by devising compensation and gratuity schemes. The rules have been developed piecemeal, only in relation to some keys areas, and no explicit provision exists for compensating loss of office suffered by licensed clergy, readers, lay workers, or musical directors, for example, all of whom may be in receipt of an emolument. Whilst the underlying rationale for compensation in civil law is the suffering of harm or unfairness by the compensated party,[208] some ecclesiastical compensation schemes operate when there has been no manifest unfair treatment of the payee.

First, compensation may be paid when loss results from an administrative decision of the church. Provision exists for 'conferring rights to compensation on incumbents of benefices, vicars in team ministries, and archdeacons whose benefices or offices are dissolved, abolished, vacated, or resigned' as a result of a pastoral reorganization scheme.[209] Loss includes that arising from ceasing to occupy the parsonage house and expenses arising from a change of residence. The right to and amount of compensation payable are determined in the first instance by the diocesan pastoral committee but the claimant has a right of appeal to a tribunal. Compensation consists of periodical payments or a lump sum payment or a mixture of these. In assessing quantum the emoluments of any ecclesiastical office to which the claimant has been or is to be appointed (or of any other regular remunerated employment in which he is or is to be engaged) must be taken into account. If a claimant refuses without 'good and

---

[206] Episcopal Endowments and Stipends Measure 1943, ss. 1, 5, 7; the Commissioners have a discretion to pay the whole or any part of the stipend of a suffragan or any chaplain to the bishop: s. 5(b); suffragan bishops may also receive augmentation: Church Property (Miscellaneous Provisions) Measure 1960, s. 21; *WAOB* recommends the establishment of a Bishoprics Committee, appointed by the proposed National Council 'to supervise and give general directions with regard to the administration by the officers of the Council for paying the stipends of, and otherwise providing financial support for, bishops' (draft Measure, c. 10); the budget for episcopal stipends, expenses, and housing would be set by the Council in consultation with the Committee (8.32).

[207] Cathedrals Measure 1963, s. 28–43; *WAOB* recommends that cathedral clergy stipends would be set by the proposed National Council (8.36).

[208] I. T. Smith and J. C. Wood, *Industrial Law* (5th edn., London, 1993) 390 ff.

[209] Pastoral Measure 1983, s. 26.

sufficient reason' to accept an ecclesiastical office which in the opinion of the committee or tribunal is reasonably comparable to the benefice or office in respect of which compensation is claimed, the committee or tribunal may take into account the emoluments of the office so refused. If a person claiming or receiving compensation under these provisions executes a deed of relinquishment of orders, becomes a member of a religious body not in communion with the Church of England, or becomes disqualified from holding preferment (under the Ecclesiastical Jurisdiction Measure 1963) the claim may be refused or, as the case may be, no further compensation shall be made. The claimant receiving periodical payments must disclose to the pastoral committee any remunerated employment for the purposes of adjusting a periodical payment; failure to do so enables the committee to direct its repayment or any excess as they think just and that amount is recoverable as a debt due to the diocesan board of finance; an appeal lies to the tribunal against such a direction.[210]

Secondly, whereas in the above arrangement compensation results from loss not arising through the 'fault' of the claimant, under the following scheme compensation is paid where loss occurs through the unwillingness of a person to accept an ecclesiastical development. The Ordination of Women (Financial Provisions) Measure 1993 was designed, as its Preamble states, 'to make provision as to the relief of hardship incurred by persons resigning from ecclesiastical service by reason of opposition to the ordination of women as priests'. Every clerk in holy orders, deaconess, or licensed lay worker who was in whole-time stipendiary and pensionable ecclesiastical service for not less than five years,[211] is entitled to receive a resettlement grant and periodical payments as compensation.[212] A payment may not be made unless and until the claimant makes within the prescribed time limit a declaration that he 'would not have resigned but for [his] opposition to the promulgation of the Canon . . . enabling a woman to be ordained to the office of priest'.[213] A resettlement grant must be a single payment of an amount equal to three-tenths of the national minimum stipend for the year in which the application for the grant was made or such greater amount as the Pensions Board may, with the concurrence of the Church Commissioners, determine. A grant must not be paid unless the Board is satisfied that the applicant was, immediately before the material time, residing in accommodation made available to undertake the service from which the person has resigned.[214] Periodical payments, made

---

[210] Ibid., Sched. 4; see para. 13 for effect on pensions and paras. 14–15 for composition of pastoral committee and the tribunal; the Commissioners may make rules prescribing the procedure to be followed in claiming and determining rights to and amounts of compensation: para. 16; legal aid is available to the claimant: para. 17; compensation payments are made by the diocesan board of finance: para. 18.

[211] S. 1(2): the claimant must not have attained retiring age and must not be in receipt of a pension; claims may be made up to 10 years after Feb. 1993.

[212] S. 1(1): such persons may also participate in a church housing scheme under s. 2.

[213] S. 7, Sched.   [214] S. 3.

monthly, cease to be payable when the person attains retiring age, receives a pension, or re-enters whole-time stipendiary ecclesiastical service.[215]

The Board may also provide such financial benefit, on application made to it by 'any person' not being an ordained minister, deaconess, or licensed lay worker, by way of periodical payments, grant, loan, or otherwise as it thinks fit. It may do so only if satisfied that, within the period of ten years immediately after the promulgation of the Canon, the applicant or any person on whom the applicant is dependent (or was dependent immediately before that person's death) has ceased to hold an office or employment or to be a member of a religious community consequent on his resignation therefrom. The person must have made the relevant declaration and the Board must be satisfied that in consequence 'the applicant has suffered or will suffer financial hardship'. The Board, in determining whether financial benefit should be provided and its amount, must have regard *inter alia* to the age and other circumstances of the applicant, any special need in respect of housing or training for suitable employment, the extent to which the applicant provides or might reasonably be expected to provide financial support for any person dependent upon him, and all other relevant circumstances.[216] Periodical payment may be refused, suspended, or reduced on account of other employment undertaken by the applicant, who must furnish the Board with details of this.[217]

The Pensions Board administers the system of benefits and the Church Commissioners must make the necessary payments to the Board out of their General Fund.[218] The applicant may appeal against the Board's determination to a special tribunal.[219] In this arrangement compensation is paid to a person for a loss caused by the church's decision to ordain women as priests. Whilst on one hand compensation may be treated as properly paid in so far as the recipient's conscientious action is without fault, on the other it may be thought that the payment is improper unless the assumption is made that the church was at fault in ordaining women (being the stimulus for the payment).

Thirdly, compensation may be paid when loss results from the fault of the payee; this model is entirely inconsistent with the normal rationale for compensation. Under the Incumbents (Vacation of Benefices) Measure 1977 (as amended), after proceedings are instituted to deal with a serious breakdown of pastoral relations, if the incumbent resigns or the bishop issues a declaration

---

[215] S. 4. [216] S. 5.

[217] S. 6(1), (3); the Board must not exercise its powers such that the total amount of the emoluments in question and the periodical payments (if any) would be less than the national minimum stipend: s. 6(2).

[218] S. 8(1); the Board must act in consultation with the Commissioners and in accordance with such general directions as the Commissioners may give; when they give directions they must cause a report thereon to be laid before General Synod: s. 8(2); these may include directions which appear to them requisite or expedient for securing a due balance between the liabilities likely to be imposed on the General Fund and the resources available to meet those liabilities.

[219] S. 10; see *supra* Ch. 5.

vacating the benefice (and here the incumbent may have contributed to the breakdown), 'the incumbent shall be entitled to compensation for any loss suffered by him in consequence of his resignation or the vacation of the benefice'.[220] Loss includes that arising from ceasing to occupy the parsonage house or other residence and any expenses arising from change of residence. The system for determining loss and quantum is the same as that for compensation for dispossession under a pastoral scheme.[221] These arrangements are unusual in that compensation is given when the payee may have contributed to the loss suffered. There is no guidance in the Measure to reduce compensation in accordance with the degree of the incumbent's contribution to the breakdown. It was decided in *Re Flenley* that compensation is payable regardless of fault on the part of the incumbent 'for it is the clear intention of this Measure that the vacation of the benefice is for pastoral reasons and is not punitive in its purpose'; in this case it was held by the Canterbury Appeal Tribunal that the plain wording of the Measure entitled the claimant to compensation for any loss incurred until the compulsory retirement age of seventy.[222]

These piecemeal Church of England provisions may be contrasted with Roman Catholic canon law. As well as a general system of financial provision in the event of removal from office,[223] Roman Catholic canon law operates a system of 'indemnification actions': '[a]nyone who unlawfully inflicts damage upon someone by a juridic act, or indeed by any other act placed with malice or culpability, is obliged to compensate for the damage inflicted.'[224] In the Church of England no equivalent provision exists for compensation payable as a result of unlawful disciplinary proceedings (such as a suspension) or action (such as the revocation of a licence). Synodical measures and canons are consistently silent on the matter. As a basic principle, the civil law principles of compensation for unfair dismissal do not apply to non-employed office-holding personnel of the church. The church's appellate courts possess no jurisdiction to order an award of compensation against a censure unlawfully imposed by a lower court; the power is simply to overturn the censure.[225]

---

[220] Ss. 4, 10, 13(1).   [221] S. 13(2), (3); Sched. 2.

[222] *Re Flenley* (1981) Fam 64 at 70 *per* Moore Ch; see also the decision of Calcutt Ch, *In re Christ Church, Albany Street* (1979) unreported (16 July).

[223] *CIC*, c. 192: a person may removed from office only 'with due regard for rights which may have been acquired by contract or by the law itself'; c. 195: 'If a person is removed from an office which is the source of financial support, not by the law itself [that is, if removal is not automatic], but by a decree of the competent authority, this same authority is to take care such support is seen to for a suitable time, unless it is provided otherwise'; *CIC: TC*, 111–12.

[224] *CIC*, c. 128; for process see cc. 57, 221; for damage as a result of unlawful alienation of property, c. 1296; for an action for reparation of damages, cc. 1729–31; for the forum, c. 1410; see also cc. 1647, 1718.   [225] See *supra* Ch. 7 for loss of licensed office and unfair dismissal.

Pensions

Roman Catholic canon law requires provision to be made for ordained ministers to have social assistance by which their needs are suitably met if they suffer from illness, incapacity, or old age: specific arrangements are supplied by particular norms.[226] As to non-ordained persons involved in ecclesiastical work, by canon administrators must observe meticulously the requirements of civil employment law.[227] With respect to the Church of England, under the Clergy Pensions Measure 1961 as amended, on retirement any clerk in holy orders, deaconess, or licensed lay worker (a 'scheme member') has a basic right to receive from the Church Commissioners a pension for the remainder of life.[228] No contribution during the period of service is required. The right arises if the scheme member has completed a qualifying period of pensionable service of not less than two years or a succession of periods with or without intervals amounting to no less than two years. The Pensions Board may, however, with the concurrence of the Church Commissioners, substitute a shorter period in exceptional circumstances.[229] Pensionable service is 'stipendiary ecclesiastical service', service rendered under the direction of a diocesan bishop or carried on in furtherance of the spiritual or administrative work of the church and recognized as such by a diocesan bishop.[230] Any period of service for which a scheme member is party to any pension or superannuation scheme other than that established under the Measure (or one approved by the Pensions Board and the Commissioners) is not treated as pensionable service.[231] The Board may enter a pension agreement with a person who ceases to be a member of the scheme, or with any prospective scheme member, with respect to any service performed which may be treated as pensionable service; the agreement may require the scheme member to make contributions.[232]

The right to a pension accrues, and its rate is fixed (by reference to office and term of years served) according to whether the person retires on or after the retiring age or if he retires before attaining the retiring age, on the ground that he has become incapable through infirmity of performing the duties of his office; as to the latter the Board must be satisfied that the infirmity is likely to

---

[226] *CIC*, c. 281(2); c. 1274: the conference of bishops must ensure that an institute exists which sufficiently provides for the social security of the clergy wherever social insurance has not been suitably arranged; c. 536: the diocesan bishop, taking into account norms issued by the conference of bishops, is to provide for the 'suitable support and housing' of resigned pastors on attaining 70; see *COCLA*, 1336 for the bishops conference of England and Wales provision, in accordance with c. 538(3), providing for the worthy maintenance and residence of retired and sick diocesan priests.

[227] *CIC*, c. 1286; see also c. 538; *CCL: TC*, 217, n. 127; J. Kinsella and W. Jenne, *Fullness in Christ: A Report on a Study of Clergy Retirement* (Washington, 1979).

[228] S. 1(1); Church of England (Pensions) Measure 1988, s. 1;see also Bishops (Retirement) Measure 1986, s. 7.   [229] S. 1(2), as amended by s. 1 of the 1988 Measure.

[230] S. 46(1).   [231] S. 1(4).   [232] S. 1(3), as amended by s. 1 of the 1988 Measure.

be permanent.[233] The rates of pension are fixed by reference to the office held and the term of years of served and may be augmented at the discretion of the Commissioners.[234] There is no general power to suspend a pension except where the scheme member accepts and resumes listed ecclesiastical offices or has not attained the age of seventy in the case of a man or sixty-five in the case of a woman and after retirement performs pensionable service.[235] The power to determine questions related to pensions, including whether pensionable service has been performed, vests in the Pensions Board itself though a right of appeal exists to the High Court, whose decision is final.[236] The Pensions Board also administers moneys for spouses and dependants.[237]

Legal Officers and Proceedings: Fees and Legal Aid

In contrast with the Roman Catholic Church, in which the responsibility falls on the diocesan episcopacy,[238] the Church of England organizes remuneration of ecclesiastical judges and legal officers on a national basis. The Fees Advisory Commission is empowered to make an order as to the annual fees to be paid to legal officers in respect of such of the duties of their office as are specified by the Commission. The legal officers covered are the provincial registrars, diocesan registrars (and their deputies), bishops' legal secretaries, and chapter clerks. The order must be laid before General Synod and cannot come into force without its approval. The order takes effect as if it were a Statutory Instrument and is subject to annulment in pursuance of resolution of either House of Parliament. The Commission may make a similar order as to the fees to be paid in respect of such duties performed by ecclesiastical judges and legal officers as are specified by the Commission (not in the case of legal officers, being duties covered by the annual fees order). Any fee payable is recoverable as a debt.[239]

---

[233] Ss. 1(1), 3: a scheme member dissatisfied with the decision has a right of appeal to a Board, of 2 or more referees appointed by the Pensions Board, the decision of which 'shall be final'; Clergy Pensions (Amendment) Measure 1972, s. 3: the Board may require further medical evidence.   [234] S. 2, Church of England (Pensions) Measure 1988, Sched. 1.

[235] S. 4, as amended by Church of England (Pensions) Measure 1988, s. 2 (diocesan and suffragan bishop, archdeacon, dean, provost, residentiary canon, or incumbent of a benefice).

[236] S. 38.

[237] Ss. 10–16, as amended by Church of England (Pensions) Measure 1988, s. 3 (for children see s. 4); SI 1988 No. 2256 governs dependents of female clergy; the position of a divorced spouse of a deceased scheme member remains unclear, as is the position of a spouse whom the scheme member might marry after divorce: see *Payne-Collins v Taylor Woodrow Construction Ltd* [1975] 1 All ER 898.

[238] *CIC*, c. 1649: the bishop responsible for the tribunal is to establish norms concerning payment or reimbursement of judicial expenses, the remuneration of advocates, experts, and interpreters, and the granting of free legal aid.

[239] Ecclesiastical Fees Measure 1986, ss. 5–7, as amended by CCEJM, Scheds. 3, 6; Legal Officers (Annual Fees) Order 1995, Ecclesiastical Judges and Legal Officers (Fees) Order 1995, GS 1157–8.

Like the state and the Roman Catholic Church,[240] the Church of England operates a system of legal aid to assist those involved in ecclesiastical legal proceedings. General Synod must continue and maintain a Legal Aid Fund to which the Synod and the Church Commissioners may contribute such sums as each from time to time decides. At every ordinary election to the General Synod its Standing Committee must appoint a Legal Aid Commission charged with the duty of administering the Fund which is held by the Central Board of Finance on behalf of the Synod.[241] Designated classes may apply to the Commission for financial assistance in respect of costs incurred in connection with designated proceedings. On an application the Commission may issue a certificate authorizing the payment out of the Fund of the whole or part of costs incurred by the applicant as well as a certificate for the payment *inter alia* of a contribution towards those costs. In deciding an application, the Commission must consider the financial resources of the applicant (including those of the applicant's spouse). Legal aid must not be granted if it appears to the Commission that the applicant could afford to proceed without legal aid. The Commission may not grant legal aid unless the applicant shows reasonable grounds for taking or defending the proceedings or being a party thereto. The Standing Committee of General Synod may make such rules as it considers necessary or desirable as to the procedure to be observed in an application, including the circumstances in which the Commission may amend, revoke, or discharge a certificate; the rules must be laid before and approved by General Synod.[242]

CONCLUSIONS

The Church of England's legal structures dealing with the regulation of finance are comprehensive but complicated (if implemented, the recommendations of the recent Turnbull Commission will simplify them). This is, in part, the result of the evolution of the church's legal system itself, and in part the existing

---

[240] *CIC*, cc. 1465, 1649.

[241] Church of England (Legal Aid) Measure 1994, s. 1(1); the Measure, amending the Church of England (Legal Aid and Miscellaneous Provisions) Measure 1988, follows the recommendations of a report by the Legal Aid Commission of 1992, GS 1028 (resulting from the expenses incurred in the *Tyler* litigation, see *supra* Ch. 5).

[242] Ss. 2–4; Church of England (Legal Aid) Rules 1995, GS 1160: by r. 11(5) the decision of the Commission is final; Sched. 1 sets out the proceedings covered: proceedings in any ecclesiastical court or before any commission, committee, or examiner in respect of an offence under EJM 1963; proceedings on an enquiry under IVBM 1977 conducted by the provincial tribunal; proceedings for compensation under that Measure and the Pastoral Measure 1983 (including an interview by pastoral committee); a minister, deaconess, lay worker, or stipendiary reader appealing against revocation of a licence by canon created under the Church of England (Legal Aid and Miscellaneous Provisions) Measure 1988, s. 7; and a person appealing against a proposed deposition from holy orders.

secular laws which are regulatory in nature. The introduction of complex internal structures has increased the financial burdens on the church. As in Roman Catholic canon law, the general schemes underlying this structure both facilitate and regulate those fund-holding institutions and bodies in terms of their powers and their accountability. However, some key areas, in contrast with Roman Catholic canon law, notably the quota system and insurance, operate without regulation by formal internal law. Diocesan norms go some way to regulate these matters. As with Roman Catholic canon law, but in substantially more detail, the law of the Church of England seeks to confer and protect basic rights to remuneration for ministry in a comprehensive fashion, though apparently no systematic rationale exists to regulate the increasing use by legislators of compensation schemes. The problem of compensation for unfair dismissal remains unaddressed.

General Conclusions

The legal framework of the Church of England is complex. A study of it is in reality the study of a legal system in its entirety, for it is a study of a society, the way it regulates its government, the obligations and rights of persons in and associated with it, its teaching, its public services, and its property. But the church is no ordinary society. Only the visible institutional church is susceptible to formal regulation. And this is as it should be. In point of fact, any study ought neither to dwell on nor to present the church and its law as static and one-dimensional. The Church of England is part of the apostolic church universal: the theological and historical roots of internal legal regulation, and its place in the fulfilment of the church's mission, must be explored fully if the true intent and purpose of that regulation is to be uncovered. It is on this basis that the rules of the Church of England may be properly compared with other churches. The canon law of Roman Catholic Church is, historically, the natural yardstick with which the law of the Church of England may be compared. The former is in more ways than one the parent of the latter. Similarly, living as it does in the wider legal environment, of which the Church of England is a legally established and significant part, law created by the church may properly be set in relation to law made by the state, not least to expose for debate the standards of each. It is a combination of these factors and possibilities which makes the study of church law such a compelling enterprise.

It is difficult to express in a paragraph the overriding legal principles of the Church of England, even on the assumption that they are ascertainable. Whilst much has been the direct result of general ecclesial planning, equally, much has not. On one hand, it is obvious that the law ought to enable the church to fulfil its mission to society. In this regard, the laws dealing with the rites of the church are paradigmatic in so far as, in mandatory terms, they make the principle of free access to the ministrations of the church a tangible reality. Equally, the law clearly operates a principle of full participation in the government of the church by both clergy and laity. Synodical government is a legal requirement and representatives from the whole church are free to be involved directly in the processes of general legislative and administrative decision-making at all levels, national, diocesan, and parochial. At the same time, the law operates a principle of episcopal oversight, and in so doing expresses the operative current theology: the functions and discipline of those in ordained and official lay ministry are directly in the keeping of the diocesan bishop, the chief pastor in the diocese. Matters of faith, doctrine, and liturgy are delicate: whilst the law protects the church's doctrinal and liturgical inheritance, it affords ample scope for conscionable intellectual freedom with respect to faith and doctrine and for experimentation in liturgical development. In connection with church property, the operative principle is one of careful management and guardianship for the benefit of future generations whilst at the same time seeking to accommodate the pastoral and liturgical needs of today's parishioners. In all this the law affords an elaborate and flexible system for the settlement of disputes and for the vindication of rights and duties.

These, needless to say, are mere generalizations. On the other hand, whilst the innovation has been effected by General Synod itself, the legal distribution of legislative and administrative powers to national and diocesan executive bodies may be thought by some not to lie comfortably with the principle of synodical government—though more often than not these bodies are legally responsible either to General Synod or the diocesan synod. Unilateral and informal rule-making by the House of Bishops and by diocesan bishops is typical of this sort of development and is considered by some to reflect the operation of a very different theological assumption about ecclesiastical government. The accountability of the Church Commissioners remains problematic. The recommendations of the Turnbull Commission—the introduction of a National Council, the stream-lining of General Synod's subordinate bodies, and changes in the Church Commissioners and the Pensions Board—will result in a debate about management but may also stimulate debate which directly addresses the question of the proper location of authority within the church. With regard to clerical discipline the terms of the principle of canonical obedience are remarkably unclear, as is the precise jurisdiction of the incumbent within the benefice. An associated problem is the overly complicated, cumbersome, and expensive court system, though this is offset by the welcome introduction of tribunals and less formal methods of dispute resolution, particularly in connection with pastoral relations. Indeed, one often wonders precisely how much ancient case law, and pre-Reformation canon law, is still applicable to and binding on the Church of England: a problem which has bedevilled much of this study has been the need to cite old judicial decisions, sometimes said with too great a degree of certainty to support what are taken for axiomatic legal propositions. Equally, it is often unclear whether the terms of a modern canon are narrower than the Canons of 1603 and, therefore, whether recourse ought still to be made to the latter to determine the meaning of the former. Of concern is the distinct lack of clarity in some key areas. This is most evident in relation to the rites of the church. With regard to baptismal, marriage, and Eucharistic discipline in particular, a closer analysis of both canonical provisions and those arising under ecclesiastical quasi-legislation discloses either (some may say alarmingly) unfettered scope for arbitrary ministerial action or else a high degree of freedom of conscience. It is in these areas that the legislator's balancing trick of regulation and liberty is perhaps most sensitive.

It is axiomatic that a formal, written legal system cannot deal with every eventuality. The increasing use of ecclesiastical quasi-legislation, in the form of both statements from the House of Bishops and diocesan pastoral regulations and norms, deserves a separate mention. Any comprehensive study of the legal framework of the church must take notice of them. Whereas prior to its introduction the areas which quasi-legislation addresses were largely unregulated, its use today may be welcomed as providing instruments of clarification, flexibility, and adaptability, often designed as they are to fill the gaps of the formal law. On the other hand, the advent of quasi-legislation reflects a marked expansion of ecclesiastical regulation. Two worries particularly deserve mention. The first concerns the degree to which these codes of practice, guidelines, and the like give rise to binding rights and duties. From an analysis of the treatment of analogous instruments in secular administrative law, it seems likely that in any future litigation, if the intention of the maker was to bind, a secular court might very well enforce their terms; at the same time the strict legality of some pieces of quasi-legislation is often uncertain. Secondly, in so far as many modern quasi-legal instruments deal with highly important and contentious matters, it may be appropriate for the legislators of the church to consider putting them on a more conspicuously legal footing, perhaps canonical. More careful drafting would then be needed, including the use of permissive language if this were desired, and this must clarify the 'guidance' sought. Having said this, whilst it rejected 'the more extreme calls . . . for the removal of the Church's legal system' ('far from "freeing the Church", that would subject its working wholly to the provisions of secular law'), the Turnbull Commission has proposed that the church should look for 'Synod legislation that was less prescriptive and detailed, giving more discretion to dioceses and those in day-to-day charge of various aspects of the Church's work to apply it in ways which best suit their local circumstances' (*Working As One Body* (1995), para. 6.40). For the future, less formal law may well mean more ecclesiastical quasi-legislation.

Comparisons between the legal framework of the Church of England and that of the Roman Catholic Church fall into two categories. On one hand, similarities are obvious. Both churches operate a maximalist regulatory culture: in the Roman Catholic Church this is achieved by means of a Code, in the Church of England by piecemeal sporadic rule-making (both formal and informal), perhaps under the influence of the common law approach. Like the Church of England, the ministrations of the Roman Catholic Church are offered to all in society. However, under the Roman Catholic Church's ecumenical canon law, access to the church's rites for non-Roman Catholics is available only in prescribed circumstances, which in reality is not far from the Church of England's arrangements of conditional rights. As with the Church of England, in the Roman Catholic Church legislative, administrative, and judicial powers are ordered hierarchically. In the Church of England the courts are most active in property-related faculty cases, whereas in the Roman Catholic Church the courts are most active with matrimonial business. Yet the advent of quasi-adjudicative dispute-settlement models in the Church of England finds some of a parallel in the Roman Catholic Church's principle of hierarchical administrative recourse. In both churches the legal organization of ministerial functions is almost identical. Finally, both churches assign to law a protective function with respect to faith, doctrine, and liturgy, though the substance of these may in key areas be very different.

Some differences between the two canonical systems are obvious, others less so. The Roman Catholic Church has developed a sophisticated canonical theory which clearly defines the place and role of law within the church. The Church of England has not: its philosophy of law must be constructed through the classification of legislative intents, in turn deduced from a sea of single instances. The law of the Church of England affords to the laity the power of governance. The canon law of the Roman Catholic Church does not: the power of governance is reserved to ordained ministers; the laity may participate only in its exercise. In legislative, administrative, and judicial contexts, canonically the laity has only a consultative vote; in the Church of England lay people enjoy determinative votes. Outside the College of Bishops, the Roman Catholic Church assigns full canonical power to one office, the papacy: the Church of England assigns it to General Synod. Roman Catholic canon law enables flexibility through powers of dispensation, to lesser or greater extents, at all levels of the church. In the Church of England rules enabling formal dispensation are rare. The Roman Catholic Church does not operate a formal system of binding judicial precedent; the Church of England does, though the practice of consulting and following persuasive precedents is shared. In the Church of England there is no express and concise compendium equivalent to the Roman Catholic Church's canonical ministry of the laity, in which fundamental rights and duties are distributed amongst all the faithful. In terms of the regulation of doctrine the two churches are somewhat different: in the Church of England there is no modern formal equivalent either to the Roman Catholic Church's general duties of assent to the teaching of the church or to the catechumenate. The formal canon law of the Roman Catholic Church is less well developed with regard to the non-office holding laity, and more restrictive with respect to ecumenical liturgical action and the questions of divorce and remarriage. Unlike the Church of England, the Roman Catholic Church operates a minimalist approach to property management and regulation: the absence of legal rules governing the quota system in the former is very different from the contribution rules in the latter. Above all, the Roman Catholic Church protects the centrality of the bishops—within the principle of subsidiarity, leadership and government rest with the bishops. In the Church of England, the formal law operates a system of episcopal leadership and synodical government.

The legal relationship between the Church of England and the state is ambiguous. Whilst the doctrine of royal supremacy lies at the legal heart of the establishment complex, at least for the purposes of analysis the key concepts must be ecclesiastial autonomy and state intrusion. Ecclesiastical autonomy involves the ability of the church to fulfil its mission, as historically set and as acted out in the contemporary world. State intrusion may be both facilitative—when legislative, executive, and judicial state bodies confer benefits on the church (perhaps at its request)—and controlling—where state bodies impose burdens on the church (perhaps against its wishes). In the light of these two concepts, the ambiguity of the Church of England's position with the state is not too difficult to discern. On one hand, and setting aside questions of historical continuity, in a legal sense the Church of England was established at the Reformation by legislative action on the part of the state. The most obvious benefits are episcopal representation in the House of Lords and the principle that synodical measures (and perhaps synodical canons) enjoy an authority equal to law enacted at the instigation of the state in the form of parliamentary statutes. Less obvious benefits include, for example, the inapplicability of certain key provisions in the Charities Act 1993 to the Church Commissioners and the ability of certain church judicial bodies to issue injunctions and similar orders. The burdens include the principle that the enactment and alteration of synodical measures require the consent of the Queen in Parliament and that appointments to episcopal office are by law royal appointments which, by constitutional convention, are made on the advice of the Prime Minister. Whether the legal requirements securing a Protestant succession to the throne and communion of the monarch with the Church of England may be treated as benefits or burdens continues to be debated.

The ambiguity of church–state relations surfaces in so many ways. The dominant secular doctrine of parliamentary supremacy is, needless to say, an ever-present source for potential state intrusion. Since 1919, however, the opportunities for such intrusion have become less evident. Whilst synodical measures still need parliamentary approval, the Enabling Act of 1919 fundamentally loosened the bonds between church and state by assigning to the church the function of initiating a legislative process which results in the creation of instruments enjoying the status of parliamentary statutes. The Enabling Act 1919 removed the need for unilateral action by Parliament to create statutes for the Church of England. The present power of General Synod, acquired from the Enabling Act 1919 through the Synodical Government Measure 1969, is, moreover, commonly used to lessen both the actuality and the possibility of state intrusion. A handful of examples may suffice.

Under the Synodical Government Measure 1969 General Synod is broadly free to make any canon it pleases (subject to royal assent and licence), but synodical canons may not be repugnant to royal prerogative, statute, or common law. Similarly, under this Measure the exclusive (rather than inclusive) provisions concerning membership of the Church of England were strengthened: only members of the Church of England are eligible for office in the church. Notably, the Church of England (Worship and Doctrine) Measure 1974 enables liturgical and doctrinal developments by promulgation of canons, without the need for parliamentary approval. Similarly, General Synod has on several occasions enacted measures, containing Henry VIII clauses, which exclude the possibility of intrusion by the state's courts. The Priests (Ordination of Women) Measure 1993 provided that the Sex Discrimination Act 1975 is not applicable, in prescribed cases, to episcopal decisions concerning ordination and appointment of women. General Synod is free to legislate for the Church of England, but in an appropriate case the state's secular judiciary may upset legislation if the prescribed procedures for its enactment have not been satisfied. The Church of England is free to organize disciplinary processes with regard to ordained office-holders, but secular industrial tribunals have recently sought to apply the state's standards for fair dismissal of employees by parliamentary statute. Finally, the canons of the Church of England, whilst conventionally treated as part of the law of the land with regard to the clergy (and possibly lay officers), are still assumed not to bind the laity, even those classified legally as members of the church. By contrast, General Synod occasionally strengthens the ties of establishment. By Standing Orders, for example, General Synod requires that any subordinate legislation (created under the authority of a parent measure) of general (as opposed to local) application, if it seeks to affect the legal rights of subjects, must be submitted to Parliament for approval.

In other words, whilst we may conclude that legally speaking the terms of establishment are clearly in the keeping of the supreme civil legislature (the Queen in Parliament), whether or not ties exist between state and church is in large measure a matter for General Synod, as representative of the church, in its exercise (or non-exercise) of the extensive legal powers which the state has committed to it. In so many areas the Church of England has, and may determine the limits of, its own legal autonomy. In any event, the Church of England alone is responsible for fulfilling its mission in society. Establishment by state-law is not necessary to achieve this. The existence of structures to enable any church to fulfil its mission is a matter solely for that church. Similarly, the state ought not to frustrate any church in its mission. Establishment is not necessary to control and limit state interference. Law, however, is necessary and, under the present constitutional system, it is a matter for the state to impose on itself laws preventing improper interference. In the European legal tradition, concordat settlements afford a negotiated definition of ecclesiastical autonomy. At the same time, the church ought not to frustrate the state in fulfilling its service of government to society. Law should provide for enforcement of both state respect for the church and church respect for the state. Structures should exist to enable vindication of both church and state rights and duties. Establishment is not necessary to achieve reciprocity. Indeed, insistence by secular courts that churches act in accordance with their internal rules and with standards set by the state is an expression of the principles of responsibility, autonomy, and reciprocity.

In the context of these personal observations, the legal position of the Roman Catholic Church in relation to the state is in some fundamentals not dissimilar to that of the Church of England. In so far as state-made law does define key elements of the relationship between the state and the Roman Catholic Church, that church bears several of the marks of establishment, in the wide judicial sense explored in Chapter 1. Before the Reformation the Roman Catholic Church may be understood, in our terms, as having been the established church: the relationship between the church and the state (although the distinction is not a happy one with regard to the medieval period) was close. The jurisdiction of the papacy was recognized, bishops participated directly in the state's legislative processes, the jurisdiction of church courts was recognized, protected, and controlled by the state, and canon law was enforceable in them. The Reformation legislation ended this. The Roman Catholic Church today is clearly not a church established in England by state law. However, whilst technically it is arguable that the Ecclesiastical Titles Act 1871 does not legalize the Roman Catholic Church's hierarchy, government, and canon law, their legality in the wider legal environment is dependent on tacit state approval. Moreover, the church's hierarchy is recognized in several notable parliamentary statutes, as some rights of Roman Catholics are expressly recognized and protected in synodical legislation. Legally, like the Church of England, the Roman Catholic Church is according to secular law a 'quasi-corporate institution'. However, unlike the Church of England, the church exists legally as a consensual society bound together as a matter of contract. Certainly, the state has conferred on the Roman Catholic Church no benefit equivalent to that under which Church of England measures enjoy the same authority as parliamentary statutes. Importantly, however, like the canons of the Church of England Roman Catholic canon law is, in the wider legal environment, inferior to state-made law: the canons of neither church may be repugnant to the law of the land. Moreover, like the law of the Church of England, but for a different reason, Roman Catholic canon law is enforceable in the secular courts, at least when property is at stake. Finally, as is the case with the Church of England, general secular law is applicable to the Roman Catholic Church.

Equally, the relationship between the Roman Catholic Church and the state is characterized by ambiguity. The national conference of bishops is free to make particular law for England and Wales, but the laws it promulgates must not be in conflict with the state's law. Like the Church of England, the Roman Catholic Church is free to share its buildings with other churches, but when it chooses to do so the matter is governed by parliamentary statute. A Roman Catholic bishop, like his Church of England counterpart, may authorize an ordained minister to serve in a state prison; but when he does so ministerial functions are regulated by parliamentary statute and subordinate legislation. The Roman Catholic Church is free to enjoy the use of property settled by way of trusts; but the matter is governed by the secular law on charities. In short, because the law of the state elucidates the relations between the Roman Catholic Church and the state, in that it protects the religious freedom of the church, it too may be said in a loose sense to be established. In so many fundamental ways, the respective legal positions of the Church of England and the Roman Catholic Church to the state are similar. With respect to the former the ties may be more obvious and explicit, with respect to the latter they are more diffuse and implicit. The key question is whether ecclesiastical regulation, in its many forms, promotes for the purposes of both churches the salvation of souls and faithfulness to the vision and commission of Jesus Christ.

Bibliography

REPORTS AND CONSULTATION DOCUMENTS

Abortion and the Church, Report of the Doctrine Commission of the Church of England (London, 1993)

An Honourable Estate, Report of a Working Party of the General Synod of the Church of England (London, 1988)

Baptism and Confirmation Today, Report of the Joint Committee of the Convocations of Canterbury and York (London, 1954)

Baptism, Eucharist, Ministry, World Council of Churches (Geneva, 1982)

Baptism, Thanksgiving and Blessing, Report of the Doctrine Commission of the Church of England (London, 1971)

Believing in the Church: The Corporate Nature of Faith, Report of the Doctrine Commission of the Church of England (London, 1981)

Care of Churches and Cathedrals, the Chichester Report (London, 1984)

Christian Initiation and Church Membership, British Council of Churches (London, 1988)

Christian Initiation: A Policy for the Church of England, Discussion Paper by M. Reardon (London, 1991)

Christian Initiation: Birth and Growth in the Christian Society, Report of the Ely Commission (London, 1971)

Church and State, Reports of the Archbishops' Commission (London, 1916, 1952)

Church as Communion, An Agreed Statement by the Second Anglican-Roman Catholic International Commission (London, 1991)

Clergy Conditions of Service, A Consultative Paper prepared by the Clergy Conditions of Service Steering Group (London, 1994)

Communion before Confirmation, Report of the General Synod the Church of England's Board of Education Working Party on Christian Initiation and Participation in the Eucharist (London, 1985)

Deacons in the Ministry of the Church, A Report to the House of Bishops of the General Synod of the Church of England (London, 1988)

Dispensation in Practice and Theory with special reference to Anglican Churches (London, 1942)

Doctrine in the Church of England, Report of the Doctrine Commission of the Church of England (London, 1938)

Episcopal Ministry, Report of the Archbishops' Commission on the Episcopate (London, 1990)

Government By Synod, Report of the Synodical Government Commission set up by the Church Assembly (London, 1966)

Heritage and Renewal, Report of the Archbishops' Commission on Cathedrals (London, 1994)

Issues in Human Sexuality, Statement by the House of Bishops of General Synod of the Church of England (London, 1991)

Local Church Unity, British Council of Churches (London, 1985)

Marriage and the Church's Task, the Lichfield Report (London, 1978)

Marriage, Divorce and the Church, the Root Report (London, 1971)

No Just Cause: The Law of Affinity in England and Wales (London, 1984)

On the Way: Towards an Integrated Approach to Christian Initiation (London 1995)

One Body, Many Members, British Council of Churches (London, 1986)

Ordination and Reception of Dr. Graham Leonard, Statement by Cardinal Hume, Canon Law Society of Great Britain and Ireland, *Newsletter*, No. 98 (1994) 54

Patterns of Worship, Report of the Liturgical Commission of the Church of England (London, 1990)

Putting Asunder (London, 1966)

Senior Church Appointments, Report of the Working Party established by the Standing Committee of the General Synod of the Church of England (London, 1992)

Subscription and Assent to the 39 Articles, Report of the Archbishops' Commission on Christian Doctrine (London, 1968)

Synodical Government, 1970–1990: The First Twenty Years, A Discussion Paper issued on behalf of the Standing Committee of the General Synod of the Church of England (London, 1990)

The Canon Law of the Church of England, Report of the Archbishops' Commission (London, 1947)

The Church and the Law of Nullity of Marriage, Report of the Archbishops' Commission (London, 1949)

The Marriage of Adherents of Other Faiths in Anglican Churches, Report of the Inter-Faith Consultative Group of the Board of Mission to the House of Bishops of the General Synod of the Church of England, Board of Mission Occasional Paper No. 1 (London, 1992)

The Nature of Christian Belief, Statement and Exposition by the House of Bishops of the General Synod of the Church of England (London, 1986)

The Political Economy of the Church, Diocese of Portsmouth (Portsmouth, 1981)

The Position of the Laity in the Church, Report of the Joint Committee of the Convocation of Canterbury (1902), with an introduction by N. Sykes (reprinted, London, 1952)

Working As One Body, Report of the Archbishops' Commission on the Organisation of the Church of England, the Turnbull Commission (London, 1995)

Working Party on Lay Office-Holders: Report and Proposed Measure and Canon, GS 1164–6 (London, 1995)

Worship in the Church, Report of the Liturgical Commission of the Church of England on its work 1986–1991 (London, 1992)

BOOKS AND ARTICLES

Alberigo, G., and Weller, A. (eds.), *Election—Consensus—Reception*, *Concilium*, 7(8) (London, 1972)

Alesandro, J. A., 'The revision of church law: conflict and reconciliation', *The Jurist*, 40 (1980), 1

—— 'Pastoral opportunities', *Chicago Studies*, 23 (1984), 97

Allen, C.K., *Law and Orders* (London, 1947)

Anandarayar, A., 'Parish and its pastors in the new code of canon law', Hite and Ward, *Readings*, 271

Atiyah, P. S., *Promises, Morals and Law* (Oxford, 1981)

Augustine, P. C., *A Commentary on the New Code of Canon Law* (St Louis, 1922)

Austin, J., *Lectures in Jurisprudence*, ed. R. Campbell (London, 1880)

Austin, R. J., 'The particular church and the universal church in the 1983 Code of Canon Law', *Studia Canonica*, 22 (1988), 339

Avis, P., *Anglicanism and the Christian Church* (Edinburgh, 1989)

Aymans, W., 'Ecclesiological implications of the new legislation', *Studia Canonica*, 17 (1983), 63

Bailey, S. H., Jones, B. L., and Mowbray, A. R., *Cases and Materials on Administrative Law* (2nd edn., London, 1992)

Baldwin, R., and Houghton, J., 'Circular arguments: the status and legitimacy of administrative rules', *Public Law* (1986) 239

Balhoff, M. J., 'Age for confirmation: canonical evidence', *The Jurist*, 45 (1985) 549

Barrett, P. L. S., *Barchester: English Cathedral Life in the Nineteenth Century* (London, 1993)

Bayley, M., *The Local Church and Mentally Handicapped People* (London, 1984)

Beal, J. P., 'The apostolic visitation of a diocese: a canonico-historical investigation', *The Jurist*, 49 (1989), 341

Beatson, J., '"Public" and "Private" in administrative law', *Law Quarterly Review*, 103 (1987), 34

Belgiorno de Stefano, M. G., 'Religious freedom in the decisions of the European Court of Human Rights', in U. Leanza (ed.), *University of Rome II Department of Public Law Yearbook* (Rome, 1989) 239

Bell, J., and Engle, G. (eds.), *Cross on Statutory Interpretation* (2nd edn., London, 1987)

Beloff, M., 'Judicial review in the sporting world', *Public Law* (1989), 95

Bennion, F., *Statutory Interpretation* (London, 1984)

Bentham, J., *Of Laws in General*, ed. H. L. A. Hart (London, 1970)

Bertrams, W., 'Subsidiarity in the church', *Catholic Mind*, 59 (1961), 358

Bianchi, E., *Reconciliation: The Function of the Church* (New York, 1969)

Bicknell, E. J., *A Theological Introduction to the Thirty-Nine Articles of the Church of England* (2nd edn., London, 1925)

Bloor, R. H., 'Clocks, bells and cockerels', *Ecclesiastical Law Journal*, 3 (1995), 393

Blunt, J. H., *The Book of Church Law* (London, 1899)

Bogdan, L. A., 'Simple convalidation of marriage in the 1983 code of canon law', *The Jurist*, 46 (1986), 511

Borras, A., 'The canonical limits of Catholic identity in some problematic situations', *Concilium* (1994), 47

Bossy, J., *The English Catholic Community* (London, 1975)

Bowers, J., *Employment Law* (London, 1990)

Box, H., *The Principles of Canon Law* (Oxford, 1949)

Boyle, P. M., 'The relationship of law to love', *The Jurist*, 25 (1965), 393

Bradley, A. W., 'The sovereignty of parliament—in perpetuity', in J. Jowell and D. Oliver (eds.), *The Changing Constitution* (2nd edn., Oxford, 1989) 25

Bradney, A., *Religions, Rights and Laws* (Leicester, 1993)

Brandwood, G. K., 'Immersion baptistries in Anglican churches, *Archeological Journal*, 147 (1990), 420

Brentford, Viscount, 'In favour of keeping Sunday "special"', *Ecclesiastical Law Journal*, 2 (1990–92), 14

Briden, T., and Hanson, B. (eds.), *Moore's Introduction to English Canon Law* (3rd edn., London, 1992)

Brock, J., 'Prelates in parliament', *Parliamentary Affairs*, 14 (1971), 222

Bromley, P. M., and Lowe, N (eds.), *Bromley's Family Law* (8th edn., London, 1992)

Broussard, G. L., 'Ecclesiastical taxation: an historical synopsis', Catholic University of America, JCL dissertation (Washington, 1966)

Brundage, J. A., *Medieval Canon Law* (London, 1995)

Bullimore, J. W., 'Where now the draft Care of Cathedrals measure?', *Ecclesiastical Law Journal*, 1 (1988), 24

Burman, P., and Stapleton, H., *The Churchyards Handbook* (3rd edn., London, 1988)

Burn, R., *Ecclesiastical Law*, 4 Volumes (9th edn., London, 1842)

Bursell, R., 'What is the place of custom in English canon law?', *Ecclesiastical Law Journal*, 1 (1989), 12

—— 'The seal of the confessional', *Ecclesiastical Law Journal*, 1 (1990), 84

Butler, B. C., *The Idea of the Church* (Baltimore, 1962)

—— 'Infallible; *authenticum*; *assensus*; *obsequium*: Christian teaching and the Christian's response', *Doctrine and Life*, 31 (1981), 77

Calvo, P. R., and Klinger, N. J. (eds.), *Clergy Procedural Manual* (Washington, 1992)

Cane, P., *An Introduction to Administrative Law* (2nd edn., Oxford, 1992)

Caparros, E., Thériault, M., and Thorn, J. (eds.), *Code of Canon Law Annotated* (Montreal, 1993)

Carlson, R., 'The parish according to the revised law', *Studia Canonica*, 19 (1985), 5

Carter, P., and Perry, M., *A Handbook of Parish Finance* (3rd edn., London, 1992)

Casado, J. H., 'Renewal and effectiveness in canon law', *Studia Canonica*, 28 (1994), 5

Casey, J., *Constitutional Law in Ireland* (2nd edn., London, 1992)

Certoma, G. L., *The Italian Legal System* (London, 1985)

Ciprotti, P., 'The Holy See: its function, form and status in international law', *Concilium*, 8(6) (1970), 63

Clarkson, A., Pix, S., Rees, J., and Sherwood, D., 'Marriage in church after divorce: a working party report', *Ecclesiastical Law Journal*, 2 (1992), 359

Clements, K. W., *Lovers of Discord: Twentieth-Century Theological Controversies in England* (London, 1988)

Cogan, P. J., 'The protection of rights in hierarchical churches: an ecumenical survey', *The Jurist*, 46 (1986), 205

Congar, Y., *The Mystery of the Church* (Baltimore, 1960)

Coningsby, T., 'An honourable estate—a personal view of the Report of the working party of General Synod', *Ecclesiastical Law Journal*, 1 (1988), 10

Cora, G., 'Team ministry: theological aspects', *American Ecclesiastical Review*, 167 (1973), 684

Corecco, E., 'Ecclesiological bases of the code', *Concilium*, 185 (1986), 3

—— *The Theology of Canon Law: A Methodological Question* (Pittsburgh, Pennsylvania, 1992)

Coriden, J. A., 'Celibacy, canon law and synod', *Concilium*, 8(8) (1972), 109
—— 'A challenge: make rights real', *The Jurist*, 45 (1987), 1
—— 'The canonical doctrine of reception', *The Jurist*, 50 (1990), 58
—— *An Introduction to Canon Law* (London, 1991)
—— 'The rights of parishes', *Studia Canonica*, 28 (1994), 293
Cotterrell, R., *The Politics of Jurisprudence: A Critical Introduction to Legal Philosophy* (London, 1989)
Coughlan, M. J., *The Vatican, the Law and the Human Embryo* (London, 1990)
Cross, R., and Harris, J. W., *Precedent in English Law* (4th edn., Oxford, 1991)
Cruickshank, M., *Church and State in English Education* (London, 1963)
Curran, C. E., *Faithful Dissent* (Kansas City, 1986)
D. Walker (ed.), *A History of the Church in Wales* (Penarth, 1976, re-issued, 1990)
Daintith, T., 'Legal analysis of economic policy', *Journal of Law and Society*, 9 (1982), 191
Dale, W., *Law of the Parish Church* (6th edn., London, 1989)
Dalton, W., 'Parish councils or parish pastoral councils', *Studia Canonica*, 22 (1988), 169
Davidson, F. P., 'Judicial review of decisions to dismiss', *Northern Ireland Legal Quarterly*, 35 (1984), 121
Davies, R., 'Church and state', *Cambrian Law Review*, 7 (1976), 11
de Bhaldraithe, E., 'Mixed marriages in the new code of canon law: can we now implement the Anglican-Roman Catholic recommendations?', *The Jurist*, 46 (1986), 419
de Paolis, V., 'Temporal goods of the church in the new code: with particular reference to institutes of religious consecrated life', *The Jurist*, 43 (1983), 343
Denning, A. T., 'The meaning of "ecclesiastical law"', *Law Quarterly Review*, 60 (1944), 235
Dias, R. W. M., *Jurisprudence* (5th edn., London, 1985)
Dicey, A. V., *Law of the Constitution* (10th edn., London, 1959)
Dix, G., *The Theology of Confirmation in Relation to Baptism* (London, 1946, reprinted, 1948)
Doe, N., 'Non-legal rules and the courts: enforceability', *Liverpool Law Review*, 9 (1987), 173
—— 'The problem of abhorrent legislation and the judicial idea of legislative supremacy', *Liverpool Law Review*, 10 (1988), 113
—— *Fundamental Authority in Late Medieval English Law* (Cambridge, 1990)
—— 'A facilitative canon law: the problem of sanctions and forgiveness', in N. Doe (ed.), *Essays in Canon Law: A Study of the Law of the Church in Wales* (Cardiff, 1992) 69
—— 'Obedience to doctrine in canon law: the legal duty of intellectual assent', *Denning Law Journal* (1992), 23
—— 'Canonical doctrines of judicial precedent: a comparative study', *The Jurist*, 54 (1994), 205
—— 'Churches in the United Kingdom and the law of data protection', in G. Robbers (ed.), *Europaisches Datenschutzrecht und die Kirchen* (Berlin, 1994), 167

Doogan, H. F. (ed.), *Catholic Tribunals: Marriage Annulment and Dissolution* (Newtown, Australia, 1990)

Doyle, T. P., 'The theology of marriage: where are we today?', *Studia Canonica*, 19 (1985), 357

Draper, J. (ed.), *Communion and Episcopacy: Essays to Mark the Centenary of the Chicago-Lambeth Quadrilateral* (Oxford, 1988)

Dudley, M., and Rowell, G., *Confession and Absolution* (London, 1990)

Dulles, A. V., *Models of the Church* (Dublin, 1976)

—— '*Ius divinum* as an ecumencial problem', *Theological Studies*, 38 (1977), 681

Edwards, Q., 'The canon law of the Church of England', *Ecclesiastical Law*, 1 (1988), 18

Elliott, D. W., 'Blasphemy and other expressions of offensive opinion', *Ecclesiastical Law Journal*, 3 (1993) 70

—— 'An evidential privilege for priest-penitent communications', *Ecclesiastical Law Journal*, 3 (1995), 272

Elton, G. R., *Policy and Policing: The Enforcement of the Reformation in the Age of Thomas Cromwell* (Cambridge, 1972)

—— *Reform and Reformation: England 1509–1558* (London, 1977)

—— *The Tudor Constitution: Documents and Commentary* (2nd edn., Cambridge, 1982)

Euart, S. A., 'Council, code and laity: implications for lay ministry', *The Jurist*, 47 (1987), 492

Evans, G. R., and Wright, J. R. (eds.), *The Anglican Tradition: A Handbook of Sources* (London, 1991)

Farran, C. d'O., 'The Royal Marriages Act 1771', *Modern Law Review*, 14 (1951), 53

Farrelly, A., 'The diocesan finance council: functions and duties according to the code of canon law', *Studia Canonica*, 23 (1989), 149

Faull, D. W., 'Shared churches', Institute for the Study of Worship and Religious Architecture, *Research Bulletin* (1973), 77

Faull, D., and Rees, J., 'The church and housing', *Ecclesiastical Law Journal*, 3 (1995), 313

Fawcett, J. E. S., *The Application of the European Convention on Human Rights* (2nd edn., Oxford, 1987)

Fisher, S., 'Judicial intervention in church affairs in New South Wales', *Law and Justice* (1992), 51

Flannery, A. (ed.), *Vatican Council II*, Vatican Collection, 2 Volumes (New York, 1982,1988)

Fordham, M., *Judicial Review Handbook* (Chichester, 1995)

Ganz, G., *Quasi-Legislation: Recent Developments in Secondary Legislation* (London, 1987)

Garbett, C. F., *The Claims of the Church of England* (London, 1947)

—— *Church and State in England* (London, 1950)

Gauthier, A., 'Juridical persons in the code of canon law', *Studia Canonica*, 25 (1991), 77

Gerosa, L., 'Penal law and ecclesial reality: the applicability of the penal sanctions laid down in the new code', *Concilium*, 185 (1986), 60

Glazebrook, P. R., 'The plea of necessity in English law', *Cambridge Law Journal*, 30 (1972A), 87

Gramunt, I., 'The essence of marriage and the code of canon law', *Studia Canonica*, 25 (1991), 318

Gramunt, I., and Wauck, A., 'Capacity and incapacity to contract marriage', *Studia Canonica*, 22 (1988) 147

Granfield, P., *The Limits of the Papacy* (London, 1987)

Gray, D., 'The revision of canon law and its application to liturgical revision in the recent history of the Church of England', *The Jurist*, 48 (1988) 638

Greeley, A., 'Sociology and church structure', *Concilium*, 8(6) (1970), 26

Green, R., *Church of England Church Schools: A Matter of Opinion*, London and Southwark Diocesan Board of Education, Schools Division (London, 1982)

Green, T. J., 'Penal law revised: the revision of the penal law schema', *Studia Canonica*, 15 (1981), 135

—— 'Reflections on the Eastern Code revision process', *The Jurist*, 51 (1991), 18

—— 'The church's teaching mission: some aspects of the normative role of episcopal conferences', *Studia Canonica*, 27 (1993), 23

Grieve, M., 'Blasphemy law; first rights or last rites?', *Counsel* (Jan/Feb 1995), 10

Griffiths, J. A., 'Cognitive faith and the problem of mental handicap in canon law', in N. Doe (ed.), *Essays in Canon Law: A Study of the Law of the Church in Wales* (Cardiff, 1992) 89

Guiry, R. W., 'Immaturity, maturity and Christian marriage', *Studia Canonica*, 25 (1991), 93

Gula, R. M., 'The right to private and public dissent from specific pronouncements of the ordinary magisterium', *Église et Théologie*, 9 (1978), 319

Halliburton, J., *The Authority of a Bishop* (London, 1987)

Halsbury, *Laws of England*, Volume 14, *Ecclesiastical Law* (London, 1975)

Hamer, J., *The Church is a Communion* (New York, 1964)

Hanford, R., 'The medieval foundations of the banns of marriage', University of Wales LL.M. dissertation (Cardiff, 1995)

Hannon, P., *Church, State, Morality and Law* (Dublin, 1992)

Hanson, B., 'Legal aspects concerning 'A Form for the Reconciliation of a Penitent''', unpublished paper, GS Misc 169, 1983

Harnack, A., *The Constitution and Law of the Church in the First Two Centuries*, trans. F. L. Pogson (London, 1910)

Harris, N., *Law and Education: Regulation, Consumerism and the Education System* (London, 1993)

Harrison, D. E. W., and Sansom, M. C., *Worship in the Church of England* (London, 1982)

Harrison, E., 'The God club', *The Times Magazine*, 19 March 1994, 16

Hart, H. L. A., *The Concept of Law* (2nd. edn., Oxford, 1994)

Harte, J. D. C., 'Church v. state in listed building control I: the faculty jurisdiction: a case for conservation', *Journal of Planning Law* (1985), 611

—— 'Doctrine, conservation and aesthetic judgments in the Court of Ecclesiastical Causes Reserved', *Ecclesiastical Law Journal*, 1 (1987), 22

—— 'Churchyards and coffin ways', *Rights of Way Law Review* (1993), 17

Hastings, A., *Church and State: The English Experience* (Exeter, 1991)

Helmholz, R. H., *Roman Canon Law in Reformation England* (Cambridge, 1990)

Hendricks, J. W. M., 'On the sacramentality of the episcopal consecration', *Studia Canonica*, 28 (1994), 231

Hill, M., *Ecclesiastical Law* (London, 1995)

Hite, J., 'Church law on property and contracts', *The Jurist*, 44 (1984), 117

—— 'The administration of church property', Hite and Ward, *Readings*, 408

Hite, J., and Ward, D. J. (eds.), *Readings, Cases, Materials in Canon Law: A Textbook for Ministerial Students* (revised edn., Collegeville, Minnesota, 1990)

Hohfeld, W. N., 'Some fundamental legal conceptions as applied in judicial reasoning', *Yale Law Journal*, 23 (1913), 16

Hollenbach, D., *Claims in Conflict: Retrieving and Renewing the Catholic Human Rights Tradition* (New York, 1979)

Hooker, R., *The Laws of Ecclesiastical Polity* (c.1594), Books I–IV, ed. R. Bayne (New York, 1907)

Horvath, T., 'A structural understanding of the magisterium of the church', *Science et Ésprit*, 29(3) (1977), 283

Howarth, D. R., 'Church and state in employment law', *Cambridge Law Journal*, 45 (1986) 404

Howes, R. G., *Creating an Effective Parish Pastoral Council* (Collegeville, Minnesota, 1991)

Huels, J. M., 'Another look at lay jurisdiction', *The Jurist*, 41 (1981), 74

—— 'The interpretation of liturgical law', *Worship*, 55 (1981), 218

—— '"Use of reason" and the reception of the sacraments by the mentally-handicapped', *The Jurist*, 44 (1984), 209

Hughes, J. J., *Absolutely Null and Utterly Void: The Papal Condemnation of Anglican Orders 1896* (London, 1968)

—— *Stewards of the Lord: A Reappraisal of Anglican Orders* (London, 1970)

Huizing, P., 'Crime and punishment in the church', *Concilium*, 8(3) (1967), 57

—— 'Church and state in public ecclesiastical law', *Concilium*, 8(6) (1970), 126

—— 'Subsidiarity', *Concilium*, 188 (1986), 118

Huizing, P., and Walf, K. (eds.), *Electing Our Own Bishops*, *Concilium* (Edinburgh, 1980)

Hull, J. M., 'Religious education and Christian values in the 1988 Education Reform Act', *Ecclesiastical Law Journal*, 2 (1990–92), 69

—— 'Church-related schools and religious education in the publicly-funded education system of England', in *Church and State in Europe: State Financial Support, Religion and the School*, Proceedings of the European Consortium for Church-State Research (Milan, 1992) 181

Huysmans, R. G. W., 'The significance of particular law and the nature of dispensation as questions on the rule of papal law', in J. H. Provost and K. Walf (eds.), *Studies in Canon Law* (Leuven, 1991) 37

Ive, A., *The Church of England in South Africa: A Study of its History, Principles and Status* (Capetown, 1966)

Jacob, G., *New Law Dictionary* (5th edn., London, 1744)

Jamieson, N. J., 'Towards a systematic ststute law', *Otago Law Review* (1976), 568

Jennings, L., 'A renewed understanding of the diocesan synod', *Studia Canonica*, 20 (1986), 319

Johnson, J. G., 'The synod of bishops: an exploration of its nature and function', *Studia Canonica*, 20 (1986), 275

Jones, T. H., *'Omnis Gallia* . . . or, the roles of the archdeacon', *Ecclesiastical Law Journal*, 2 (1990–92), 236

—— 'Law and the suppression of heresy in the English church: an historical survey', University of Wales LL.M. dissertation (Cardiff, 1994)

Jones, N. L., *Parliament and the Settlement of Religion* (London, 1982)

Jong, A. de., 'Concordats and international law', *Concilium*, 8(6) (1970), 104

Jukes, J., *'Regolamento* for employment by Roman Curia', Canon Law Society of Great Britain and Ireland, *Newsletter*, No. 91 (1992), 30

—— 'A comment on the divorced and remarried within the Christian community', Canon Law Society of Great Britain and Ireland, *Newsletter*, No. 93 (1994), 27

Kelley, W., 'The authority of liturgical law', *The Jurist*, 28 (1968), 397

Kenny, C., 'The evolution of the law of blasphemy', *Cambridge Law Journal*, 1 (1922), 127

Khan, A. N., 'Employment of church minister', *Solicitors Journal*, 131 (1987), 38

Kilmartin, E. J., 'Lay participation in the apostolate of the hierarchy', in J. H. Provost (ed.), *Official Ministry in a New Age* (Washington, 1981)

Kinsella, J., and Jenne, W., *Fullness in Christ: A Report on a Study of Clergy Retirement* (Washington, 1979)

Knox, J., *The Ethic of Jesus in the Teaching of the Church* (London, 1961)

Komonchack, J., 'The status of the faithful in the revised code of canon law', *Concilium* (1981), 37

Koury, J., 'From prohibited to permitted: transitions in the code of canon law', *Studia Canonica*, 24 (1990), 147

—— 'Hard and soft canons continued: canonical institutes for legal flexibility and accommodation', *Studia Canonica*, 25 (1991), 325

Krause, H., *'Cessante causa cessat lex'*, *Zeitschrift der Savigny-Stiftung fur Rechtsgesechichte*, kanontistische Abteilung, 46 (1960), 81

Kuhrt, G. W., *Believing in Baptism* (London, 1987)

Kung, H., *The Church* (London, 1968)

Kunz, J. L., 'The status of the Holy See in international law', *American Journal of International Law*, 46 (1952), 308

Lampe, G. W. H., *The Seal of the Spirit* (London, 1951)

Langan, J., 'Human rights in Catholicism', *Journal of Ecumenical Studies*, 19 (1982), 25

Lara, C., 'Some general reflections on the rights and duties of the Christian faithful', *Studia Canonica*, 20 (1986), 7

Lawler, M. G., 'Indissolublity, divorce and holy communion', *New Blackfriars*, 76 (1995), 229

Leeder, L., 'The diaconate in the Church of England: a legal perspective', in C. Hall (ed.), *The Deacon's Ministry* (Leominster, 1992) 123

Legal Opinions Concerning the Church of England, Opinions of the Legal Advisory Commission (London, 1994)

Lehmberg, S. E., *The Reformation Parliament, 1529–1536* (Cambridge, 1970)

Lejeune, M., 'Demythologizing canon law', *Studia Canonica*, 21 (1987), 5

Lewis, C., 'The idea of the church in the parish communion', *Crucible* (July–September 1982), 119

Lewis, N., 'De-legalisation in Britain in the 1980s', in P. McAuslan and J. F. McEldowney, *Law, Legitimacy and the Constitution* (London, 1985) 107

Lobo, G., 'The Christian and canon law', Hite and Ward, *Readings*, 30

Lorenzen, T., 'The theological basis for religious liberty: a Christian perspective', *Journal of Church and State*, 20 (1979), 425

Lyall, F., *Of Presbyters and Kings: Church and State in the Law of Scotland* (Aberdeen, 1980)

Lynch, J., 'Mixed marriages in the aftermath of *Matrimonia mixta*', *Journal of Ecumenical Studies*, 11 (1974), 643

Lyon, J. N., 'Privileged communications—penitent and priest', *Criminal Law Quarterly* (Toronto) (1964–5), 327

MacMorran, K. M., Moore E. G., and Briden, T., *A Handbook for Churchwardens and Parochial Church Councillors* (9th edn., London, 1989)

Maida, A. J., 'The Code of Canon Law of 1983 and the property of the local church', in M. Thériault and J. Thorn (eds.), *The New Code of Canon Law*, Proceedings of the Fifth International Congress of Canon Law, 2 Volumes (Ottawa, 1986) II, 743

Maitland, F. W., *Roman Canon Law in the Church of England* (London, 1898)

Manchester, A. H., *Modern Legal History* (London, 1980)

Marshall, G., *Constitutional Conventions* (Oxford, 1984)

Martos, J., *Doors to the Sacred* (London, 1981)

Mason, A. J., *The Relation of Confirmation to Baptism* (London, 1891)

Matthews, K., 'Procedures of compromise for the resolution of conflict', *Studia Canonica*, 18 (1984), 55

———'Extra-judicial appeal and hierarchical recourse', *Studia Canonica*, 18 (1984), 95

May, G., 'Ecclesiastical law', in K. Rahner (ed.), *Encyclopedia of Theology* (London, 1981) 395

McAreavey, J., 'Abortion and the sacrament of penance', *The Furrow* (1993), 230

McBrien, R., 'The church: sign and instrument of unity', *Concilium*, 8(6) (1970), 26

McClean, D., 'State financial support for the church: the United Kingdom', in *Church and State in Europe: State Financial Support, Religion and the School*, Proceedings of the European Consortium for Church-State Research (Milan, 1992) 77

———'Marriage in England', in *Marriage and Religion in Europe*, Proceedings of the European Consortium for Church-State Research (Milan, 1993) 187

McEldowney, J. F., *Public Law* (London, 1994)

McGrath, A., 'On the gravity of causes of a psychological nature in the proof of inability to assume the essential obligations of marriage', *Studia Canonica*, 22 (1988), 67

McHenry, B., 'The future of synodical government in the Church of England', *Ecclesiastical Law Journal*, 3 (1993), 86

McIntyre, J. P., 'The acquired right: a new context', *Studia Canonica*, 26 (1992), 25

———'Optional priestly celibacy', *Studia Canonica*, 29 (1995), 103

McKenna, K. E., 'Confidential clergy matters and the secret archives', *Studia Canonica*, 26 (1992), 191

McManus, F. R., 'Liturgical law and difficult cases', *Worship*, 48 (1974), 347

Megarry, R. E., 'Administrative quasi-legislation', *Law Quarterly Review*, 60 (1944), 125

Mendoca, A., 'Effects of personality disorders on matrimonial consent', *Studia Canonica*, 21 (1987), 66

Minear, P. S., *Commands of Christ* (Edinburgh, 1972)

Moffat, G., and Chesterman, M., *Trusts Law: Texts and Materials* (London, 1988)

Moodie, M., 'The administrator and the law: authority and its exercise in the code', Hite and Ward, *Readings*, 444

Moore, P., 'Legal references: a simple guide', *Ecclesiastical Law Journal*, 3 (1994), 183

Morgan, K. O., *Rebirth of a Nation: Wales 1880–1980* (2nd edn., Oxford, 1982)

Morrisey, F. G., 'The conveyance of ecclesiastical property', *Proceedings of the Canon Law Society of America* (Washington, 1976) 123

——— 'Is the new code an improvement for the law of the Catholic Church?', *Concilium*, 185 (1986), 32

——— 'Papal and curial pronouncements: their canonical significance in the light of the 1983 code of canon law', *The Jurist*, 50 (1990), 102

——— 'The laity in the new code of canon law', Hite and Ward, *Readings*, 323

——— 'Recent studies concerning clerics and sexual abuse of minors', Canon Law Society of Great Britain and Ireland, *Newsletter*, No. 91 (1992), 6

Munro, C., 'Laws and conventions distinguished', *Law Quarterly Review*, 91 (1975), 218

Murphy, J., *Church, State and Schools in Britain* (London, 1971)

Muthig, J., 'The Roman curia: how the church is run', Hite and Ward, *Readings*, 221

Nedungatt, G., 'The title of the new canonical legislation', *Studia Canonica*, 19 (1985), 61

——— 'The title of the oriental code', *Studia Canonica*, 25 (1991) 465

Neill, S., *Anglicanism* (Harmondsworth, 1958)

Neumann, J., 'The specific social nature of the church and its consequences for canon law', *Concilium*, 8(5) (1969), 7

Newsom, G. H., and Newsom, G. L., *Faculty Jurisdiction of the Church of England* (2nd edn., London, 1993)

Nokes, G. D., 'Professional privilege', *Law Quarterly Review*, 66 (1950), 88

Norman, E. R., *Roman Catholicism in England* (Oxford, 1985)

North, P. M., and Fawcett, J. J. (eds.), *Cheshire and North: Private International Law* (12th edn., London, 1992)

Nurser, J., 'The European Community and the Church of England', *Ecclesiastical Law Journal*, 3 (1995), 103

O'Connor, W., 'The indissolubility of a ratified, consummated marriage', *Ephemerides Theologiae Louvaniensis*, 13 (1936), 692

O'Dea, T., 'The church as *sacramentum mundi*', *Concilium*, 8(6) (1970) 36

O'Rourke, J. J., 'Considerations on the convalidation of marriage', *The Jurist*, 43 91983) 387

Ogilvie, M. H., 'What is a church by law established?', *Osgoode Hall Law Journal*, 28 (1990), 179

Ombres, R., 'Why then the law?', *New Blackfriars* (1974), 296

——— 'Faith, doctrine and Roman Catholic canon law', *Ecclesiastical Law Journal*, 1 (1989), 33

Örsy, L., 'Matrimonial consent in the new code', *The Jurist*, 43 (1983), 29

——— 'Ecumenism and marriage', in M. Thériault and J. Thorn (eds.), *The New Code of Canon Law*, Proceedings of the Fifth International Congress of Canon Law, 2 Volumes (Ottawa, 1986) II, 1041

——— *The Church: Learning and Teaching* (Wilmington, Delaware, 1987)

——— 'Towards a theological conception of canon law', Hite and Ward, *Readings*, 10

——— *The Profession of Faith and the Oath of Fidelity: A Theological and Canonical Analysis* (Wilmington, Delaware, 1990)

——— *Theology and Canon Law: New Horizons for Legislation and Interpretation* (Collegeville, Minnesota, 1992)

Otero, J. C., 'Church-state relations in the light of Vatican II', *Concilium*, 8(6) (1970), 113

Palmer, B., *High and Mitred: Prime Ministers as Bishop Makers, 1837–1977* (London, 1992)

Pannick, D., 'What is a public authority for the purposes of judicial review?', in J. Jowell and D. Oliver (eds.), *New Directions in Judicial Review* (London, 1988) 23

Paprocki, T. J., 'Rights of Christians in the local church: canon law procedures in the light of civil law principles of administrative justice', *Studia Canonica*, 24 (1990), 427

Parry, C., 'Further considerations upon the Prince of Hanover's case', *International and Comparative Law Quarterly*, 5 (1956), 61

Peay, J., *Tribunals on Trial* (Oxford, 1989)

Peter, C. J., 'Dimensions of *ius divinum* in Roman Catholic theology', *Theological Studies*, 34 (1973), 227

Phillimore, R., *The Ecclesiastical Law of the Church of England*, 2 Volumes (2nd edn., London, 1895)

Picarda, H., *The Law and Practice Relating to Charities* (London, 1977)

——— 'New religions as charities', *New Law Journal*, 131 (1983), 436

Poole, D., 'Janaway: a comment', *Law and Justice* (1988), 82

Potz, R., 'The concept and development of law according to the 1983 *Corpus Iuris Canonici*', *Concilium*, 185 (1986), 14

Poulter, S., 'The definition of marriage in English law', *Modern Law Review*, 42 (1979), 409

Poulter, S., 'The religious education provisions of the Education Act 1988', *Education and the Law*, 2 (1990), 1

Power, D., 'The funeral rites of suicide and liturgical developments', *Concilium*, 179 (1985), 75

Provost, J. H., 'The revision of Book V of the code of canon law', *Studia Canonica*, 9 (1975), 135

——— 'First penance and first Eucharist', *The Jurist*, 43 (1983), 450

—— 'The participation of the laity in the governance of the church', *Studia Canonica*, 17 (1983), 417

—— 'Protecting and promoting the rights of Christians: some implications for church structure', *The Jurist*, 46 (1986), 289

—— 'Suggested operative principles for apostolic visitation', *The Jurist*, 49 (1989), 543

—— 'Approaches to Catholic identity in church law', *Concilium* (1994), 15

Provost, J., and Walf, K. (eds.), *Collegiality Put to the Test* (Edinburgh, 1990)

Quick, O. C., *The Christian Sacraments* (London, 1927, reprinted, 1955)

Quinlan, M. R., 'Parental rights and admission of children to the sacraments of initiation', *Studia Canonica*, 25 (1991), 385

Rahner, K., *Theological Investigations* (Baltimore, 1966), Volume 4, 'The concept of mystery in Catholic theology', 36, Volume 5, 'Reflections on the concept of *ius divinum* in Catholic thought', 219

—— 'Magisterium', in K. Rahner (ed.), *Encyclopedia of Theology* (London, 1981) 871

Ravenscroft, R. L., 'The role of the archdeacon today', *Ecclesiastical Law Journal*, 3 (1995), 379

Raz, J., *The Concept of a Legal System* (Oxford, 1970)

—— 'Legal principles and the limits of law', *Yale Law Journal*, 81 (1972), 823

Ridderbos, H., *Paul: An Outline of His Theology* (London, 1975)

Ritty, C., 'Changing economy and the new code of canon law', *The Jurist*, 26 (1966), 469

Robertson, J. W., 'Canons 867 and 868 and baptizing infants against the will of parents', *The Jurist*, 45 (1985), 631

Robilliard, St J. A., 'Should parliament enact a religious discrimination act?', *Public Law* (1978), 379

—— *Religion and the Law: Religious Liberty in Modern English Law* (Manchester, 1984)

Robinson, G., 'Law in the life of the church', *Studia Canonica*, 17 (1983), 47

Robinson, W. A., *Justice and Administrative Law* (3rd edn., 1951).

Roche, G. J., 'Consent is a union of wills: a study of the bilateral dimension of matrimonial consent', *Studia Canonica*, 18 (1984), 415

Rogers, W. V. H., *Winfield and Jolowicz on Tort* (14th edn., London, 1994)

Routledge, K. G., 'Blasphemy: the report of the Archbishop of Canterbury's Working Party on offences against religion and public worship—a personal view', *Ecclesiastical Law Journal*, 1 (1989), 27

Rowland, S., *A Local Church of England Parish and Registration*, The Office of Data Protection (London, 1994)

Russell, A., *The Clerical Profession* (London, 1980)

Rutherford, R., *The Death of a Christian: The Rite of Funerals* (New York, 1980)

Santer, M. (ed.), *Their Lord and Ours* (London, 1982)

Scarisbrick, J. J., *Henry VIII* (London, 1968)

Schillebeeckx, E., *Ministry—A Case for Change* (London, 1981)

Schramm, P. E., *A History of the English Coronation* (London, 1937)

Schwarzenberger, G., and Brown, E. D., *A Manual of International Law* (6th edn., London, 1976)

Seasoltz, R. K., *New Liturgy, New Laws* (Collegeville, Minnesota, 1980)

Setien, J., 'Tensions in the church', *Concilium*, 8(5) (1969), 35

Slaughter, I. E., 'Functions of the Ecclesiastical Committee under Section 3(3) of the Church of England Assembly (Powers) Act 1919', unpublished paper, Church House, 20 April 1989, LC(89)12

Smale, D. A.(ed.), *Davies' Law of Burial, Cremation and Exhumation* (6th edn., Crayford, 1993)

Smethurst, A. F., Wilson, H.R., and Riley, H (eds.), *Acts of the Convocations of Canterbury and York* (London, 1961)

Smiddy, T., *'Negotiatio'*, *The Jurist*, 11 (1951), 486

Smith, I. T., and Wood, J. C., *Industrial Law* (5th edn., London, 1993)

Smith, M. G., and Others, 'Report of the Working Party on the legal preliminaries to marriage', *Ecclesiastical Law Journal*, 3 (1995), 323

Smith, P., 'Lack of due discretion and suitability for ordination', *Studia Canonica*, 21 (1987), 125

Smith, P., 'Points of law and practice concerning ecclesiastical visitation', *Ecclesiastical Law Journal*, 2 (1990–92), 189

Sparkes, P., 'Exclusive burial rights', *Ecclesiastical Law Journal*, 2 (1991), 133

Spencer, J. R., 'Blasphemy: the Law Commission's Working Paper', *Criminal Law Review* (1981), 810

Stake, R. S., 'Professionalism and confidentiality in the practice of spiritual direction', *The Jurist*, 43 (1983), 214

Stancliffe, D., 'Baptism and fonts', *Ecclesiastical Law Journal*, 3 (1994), 141

Stanton, K. M., *The Modern Law of Tort* (London, 1994)

Starke, J. G., *Introduction to Internationl Law* (9th edn., London, 1984)

Steinmuller, W., 'Divine law and its dynamism in Protestant theology of law', *Concilium*, 8(5) (1969), 13

Stenson, A., 'Penalties in the new code of canon law: the role of the confessor', *The Jurist*, 43 (1983) 406

—— 'The concept and implications of the formal act of defection of Canon 1117', *Studia Canonica*, 21 (1987) 175

Stevas, N. St.J., *The Agonising Choice: Birth Control, Religion and the Law* (London, 1971)

Stone, L., 'The political programme of Thomas Cromwell', *Bulletin of the Institute of Historical Research*, 24 (1951), 1

—— *The Family, Sex and Marriage in England: 1500–1800* (London, 1977)

Stone, R., *Civil Liberties* (London, 1994)

Sullivan, F. A., *Magisterium: Teaching Authority in the Catholic Church* (Dublin, 1983)

—— 'Magisterium', in J. A. Komonchack, M. Collins and D. A. Lane (eds.), *The New Dictionary of Theology* (London, 1987) 617

—— 'The response due to the non-definitive exercise of magisterium', *Studia Canonica*, 23 (1989), 267

Sykes, S. W., *The Integrity pf Anglicanism* (London, 1978)

Taunton, E., *The Law of the Church* (London, 1906)

Teissier, H., 'Bishops conferences and their function in the church', *Concilium*, 188 (1986), 110

Thomas, E. L. (ed.), *Baker's Law Relating to Burials* (6th edn., London, 1901)

Thomas, P. K., 'Marriage annulments for gay men and lesbian women: new canonical and psychological insights', *The Jurist*, 43 (1983), 318

Thompson, W. M., 'Authority and *magisterium* in recent Catholic thought', *Chicago Studies* (1977), 278

Tiemann, W. H., and Bush, J. C., *The Right to Silence: Privileged Clergy Communication and the Law* (2nd edn., Nashville, 1983)

Tierney, T., 'The right of the faithful to the sacraments', *Catholic Lawyer*, 23 (1977), 57

Till, B., *York Against Durham: The Guardianship of the Spiritualities in the Diocese of Durham Sede Vacante* (York, 1993)

Tiller, J., *A Strategy for the Church's Ministry* (London, 1985)

Treitel, G. H., *The Law of Contract* (8th edn., London, 1991)

Trisco, R., 'The variety of procedures in modern history', in W. Bassett (ed.), *The Choosing of Bishops* (Hartford, 1971)

Tuché, A., 'The code of canon law of 1983 and ecumenical relations', in M. Thériault and J. Thorn (eds.), *The New Code of Canon Law*, Proceedings of the Fifth International Congress of Canon Law, 2 Volumes (Ottawa, 1986) I, 401

Turner, R., 'Bonds of discord: alternative episcopal oversight examined in the light of the nonjuring consecrations', *Ecclesiastical Law Journal*, 3 (1995), 398

Twining, W., and Miers, D., *How To Do Things With Rules* (2nd edn., London, 1982)

Urresti, T., 'Canon law and theology: two different sciences', *Concilium*, 8(3) (1967), 10

——— 'The theologian in interface with canonical reality', *Journal of Ecumenical Studies*, 19 (1982), 146

Urrutia, F., 'Delegation and the executive power of governance', *Studia Canonica*, 19 (1985), 339

——— 'Administrative power in the church according to the code of canon law', *Studia Canonica*, 20 (1986), 253

Vella, D. J., 'Canon law and the mystical body', *The Jurist*, 22 (1962), 412

Vidler, A., 'The relations of church and state with special reference to England', *Quis Custodiet*, 30 (1971) 6

Wade, E. C. S., and Bradley, A. W., *Constitutional and Administrative Law* (10th edn., London, 1985)

Wadham, J. (ed.), *Your Rights: The Liberty Guide* (London, 1994)

Walf, K., 'Gospel, church law and human rights: foundations and deficiencies', *Concilium* (1990), 32

Walter, N., *Blasphemy: Ancient and Modern* (London, 1990)

Wamboldt, W. J. S., 'Canon law on the indissolubility of marriage in the Roman Catholic Church', *Studia Canonica*, 21 (1987), 265

Ward, D. J., 'Trust management under the new code of canon law', *The Jurist*, 44 (1984), 134

——— 'Liturgy and law', Hite and Ward, *Readings*, 396

Waterhouse, J., *The Power of the Local Ordinary to Impose a Matrimonial Ban* (Washington, 1952)

Watkin, T. G., 'Vestiges of establishment: the ecclesiastical and canon law of the Church in Wales', *Ecclesiastical Law Journal*, 2 (1990), 110

Webster, R., *A Brief History of Blasphemy* (Southwold, 1990)

Whitehouse, C., and Stuart-Buttle, E., *Revenue Law: Principles and Practice* (8th edn., London, 1990)

Wijlens, M., *Theology and Canon Law: The Theories of Klaus Morsdorf and Eugenio Corecco* (Lanham, Md, 1992)

Wilkinson, J. T., *1662 and After: Three Centuries of English Nonconformity* (London, 1962)

Wilson, D., 'Symbols and readings—reflections from celebrating mass with mentally handicapped people', *Liturgy*, 9(5) (1985), 181

Winninger, P., 'A pastoral canon law', *Concilium*, 8(5) (1969), 28

Woestman, W. H. (ed.), 'Dissolution of a ratified non-consummated marriage: a procedure sinking into oblivion', *Studia Canonica*, 21 (1987), 195

——'Too many invalid marriages', *Studia Canonica*, 24 (1990), 193

——(ed.) *Papal Allocutions to the Roman Rota 1939–1994* (Ottawa, 1994)

Wood, S., 'The theological foundation of episcopal conferences and collegiality', *Studia Canonica*, 22 (1988), 327

Woolf, H., 'Public law—private law: why the divide?', *Public Law* (1986), 220

Zielinski, P., 'Pious wills and mass stipends in relation to canons 1299–1310', *Studia Canonica*, 19 (1985), 115

INDEX